CULTURAL THEORY

AND

POPULAR CULTURE

for Jannette, my oldest friend

CULTURAL THEORY

AND

POPULAR CULTURE

A Reader

Second edition

edited and
introduced by
JOHN STOREY

PEARSON

Prentice
Hall

Harlow, England • London • New York • Boston • San Francisco • Toronto
Sydney • Tokyo • Singapore • Hong Kong • Seoul • Taipei • New Delhi
Cape Town • Madrid • Mexico City • Amsterdam • Munich • Paris • Milan

Pearson Education Limited
Edinburgh Gate
Harlow
Essex CM20 2JE
England

and Associated Companies throughout the world

Visit us on the World Wide Web at:
http://www.pearsoned.co.uk

First published 1994
This second edition published 1998

Typeset in 10/12pt Sabon
by Mathematical Composition Setters Ltd, Salisbury

Printed and bound in Great Britain by
Henry Ling Limited, at the Dorset Press, Dorchester, DT1 1HD

Library of Congress Cataloging-in-Publication Data

Cultural theory and popular culture : a reader / edited and introduced
  by John Storey. — 2nd ed.
      p.   cm.
    "Companion volume to An introductory guide to cultural theory and
popular culture, second edition"—Pref. to 2nd ed.
    Includes bibliographical references and index.
    ISBN 0-13-776121-X (alk. paper)
    1. Popular culture. 2. Popular culture—Philosophy.   3. Culture–
–Philosophy. I. Storey, John 1950–
  CB19.C83   1997
  306—dc21   97-29547
                                                             CIP

British Library Cataloguing in Publication Data

A catalogue record for this book is available from
the British Library

ISBN 0-13-776121-X
10 9 8
08 07 06 05 04

Contents

Preface

This book is a companion volume to *An Introduction to Cultural Theory and Popular Culture*, second edition (Prentice Hall/Harvester Wheatsheaf, 1997). In that book my intention was to map the study of popular culture across the field of cultural theory from my own postdisciplinary location in cultural studies. However, the book was not intended to be a substitute for reading first hand the theorists and critics I discussed. *Cultural Theory and Popular Culture: A Reader* (second edition) collects together work by most of the critics and theorists discussed in *An Introduction to Cultural Theory and Popular Culture*, and also contains work by other critics and theorists, which together supplement and extend the conceptual terrain of the first book. My hope is that the 55 readings collected here, together with the general introduction and the introductions to the seven individual sections, will be interesting and useful both to those familiar with the field and to those for whom – as an academic subject at least – it is all very new.

In preparing the second edition I have made a number of changes. I have removed six existing texts and I have added nine new readings. I have revised and rewritten the general introduction and the seven section introductions. The bibliography has been updated.

There are a number of people I would like to take this opportunity to thank. First and foremost, I would like to thank students on the 'Cultural Theory and Popular Culture' module (1990–7) on both the BA (Hons) Communication Studies and BA (Hons) Media and Cultural Studies degrees at the University of Sunderland, with whom I have studied many of the readings collected here. I would also like to thank colleagues both in the Media and Cultural Studies subject group and at the Raman Selden Centre for the Study of Textual and Cultural Theory for their encouragement and support. Thanks also to Christina Wipf Perry at Prentice Hall for suggesting a second edition. But last, and most of all, I would like to thank Kate and Jenny for their help and support.

Introduction: The Study of Popular Culture and Cultural Studies

The aim of this book is to provide a map of the development of the study of popular culture across the field of cultural theory from the postdisciplinary perspective of cultural studies. It is, of course, difficult to draw a clear borderline between the study of popular culture in cultural studies and, say, the study of popular culture in historical studies, literary studies, anthropology or sociology. Some of the readings included here might, for example, just as easily be found in a book called *History and Popular Culture: A Reader*. However, although the borderline might be difficult to draw, it does exist. Perhaps the best way to register this difference is to describe the history and the assumptions of cultural studies.

What Is (British) Cultural Studies?[1]

Although it is possible to point to degree programmes, to journals, to conferences and associations, there is no simple answer to this question. The first problem any attempt at definition encounters is whether or not cultural studies is simply the study of contemporary culture. Richard Johnson, for example, describes cultural studies as 'a process, a kind of alchemy for producing useful knowledge; codify it and you might halt its reaction'.[2] However, it has recently become increasingly fashionable for the term cultural studies to be used to describe any approach to the study of culture. At the risk of seeming sectarian (and out of step with the postdisciplinary aims and spirit of cultural studies), I find it very difficult to accept this usage. I think there is a difference between cultural studies and other ways to study culture ('culture studies' or the 'sociology of culture', for example).

Traditionally, an academic field of inquiry is defined by three criteria: first, there is the object of study; second, there is the method of approach to the object of study; third, there is the history of the field of inquiry itself. While there is little difficulty in addressing the first and third criteria (which I shall do shortly), the second does create a problem. The problem is this: cultural studies has never had one distinct method of approach to its object of study. Therefore, in order to avoid difficulties I cannot possibly deal with here, I intend to substitute 'basic assumptions' for methodology.

John Fiske maintains that 'culture' in cultural studies 'is neither aesthetic nor humanist in emphasis, but political'.[3] What he means by this is that the object of study in cultural studies is not culture defined in a narrow sense, as the objects of supposed aesthetic excellence ('high art'); nor, in an equally narrow sense, as a process of aesthetic, intellectual and spiritual development; but culture understood, in Raymond Williams's phrase, as 'a particular way of life, whether of a people, a period or a group' (Reading 5). This is a definition of culture which can embrace the first two definitions, but also, and crucially, it can range beyond the social exclusivity and narrowness of these, to include popular culture – the cultures of everyday life. Therefore, although cultural studies cannot (and should not) be reduced to the study of popular culture, it is certainly the case that the study of popular culture is central to the project of cultural studies. As Cary Nelson explains, 'people with ingrained contempt for popular culture will never fully understand the cultural studies project'.[4]

When asked to say what is distinctive about the cultural studies perspective, Stuart Hall responded 'I think the question of the politics of culture or the culture of politics is somewhere close to ... what is at the centre of cultural studies'.[5] Cultural studies regards culture as political in another quite specific sense, one which reveals the dominant political position in cultural studies. Here is part of the conclusion to Hall's essay 'Notes on Deconstructing "the Popular"' (Reading 42):

> Popular culture ... is an arena of consent and resistance. It is partly where hegemony arises, and where it is secured. It is not a sphere where socialism, a socialist culture already fully formed – might be simply 'expressed'. But it is one of the places where socialism might be constituted. That is why 'popular culture' matters.

Others working in cultural studies might not express their attitude to popular culture quite in these terms, but they would certainly share Hall's concern to think culture politically.

All the basic assumptions of British cultural studies are Marxist. This is not to say that all practitioners of cultural studies are Marxists, but that cultural studies is itself grounded in Marxism. All its major texts are informed, one way or another, by Marxism; whether or not their authors regard themselves as Marxist, post-Marxist or rhetorical Marxists (using the rhetoric, vocabulary, models, etc., without, necessarily, a commitment to the politics).

Marxism informs cultural studies in two basic ways. First, to understand the meaning(s) of culture we must analyse it in relation to the social structure and its history. Although it is constituted (made possible) by a particular social structure with a specific history, it is not studied as a reflection of this structure and history. On the contrary, cultural studies argues that culture's importance derives from the fact that it helps to constitute the structure and shape the history. Second, cultural studies assumes that capitalist industrial societies are societies divided unequally along, for example, ethnic, gender and class lines. It is argued that culture is one of the principal sites where these divisions are established and contested: culture is a terrain on which there takes place a continual struggle over meaning(s), in which subordinate groups attempt to resist the imposition of meanings which bear the interests of dominant groups. As Tony Bennett explains, cultural studies is committed 'to examining cultural practices from the point of view of their intrication with, and within, relations of power'.[6] It is this which makes culture ideological. Ideology is the central concept in cultural studies. James Carey even suggests that 'British cultural studies could be described just as easily and perhaps more accurately as ideological studies'.[7]

There are many competing definitions of ideology, but it is the formulation established by Hall in the early 1980s,[8] which is generally accepted as the dominant working definition in cultural studies: 'By ideology I mean the mental frameworks – the languages, the concepts, categories, imagery of thought, and the systems of representation – which different classes and social groups deploy in order to make sense of, define, figure out and render intelligible the way society works.'[9] Working from Antonio Gramsci's concept of hegemony (see Readings 21, 22, 23, 24, 42), Hall developed a theory of 'articulation' to explain the processes of ideological struggle (Hall's use of 'articulation' plays on the term's double meaning: to express and to join together). He argues that cultural texts and practices are not inscribed with meaning, guaranteed once and for all by the intentions of production; meaning is always the result of an act of 'articulation'. The process is called 'articulation' because meaning has to be expressed, but it is always expressed in a specific context, a specific historical moment, within a specific discourse(s). Thus expression is always connected (articulated) to and conditioned by context.

Hall's formulation also draws on the work of the Russian theorist Valentin Volosinov.[10] Volosinov argues that meaning is determined by the social context in which it is articulated. Cultural texts and practices are 'multi-accentual'; that is, they can be articulated with different 'accents' by different people in different contexts for different politics. A text or practice or event is not the issuing source of meaning, but a site where the articulation of meaning – variable meaning(s) – can take place. And because different meanings can be ascribed to the same text or practice or event, meaning is always a potential site of conflict. When, for example, a radical rap group use the word 'nigger' to attack an embedded institutional racism, it is articulated with an 'accent' very different from the 'accent' given the word in, say, the Neanderthal ramblings of a neo-Nazi. This, of course, is not simply a question of linguistic struggle – a conflict over semantics – but a sign of political struggle about who can claim the power and the authority to define social reality. As Hall explains,

> The meaning of a cultural form and its place or position in the cultural field is not inscribed inside its form. Nor is its position fixed once and forever. This year's radical

symbol or slogan will be neutralized into next year's fashion; the year after, it will be the object of a profound cultural nostalgia. (Reading 42)

The cultural field is defined by this struggle to articulate, disarticulate and rearticulate cultural texts and practices for particular ideologies, particular politics. Hall contends that 'meaning is always a social production, a practice. The world has to be *made* to mean.'[11] A key question for cultural studies is: Why do particular meanings get regularly constructed around particular cultural texts and practices and achieve the status of 'common sense', acquire a certain taken-for-granted quality? However, although it recognises that the culture industries are a major site of ideological production, constructing powerful images, descriptions, definitions, frames of reference for understanding the world, cultural studies rejects the view that 'ordinary' people who consume these productions are cultural dupes, victims of 'an up-dated form of the opium of the people'. As Hall insists:

> That judgement may make us feel right, decent and self-satisfied about our denunciations of the agents of mass manipulation and deception – the capitalist cultural industries: but I don't know that it is a view which can survive for long as an adequate account of cultural relationships; and even less as a socialist perspective on the culture and nature of the working class. Ultimately, the notion of the people as a purely passive, outline force is a deeply unsocialist perspective. (Reading 42)

In contrast, for Hall the field of culture is a major site of ideological struggle; a terrain of 'incorporation' and 'resistance': one of the sites where hegemony is to be won or lost. The consumption of cultural texts and practices – or 'secondary production', as Michel de Certeau (Reading 45) calls it – is therefore always, at some level, the articulation and activation of meaning. As Fiske points out: 'If the cultural commodities or texts do not contain resources out of which the people can make their own meanings of their social relations and identities, they will be rejected and will fail in the marketplace. They will not be *made* popular.'[12] But as he also makes clear: 'Popular culture is made by subordinate peoples in their own interests out of resources that also, contradictorily, serve the economic interests of the dominant.'[13]

Gramscian cultural studies insists that there is a dialectic between the processes of production and the activities of consumption. The consumer always confronts a text or practice in its material existence as a result of determinate conditions of production. But in the same way, the text or practice is confronted by a consumer who in effect 'produces in use' the range of possible meaning(s) – these cannot just be read off from the materiality of the text or practice, or the means or relations of its production.

There are different ways of thinking, different ways of using, what Hall calls 'the enormously productive metaphor of hegemony'.[14] Hegemony theory in cultural studies operates not always quite as formulated by Gramsci. The concept has been expanded and elaborated to take into account other areas of struggle. Whereas for

Gramsci, the concept is used to explain and explore relations of power articulated in terms of class, recent formulations in cultural studies have extended the concept to include, for example, gender, race, meaning and pleasure. What has remained constant (or relatively constant under the impact of political and theoretical change, from left-Leavisism to postmodernism and post-colonialism) is a particular guiding principle of cultural analysis. It is first found in what Michael Green quite rightly calls Hoggart's 'remarkably enduring formulation',[15] 'Against this background may be seen how much the more generally diffused appeals of the mass publications connect with commonly accepted attitudes, *how they are altering those attitudes and how they are meeting resistance*' (my italics).[16] In the 1960s it is given a culturalist accent by Hall and Whannel, 'Teenage culture is a contradictory mixture of the authentic and the manufactured: it is *an area of self-expression for the young and a lush grazing pasture for the commercial providers*' (my italics, Reading 7). In the 1970s it is found in the Gramscian tones of John Clarke *et al.*: 'Men and women are... *formed, and form themselves* through society, culture and history. So the existing cultural patterns form a sort of historical reservoir – a pre-constituted "field of possibilities" – which groups take up, transform, develop. Each group *makes something of its starting conditions* – and through this "making", through this practice, culture is reproduced and transmitted' (my italics).[17] In the 1980s we hear it in the Foucauldian analysis of Mica Nava: 'Consumerism is far more than just economic activity: it is also about dream and consolation, communication and confrontation, image and identity.... Consumerism is a discourse through which *disciplinary power is both exercised and contested*' (my italics).[18] In the 1990s it is there in Marie Gillespie's account of the relationship between media consumption and the cultures of migrant and diasporic communities, demonstrating how young Punjabi Londoners are '*shaped by but at the same time reshaping the images and meanings* circulated in the media' (my italics) – what she calls 're-creative consumption'.[19] In every decade in the history of cultural studies the point has been made and repeated. It is the 'Gramscian insistence' (before, with and after Gramsci), learned from Marx, that we make culture and we are made by culture; there is agency and there is structure.[20] It is not enough to celebrate agency; nor is it enough to detail the structure(s) of power, we must always keep in mind the dialectical play between resistance and incorporation. The best of cultural studies has always been mindful of this.

There are those, within and without cultural studies, who believe that Hall's model of ideological struggle has led to an uncritical celebration of popular culture: 'resistance' is endlessly elaborated in terms of empowerment and pleasure, while 'incorporation' is quietly forgotten. Nicholas Garnham (see Reading 54) argues that to reverse this trend requires a 'return' to the procedures of political economy. Lawrence Grossberg (Reading 55) offers a response to Garnham's argument. Jim McGuigan (Reading 53) contends that the work of John Fiske (see Reading 47) has reduced the study of popular culture in cultural studies to an uncritical celebration of the 'popular' reading. The work of Paul Willis (see Reading 50) and that of len Ang (see Readings 26 and 48) are also cited as examples of this uncritical drift. From different perspectives, both Michael Schudson (Reading 46) and Duncan Webster (Reading 51) provide overviews of some of the issues involved in the debate between what might be called 'cultural populism' and 'cultural pessimism'. My own view (and I draw attention to it because it has almost certainly informed the selection of the 55 readings collected here in this book) is that people *make* popular culture from the repertoire of commodities supplied by the culture industries (film, television, music, publishing, sporting, etc.). I also believe that making popular culture ('production in use') can be empowering to subordinate and resistant to dominant understandings of the world. But this is not to say that it is always empowering and resistant. To deny that the consumers of popular culture are cultural dupes is not to deny that the culture industries seek to manipulate; but it is to deny that popular culture is little more than a degraded landscape of commercial and ideological manipulation, imposed from above in order to make profit and secure ideological control. To decide these matters requires vigilance and attention to the details of the production, distribution and consumption of culture. These are not matters that can be decided once and for all (outside the contingencies of history and politics) with an elitist glance and a condescending sneer. Nor can they be read off from the moment of production (locating meaning, pleasure, ideological effect, etc., in, variously, the intention, the means of production or the production itself); these are only aspects of the contexts for 'production in use', and it is, ultimately, in 'production in use' that questions of meaning, pleasure, ideological effect, and so on, can be (contingently) decided.

Whatever else cultural studies is, it is certainly not the monolithic unity conjured up by critics such as McGuigan and Garnham.[21] Cultural studies has always been an unfolding discourse, responding to changing historical and political conditions and always marked by debate, disagreement and intervention. Hall makes this very clear:

> Cultural Studies has multiple discourses; it has a number of different histories. It is a whole set of formations; it has its own different conjunctures and moments in the past. It included many different kinds of work. I want to insist on that! It always was a set of unstable formations. It was 'centred' only in quotation marks.... It had many trajectories; many people had and have different theoretical positions, all of them in contention.[22]

For example, the centrality of class in cultural studies was disrupted first by feminism's insistence on the importance of gender(see Readings 16, 24, 26, 27, 28, 29, 30, 31, 32, 34, 35, 38, 40, 48), and then by black students raising questions about the invisibility of race in much cultural studies analysis (see Readings 9, 29, 37, 40).[23] Similarly, there can be no doubt that in recent years cultural studies has been radically transformed as debates about postmodernism and postmodernity have threatened to replace the more familiar debates about ideology and hegemony.[24]

According to Hall's influential account of the formation and development of cultural studies, the key point to understand is that 'there are no "absolute beginnings" and few unbroken continuities....What is important are the significant breaks – where old lines of thought are disrupted, older constellations displaced, and elements, old and new, are regrouped around a different set of premises and themes.'[25] Hall charts the formation of British cultural studies around three 'significant breaks'. First, there is the break with Leavisism and mechanistic forms of Marxism, which results in the birth of culturalism (late 1950s/early 1960s). Then, there is the encounter with French structuralism and poststructuralism (1960s/early 1970s). Finally, there is the discovery of the work of Gramsci and the concept of hegemony (mid-1970s), enabling a synthesis of the best of culturalism and structuralism. It is at this moment that the postdisciplinary approach to contemporary culture – now known internationally, as British cultural studies – is born. British cultural studies continues to be Gramscian in its critical focus, but debates in and about postmodernism have increasingly threatened to dislodge its prominence. Whether this challenge has produced a 'paradigm crisis' is not yet clear. Some of the readings collected here, especially in Parts 6 and 7, directly and indirectly address this question.

About This Book

The 55 readings gathered here collectively map the development of the study of popular culture in cultural studies. Although I have grouped them in seven parts to suggest a certain chronology of development, I am aware that the story of cultural studies (or, for that matter, the story of the study of popular culture from the perspective of cultural studies) cannot be easily told within a linear narrative. There are many moments of overlap, many occasions when the story turns back on itself to reconsider and sometimes reactivate what had seemed dead and gone. The upshot of this is that some readings might have been situated in more than one part; and, moreover, that some readings sit very uncomfortably in only one part. Having said this, the book is organised 'chronologically' into seven parts. Each part marks a particular moment in the history of the study of popular culture in cultural studies. Part One contains work from the 'pre-history' of the study of popular culture in cultural studies. This is the approach known as the 'culture and civilisation' tradition. The next five parts contain examples of work from the approaches of culturalism, structuralism and poststructuralism, Marxism, feminism and postmodernism. Although feminism and Marxism have their own separate parts, so central have been these approaches to the elaboration of cultural studies that examples of them appear in many of the other parts as well. The final part addresses recent debates around 'the politics of the popular' – questions of value, meaning, ideology, pessimism, populism and pleasure.

Readers always tell particular stories, establish narrative paths through a field of study. This Reader is no different. Readers are also classic examples of the play of 'intertextuality': they tell stories intended by an author, but are inscribed with, constantly pushed and jostled by, other stories, other authors. In this Reader I have tried to draw a particular route through the development of the study of popular culture in cultural studies. I am aware that there are other ways to tell this story, and that at specific stages in my own telling some of these other ways demand the greater attention. I am also aware that although you may recognise the general features of the map this Reader offers, you may not at times feel entirely satisfied with the details. Other Readers (with other details) will tell it differently. When one is making a Reader, it is not always possible to tell exactly the story first intended. For a variety of reasons (financial constraints and non-availability of material, etc.), one cannot always reproduce the details of the narrative one would have liked. But having said that, I am happy with what I have been able to reproduce. I might have related it differently, but I stand by the telling I have told. My hope is that you find it as pleasurable and as useful to read as I have found it useful and pleasurable to tell.

Notes

1. I use the term 'British' cultural studies to specify the location from which I write and thus to refuse any tendency to universalise this location as *the* location of cultural studies as it continues to develop as an international field of critical inquiry.
2. Richard Johnson, 'What is cultural studies anyway?', *What is Cultural Studies: A reader*, ed. John Storey, London: Edward Arnold, 1996, p. 75.
3. John Fiske, 'British cultural studies and television', *What is Cultural Studies: A reader*, ed. John Storey, London: Edward Arnold, 1996, p. 115.
4. Cary Nelson, 'Always already cultural studies: academic conferences and a manifesto', *What is Cultural Studies: A reader*, ed. John Storey, London: Edward Arnold, 1996, p. 279.
5. Stuart Hall, 'Cultural studies and the politics of internationalization (An interview with Stuart Hall by Kuan-Hsing Chen)', *Stuart Hall: Critical dialogues in cultural studies*, ed. Dave Morley and Kuan-Hsing Chen, London: Routledge, 1996, p. 396.
6. Tony Bennett, 'Pulling policy into cultural studies', *What is Cultural Studies: A reader*, ed. John Storey, London: Edward Arnold, 1996, p. 307.
7. James W. Carey, 'Overcoming resistance to cultural studies', *What is Cultural Studies: A reader*, ed. John Storey, London: Edward Arnold, 1996, p. 65.
8. Stuart Hall, 'The rediscovery of ideology: the return of the repressed in media studies', *Subjectivity and Social Relations*, ed. Veronica Beechey and James Donald, Milton Keynes: Open University Press, 1985; Stuart Hall, 'The problem of ideology: Marxism without guarantees' and 'On postmodernism and articulation: an interview with Stuart Hall (edited by Lawrence Grossberg)', *Stuart Hall: Critical dialogues in cultural studies*, ed. David Morley and Kuan-Hsing Chen, London: Routledge, 1996.
9. Hall, 'The problem of ideology: Marxism without guarantees', p. 26.
10. Valentin Volosinov, *Marxism and the Philosophy of Language*, London: Seminar Press, 1973. Another major influence on Hall's position is Ernesto Laclau, especially *Politics and Ideology in Marxist Theory*, London: Verso, 1977.

11. Hall, 'The rediscovery of ideology', p. 34.
12. John Fiske, *Reading the Popular*, London: Unwin Hyman, 1989, p. 2.
13. *Ibid*. See also Readings 23 and 47.
14. Stuart Hall, 'Cultural Studies and its theoretical legacies', *Cultural Studies*, ed. Lawrence Grossberg, Cary Nelson and Paula Treichler, London: Routledge, 1992, p. 280.
15. Michael Green, 'The Centre for Contemporary Cultural Studies', *What Is Cultural Studies: A reader*, ed. John Storey, London: Edward Arnold, 1996, p. 52.
16. Richard Hoggart, *The Uses of Literacy*, Harmondsworth: Penguin, 1957, p. 19.
17. John Clarke, Stuart Hall, Tony Jefferson and Brian Roberts, 'Subculture, cultures and classes', *Resistance Through Rituals*, ed. Stuart Hall and Tony Jefferson, London: Hutchinson, 1976, p. 11.
18. Mica Nava, 'Consumerism and its contradictions', *Cultural Studies* 1:2, 1987, pp. 209–10.
19. Marie Gillespie, *Television, Ethnicity and Cultural Change*, London: Routledge, 1995, p. 2.
20. Karl Marx, *The Eighteenth Brumaire of Louis Bonaparte*, Moscow: Progress Publishers, 1977, p. 10.
21. For an interesting critique of these critics, see Angela McRobbie, 'Looking back at New Times and its critics', *Stuart Hall: Critical dialogues in cultural studies*, ed. David Morley and Kuan-Hsing Chen, London: Routledge, 1996.
22. Hall, 'Cultural studies and its theoretical legacies', p. 278.
23. See Women's Studies Group, Centre for Contemporary Cultural Studies, *Women Take Issue*, London: Hutchinson, 1978; Centre for Contemporary Cultural Studies, *The Empire Strikes Back*, London: Hutchinson, 1982; Paul Gilroy, *There Ain't No Black in the Union Jack*, London: Hutchinson, 1987.
24. For an enthusiastic discussion of postmodern cultural studies see Kuan-Hsing Chen, 'Post-Marxism: between/beyond critical postmodernism and cultural studies', *Stuart Hall: Critical dialogues in cultural studies*, ed. David Morley and Kuan-Hsing Chen, London: Routledge, 1996.
25. Stuart Hall, 'Cultural studies: two paradigms', *What is Cultural Studies: A reader*, ed. John Storey, London: Edward Arnold, 1996, p. 31.

PART ONE

The 'Culture and Civilisation' Tradition

Introduction

The 'culture and civilisation' tradition represents the 'pre-history' of the study of popular culture in cultural studies. It is a tradition founded on the assumptions of Matthew Arnold and elaborated in the theory and practice of F. R. Leavis and the Leavisites gathered around the journal *Scrutiny*. The American version also includes aspects drawn from the analysis of the Frankfurt School.

Arnold's attitude to culture is organised around the binary opposition, which is also the title of his most famous work, *Culture and Anarchy* (Reading 1). Although Arnold had very little to say directly about popular culture, his importance for the student of popular culture is that he inaugurates a particular way of seeing, a particular way of mapping the field of culture. Arnold established a cultural agenda which remained dominant from the 1860s to the 1950s. At the centre of the Arnoldian perspective is his celebrated definition of culture as 'the best that has been thought and said in the world'. The work of the men and women of culture is to know the best and then to make the best prevail. Knowledge of the best will result from 'disinterested and active use of reading, reflection, and observation'. Once this is achieved, the men and women of culture must endeavour to get 'our countrymen to seek culture'. Although Arnold never defined popular culture, reading across his work, it is clear that what he calls 'anarchy' operates as a synonym for popular culture defined as working-class culture. More specifically, he uses anarchy to refer both to the lived culture of the new urban and industrial working class, and to their unwelcomed eruption into formal politics in 1867. For Arnold, working-class culture is significant in that it signals social and cultural decline – a breakdown in social and cultural authority. When he describes culture as 'the great help out of our present difficulties', he is referring to the particular problems of the suffrage campaign of 1866–7, in which 'the working class ... raw and half-developed ... long lain half-hidden amidst its poverty and squalor ... now issuing from its hiding-place to assert an Englishman's heaven-born privilege of doing as he likes, and beginning to perplex *us* by marching where it likes, meeting where it likes, bawling what it likes, breaking what it likes' (my italics). But he is also referring to the general problem of working-class lived

3

culture: the 'raw and uncultivated ... masses'; 'the raw and unkindled masses'; 'our masses ... quite ... raw and uncultivated'; 'those vast, miserable, unmanageable masses of sunken people'

The function of culture is to produce a cultured middle class; a class with the necessary cultural authority to be hegemonic. The working class are always to be on the side of 'anarchy', always in a relation of binary opposition to 'culture'. All that is required of them is that they recognise their cultural difference and acknowledge cultural deference. Arnold is very clear on this point:

> The mass of mankind will never have any ardent zeal for seeing things as they are; very inadequate ideas will always satisfy them. On these inadequate ideas reposes, and must repose, the general practice of the world. That is as much as saying that whoever sets himself to see things as they are will find himself one of a very small circle; but it is only by this small circle resolutely doing its own work that adequate ideas will ever get current at all.[1]

> The highly-instructed few, and not the scantily-instructed many, will ever be the organ of the human race of knowledge and truth. Knowledge and truth in the full sense of the words, are not attainable by the great mass of the human race at all.[2]

If the mass of humankind is to be always satisfied with inadequate ideas, never able to attain truth and knowledge, for whom are the men and women of culture working? And what of the adequate ideas they will make current – current for whom? Culture, as the best that has been thought and said, is not there to be embraced by all; its function is twofold: first to enable middle-class hegemony; and second, to police, through strategies of difference and deference, the unruly and disruptive forces of the popular.

F. R. Leavis takes these Arnoldian assumptions and develops them in actual accounts of, and encounters with, popular culture. Although his work spans a forty-year period, his attitude to popular culture is formed in the 1930s, with the publication of three works: *Mass Civilisation and Minority Culture* (Reading 2), *Fiction and the Reading Public* (by Q. D. Leavis) and *Culture and Environment* (written with Denys Thompson). Together these three books establish the basis of the Leavisite approach to popular culture. Like Arnold, the Leavisites believe that 'culture has always been a minority keeping'. The problem, however, is that the cultured minority can no longer command deference for their values and their judgements. There has been what Q. D. Leavis refers to as a 'collapse of authority'.[3] The minority find themselves in 'a hostile environment'. The Arnoldian project has faltered; 'mass civilisation' and its 'mass culture' pose a subversive challenge, threatening 'to land *us* in irreparable chaos' (my italics).

The resistance of the Leavisites was tempered by a very particular (perhaps mythic) reading of the past. It is claimed that prior to the nineteenth century, and certainly in and before the seventeenth, England had a vigorous common culture. However, as a result of the changes brought about by the Industrial Revolution, this culture fractured into two cultures. On the one hand, a minority culture, on the other, a mass civilisation. The minority culture is the embodiment of the values and standards of 'the best that has been thought and said' (now more or less reduced by the Leavisites to a literary tradition). In contrast to this is the mass culture of mass civilisation: 'commercial' culture consumed unthinkingly by the 'uneducated' majority – cinema, radio, popular fiction, the popular press, advertising, and so on. It is against this threat that Leavisism proposes 'resistance by an armed and active minority'.[4]

The first fifteen years following the Second World War witnessed a very public debate among American intellectuals about the past, present and future of so-called 'mass culture'. Mass culture was seen by some as a typically American phenomenon, and by others as a foreign import which threatened the very well-being of the American way of life. Dwight Macdonald is a key figure in this debate. Influenced by both Leavisism and the Frankfurt School (see Reading 20), he contends, in his very influential essay 'A Theory of Mass Culture' (Reading 3), that mass culture should be condemned for a number of reasons. First, it is parasitic culture, feeding on high culture while offering nothing in return. Second, it is a culture imposed from above on the 'masses'. Whereas folk culture was a culture of the people, mass culture is a culture *for* the people. It is a culture 'fabricated by technicians hired by businessmen; its audience are passive consumers, their participation limited to the choice between buying and not buying'. Moreover, it is a culture fabricated by the dominant class to 'exploit the cultural needs of the masses in order to make profit and/or to maintain their class rule'. What makes Macdonald different from the other writers of the 'culture and civilisation' tradition is his suggestion that mass culture might actually maintain rather than undermine the inequalities of a class society (evidence of the influence of the Frankfurt School). But he shares the tradition's despair at the absence of 'a clearly defined cultural elite'. He also shares their disgust for the new cultural forms, an 'homogenized culture ... that threatens to engulf everything in its spreading ooze'. He also shares their pessimism: 'far from mass culture getting better, we will be lucky if it doesn't get worse'.

It is easy to be critical of the 'culture and civilisation' tradition's approach to popular culture. Given the recent developments in the field of cultural theory, it is almost enough to present a narrative of its approach to condemn it to 'populist' disapproval. However, it must be remembered that from a historical point of view, the tradition's work is absolutely foundational to the project of the study of popular culture in cultural studies. Moreover, the impact of the tradition is difficult to underestimate: for almost a hundred years it was undoubtedly the dominant paradigm in cultural analysis. Indeed, it could be argued that it still forms a kind of repressed 'common sense' in certain areas of British and American academic and non-academic life.

Notes

1. Matthew Arnold, *Poetry and Prose*, London: Rupert Hart Davis, 1954, pp. 364–5.
2. Matthew Arnold, *Complete Prose Works*, vol. III, Ann Arbor: University of Michigan Press, 1960–77, pp. 43–4.
3. Q. D. Leavis, *Fiction and the Reading Public*, London: Chatto & Windus, 1978, p. 187.
4. *Ibid.*, p. 270.

1 □ *Culture and Anarchy*

Matthew Arnold

[...]

The whole scope of the essay is to recommend culture as the great help out of our present difficulties; culture being a pursuit of our total perfection by means of getting to know, on all the matters which most concern us, the best which has been thought and said in the world; and through this knowledge, turning a stream of fresh and free thought upon our stock notions and habits, which we now follow staunchly but mechanically, vainly imagining that there is a virtue in following them staunchly which makes up for the mischief of following them mechanically. This, and this alone, is the scope of the following essay. I say again here, what I have said in the pages which follow, that from the faults and weaknesses of bookmen a notion of something bookish, pedantic, and futile has got itself more or less connected with the word culture, and that it is a pity we cannot use a word more perfectly free from all shadow of reproach. And yet, futile as are many bookmen, and helpless as books and reading often prove for bringing nearer to perfection those who use them, one must, I think, be struck more and more, the longer one lives, to find how much, in our present society, a man's life of each day depends for its solidity and value on whether he reads during that day, and, far more still, on what he reads during it. More and more he who examines himself will find the difference it makes to him, at the end of any given day, whether or no he has pursued his avocations throughout it without reading at all; and whether or no, having read something, he has read the newspapers only. This, however, is a matter for each man's private conscience and experience. If a man without books or reading, or reading nothing but his letters and the newspapers, gets nevertheless a fresh and free play of the best thoughts upon his stock notions and habits, he has got culture. He has got that for which we prize and recommend culture; he has got that which at the present moment we seek culture that it may give us. This inward operation is the very life and essence of

From Arnold, M., *Culture and Anarchy*, Cambridge University Press, London, 1932, pp. 6–7, 68–71, 76–7, 80–82, 106–9, 206–7.

culture, as we conceive it. Nevertheless, it is not easy so to frame one's discourse concerning the operation of culture, as to avoid giving frequent occasion to a misunderstanding whereby the essential inwardness of the operation is lost sight of.

[...]

Culture [...] has one great passion, the passion for sweetness and light. It has one even yet greater! – the passion for making them *prevail*. It is not satisfied till we *all* come to a perfect man; it knows that the sweetness and light of the few must be imperfect until the raw and unkindled masses of humanity are touched with sweetness and light. If I have not shrunk from saying that we must work for sweetness and light, so neither have I shrunk from saying that we must have a broad basis, must have sweetness and light for as many as possible. Again and again I have insisted how those are the happy moments of humanity, how those are the marking epochs of a people's life, how those are the flowering times for literature and art and all the creative power of genius, when there is a *national* glow of life and thought, when the whole of society is in the fullest measure permeated by thought, sensible to beauty, intelligent and alive. Only it must be *real* thought and *real* beauty; *real* sweetness and *real* light. Plenty of people will try to give the masses, as they call them, an intellectual food prepared and adapted in the way they think proper for the actual condition of the masses. The ordinary popular literature is an example of this way of working on the masses. Plenty of people will try to indoctrinate the masses with the set of ideas and judgments constituting the creed of their own profession or party. Our religious and political organisations give an example of this way of working on the masses. I condemn neither way; but culture works differently. It does not try to teach down to the level of inferior classes; it does not try to win them for this or that sect of its own, with ready-made judgments and watchwords. It seeks to do away with classes; to make the best that has been thought and known in the world current everywhere; to make all men live in an atmosphere of sweetness and light, where they may use ideas, as it uses them itself, freely – nourished and not bound by them.

This is the *social idea*; and the men of culture are the true apostles of equality. The great men of culture are those who have had a passion for diffusing, for making prevail, for carrying from one end of society to the other, the best knowledge, the best ideas of their time; who have laboured to divest knowledge of all that was harsh, uncouth, difficult, abstract, professional, exclusive; to humanise it, to make it efficient outside the clique of the cultivated and learned, yet still remaining the *best* knowledge and thought of the time, and a true source, therefore, of sweetness and light.

[...]

For a long time, [...] the strong feudal habits of subordination and deference continued to tell upon the working class. The modern spirit has now almost entirely dissolved those habits, and the anarchical tendency of our worship of freedom in and for itself, of our superstitious faith, as I say, in machinery, is becoming very manifest. More and more, because of this our blind faith in machinery, because of our want of light to enable us to look beyond machinery to the end for which machinery is valuable, this and that man, and this and that body of men, all over the country, are beginning to assert and put in practice an Englishman's right to do what he likes; his right to march where he likes, meet where he likes, enter where he likes, hoot as he likes, threaten as he likes, smash as he likes. All this, I say, tends to anarchy [.]

[. . .]

He [the Hyde Park rough] has no visionary schemes of revolution and trans-formation, though of course he would like his class to rule, as the aristocratic class like their class to rule, and the middle class theirs. But meanwhile our social machine is a little out of order; there are a good many people in our paradisiacal centres of industrialism and individualism taking the bread out of one another's mouths. The rough has not yet quite found his groove and settled down to his work, and so he is just asserting his personal liberty a little, going where he likes, assembling where he likes, bawling as he likes, hustling as he likes. Just as the rest of us, – as the country squires in the aristocratic class, as the political dissenters in the middle class, – he has no idea of a *State*, of the nation in its collective and corporate character controlling, as government, the free swing of this or that one of its members in the name of the higher reason of all of them, his own as well as that of others. He sees the rich, the aristocratic class, in occupation of the executive government, and so if he is stopped from making Hyde Park a bear-garden or the streets impassable, he says he is being butchered by the aristocracy.

His apparition is somewhat embarrassing, because too many cooks spoil the broth; because, while the aristocratic and middle classes have long been doing as they like with great vigour, he has been too undeveloped and submissive hitherto to join in the game; and now, when he does come, he comes in immense numbers, and is rather raw and rough. But he does not break many laws, or not many at one time; and, as our laws were made for very different circumstances from our present (but always with an eye to Englishmen doing as they like) [.]

[. . .]

[Moreover] it is evident our laws give our playful giant, in doing as he likes, considerable advantage. [. . .] So he has his way, and if he has his way he is soon satisfied for the time. However, he falls into the habit of taking it oftener and oftener, and at last begins to create by his operations a confusion of which mischievous people can take advantage, and which at any rate, by troubling the common course of business throughout the country, tends to cause distress, and so to increase the sort of anarchy and social disintegration which had previously commenced. And thus that profound sense of settled order and security, without which a society like ours cannot live and grow at all, sometimes seems to be beginning to threaten us with taking its departure.

Now, if culture, which simply means trying to perfect oneself, and one's mind as part of oneself, brings us light, and if light shows us that there is nothing so very blessed in merely doing as one likes, that the worship of the mere freedom to do as one likes is worship of machinery, that the really blessed thing is to like what right reason ordains, and to follow her authority, then we have got a practical benefit out of culture. We have got a much wanted principle, a principle of authority, to counteract the tendency to anarchy which seems to be threatening us.

[. . .]

[Arnold redefines the aristocracy as Barbarians, and the middle class and labour aristocracy as Philistines.] But that vast portion, lastly, of the working class which, raw and half-developed, has long lain half-hidden amidst its poverty and squalor, and is now issuing from its hiding-place to assert an Englishman's heaven-born privilege of doing as he likes, and is beginning to perplex us by marching where it likes, meeting where it likes, bawling what it likes, breaking what it likes, – to this vast residuum we may with great propriety give the name of *Populace*.

[. . .]

And as to the Populace, who, whether he be Barbarian or Philistine, can look at them without sympathy, when he remembers how often, – every time that we snatch up a vehement opinion in ignorance and passion, every time that we long to crush an adversary by sheer violence, every time that we are envious, every time that we are brutal, every time that we adore mere power or success, every time that we add our voice to swell a blind clamour against some unpopular personage, every time that we trample savagely on the fallen, – he has found in his own bosom the eternal spirit of the Populace, and that there needs only a little help from circumstances to make it triumph in him untameably? [. . .] All of us, so far as we are Barbarians, Philistines, or Populace, imagine happiness to consist in doing what one's ordinary self likes. What one's ordinary self likes differs according to the class to which one belongs, and has its severer and its lighter side; always, however, remaining machinery, and nothing more. The graver self of the Barbarian likes honours and consideration; his more relaxed self, field-sports and pleasure. The graver self of one kind of Philistine likes fanaticism, business, and money-making; his more relaxed self, comfort and tea-meetings. Of another kind of Philistine, the graver self likes rattening; the relaxed self, deputations, or hearing Mr Odger speak. The sterner self of the Populace likes bawling, hustling, and smashing; the lighter self, beer. But in each class there are born a certain number of natures with a curiosity about their best self, with a bent for seeing things as they are, for disentangling themselves from machinery, for simply concerning themselves with reason and the will of God, and doing their best to make these prevail; – for the pursuit, in a word, of perfection.

[. . .]

Natures with this bent emerge in all classes, – among the Barbarians, among the

Philistines, among the Populace. And this bent always tends to make them out of their class, and to make their distinguishing characteristic not their Barbarianism or their Philistinism, but their *humanity*.

[. . .]

Therefore, when we speak of ourselves as divided into Barbarians, Philistines, and Populace, we must be understood always to imply that within each of these classes there are a certain number of *aliens*, if we may so call them, – persons who are mainly led, not by their class spirit, but by a general *humane* spirit, by the love of human perfection; and that this number is capable of being diminished or augmented. I mean, the number of those who will succeed in developing this happy instinct will be greater or smaller, in proportion both to the force of the original instinct within them, and to the hindrance or encouragement which it meets with from without. In almost all who have it, it is mixed with some infusion of the spirit of an ordinary self, some quantity of class-instinct, and even, as has been shown, of more than one class-instinct at the same time; so that, in general, the extrication of the best self, the predominance of the *humane* instinct, will very much depend upon its meeting, or not, with what is fitted to help and elicit it.

[. . .]

And so we bring to an end what we had to say in praise of culture, and in evidence of its special utility for the circumstances in which we find ourselves, and the confusion which environs us. Through culture seems to lie our way, not only to perfection, but even to safety.

[. . .]

[Culture teaches that] the framework of society, that theatre on which this august drama has to unroll itself, is sacred; and whoever administers it, and however we may seek to remove them from their tenure of administration, yet, while they administer, we steadily and with undivided heart support them in repressing anarchy and disorder; because without order there can be no society, and without society there can be no human perfection.

With me, indeed, this rule of conduct is hereditary. I remember my father, in one of his unpublished letters written more than forty years ago, when the political and social state of the country was gloomy and troubled, and there were riots in many places, goes on, after strongly insisting on the badness and foolishness of the government, and on the harm and dangerousness of our feudal and aristocratical constitution of society, and ends thus: 'As for rioting, the old Roman way of dealing with *that* is always the right one; flog the rank and file, and fling the ringleaders from the Tarpeian Rock!' And this opinion we can never forsake, however our Liberal friends may think a little rioting, and that they call popular demonstrations, useful sometimes to their own interests and to the interests of the valuable practical operations they have in hand[.] [. . .] And even when they artfully show us operations which are undoubtedly precious, such as the abolition of the slave-trade, and ask us if, for their sake, foolish and obstinate governments may not wholesomely be frightened by a little disturbance, the good design in view and the difficulty of overcoming opposition to it being considered, – still we say no, and that monster processions in the streets and forcible irruptions into the parks, even in professed support of this good design, ought to be unflinchingly forbidden and repressed; and that far more is lost than is gained by permitting them.

Because a State in which law is authoritative and sovereign, a firm and settled course of public order, is requisite if man is to bring to maturity anything precious and lasting now, or to found anything precious and lasting for the future.

Thus, in our eyes, the very framework and exterior order of the State, whoever may administer the State, is sacred; and culture is the most resolute enemy of anarchy, because of the great hopes and designs for the State which culture teaches us to nourish. But as, believing in right reason, and having faith in the progress of humanity towards perfection, and ever labouring for this end, we grow to have clearer sight of the ideas of right reason, and of the elements and helps of perfection, and come gradually to fill the framework of the State with them, to fashion its internal composition and all its laws and institutions conformably to them, and to make the State more and more the expression, as we say, of our best self, which is not manifold, and vulgar, and unstable, and contentious, and ever-varying, but one, and noble, and secure, and peaceful, and the same for all mankind, – with what aversion shall we not *then* regard anarchy, with what firmness shall we not check it, when there is so much that is so precious which it will endanger!

[. . .]

Therefore, however great the changes to be accomplished, and however dense the array of Barbarians, Philistines, and Populace, we will neither despair on the one hand, nor, on the other, threaten violent revolution and change. But we will look forward cheerfully and hopefully to 'a revolution', as the Duke of Wellington said, 'by due course of law'; though not exactly such laws as our Liberal friends are now, with their actual lights, fond of offering to us.

2 □ *Mass Civilisation and Minority Culture*

F. R. Leavis

> And this function is particularly important in our modern
> world, of which the whole civilisation is, to a much greater
> degree than the civilisation of Greece and Rome, mechanical
> and external, and tends constantly to become more so.
>
> (*Culture and Anarchy*, 1869)

For Matthew Arnold it was in some ways less difficult. I am not thinking of the so much more desperate plight of culture today,[1] but (it is not, at bottom, an unrelated consideration) of the freedom with which he could use such phrases as 'the will of God' and 'our true selves'. Today one must face problems of definition and formulation where Arnold could pass lightly on. When, for example, having started by saying that culture has always been in minority keeping, I am asked what I mean by 'culture', I might (and do) refer the reader to *Culture and Anarchy*; but I know that something more is required.

In any period it is often a very small minority that the discerning appreciation of art and literature depends: it is (apart from cases of the simple and familiar) only a few who are capable of unprompted, first-hand judgment. They are still a small minority, though a larger one, who are capable of endorsing such first-hand judgment by genuine personal response. The accepted valuations are a kind of paper currency based upon a very small proportion of gold. To the state of such a currency the possibilities of fine living at any time bear a close relation. There is no need to elaborate the metaphor: the nature of the relation is suggested well enough by this passage from Mr I. A. Richards, which should by now be a *locus classicus*:

> But it is not true that criticism is a luxury trade. The rearguard of Society cannot be extricated until the vanguard has gone further. Goodwill and intelligence are still too

From Leavis, F. R.. *Mass Civilisation and Minority Culture*, Minority Press, Cambridge, 1930, pp. 3–30.

little available. The critic, we have said, is as much concerned with the health of the mind as any doctor with the health of the body. To set up as a critic is to set up as a judge of values. . . . For the arts are inevitably and quite apart from any intentions of the artist an appraisal of existence. Matthew Arnold, when he said that poetry is a criticism of life, was saying something so obvious that it is constantly overlooked. The artist is concerned with the record and perpetuation of the experiences which seem to him most worth having. For reasons which we shall consider . . . he is also the man who is most likely to have experiences of value to record. He is the point at which the growth of the mind shows itself.[2]

This last sentence gives the hint for another metaphor. The minority capable not only of appreciating Dante, Shakespeare, Donne, Baudelaire, Hardy (to take major instances) but of recognising their latest successors constitute the consciousness of the race (or of a branch of it) at a given time. For such capacity does not belong merely to an isolated aesthetic realm: it implies responsiveness to theory as well as to art, to science and philosophy in so far as these may affect the sense of the human situation and of the nature of life. Upon this minority depends our power of profiting by the finest human experience of the past; they keep alive the subtlest and most perishable parts of tradition. Upon them depend the implicit standards that order the finer living of an age, the sense that this is worth more than that, this rather than that is the direction in which to go, that the centre[3] is here rather than there. In their keeping, to use a metaphor that is metonymy also and will bear a good deal of pondering, is the language, the changing idiom, upon which fine living depends, and without which distinction of spirit is thwarted and incoherent. By 'culture' I mean the use of such a language. I do not suppose myself to have produced a tight definition, but the account, I think, will be recognised as adequate by anyone who is likely to read this pamphlet.

It is a commonplace today that culture is at a crisis. It is a commonplace more widely accepted than understood: at any rate, realisation of what the crisis portends does not seem to be common. [. . .]

It seems, then, not unnecessary to restate the obvious. In support of the belief that the modern phase of human history is unprecedented it is enough to point to the machine. The machine, in the first place, has brought about change in habit and the circumstances of life at a rate for which we have no parallel. The effects of such change may be studied in *Middletown*, a remarkable work of anthropology, dealing (I am afraid it is not superfluous to say) with a typical community of the Middle West. There we see in detail how the automobile (to take one instance) has, in a few years, radically affected religion,[4] broken up the family, and revolutionised social custom. Change has been so catastrophic that the generations find it hard to adjust themselves to each other, and parents are helpless to deal with their children. It seems unlikely that the conditions of life can be transformed in this way without some injury to the standard of living (to wrest the phrase from the economist): improvisation can hardly replace the delicate traditional adjustments, the mature. inherited codes of habit and valuation, without severe loss, and loss that may be more than temporary. It is a breach in continuity that threatens: what has been inadvertently dropped may be irrecoverable or forgotten.

To this someone will reply that Middletown is America and not England. And it is true that in America change has been more rapid, and its effects have been intensified by the fusion of peoples. But the same processes are at work in England and the Western world generally, and at an acceleration. It is a commonplace that we are being Americanised, but again a commonplace that seems, as a rule, to carry little understanding with it. Americanisation is often spoken of as if it were something of which the United States are guilty. But it is something from which Lord Melchett, our 'British-speaking'[5] champion, will not save us even if he succeeds in rallying us to meet that American enterprise which he fears, 'may cause us to lose a great structure of self-governing brotherhoods whose common existence is of infinite importance to the future continuance of the Anglo-Saxon race, and of the gravest import to the development of all that seems best in our modern civilisation.'[6] For those who are most defiant of America do not propose to reverse the processes consequent upon the machine. We are to have greater efficiency, better salesmanship, and more mass-production and standardisation. Now, if the worst effects of mass-production and standardisation were represented by Woolworth's there would be no need to despair. But there are effects that touch the life of the community more seriously. When we consider, for instance, the processes of mass-production and standardisation in the form represented by the Press, it becomes obviously of sinister significance that they should be accompanied by a process of levelling-down.

[. . .]

It applies even more disastrously to the films: more disastrously, because the films have a so much more potent influence.[7] They provide now the main form of recreation in the civilised world; and they involve surrender, under conditions of hypnotic receptivity, to the cheapest emotional appeals, appeals the more insidious because they are associated with a compellingly vivid illusion of actual life. It would be difficult to dispute that the result must be serious damage to the 'standard of living' (to use the phrase as before). All this seems so obvious that one is diffident about insisting on it. And yet people will reply by adducing the attempts that have been made to use the film as a serious medium of art. Just as, when broadcasting is in question, they will point out that they have heard good music broadcasted and intelligent lectures. The standardising influence of broadcasting hardly admits of doubt, but since there is here no Hollywood engaged in purely commercial exploitation the levelling-down is not so obvious. But perhaps it will not be disputed that broadcasting, like the films, is in practice mainly a means of passive diversion, and that it tends to make active recreation, especially active use of the mind, more difficult.[8] And such agencies are only a beginning. The near future holds rapid developments in store.

Contemplating this deliberate exploitation of the cheap response which characterises our civilisation we may say that a new factor in history is an unprecedented use of applied psychology. This might be thought to flatter Hollywood, but, even so, there can be no room for doubt when we consider advertising, and the progress it has made in two or three decades. (And 'advertising' may be taken to cover a great deal more than comes formally under that head.)

[. . .]

Mr Gilbert Russell, who includes in his list of books for 'A Copy Writer's Bookshelf' the works of Shakespeare, the Bible, *The Forsyte Saga*, *The Oxford Book of English Verse*, *Fiery Particles* by C. E. Montague and Sir Arthur Quiller-Couch's *The Art of Writing*, tells us that:

> Competent copy cannot be written except by men who have read lovingly, who have a sense of the romance of words, and of the picturesque and the dramatic phrase; who have versatility enough and judgment enough to know how to write plainly and pungently, or with a certain affectation. Briefly, competent copy is a matter not only of literary skill of a rather high order, but also skill of a particular specialised kind.

The influence of such skill is to be seen in contemporary fiction. For if, as Mr Thomas Russell (author of 'What did you do in the Great War, daddy?'), tells us, 'English is the best language in the world for advertising', advertising is doing a great deal for English. It is carrying on the work begun by Mr Rudyard Kipling, and, where certain important parts of the vocabulary are concerned, making things more difficult for the fastidious. For what is taking place is not something that affects only the environment of culture, stops short, as it were, at the periphery. This should be obvious, but it does not appear to be so to many who would recognise the account I have given above as matter of commonplace. Even those who would agree that there has been an overthrow of standards, that authority has disappeared, and that the currency has been debased and inflated, do not often seem to realise what the catastrophe portends. My aim is to bring this home, if possible, by means of a little concrete evidence. I hope, at any rate, to avert the charge of extravagant pessimism.

[. . .]

In the *Advertisement* to the first edition of *Lyrical Ballads* I light on this:

> An accurate taste in poetry, as in all other arts, Sir Joshua Reynolds has observed, is an acquired talent, which can only be produced by severe thought, and a long continued intercourse with the best models of composition.

When Wordsworth wrote that, severe thought and long-continued intercourse with the best models were more widely possible than now. What distractions have come to beset the life of the mind since then! There seems every reason to believe that the average cultivated person of a century ago was a very much more competent reader than his modern representative. Not only does the modern dissipate himself upon so much more reading of all kinds: the task of acquiring discrimination is much more difficult. A reader who grew up with Wordsworth moved among a limited set of signals (so to speak): the variety was not overwhelming. So he was able to acquire discrimination as he went along. But the modern is exposed to a concourse of signals so bewildering in their variety and number that, unless he is especially gifted or especially favoured, he can hardly begin to discriminate. Here we have the plight of culture in general. The landmarks have shifted, multiplied and crowded upon one another, the distinctions and dividing lines have blurred away, the boundaries are gone, and the arts and literatures of different countries and periods have flowed together, so that, if we revert to the metaphor of 'language' for culture, we may, to describe it, adapt the sentence in which Mr T. S. Eliot describes the intellectual situation: 'When there is so much to be known, when there are so many fields of knowledge in which the same words are used with different meanings, when every one knows a little about a great many things, it becomes increasingly difficult for anyone to know whether he knows what he is talking about or not.'

[...]

The critically adult public, then, is very small indeed: they are a very small minority who are capable of fending for themselves amid the smother of new books.

[...]

The reader must have a great deal more done for him. Again we have to learn from America: the problem has been solved there by the Book of Month Club and similar organisations. The problem is now rapidly being solved here, where The Book Society has already been followed by The Book Guild.

> 'Out of the thousands of books published every year,' writes Miss Ethel Mannin for the Book Guild, '– there are between 12,000 and 14,000 – how on earth is the ordinary person to sift the sheep from the goats? Distinguished critics attempt to guide the public, but they are often so hopelessly 'high brow' and 'precious,' and simply add to the general confusion and bewilderment.
>
> When the aims of The Book Guild were explained to me, therefore, it seemed too good to be true – an organisation which would cater *for the ordinary intelligent reader*, not for the highbrows – an organisation which would realise that *a book can have a good story and a popular appeal and yet be good literature* – be good literature and yet be absorbingly interesting, of the kind you can't put down once you've started, an organisation which would not recommend a book as a work of genius simply because it had been eulogised by some pedantic critic or other, but which would conscientiously sift really good stuff out of the mass of the affected and pretentious which is just as tiresome as the blatantly third rate.

[...]

[T]he attitude behind the word 'high-brow' is exhibited with commendable guilessness by Mr George A. Birmingham (Canon Hannay) of The Book Guild. This reverend gentleman writes in *The Book Guild Bulletin* for July 14, 1930:

> The detective novel writers have their own clientele, though they make no appeal to the young ladies who throng the counters of Boots' libraries and but little to the sheep-like crowd who follow the dictates of high-brow literary critics.

Lest the point should be missed he repeats it:

> ...not food for the Messrs Boots' young ladies or for the literary sheep whom I have already mentioned.

[...]

'High-brow' is an ominous addition to the English language. I have said earlier that culture has always been in minority keeping. But the minority now is made conscious, not merely of an uncongenial, but of a hostile environment. 'Shakespeare', I once heard Mr Dover Wilson say, 'was not a high-brow.' True: there were no 'high-brows' in Shakespeare's time. It was possible for Shakespeare to write plays that were at once popular drama and poetry that could be appreciated only by an educated minority. *Hamlet* appealed at a number of levels of response, from the highest downwards. The same is true of *Paradise Lost*, *Clarissa*, *Tom Jones*, *Don Juan*, *The Return of the Native*. The same is not true, Mr George A. Birmingham might point out, of *The Waste Land*, *Hugh Selwyn Mauberley*, *Ulysses* or *To the Lighthouse*. These works are read only by a very small specialised public and are beyond the reach of the vast majority of those who consider themselves educated. The age in which the finest creative talent tends to be employed in works of this kind is the age that has given currency to the term 'high-brow'. But it would be as true to say that the attitude implicit in 'high-brow' causes this use of talent as the converse. The minority is being cut off as never before from the powers that rule the world; and as Mr George A. Birmingham and his friends succeed in refining and standardising and conferring authority upon 'the taste of the bathos implanted by nature in the literary judgments of man' (to use Matthew Arnold's phrase), they will make it more and more inevitable that work expressing the finest consciousness of the age should be so specialised as to be accessible only to the minority.

'Civilisation' and 'culture' are coming to be antithetical terms. It is not merely that the power and the sense of authority are now divorced from culture, but that some of the most disinterested solicitude for civilisation is apt to be, consciously or unconsciously, inimical to culture.

[...]

The prospects of culture, then, are very dark. There is the less room for hope in that a standardised civilisation is rapidly enveloping the whole world. The glimpse of Russia that is permitted us does not afford the comfort that we are sometimes invited to find there. Anyone who has seen Eisenstein's film, *The General Line*, will appreciate the comment made by a writer in the *New Republic* (June 4, 1930), comparing it with an American film:

> One fancies, thinking about these things, that America might well send *The Silent Enemy* to Russia and say, 'This is what living too long with too much machinery does to people. Think twice, before you commit yourselves irrevocably to the same course.'

But it is vain to resist the triumph of the machine. It is equally vain to console us with the promise of a 'mass culture' that shall be utterly new. It would, no doubt, be possible to argue that such a 'mass culture' might be better than the culture we are losing, but it would be futile: the 'utterly new' surrenders everything that can interest us.[9]

What hope, then, is there left to offer? The vague hope that recovery *must* come, somehow, in spite of all? Mr I. A. Richards, whose opinion is worth more than most people's, seems to authorise hope: he speaks of 'reasons for thinking that this century is in a cultural trough rather than upon a crest'; and says that 'the situation is likely to get worse before it is better'.[10] 'Once the basic level has been reached,' he suggests, 'a slow climb back may be possible. That at least is a hope that may be reasonably entertained.'[11] But it is a hope that looks very desperate in face of the downward acceleration described above, and it does not seem to point to any factor that might be counted upon to reverse the process.

Are we then to listen to Spengler's[12] (and Mr Henry Ford's[13]) admonition to cease bothering about the inevitable future? That is impossible. Ridiculous, priggish and presumptuous as it may be, if we care at all about the issues we cannot help believing that, for the immediate future, at any rate, we have some responsibility. We cannot help clinging to some such hope as Mr Richards offers; to the belief (unwarranted, possibly) that what we value most matters too much to the race to be finally abandoned, and that the machine will yet be made a tool.

It is for us to be as aware as possible of what is happening, and, if we can, to 'keep open our communications with the future'.

Notes

1. 'The word, again, which we children of God speak, the voice which most hits our collective thought, the newspaper with the largest circulation in England, nay with the largest circulation in the whole world, is the *Daily Telegraph*!' – *Culture and Anarchy*.
   It is the *News of the World* that has the largest circulation today.
2. *The Principles of Literary Criticism*, p. 61.
3. '...the mass of the public is without any suspicion that the value of these organs is relative to their being nearer a certain ideal centre of correct information, taste and intelligence, or farther away from it.' – *Culture and Anarchy*.
4. 'One gains a distinct impression that the religious basis of all education was more taken for granted if less talked about thirty-five years ago, when high school "chapel" was a

religio-inspirational service with a "choir" instead of the "pep session" which it tends to become to-day.' *Middletown*, by R. S. and H. M. Lynd, p. 204. This kind of change, of course, is not due to the automobile alone.

5. 'That would be one of the greatest disasters to the British-speaking people, and one of the greatest disasters to civilisation.' – Lord Melchett, *Industry and Politics*, p. 278.

6. *Ibid.*, p. 281.

7. 'The motion picture, by virtue of its intrinsic nature, is a species of amusing and informational Esperanto, and, potentially at least, a species of aesthetic Esperanto of all the arts; if it may be classified as one, the motion picture has in it, perhaps more than any other, the resources of universality. . . . The motion picture tells its stories directly, simply, quickly and elementally, not in words but in pictorial pantomime. To see is not only to believe; it is also in a measure to understand. In theatrical drama, seeing is closely allied with hearing, and hearing, in turn, with mental effort. In the motion picture, seeing is all – or at least nine-tenths of all.' – *Encyclopaedia Britannica*, 14th edn – 'Motion Pictures: A Universal Language'.

   The *Encyclopaedia Britannica*, fourteenth edition, is itself evidence of what is happening: 'humanised, modernised, pictorialised', as the editors announce.

8. Mr Edgar Rice Burroughs (creator of Tarzan), in a letter that I have been privileged to see, writes: 'It has been discovered through repeated experiments that pictures that require thought for appreciation have invariably been box-office failures. The general public does not wish to think. This fact, probably more than any other, accounts for the success of my stories, for without this specific idea in mind I have, nevertheless, endeavoured to make all of my descriptions so clear that each situation could be visualised readily by any reader precisely as I saw it. My reason for doing this was not based upon a low estimate of general intelligence, but upon the realisation that in improbable situations, such as abound in my work, the greatest pains must be taken to make them appear plausible. I have evolved, therefore, a type of fiction that may be read with the minimum of mental effort.' The significance of this for my argument does not need comment. Mr Burroughs adds that his books sell at over a million copies a year. There is not room here to make the comparisons suggested by such documents as the *Life of James Lackington* (1791).

9. '. . . indeed, this gentleman, taking the bull by the horns, proposes that we should for the future call industrialism culture, and then of course there can be no longer any misapprehension of their true character; and besides the pleasure of being wealthy and comfortable, they will have authentic recognition as vessels of sweetness and light.' – *Culture and Anarchy*.

10. *Practical Criticism*, p. 320.

11. *Ibid.*, p. 249.

12. 'Up to now everyone has been at liberty to hope what he pleased about the future. Where there are no facts, sentiment rules. But henceforward it will be every man's business to inform himself of what *can* happen and therefore of what with the unalterable necessity of destiny and irrespective of personal ideals, hopes or desires, *will* happen.' – *The Decline of the West*, vol. I, p. 39.

13. 'But what of the future? Shall we not have over-production? Shall we not some day reach a point where the machine becomes all powerful, and the man of no consequence?

   No man can say anything of the future. We need not bother about it. The future has always cared for itself in spite of our well-meant efforts to hamper it. If to-day we do the task we can best do, then we are doing all that we can do.

Perhaps we may over-produce, but that is impossible until the whole world has all its desires. And if that should happen, then surely we ought to be content.' – Henry Ford, *To-day and To-morrow*, pp. 272–3.

3 □ A Theory of Mass Culture

Dwight Macdonald

For about a century, Western culture has really been two cultures: the traditional kind – let us call it 'High Culture' – that is chronicled in the textbooks, and a 'Mass Culture' manufactured wholesale for the market. In the old art forms, the artisans of Mass Culture have long been at work: in the novel, the line stretches from Eugène Sue to Lloyd C. Douglas; in music, from Offenbach to Tin-Pan Alley; in art from the chromo to Maxfield Parrish and Norman Rockwell; in architecture, from Victorian Gothic to suburban Tudor. Mass Culture has also developed new media of its own, into which the serious artist rarely ventures: radio, the movies, comic books, detective stories, science fiction, television.

It is sometimes called 'Popular Culture',[1] but I think 'Mass Culture' a more accurate term, since its distinctive mark is that it is solely and directly an article for mass consumption, like chewing gum. A work of High Culture is occasionally popular, after all, though this is increasingly rare. Thus Dickens was even more popular than his contemporary, G. A. Henty, the difference being that he was an artist, communicating his individual vision to other individuals, while Henty was an impersonal manufacturer of an impersonal commodity for the masses.

The Nature of Mass Culture

The historical reasons for the growth of Mass Culture since the early 1800s are well known. Political democracy and popular education broke down the old upper-class monopoly of culture. Business enterprise found a profitable market in the cultural demands of the newly awakened masses, and the advance of technology made possible the cheap production of books, periodicals, pictures, music, and furniture, in sufficient quantities to satisfy this market. Modern technology also created new

From Rosenberg, B. and White, D. W. (eds), *Mass Culture: The popular arts in America*, Macmillan, New York, 1957, pp. 59–73.

media such as the movies and television which are specially well adapted to mass manufacture and distribution.

The phenomenon is thus peculiar to modern times and differs radically from what was hitherto known as art or culture. It is true that Mass Culture began as, and to some extent still is, a parasitic, a cancerous growth on High Culture. As Clement Greenberg pointed out in 'Avant-garde and *kitsch*' (*Partisan Review*, Fall, 1939): 'The precondition of *kitsch* (a German term for "Mass Culture") is the availability close at hand of a fully matured cultural tradition, whose discoveries, acquisitions, and perfected self-conscious *kitsch* can take advantage of for its own ends.' The connection, however, is not that of the leaf and the branch but rather that of the caterpillar and the leaf. *Kitsch* 'mines' High Culture the way improvident frontiersmen mine the soil, extracting its riches and putting nothing back. Also, as *kitsch* develops, it begins to draw on its own past, and some of it evolves so far away from High Culture as to appear quite disconnected from it.

It is also true that Mass Culture is to some extent a continuation of the old Folk Art which until the Industrial Revolution was the culture of the common people, but here, too, the differences are more striking than the similarities. Folk Art grew from below. It was a spontaneous, autochthonous expression of the people, shaped by themselves, pretty much without the benefit of High Culture, to suit their own needs. Mass Culture is imposed from above. It is fabricated by technicians hired by businessmen; its audiences are passive consumers, their participation limited to the choice between buying and not buying. The Lords of *kitsch*, in short, exploit the cultural needs of the masses in order to make a profit and/or to maintain their class rule – in Communist countries, only the second purpose obtains. (It is very different to *satisfy* popular tastes, as Robert Burns' poetry did, and to *exploit* them, as Hollywood does.) Folk Art was the people's own institution, their private little garden walled off from the great formal park of their masters' High Culture. But Mass Culture breaks down the wall, integrating the masses into a debased form of High Culture and thus becoming an instrument of political domination. If one had no other data to go on, the nature of Mass Culture would reveal capitalism to be an exploitative class society and not the harmonious commonwealth it is sometimes alleged to be. The same goes even more strongly for Soviet Communism and *its* special kind of Mass Culture.

Mass Culture: USSR

'Everybody' knows that America is a land of Mass Culture, but it is not so generally recognized that so is the Soviet Union. Certainly not by the Communist leaders, one of whom has contemptuously observed that the American people need not fear the peace-loving Soviet state which has absolutely no desire to deprive them of their Coca-Cola and comic books. Yet the fact is that the USSR is even more a land of Mass Culture than is the USA. This is less easily recognizable because their Mass Culture is *in form* just the opposite of ours, being one of propaganda and pedagogy rather than of entertainment. None the less, it has the essential quality of Mass, as against High or Folk, Culture: it is manufactured for mass consumption by technicians employed by the ruling class and is not an expression of either the individual artist or the common people themselves. Like our own, it exploits rather than satisfies the cultural needs of the masses, though for political rather than commercial reasons. Its quality is even lower: our Supreme Court building is tasteless and pompous, but not to the lunatic degree of the proposed new Palace of the Soviets – a huge wedding cake of columns mounting up to an eighty-foot statue of Lenin; Soviet movies are so much duller and cruder than our own that even the American comrades shun them; the childish level of *serious* Soviet magazines devoted to matters of art or philosophy has to be read to be believed, and as for the popular press, it is as if Colonel McCormick ran every periodical in America.

Gresham's Law in Culture

The separation of Folk Art and High Culture in fairly watertight compartments corresponded to the sharp line once drawn between the common people and the aristocracy. The eruption of the masses on to the political stage has broken down this compartmentation, with disastrous cultural results. Whereas Folk Art had its own special quality, Mass Culture is at best a vulgarized reflection of High Culture. And whereas High Culture could formerly ignore the mob and seek to please only the *cognoscenti*, it must now compete with Mass Culture or be merged into it.

The problem is acute in the United States and not just because a prolific Mass Culture exists here. If there were a clearly defined cultural elite, then the masses could have their *kitsch* and the elite could have its High Culture, with everybody happy. But the boundary line is blurred. A statistically significant part of the population, I venture to guess, is chronically confronted with a choice between going to the movies or to a concert, between reading Tolstoy or a detective story, between looking at old masters or at a TV show; i.e. the pattern of their cultural lives is 'open' to the point of being porous. Good art competes with *kitsch*, serious ideas compete with commercialized formulae – and the advantage lies all on one side. There seems to be a Gresham's Law in cultural as well as monetary circulation: bad stuff drives out the good, since it is more easily understood and enjoyed. It is this facility of access which at once sells *kitsch* on a wide market and also prevents it from achieving quality.[2] Clement Greenberg writes that the special aesthetic quality of *kitsch* is that it 'predigests art for the spectator and spares him effort, provides him with a shortcut to the pleasures of art that detours what is necessarily difficult in genuine art' because it includes the spectator's reactions in the work of art itself instead of forcing him to make his own responses. Thus 'Eddie Guest and the Indian Love Lyrics are more "poetic" than T. S. Eliot and Shakespeare.' And so, too, our 'collegiate Gothic' such as the Harkness Quadrangle at Yale is more picturesquely Gothic than Chartres, and a pinup girl smoothly airbrushed by Petty is more sexy than a real naked woman.

When to this ease of consumption is added *kitsch*'s ease of production because of its standardized nature, its prolific growth is easy to understand. It threatens High Culture by its sheer pervasiveness, its brutal, overwhelming *quantity*. The upper classes, who begin by using it to make money from the crude tastes of the masses and to dominate them politically, end by finding their own culture attacked and even threatened with destruction by the instrument they have thoughtlessly employed. (The same irony may be observed in modern politics, where most swords seem to have two edges; thus Nazism began as a tool of the big bourgeoisie and the army *Junkers* but ended by using *them* as *its* tools.)

Homogenized Culture

Like nineteenth-century capitalism, Mass Culture is a dynamic, revolutionary force, breaking down the old barriers of class, tradition, taste, and dissolving all cultural distinctions. It mixes and scrambles everything together, producing what might be called homogenized culture, after another American achievement, the homogenization process that distributes the globules of cream evenly throughout the milk instead of allowing them to float separately on top. It thus destroys all values, since value judgments imply discrimination. Mass Culture is very, very democratic: it absolutely refuses to discriminate against, or between, anything or anybody. All is grist to its mill, and all comes out finely ground indeed.

Consider *Life*, a typical homogenized mass-circulation magazine. It appears on the mahogany library tables of the rich, the glass end-tables of the middle-class and the oilcloth-covered kitchen tables of the poor. Its contents are as thoroughly homogenized as its circulation. The same issue will contain a serious exposition of atomic theory alongside a disquisition on Rita Hayworth's love life; photos of starving Korean children picking garbage from the ruins of Pusan and of sleek models wearing adhesive brassieres; an editorial hailing Bertrand Russell on his eightieth birthday ('A GREAT MIND IS STILL ANNOYING AND ADORNING OUR AGE') across from a full-page photo of a housewife arguing with an umpire at a baseball game ('MOM GETS THUMB'); a cover announcing in the same size type 'A NEW FOREIGN POLICY, BY JOHN FOSTER DULLES' and 'KERIMA: HER MARATHON KISS IS A MOVIE SENSATION'; nine color pages of Renoirs plus a memoir by his son, followed by a full-page picture of a roller-skating horse. The advertisements, of course, provide even more scope for the editor's homogenizing talents, as when a full-page photo of a ragged Bolivian peon grinningly drunk on coca leaves (which Mr Luce's conscientious reporters tell us he chews to narcotize his chronic hunger pains) appears opposite an ad of a pretty, smiling, well-dressed American mother with her two pretty, smiling, well-dressed children (a boy and a girl, of course – children are always homogenized in American ads) looking raptly at a clown on a TV set ('RCA VICTOR BRINGS YOU A NEW KIND OF TELEVISION – SUPER SETS WITH "PICTURE POWER"'). The peon would doubtless find the juxtaposition piquant if he could afford a copy of *Life* which, fortunately for the Good Neighbor Policy, he cannot.

Academicism and Avant-gardism

Until about 1930, High Culture tried to defend itself against the encroachments of Mass Culture in two opposite ways: Academicism, or an attempt to compete by imitation; and Avant-gardism, or a withdrawal from competition.

Academicism is *kitsch* for the elite: spurious High Culture that is outwardly the real thing but actually as much a manufactured article as the cheaper cultural goods produced for the masses. It is recognized at the time for what it is only by the Avant-gardists. A generation or two later, its real nature is understood by everyone and it quietly drops into the same oblivion as its franker sister-under-the-skin. Examples are painters such as Bougereau and Rosa Bonheur, critics such as Edmund Clarence Stedman and Edmund Gosse, the Beaux-Arts school of architecture, composers such as the late Sir Edward Elgar, poets such as Stephen Phillips, and novelists such as Alphonse Daudet, Arnold Bennett, James Branch Cabell and Somerset Maugham.

The significance of the Avant-garde movement (by which I mean poets such as Rimbaud, novelists such as Joyce, composers such as Stravinsky, and painters such as Picasso) is that it simply refused to compete. Rejecting Academicism – and thus, at a second remove, also Mass Culture – it made a desperate attempt to fence off some area where the serious artist could still function. It created a new compartmentation of culture, on the basis of an intellectual rather than a social elite. The attempt was remarkably successful: to it we owe almost everything that is living in the art of the last fifty or so years. In fact, the High Culture of our times is pretty much identical with Avant-gardism. The movement came at a time (1890–1930) when bourgeois values were being challenged both culturally and politically. (In this country, the cultural challenge did not come until World War I, so that our Avant-garde flourished only in the twenties.) In the thirties the two streams mingled briefly, after each had spent its real force, under the aegis of the Communists, only to sink together at the end of the decade into the sands of the wasteland we still live in. The rise of Nazism and the revelation in the Moscow Trials of the real nature of the new society in Russia inaugurated the present period, when men cling to the evils they know rather than risk possibly greater ones by pressing forward. Nor has the chronic state of war, hot or cold, that the world has been in since 1939 encouraged rebellion or experiment in either art or politics.

A Merger Has Been Arranged

In this new period, the competitors, as often happens in the business world, are merging. Mass Culture takes on the color of both varieties of the old High Culture,

Academic and Avant-garde, while these latter are increasingly watered down with Mass elements. There is slowly emerging a tepid, flaccid Middlebrow Culture that threatens to engulf everything in its spreading ooze. Bauhaus modernism has at last trickled down, in a debased form of course, into our furniture, cafeterias, movie theatres, electric toasters, office buildings, drug stores, and railroad trains. Psycho-analysis is expounded sympathetically and superficially in popular magazines, and the psychoanalyst replaces the eccentric millionaire as the *deus ex machina* in many a movie. T. S. Eliot writes *The Cocktail Party* and it becomes a Broadway hit. (Though in some ways excellent, it is surely inferior to his *Murder in the Cathedral*, which in the unmerged thirties had to depend on WPA to get produced at all.)

The typical creator of *kitsch* today, at least in the old media, is an indeterminate specimen. There are no widely influential critics so completely terrible as, say, the last William Lyon Phelps was. Instead we have such gray creatures as Clifton Fadiman and Henry Seidel Canby. The artless numbers of an Eddie Guest are drowned out by the more sophisticated though equally commonplace strains of Benet's *John Brown's Body*. Maxfield Parrish yields to Rockwell Kent, Arthur Brisbane to Walter Lippman, Theda Bara to Ingrid Bergman. We even have what might be called *l'avant-garde pompier* (or, in American, 'phoney Avant-gardism'), as in the buildings of Raymond Hood and the later poetry of Archibald MacLeish, as there is also an academic Avant-gardism in *belles lettres* so that now the 'little' as well as the big magazines have their hack writers.

All this is not a raising of the level of Mass Culture, as might appear at first, but rather a corruption of High Culture. There is nothing more vulgar than sophisticated *kitsch*. Compare Conan Doyle's workmanlike and unpretentious Sherlock Holmes stories with the bogus 'intellectuality' of Dorothy M. Sayers, who, like many contemporary detective-story writers, is a novelist *manquée* who ruins her stuff with literary attitudinizing. Or consider the relationship of Hollywood and Broadway. In the twenties, the two were sharply differentiated, movies being produced for the masses of the hinterland, theatre for an upper-class New York audience. The theatre was High Culture, mostly of the Academic variety (Theatre Guild) but with some spark of Avant-garde fire (the 'little' or 'experimental' theatre movement). The movies were definitely Mass Culture, mostly very bad but with some leaven of Avant-gardism (Griffith, Stroheim) and Folk Art (Chaplin and other comedians). With the sound film, Broadway and Hollywood drew closer together. Plays are now produced mainly to sell the movie rights, with many being directly financed by the film companies. The merger has standardized the theatre to such an extent that even the early Theatre Guild seems vital in retrospect, while hardly a trace of the 'experimental' theatre is left. And what have the movies gained? They are more sophisticated, the acting is subtler, the sets in better taste. But they too have become standardized: they are never as awful as they often were in the old days, but they are never as good either. They are better entertainment and worse art. The cinema of the twenties occasionally gave us the fresh charm of Folk Art or the imaginative intensity of Avant-gardism. The coming of sound, and with it Broadway, degraded the camera to a recording instrument for an alien art form, the spoken play. The silent film had at least the *theoretical possibility*, even within the limits of Mass Culture, of being artistically significant. The sound film, within those limits, does not.

Division of Labor

The whole field could be approached from the standpoint of the division of labor. The more advanced technologically, the greater the division. Cf. the great Blackett-Semple-Hummert factory – the word is accurate – for the mass production of radio 'soap operas'. Or the fact that in Hollywood a composer for the movies is not *permitted* to make his own orchestrations any more than a director can do his own cutting. Or the 'editorial formula' which every big-circulation magazine tailors its fiction and articles to fit, much as automobile parts are machined in Detroit. *Time* and *Newsweek* have carried specialization to its extreme: their writers don't even sign their work, which in fact is not properly theirs, since the gathering of data is done by a specialized corps of researchers and correspondents and the final article is often as much the result of the editor's blue-pencilling and rewriting as of the original author's efforts. The '*New Yorker* short story' is a definite genre – smooth, minor-key, casual, suggesting drama and sentiment without ever being crude enough to actually create it – which the editors have established by years of patient, skilful selection the same way as a gardener develops a new kind of rose. They have, indeed, done their work all too well: would-be contributors now deluge them with lifeless imitations, and they have begun to beg writers not to follow the formula *quite* so closely.

Such art workers are as alienated from their brainwork as the industrial worker is from his handwork. The results are as bad qualitatively as they are impressive quantitatively. The only great films to come out of Hollywood, for example, were made before industrial elephantiasis had reduced the director to one of a number of technicians all operating at about the same level of authority. Our two greatest directors, Griffith and Stroheim, were artists, not specialists; they did everything themselves, dominated everything personally: the scenario, the actors, the camera work, and above all the cutting (or *montage*). Unity is essential in art; it cannot be achieved by a production line of specialists, however competent. There have been successful collective creations (Greek temples, Gothic churches, perhaps the *Iliad*) but their creators were part of a tradition which was strong enough to impose unity on their work. We have no such tradition today, and so art – as against *kitsch* – will result only when a single brain and sensibility is in full command. In the movies, only the director can even theoretically be in such a position; he was so in the pre-1930 cinema of this country, Germany, and the Soviet Union.

Griffith and Stroheim were both terrific egoists – crude, naïve, and not without charlatanry – who survived until the industry became highly enough organized to resist their vigorous personalities. By about 1925, both were outside looking in; the manufacture of commodities so costly to make and so profitable to sell was too serious a matter to be entrusted to artists.

'One word of advice, Von,' Griffith said to Stroheim, who had been his assistant on *Intolerance*, when Stroheim came to him with the news that he had a chance to make a picture himself. 'Make your pictures in your own way. Put your mark on them. Take a stand and stick to your guns. You'll make some enemies, but you'll make good pictures.' Could that have been only thirty years ago?

Adultized Children and Infantile Adults

The homogenizing effects of *kitsch* also blurs age lines. It would be interesting to know how many adults read the comics. We do know that comic books are by far the favorite reading matter of our soldiers and sailors, that some forty million comic books are sold a month, and that some seventy million people (most of whom must be adults, there just aren't that many kids) are estimated to read the newspaper comic strips every day. We also know that movie Westerns and radio and TV programs such as 'The Lone Ranger' and 'Captain Video' are by no means enjoyed only by children. On the other hand, children have access to such grown-up media as the movies, radio and TV. (Note that these newer arts are the ones which blur age lines because of the extremely modest demands they make on the audience's cultural equipment; thus there are many children's books but few children's movies.)

This merging of the child and grown-up audience means: (1) infantile regression of the latter, who, unable to cope with the strains and complexities of modern life, escapes via *kitsch* (which, in turn, confirms and enhances their infantilism); (2) 'overstimulation' of the former, who grow up too fast. Or, as Max Horkheimer well puts it: 'Development has ceased to exist. The child is grown up as soon as he can walk, and the grown-up in principle always remains the same.' Also note (a) our cult of youth, which makes 18–22 the most admired and desired period of life, and (b) the sentimental worship of Mother ('Momism') as if we couldn't bear to grow up and be on our own. Peter Pan might be a better symbol of America than Uncle Sam.

Idols of Consumption

Too little attention has been paid to the connection of our Mass Culture with the historical evolution of American Society. In *Radio Research, 1942–43* (Paul F. Lazarsfeld, ed.), Leo Lowenthal compared the biographical articles in *Collier's* and *The Saturday Evening Post* for 1901 and 1940–41 and found that in the forty-year interval the proportion of articles about business and professional men and political leaders had declined while those about entertainers had gone up 50 per cent. Furthermore, the 1901 entertainers are mostly serious artists – opera singers, sculptors, pianists, etc. – while those of 1941 are *all* movie stars, baseball players, and such; and even the 'serious' heroes in 1941 aren't so very serious after all: the businessmen and politicians are freaks, oddities, not the really powerful leaders as in 1901. The 1901 *Satevepost* heroes he calls 'idols of production', those of today 'idols of consumption'.

Lowenthal notes that the modern *Satevepost* biographee is successful not because of his own personal abilities so much as because he 'got the breaks'. The whole competitive struggle is presented as a lottery in which a few winners, no more talented or energetic than anyone else, drew the lucky tickets. The effect on the mass reader is at once consoling (it might have been me) and deadening to effort, ambition (there are no rules, so why struggle?). It is striking how closely this evolution parallels the country's economic development. Lowenthal observes that the 'idols of production' maintained their dominance right through the twenties. The turning point was the 1929 depression when the problem became how to consume goods rather than how to produce them, and also when the arbitrariness and chaos of capitalism was forcefully brought home to the mass man. So he turned to 'idols of consumption', or rather these were now offered him by the manufacturers of Mass Culture, and he accepted them. 'They seem to lead to a dream world of the masses,' observes Lowenthal,

> who are no longer capable or willing to conceive of biographies primarily as a means of orientation and education. . . . He, the American mass man, as reflected in his 'idols of consumption' appears no longer as a center of outwardly directed energies and actions on whose work and efficiency might depend mankind's progress. Instead of the 'givers' we are faced with the 'takers'. . . . They seem to stand for a phantasmagoria of world-wide social security – an attitude which asks for no more than to be served with the things needed for reproduction and recreation, an attitude which has lost every primary interest in how to invent, shape, or apply the tools leading to such purposes of mass satisfaction.

Sherlock Holmes to Mike Hammer

The role of science in Mass Culture has similarly changed from the rational and the purposive to the passive, accidental, even the catastrophic. Consider the evolution of the detective story, a genre which can be traced back to the memoirs of Vidocq, the master-detective of the Napoleonic era. Poe, who was peculiarly fascinated by scientific method, wrote the first and still best detective stories: *The Purloined Letter*, *The Gold Bug*, *The Mystery of Marie Roget*, *The Murders in the Rue Morgue*. Conan Doyle created the great folk hero, Sherlock Holmes, like Poe's Dupin a sage whose wizard's wand was scientific deduction (Poe's 'ratiocination'). Such stories could only appeal to – in fact, only be *comprehensible* to – an audience accustomed to think in scientific terms: to survey the data, set up a hypothesis, test it by seeing whether it caught the murderer. The very idea of an art genre cast in the form of a problem to be solved by purely intellectual means could only have arisen in a scientific age. This kind of detective fiction, which might be called the 'classic' style, is still widely practiced (well by Agatha Christie and John Dickson Carr, badly by the more popular Erle Stanley Gardiner) but of late it has been overshadowed by the rank, noxious growth of works in the 'sensational' style. This was inaugurated by Dashiel Hammett (whom André Gide was foolish enough to admire) and has recently been enormously stepped up in voltage by Mickey Spillane, whose six books to date have sold thirteen million copies. The sensationalists use what for the classicists was the point – the uncovering of the criminal – as a mere excuse for the minute description of scenes of bloodshed, brutality, lust, and alcoholism. The cool, astute, subtle Dupin–Holmes is replaced by the crude man of action whose prowess is measured not by intellectual mastery but by his capacity for liquor, women, and mayhem (he can 'take it' as well as 'dish it out' – Hammett's *The Glass Key* is largely a chronicle of the epic beatings absorbed by the hero before he finally staggers to the solution). Mike Hammer, Spillane's aptly named hero, is such a monumental blunderer that even Dr Watson would have seen through him. According to Richard W. Johnston (*Life*, June 23, 1952), 'Mike has one bizarre and memorable characteristic that sets him apart from all other fictional detectives: sheer incompetence. In the five Hammer cases, 48 people have been killed, and there is reason to believe that if Mike had kept out of the way, 34 of them – all innocent of the original crime – would have survived.' A decade ago, the late George Orwell, apropos a 'sensationalist' detective story of the time, *No Orchids for Miss Blandish*, showed how the brutalization of this genre mirrors the general degeneration in ethics from nineteenth-century standards. What he would have written had Mickey Spillane's work been then in existence I find hard to imagine.

Frankenstein to Hiroshima

The real heirs of the 'classic' detective story today, so far as the exploitation of science is concerned, are the writers of science fiction, where the marvels and horrors of the future must always be 'scientifically possible' – just as Sherlock Holmes drew on no supernatural powers. This is the approach of the bourgeoisie, who think of science as their familiar instrument. The masses are less confident, more awed in their approach to science, and there are vast lower strata of science fiction where the marvellous is untrammeled by the limits of knowledge. To the masses, science is the modern *arcanum arcanorum*, at once the supreme mystery and the philosopher's stone that explains the mystery. The latter concept appears in comic strips such as 'Superman' and in the charlatan-science exploited by 'health fakers' and 'nature fakers'. Taken this way, science gives man mastery over his environment and is beneficent. But science itself is not understood, therefore not mastered, therefore terrifying because of its very power. Taken *this* way, as the supreme mystery, science becomes the stock in trade of the 'horror' pulp magazines and comics and movies. It has got to the point, indeed, that if one sees a laboratory in a movie, one shudders, and the white coat of the scientist is as blood-chilling a sight as Count Dracula's black cloak. These 'horror' films have apparently an indestructible popularity: *Frantenstein* is still shown, after twenty-one years, and the current revival of *King Kong* is expected to gross over two million dollars.

If the scientist's laboratory has acquired in Mass Culture a ghastly atmosphere, is this perhaps not one of those deep popular intuitions? From Frankenstein's laboratory to Maidenek and Hiroshima is not a long journey. Was there a popular suspicion, perhaps only half conscious, that the nineteenth-century trust in science, like the nineteenth-century trust in popular education, was mistaken, that science can as easily be used for antihuman as for prohuman ends, perhaps even more easily? For Mrs Shelley's Frankenstein, the experimenter who brought disaster by pushing his science too far, is a scientific folk hero older than and still as famous as Mr Doyle's successful and beneficent Sherlock Holmes.

The Problem of the Masses

Conservatives such as Ortega y Gasset and T. S. Eliot argue that since 'the revolt of the masses' has led to the horrors of totalitarianism (and of California roadside architecture), the only hope is to rebuild the old class walls and bring the masses once more under aristocratic control. They think of the popular as synonymous with cheap and vulgar. Marxian radicals and liberals, on the other hand, see the masses as intrinsically healthy but as the dupes and victims of cultural exploitation by the Lords of *kitsch* – in the style of Rousseau's 'noble savage' idea. If only the masses were offered good stuff instead of *kitsch*, how they would eat it up! How the level of Mass Culture would rise! Both these diagnoses seem to me fallacious: they assume that Mass Culture is (in the conservative view) or could be (in the liberal view) an expression of *people*, like Folk Art, whereas actually it is an expression of *masses*, a very different thing.

There are theoretical reasons why Mass Culture is not and can never be any good. I take it as axiomatic that culture can only be produced by and for human beings. But in so far as people are organized (more strictly, disorganized) as masses, they lose their human identity and quality. For the masses are in historical time what a crowd is in space: a large quantity of people unable to express themselves as human beings because they are related to one another neither as individuals nor as members of communities – indeed, they are not related *to each other* at all, but only to something distant, abstract, nonhuman: a football game or bargain sale in the case of a crowd, a system of industrial production, a party or a State in the case of the masses. The mass man is a solitary atom, uniform with and undifferentiated from thousands and millions of other atoms who go to make up 'the lonely crowd', as David Riesman well calls American society. A folk or a people, however, is a community, i.e. a group of individuals linked to each other by common interests, work, traditions, values, and sentiments; something like a family, each of whose members has a special place and function as an individual while at the same time sharing the group's interests (family budget) sentiments (family quarrels), and culture (family jokes). The scale is small enough so that it 'makes a difference' what the individual does, a first condition for human – as against mass – existence. He is at once more important as an individual than in mass society and at the same time more closely integrated into the community, his creativity nourished by a rich combination of individualism and communalism. (The great culture-bearing elites of the past have been communities of this kind.) In contrast, a mass society, like a crowd, is so undifferentiated and loosely structured that its atoms, in so far as human values go, tend to cohere only along the line of the least common denominator; its morality sinks to that of its most brutal and primitive members, its taste to that of the least sensitive and most ignorant. And in addition to everything else, the scale is simply too big, there are just *too many people*.

Yet this collective monstrosity, 'the masses', 'the public', is taken as a human norm by the scientific and artistic technicians of our Mass Culture. They at once degraded the public by treating it as an object, to be handled with the lack of ceremony and the objectivity of medical students dissecting a corpse, and at the same time flatter it, pander to its level of taste and ideas by taking these as the criterion of reality (in the case of questionnaire-sociologists and other 'social scientists') or of art (in the case of the Lords of *kitsch*). When one hears a questionnaire-sociologist talk about how he will 'set up' an investigation, one feels he regards people as a herd of dumb animals, as mere congeries of conditioned reflexes, his calculation being which reflex will be stimulated by which question. At the same time, of necessity, he sees the statistical majority as the great Reality, the secret of life he is trying to find out; like the *kitsch* Lords, he is wholly without values, willing to accept any idiocy if it is held by many people. The aristocrat and the democrat both criticize and argue with popular taste, the one with hostility, the other in friendship, for both attitudes proceed from a set of values. This is less degrading to the masses than the 'objective' approach of Hollywood and the questionnaire-sociologists, just as it is less degrading to a man to be shouted at in anger than to be quietly assumed to be part of a machine. But the *plebs* have their dialectical revenge: complete indifference to their human *quality* means complete prostration before their statistical *quantity*, so that a movie magnate who cynically 'gives the pubic what it wants' – i.e. assumes it wants trash – sweats with terror if box-office returns drop 10 per cent.

The Future of High Culture: Dark

The conservative proposal to save culture by restoring the old class lines has a more solid historical base than the Marxian hope for a new democratic, classless culture, for, with the possible (and important) exception of Periclean Athens, all the great cultures of the past were elite cultures. Politically, however, it is without meaning in a world dominated by the two great mass nations, USA and USSR, and becoming more industrialized, more massified all the time. The only practical thing along those lines would be to revive the *cultural elite* which the Avant-garde created. As I have already noted, the Avant-garde is now dying, partly from internal causes, partly suffocated by the competing Mass Culture, where it is not being absorbed into it. Of course this process has not reached 100 per cent, and doubtless never will unless the country goes either Fascist or Communist. There are still islands above the flood for those determined enough to reach them, and to stay on them: as Faulkner has shown, a writer can even use Hollywood instead of being used by it, if his purpose is firm enough. But the homogenization of High and Mass Culture has gone far and is going farther all the time, and there seems little reason to expect a revival of Avant-gardism, that is, of a successful countermovement to Mass Culture. Particularly not in this country, where the blurring of class lines, the absence of a stable cultural tradition, and the greater facilities for manufacturing and marketing *kitsch* all work in the other direction. The result is that our intelligentsia is remarkably small, weak, and disintegrated. One of the odd things about the American cultural scene is how many brainworkers there are and how few intellectuals, defining the former as specialists whose thinking is pretty much confined to their limited 'fields' and the latter as persons who take all culture for their province. Not only are there few intellectuals, but they don't hang together, they have very little *esprit de corps*, very little sense of belonging to a community; they are so isolated from each other they don't even bother to quarrel – there hasn't been a really good fight among them since the Moscow Trials.

The Future of Mass Culture: Darker

If the conservative proposal to save our culture via the aristocratic Avant-garde seems historically unlikely, what of the democratic-liberal proposal? Is there a reasonable prospect of raising the level of Mass Culture? In his recent book *The Great Audience*, Gilbert Seldes argues there is. He blames the present sad state of our Mass Culture on the stupidity of the Lords of *kitsch*, who underestimate the mental age of the public; the arrogance of the intellectuals, who make the same mistake and so snobbishly refuse to work for such mass media as radio, TV and movies; and the passivity of the public itself, which doesn't insist on better Mass Cultural products. This diagnosis seems to me superficial in that it blames everything on subjective, moral factors: stupidity, perversity, failure of will. My own feeling is that, as in the case of the alleged responsibility of the German (or Russian) people for the horrors of Nazism (or Soviet Communism), it is unjust to blame social groups for this result. Human beings have been caught up in the inexorable workings of a mechanism that forces them, with a pressure only heroes can resist (and one cannot *demand* that anybody be a hero, though one can *hope* for it), into its own pattern. I see Mass Culture as a reciprocating engine, and who is to say, once it has been set in motion, whether the stroke or the counterstroke is 'responsible' for its continued action?

The Lords of *kitsch* sell culture to the masses. It is a debased trivial culture that voids both the deep realities (sex, death, failure, tragedy) and also the simple, spontaneous pleasures, since the realities would be too real and the pleasures too *lively* to induce what Mr Seldes calls 'the mood of consent', i.e. a narcotized acceptance of Mass Culture and of the commodities it sells as a substitute for the unsettling and unpredictable (hence unsaleable) joy, tragedy, wit, change, originality and beauty of real life. The masses, debauched by several generations of this sort of thing, in turn come to demand trivial and comfortable cultural products. Which came first, the chicken or the egg, the mass demand or its satisfaction (and further stimulation) is a question as academic as it is unanswerable. The engine is reciprocating and shows no signs of running down.

Indeed, far from Mass Culture getting better, we will be lucky if it doesn't get worse. When shall we see another popular humorist like Sholem Aleichem, whose books are still being translated from the Yiddish and for whose funeral in 1916 a hundred thousand inhabitants of the Bronx turned out? Or Finlay Peter Dunne, whose Mr Dooley commented on the American scene with such wit that Henry Adams was a faithful reader and Henry James, on his famous return to his native land, wanted to meet only one American author, Dunne? Since Mass Culture is not an art form but a manufactured commodity, it tends always downward, towards cheapness – and so standardization – of production. Thus, T. W. Adorno has noted, in his brilliant essay 'On popular music' (*Studies in Philosophy and Social Science*, New York, No. 1, 1941), that the chorus of every popular song *without* exception has the same number of bars, while Mr Seldes remarks that Hollywood movies are cut in a uniformly rapid tempo, a shot rarely being held more than forty-five seconds, which gives them a standardized effect in contrast to the varied tempo of European film cutting. This sort of standardization means that what may have begun as something fresh and original is repeated until it becomes a nerveless routine – *vide* what happened to Fred Allen as a radio comedian. The only time Mass Culture is good is at the very beginning, before the 'formula' has hardened, before the money boys and efficiency experts and audience-reaction analysts have moved in. Then for a while it may have the quality of real Folk Art. But the Folk artist today lacks the cultural roots and the intellectual toughness (both of which the Avant-garde artist has relatively more of) to resist for long the pressures of Mass Culture. His taste can easily be corrupted, his sense of his own special talent and limitations obscured, as in what happened to Disney between the gay, inventive early Mickey Mouse and Silly Symphony cartoons and the vulgar pretentiousness of *Fantasia* and heavy-handed sentimentality of *Snow White*, or to Westbrook Pegler, who has regressed from an excellent sports writer, with a sure sense of form and a mastery of coloquial satire, into the rambling, course-grained, garrulous political pundit of today. Whatever virtues the Folk artist has, and they are many, staying power is not one of them. And staying power is the essential virtue of one who would hold his own against the spreading ooze of Mass Culture.

Notes

1. As I did myself in 'A theory of popular culture' (*Politics*, February 1944), parts of which have been used or adapted in the present article.

2. The success of *Reader's Digest* illustrates the law. Here is a magazine that has achieved a fantastic circulation – some fifteen millions, much of which is accounted for by its foreign editions, thus showing that *kitsch* by no means appeals only to Americans – simply by reducing to even lower terms the already superficial formulae of other periodicals. By treating a theme in two pages which they treat in six, the *Digest* becomes three times as 'readable' and three times as superficial.

PART TWO

Culturalism

Introduction

The readings collected in this section represent the founding texts of culturalism. Culturalism was born in critical dialogue with both Leavisism and mechanistic and economistic versions of Marxism. The educational space opened up by the Leavisites was occupied by the culturalists in ways which eventually challenged many of the basic assumptions of Leavisism. Culturalism is an approach which insists that by analysing the culture of a society, the textual forms and documented practices of a culture, it is possible to reconstitute the patterned behaviour and constellations of ideas shared by the men and women who produce and consume the texts and practices of that society. It is an approach which stresses 'human agency', the active production of culture, rather than its passive consumption. Taken together as a body of work, the contributions of Richard Hoggart, Raymond Williams, E. P. Thompson, and Stuart Hall and Paddy Whannel clearly mark the emergence of what is now known as the cultural studies approach to popular culture. The early institutional home of these developments, established in 1964, was the Centre for Contemporary Cultural Studies at the University of Birmingham .

The Uses of Literacy (Reading 4) is a book of two halves. The first half describes the working-class culture of Hoggart's youth (the 1930s); the second half describes this culture under threat from the new forms of mass entertainment (especially American) of the 1950s. Dividing the book in this way produces a 'before and after' effect: a Leavisite scenario in which 'good' culture gives way to 'bad' culture. In this way, Hoggart's approach to popular culture has much in common with the approach of Leavisism. Hoggart shares with the Leavisites a belief in a cultural Fall – from healthy culture to a corrupt and corrupting mass culture. He also shares with the Leavisites the belief that this can be resisted by education in discrimination. However, what marks the difference between Hoggart and the Leavisites is the former's detailed preoccupation with – and above all, his clear commitment to – working-class culture. The distance between the two positions is most evident in the difference between their respective 'good past/bad present' binary. Instead of the Leavisite 'organic community' of the seventeenth century, Hoggart's 'good past' is the working-class culture of the 1930s. In short, the culture he celebrates is the very culture the Leavisites were 'armed' to resist. This alone makes Hoggart's approach an implicit critique of – and advance on – Leavisism. Moreover, he does not see the working class as the passive and helpless victims of a manipulative mass culture. For example, he defines working-class appreciation of popular song, against the dismissive hostility of the Leavisite longing for the 'purity' of folk song, in terms which have become central to the project of cultural studies. Popular songs become successful, he maintains – 'no matter how much Tin Pan Alley plugs them' – only if they can be made to meet the emotional requirements of their popular audiences. Hoggart never quite says it, but the implication is there: popular culture is culture made popular by ordinary working people. He identifies a 'popular aesthetic', one which values culture that 'shows' rather than 'explores'; one which values not culture which offers 'an escape from ordinary life', but a culture of intensification, premised on the belief 'that ordinary life is intrinsically interesting'. The problem with the mass culture becoming available in the 1950s is that it is a culture 'full of corrupt brightness, of improper appeals and moral evasions'. Moreover, it is a culture which actively threatens 'a gradual drying-up of the more positive, the fuller, the more cooperative kinds of enjoyment, in which one gains much by giving much'. Hoggart's account of the working-class culture of the 1950s presents a picture of a culture under attack from the 'shiny barbarism' of a new mass culture. It is an attack under which many of the young have already withered. These 'barbarians in wonderland' demand more, and are given more, than their parents and grandparents had or expected. Succumbing to this mindless hedonism, according to Hoggart, leads only to a cycle of debilitating excess. The pleasures of mass culture do not so much 'debase' taste, 'they over-excite it, eventually dull it, and finally kill it'.

Stuart Hall and Paddy Whannel's *The Popular Arts* was written against a background of concern about the influence of popular culture in the classroom. The book has a complex relationship with both Leavisism and the emerging forms of cultural analysis represented by Hoggart and Williams. Rather than accepting the Leavisite position that all popular culture is bad, or Hoggart's position that this is true only of contemporary popular culture, Hall and Whannel advocate 'training in discrimination' from *within* popular culture rather than *against* it. Their aim is to 'train a more demanding audience', one that will demand 'good' popular culture rather than 'bad'. As they put it: 'the struggle [in terms of actual quality] between what is good and worthwhile and what is shoddy and debased is not a struggle against the modern forms of communication, but a conflict within these media'. However, when the focus of the book turns to youth culture (see Reading 7) there are clear changes in its method of approach and in its attitude to popular culture. Popular culture is now itself seen as a site of conflict: 'Teenage culture is a contradictory mixture of the authentic and the manufactured: it is an area of self-expression for the young and a lush grazing pasture for the commercial providers.'

Raymond Williams's 'The Analysis of Culture' (Reading 5) is perhaps the founding text of culturalism. Its detailed attention to the category of culture has had enormous influence. Williams distinguishes between three ways of thinking about culture. First, there is 'the "ideal" in which culture is a state or process of human perfection, in terms of certain absolute or universal values'. Second, there is the 'documentary' record; the recorded texts and practices of culture. Third, 'there is the "social" definition of culture, in which culture is a description of a particular way of life'. It is the third definition which proved fundamental to the founding of culturalism. On the basis of the 'social' definition of culture, Williams introduces three new ways of thinking about contemporary urban culture. First, the 'anthropological' claim that culture is a description of a particular way of life. Second, the claim that culture 'expresses certain meanings and values'. Third, the claim that the work of cultural analysis should be the 'clarification of the meanings and values implicit and explicit in a particular way of life, a particular culture'. In addressing the 'complex organisation' of culture as a particular way of life, the purpose of cultural analysis is always to understand what a culture is saying, what a culture is expressing: 'the actual experience through which a culture was lived'; the 'important common element'; 'a particular community of experience'. In brief, to reconstitute what Williams calls the 'structure of feeling'; the shared values of a particular group, class or society. Taken together, the three aspects embodied in the 'social' definition of culture – culture as a particular way of life, culture as an expression of a particular way of life, and cultural analysis as a method of reconstituting a particular way of life – establish both the general perspective and the basic procedures of culturalism.

This perspective and this set of procedures are evident in E. P. Thompson's monumental *The Making of the English Working Class* (the 'Preface' is reproduced here as Reading 6). Although Thompson rejects culturalism as a description of his work, it is certainly the case that his commitment to human agency, to the historical situatedness of culture, to working-class experience, to the plurality of cultures, and to a history written on the basis of radical listening (to the voices usually excluded from conventional accounts of the past) place him, in terms of attitude and method (if not formal politics), with Hoggart, Williams, Hall and Whannel – and with others who made the break from Leavisism and mechanical forms of Marxism. Where he goes beyond these writers is in his insistence that cultures always exist in conflict and struggle to establish 'particular ways of life' rather than evolve to form a 'particular *way* of life'.

Finally, culturalism is also the defining approach of the readings collected here by Gareth Stedman Jones (Reading 8) and Paul Gilroy (Reading 9). Both are also examples of debate within culturalism. Each, in a different way (Gilroy in terms of race; Stedman Jones in terms of class), seeks to extend the founding assumptions of the culturalist perspective.

4 □ *The Full Rich Life*
& The Newer Mass Art:
Sex in Shiny Pockets

Richard Hoggart

The Full Rich Life

[...]

Outdoors, and especially in the more public parts of the cities, the cleaner lines of
the twentieth century have made their impression, in the post-offices, the telephone
kiosks, the bus stations. But in the working-class shopping and amusement areas the
old idiom – in its modern style – persists; it persists, for example, in the huge
furniture stores, in the marzipan super-cinemas, and in the manner of window-
dressing retained by the cheaper clothiers and outfitters. There is a working-class
city centre as there is one for the middle classes. They are geographically united, they
overlap, they have concurrent lives; but they also have distinctive atmospheres. The
centre belongs to all groups, and each takes what it wants and so makes its own
centre – favourite streets, popular shops (with 'Wooley's' – Woolworth's – a clear
favourite with working-class people), tram stops, parts of the market, places of
amusement, places for cups of tea.

In the working-class area itself, in those uneven cobbled streets to which until
recently motor-cars seldom penetrated, the world is still that of fifty years ago. It
is an untidy, messy, baroque, but on the whole drably baroque, world. The shop
windows are an indiscriminate tangle of odds-and-bobs at coppers each; the counter
and every spare stretch of upper space is festooned with cards full of proprietary
medicines. The outer walls are a mass of small advertisements, in all colours. There
are hundreds of them, in all stages of wear-and-tear, some piled a quarter of an inch
thick on the bodies of their predecessors.

In those towns where they are still retained, the trams are obviously much more
in place in the working-class areas than when they run up to the 'good residential'
districts. Their improbable 'Emmett' shape, their extraordinary noisiness, which

From Hoggart, R., *The Uses of Literacy*, Chatto & Windus, London, 1957, pp. 144–9,
246–500.

makes two or three together sound like a small fairground, the mass of tiny advertisements which surround their interiors, their wonderful double necklace of lights at night – all make them representative working-class vehicles, the gondolas of the people.

All this is the background to specific acts of baroque living. Most working-class pleasures tend to be mass-pleasures, overcrowded and sprawling. Everyone wants to have fun at the same time, since most buzzers blow within an hour of each other. Special occasions – a wedding, a trip to the pantomime, a visit to the fair, a charabanc outing – assume this, and assume also that a really special splendour and glitter must be displayed. Weddings are more often than not attempts for once to catch some of the splendour associated with the idea of upper-class life. The large cake is no doubt 'good', but the elaborate white dress and veil can only be poor imitations of a real thing which would cost a hundred guineas. The bridesmaids are all dressed alike, down to little arm-bands, long net gloves, and large hats; but the finish and the fit are not good. The drink flows freely and includes the richer varieties – port, especially.

The fairgrounds, like the furniture, have an intensely conscious modernity. The lovely stylized horses have almost gone, and so have the fantastic mechanical organs; each year bigger and louder relay-systems and more and more Coney Island-style coloured lights appear. But again the new materials are adapted to the old demands for a huge complication and exotic involution of colour, noise, and movement. The same demands are met in the large holiday camps; if you look closely at the interiors of the great public halls there, you may see the steel girders and bare corrugations of the roofs: but you will have to peer through a welter of artificial trees, imitation half-timbering, great dazzling chandeliers.

Most illuminating of all is the habit of the 'chara' trip. For the day trip by 'chara' has been particularly taken up by working-class people, and made into one of their peculiar – that is, characteristic – kinds of pleasure-occasion. Some even take their week's holiday in this way, in successive outings. In its garishness and cheerfulness the 'chara' trip today still speaks the language of:

Oh, I do like to be beside the seaside.

These buses, sometimes from a big town fleet, but often one of a couple owned by a local man, are the super-cinemas of the highways. They are, and particularly if they belong to a small firm specializing in day trips for working-class people, plushily over-upholstered, ostentatiously styled inside and out; they have lots of chrome bits, little flags on top, fine names, and loud radios. Every day in summer the arterial roads out of the big towns are thick with them humming towards the sea, often filled, since this is a pleasure which particularly appeals to mothers who want a short break and lots of company, with middle-aged women, dressed in their best, out on a pub, club, or street excursion. Their hair has been in curlers the night before; they have eased themselves into the creaking corsets they do not wear every day, have put on flowered summer dresses and fancy shoes. One year, I remember, the fashion, except on really warm days, was for fur-lined bootees, the kind which show thick fur round the upper edges but are not so thickly lined throughout. They have gathered together all the bits-and-bobs of equipment which give a working-class woman, when she is dressed up, a somewhat cluttered and over-dressed air – things around the neck, a prized item of jewellery, such as a brooch or a cameo, pinned to the centre of the bodice, and a tightly clutched handbag.

The 'charas' go rolling out and across the moors for the sea, past the road-houses which turn up their noses at coach-parties, to one the driver knows where there is coffee and biscuits or perhaps a full egg-and-bacon breakfast. Then on to a substantial lunch on arrival, and after that a fanning-out in groups. But rarely far from one another, because they know their part of the town and their bit of beach, where they feel at home. At Scarborough they leave the north side to the lower middle-classes who come for a week or two, and take rooms in the hundreds of little red villas. They leave the half-alive Edwardian elegance of the south end (it hasn't a beach anyway; the sea is a splendid frame for an esplanade and formal cliff-gardens) to middle-aged professionals, West Riding businessmen who are doing quite well and have come in their Rovers. They walk down Westborough to the half-mile-long centre-piece around the harbour, where Jews up from Leeds for the season with van-loads of gaudy knick-knacks jostle for space with lavatorially tiled fish-and-chip saloons ('Fish, chips, tea, bread and butter – 3/-: No Tea with own Eatables'). Here again the same clutter, the same extraordinary Bartholomew Fair of a mess, but even messier and more colourful than that they are used to in their own shopping-areas at home. They have a nice walk past the shops; perhaps a drink; a sit in a deck-chair eating an ice-cream or sucking mint-humbugs; a great deal of loud laughter – at Mrs Johnson insisting on a paddle with her dress tucked in her bloomers, at Mrs Henderson pretending she has 'got off' with the deck-chair attendant, or in the queue at the ladies' lavatory. Then there is the buying of presents for the family, big meat-tea, and the journey home with a stop for drinks on the way. If the men are there, and certainly if it is a men's outing, there will probably be several stops and a crate or two of beer in the back for drinking on the move. Somewhere in the middle of the moors the men's parties all tumble out, with much horseplay and noisy jokes about bladder-capacity. The driver knows exactly what is expected of him as he steers his warm, fuggy, and singing community back to the town; for his part he gets a very large tip, collected during the run through the last few miles of town streets.

[. . .]

The Newer Mass Art: Sex in Shiny Packets

The Juke-box Boys

This regular, increasing, and almost entirely unvaried diet of sensation without commitment is surely likely to help render its consumers less capable of responding openly and responsibly to life, is likely to induce an underlying sense of purpose-lessness in existence outside the limited range of a few immediate appetites. Souls which may have had little opportunity to open will be kept hard-gripped, turned in upon themselves, looking out 'with odd dark eyes like windows' upon a world which is largely a phantasmagoria of passing shows and vicarious stimulations. That this is not today the position of many working-class people is due mainly to the capacity of the human spirit to resist; to resist from a sense, even though it is not usually defined, that there are other things which matter and which are to be obeyed.

But it may be useful to look now at some of those points in English life at which the cultural process described [. . .] is having its strongest effect. We should see there the condition which might already have been reached were it not for the resistances [. . .]. One such illustration is to be found in the reading of young men on National Service. For two years many of them are, on the whole, bored; they are marking time until they go back to their jobs; they are adolescent and have money to spare. They are cut off from the unconsciously felt but important steadying effect of home, of the web of family relationships; perhaps also from the sense, at their place of work, of being part of an organization which has a tradition in its own kind of skill. They are as a result open to the effects of the reading, both fragmentary and sensational, so freely provided for them. The only bound books read by a great many, my own experience strongly suggests, are likely to be those written by the most popular crime novelists. Otherwise, they read comics, gangster novelettes, science and crime magazines, the newer-style magazines or magazine/newspapers, and the picture-dailies. Luckily, National Service lasts only two years; after that, they go home and back to work, still readers of these publications, but soon also men with commitments, with more demands on their time and money, probably with a good chance of picking up older, neighbourhood rhythms, with a good chance of escaping from the worst effects of what can be a glassily hermaphrodite existence ('life like a permanent wank [masturbation] inside you,' as a soldier once described it to me), and one not connected to any meaningful sense of personal aim. I know there are exceptions and that much is being done to improve matters; but, given the background described in the preceding chapters, this is for many the predominant atmosphere during the period of National Service.

Perhaps even more symptomatic of the general trend is the reading of juke-box boys, of those who spend their evening listening in harshly lighted milk-bars to the 'nickelodeons'. There are, of course, others who read the books and magazines now to be discussed – some married men and women, perhaps in particular those who are finding married life a somewhat jaded affair, 'dirty old men', some schoolchildren – but one may reasonably take those who, night after night, visit these bars as typical or characteristic readers of these most developed new-style popular journals.

[. . .] The milk-bars indicate at once, in the nastiness of their modernistic knick-knacks, their glaring showiness, an aesthetic breakdown so complete that, in comparison with them, the layout of the living-rooms in some of the poor homes from which the customers come seems to speak of a tradition as balanced and civilized as an eighteenth-century town house. I am not thinking of those milk-bars which are really quick-service cafés where one may have a meal more quickly than in a café with table-service. I have in mind rather the kind of milk-bar – there is one in almost every northern town with more than, say, fifteen thousand inhabitants – which has become the regular evening rendezvous of some of the young men. Girls go to some, but most of the customers are boys aged between fifteen and twenty, with drape-suits, picture ties, and an American slouch. Most of them cannot afford a succession of milk-shakes, and make cups of tea serve for an hour or two whilst – and this is their main reason for coming – they put copper after copper into the mechanical record-player. About a dozen records are available at any time; a numbered button is pressed for the one wanted, which is selected from a key to titles. The records seem to be changed about once a fortnight by the hiring firm; almost all are American; almost all are 'vocals' and the styles of singing much advanced beyond what is normally heard on the Light Programme of the BBC. Some of the tunes are catchy; all have been doctored for presentation so that they have the kind of beat which is currently popular; much use is made of the 'hollow-cosmos' effect which echo-chamber recording gives. They are delivered with great precision and competence, and the 'nickelodeon' is allowed to blare out so that the noise would be sufficient to fill a good-sized ballroom, rather than a converted shop in the main street. The young men waggle one shoulder or stare, as desperately as Humphrey Bogart, across the tubular chairs.

Compared even with the pub around the corner, this is all a peculiarly thin and pallid form of dissipation, a sort of spiritual dry-rot amid the odour of boiled milk. Many of the customers – their clothes, their hair-styles, their facial expressions all indicate – are living to a large extent in a myth-world compounded of a few simple elements which they take to be those of American life.

They form a depressing group and one by no means typical of working-class people; perhaps most of them are rather less intelligent than the average, and are therefore even more exposed than others to the debilitating mass-trends of the day. They have no aim, no ambition, no protection, no belief. They are the modern equivalents of Samuel Butler's mid-nineteenth-century ploughboys, and in as unhappy a position as theirs:

> The row of stolid, dull, vacant plough-boys, ungainly in build, uncomely in face, lifeless, apathetic, a race a good deal more like the pre-Revolution French peasant as described by Carlyle than is pleasant to reflect upon – a race now supplanted...

For some of them even the rough sex-life of many of their contemporaries is not yet possible; it requires more management of their own personalities and more meeting with other personalities than they can compass.

From their education at school they have taken little which connects with the realities of life as they experience it after fifteen. Most of them have jobs which require no personal outgoing, which are not intrinsically interesting, which encourage no sense of personal value, of being a maker. The job is to be done day by day, and after that the rest is amusement, is pleasure; there is time to spare and some money in the pocket. They are ground between the millstones of technocracy and democracy; society gives them an almost limitless freedom of the sensations, but makes few demands on them – the use of their hands and of a fraction of their brains for forty hours a week. For the rest they are open to the entertainers and their efficient mass-equipment. The youth clubs, the young people's institutes, the sports clubs, cannot attract them as they attract many in their generation; and the commercial people ensure, by the inevitable processes of development in commercial entertainment, that their peculiar grip is retained and strengthened. The responsibilities of marriage may gradually change them. Meanwhile, they have no responsibilities, and little sense of responsibilities, to themselves or to others. They are in one dreadful sense the new workers; if, by extrapolation simply from a reading of newer working-class entertainment literature, one were to attempt to imagine the ideal readers for that literature, these would be the people. It is true, as I have said, that they are not typical. But these are the figures some important contemporary forces are tending to create, the directionless and tamed helots of a machine-minding class. If they seem to consist so far chiefly of those of poorer intelligence or from homes subject to special strains, that is probably due to the strength of a moral fibre which most cultural providers for working-class people are helping to de-nature. The hedonistic but passive barbarian who rides in a fifty-horse-power bus for threepence, to see a five-million-dollar film for one-and-eightpence, is not simply a social oddity; he is a portent.

5 □ The Analysis of Culture

Raymond Williams

There are three general categories in the definition of culture. There is, first, the 'ideal', in which culture is a state or process of human perfection, in terms of certain absolute or universal values. The analysis of culture, if such a definition is accepted, is essentially the discovery and description, in lives and works, of those values which can be seen to compose a timeless order, or to have permanent reference to the universal human condition. Then, second, there is the 'documentary', in which culture is the body of intellectual and imaginative work, in which, in a detailed way, human thought and experience are variously recorded. The analysis of culture, from such a definition, is the activity of criticism, by which the nature of the thought and experience, the details of the language, form and convention in which these are active, are described and valued. Such criticism can range from a process very similar to the 'ideal' analysis, the discovery of 'the best that has been thought and written in the world', through a process which, while interested in tradition, takes as its primary emphasis the particular work being studied (its clarification and valuation being the principal end in view) to a kind of historical criticism which, after analysis of particular works, seek to relate them to the particular traditions and societies in which they appeared. Finally, third, there is the 'social' definition of culture, in which culture is a description of a particular way of life, which expresses certain meanings and values not only in art and learning but also in institutions and ordinary behaviour. The analysis of culture, from such a definition, is the clarification of the meanings and values implicit and explicit in a particular way of life, a particular culture. Such analysis will include the historical criticism always referred to, in which intellectual and imaginative works are analysed in relation to particular traditions and societies, but will also include analysis of elements in the way of life that to followers of the other definitions are not 'culture' at all: the organization of production, the structure of the family, the structure of institutions which express or govern social relationships, the characteristic forms through which members of the society communicate. Again, such analysis ranges from an 'ideal'

From Williams, R., *The Long Revolution*, Chatto & Windus, London, 1961, pp. 57–70.

emphasis, the discovery of certain absolute or universal, or at least higher and lower, meanings and values, through the 'documentary' emphasis, in which clarification of a particular way of life is the main end in view, to an emphasis which, from studying particular meanings and values, seeks not so much to compare these, as a way of establishing a scale, but by studying their modes of change to discover certain general 'laws' or 'trends', by which social and cultural development as a whole can be better understood.

It seems to me that there is value in each of these kinds of definition. For it certainly seems necessary to look for meanings and values, the record of creative human activity, not only in art and intellectual work, but also in institutions and· forms of behaviour. At the same time, the degree to which we depend, in our knowledge of many past societies and past stages of our own, on the body of intellectual and imaginative work which has retained its major communicative power, makes the description of culture in these terms, if not complete, at least reasonable. It can indeed be argued that since we have 'society' for the broader description, we can properly restrict 'culture' to this more limited reference. Yet there are elements in the 'ideal' definition which also seem to me valuable, and which encourage the retention of the broad reference. I find it very difficult, after the many comparative studies now on record, to identify the process of human perfection with the discovery of 'absolute' values, as these have been ordinarily defined. I accept the criticism that these are normally an extension of the values of a particular tradition or society. Yet, if we call the process, not human perfection, which implies a known ideal towards which we can move, but human evolution, to mean a process of general growth of man as a kind, we are able to recognize areas of fact which the other definitions might exclude. For it seems to me to be true that meanings and values, discovered in particular societies and by particular individuals, and kept alive by social inheritance and by embodiment in particular kinds of work, have proved to be universal in the sense that when they are learned, in any particular situation, they can contribute radically to the growth of man's powers to enrich his life, to regulate his society, and to control his environment. We are most aware of these elements in the form of particular techniques, in medicine, production, and communications, but it is clear not only that these depend on more purely intellectual disciplines, which had to be wrought out in the creative handling of experience, but also that these disciplines in themselves, together with certain basic ethical assumptions and certain major art forms, have proved similarly capable of being gathered into a general tradition which seems to represent, through many variations and conflicts, a line of common growth. It seems reasonable to speak of this tradition as a general human culture, while adding that it can only become active within particular societies, being shaped, as it does so, by more local and temporary systems.

The variations of meaning and reference, in the use of culture as a term, must be seen, I am arguing, not simply as a disadvantage, which prevents any kind of neat and exclusive definition, but as a genuine complexity, corresponding to real elements in experience. There is a significant reference in each of the three main kinds of definition, and, if this is so, it is the relations between them that should claim our attention. It seems to me that any adequate theory of culture must include the three areas of fact to which the definitions point, and conversely that any particular definition, within any of the categories, which would exclude reference to the others, is inadequate. Thus an 'ideal' definition which attempts to abstract the process it describes from its detailed embodiment and shaping by particular societies – regarding man's ideal development as something separate from and even opposed to his 'animal nature' or the satisfaction of material needs – seems to me unacceptable. A 'documentary' definition which sees value only in the written and painted records, and marks this area off from the rest of man's life in society, is equally unacceptable. Again, a 'social' definition, which treats either the general process or the body of art and learning as a mere by-product, a passive reflection of the real interests of the society, seem to me equally wrong. However difficult it may be in practice, we have to try to see the process as a whole, and to relate our particular studies, if not explicitly at least by ultimate reference, to the actual and complex organization.

We can take one example, from analytic method, to illustrate this. If we take a particular work of art, say the *Antigone* of Sophocles, we can analyse it in ideal terms – the discovery of certain absolute values, or in documentary terms – the communication of certain values by certain artistic means. Much will be gained from either analysis, for the first will point to the absolute value of reverence for the dead; the second will point to the expression of certain basic human tensions through the particular dramatic form of chorus and double *kommos*, and the specific intensity of the verse. Yet it is clear that neither analysis is complete. The reverence, as an absolute value, is limited in the play by the terms of a particular kinship system and its conventional obligations – Antigone would do this for a brother but not for a husband. Similarly, the dramatic form, the metres of the verse, not only have an artistic tradition behind them, the work of many men, but can be seen to have been shaped, not only by the demands of the experience, but by the particular social forms through which the dramatic tradition developed. We can accept such extensions of our original analysis, but we cannot go on to accept that, because of the extensions, the value of reverence, or the dramatic form and the specific verse, have meaning only in the contexts to which we have assigned them. The learning of reverence, through such intense examples, passes beyond its context into the general growth of human consciousness. The dramatic form passes beyond its context, and becomes an element in a major and general dramatic tradition, in quite different societies. The play itself, a specific communication, survives the society and the religion which helped to have it, and can be re-created to speak directly to unimagined audiences. Thus, while we could not abstract the ideal value or the specific document, neither could we reduce these to explanation within the local terms of a particular culture. If we study real relations, in any actual analysis, we reach the point where we see that we are studying a general organization in a particular example, and in this general organization there is no element that we can abstract and separate from the rest. It was certainly an error to suppose that values or art-works could be adequately studied without reference to the particular society within which they were expressed, but it is equally an error to suppose that the social explanation is determining, or that the values and works are mere by-products. We have got into the habit, since we realized how deeply works or values could be determined by the whole situation in which they are expressed, of asking about these relationships in a standard form: 'what is the relation of this art to this society?' But 'society', in this question, is a specious whole. If the art is part of the society, there is no solid whole, outside it, to which, by the form of our question, we concede priority. The art is there, as an activity, with the production, the trading, the politics, the raising of families. To study the relations adequately we must study them actively, seeing all the activities as particular and contemporary forms of human energy. If we take any one of these activities, we can see how many of the others are reflected in it, in various ways according to the nature of the whole organization. It seems likely, also, that the very fact that we can distinguish any particular activity, as serving certain specific ends, suggests that without this activity the whole of the human organization at that place and time could not have been realized. Thus art, while clearly related to the other activities, can be seen as expressing certain elements in the organization which, within that organization's terms, could only have been expressed in this way. It is then not a question of relating the art to the society, but of studying all the activities and their inter-relations, without any concession of priority to any one of them we may choose to abstract. If we find, as often, that a particular activity came radically to change the whole organization, we can still not say that it is to this activity that all the others must be related; we can only study the varying ways in which, within the changing organization, the particular activities and their interrelations were affected. Further, since the particular activities will be serving varying and sometimes conflicting ends, the sort of change we must look for will rarely be of a simple kind: elements of persistence, adjustment, unconscious assimilation, active resistance, alternative effort, will all normally be present, in particular activities and in the whole organization.

The analysis of culture, in the documentary sense, is of great importance because it can yield specific evidence about the whole organization within which it was expressed. We cannot say that we know a particular form or period of society, and that we will see how its art and theory relate to it, for until we know these, we cannot really claim to know the society. This is a problem of method, and is mentioned here because a good deal of history has in fact been written on the assumption that the bases of the society, its political, economic, and 'social' arrangements, form the central core of facts, after which the art and theory can be adduced, for marginal illustration or 'correlation'. There has been a neat reversal of this procedure in the histories of literature, art, science, and philosophy, when these are described as developing by their own laws, and then something called the 'background' (what in general history was the central core) is sketched in. Obviously it is necessary, in exposition, to select certain activities for emphasis, and it is entirely reasonable to trace particular lines of development in temporary isolation.

But the history of a culture, slowly built up from such particular work, can only be written when the active relations are restored, and the activities seen in a genuine parity. Cultural history must be more than the sum of the particular histories, for it is with the relations between them, the particular forms of the whole organization, that it is especially concerned. I would then define the theory of culture as the study of relationships between elements in a whole way of life. The analysis of culture is the attempt to discover the nature of the organization which is the complex of these relationships. Analysis of particular works or institutions is, in this context, analysis of their essential kind of organization, the relationships which works or institutions embody as parts of the organization as a whole. A key-word, in such analysis, is pattern: it is with the discovery of patterns of a characteristic kind that any useful cultural analysis begins, and it is with the relationships between these patterns, which sometimes reveal unexpected identities and correspondences in hitherto separately considered activities, sometimes again reveal discontinuities of an unexpected kind, that general cultural analysis is concerned.

It is only in our own time and place that we can expect to know, in any substantial way, the general organization. We can learn a great deal of the life of other places and times, but certain elements, it seems to me, will always be irrecoverable. Even those that can be recovered are recovered in abstraction, and this is of crucial importance. We learn each element as a precipitate, but in the living experience of the time every element was in solution, an inseparable part of a complex whole. The most difficult thing to get hold of, in studying any past period, is this felt sense of the quality of life at a particular place and time: a sense of the ways in which the particular activities combined into a way of thinking and living. We can go some way in restoring the outlines of a particular organization of life; we can even recover what Fromm calls the 'social character' or Benedict the 'pattern of culture'. The social character – a valued system of behaviour and attitudes – is taught formally and informally; it is both an ideal and a mode. The 'pattern of culture' is a selection and configuration of interests and activities, and a particular valuation of them, producing a distinct organization, a 'way of life'. Yet even these, as we recover them, are usually abstract. Possibly, however, we can gain the sense of a further common element, which is neither the character nor the pattern, but as it were the actual experience through which these were lived. This is potentially of very great importance, and I think the fact is that we are most conscious of such contact in the arts of a period. It can happen that when we have measured these against the external characteristics of the period, and then allowed for individual variations, there is still some important common element that we cannot easily place. I think we can best understand this if we think of any similar analysis of a way of life that we ourselves share. For we find here a particular sense of life, a particular community of experience hardly needing expression, through which the characteristics of our way of life that an external analyst could describe are in some way passed, giving them a particular and characteristic colour. We are usually most aware of this when we notice the contrasts between generations, who never talk quite 'the same language', or when we read an account of our lives by someone from outside the community, or watch the small differences in style, of speech or behaviour, in someone who has learned our ways yet was not bred in them. Almost any formal description would be too crude to express this nevertheless quite distinct sense of a particular and native style. And if this is so, in a way of life we know intimately, it will surely be so when we ourselves are in the position of the visitor, the learner, the guest from a different generation: the position, in fact, that we are all in, when we study any past period. Though it can be turned to trivial account, the fact of such a characteristic is neither trivial nor marginal; it feels quite central.

The term I would suggest to describe it is *structure of feeling*: it is as firm and definite as 'structure' suggests, yet it operates in the most delicate and least tangible parts of our activity. In one sense, this structure of feeling is the culture of a period: it is the particular living result of all the elements in the general organization. And it is in this respect that the arts of a period, taking these to include characteristic approaches and tones in argument, are of major importance. For here, if anywhere, this characteristic is likely to be expressed; often not consciously, but by the fact that here, in the only examples we have of recorded communication that outlives its bearers, the actual living sense, the deep community that makes the communication possible, is naturally drawn upon. I do not mean that the structure of feeling, any more than the social character, is possessed in the same way by the many individuals in the community. But I think it is a very deep and very wide possession, in all actual communities, precisely because it is on it that communication depends. And what is particularly interesting is that it does not seem to be, in any formal sense, learned. One generation may train its successor, with reasonable success, in the social character or the general cultural pattern, but the new generation will have its own structure of feeling, which will not appear to have come 'from' anywhere. For here, most distinctly, the changing organization is enacted in the organism: the new generation responds in its own ways to the unique world it is inheriting, taking up many continuities, that can be traced, and reproducing many aspects of the organization, which can be separately described, yet feeling its whole life in certain ways differently, and shaping its creative response into a new structure of feeling.

Once the carriers of such a structure die, the nearest we can get to this vital element is in the documentary culture, from poems to buildings and dress-fashions, and it is this relation that gives significance to the definition of culture in documentary terms. This in no way means that the documents are autonomous. It is simply that, as previously argued, the significance of an activity must be sought in terms of the whole organization, which is more than the sum of its separable parts. What we are looking for, always, is the actual life that the whole organization is there to express. The significance of documentary culture is that, more clearly than anything else, it expresses that life to us in direct terms, when the living witnesses are silent. At the same time, if we reflect on the nature of a structure of feeling, and see how it can fail to be fully understood even by living people in close contact with it, with ample material at their disposal, including the contemporary arts, we shall not suppose that we can ever do more than make an approach, an approximation, using any channels.

We need to distinguish three levels of culture, even in its most general definition. There is the lived culture of a particular time and place, only fully accessible to those living in that time and place. There is the recorded culture, of every kind, from art to the most everyday facts: the culture of a period. There is also, as the factor connecting lived culture and period cultures, the culture of the selective tradition.

When it is no longer being lived, but in a narrower way survives in its records, the culture of a period can be very carefully studied, until we feel that we have reasonably clear ideas of its cultural work, its social character, its general patterns of activity and value, and in part of its structure of feeling. Yet the survival is governed, not by the period itself, but by new periods, which gradually compose a tradition. Even most specialists in a period know only a part of even its records. One can say with confidence, for example, that nobody really knows the nineteenth-century novel; nobody has read, or could have read, all its examples, over the whole range from printed volumes to penny serials. The real specialist may know some hundreds; the ordinary specialist somewhat less; educated readers a decreasing number: though all will have clear ideas on the subject. A selective process, of a quite drastic kind, is at once evident, and this is true of every field of activity. Equally, of course, no nineteenth-century reader would have read all the novels; no individual in the society would have known more than a selection of its facts. But everyone living in the period would have had something which, I have argued, no later individual can wholly recover: that sense of the life within which the novels were written, and which we now approach through our selection. Theoretically, a period is recorded; in practice, this record is absorbed into a selective tradition; and both are different from the culture as lived.

It is very important to try to understand the operation of a selective tradition. To some extent, the selection begins within the period itself; from the whole body of activities, certain things are selected for value and emphasis. In general this selection will reflect the organization of the period as a whole, though this does not mean that the values and emphases will later be confirmed. We see this clearly enough in the case of past periods, but we never really believe it about our own. We can take an example from the novels of the last decade. Nobody has read all the English novels of the 1950s; the fastest reader, giving twenty hours a day to this activity alone, could not do it. Yet it is clear, in print and in education, not only that certain general characteristics of the novel in this period have been set down, but also that a reasonably agreed short list has been made, of what seem to be the best and most relevant works. If we take the list as containing perhaps thirty titles (already a very drastic selection indeed) we may suppose that in fifty years the specialist in the novel of the 1950s will know these thirty, and the general reader will know perhaps five or six. Yet we can surely be quite certain that, once the 1950s have passed, another selective process will be begun. As well as reducing the number of works, this new process will also alter, in some cases drastically, the expressed valuations. It is true that when fifty years have passed it is likely that reasonably permanent valuations will have been arrived at, though these may continue to fluctuate. Yet to any of us who had lived this long process through, it would remain true that elements important to us had been neglected. We would say, in a vulnerable elderly way, 'I don't understand why these young people don't read X any more', but also, more firmly, 'No, that isn't really what it was like; it is your version'. Since any period includes at least three generations, we are always seeing examples of this, and one complicating factor is that none of us stay still, even in our most significant period: many of the adjustments we should not protest against, many of the omissions, distortions and reinterpretations we should accept or not even notice, because we had been part of the change which brought them about. But then, when living witnesses had gone, a further change would occur. The lived culture would not only have been fined down to selected documents; it would be used, in its reduced form, partly as a contribution (inevitably quite small) to the general line of human growth; partly for historical reconstruction; partly, again, as a way of having done with us, of naming and placing a particular stage of the past. The selective tradition thus creates, at one level, a general human culture; at another level, the historical record of particular society; at a third level, most difficult to accept and assess, a rejection of considerable areas of what was once a living culture.

Within a given society, selection will be governed by many kinds of special interest, including class interests. Just as the actual social situation will largely govern contemporary selection, so the development of the society, the process of historical change, will largely determine the selective tradition. The traditional culture of a society will always tend to correspond to its *contemporary* system of interests and values, for it is not an absolute body of work but a continual selection and interpretation. In theory, and to a limited extent in practice, those institutions which are formally concerned with keeping the tradition alive (in particular the institutions of education and scholarship) are committed to the tradition as a whole, and not to some selection from it according to contemporary interests. The importance of this commitment is very great, because we see again and again, in the workings of a selective tradition, reversals and re-discoveries, returns to work apparently abandoned as dead, and clearly this is only possible if there are institutions whose business it is to keep large areas of past culture, if not alive, at least available. It is natural and inevitable that the selective tradition should follow the lines of growth of a society, but because such growth is complex and continuous, the relevance of past work, in any future situation, is unforeseeable. There is a natural pressure on academic institutions to follow the lines of growth of a society, but a wise society, while ensuring this kind of relevance, will encourage the institutions to give sufficient resources to the ordinary work of preservation, and to resist the criticism, which any particular period may make with great confidence, that much of this activity is irrelevant and useless. It is often an obstacle to the growth of a society that so many academic institutions are, to an important extent, self-perpetuating and resistant to change. The changes have to be made, in new institutions if necessary, but if we properly understand the process of the selective tradition, and look at it over a sufficiently long period to get a real sense of historical change and fluctuation, the corresponding value of such perpetuation will be appreciated.

In a society as a whole, and in all its particular activities, the cultural tradition can be seen as a continual selection and re-selection of ancestors. Particular lines will be drawn, often for as long as a century, and then suddenly with some new stage in growth these will be cancelled or weakened, and new lines drawn. In the analysis of contemporary culture, the existing state of the selective tradition is of vital importance, for it is often true that some change in this tradition – establishing new lines with the past, breaking or re-drawing existing lines – is a radical kind of *contemporary* change. We tend to underestimate the extent to which the cultural tradition is not only a selection but also an interpretation. We see most past work through our own experience, without even making the effort to see it in something like its original terms. What analysis can do is not so much to reverse this, returning a work to its period, as to make the interpretation conscious, by showing historical alternatives; to relate the interpretation to the particular contemporary values on which it rests; and, by exploring the real patterns of the work, confront us with the real nature of the choices we are making. We shall find, in some cases, that we are keeping the work alive because it is a genuine contribution to cultural growth. We shall find, in other cases, that we are using the work in a particular way for our own reasons, and it is better to know this than to surrender to the mysticism of the 'great valuer, Time'. To put on to Time, the abstraction, the responsibility for our own active choices is to suppress a central part of our experience. The more actively all cultural work can be related, either to the whole organization within which it was expressed, or to the contemporary organization within which it is used, the more clearly shall we see its true values. Thus 'documentary' analysis will lead out to 'social' analysis, whether in a lived culture, a past period, or in the selective tradition which is itself a social organization. And the discovery of permanent contributions will lead to the same kind of general analysis, if we accept the process at this level, not as human perfection (a movement towards determined values), but as a part of man's general evolution, to which many individuals and groups contribute. Every element that we analyse will be in this sense active: that it will be seen in certain real relations, at many different levels. In describing these relations, the real cultural process will emerge.

6 □ *Preface from* The Making of the English Working Class

E. P. Thompson

This book has a clumsy title, but it is one which meets its purpose. *Making*, because it is a study in an active process, which owes as much to agency as to conditioning. The working class did not rise like the sun at an appointed time. It was present at its own making.

Class, rather than classes, for reasons which it is one purpose of this book to examine. There is, of course, a difference. 'Working classes' is a descriptive term, which evades as much as it defines. It ties loosely together a bundle of discrete phenomena. There were tailors here and weavers there, and together they make up the working classes.

By class I understand a historical phenomenon, unifying a number of disparate and seemingly unconnected events, both in the raw material of experience and in consciousness. I emphasize that it is a *historical* phenomenon. I do not see class as a 'structure', nor even as a 'category', but as something which in fact happens (and can be shown to have happened) in human relationships.

More than this, the notion of class entails the notion of historical relationship. Like any other relationship, it is a fluency which evades analysis if we attempt to stop it dead at any given moment and anatomize its structure. The finest-meshed sociological net cannot give us a pure specimen of class, any more than it can give us one of deference or of love. The relationship must always be embodied in real people and in a real context. Moreover, we cannot have two distinct classes, each with an independent being, and then bring them *into* relationship with each other. We cannot have love without lovers, nor deference without squires and labourers. And class happens when some men, as a result of common experiences (inherited or shared), feel and articulate the identity of their interests as between themselves, and as against other men whose interests are different from (and usually opposed to) theirs. The class experience is largely determined by the productive relations into which men are born – or enter involuntarily. Class-consciousness is the way in

From Thompson, E. P., *The Making of the English Working Class*, Victor Gollancz, London, 1963, pp. 8–13.

which these experiences are handled in cultural terms; embodied in traditions, value-systems, ideas, and institutional forms. If the experience appears as determined, class-consciousness does not. We can see a *logic* in the responses of similar occupational groups undergoing similar experiences, but we cannot predicate any *law*. Consciousness of class arises in the same way in different times and places, but never in just the same way.

There is today an ever-present temptation to suppose that class is a thing. This was not Marx's meaning, in his own historical writing, yet the error vitiates much latter-day 'Marxist' writing. 'It', the working class, is assumed to have a real existence, which can be defined almost mathematically – so many men who stand in a certain relation to the means of production. Once this is assumed it becomes possible to deduce the class-consciousness which 'it' ought to have (but seldom does have) if 'it' was properly aware of its own position and real interests. There is a cultural superstructure, through which this recognition dawns in inefficient ways. These cultural 'lags' and distortions are a nuisance, so that it is easy to pass from this to some theory of substitution: the party, sect, or theorist, who disclose class-consciousness, not as it is, but as it ought to be.

But a similar error is committed daily on the other side of the ideological divide. In one form, this is a plain negative. Since the crude notion of class attributed to Marx can be faulted without difficulty, it is assumed that any notion of class is a pejorative theoretical construct, imposed upon the evidence. It is denied that class has happened at all. In another form, and by a curious inversion, it is possible to pass from a dynamic to a static view of class. 'It' – the working class – exists, and can be defined with some accuracy as a component of the social structure. Class-consciousness, however, is a bad thing, invented by displaced intellectuals, since everything which disturbs the harmonious coexistence of groups performing different 'social roles' (and which thereby retards economic growth) is to be deplored as an 'unjustified disturbance-symptom'.[1] The problem is to determine how best 'it' can be conditioned to accept its social role, and how its grievances may best be 'handled and channelled'.

If we remember that class is a relationship, and not a thing, we cannot think in this way. 'It' does not exist, either to have an ideal interest or consciousness, or to lie as a patient on the Adjustor's table. Nor can we turn matters upon their heads, as has been done by one authority who (in a study of class obsessively concerned with methodology, to the exclusion of the examination of a single real class situation in a real historical context) has informed us:

> Classes are based on the differences in legitimate power associated with certain positions, i.e. on the structure of social rôles with respect to their authority expectations.... An individual becomes a member of a class by playing a social rôle relevant from the point of view of authority.... He belongs to a class because he occupies a position in a social organization; i.e. class membership is derived from the incumbency of a social rôle.[2]

The question, of course, is how the individual got to be in this 'social rôle', and how the particular social organization (with its property-rights and structure of authority) got to be there. And these are historical questions. If we stop history at a given point, then there are no classes but simply a multitude of individuals with a multitude of experiences. But if we watch these men over an adequate period of social change, we observe patterns in their relationships, their ideas, and their institutions. Class is defined by men as they live their own history, and, in the end, this is its only definition.

If I have shown insufficient understanding of the methodological preoccupations of certain sociologists, nevertheless I hope this book will be seen as a contribution to the understanding of class. For I am convinced that we cannot understand class unless we see it as a social and cultural formation, arising from processes which can only be studied as they work themselves out over a considerable historical period. In the years between 1780 and 1832 most English working people came to feel an identity of interests as between themselves, and as against their rulers and employers. This ruling class was itself much divided, and in fact only gained in cohesion over the same years because certain antagonisms were resolved (or faded into relative insignificance) in the face of an insurgent working class. Thus the working-class presence was, in 1832, the most significant factor in British political life.

The book is written in this way. In Part One I consider the continuing popular traditions in the eighteenth century which influenced the crucial Jacobin agitation of the 1790s. In Part Two I move from subjective to objective influences – the experiences of groups of workers during the Industrial Revolution which seem to me to be of especial significance. I also attempt an estimate of the character of the new industrial work-discipline, and the bearing upon this of the Methodist Church. In Part Three I pick up the story of plebeian Radicalism, and carry it through Luddism to the heroic age at the close of the Napoleonic Wars. Finally, I discuss some aspects of political theory and of the consciousness of class in the 1820s and 1830s.

This is a group of studies, on related themes, rather than a consecutive narrative. In selecting these themes I have been conscious, at times, of writing against the weight of prevailing orthodoxies. There is the Fabian orthodoxy, in which the great majority of working people are seen as passive victims of *laissez faire*, with the exception of a handful of far-sighted organizers (notably, Francis Place). There is the orthodoxy of the empirical economic historians, in which working people are seen as a labour force, as migrants, or as the data for statistical series. There is the 'Pilgrim's Progress' orthodoxy, in which the period is ransacked for forerunners– pioneers of the Welfare State, progenitors of a Socialist Commonwealth, or (more recently) early exemplars of rational industrial relations. Each of these orthodoxies has a certain validity. All have added to our knowledge. My quarrel with the first and second is that they tend to obscure the agency of working people, the degree to which they contributed by conscious efforts, to the making of history. My quarrel with the third is that it reads history in the light of subsequent preoccupations, and not as in fact it occurred. Only the successful (in the sense of those whose aspirations anticipated subsequent evolution) are remembered. The blind alleys, the lost causes, and the losers themselves are forgotten.

I am seeking to rescue the poor stockinger, the Luddite cropper, the 'obsolete' hand-loom weaver, the 'utopian' artisan, and even the deluded follower of Joanna Southcott, from the enormous condescension of posterity. Their crafts and traditions may have been dying. Their hostility to the new industrialism may have been backward-looking. Their communitarian ideals may have been fantasies. Their insurrectionary conspiracies may have been foolhardy. But they lived through these times of acute social disturbance, and we did not. Their aspirations were valid in terms of their own experience; and, if they were casualties of history, they remain, condemned in their own lives, as casualties.

Our only criterion of judgement should not be whether or not a man's actions are justified in the light of subsequent evolution. After all, we are not at the end of social evolution ourselves. In some of the lost causes of the people of the Industrial Revolution we may discover insights into social evils which we have yet to cure. Moreover, the greater part of the world today is still undergoing problems of industrialization, and of the formation of democratic institutions, analogous in many ways to our own experience during the Industrial Revolution. Causes which were lost in England might, in Asia or Africa, yet be won.

Finally, a note of apology to Scottish and Welsh readers. I have neglected these histories, not out of chauvinism, but out of respect. It is because class is a cultural as much as an economic formation that I have been cautious as to generalizing beyond English experience. (I have considered the Irish, not in Ireland, but as immigrants to England.) The Scottish record, in particular, is quite as dramatic, and as tormented, as our own. The Scottish Jacobin agitation was more intense and more heroic. But the Scottish story is significantly different. Calvinism was not the same thing as Methodism, although it is difficult to say which, in the early nineteenth century, was worse. We had no peasantry in England comparable to the Highland migrants. And the popular culture was very different. It is possible, at least until the 1820s, to regard the English and Scottish experiences as distinct, since trade union and political links were impermanent and immature.

Notes

1. An example of this approach, covering the period of this book, is to be found in the work of a colleague of Professor Talcott Parsons: N. J. Smelser, *Social Change in the Industrial Revolution* (1959).
2. R. Dahrendorf, *Class and Class Conflict in Industrial Society* (1959), pp. 148–9.

7 □ The Young Audience

Stuart Hall and Paddy Whannel

We have no delinquent generation of young people; we have a most selfish generation of young people. We have a materialistic generation of young people. We have a greedy generation of young people; having been given so much on a plate they expect the lot for the taking.

(*Teachers' World* editorial, 8 December 1961)

Go for the youngsters, go for as much sex as you can, go for as much violence as you can – and we are going to succeed. (Mr J. Goodlatte, Managing Director of ABC: reported in the *Daily Cinema*, April 1963)

The main emphasis in this book is on the content and forms of mass communication and the popular arts, rather than the sociology of audiences. But when we come to deal with 'teenage' entertainments and culture, the distinction between media and audience is difficult to maintain. For one thing, the postwar spurt in the growth of the media and the change in adolescent attitudes have gone hand in hand – apparently two aspects of the same social trend. Secondly, we are dealing with a whole culture from one specialized point of view: in our study particular weight is given to the nature and quality of popular entertainment for young people, whereas a full account of the culture would place more emphasis on other aspects of life – such as work, politics, the relation to the family, social and moral beliefs, and so on. Thirdly, we are dealing with the complex interaction between the attitudes of the young and what is provided for their consumption by the world of commercial entertainments. The picture of young people as innocents exploited by the sharp merchants of Denmark Street has some truth in it, but is over-simplified. We have a situation in some ways more similar to that of television, where the use intended

From Hall, S. and Whannel, P., *The Popular Arts*, Hutchinson, London, 1964, pp. 269–83, 294–7, 310–12.

by the provider and the use actually made by the audience of the particular style never wholly coincide, and frequently conflict. This conflict is particularly marked in the field of teenage entertainments, though it is to some extent common to the whole area of mass entertainment in a commercial setting. Our main purpose here is to show how these two aspects of the culture interact, and then to attempt an evaluation of the quality of the culture itself. Thus, in looking at the field of pop music, we shall have to consider the boom in teenage music, but also the role of the performers, their social biographies, the quality of their popular appeal, the music industry which promotes them to stardom, the publications, depending on the teenage reader, which support them, and the attitudes and feelings which are caught up and transposed by the beat of the music, the words of the lyrics and the vocal texture of the performers.

[. . .]

For many young people, Britain in the fifties and sixties has been a society in transition, a society throwing out a number of confusing signals. Teenage culture is, in part, an authentic response to this situation, an area of common symbols and meanings, shared in part or in whole by a generation, in which they can work out or work through not only the natural tensions of adolescence, but the special tensions of being an adolescent in our kind of society.

[. . .]

Of course, there is always a gap between the generations and it is difficult to judge whether the gap is now wider than it has been in the past. The conflict between generations is really one form of the maturing process in adolescence, and should trouble us only when it is so wide that the maturing process itself is disrupted. But it does seem likely that when we have, on the one hand, parents occupied with making the adjustment to a new tempo of life, and, on the other, a young generation which is itself the product of those changes to which adults are adjusting, the gap in social experience and feeling between the generations can become dangerously wide. Parents are always one generation behind their children: today they seem to be two generations behind. Naturally, there are many young people who don't experience these tensions at all, and one must be constantly aware of how varied the pattern is. But there is something like a majority feeling, even if the trends are really set by a small minority, and in the age of the mass media these tensions communicate themselves much more rapidly from place to place, group to group. One of the special features of this is the role of the media in speeding up the fashion-cycle among the young.

This helps to isolate teenagers as a distinct grouping from the rest of society. Paul Goodman suggests that youth is the only subculture which behaves as if it were a class. And this isolation is often stressed and validated by the media themselves. Some teenagers are genuinely 'misunderstood': Dr Winnicott has suggested that at this stage of adolescence they don't really want to be understood. But many more learn to feel misunderstood because they are told so often that they are. One could cite a host of articles, features and reports which, without trying to probe to the heart of the problem, loosely glamorize this feeling of group isolation. As an example of the trend in journalism, one selects almost at random an early edition of the magazine *Today*, still during this period in search of a new audience and format (12 March 1962; *Today* used to be *John Bull*). A rather jazzed-up 'Teenage Report to the Nation' ends with a familiar warning to adult squares: 'We're interesting people when you get to know us. Only you never will.' Earlier in the same article, in the section on teenage slang, we find the same emphasis: 'I'm giving all this knowledge away, but it will do you no good.' (Incidentally, judging from the jiving couple on the cover, this whole issue of *Today* was angled at the younger generation, but the list of contents provides a very strange glimpse of the composite editorial image of its audience: Today's Post – 'Anybody Want a Dream Home?'; 'How to Play the Stock Market' – 'Hitch your wagon to the big-money boys, the takeover bid specialists, who know where the profits are to be found'; 'The Snobs Who Come to My Parties' – by the Duke of Bedford; the Teenage Report; a feature entitled 'Look at the Accidents Pedestrians Cause'; 'Of Course I Believe in Luck' – by Gilbert Harding; a colour spread on the film *Can-Can*; 'When the Killer Strikes . . .'; and a story by Nevil Shute entitled 'Departure into Danger'. James Bond was promised for the following issue.)

The isolation of the subculture also becomes a major emphasis in the songs, lyrics, interviews with pop stars, teenage films, comics and stories. The culture provided by the commercial entertainment market therefore plays a crucial role. It mirrors attitudes and sentiments which are already there, and at the same time provides an expressive field and a set of symbols through which these attitudes can be projected. But it also gives those attitudes a certain stress and shape, particularizing a background of feelings by the choice of a certain style of dress, a particular 'look', by the way a typical emotion is rendered in a song or depicted in a drawing or photograph.

Teenage entertainments, therefore, play a cultural and educative role which commercial providers seem little aware of. Their symbols and fantasies have a strong hold upon the emotional commitment of the young at this stage in their development, and operate more powerfully in a situation where young people are tending to learn less from established institutions, such as the family, the school, the church and the immediate adult community, and more from one another. They rely more on themselves and their own culture, and they are picking up signals all the time, especially from the generation just ahead.

Teenage culture is a contradictory mixture of the authentic and the manufactured: it is an area of self-expression for the young and a lush grazing pasture for the commercial providers. One might use the cult figure of the pop singer as an illustration. He is usually a teenager, springing from the familiar adolescent world, and sharing a whole set of common feelings with his audience. But once he is successful, he is transformed into a commercial entertainer by the pop-music business. Yet in style, presentation and the material he performs, he must maintain his close involvement with the teenage world, or he will lose his popularity. The record companies see him as a means of marketing their products – he is a living, animated, commercial image. The audience will buy his records if they like his performances, and thus satisfy the provider's need to keep sales high: but they will also regard the pop singer as a kind of model, an idealized image of success, a glamorized version of themselves.

[. . .]

This apparent self-sufficiency in teenage culture is not simply a matter of keeping adult experience at arm's length; it is also a by-product of the limited subject matter and emotions dealt with in commercial entertainments. A study of the lyrics of teenage songs and the situations dramatized in them shows the recurrence of certain set patterns. These all deal with romantic love and sexual feeling. The emotion is intensely depicted, but the set-ups recur with monotonous regularity and the rendered style stereotypes the emotion. They deal exclusively with falling in love, falling out of love, longing for the fulfilment of love, the magic of love fulfilled. Of course, this has been the typical subject matter of popular song throughout the ages. But one has then to compare the actual quality of the statement in pop music with, say, the folk song or the blues or even the pointed Johnny Mercer lyric of the twenties to appreciate the particular flavour, the generalized loneliness and yearning – a yearning of 'nobody in particular for anyone-at-all', as Philip Oakes one wrote.

> Johnny An-gel
> He doesn't even know I exist
> . . . I pray someday he'll love me
> And together we will see
> How lovely Heaven will be.

These songs, and the romantic stories with which they have so much in common, portray what Francis Newton calls 'the condition, the anxieties, the bragging and uncertainty of school-age love and increasingly school-age sex'. They reflect adolescent difficulties in dealing with a tangle of emotional and sexual problems. They invoke the need to experience life directly and intensely. They express the drive for security in an uncertain and changeable emotional world. The fact that they are produced for a commercial market means that the songs and settings lack a certain authenticity. Yet they also dramatize authentic feelings. They express vividly the adolescent emotional dilemma. And since they are often written on behalf of the adult providers of the entertainment world by teenage stars and songwriters, who share the cultural ethos of their audiences, there is a good deal of interaction and feedback going on all the time.

These emotions, symbols and situations drawn off from the provided teenage culture contain elements both of emotional realism and of fantasy fulfilment. There is a strong impulse at this age to identify which these collective representations and to use them as guiding fictions. Such symbolic fictions are the folklore by means of which the teenager, in part, shapes and composes his mental picture of the world.

[...]

Because of its high emotional content, teenage culture is essentially non-verbal. It is more naturally expressed in music, in dancing, in dress, in certain habits of walking and standing, in certain facial expressions and 'looks' or in idiomatic slang. Though there is much to be learned from the lyrics of pop songs, there is more in the *beat* (loud, simple, insistent), the *backing* (strong, guitar-dominated), the *presentation* (larger-than-life, mechanically etherealized), the *inflections* of voice (sometimes the self-pitying, plaintive cry, and later the yeah-saying, affirmative shouting) or the *intonations* (at one stage mid-Atlantic in speech and pronunciation, but more recently rebelliously northern and provincial). One can trace a whole line of development in popular music by listening to intonations – Louis Armstrong's gravelly rasp on the last word in 'I Can't Give You Anything But Love, Baby' becomes Elvis Presley's breathy, sensual invocation, 'Bab-eh' is then anglicized into Adam Faith's 'Boi-by', with a marked Cockney twist (in 'What Do You Want If You Don't Want Money?') and provincialized by groups like The Beatles.

Certain attitudes seem not only to recur with emphasis in the provided culture, but to have found some specially appropriate physical image or presence among teenagers themselves. This teenage 'look' can be partly attributed to the designers of mass-produced fashions and off-the-peg clothes and to the cosmetic advice syndicated in girls' and women's magazines. C & A's and Marks and Spencer's, by marketing fashionable styles at reasonable prices, have played a significant role here. But these styles have a deeper social basis. The very preoccupation with the image of the self is important – pleasing, though often taken to extremes. Dress has become, for the teenager, a kind of minor popular art, and is used to express certain contemporary attitudes. There is, for example, a strong current of social nonconformity and rebelliousness among teenagers. At an early stage these antisocial feelings were quite active – the rejection of authority in all its forms, and a hostility towards adult institutions and conventional moral and social customs. During this period, adult commentators often misread this generalized nonconformism as a type of juvenile delinquency, though it had little to do with organized crime and violence. The 'Teddy Boy' style, fashionable some years ago, with its tumbling waterfall hairstyle, fetishistic clothes, long jackets, velvet collars, thick-soled shoes, and the accoutrements which went along with them – string ties with silver medallions, lengthy key-chains, studded ornamental belts – was a perfect physical expression of this spirit. Contrary to expectations, this style did not disappear, but persisted in the dress of motorcycle addicts and 'ton-up' kids, and reappeared with the 'rockers'. A variant of this nonconformity could be found among 'ravers' or beatniks, with the trend to long hair, heavy sweaters, drainpiped jeans and boots or black stockings and high heels. The Teddy Boy look, an historical throwback, with its recall of Edwardian times, matched exactly the primitivism of the attitudes it expressed.

[. . .]

In what terms it is possible to establish even rough standards of judgement about this kind of music? There are many forces at work which inhibit any judgement whatsoever: pop music is regarded as the exclusive property of the teenager, admission to outsiders reserved. In these terms, disqualification is by age limit. But, of course, this is nonsense. Like any other popular commercial music, teenage pop is light entertainment music, intended for dancing, singing, leisure and enjoyment. It differs in character, but not in *kind*, from other sorts of popular music which have provided a base for commercial entertainment since the advent of jazz, and before. If we are unable to comment on its quality and to make meaningful distinctions, it is largely because we lack a vocabulary of criticism for dealing with the lighter and more transient qualities which are part of a culture of leisure. We need that vocabulary very much indeed now, since this is the area in which the new media are at play.

On the other hand, there are counter-forces at work which dismiss *all* pop music simply because of its teenage connections and its cult qualities. This reaction is just as dangerous since it is based upon prejudice. It springs in part from the inability of adults to establish their own points of reference in relation to popular culture – even though, lying behind the rejection of Elvis Presley, there is often a secret addiction to Gracie Fields or Vera Lynn or the Charleston or Al Jolson or Nelson Eddy. (One needs to listen carefully to the older Tin Pan Alley tunes which survive in the repertoire of any pub sing-song to detect the connections.) There must also remain the suspicion that pop music provides a sitting target for those who have, for some unaccountable reason, to work off social envy or aggression against the younger generation. From this point of view, contemporary pops could not be better designed, since they are basically loud, raucous, always played at full volume, an obvious affront to good taste. They are frankly sensual in appeal, with persistent themes of youth, love and sex (but then, look again at the lyrics in Reeves's *Idiom of the People*): and these themes are given a physical image in the pop singer himself, whose behaviour on and off stage is a challenge to British modesty and reserve. Worst of all, the music itself is an affirmation of a spirit of adolescent rebelliousness and independence, and therefore, it is supposed, symbolizes some sort of deep undermining of adult authority and tastes.

Pop music may well be all of these things, but that does not help us much at the end of the day. For it is more difficult to judge, keeping one's respect both for the lively qualities embodied and the standards of light entertainment generally, the quality of a music which is so entwined with the cult of its own presentation, so mixed in with the mystic rites of the pop singer and his mythology and so shot through with commercialism. It might be said, then, that the pops cannot be judged at all – but have rather to be seen as part of a whole subculture, and handled as one would the chants and ceremonies of a primitive tribe. Are these standards anthropological?

This method, too, has its pitfalls. It invites a slack relativism, whereby pop music of any kind is excused because it plays a functional role in the teenage world. Functional it is – but the relationship between what is authentically part of teenage culture and what is provided for that culture by an adult and organized industry is not a simple one. If we add the evidence of the first part of this chapter, which deals with authentic features of the culture, to the second part, which describes the organization of the industry, we see how necessary it is to view this phenomenon both from within and without teenage culture itself. And this consideration brings us back to one of the basic problems in popular culture – does the audience get what it likes (in which case, are those likes enough?) and needs (in which case, are the needs healthy ones?), or is it getting to like what it is given (in which case, perhaps tastes can be extended)? Nowhere in this whole field is it so true that the real answer lies in an understanding of how these two factors interact in contemporary popular culture.

[. . .]

Throughout we have constantly made comparisons between pop music and jazz. This is because, though there are many individual pop songs worth listening to, in general jazz seems an infinitely richer kind of music, both aesthetically and emotionally. The comparison this way seems much more rewarding than the more typical confrontation which is so frequently made between pop music and classical music. The reference to jazz helps us to make comparisons with another entertainment music, which nevertheless has legitimate uses and discernible standards. The point behind such comparisons ought not to be simply to wean teenagers away from the juke-box heroes, but to alert them to the severe limitations and the ephemeral quality of music which is so formula-dominated and so directly attuned to the standards set by the commercial market. It is a genuine widening of sensibility and emotional range which we should be working for – an extension of tastes which might lead to an extension of pleasure. The worst thing which we would say of pop music is not that it is vulgar, or morally wicked, but, more simply, that much of it is not very good.

8 □ Working-Class Culture and Working-Class Politics in London, 1870–1900: Notes on the Remaking of a Working Class

Gareth Stedman Jones

[...]

The traditional culture of all London artisans had been work-centered. In the first half of the nineteenth century, most London trades worked a twelve-hour day, six days a week, with a daily break of two hours for meals. Workers generally lived in the immediate vicinity of their work. Political discussion, drinking and conviviality took place either at the workplace itself or at a local pub which generally served as a house of call and a center of union organization. Trade feasts, carnivals and outings were normal. Intermarriage, a hereditary tendency in apprenticeship and a distinctive language and dress all reinforced trade solidarity; even broad political movements like Chartism were to some extent organized on a trade basis. If this was the 'republic of artisans', it was a very masculine republic. Homes were cramped and uncomfortable; where they were not the place of work, they were little more than places to sleep and eat in. Even if some artisans discussed politics with their wives, women were *de facto* excluded from the focal institutions of this culture.

In the second half of the century, this work-centered culture began to yield to a culture oriented towards the family and the home. By the mid-1870s, weekly hours of work had been substantially reduced in most skilled trades. A $54–56\frac{1}{2}$-hour week, or a nine-hour day and a Saturday half holiday became general. The growth of sporting interests, seaside excursions, working men's clubs and music halls from

From *Journal of Social History*, vol. 7, 1973–4, pp. 460–508.

about this time is therefore not accidental. In London, however, this increase in leisure time should be seen in connection with another tendency – the growing geographical separation between home and workplace.

[. . .]

From the 1870s, the migration of the skilled working class to the suburbs became a mass phenomenon. While the residential population of the City declined from 75,000 in 1871 to 38,000 in 1891, its daytime population increased from 170,000 in 1866 to 301,000 in 1891. The old skilled artisan centre of Holborn and Finsbury was reduced from 93,423 to 66,781 in the same period. By the time of the Booth survey, the majority of workers commanding skilled wage rates commuted to work on a tram, a workman's train or on foot.[1]

This combination of increased leisure time and suburban migration would alone have eroded the strength of the work-centered culture. But it was combined with a number of other factors which further reinforced this process. The fall of prices in the Great Depression period produced a rise in real wages spread over the whole employed population. This increased spending power again strengthened the importance of home and family.

[. . .]

Yet despite its growing ideological significance the home remained a crowded and unrelaxing environment. After the evening meal, therefore, men and to some extent women continued to pass a high proportion of their evenings in the pub. If the man commuted to work, however, the regular pub visited would no longer be the trade pub near the workplace, but the 'local'. At the 'local' they would mingle with men of different trades and occupations. Conversation was less likely to concern trade matters, more likely to reflect common interests, politics to a certain extent, but more often, sport and entertainment.

[. . .]

If we wish to find a peculiarly metropolitan form of the new working-class culture, it is to the music hall that we must look.

[. . .]

Despite the repeated claims made for its educational value by its promoters, the music hall, like the fairs and the races, was subject to constant evangelical disapproval. Music halls began as extensions to public houses and the sale of drink remained the mainstay of their profits. Added to this there were frequent allegations – often well-founded – that the halls were used by prostitutes to pick up clients. Yet, despite the efforts of campaigners for temperance, moral purity or a more intelligent use of leisure time, not to mention determined attempts by theatre managers to crush a dangerous rival, the number of music halls increased dramatically between 1850 and 1900. The first music hall was built as an extension to the Canterbury Arms, Lambeth by the publican, Charles Morton, in 1849 and housed 100 people. Its success was immediate, and by 1856 it had both been enlarged to hold 700 and then rebuilt to hold 1,500. By 1866, there were 23 halls in addition to innumerable pub rooms where music hall entertainment was held. In the 1870s the number of halls continued to increase at a prodigious rate even though 200 halls were closed after strict fire precautions had been imposed in 1878. In the 1880s it was estimated that there were 500 halls in London, and at the beginning of the 1890s it was calculated that the 35 largest halls alone were catering to an average audience of 45,000 nightly.

Although music hall entertainment spread to the provinces, it began and remained a characteristically London creation. According to a Parliamentary Commission in 1892, 'the large collection of theatres and music halls gathered together, the amount of capital used in the enterprise, the great number of persons, directly and indirectly provided with employment, the multitudes of all classes of the people who attend theatres and music halls of London, find no other parallel in any other part of the country.' Apart from the central palaces which particularly from the 1880s onwards began to attract sporting aristocrats, military officers, students, clerks and tourists, the music hall was predominantly working-class, both in the character of its audience, the origins of its performers and the content of its songs and sketches.

[. . .]

In general the music hall appealed to all sectors of the working class from the casual labourer to the highly paid artisan. Its importance as a social and cultural institution in proletarian districts was second only to that of the pub.

[. . .]

[I]t is clear that by the beginning of the twentieth century a new working-class culture had emerged in London. Many of its institutions dated back to the middle of the century, but its general shape had first become visible in the 1870s, and dominant in the 1890s. [. . .] This culture was clearly distinguished from the culture of the middle class and had remained largely impervious to middle-class attempts to dictate its character or direction. Its dominant cultural institutions were not the school, the evening class, the library, the friendly society, the church or the chapel, but the pub, the sporting paper, the race course and the music hall.

[. . .]

Once the evidence is sifted critically, the music hall can give us a crucial insight into the attitudes of working-class London. But this can only be done if working-class music hall is disentangled from its West End variant with which it is generally confused.

Music hall has both a reflection and a reinforcement of the major trends in London working-class life from the 1870s to the 1900s. [. . .] Music hall was a participatory form of leisure activity, but not a demanding one. The audience joined in the chorus, but if they didn't like the song or the sentiments expressed, they 'gave it the bird', and it was unlikely to be heard again. Top stars could earn up to £100 a week by rushing from one hall to another in the course of each evening. But the profession was also crowded with less successful aspirants. The vast majority of performers came from poor backgrounds and began by doing turns in pubs or trying themselves out in a newcomer's spot in one of the smaller halls. Since most singers were generally too poor to pay a song writer, they composed the lyrics themselves, usually adapting it to an already known tune. Until it was transformed by the coming of the more pretentious palaces of variety in the Edwardian period, the atmosphere of the halls was more like that of the pub than the theatre. Indeed, many of the smaller halls were simply extensions to pub premises. Performances were continuous from 6 to 11, but the audience could move freely to and from the bar which was responsible for half the profits of the proprietor. The great boast of music hall and of Charles Morton, its self-appointed 'father', was that it was a 'family entertainment'. Unlike the old 'free and easies' and pub sing-songs which had been popular in the 1840s, the music hall admitted women, and avoided overtly obscene songs. In fact, the bulk of the audiences were composed of young unmarried workers, male and female; but all witnesses agreed that there was always a fair sprinkling of families as well.

In working-class districts, where the multiplicity of occupations, the separation of home from workplace and the overcrowding and impermanence of apartments made any stable community life very difficult, the local hall with its blaze of light and sham opulence, its laughter and its chorus singing, fulfilled, if only in an anonymous way, a craving for solidarity in facing the daily problems of poverty and family life. Music hall stood for the small pleasures of working-class life – a glass of 'glorious English beer', a hearty meal of 'boiled beef and carrots', a day by the seaside, Derby Day and the excitements and tribulations of betting, a bank holiday spent on Hampstead Heath or in Epping Forest, the pleasures of courtship and the joys of friendship.[2] Its attitude was *a little bit of what you fancy does you good*. Music hall was perhaps the most unequivocal response of the London working class to middle-class evangelism. As Marie Lloyd told her critics in 1897:

> You take the pit on a Saturday night or a Bank Holiday. You don't suppose they want Sunday school stuff do you? They want lively stuff with music they can learn quickly. Why, if I was to try and sing highly moral songs they would fire ginger beer bottles and beer mugs at me. They don't pay their sixpences and shillings at a Music Hall to hear the Salvation Army.[3]

Or, as the *Era* had put it in 1872:

> The artisan tired with his day's labour, wants something to laugh at. He neither wants to be preached to. nor is he anxious to listen to the lugubrious effusions of Dr. Watts or the poets of the United Kingdom Alliance.[4]

Music hall appealed to the London working class because it was both escapist *and yet* strongly rooted in the realities of working-class life. This was particularly true of its treatment of the relations between the sexes. While its attitude towards courtship could be rhapsodic, there were few illusions about marriage.

[. . .]

Among the poor, marriage was normally the result of pregnancy, but among all sectors of the working class, marriage meant children and the constant drudgery of work on a declining standard of living until they were old enough to bring money into the home. Marriage as a 'comic disaster' is an endless refrain of music-hall songs. The titles of the best-known male songs are self-explanatory: Tom Costello's 'At Trinity Church I met my doom', Charles Coburn's 'Oh what an Alteration', Gus Elen's 'It's a great big shame', or George Beauchamp's 'She was one of the early birds and I was one of the worms'. The lead in translating courtship into marriage was normally taken by the woman. For working-class women, marriage was an economic necessity and unlikely to happen after the age of 25. Booth stated that among the poor, marriage banns were almost invariably put up by the woman.[5] The anxiety of girls to get married was the theme of many female songs like Lily Morris's 'Why am I always the bridesmaid, never the blushing bride?' or Vesta Victoria's 'Waiting at the Church'. According to Dan Leno, in his sketch of the lodger entitled 'Young Men taken in and Done for':

> I'll tell you how the misfortune happened. One morning Lucy Jagg's mother came upstairs to my room, knocked at the door and said, 'Mr. Skilley are you up?' I said, 'No, what for?' Mrs. Jaggs said, 'Come along get up, you're going to be married.' I said, 'No, I don't know anything about it.' She said, 'Yes you do, you spoke about it last night, when you'd had a little drink.' Well, I thought, if I did say so, I suppose I did, so I came downstairs half asleep (in fact I think every man's half asleep when he going to be married).[6]

But despite their determination to achieve wedlock, the attitude of women to marriage was no more romantic than that of men. The pros and cons were summed up by Marie Loftus in 'Girls, we would never stand it':

> When first they come courting,
>   how nice they behave,
> For a smile or a kiss,
>   how humbly they crave
> But when once a girl's wed,
>   she's a drudge and a slave.

Nevertheless, she concludes,

> I think we would all prefer
>   marriage with strife
> Than be on the shelf
>   and be nobody's wife.[7]

The same comic realism dominated the depiction of relations between husband and wife. Husbands make themselves out to be dominated by the tyranny of their wives. They escape to the pub, go off to the races and lose money on horses or are cheated out of it by 'welshers', they get drunk and return home to face the consequences. Males are generally represented as incompetent at spending money and are endlessly getting 'done'. But if a wife is incompetent at managing the household, the results are much more serious. In the end the wife who 'jaws' is preferable to the wife who drinks. The problems of the lodger, the landlord and the pawnbroker shop are also constantly discussed. Finally, the threat of destitution in old age, once children no longer contribute to the family income and the man is too old to work, is not evaded. The whole point of Albert Chevalier's famous song 'My Old Dutch' is that it is sung in front of the backdrop representing the workhouse with its separate entrances for men and women.

In music hall, work is an evil to be avoided when possible. But the only real escape suggested in the songs is the surprise inheritance or the lucky windfall. [. . .] when such an escape is made in the songs, the result is consternation; the former friend begins 'to put on airs', as Gus Elen sang: ' 'E don't know where 'e are.' Class is a life sentence, as final as any caste system. The pretensions of those who feigned escape aroused particular scorn, as did those who suggested that education would change this state of affairs. According to a *Daily Telegraph* report of Mrs Lane's Britannia Theatre in Hoxton in 1883:

> Here is a large audience mainly composed of the industrious classes, determined to enjoy itself to the utmost. . . . Mrs. Lane's friends feel the disgrace which attaches to a fulfilling of the requirements of the School Board so that when one of the characters upon the stage pertinently asks, 'if every kid's brought up to be a clerk, what about labour? Who's to do the work?' there rises a mighty outburst of applause.[8]

There was no political solution to the class system. It was simply a fact of life. They certainly did not consider it to be just, for as Billy Bennett sang, 'It's the rich what gets the pleasure, It's the poor what gets the blame'. But socialism was just a lot of hot air. As Little Tich put it, in his sketch of the gas-meter collector, 'My brother's in the gas trade too, you know. In fact he travels on gas. He's a socialist orator.' Music hall never gave class a political definition. Trade unionism was accepted as an intrinsic part of working-class life and the music-hall songs of 1889 supported the 'Docker's tanner'.[9] But music hall didn't generally sing about the relationship between workers and employers, and the capitalist is completely absent as a music-hall stereotype. The general music-hall attitude was that if a worker could get a fair day's wage for a fair day's work, that was a good thing, but if the worker could get a fair day's wage without doing a fair day's work, that was even better. The attitude towards the rich was similarly indulgent. The general depiction of the upper class was, as MacInnes has remarked, not hostile but comic.[10] Upper-class figures like Champagne Charlie, Burlington Bertie, the 'toff' and the galloping major were incompetent and absurd, but there was no reference to the source of their income.

Music hall has often been associated with a mood of bombastic jingoism, associated with MacDermott's 1878 song 'We don't want to fight but by jingo if we do', or 'Soldiers of the Queen', sung at the time of the Boer war.[11] The audiences of Piccadilly and Leicester Square sang these songs with undoubted gusto, and, judging by the innumerable song sheets on these themes, could never get enough of them. But the predominant mood of the working-class halls was anti-heroic. Workers were prepared to admire and sing about the bravery of the common soldier or the open-handed generosity of the sailor, but they did not forget the realities of military life. Men joined the army usually to escape unemployment, and if they survived their years of service, it was to unemployment that they would return. According to one song of the 1890s which recounts a conversation between Podger and his lodger, a soldier on leave:

> Said he, now Podger, Why don't you enlist,
>   you'll get cheap beer
> The glories too, of war in view
>   Come be a soldier bold
> Said I, not me. No not me,
>   I'm not having any don't you see
> Might lose my legs, come home on pegs.
>   Then when I'm O-L-D
> Not wanted more.
>   Workhouse door
> Not, not, not, not me.[12]

In a song which was enormously popular in the 1890s, Charles Godfrey's 'On Guard', an old Crimean veteran asks for a night's shelter in the workhouse casual ward. 'Be off, you tramp,' exclaims the harsh janitor. 'You are not wanted here.' 'No,' thunders the tattered veteran, 'I am *not* wanted *here*, but at Balaclava, I *was* wanted *there*.' This scene, which was a working-class favorite, was apparently curtailed in the West End because officers from the household brigade complained that it was bad for recruiting.[13]

Working-class music hall was conservative in the sense that it accepted class divisions and the distribution of wealth as part of the natural order of things. By the 1890s, the class resentment expressed in Godfrey's sketch was as near as it came to political criticism. But the music-hall industry was not merely a passive barometer of working-class opinion. And here lies the difficulty of using it simply as an index of working-class attitudes. For in the period between 1870 and 1900 it became actively and self-consciously Tory. There were two major reasons for this development.

The first reason was the growth of a second audience for music-hall entertainment, alongside that of the working class. This new audience consisted of sporting aristocrats, from the Prince of Wales downwards, guards officers from St James's, military and civil officials on leave from imperial outposts, clerks and white-collar workers, university, law and medical students and the growing number of tourists from the white Dominions. This audience can be dated back to the 1860s, but it first reached boom proportions in the 1880s, as witnessed by the opening of the new Pavilion in 1884, rapidly followed by the Empire, the Trocadero, the Tivoli and the Palace. The Empire was the most famous centre of this new audience. It provided a natural focus for jingoism, upper-class rowdyism and high-class prostitution. The most popular event in its annual calendar was boat race night, a drunken saturnalia in which all breakable objects had to be removed from the reach of its tipsy 'swells'. There was little in common between these imperial playgrounds and the working-class halls, except for the important fact that these new palaces drew upon the working-class halls for many of their performers. Furthermore, as the entertainment business became more organized and monopolistic, and combines began to take over the proletarian halls, the turns offered in Hackney or Piccadilly to some extent converged.[14]

In the 1860s many of the songs sung in the working-class halls were still anti-aristocratic and populist in tone. They were still at a halfway stage between the old street ballad and the mature music-hall song. Even Frederick Stanley, defending music-hall interests before a Parliamentary enquiry in 1866, conceded as the one valid objection to the music hall 'the immense difficulty of improving the comic element'. 'I believe', he stated, 'it is impossible to get a comic song written worthy of the present age.' But the atmosphere changed in the 1870s with the appearance of stars like Leybourne, Vance and MacDermott. The anti-aristocratic element in the songs disappeared, the intellectual level fell and a jingoist tone became prominent. The effects of the new audience were clearly evident by the late 1880s, when Vesta Tilley stated:

> Nowadays, nothing goes down better than a good patriotic song, for politics are played out as they are far too common. Talking of that suggests the oddity of the music hall audience in their political bent. Every such allusion must be Conservative.[15]

This first reason for music-hall Toryism, the growth of an aristocratic and jingoist clientele, had little to do with any marked shift in working-class opinion. But the second reason affected slum and West End music halls alike. This was the increasing association between Toryism and the drink trade. In the first half of the nineteenth century, as Brian Harrison has shown, the pub was not the exclusive property of any particular political interest and in fact London brewing magnates tended to be Whig or Liberal rather than Conservative. But the rise of the teetotal movement and its growing tendency to operate as a pressure group on the flank of the Liberal Party began to push publicans and music-hall proprietors towards Toryism. This tendency became increasingly apparent after the 1871 Liberal Licensing Act.[16] In the 1880s, liberals, teetotallers and radical temperance advocates attacked both the central pleasure palaces and the working-class halls with equal vigor, for both were associated, although in unequal proportions, with drinking, gambling, prostitution, crude chauvinism and the absence of educational content. In the early 1880s, the temperance crusader, F. N. Charrington, launched his attack on Lusby's Music Hall on the Mile End Road and the Salvation Army made an unsuccessful attempt to close down the Eagle in the City Road. But reformers did not confine their assaults to the working-class halls. In 1894, Mrs Ormiston Chant of the Social Purity League challenged the license of the Empire in the name of 'the calm steady voice of righteous public opinion, the non-conformist conscience'.[17] Supported by the Progressive party and the Labour bench on the London County Council, Mrs Chant was successful in getting a screen erected between the auditorium and the bars, thus fencing off the audience from the provision of drink and the solicitation of prostitutes. But the young 'swells' and 'toffs' of the period, who regarded the Empire as their spiritual home, violently resisted this restriction of their prerogatives. On the Saturday following the erection of the screen, 200–300 aristocratic rowdies smashed it down again with their walking sticks and paraded in triumph around Leicester Square, waving its fragments at the passers-by. [. . .] This incident was no doubt the origin of the myth, assiduously cultivated by the upper class after the war, of an affinity of outlook between the 'top and bottom drawer' against the 'kill-joys' in between. It is true, however, that for different reasons, both the proletarian halls and the West End pleasure strip were devitalized in the succeeding twenty years. The West End became more decorous after the Wilde scandal, while the working-class halls were bought up by the Moss-Stoll syndicate, whose policy was to replace the 'coarseness and vulgarity' of the halls by the gentility and decorum of the Palace of Variety. Music-hall entertainment was given its final kiss of death with the achievement of a Royal Command Performance in 1912. Music-hall artistes removed from their acts any allusions that could be considered offensive or coarse and vainly tried to win the approval of King George V – 'a lover of true Bohemianism', according to Conan Doyle's unctuous description of the proceedings.

If these had been the only tendencies at work in music hall since the 1870s, it would be difficult to explain its prominent position in London working-class culture. But it was the mid-eighties which also witnessed the emergence of the greatest and best-loved music-hall performers – Dan Leno, Marie Lloyd, Gus Elen, Little Tich, Kate Karney and others. These artistes, who all sprang from poor London backgrounds, articulated with much greater accuracy than their predecessors the mood and attitudes of the London masses. Although they were popular in both the West and the East End, they sang or spoke not about the Empire or the Conservative Party, but about the occupations, food, drink, holidays, romances, marriages and misfortunes of the back streets. It is from their songs that the specificity of London working-class culture can best be assessed.

Unlike the ballad, the songs of these performers expressed neither deep tragedy nor real anger. They could express wholehearted enjoyment of simple pleasures or unbounded sentimentality in relation to objects of affection. But when confronted with the daily oppressions of the life of the poor, their reactions were fatalistic. In the middle of the century, Mayhew had written:

> Where the means of sustenance and comfort are fixed, the human being becomes conscious of what he has to depend upon.
>   If, however his means be uncertain – abundant at one time, and deficient at another – a spirit of speculation or gambling with the future will be induced, and the individual gets to believe in 'luck' and 'fate' as the arbiters of his happiness rather than to look upon himself as 'the architect of his fortunes' – trusting to 'chance' rather than his own powers and foresight to relieve him at the hour of necessity.[18]

This was precisely the attitude to life projected by the London music hall. The two greatest products of that culture, Dan Leno and Charlie Chaplin, play little men, perpetually 'put upon'; they have no great ideals or ambitions; the characters they play are undoubtedly very poor, but not obviously or unmistakably proletarian; they are unmistakably products of city life, but their place within it is indeterminate; their exploits are funny but also pathetic; they are forever being chased by men or women, physically larger than themselves, angry foremen, outraged husbands, domineering landladies or burly wives; but it is usually chance circumstances, unfortunate misunderstandings, not of their own making, which have landed them in these situations; and it is luck more than their own efforts which finally comes to the rescue.

The art of Leno and Chaplin brings us back again to the situation of the poor and the working class in late Victorian and Edwardian London; to that vast limbo of semi-employed labourers, casualized semi-skilled artisans, sweated home workers, despised foreigners, tramps and beggars.

[...]

Music hall highlighted the peculiarities of the working-class situation in London. But it also reflected the general development of the English working class after 1870. Fatalism, political scepticism, the evasion of tragedy or anger and a stance of comic stoicism were pre-eminently Cockney attitudes because the decline of artisan traditions, the tardiness of factory development, the prevalence of casual work and the shifting amorphous character of the new proletarian suburbs were particularly marked features of London life. But it would be a mistake to overemphasize the purely local significance of these themes. In industrial areas more homogeneous than London, trade unionism tended to occupy a much more commanding place in working-class culture. In such communities, co-ops, friendly societies, choral clubs and football teams were also more likely to flourish. But these were differences of degree, not of kind. There are good historical reasons why after 1870 London pioneered music hall, while coal, cotton and ship-building areas in the north generated the most solid advances in trade unionism.

Trapped in the twilight world of small workshop production, London was not well-placed to sustain the defensive corporate forms of solidarity upon which working-class politics was increasingly to be based. The strength of its own political tradition had not been founded on the factory. It therefore registered the new situation in predominantly cultural forms. But music hall did spread to the provinces and trade unions were slowly able to secure important pockets of strength in certain areas of London. There was great diversity of local experience, but no unbridgeable gulf. What is finally most striking is the basic consistency of outlook reflected in the new working-class culture which spread over England after 1870.

If the 'making of the English working class' took place in the 1790–1830 period, something akin to a remaking of the working class took place in the years between 1870 and 1900. For much of the cluster of 'traditional' working-class attitudes analyzed by contemporary sociologists and literary critics, dates not from the first third, but from the last third of the nineteenth century. This remaking process did not obliterate the legacy of that first formative phase of working-class history, so well described by Edward Thompson. But it did transform its meaning. In the realm of working-class ideology, a second formative layer of historical experience was superimposed upon the first, thereby coloring the first in the light of its own changed horizons of possibility. The struggles of the first half of the century were not forgotten, but they were recalled selectively and re-interpreted. The solidarity and organizational strength achieved in social struggles were channeled into trade union activity and eventually into a political party based upon that activity and its goals. The distinctiveness of a working-class way of life was enormously accentuated. Its separateness and impermeability were now reflected in a dense and inward-looking culture, whose effect·was both to emphasize the distance of the working class from the classes above it and to articulate its position within an apparently permanent social hierarchy.

The growth of trade unionism on the one hand and the new working-class culture on the other were not contradictory but interrelated phenomena. Both signified a major shift in the predominant forms of working-class activity. What above all differentiated the Chartist period from the post-1870 period was the general belief that the economic and political order brought into being by the Industrial Revolution was a temporary aberration, soon to be brought to an end. This belief sustained the activities of moderate Chartists like Lovett and Vincent no less than Harney and O'Connor. It was this half articulated conviction that had made Chartism into a mass force.

Once the defeat of Chartism was finally accepted, this conviction disappeared. Working people ceased to believe that they could shape society in their own image. Capitalism had become an immovable horizon. Demands produced by the movements of the pre-1850 period – republicanism, secularism, popular self-education, co-operation, land reform, internationalism, etc. – now shorn of the conviction which had given them point, eventually expired from sheer inanition, or else, in a diluted form, were appropriated by the left flank of Gladstonian liberalism. The main impetus of working-class activity now lay elsewhere. It was concentrated into trade unions, co-ops, friendly societies, all indicating a *de facto* recognition of the existing social order as the inevitable framework of action. The same could be said of music hall. It was a culture of consolation.

Notes

1. See C. Booth, *Life and Labour of the People in London* (1902), Series 2 (industry series) *passim*, for commuting habits skilled workers in various trades, and see Series 2, vol. 5, ch. III, for summary.
2. See Colin MacInnes, *Sweet Saturday Night* (1967), pp. 106–23.
3. Quoted in D. Farson, *Marie Lloyd and Music Hall* (1972), p. 57.
4. A. E. Wilson, *East End Entertainment* (1954), p. 215.
5. Booth, op. cit., final volume, p. 45.
6. *McGlennon's Star Song Book* (1888), No. 10, p. 4.
7. *Ibid.*, No. 4, p. 3.
8. Wilson, *East End Entertainment*, p. 183.
9. See 'The Dock Labourers' Strike' and the 'Dock Labourer' in *New and Popular Songs* (1889).
10. MacInnes, *Sweet Saturday Night*, p. 108.
11. According to one report, Disraeli used to send his secretary, Monty Corry, to the music hall to listen in on MacDermott's song to assess the extent of support for his foreign policy. See J. B. Booth (ed.), *Seventy Years of Song* (1943), p. 38.
12. *MacGlennon's Star Song Book* (1896–7), No. 105.
13. Harold Scott, *The Early Doors* (1946), p. 215.
14. Real convergence was more possible in variety than in music hall. Even Marie Lloyd found herself booed in the East End music hall when she attempted to sing some of her more risqué West End numbers. See Farson, *Marie Lloyd and Music Hall*, p. 75.
15. *McGlennon's Star Song Book*, No. 8, p. 2.
16. Royden Harrison, *Before the Socialists* (1965), pp. 319–48.
17. Mrs Ormiston Chant, *Why We Attacked the Empire* (1895), p. 5.
18. H. Mayhew, *London Labour and the London Poor* (1861), vol. 2, p. 325.

9 □ 'Get up, get into it and get involved' – Soul, Civil Rights and Black Power

Paul Gilroy

[...]

This section turns away from the relationship between Britain and the Caribbean to focus on Afro-America, a second source of cultural and political raw-material for UK blacks in the postwar period.

[...]

James Brown's 'Say It Loud I'm Black and I'm Proud', the ChiLites 'Power To The People' and various versions of Weldon Irvine jnr's 'Young Gifted and Black' were all taken to the heart of black communities many miles from those in which they were created. These recordings are only the most obvious illustrations of the character of a period in which soul was revered as the principal criterion for affiliation to the Black Power movement. *Ebony* pronounced 1967 the year of 'Retha, Rap and Revolt' and during this time, singers, typified by James Brown, 'Soul Brother no. 1', and Aretha Franklin, 'The First Lady', were identified as the spiritual and moral guardians of the inner meanings not merely of black music but of black American culture as a whole. They were a priestly caste guarding the spirit in the dark which represented a political community's sense of its history (Jones, 1967). These singers did not simply provide a soundtrack for the political actions of their soul sisters and brothers. They were mandated to speak on behalf of the community in elaborate, celebratory, ritual performances. The privileged position which flowed from enjoying a public voice was used by artists to blend the contradictory elements of the Black Power movement into an uneasy unity and to

From Gilroy, P., *There Ain't No Black in the Union Jack*, Hutchinson, London, 1987, pp. 171–221.

create an anti-racist current among whites, particularly the young. Song after song from this era urges the oppressors to 'think' while simultaneously warning them of the dire consequences which would develop if freedom did not follow.[1] The most powerful songs from these years provide a musical counterpart to the urgent definitions of Black Power which were being advanced as 'the last reasonable opportunity' for American society to work out its racial problems (Carmichael and Hamilton, 1967). The Impressions were, like many others, swept along by the tide of black pride and articulated these aspirations in their late-1960s hits 'We're Rolling On' and 'We're a Winner': 'No more tears do we cry, We have finally dried our eyes and We're moving on up.'

The reformist strategies of the Civil Rights period had developed hand in hand with the movement's espousal of non-violence, creating, indeed requiring, a musical culture which pointed to the patience, dignity and determination of blacks in the furtherance of racial justice. With Black Power, both the tone and the tactics changed. The political focus shifted towards the idea that civil disobedience had to be supplemented by a capacity for defensive violence which was symbolized by Huey Newton's armed Panthers on patrol in Oakland (Newton, 1974).

The defensive militarization of elements within the Black Power movement may have started as a simple response to police harassment and repressive use of the legal system. However, once blacks were speaking the contending revolutionary languages of Marxism–Leninism and cultural–nationalism, in public and seen to be armed, bold and confident, the full weight of state violence descended upon them. The FBI's Counter-Intelligence Programme (Cointelpro) spearheaded the governmental response but other less overt forms of harassment were employed ranging from assassination to petty persecution, surveillance and dis-information or 'smearing'. In 1969 alone, twenty-seven members of the Black Panther Party were killed by the police and another 749 arrested. The effects of these repressive operations can be judged from the relative decline of the more overt expressions of commitment to revolutionary black struggle in either of its principal forms. Clear open statements were replaced, in musical culture at least, by more oblique forms of signification often more stylized and satirical in their stance. The iconography of soul shifted away from the pseudo-military macho imagery of clenched fists in black leather towards the dress and cultural emblems of ancient Africa. The forthright photographs of Aretha Franklin as a militant African queen which appeared on the cover of her 1972 album *Young, Gifted and Black* were replaced on her next set, *Hey Now Hey The Other Side Of The Sky* by drawings depicting her as a winged Egyptian deity, her microphone plugged into the roots of an African tree in a red, green and black pot. These and other more elliptical statements, like Roy Ayers's memorable 1973 album *Red, Black and Green*, spoke to blacks directly and repeatedly on the subject of their African heritage but withdrew from direct communication with a white audience. Sly Stone, whose Family had been the first multiracial band to achieve any kind of prominence, commented on the transition from Black Power to mystical Pan-Africanism by seguing the track 'Africa Talks To You (The Ashphalt Jungle)' into a non-existent cut entitled 'There's A Riot Going

On'. Griel Marcus (1977, p. 97) has pointed out that Sly's album of the same name

> represented . . . the attempt to create a new music appropriate to new realities. It was music that had as much to do with the Marin shootout and the death of George Jackson as [Sly's] earlier sound had to do with the pride of the riot the title track of his album said was no longer going on. '[F]rightened faces to the wall' Sly moans. 'Can't you hear your Mama call? The Brave and Strong – Survive! Survive!' I think those faces up against the wall belonged to Black Panthers, forced to strip naked on the streets of Philadelphia so Frank Rizzo and his cops could gawk and laugh and make jokes about big limp cocks while Panther women, lined up with the men, were psychologically raped.

There were still, particularly at election time, records which – like James Brown's 'Payback' and 'Funky President' – addressed themselves to the political conjuncture and correctly recognized its significance as a 'second reconstruction':

> It all started with 40 acres and a mule. . . . But nothing good is simple. . . . As yesterday's windmills turned to today's skyscrapers and farms to parking lots . . . anger and revenge increased. As time ran out, putting politicians and hustlers in the same bag. . . . Backstabbin' scrappin but never rappin' the message cried to live and let live. . . .[2]

Political and cultural activists who were not primarily known as musicians had also been drawn towards popular black music as a result of its interventionist potential. Amiri Baraka (Leroi Jones), chairman of the Congress of African People in Newark, enlisted members of The Commodores, Kool and The Gang, and Parliament to support his own bands, The Advanced Workers and The Revolutionary Singers. Together they issued 'You Was Dancin' Need To Be Marchin' So You Can Dance Later On' on the People's War label.[3] These assertive statements would reappear in the wake of Reagan's 1980 election victory, but they declined steadily after 1972. Instead, as the war in Vietnam developed, Uncle Sam's imperial adventures were satirized by references to 'Uncle Jam's Army' and tales of 'specially trained Afronauts capable of funketizing galaxies'. The vision of a black homeland, whether in Africa or in an independent republic inside the southern borders of the USA, was secularized and modernized. The dream of life beyond the reach of racism acquired an other-worldly, utopian quality and then manifested itself in a flash hi-tech form deliberately remote from the everyday realities of the ghetto lifeworld.[4] If the repressive and destructive forces unleashed by a 'maggot brained' and infanticidal America were rapidly acquiring a global character, the answer to them was presented as flight, not back to the African motherland, for that too was tainted by Americanism, but into space. The cover of Funkadelic's 1978 set 'One Nation Under a Groove', for example, showed a squad of 'Afronauts' raising the red, black and green standard of Africa as they stepped off the planet earth. The celestial and interplanetary themes in the soul and funk of this period provided a means to satirize American imperialism and to advance utopian visions of a reconstructed society in which the black nation, united under a groove, would thrive in peace. The destructive capacity of America's technological rationality would be held in check by mystic, natural forces contained within the pyramids of ancient Egypt, a durable symbol of black pride and creativity most powerfully evoked by the Jones Girls' 'Nights Over Egypt'.[5] The futuristic emphasis in these images served to underline the impossibility of strategic political calculation. The means by which black America was to get from where it was to its reconstituted future was as inconceivable as time travel itself. The political repertoire which stretched between mass non-violent direct action to open militarization appeared to have been exhausted.

This period also witnessed the re-emergence of jazz as a truly popular music (Palmer, 1974; Siggerson, 1977), a development which had been foreseen by Leroi Jones (1967). This shift, spearheaded by Pharoah Sanders and Albert Ayler in the late 1960s and developed to its logical conclusion by Miles Davis, Herbie Hancock, John Handy and others during the 1970s, connected the most innovative players directly to the dance-floors and gave an added impetus to the work of popular funk musicians who had few pretensions to jazz-based respectability. The most important exponents of this fusion of jazz, nationalism, satire and dance-orientation were also two of the most popular black bands of the 1970s: Earth Wind and Fire and Parliament/Funkadelic. In 1975, the latter, a loose aggregate of musicians led by refugees from James Brown's backing band, the JBs, cut what is arguably the greatest of all black nationalist dance records, 'Chocolate City'. This was a ruminative piece of funk set to a relentless drum machine beat and decorated freely with Bernie Worrell's piano, Bootsy Collins's base and some free, meandering saxophone solos. The rap vocal from George Clinton, which gave the record its title, explored the post-Black Power situation by speculating about the effects of black inner-city residents electing black local governments and looked at the implications of the move from open protest to electoral politics. 'You don't need the bullet when you've got the ballot,' argued Clinton, suggesting that the latter had become a more appropriate tactical vehicle for black liberation than the former in the aftermath of Cointelpro. The Chocolate City referred to was not simply Washington DC, the national capital in which 'vanilla suburbs' surrounded an inner core populated by impoverished blacks, but rather all cities in which blacks had been able to capture control of municipal government:

> There's a lot of Chocolate Cities around
> We got Newark
> We got Gary
> Somebody told me we got LA
> And we' working on Atlanta

The record climaxes in some frenetic interplay between saxophone and bass. This instrumental passage is introduced by the idea that the transformation of American Democracy is itself within the grasp of blacks. The proposition is made concrete by Clinton's nominations for a new set of leaders: Mohammed Ali for President,

Reverend Ike (a well-known evangelist noted for his ability to extract money from his ghetto flock) as Secretary of the Treasury, Richard Pryor as Minister of Education, Stevie Wonder as Secretary of Fine Arts, and Aretha Franklin, as ever, the First Lady. This record was still being played on London's pirate black music radio stations (Mosco and Hind, 1985) in 1985. To the further delight of black audiences on both sides of the Atlantic, the band which made it signified their political contempt for the music business in which they were forced to operate by signing to competing record conglomerates under a variety of different names.

Earth Wind and Fire's political development covers the same ground as Parliament/Funkadelic, but their movement was in precisely the opposite direction. They began in the early 1970s with mystical, veiled statements of Pan-African themes. These were presented in arrangements which were heavily reliant on the sound of the African thumb piano or Kalimba, which was to become the group's trademark. The group's unique solution also drew on the jazz tradition. Their arrangers, particularly the Chicagoan Tom Washington, attempted to adapt the big-band sounds of Ellington and Basie to a dance funk context. Later on, the mystical material gave way to open political commentary on songs like 'Stand Tall (Let Me Talk)', which harked back to 'Stand' by Sly and the Family Stone, and 'Freedom Of Choice', a forthright attack on monetarism which was banned by several radio stations. The band's early work was dominated by a desire to represent *in their music* the continuity between black American and African cultural creation. This project was fully realized later on by other artists, particularly Ralph MacDonald, who created a musical equivalent to Alex Haley's *Roots* with his 1978 set *The Path*. Earth Wind and Fire took Jesse Jackson's Black Litany, 'I am Somebody' (which would have been known to their audience from the film *Wattstax* and the JBs' dance classic 'Same Beat', if not from any immediate political experience), and pared it down to its essential context – a potent affirmation of black humanity and dignity. It became simply 'I am', the title of their 1979 album.

Jackson was a central figure in the relationship between Afro-American music and politics long before a legion of rappers, singers, producers and musicians lent their talents to support his presidential candidacy in 1984. An ex-CORE student leader and aide to Martin Luther King, Jackson had worked in Chicago during the 1960s creating 'Operation Breadbasket', a programme for boycotting ghetto supermarkets which refused to hire local black staff or lodge their profits in ghetto banks. The idea had spread to seven other cities by 1970 and claimed to have created 5,000 new jobs for ghetto dwellers.[6] In 1967, the Operation Breadbasket activists under Jackson's direction in Cleveland had become involved in the campaign to elect the city's first black mayor, Carl Stokes. It was the power of soul music which helped to secure the articulation of the mass movement of blacks with this comparatively narrow electoral aim. Breadbasket's own band toured the ghetto early on election day instructing registered voters to get up early and vote for Stokes (Preston *et al.*, 1982). Jackson was again prominent in the campaign to elect a black mayor in Newark. This time, the candidate, Kenneth Gibson, enjoyed the support of James Brown and Stevie Wonder, who both performed on his behalf. By 1970 black mayors had been installed in Washington and Gary as well. Jackson's combination of black capitalism and militant self-held rhetoric, 'we do not want a welfare state. We have potential. We can produce. We can feed outselves' (Haralambos, 1974) was appealing. However, the cultural dimension to his political interventions was an important element in their success which has been overlooked by some commentators (Marable, 1985).

The extraordinary level of support for Jackson which was expressed by musicians, artists and performers in 1984 had been triggered by the election of Reagan and the subsequent erosion of black living standards which followed it. In 1981, Gil Scott-Heron's commentary on the Reagan victory, 'B Movie', had been a surprise hit, demonstrating that as far as the soul charts were concerned, it was possible to be simultaneously radical and successful. The Fatback Band, the Valentine Brothers and Syl Johnson, whose early classic, 'Is It Because I'm Black?' had been sung over in reggae style by Ken Boothe, were some of the artists who came forward with denunciations of Reaganomics.[7] Their statements were all underground hits on the British soul scene and significantly drew additional strength from a re-examination of the black militancy of the 1960s. This was an early product of the explosion in New York which created rap, electro and hip-hop in the context of a street culture centred on dance, graffiti and new forms of music-making which will be discussed in detail below.

The rappers and breakdancers who once again established America as the primary source of material for the cultural syncretisms of black Britain articulated a clear political line which was well received here. 'Rappers' Delight', the Sugar Hill Gang's version of Chic's hit 'Good Times', reached Britain in the summer of 1979. There were better rap records to follow. In late 1980, Brother D, a maths teacher and community activist from Brooklyn, issued 'How We Gonna Make The Black Nation Rise?' with his group Collective Effort on the radical reggae label 'Clappers'. Taking their cues as much from the success of Rappers' Delight as from the rap genre's emergent tradition of signovers and cover versions, the group used the backing track from an established dance-floor favourite, Cheryl Lynn's 'To Be Real'. The original chant chorus – the phrase 'to be real' – was left intact between the rapped segments, giving the didactic and pedagogic elements in the second version authenticity and urgency, as well as emphasizing their organic relationship to the underground culture which had made 'To Be Real' into a classic. The rap was a strident and provocative call for solidarity and organization in the Reagan era. It denounced the drug abuse and passivity which Brother D discerned in ghetto life and sought to warn his listeners of the danger they were in.

> As you're moving to the beat till the early light
> The country's moving too, moving to the right
> Prepare now, or get high and wait
> 'cause there ain't no party in a police state

The lyric went beyond a nationalist stance. It noted the rise of the Klan and the possibility of 'racial' genocide but made a clear statement on the ecological crisis, suggesting, rather as Bahro (1982, 1984) has done, that the crisis in the biosphere could achieve the unification of political forces across the conflictual lines of 'race':

> Cancer in the water, pollution in the air
> But you're partying hearty like you just don't care
> Wake up y'all you know it ain't right
> That hurts everybody black and white

Though stylistically a fast soul piece aimed at the very discos it denounced, the record made conspicuous attempts to open a dialogue with the reggae world in which 'Clappers' were established: 'there's a message in our music for I n I'. Picked up for British release in a licensing deal by Island Records, the disc was a dance-floor hit in the soul and hip-hop clubs twice between 1982 and 1985. It also picked up substantial sales in the rock market.

As the smoke from the uprisings of 1981 hung in the inner-city air, young Britons were absorbing the 'Don't push me, 'cause I'm close to the edge' message transmitted by Grandmaster Flash and the Furious Five, and pondering the relevance of Afrika Bambaataa's 'Zulu Nation' to their own experience of structural unemployment, police harassment, drug abuse and racial disadvantage. In both America and Britain, a rediscovery of the black politics of the 1960s has been a consistent feature of hip-hop culture. It has been expressed in a variety of ways including, most obviously, an enthusiasm for politically articulate dance music of the period. James Brown's 'Get Up, Get Into It and Get Involved' was a favourite, and the same trend may explain the British popularity of many political waxings on the Philadelphia International label. Of these, 'Let's Clean Up The Ghetto' was so sought after that it was eventually re-released in 1985. Originally produced in 1977 by label bosses Gamble, a Muslim, and Huff, the record used the combined talents of Teddy Pendergrass, Billy Paul, Lou Rawls and others to comment on the need for self-reliance and political autonomy in the context of the municipal strikes in New York City. More significantly, records in this vein exported to Europe the idea that black communities in the inner city, particularly the young, could define themselves politically and philosophically as an oppressed 'nation' bound together in the framework of the diaspora by language and history.

The Pan-African desire to reconstitute and unify New World blacks into a single self-conscious people was given a further musical boost in the summer of 1983 by the release of 'The Crown', a rap on the themes of black history and pride which had been produced by Gary Byrd, an early rapper, lyricist and radio DJ, and Stevie Wonder, the soul musician who had pioneered the adaptation of reggae to black American tastes. The record passed largely unnoticed in the US but was a major hit in Britain, a remarkable development because it was over ten minutes long and its creators refused to issue it in an edited format, thus denying the record any airplay on the legal radio stations. This was a wholly underground success popularized by the clubs and the pirate broadcasters. It remains significant because it demonstrated that the Ethiopianist and Pan-African ideas associated with reggae could be perfectly integrated into a soul setting, and that the results could be popular.

I do recall so very well
when I was just a little boy
I used to hurry home from school
I used to always feel so blue
because there was no mention in the books
we read about our heritage
So therefore any information that I got was education
Bums, hobos at depot stations
I would listen with much patience
Or to relatives who told the tales
that they were told to pass ahead
And then one day from someone old
I heard a story never told
of all the kingdoms of my people
And how they fought for freedom
All about the many things we have unto the world contributed
You wear the crown. . . .
Its not Star Wars, its not Superman
Its not the story of the Ku Klux Klan. . . .

Stevie Wonder's involvement in the campaign to secure a US public holiday for Martin Luther King's birthday provided a further opportunity for black music to become politically engaged and, of course, drew attention to the political legacy of the 1960s which was being commemorated. In support of this campaign, a number of records, including Wonder's own 'Happy Birthday' (issued with selections of King's speeches on the b-side), addressed themselves to both King's death and the continuing relevance of his political achievements. In both rap and more conventional soul styles, some of these tunes even used tapes of King's own voice to develop their arguments. The most interesting of these were Bobby Womack's 'American Dream' and 'Martin Luther' by Hurt 'em Bad and the SC Band. Both featured extracts from the 'I Have A Dream' speech, the latter setting the scene with a rap about the struggle for desegregation.

King's was not the only black radical voice which was retrieved and woven into rap and electro records. The general revival of interest in the struggles of the 1960s was conveyed in particular by 'No Sellout', a record issued by Tommy Boy, a leading rap and electro label and credited to Malcolm X. Keith Le Blanc, the white drummer with the house band at Sugar Hill records, the company which had spearheaded the commercial exploitation of radical raps, edited together a number of Malcolm's aphorisms and observations into a political commentary which was set to a fragmented electronic rhythm track and punctuated by the spoken chorus 'Malcolm X, no sellout'. The record was an underground hit in Britain during 1984 and received the support of Malcolm's widow, Dr Betty Shabazz. She told the British paper *Black Music*: 'This recording documents Malcolm's voice at a time and space in history some 19 years ago. Its meaning is just as relevant today as it was then.'[8]

The 1983 election provided the first opportunity for Britain's soul and electro subculture to implement the political tactics which had been transmitted across the Atlantic with these new forms. One London rapper, calling himself Newtrament after the milky drink popular with the Afro-Caribbean community, recorded 'London Bridge Is Falling Down', a rap based on the nursery rhyme previously adapted for radical purposes by the reggae group Culture. His version chronicled police malpractice and inner-city decay while suggesting that electoral politics were a sham. Whoever won the contest, he argued, the political processes of significance would take place far from Parliament and the plight of the dispossessed, and the poor would be essentially unaffected:

> Election Fever on all four channels
> . . . Red or Blue. . . .
> Win or lose, lose or win
> jobs will still be getting thin

A speech by Labour Party leader Michael Foot could be heard faintly in the background while a voice chanted 'vote vote vote, there ain't no hope'. A second more orthodox soul record which appeared at this time was 'Thatcher Rap' by the Phantom, an anonymous artist who had cut an anti-NF reggae 45 at the time of the first ANL carnival. Here again, snippets of a politician's speeches were assembled so that they became the vocal in a funky dance piece. Mrs Thatcher's lines were interspersed with the chorus – 'they tell me there's a crisis going on'.

Reagan's decision to seek a second presidential term and Jesse Jackson's tactical campaign for the Democratic Party nomination both generated a number of overtly political soul, rap and funk records during 1983–4. Tunes denounced Reagan and praised Jackson in almost equal measure.[9] Some of them used Reagan's voice, either mimicked or recorded, and even rearranged his words to emphasize the unpleasant features concealed behind his avuncular exterior. Several took Reagan's well-publicized *faux pas*, 'we begin bombing in five minutes', and transformed it into the centrepiece of satirical synthesized dance music. The best of these records, significantly perhaps the furthest away from a distorted but none the less realist presentation of his opinions, was Air Force One's 'See The Light Feel the Heat'. This gave the President some surreal lines: 'We still have a lot further to tango', and cut them into a chilling invocation of the nuclear holocaust and a mumbling discourse on the defence budget.

Once again the detail of these records is less significant than the fact that they were enthusiastically received by the inhabitants of Britain's black music subcultures. Those who could not afford to pay inflated prices for imported discs could look forward to hearing them on and taping them from the pirate radio stations which had begun to transmit regularly in the autumn of 1981. These outlets were important sites in which the black cultures of the US and the Caribbean were diverted into the working-class mainstream of southeast England. Their illegal status carried over into the soul scene through a close relationship between the radio DJs and the clubs where they worked when they were not on the air. A mood of opposition was cultivated by the stations who were frequently shut down by the Department of Trade inspectors. Their resistance of the government's attempts to regulate their broadcasting added substantially to the underground connotations attached to the music itself.

Notes

1. The lyrics from Aretha Franklin's 'Think' which are reproduced below typify this mood.
2. These words come from the sleeve note to James Brown's double album *The Payback* (Polydor 2679 025, 1973).
3. *Rolling Stone*, 10 February 1977.
4. The sleeve illustration to any of the Parliament releases after 'Chocolate City' bear this out. The best examples apart from their 'Mothership Connection' are two Dexter Wansell album sleeves, *Life On Mars* and *Voyager*, which depicts him in a space suit preparing to leave earth.
5. The Jones Girls, 'Get As Much Love As You Can' (Philadelphia International 85347, 1981).
6. *Time*, 6 April 1970.
7. The Valentine Brothers, 'Money's Too Tight To Mention' and Syl Johnson, 'Keep On Loving Me' (Epic 25300) are two songs which make overt reference to Reaganomics.
8. *Black Music*, February 1984, p. 10.
9. Face 2000, 'Run Jesse Run' (RSP 1001); Melle Mel, 'Jesse' (Sugar Hill 32016); Reathel Bean and the Doonesbury Break Crew, 'Rap Master Ronnie' (Silver Screen SSR115); Gil Scott Heron, 'Rerun' (Arista AD1-9216); Bonzo Goes To Washington, 'Bombing In Five Minutes' (Sleeping Bag SLX13); Uncle Sham and The Politicians, 'Vote For me' (Easy Street EZS 7509); and Captain Rapp, 'Bad Times (I Can't Stand It)' (Becket KSL 10) are some of the better politically articulate discs of the 1984 election period.

References

Bahro, R. (1982) *Socialism and Survival*, London: Heretic Books.
Bahro, R. (1984) *From Red to Green*, London: New Left Books.
Carmichael, S. and Hamilton, C. (1967) *Black Power: The politics of liberation in America*, New York: Vintage.
Haralambos, M. (1974) *Right On: From blues to soul in black America*, Eddison Bluesbooks
Jones, L. (1967) *Black Music*, New York: Quill.
Marable, M. (1985) *Black American Politics from The Washington Marches to Jesse Jackson*, London: Verso.
Marcus, G. (1977) *Mystery Train: Images of America in rock 'n' roll music*, London: Omnibus Press.

Mosco, S. and Hind, J. (1985) *Rebel Radio: The Full Story of British Pirate Radio*, London: Pluto Press.

Newton, H. (1974) *Revolutionary Suicide*, London: Wildwood House.

Palmer, R. (1974) 'Avant garde funk', Black Music, October.

Preston, M. B. *et al.* (eds) (1982) *The New Black Politics: The search for political power*, Brentwood: Longman.

Siggerson, D. (1977) 'Love and money – crossover jazz in the Seventies', pts 1 and 2, *Black Music*, March and April.

PART THREE

Structuralism and Poststructuralism

Introduction

Structuralism

Structuralism is a method of approaching cultural texts and practices which is derived from the theoretical work of the Swiss linguist Ferdinand de Saussure.[1] Certain key ideas and a particular vocabulary from Saussure have passed from linguistics into cultural studies. Structuralism takes two basic ideas from Saussure's work. First, a concern with the underlying relations of cultural texts and practices – the 'grammar' which makes meaning possible. This perspective is derived from Saussure's division of language into '*langue*' and '*parole*'. *Langue* is used to refer to the system of language; the rules and conventions which organise it. *Parole* is used to refer to the individual utterance. To clarify this distinction Saussure refers us to a game of chess. He points out that without a body of rules there could not be a game of chess, but that it is only in an actual game that these rules are made manifest. Therefore, there is *langue* (the rules) and there is *parole* (an individual game). It is the homogeneity of the underlying structure which makes the heterogeneity of the performance possible.

The second basic idea taken by structuralists from Saussure's work is the view that meaning is always the result of an interplay of relationships of opposition and combination, made possible by the underlying structure. This derives from Saussure's contention that languages consist of 'signs', which in turn can be divided into two component parts, 'signifier' and 'signified'. When I write the word 'cat' it produces the inscription 'cat', but also the concept or mental image 'cat': a four-legged feline creature. For Saussure the inscription (it could also be the acoustic sound 'cat') is the signifier, and the concept or mental image is the signified; together (like two sides of a coin) they make up the sign. Saussure argues that the relationship between signifier and signified is arbitrary. That is to say, there is no reason why the inscription 'cat' should produce the concept or mental image of an actual cat. It might just as easily produce the concept or mental image of an actual dog. What prevents this is convention. We live in a language community in which the inscription 'cat' refers to four-legged feline animals. Other language communities have different inscriptions to refer to this animal. It follows from this, according to Saussure, that meaning is the result of differences and relationships within the system of language itself, rather than the result of a natural correspondence between signifier and signified. Traffic lights are a good example of this process. There is no necessary correspondence between, say, green and 'go'; red, for example, would do just as well. The system works through difference and relationship (contrast and opposition), rather than the assertion of a positive relationship between colour and command. It also follows from Saussure's formulation that language does not reflect an already existing reality. On the contrary, language constructs and organises our sense of reality. When a European gazes at a snowscape and sees only snow, an Eskimo, with over fifty words for snow, sees a very different landscape. What this demonstrates to a structuralist is that the language we use permits us to conceptualise the world in different ways. Structuralists study the texts and practices of culture, by analogy, as examples of language. Each is seen as a performance generated by a structure.

Roland Barthes's *Mythologies* represents the most significant attempts to bring the methodology of semiology (the structuralist study of 'signs') to bear on popular culture. It is also one of the founding texts of cultural studies. The book is a collection of essays on French popular culture, written by Barthes in the 1950s. The aim of the book is to make explicit what too often remains implicit and unnoticed in the texts and practices of popular culture. Its guiding principle is always to interrogate 'the falsely obvious' the 'what-goes-without-saying'. As the 'Preface' makes clear Barthes 'resented seeing Nature and History confused at every turn'. The book concludes with a theoretical essay called 'Myth Today' (Reading 11). It is in this essay that Barthes outlines the theoretical assumptions that inform his approach to popular culture. Barthes's method is an elaboration of Saussure's model of language He takes the schema 'signifier/signified = sign' and adds to it a second level of signification. The first level of signification (identified by Saussure) he calls 'primary signification' or 'denotation'; the second level he calls 'secondary signification' or 'connotation'. He then argues that it is at the second level of signification that what he calls 'myth' is produced and consumed. By myth Barthes means ideology understood as ideas and practices which defend the status quo – the 'bourgeois norm' – and actively promote the interests and values of the dominant classes in society. Myth is the turning of the cultural and the historical into the natural, the taken-for-granted. Barthes's most famous example of this process (included in Reading 11) is his analysis of the photograph of a black soldier saluting the French flag, which appeared on the cover of Paris Match in 1955. The 'secondary signification' or 'connotations' of the photograph represent, according to Barthes, an attempt, during a moment of political crisis (following defeat in Vietnam and pending defeat in Algeria), to give French imperialism a positive image.

Will Wright's structuralist account of the Hollywood Western (Reading 12) also draws on the theoretical foundations supplied by Saussure, but develops these through the work on 'primitive myth' by the French anthropologist Claude Lévi-

Strauss.[2] Lévi-Strauss claims that beneath the vast heterogeneity of myths can be discovered a homogeneous structure. In structuralist terminology, individual myths are examples of '*parole*', expressions of an underlying system of '*langue*'. Myths work like language; comprised of 'mythemes', analogous to individual units of language, 'morphemes' and 'phonemes'. Like morphemes and phonemes, mythemes take on meaning only when they are combined in particular patterns. The task of the anthropologist is to discover and understand the underlying 'grammar' of myth; the rules and regulations which make it possible for individual myths to be meaningful. He argues that myths are structured in terms of 'binary oppositions', dividing the world into mutually exclusive categories: culture/nature, man/woman, black/white, good/bad, us/them, and so on. Drawing on Saussure, he sees meaning as the result of the process of interplay between similarity and difference.

Lévi-Strauss also claims that besides sharing an underlying structure, myths share the same social function; that is, they make the world explicable, they magically resolve its problems and contradictions. Wright uses Lévi-Strauss's structuralist methodology to analyse the Hollywood Western. He argues that much of its narrative power derives from its structure of binary oppositions. But in a move beyond Lévi-Strauss (and borrowing from Vladimir Propp[3]), he contends that in order to understand fully the mythic structure of the Western we must also pay attention to its narrative structure. According to Wright, the Hollywood Western has evolved through three stages: 'classic' (including a variation he calls 'vengeance'), 'transition theme' and 'professional'. Each of these stages has produced variations in the structure of binary oppositions and in the ordering of narrative 'functions'.

Sigmund Freud's analysis of what he calls the 'dream-work' (Reading 10) may also be considered as an example of a structuralist methodology. Whereas Saussure distinguishes between *langue* and *parole*, Freud presents the individual dream as an expression of an underlying structure – the unconscious. His analysis of the dream-work, the processes (condensation, displacement, symbolism and secondary revision) which transform the latent dream into its manifest content, is, ultimately, of value to Freud because of the 'unimaginably broad access [it makes possible] to a knowledge of unconscious mental life'.

Poststructuralism

Like structuralism, poststructuralism is largely a French invention. The key figures are Jacques Derrida, Michel Foucault, Jacques Lacan, the later work of Roland Barthes, and within Marxism, the work of Louis Althusser and Pierre Macherey. Poststructuralism rejects the idea that meaning is generated and guaranteed by an underlying structure. For poststructuralists, meaning is always a process. What we call meaning is a momentary halt in a continuing process of interpretations of interpretations. Whereas Saussure saw meaning in language as a result of a process of 'signifier/signified = sign', poststructuralists argue that signifiers do not produce signifieds, they produce more signifiers. Jacques Derrida has invented a new word to describe this process: différance, meaning both to defer and to differ. Saussure argued that meaning is the result of difference; Derrida adds to this that meaning is also always deferred, never fully present, always both absent and present. For example, if we track the meaning of a word through a dictionary we encounter a relentless deferment of meaning in which there is 'indefinite referral of signifier to signifier ... which gives the signified meaning no respite ... so that it always signifies again'.[4] It is only when a word is located in a discourse and read in a context that there is a temporary halt to the play of signifier to signifier. But even discourses and contexts cannot fully control the play of meaning; 'traces' will always be carried from other discourses and from other contexts.

Marxist poststructuralism entered cultural studies in the early 1970s with the translation into English of the work of Louis Althusser. In a poststructuralist rereading of Marx, Althusser formulated two new concepts: the 'problematic' and the 'symptomatic reading'. A problematic is the discursive structure which underlines, frames and produces the repertoire of crisscrossing and competing discourses out of which a text is materially organised. The problematic of a text relates to its moment of historical production as much by what it attempts to exclude as by what it includes. That is to say, it encourages a text to answer questions posed by itself, but at the same time it generates the production of 'deformed' answers to questions it attempts to exclude. Thus the problematic of a text is structured as much by what is absent (what is not said) as by what is present (what is said). The task of an Althusserian critical practice is to deconstruct the text's problematic; to perform what Althusser calls a 'symptomatic reading'.

In *Reading Capital*, he characterises Marx's method of reading the political economy of Adam Smith as a 'symptomatic reading' in that

> it divulges the undivulged event in the text it reads, and in the same movement relates it to a *different* text, present as a necessary absence in the first. Like his first reading, Marx's second reading presupposes the existence of *two* texts, and the measurement of the first against the second. But what distinguishes this new reading from the old is the fact that in the new one the second text is articulated with the lapses in the first text.[5]

By a symptomatic reading of Smith, Marx is able to measure 'the problematic contained in the paradox of an answer which does not correspond to any question posed'.[6] Therefore, to read a text symptomatically is to perform a double reading: reading first the manifest text, and then, through the lapses, distortions, silences and absences (the 'symptoms' of a problem struggling to be posed) in the manifest text, to produce and read the latent text.[7] Undoubtedly the most sustained attempt to apply this method of reading is Pierre Macherey's *A Theory of Literary Production* (Reading 13). In an analysis of Jules Verne's popular fiction, Macherey shows how Verne's novels and stories gain their fictional form from the workings of a particular historical problematic; and that when read symptomatically, this work can be made to 'stage' the contradictions between the myth and the reality of late nineteenth-century French imperialism.

In 'Ideology and Ideological State Apparatuses' (Reading 14) Althusser retheorises the Marxist concept of ideology as a material practice (rituals, customs, patterns of behaviour, ways of thinking which take practical form) reproduced in and through the practices and productions of the Ideological State Apparatuses (education, organised religion, the mass media, the family, organised politics, the culture industries, etc.). In this formation, 'all ideology has the function (which defines it) of "constructing" concrete individuals as subjects'. Ideological subjects are generated by acts of 'hailing' or 'interpellation'; that is, made subjects of, and subjected to, specific ideological discourses and subject positions. In this way, ideology captures our attention and provides us with a language to speak. When, for example, I am told by an advertisement that 'people like you' are turning to this or that product, I am being interpellated as a member of a group, but, more importantly, as an individual 'you' of that group. I am addressed as an individual who can recognise myself in the imaginary space opened up by the pronoun 'you'. Thus I am invited to become the 'you' spoken to in the advertisement. But for Althusser, my response to the advertisement's invitation is an act of ideological 'misrecognition'. First, it is an act of misrecognition in the sense that in order for the advertment to work, it must invite many others who must also (mis)recognise themselves in the 'you' of its discourse. Second, it is a misrecognition in another sense: the 'you' I (mis)recognise in the advertisement is in fact a 'you' created by the advertisement. Advertising thus flatters us into thinking we are the special 'you' of its discourse and, by so doing, interpellates us as subjects of, and subjected to, its material practices.

The work of Michel Foucault has had a major impact on cultural studies in recent years. Foucault is concerned with the relationship between knowledge and power and how this relationship operates within what he calls discursive formations, the conceptual frameworks which allow some modes of thought and deny the possibility of others. Foucault does not see power as a negative force, something which denies, represses, negates; for Foucault, power is a productive force. 'We must cease once and for all', he argues, 'to describe the effects of power in negative terms: it "excludes", it "represses", it "censors", it "abstracts", it "masks", it "conceals". In fact, power produces; it produces reality; it produces domains of objects and rituals of truth.'[8] In Reading 15, Foucault elaborates the procedures and the protocols of power with reference to a history of sexuality. He analyses power as a 'discursive field' in which a 'multiplicity of force relations' are confronted by a 'multiplicity of points of resistance'. In an authoritative overview of poststructuralist theory (Reading 16), Chris Weedon addresses the usefulness of Foucault's concept of the discursive field for a feminist politics of culture. She concludes that Foucault's mode of analysis enables feminist poststructuralism, 'in detailed, historically specific analysis, to explain the working of power on behalf of specific interests and to analyse the opportunities for resistance to it'.

Notes

1. See Ferdinand de Saussure, *Course in General Linguistics*, London: Fontana, 1974.
2. See especially Claude Lévi-Strauss, *Structural Anthropology*, London: Allen Lane, 1968.
3. Vladimir Propp, *The Morphology of the Folk Tale*, Austin: University of Texas Press, 1975.
4. Jacques Derrida, *Writing and Difference*, London: Routledge & Kegan Paul, 1978, p. 25.
5. Louis Althusser and Etienne Balibar, *Reading Capital*, London: Verso, 1979, p. 28. This is Marx's comment on Smith: 'Adam Smith's contradictions are of significance because they contain problems which it is true he does not solve, but which he reveals by contradicting himself.' *Theories of Surplus Value*, London: Lawrence and Wishart, 1951, p. 146.
6. Althusser and Balibar, *Reading Capital*, p. 28.
7. There is an acknowledged relationship between this method and Freud's analysis of the dream-work; for its basis in Freud's work see Reading 10.
8. Michel Foucault, *Discipline and Punish*, Harmondsworth: Penguin, 1979, p. 194.

10 □ *The Dream-Work*

Sigmund Freud

Ladies and Gentlemen, – When you have thoroughly grasped the dream-censorship and representation by symbols, you will not yet, it is true, have completely mastered the distortion in dreams, but you will nevertheless be in a position to understand most dreams. In doing so you will make use of both of the two complementary techniques: calling up ideas that occur to the dreamer till you have penetrated from the substitute to the genuine thing and, on the ground of your own knowledge, replacing the symbols by what they mean. Later on, we shall discuss some uncertainties that arise in this connection.

We can now take up once more a task that we tried to carry out previously with inadequate means, when we were studying the relations between the elements of dreams and the genuine things they stood for. We laid down four main relations of the kind: the relation of a part to a whole, approximation or allusion, the symbolic relation and the plastic representation of words. We now propose to undertake the same thing on a larger-scale, by comparing the manifest content of a dream *as a whole* with the latent dream as it is revealed by interpretation.

I hope you will never again confuse these two things with each other. If you reach that point, you will probably have gone further in understanding dreams than most readers of my *Interpretation of Dreams*. And let me remind you once again that the work which transforms the latent dream into the manifest one is called the *dream-work*. The work which proceeds in the contrary direction, which endeavours to arrive at the latent dream from the manifest one, is our *work of interpretation*. This work of interpretation seeks to undo the dream-work. The dreams of infantile type which we recognize as obvious fulfilments of wishes have nevertheless experienced some amount of dream-work – they have been transformed from a wish into an actual experience and also, as a rule, from thoughts into visual images. In their case there is no need for interpretation but only for undoing these two transformations. The additional dream-work that occurs in other dreams is called 'dream-distortion', and this has to be undone by our work of interpretation.

Having compared the interpretations of numerous dreams, I am in a position to give you a summary description of what the dream-work does with the material of the latent dream-thoughts. I beg you, however, not to try to understand too much of what I tell you. It will be a piece of description which should be listened to with quiet attention.

The first achievement of the dream-work is *condensation*. By that we understand the fact that the manifest dream has a smaller content than the latent one, and is thus an abbreviated translation of it. Condensation can on occasion be absent; as a rule it is present, and very often it is enormous. It is never changed into the reverse; that is to say, we never find that the manifest dream is greater in extent or content than the latent one. Condensation is brought about (1) by the total omission of certain latent elements, (2) by only a fragment of some complexes in the latent dream passing over into the manifest one and (3) by latent elements which have something in common being combined and fused into a single unity in the manifest dream.

If you prefer it, we can reserve the term 'condensation' for the last only of these processes. Its results are particularly easy to demonstrate. You will have no difficulty in recalling instances from your own dreams of different people being condensed into a single one. A composite figure of this kind may look like A perhaps, but may be dressed like B, may do something that we remember C doing, and at the same time we may know that he is D. This composite structure is of course emphasizing something that the four people have in common. It is possible, naturally, to make a composite structure out of things or places in the same way as out of people, provided that the various things and places have in common something which is emphasized by the latent dream. The process is like constructing a new and transitory concept which has this common element as its nucleus. The outcome of this superimposing of the separate elements that have been condensed together is as a rule a blurred and vague image, like what happens if you take several photographs on the same plate.

The production of composite structures like these must be of great importance to the dream-work, since we can show that where in the first instance the common elements necessary for them were missing, they are deliberately introduced – for instance, through the choice of the words by which a thought is expressed. We have already come across condensations and composite structures of this sort. They played a part in the production of some slips of the tongue. You will recall the young man who offered to *'begleitdigen'* ['*begleiten* (accompany)' + '*beleidigen* (insult)'] a lady. Moreover, there are jokes of which the technique is based on a condensation like this. But apart from these cases, it may be said that the process is something quite unusual and strange. It is true that counterparts to the construction of these composite figures are to be found in some creations of our imagination, which is ready to combine into a unity components of things that do not belong together in our experience – in the centaurs, for instance, and the fabulous beasts which appear in ancient mythology or in Böcklin's pictures. The 'creative' imagination, indeed, is quite incapable of *inventing* anything; it can only combine components that are strange to one another. But the remarkable thing about the procedure of the dream-work lies in what follows. The material offered to the dream-work consists of thoughts – a few of which may be objectionable and unacceptable, but which are correctly constructed and expressed. The dream-work puts these thoughts into another form, and it is a strange and incomprehensible fact that in making this translation (this rendering, as it were, into another script or language) these methods of merging or combining are brought into use. After all, a translation normally endeavours to preserve the distinctions made in the text and particularly to keep things that are similar separate. The dream-work, quite the contrary, tries to condense two different thoughts by seeking out (like a joke) an ambiguous word in which the two thoughts may come together. We need not try to understand this feature all at once, but it may become important for our appreciation of the dream-work.

But although condensation makes dreams obscure, it does not give one the impression of being an effect of the dream-censorship. It seems traceable rather to some mechanical or economic factor, but in any case the censorship profits by it.

The achievements of condensation can be quite extraordinary. It is sometimes possible by its help to combine two quite different latent trains of thought into one manifest dream, so that one can arrive at what appears to be a sufficient interpretation of a dream and yet in doing so can fail to notice a possible 'over-interpretation'.

In regard to the connection between the latent and the manifest dream, condensation results also in no simple relation being left between the elements in the one and the other. A manifest element may correspond simultaneously to several latent ones, and, contrariwise, a latent element may play a part in several manifest once – there is, as it were, a criss-cross relationship. In interpreting a dream, moreover, we find that the associations to a single manifest element need not emerge in succession: we must often wait till the whole dream has been interpreted.

Thus the dream-work carries out a very unusual kind of transcription of the dream-thoughts: it is not a word-for-word or a sign-for-sign translation; nor is it a selection made according to fixed rules – as though one were to reproduce only the consonants in a word and to leave out the vowels; nor is it what might be described as a representative selection – one element being invariably chosen to take the place of several; it is something different and far more complicated.

The second achievement of the dream-work is *displacement*. Fortunately we have made some preliminary examination of this: for we know that it is entirely the work of the dream-censorship. It manifests itself in two ways: in the first, a latent element is replaced not by a component part of itself but by something more remote – that is, by an allusion; and in the second, the psychical accent is shifted from an important element on to another which is unimportant, so that the dream appears differently centred and strange.

Replacing something by an allusion to it is a process familiar in our waking thought as well, but there is a difference. In waking thought the allusion must be easily intelligible, and the substitute must be related in its subject-matter to the genuine thing it stands for. Jokes, too, often make use of allusion. They drop the precondition of there being an association in subject-matter, and replace it by unusual external associations such as similarity of sound, verbal ambiguity, and so on. But they retain the precondition of intelligibility: a joke would lose all its efficiency if the path back from the allusion to the genuine thing could not be followed easily. The allusions employed for displacement in dreams have set themselves free from both of these restrictions. They are connected with the element they replace by the most external and remote relations and are therefore unintelligible; and when they are undone, their interpretation gives the impression of being a bad joke or of an arbitrary and forced explanation dragged in by the hair of its head. For the dream-censorship only gains its end if it succeeds in making it impossible to find the path back from the allusion to the genuine thing.

Displacement of accent is unheard-of as a method of expressing thoughts. We sometimes make use of it in waking thought in order to produce a comic effect. I can perhaps call up the impression it produces of going astray if I recall an anecdote. There was a blacksmith in a village, who had committed a capital offence. The Court decided that the crime must be punished; but as the blacksmith was the only one in the village and was indispensable, and as on the other hand there were three tailors living there, one of *them* was hanged instead.

The third achievement of the dream-work is psychologically the most interesting. It consists in transforming thoughts into visual images. Let us keep it clear that this transformation does not affect *everything* in the dream-thoughts; some of them retain their form and appear as thoughts or knowledge in the manifest dream as well; nor are visual images the only form into which thoughts are transformed. Nevertheless they comprise the essence of the formation of dreams; this part of the dream-work is, as we already know, the second most regular one and we have already made the acquaintance of the 'plastic' representation of words in the case of individual dream-elements.

It is clear that this achievement is not an easy one. To form some idea of its difficulties, let us suppose that you have undertaken the task of replacing a political leading article in a newspaper by a series of illustrations. You will thus have been thrown back from alphabetic writing to picture writing. In so far as the article mentioned people and concrete objects you will replace them easily and perhaps even advantageously by pictures; but your difficulties will begin when you come to the representation of abstract words and of all those parts of speech which indicate relations between thoughts – such as particles, conjunctions and so on. In the case of abstract words you will be able to help yourselves out by means of a variety of devices. For instance, you will endeavour to give the text of the article a different wording, which may perhaps sound less usual but which will contain more components that are concrete and capable of being represented. You will then recall that most abstract words are 'watered-down' concrete ones, and you will for that reason hark back as often as possible to the original concrete meaning of such words. Thus you will be pleased to find that you can represent the 'possession' of an object by a real, physical sitting down on it.[1] And the dream-work does just the same thing. In such circumstances you will scarcely be able to expect very great accuracy from your representation: similarly, you will forgive the dream-work for replacing an element so hard to put into pictures as, for example, 'adultery' ['*Ehebruch*', literally, 'breach of marriage'], by another breach – a broken leg ['*Beinbruch*'].[2] And in this way you will succeed to some extent in compensating for the clumsiness of the picture writing that is supposed to take the place of the alphabetic script.

For representing the parts of speech which indicate relations between thoughts – 'because', 'therefore', 'however', etc. – you will have no similar aids at your disposal; those constituents of the text will be lost so far as translation into pictures goes. In the same way, the dream-work reduces the content of the dream-thoughts to its raw material of objects and activities. You will feel pleased if there is a possibility of in some way hinting, through the subtler details of the pictures, at certain relations not in themselves capable of being represented. And just so does the dream-work succeed in expressing some of the content of the latent dream-thoughts by peculiarities in the *form* of the manifest dream – by its clarity or obscurity, by its division into several pieces, and so on. The number of part-dreams into which a dream is divided usually corresponds to the number of main topics or groups of thoughts in the latent dream. A short introductory dream will often stand in the relation of a prelude to a following, more detailed, main dream or may give the motive for it; a subordinate clause in the dream-thoughts will be replaced by the interpolation of a change of scene into the manifest dream, and so on. Thus the form of dreams is far from being without significance and itself calls for interpretation. When several dreams occur during the same night, they often have the same meaning and indicate that an attempt is being made to deal more and more efficiently with a stimulus of increasing insistence. In individual dreams a particularly difficult element may be represented by several symbols – by 'doublets'.[3]

If we make a series of comparisons between the dream-thoughts and the manifest dreams which replace them, we shall come upon all kinds of things for which we are unprepared: for instance, that nonsense and absurdity in dreams have their meaning. At this point, indeed, the contrast between the medical and the psychoanalytic view of dreams reaches a pitch of acuteness not met with elsewhere. According to the former, dreams are senseless because mental activity in dreams has abandoned all its powers of criticism; according to our view, on the contrary, dreams become senseless when a piece of criticism included in the dream-thoughts – a judgement that 'this is absurd' – has to be represented. The dream you are familiar with of the visit to the theatre (' three tickets for 1 florin 50') is a good example of this. The judgement it expressed was: 'it was absurd to marry so early.'[4]

Similarly, in the course of our work of interpretation we learn what it is that corresponds to the doubts and uncertainties which the dreamer so often expresses as to whether a particular element occurred in a dream, whether it was this or whether, on the contrary, it was something else. There is as a rule nothing in the latent dream-thoughts corresponding to these doubts and uncertainties; they are entirely due to the activity of the dream-censorship and are to be equated with an attempt at elimination which has not quite succeeded.

Among the most surprising findings is the way in which the dream-work treats contraries that occur in the latent dream. We know already that conformities in the latent material are replaced by condensations in the manifest dream. Well, contraries are treated in the same way as conformities, and there is a special preference for expressing them by the same manifest element. Thus an element in the manifest dream which is capable of having a contrary may equally well be expressing either itself or its contrary or both together: only the sense can decide which translation is to be chosen. This connects with the further fact that a representation of 'no' – or at any rate an unambiguous one – is not to be found in dreams.

A welcome analogy to this strange behaviour of the dream-work is provided for us in the development of language. Some philologists have maintained that in the most ancient language contraries such as 'strong–weak', 'light–dark', 'big–small' are expressed by the same verbal roots. (What we term 'the antithetical meaning of primal words'.) Thus in Ancient Egyptian '*ken*' originally meant 'strong' and 'weak'. In speaking, misunderstanding from the use of such ambivalent words was avoided by differences of intonation and by the accompanying gesture, and in writing, by the addition of what is termed a 'determinative' – a picture which is not itself intended to be spoken. For instance, '*ken*' meaning 'strong' was written with a picture of a little upright man after the alphabetic signs; when '*ken*' stood for 'weak', what followed was the picture of a man squatting down limply. It was only later, by means of slight modifications of the original homologous word, that two distinct representations were arrived at of the contraries included in it. Thus from '*ken*' 'strong–weak' were derived '*ken*' 'strong' and '*kan*' 'weak'. The remains of this ancient antithetical meaning seem to have been preserved not only in the latest developments of the oldest languages but also in far younger ones and even in some that are still living.

In Latin, words that remained ambivalent in this way are '*altus*' ('high' and 'deep') and '*sacer*' ('sacred' and 'accursed').

As instances of modifications of the same root I may mention '*clamare*' ('to cry'), '*calm*' ('softly', 'quietly', 'secretly'); '*siccus*' ('dry'), '*succus*' ('juice'). And in German: '*Stimme*' ['voice'], '*stumm*' ['dumb'].

If we compare related languages, there are numerous examples. In English, 'to lock'; in German, '*Loch*' ['hole'] and '*Lücke*' ['gap']. In English, 'to cleave'; in German, '*kleben*' ['to stick'].

The English word 'without' (which is really 'with–without') is used today for 'without' alone. 'With', in addition to its combining sense, originally had a removing one; this is still to be seen in the compounds 'withdraw' and 'withhold'. Similarly with the German '*wieder*' ['together with' and '*wider*' 'against'].

Another characteristic of the dream-work also has its counterpart in the development of language. In Ancient Egyptian, as well as in other, later languages, the order of the sounds in a word can be reversed, while keeping the same meaning. Examples of this in English and German are: '*Topf*' ['pot']–'pot'; 'boat'–'tub'; 'hurry'–'*Ruhe*' ['rest']; '*Balken*' ['beam']–'*Kloben*' ['log'] and 'club'; 'wait'–'*täuwen*' ['tarry']. Similarly in Latin and German: '*capere*'–'*packen*' ['to seize']; '*ren*'–'*Niere*' ['kidney'].

Reversals like this, which occur here with individual words, take place in various ways in the dream-work. We already know reversal of meaning, replacement of something by its opposite. Besides this we find in dreams reversals of situation, of the relation between two people – a 'topsy-turvy' world. Quite often in dreams it is the hare that shoots the sportsman. Or again we find a reversal in the order of events, so that what precedes an event causally comes after it in the dream – like a theatrical production by a third-rate touring company, in which the hero falls down dead and the shot that killed him is not fired in the wings till afterwards. Or there are dreams where the whole order of the elements is reversed, so that to make sense in interpreting it we must take the last one first and the first one last. You will remember too from our study of dream-symbolism that going or falling into the water means the same as coming out of it – that is, giving birth or being born and that climbing up a staircase or a ladder is the same thing as coming down it. It is not hard to see the advantage that dream-distortion can derive from this freedom of representation.

These features of the dream-work may be described as *archaic*. They are equally characteristic of ancient systems of expression by speech and writing and they involve the same difficulties, which we shall have to discuss again later in a critical sense.

And now a few more considerations. In the case of the dream-work it is clearly a matter of transforming the latent thoughts which are expressed in words into sensory images, mostly of a visual sort. Now our thoughts originally arose from sensory images of that kind: their first material and their preliminary stages were sense impressions, or, more properly, mnemic images of such impressions. Only later were words attached to them and the words in turn linked up into thoughts. The dream-work thus submits thoughts to a *regressive* treatment and undoes their development; and in the course of the regression everything has to be dropped that had been added as a new acquisition in the course of the development of the mnemic images into thoughts.

Such then, it seems, is the dream-work. As compared with the processes we have come to know in it, interest in the manifest dream must pale into insignificance. But I will devote a few more remarks to the latter, since it is of it alone that we have immediate knowledge.

It is natural that we should lose some of our interest in the manifest dream. It is bound to be a matter of indifference to us whether it is well put together, or is broken up into a series of disconnected separate pictures. Even if it has an apparently sensible exterior, we know that this has only come about through dream-distortion and can have as little organic relation to the internal content of the dream as the façade of an Italian church has to its structure and plan. There are other occasions when this façade of the dream *has* its meaning, and reproduces an important component of the latent dream-thoughts with little or no distortion. But we cannot know this before we have submitted the dream to interpretation and have been able to form a judgement from it as to the amount of distortion that has taken place. A similar doubt arises when two elements in a dream appear to have been brought into a close relation to each other. This may give us a valuable hint that we may bring together what corresponds to these elements in the latent dream as well; but on other occasions we can convince ourselves that what belongs together in the dream-thoughts has been torn apart in the dream.

In general one must avoid seeking to explain one part of the manifest dream by another, as though the dream had been coherently conceived and was a logically arranged narrative. On the contrary, it is as a rule like a piece of breccia, composed of various fragments of rock held together by a binding medium, so that the designs that appear on it do not belong to the original rocks imbedded in it. And there is in fact one part of the dream-work, known as 'secondary revision', whose business it is to make something whole and more or less coherent out of the first products of the dream-work. In the course of this, the material is arranged in what is often a completely misleading sense and, where it seems necessary, interpolations are made in it.

On the other hand, we must not over-estimate the dream-work and attribute too much to it. The achievements I have enumerated exhaust its activity; it can do no more than condense, displace, represent in plastic form and subject the whole to a secondary revision. What appear in the dream as expressions of judgement, of criticism, of astonishment or of inference – none of these are achievements of the dream-work and they are very rarely expressions of afterthoughts about the dream; they are for the most part portions of the latent dream-thoughts which have passed over into the manifest dream with a greater or less amount of modification and adaptation to the context. Nor can the dream-work compose speeches. With a few assignable exceptions, speeches in dreams are copies and combinations of speeches which one has heard or spoken oneself on the day before the dream and which have been included in the latent thoughts either as material or as the instigator of the dream. The dream-work is equally unable to carry out calculations. Such of them as appear in the manifest dream are mostly combinations of numbers, sham calculations which are quite senseless *quâ* calculations and are once again only copies of calculations in the latent dream-thoughts. In these circumstances it is not to be wondered at that the interest which had turned to the dream-work soon tends to move away from it to the latent dream-thoughts, which are revealed, distorted to a greater or less degree, by the manifest dream. But there is no justification for carrying this shift of interest so far that, in looking at the matter theoretically, one replaces the dream entirely by the latent dream-thoughts and makes some assertion about the former which only applies to the latter. It is strange that the findings of psychoanalysis could be misused to bring about this confusion. One cannot give the name of 'dream' to anything other than the product of the dream-work – that is to say, the *form* into which the latent thoughts have been transmuted by the dream-work.

The dream-work is a process of quite a singular kind, of which the like has not yet become known in mental life. Condensations, displacements, regressive transformations of thoughts into images – such things are novelties whose discovery has already richly rewarded the labours of psychoanalysis. And you can see once more, from the parallels to the dream-work, the connections which have been revealed between psychoanalytic studies and other fields – especially those concerned in the development of speech and thought. You will only be able to form an idea of the further significance of these discoveries when you learn that the mechanism of dream-construction is the model of the manner in which neurotic symptoms arise.

I am also aware, that we are not yet able to make a survey of the whole of the new acquisitions which these studies have brought to psychology. I will only point out the fresh proofs they have provided of the existence of unconscious mental acts – for this is what the latent dream-thoughts are – and what an unimaginably broad access to a knowledge of unconscious mental life we are promised by the interpretation of dreams.

But now the time has no doubt come for me to demonstrate to you from a variety of small examples of dreams what I have been preparing you for in the course of these remarks.

Notes

1. [The German word '*besitzen*' ('to possess') is more obviously connected with sitting than its English equivalent ('*sitzen*' = 'to sit'.)]
2. While I am correcting the proofs of these pages chance has put into my hands a newspaper cutting which offers an unexpected confirmation of what I have written above:

'DIVINE PUNISHMENT

'A Broken Arm for a Broken Marriage.

'Frau Anna M., wife of a militiaman, sued Frau Klementine K. for adultery. According to the statement of claim, Frau K. had carried on an illicit relationship with Karl M., while her own husband was at the front and was actually making her an allowance of 70 Kronen [about £3.50] a month. Frau K. had already received a considerable amount of money from the plaintiff's husband, while she and her child had to live in hunger and poverty. Fellow-soldiers of her husband had informed her that Frau K. had visited taverns with M. and had sat there drinking till far into the night. On one occasion the defendant had asked the plaintiff's husband in the presence of several other soldiers whether he would not get a divorce soon from "his old woman" and set up with here. Frau K.'s caretaker also reported that she had repeatedly seen the plaintiff's husband in the house most incompletely dressed.

'Before a court in the Leopoldstadt [district of Vienna] Frau K. yesterday denied knowing M., so that there could be no question of her having intimate relations with him.

'A witness, Albertine M., stated, however, that she had surprised Frau K. kissing the plaintiff's husband.

'At a previous hearing, M., under examination as a witness, had denied having intimate relations with the defendant. Yesterday the Judge received a letter in which the witness withdrew the statements he had made on the earlier occasion and admitted that he had had a love-affair with Frau K. up till the previous June. He had only denied his relations with the defendant at the former hearing because she had come to him before the hearing and begged him on her knees to save her and say nothing. "Today, the witness wrote, "I feel compelled to make a full confession to the Court, for I have broken my left arm and this seems to me to be a divine punishment for my wrongdoing."

'The Judge stated that the penal offence had lapsed under the statute of limitations. The plaintiff then withdrew her claim and the defendant was discharged.'

3. [In philology the term is used of two different words with the same etymology: e.g. 'fashion' and 'faction', both from the Latin '*factio*'.]
4. See Sigmund Freud, *Introductory Lectures on Psychoanalysis*, Harmondsworth: Penguin, 1973, p. 153.

11 □ *Myth Today*

Roland Barthes

What is a myth, today? I shall give at the outset a first, very simple answer, which is perfectly consistent with etymology: *myth is a type of speech*.[1]

Myth is a Type of Speech

Of course, it is not *any* type: language needs special conditions in order to become myth: we shall see them in a minute. But what must be firmly established at the start is that myth is a system of communication, that it is a message. This allows one to perceive that myth cannot possibly be an object, a concept, or an idea; it is a mode of signification, a form. Later, we shall have to assign to this form historical limits, conditions of use, and reintroduce society into it: we must nevertheless first describe it as a form.

It can be seen that to purport to discriminate among mythical objects according to their substance would be entirely illusory: since myth is a type of speech, everything can be a myth provided it is conveyed by a discourse. Myth is not defined by the object of its message, but by the way in which it utters this message: there are formal limits to myth, there are no 'substantial' ones. Everything, then, can be a myth? Yes, I believe this, for the universe is infinitely fertile in suggestions. Every object in the world can pass from a closed, silent existence to an oral state, open to appropriation by society, for there is no law, whether natural or not, which forbids talking about things.

[...]

Naturally, everything is not expressed at the same time: some objects become the prey of mythical speech for a while, then they disappear, others take their place and attain the status of myth. [...] for it is human history which converts reality into

From Barthes, R., *Mythologies*, Jonathan Cape, London, 1972, pp. 117–42, 154–7.

speech, and it alone rules the life and the death of mythical language. Ancient or not, mythology can only have an historical foundation, for myth is a type of speech chosen by history: it cannot possibly evolve from the 'nature' of things.

Speech of this kind is a message. It is therefore by no means confined to oral speech. It can consist of modes of writing or of representations; not only written discourse, but also photography, cinema, reporting, sport, shows, publicity, all these can serve as a support to mythical speech. Myth can be defined neither by its object nor by its material, for any material can arbitrarily be endowed with meaning: the arrow which is brought in order to signify a challenge is also a kind of speech.

[. . .]

Mythical speech is made of a material which has *already* been worked on so as to make it suitable for communication: it is because all the materials of myth (whether pictorial or written) presuppose a signifying consciousness, that one can reason about them while discounting their substance. This substance is not unimportant: pictures, to be sure, are more imperative than writing, they impose meaning at one stroke, without analysing or diluting it. But this is no longer a constitutive difference. Pictures become a kind of writing as soon as they are meaningful: like writing, they call for a *lexis*.

We shall therefore take *language, discourse, speech*, etc., to mean any significant unit or synthesis, whether verbal or visual: a photograph will be a kind of speech for us in the same way as a newspaper article; even objects will become speech, if they mean something. [. . .] This does not mean that one must treat mythical speech like language; myth in fact belongs to the province of a general science, coextensive with linguistics, which is *semiology*.

Myth as a Semiological System

For mythology, since it is the study of a type of speech, is but one fragment of this vast science of signs which Saussure postulated some forty years ago under the name of *semiology*. [. . .] Now to postulate a signification is to have recourse to semiology.

[. . .]

Semiology is a science of forms, since it studies significations apart from their content. I should like to say one word about the necessity and the limits of such a formal science. [. . .] Less terrorized by the spectre of 'formalism', historical criticism might have been less sterile; it would have understood that the specific study of forms does not in any way contradict the necessary principle of totality and History. On the contrary: the more a system is specifically defined in its forms, the more amenable it is to historical criticism. To parody a well-known saying, I shall say that a little formalism turns one away from History, but that a lot brings one back to it.

[...]

Semiology, once its limits are settled, is not a metaphysical trap: it is a science among others, necessary but not sufficient. The important thing is to see that the unity of an explanation cannot be based on the amputation of one or other of its approaches, but, as Engels said, on the dialectical co-ordination of the particular sciences it makes use of. This is the case with mythology: it is a part both of semiology inasmuch as it is a formal science, and of ideology inasmuch as it is an historical science: it studies ideas-in-form.[2]

Let me therefore restate that any semiology postulates a relation between two terms, a signifier and a signified. This relation concerns objects which belong to different categories, and this why it is not one of equality but one of equivalence. We must here be on our guard, for despite common parlance which simply says that the signifies *expresses* the signified, we are dealing, in any semiological system, not with two, but with three different terms. For what we grasp is not at all one term after the other, but the correlation which unites them: there are, therefore, the signifier, the signified and the sign, which is the associative total of the first two terms. Take a bunch of roses: I use it to *signify* my passion. Do we have here, then, only a signifier and a signified, the roses and my passion? Not even that: to put it accurately, there are here only 'passionified' roses. But on the plane of analysis, we do have three terms; for these roses weighted with passion perfectly and correctly allow themselves to be decomposed into roses and passion: the former and the latter existed before uniting and forming this third object, which is the sign. It is as true to say that on the plane of experience I cannot dissociate the roses from the message they carry, as to say that on the plane of analysis I cannot confuse the roses as signifier and the roses as sign: the signifier is empty, the sign is full, it is a meaning. Or take a black pebble: I can make it signify in several ways, it is a mere signifier; but if I weigh it with a definite signified (a death sentence, for instance, in an anonymous vote), it will become a sign. Naturally, there are between the signifier, the signified and the sign, functional implications (such as that of the part to the whole) which are so close that to analyse them may seem futile; but we shall see in a moment that this distinction has a capital importance for the study of myth as semiological schema.

Naturally these three terms are purely formal, and different contents can be given to them. Here are a few examples: for Saussure, who worked on a particular but methodologically exemplary semiological system – the language or *langue* – the signified is the concept, the signifier is the acoustic image (which is mental) and the relation between concept and image is the sign (the word, for instance), which is a concrete entity.[3]

[...]

In myth, we find again the tri-dimensional pattern which I have just described:

the signifier, the signified and the sign. But myth is a peculiar system, in that it is constructed from a semiological chain which existed before it: it *is a second-order semiological system*. That which is a sign (namely the associative total of a concept and an image) in the first system, becomes a mere signifier in the second. We must here recall that the materials of mythical speech (the language itself, photography, painting, posters, rituals, objects, etc.), however different at the start, are reduced to a pure signifying function as soon as they are caught by myth. Myth sees in them only the same raw material; their unity is that they all come down to the status of a mere language. Whether it deals with alphabetical or pictorial writing, myth wants to see in them only a sum of signs, a global sign, the final term of a first semiological chain. And it is precisely this final term which will become the first term of the greater system which it builds and of which it is only a part. Everything happens as if myth shifted the formal system of the first significations sideways. As this lateral shift is essential for the analysis of myth, I shall represent it in the following way, it being understood, of course, that the spatialization of the pattern is here only a metaphor:

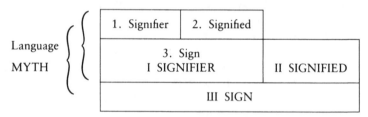

It can be seen that in myth there are two semiological systems, one of which is staggered in relation to the other: a linguistic system, the language (or the modes of representation which are assimilated to it), which I shall call the *language-object*, because it is the language which myth gets hold of in order to build its own system; and myth itself, which I shall call *metalanguage*, because it is a second language, *in which* one speaks about the first. When he reflects on a metalanguage, the semiologist no longer needs to ask himself questions about the composition of the language-object, he no longer has to take into account the details of the linguistic schema; he will only need to know its total term, or global sign, and only inasmuch as this term lends itself to myth. This is why the semiologist is entitled to treat in the same way writing and pictures: what he retains from them is the fact that they are both *signs*, that they both reach the threshold of myth endowed with the same signifying function, that they constitute, one just as much as the other, a language-oject.

It is now time to give one or two examples of mythical speech. [. . .] I am a pupil in the second form in a French *lycée*. I open my Latin grammar, and I read a sentence, borrowed from Aesop or Phaedrus: *quia ego nominor leo*. I stop and think. There is something ambiguous about this statement: on the one hand, the words in it do have a simple meaning: *because my name is lion*. And on the other hand, the sentence is evidently there in order to signify something else to me.

Inasmuch as it is addressed to me, a pupil in the second form, it tells me clearly: I am a grammatical example meant to illustrate the rule about the agreement of the predicate. I am even forced to realize that the sentence in no way *signifies* its meaning to me, that it tries very little to tell me something about the lion and what sort of name he has; its true and fundamental signification is to impose itself on me as the presence of a certain agreement of the predicate. I conclude that I am faced with a particular, greater, semiological system, since it is co-extensive with the language: there is, indeed, a signifier, but this signifier is itself formed by a sum of signs, it is in itself a first semiological system (*my name is lion*). Thereafter, the formal pattern is correctly unfolded: there is a signified (*I am a grammatical example*) and there is a global signification, which is none other than the correlation of the signifier and the signified; for neither the naming of the lion nor the grammatical example are given separately.

And here is now another example: I am at the barber's, and a copy of *Paris-Match* is offered to me. On the cover, a young Negro in a French uniform is saluting, with his eyes uplifted, probably fixed on a fold of the tricolour. All this is the *meaning* of the picture. But, whether naïvely or not, I see very well what it signifies to me: that France is a great Empire, that all her sons, without any colour discrimination, faithfully serve under her flag, and that there is no better answer to the detractors of an alleged colonialism than the zeal shown by this Negro in serving his so-called oppressors. I am therefore again faced with a greater semiological system: there is a signifier, itself already formed with a previous system (*a black soldier is giving the French salute*); there is a signified (it is here a purposeful mixture of Frenchness and militariness); finally, there is a presence of the signified through the signifier.

Before tackling the analysis of each term of the mythical system, one must agree on terminology. We now know that the signifier can be looked at, in myth, from two points of view: as the final term of the linguistic system, or as the first term of the mythical system. We therefore need two names. On the plane of language, that is, as the final term of the first system, I shall call the signifier: *meaning* (*my name is lion, a Negro is giving the French salute*); on the plane of myth, I shall call it: *form*. In the case of the signified, no ambiguity is possible: we shall retain the name *concept*. The third term is the correlation of the first two: in the linguistic system, it is the *sign*; but it is not possible to use this word again without ambiguity, since in myth (and this is the chief peculiarity of the latter), the signifier is already formed by the *signs* of the language. I shall call the third term of myth the *signification*. This word is here all the better justified since myth has in fact a double function: it points out and it notifies, it makes us understand something and it imposes it on us.

[. . .]

The Signification

We now know that myth is a type of speech defined by its intention (*I am a grammatical example*) much more than by its literal sense (*my name is lion*); and that in spite of this, its intention is somehow frozen, purified, eternalized, *made absent* by this literal sense (*The French Empire? It's just a fact: look at this good Negro who salutes like one of our own boys*). This constituent ambiguity of mythical speech has two consequences for the signification, which henceforth appears both like a notification and like a statement of fact.

Myth has an imperative, buttonholing character: stemming from an historical concept, directly springing from contingency (a Latin class, a threatened Empire), it is *I* whom it has come to seek. It is turned towards me, I am subjected to its intentional force, it summons me to receive its expansive ambiguity.

[...]

[T]his interpellant speech is at the same time a frozen speech: at the moment of reaching me, it suspends itself, turns away and assumes the look of a generality: it stiffens, it makes itself look neutral and innocent. The appropriation of the concept is suddenly driven away once more by the literalness of the meaning. This is a kind of *arrest*, in both the physical and the legal sense of the term: French imperiality condemns the saluting Negro to be nothing more than an instrumental signifier, the Negro suddenly hails me in the name of French imperiality; but at the same moment the Negro's salute thickens, becomes vitrified, freezes into an eternal reference meant to *establish* French imperiality. On the surface of language something has stopped moving: the use of the signification is here, hiding behind the fact, and conferring on it a notifying look; but at the same time, the fact paralyses the intention, gives it something like a malaise producing immobility: in order to make it innocent, it freezes it.

[...]

One last element of the signification remains to be examined: its motivation. We know that in a language, the sign is arbitrary: nothing compels the acoustic image *tree* 'naturally' to mean the concept *tree*: the sign, here, is unmotivated. Yet this arbitrariness has limits, which come from the associative relations of the word: the language can produce a whole fragment of the sign by analogy with other signs (for instance one says *aimable* in French, and not *amable*, by analogy with *aime*). The mythical signification, on the other hand, is never arbitrary; it is always in part motivated, and unavoidably contains some analogy. For Latin exemplarity to meet the naming of the lion, there must be an analogy, which is the agreement of the predicate; for French imperiality to get hold of the saluting Negro, there must be identity between the Negro's salute and that of the French soldier. Motivation is necessary to the very duplicity of myth: myth plays on the analogy between meaning and form, there is no myth without motivated form.

[...]

Motivation is unavoidable. It is none the less very fragmentary. To start with, it is not 'natural': it is history which supplies its analogies to the form. Then, the analogy between the meaning and the concept is never anything but partial: the form drops many analogous features and keeps only a few [.] [. . .] Finally, the motivation is chosen among other possible ones: I can very well give to French imperiality many other signifiers beside a Negro's salute: a French general pins a decoration on a one-armed Senegalese, a nun hands a cup of tea to a bed-ridden Arab, a white schoolmaster teaches attentive piccaninnies: the press undertakes every day to demonstrate that the store of mythical signifiers is inexhaustible.

[. . .]

Reading and Deciphering Myth

How is a myth received? We must here once more come back to the duplicity of its signifier, which is at once meaning and form. I can produce three different types of reading by focusing on the one, or the other, or both at the same time.[4]

1. If I focus on an empty signifier, I let the concept fill the form of the myth without ambiguity, and I find myself before a simple system, where the signification becomes literal again: the Negro who salutes is an *example* of French imperiality, he is a *symbol* for it. This type of focusing is, for instance, that of the producer of myths, of the journalist who starts with a concept and seeks a form for it.[5]
2. If I focus on a full signifier, in which I clearly distinguish the meaning and the form, and consequently the distortion which the one imposes on the other, I undo the signification of the myth, and I receive the latter as an imposture: the saluting Negro becomes the *alibi* of French imperiality. This type of focusing is that of the mythologist: he deciphers the myth, he understands a distortion.
3. Finally, if I focus on the mythical signifier as on an inextricable whole made of meaning and form, I receive an ambiguous signification: I respond to the constituting mechanism of myth, to its own dynamics, I become a reader of myths. The saluting Negro is no longer an example or a symbol, still less an alibi: he is the very *presence* of French imperiality.

The first two types of focusing are static, analytical; they destroy the myth, either by making its intention obvious, or by unmasking it: the former is cynical, the latter demystifying. The third type of focusing is dynamic, it consumes the myth according to the very ends built into its structure: the reader lives the myth as a story at once true and unreal.

If one wishes to connect a mythical schema to a general history, to explain how it corresponds to the interests of a definite society – in short, to pass from semiology to ideology, it is obviously at the level of the third type of focusing that one must place oneself: it is the reader of myths himself who must reveal their essential function. How does he receive this particular myth *today*? If he receives it in an innocent fashion, what is the point of proposing it to him? And if he reads it using his powers of reflection, like the mythologist, does it matter which alibi is presented? If the reader does not see French imperiality in the saluting Negro, it was not worth weighting the latter with it; and if he sees it, the myth is nothing more than a political proposition, honestly expressed. In one word, either the intention of the myth is too obscure to be efficacious, or it is too clear to be believed. In either case, where is the ambiguity?

This is but a false dilemma. Myth hides nothing and flaunts nothing: it distorts; myth is neither a lie nor a confession; it is an inflexion. Placed before the dilemma which I mentioned a moment ago, myth finds a third way out. Threatened with disappearance if it yields to either of the first two types of focusing, it gets out of this tight spot thanks to a compromise – it *is* this compromise. Entrusted with 'glossing over' an intentional concept, myth encounters nothing but betrayal in language, for language can only obliterate the concept if it hides it, or unmask it if it formulates it. The elaboration of a second-order semiological system will enable myth to escape this dilemma: driven to having either to unveil or to liquidate the concept, it will *naturalize* it.

We reach here the very principle of myth: it transforms history into nature. We now understand why, *in the eyes of the myth-consumer*, the intention, the adhomination of the concept can remain manifest without, however, appearing to have an interest in the matter: what causes mythical speech to be uttered is perfectly explicit, but it is immediately frozen into something natural; it is not read as a motive, but as a reason. If I read the Negro-saluting as symbol pure and simple of imperiality, I must renounce the reality of the picture, it discredits itself in my eyes when it becomes an instrument. Conversely, if I decipher the Negro's salute as an alibi of coloniality, I shatter the myth even more surely by the obviousness of its motivation. But for the myth-reader, the outcome is quite different: everything happens as if the picture *naturally* conjured up the concept, as if the signifier *gave a foundation* to the signified: the myth exists from the precise moment when French imperiality achieves the natural state: myth is speech justified *in excess*.

[...]

[T]he naturalization of the concept [is] the essential function of myth, [...] This is why myth is experienced as innocent speech: not because its intentions are hidden – if they were hidden, they could not be efficacious – but because they are naturalized.

In fact, what allows the reader to consume myth innocently is that he does not see it as a semiological system but as an inductive one. Where there is only an equivalence, he sees a kind of causal process: the signifier and the signified have, in his eyes, a natural relationship. This confusion can be expressed otherwise: any semiological system is a system of values; now the myth-consumer takes the signification for a system of facts: myth is read as a factual system, whereas it is but a semiological system.

[. . .]

Myth is Depoliticized Speech

And this is where we come back to myth. Semiology has taught us that myth has the task of giving an historical intention a natural justification, and making contingency appear eternal. Now this process is exactly that of bourgeois ideology. If our society is objectively the privileged field of mythical significations, it is because formally myth is the most appropriate instrument for the ideological inversion which defines this society: at all the levels of human communication, myth operates the inversion of *anti-physis* into *pseudo-physis*.

What the world supplies to myth is an historical reality, defined, even if this goes back quite a while, by the way in which men have produced or used it; and what myth gives in return is a *natural* image of this reality. And just as bourgeois ideology is defined by the abandonment of the name 'bourgeois', myth is constituted by the loss of the historical quality of things: in it, things lose the memory that they once were made. The world enters language as a dialectical relation between activities, between human actions; it comes out of myth as a harmonious display of essences. A conjuring trick has taken place; it has turned reality inside out, it has emptied it of history and has filled it with nature, it has removed from things their human meaning so as to make them signify a human insignificance. The function of myth is to empty reality: it is, literally, a ceaseless flowing out, a haemorrhage, or perhaps an evaporation, in short a perceptible absence.

It is now possible to complete the semiological definition of myth in a bourgeois society: *myth is depoliticized speech*. One must naturally understand *political* in its deeper meaning, as describing the whole of human relations in their real, social structure, in their power of making the world; one must above all give an active value to the prefix *de-*: here it represents an operational movement, it permanently embodies a defaulting. In the case of the soldier-Negro, for instance, what is got rid of is certainly not French imperiality (on the contrary, since what must be actualized is its presence); it is the contingent, historical, in one word: *fabricated*, quality of colonialism. Myth does not deny things, on the contrary, its function is to talk about them; simply, it purifies them, it makes them innocent, it gives them a natural and eternal justification, it gives them a clarity which is not that of an explanation but that of a statement of fact. If I *state the fact* of French imperiality without explaining it, I am very near to finding that it is natural and *goes without saying*: I am reassured. In passing from history to nature, myth acts economically: it abolishes the complexity of human acts, it gives them the simplicity of essences, it does away with all dialectics, with any going back beyond what is immediately visible, it organizes a world which is without contradictions because it is without depth, a world wide open and wallowing in the evident, it establishes a blissful clarity; things appear to mean something by themselves.[6]

Notes

1. Innumerable other meanings of the word 'myth' can be cited against this. But I have tried to define things, not words.
2. The development of publicity, of a natural press, of radio, of illustrated news, not to speak of the survival of a myriad rites of communication which rule social appearances, makes the development of a semiological science more urgent than ever. In a single day, how many really non-signifying fields do we cross? Very few, sometimes none. Here I am, before the sea; it is true that it bears no message. But on the beach, what material for semiology! Flags, slogans, signals, sign-boards, clothes, suntan even, which are so many messages to me.
3. The notion of *word* is one of the most controversial in linguistics. I keep it here for the sake of simplicity.
4. The freedom in choosing what one focuses on is a problem which does not belong to the province of semiology: it depends on the concrete situation of the subject.
5. We receive the naming of the lion as a pure *example* of Latin grammar because we are, *as grown-ups*, in a creative position in relation to it. I shall come back later to the value of the context in this mythical schema.
6. To the pleasure-principle of Freudian man could be added the clarity-principle of mythological humanity. All the ambiguity of myth is there: its clarity is euphoric.

12 □ The Structure of Myth & The Structure of the Western Film

Will Wright

The Structure of Myth

A myth is a communication from a society to its members: the social concepts and attitudes determined by the history and institutions of a society are communicated to its members through its myths. One of the tasks of this study is to examine this assertion. To do so, it is necessary to discover the meaning of a myth and to find out how a myth communicates its meaning. Like any communication, a myth must be heard (or viewed) and interpreted correctly; this means that myth must have a structure, like the grammar of language, that is used and understood automatically and through which meaning is communicated. In this chapter, I shall present a theory of the structure of myth and discuss how abstract social ideas are established in and communicated by this structure.

My discussion will rely to a considerable extent on the structural studies of Claude Lévi-Strauss. In fact, the idea and inspiration for my study of the Western comes almost entirely from his work. His analysis of tribal myths is primarily responsible for current anthropological interest in cognitive and structural approaches to myth and ritual. Since I cannot agree completely with his ideas on myth, however, will develop a somewhat different theoretical perspective. Essentially, I will be less concerned with structure and more concerned with order and communication. Lévi-Strauss demonstrates exhaustively the existence of a formal, conceptual structure in tribal myths for the purpose of proving that this structure is inherent in the human mind.

[. . .]

My interest, however, is not to reveal a mental structure but to show how the myths of a society, through their structure, communicate a conceptual order to the members of that society; that is, I want to establish that a myth orders the everyday

From Wright, W., *Sixguns and Society*, University of California Press, Berkeley, 1975, pp. 16–25, 29–58.

experiences of its hearers (or viewers) and communicates this order through a formal structure that is understood like language. Thus, there is an important difference of emphasis between the concerns of my study and those of Lévi-Strauss. Lévi-Strauss wants to discover the meaning of a myth in order to exhibit its mental structure, while I want to exhibit the structure of a myth in order to discover its social meaning. [...] To do this, to relate myth to the ordinary responsibilities of people who act and must understand their actions, we need a theory that attempts to explain the interaction between symbolic structures and the possibility of human action. For such a theory, we can turn briefly to the literary analysis of Kenneth Burke, who suggests that certain basic aspects of human communication are determined by the use of symbols.

[...]

Burke interprets the characters of a narrative as representing social types acting out a drama of social order. In this way, interaction – such as conflict or sexual attraction – is never simply interaction between individuals but always involves the social principles that the characters represent. Thus, a fight in a narrative would not simply be a conflict of men but a conflict of principles – good versus evil, rich versus poor, black versus white.

This interpretation of narrative seems particularly appropriate to myths, and I will adopt it as a working hypothesis for my analysis of the Western. However, Burke's analysis is essentially literary, since he presents no systematic method for discovering the ideas of social classification and order inherent in narrative works. [...] Lévi-Strauss, on the other hand, utilizes a well-thought-out method of analysis and offers a remarkable amount of data to support the validity of his method. Therefore, an adroit merger of the theoretical insights of Burke with the method-ological suggestions of Lévi-Strauss might provide an appropriate framework for an analysis of myth and social action.

[...]

Lévi-Strauss's method is to look for the structure of myth in terms of binary oppositions. An image of something (a man, say) is structurally opposed in a myth to an image of something else (a jaguar, say). In this way the sensible differences between things (like man/not like man) become symbols of conceptual differences (culture/nature). An image of a character (man) in a myth does not come to represent a concept (culture) because of any inherent properties of the image, but only because of the differences between it and the image or character (jaguar) it is opposed to.

[...]

[According to Ferdinand de Saussure] – 'concepts are...defined...negatively by their relations with other terms of the system. Their most precise characteristic is in being what others are not'. The word 'jaguar', for example, has meaning because it separates those things that are jaguars from those things that are not. Thus, every symbol divides the world into two sets, those things it does refer to and those things it does not. Distinguishing jaguars from everything else does not tell us much about jaguars, however. If we distinguished them from all other animals, or even from all wild animals, we would know a great deal more about jaguars; that is, the domain that a symbol divides influences the meaning of the symbol.

[...]

Similarly, when an image of a thing becomes a symbol, we know more about what it does if we know exactly what it does not mean. This is because the symbolic meaning created by an assumed dichotomy of images is determined only by the differences in the images; their similarities are irrelevant. When a man is contrasted to a jaguar in a myth, this can represent humanity as opposed to animality, culture as opposed to nature. The symbolism is derived from their differences. As things, they have many similarities – alive, carnivorous, earth-bound – but these are unimportant in a binary structure of meaning. Clearly, if the jaguar were opposed to an eagle instead of a man, it would no longer represent nature but probably earth as opposed to sky, or perhaps even humanity as opposed to gods. The important point is that if a man, a jaguar, and an eagle were contrasted in a tertiary structure, the meaning of each image would be far less obvious and general. In this case, an understanding of the symbolism would require much more knowledge of the particular qualities of each character involved. Specifically, it would require the interpreter to recognize the similarities as well as the differences between the characters, since for an image to be a symbol its meaning must be unique. This means, of course, that when three or more characters are structurally opposed, their symbolic reference becomes more restricted and obscure because of the fine distinctions required; thus, their interpretation becomes more difficult. On the other hand, when two characters are opposed in a binary structure, their symbolic meaning is virtually forced to be both general and easily accessible because of the simplicity of the differences between them.

This explains the prominence of binary structure in myths. In literary works by individual artists – such as novels or dramas – the desire is usually for complex, realistic characters in situations that challenge social attitudes. For this purpose, a binary structure is not appropriate. But myth depends on simple and recognizable meanings which reinforce rather than challenge social understanding. For this purpose, a structure of oppositions is necessary. The Western is structured this way, and, as we shall see, it presents a symbolically simple but remarkably deep conceptualization of American social beliefs.

[...]

Of course, more than two characters can appear in a myth. But when three or more characters do appear, they appear as contrasting pairs, not as coequal representatives of alternative positions. In the classical Western, a typical cast would include a wandering gunfighter, a group of homesteaders, and a rancher. Instead of representing equally valid, conflicting life-styles, these characters .would be presented as pairs of oppositions with each pair having a different meaning. The gunfighter is opposed to the homesteaders, a contrast representing individual independence versus social domesticity. The rancher, who is settled and domestic like the farmers, is opposed to them, but on another level or axis: the farmers represent progress and communal values in opposition to the rancher's selfish, monetary values – a contrast between good and bad. In this way, the generality of the binary structure is maintained, while the possibility for rather complicated symbolic action is created. Each two characters are identified on one axis and contrasted on another; this structure permits interaction between social types and resolutions of conflicts between social principles but prohibits the more realistic and tragic situation of all three characters being equally good, equally domestic, and equally opposed.

In this study, then, I will examine the basic oppositions of characters in the Western in order to make explicit the conceptual reference inherent in this structure. This analysis, however, will only tell us what the characters *mean*; it will not tell us what they *do*. The opposition of characters creates the conceptual image of social types; but to understand how myth presents a model of appropriate social action between these types, we must know what they do, how they act. This is the narrative dimension of the myth, or the story.

[...]

Now social action requires interaction, and interaction takes place in the story of a myth, not in the structure of oppositions. Thus, in order to fully understand the social meaning of a myth, it is necessary to analyze not only its binary structure but its narrative structure – the progression of events and the resolution of conflicts. The narrative structure tells us what the characters do, and unless we know what they do, we can never know what they mean to people who not only think but act.

[...]

My method of narrative analysis will be to reduce the stories in a set of similar films to a single list of shared functions. These functions will be one-sentence statements that describe either a single action or a single attribute of a character. Thus, for example the statement 'The hero fights the villains' would be a function, while the statement 'The hero fights and defeats the villains' would not be. Similarly, 'The hero is unknown to the society' would be a function, but 'The hero is unknown and a gunfighter' would not. The characters whose actions and attributes are decribed by these functions are generic, not specific – that is, the functions do not refer to particular heroes, such as Shane or the Ringo Kid, but to the role of the hero as a character in all the stories. Also, the character referred to by the functions need not be only one individual. The generalized character in a function can be, and often is, a group of characters in a film, all of whom share a single meaning in an opposition. Thus, a function will refer to 'the villains' or 'the society' as a single character with respect to structural action.

This method of narrative analysis is a liberalized version of a method originated by Vladimir Propp for the analysis of Russian folk tales. His tales were much simpler than the Western, and he restricted his functions to descriptions of actions, whereas I have included attributes; moreover, his tales were folk, popularized and standardized by many retellings, whereas my tales are films – stories based on a social myth, but created by specific individuals for popular acceptance and never changed or standardized by public retelling. From a study of folk tales, Propp showed that the functions that characterize a set of stories occur in a rigid, unchangeable order; in each tale every function – that is, every action – must appear in exactly the same sequence. But this approach is unnecessarily restricting, for it is easy to recognize a set of essentially similar stories with slightly differing orders of events. The order of the functions that characterize a Western plot will not always correspond exactly to the order of events in a particular film; in fact, some functions, such as 'The hero fights the villains', may occur more than once in some films.

[. . .]

The Structure of the Western Film

[. . .]

The Classical Plot

The classical Western is the prototype of all Westerns, the one people think of when they say, 'All Westerns are alike.' It is the story of the lone stranger who rides into a troubled town and cleans it up, winning the respect of the townsfolk and the love of the schoolmarm. There are many variations on this theme, which saturate Western films from 1930 to 1955, from *Cimarron* and the saving of Oklahoma to *Vera Cruz* and the saving of Mexico. The classical plot defines the genre: [. . .] the other plots – vengeance, transition, professional – are all built upon its symbolic foundation and depend upon this foundation for their meaning.

[. . .]

Shane

Shane is the classic of the classic Westerns. It was directed by George Stevens from a screenplay by A. B. Guthrie, Jr, based on the novel by Jack Schaefer. It was filmed in the Jackson Hole Valley, which is framed by the magnificent Grand Teton Mountains. In this film, Alan Ladd stars as Shane, Van Heflin as Starrett, Jean Arthur as Marion, Brandon de Wilde as Joey, and Jack Palance as Jack Wilson.

The story begins with Shane riding out of the mountains into a beautiful valley. He asks for water at the farm of Joe and Marion Starrett, who are friendly at first but then hostile, telling Shane to leave at gunpoint, as the Rikers ride up. Shane leaves and the Rikers arrive to tell Starrett to get off the land or be driven off. They have a ranch, and they need all the land for cattle. Starrett is indignant but unnerved, when Shane suddenly reappears and announces to the Rikers that he is a friend of Joe Starrett's. He is wearing a gun, and now the Riker brothers and their men are confused. After a final warning, they leave. Shane is invited for dinner, and after becoming friendly with the family, he is given a job on the farm.

The next day, Shane rides into the small town for supplies, is insulted in the saloon by one of Riker's cowboys, and backs down, avoiding a fight. That night, the seven or eight farmers in the valley gather at Starrett's to plan strategy against Riker. Shane is introduced, but one of the farmers accuses him of cowardice and Shane leaves the meeting. Sunday, all the farmers go to town together for strength, and Shane intentionally enters the saloon. He is insulted again, but this time he fights and defeats a cowboy named Chris. Riker offers him a job, he refuses, and all the cowboys in the saloon attack him. Starrett comes to his aid, and together they defeat the cowboys. Riker, in anger, sends for a gunfighter.

The gunfighter Wilson arrives in town, and Shane recognizes him as a fast draw. Riker once more tries to buy out Starrett, but the farmer refuses. The next day, Wilson forces one of the farmers into a gunfight and kills him. The following day, Riker burns one of the farms. At this point, the farmers are ready to leave the valley in defeat, but Starrett convinces them to stay one more day. He decides to go to town and kill Riker, and Riker sends for him to talk. Marion, Starrett's wife, pleads with him not to go and asks Shane to persuade him not to, but Shane refuses to interfere and goes to the barn. In the barn Chris, who has had a change of sympathy, tells Shane that Starrett is heading into a trap. Shane puts on his gun, tells Starrett he is going to town, and advises the farmer to stay home. When Starrett refuses, they fight and Shane knocks him out. After saying goodbye to Marion, for whom he has a romantic attraction, which she shares, Shane rides to town. There, in the saloon, he beats Wilson to the draw and kills him. Then he kills the two Riker brothers. Wounded, he rides out of the valley for ever, into the dark mountains, while little Joey Starrett shouts after him to 'come back.'

[. . .]

I will now attempt to extract from these stories [Wright has given plot summaries of four other classical Westerns, *Dodge City*, *Canyon Passage*, *Duel in the Sun*, *The Far Country*] a list of functions that describe common actions and situations. This list will characterize these five films as well as the other classical Westerns on the list. Not all the functions will apply to all the films; most of them will, but a few, as we will see, may be optional. More importantly, the functions need not occur in the stories in exactly the order in which I will list them. Some occur more than once in certain films and in different places in the narrative[.] [. . .] Each film is the story of a hero who is somehow estranged from his society but on whose ability rests the fate of that society. The villains threaten the society until the hero acts to protect and save it. Thus, for analysis, we can reduce each story to three sets of characters: the hero, the society, and the villains. This is possible because each of the latter groups is undifferentiated – that is, the members of society always share common interests and have no internal conflicts, and the villains always share common interests and have no internal conflicts, except over money. Each group of characters, then, acts essentially as one with respect to the other group or the hero, and therefore we need only consider these three basic characters for a general description of the action.

In each film the story opens with the hero coming into a social group, a fledgling society consisting of families and elderly people with a settled, domestic life. In *Shane*, the hero rides into the valley and meets the farmers – specifically Starrett, his wife and son[.] [...] Thus, our first function can be:

1. *The hero enters a social group.*

In each film the hero is a stranger to this society. Shane is so much a stranger that he has no last name and no past. [...]

2. *The hero is unknown to the society.*

In three of the five films, the town discovers that the new arrival is a skilled gunfighter. Shane gives himself away when he twice reaches suddenly for his gun in reaction to unexpected noises after he arrives at the peaceful Starrett farm. Later, in a scene that is not mentioned in my summary, he demonstrates his fast draw and accuracy while giving Joey, Starrett's son, a shooting lesson. Finally he proves his ability in the climactic gunfight. [...]

3. *The hero is revealed to have an exceptional ability.*

As a consequence of this ability, the society recognizes the hero as a special and different kind of person. Shane, after revealing himself as a gunfighter, is first suspected by Starrett; then, after he confronts Riker, he is respected by Starrett, admired by Marion, and worshipped by Joey. He is thought to be different by the other farmers – some suspect him of being a gunfighter – because he is the only man in the entire valley without an understandable reason for being there. He is not a farmer, but he is farming. He does not want land, and he refuses an offer from Riker for much better money. Thus, he is an enigma, who is given a special standing in the community. [...]

4. *The society recognizes a difference between themselves and the hero; the hero is given a special status.*

Another consequence of the hero's ability – or, to be exact, of the recognition of that ability by society – is that society does not fully accept the hero. Shane is immediately distrusted by Starrett, and then later, when he tries to avoid a fight, he is accused of being a coward by the farmers. When he tries to rehabilitate himself by picking a fight, the farmers are upset by the fight and try to ignore it, mumbling 'This is bad, this is bad.' Even Marion, after Joey's shooting lesson and Shane's attempt to explain to her that a gun is just like any other tool, tells him, 'This valley would be better off if there were no more guns left in it, including yours.' This means Shane himself, so, as his expression tells us, he is chastened and ashamed. Joey, who is Shane's strongest defender, turns on him and exclaims, 'I hate you,' when Shane uses his gun to knock out the boy's father. Perhaps the strongest indication in any classical Western of the society's nonacceptance of the hero comes when Shane and Starrett fight[.] [. . .]

   5. *The society does not completely accept the hero.*

In each film there is a conflict between society and the villains, the good guys and the bad guys. In *Shane*, Riker wants the land for cattle and the farmers want it for farms. [. . .]

   6. *There is a conflict of interests between the villains and the society.*

In this conflict the villains always prove themselves to be far more capable of winning. Riker is an old Indian-fighter, his men are cowboys, and Wilson, his hired gun, is a professional killer. Their opponents, the farmers, are middle-aged men and women who are unfamiliar with guns and afraid of violence[.] [. . .]

   7. *The villains are stronger than the society; the society is weak.*

Function 8 is another one that appears in only some Westerns. [. . .] It states that the hero and the villain have a strong friendship or mutual respect. [. . .]

   8. *There is a strong friendship or respect between the hero and a villain.*

Because the villains are stronger, they endanger the existence of society. Riker kills one farmer, drives another off, and almost succeeds in forcing all of them out of the valley[.] [. . .]

   9. *The villains threaten the society.*

Functions 10 and 11 are, again, like 2 and 8, optional. They state that the hero tries to stay out of the fight between the villains and society and only decides to join in when a friend of his is endangered. [...] Shane does not fight for Starrett, or even put on his guns, until Chris warns him of a trap. [...]

10. *The hero avoids involvement in the conflict.*
11. *The villains endanger a friend of the hero.*

The next two functions are obviously required: the hero fights and defeats the villains. What is interesting, however, and needs a little documentation, is the fact that the hero always fights alone, without help from the society. Shane rides to town alone to face three men, leaving the farmers at home[.] [...]

12. *The hero fights the villains.*
13. *The hero defeats the villains.*

After the fight, the society is safe. Shane wins the valley for the farmers. As he tells Joey after he kills Wilson and the Rikers, 'Ride on home to your mother and tell her...tell her everything's all right, that there are no more guns in the valley.' [...]

14. *The society is safe.*

After the fight, or after the hero decides to make the fight, society finally accepts him. [...] Shane leaves the valley after the fight, thus avoiding the probable gratitude and acceptance of the farmers. He tells Joey, who begs him to stay, that he is leaving because 'there is no living with a killing', but we know, from Starrett's comments about his wife and Shane as well as from their tender and restrained parting, that Shane is really leaving because of the love that has grown between him and his friend's wife, a love that is only indicated after he has put on his guns and decided to fight Riker. [...]

15. *The society accepts the hero.*

Our last function describes the hero losing in some way the special status he has had in the society. What this means is that he is no longer either willing or able to take the role of special person that was conferred because of his unique ability. Shane leaves, relinquishing his newly acquired position as the deadliest man in the valley. There is no law for a hundred miles, and he could, of course, stay in the valley and maximize the rewards of his power and the farmers' gratitude; but he gives up his status as gunfighter and savior and chooses instead the dark night and the cold mountains. [...]

It [the society] no longer needs his special ability, and thus whether he stays or goes, he will inevitably lose his special status. This ending – the hero marrying and settling in the now peaceful community, becoming just like everybody else – is the most common ending throughout the classical Western, though not among the five we have discussed.

16. *The hero loses or gives up his special status.*

This completes the functions for the classical plot, which I will list here for convenience

1. The hero enters a social group.
2. The hero is unknown to the society.
3. The hero is revealed to have an exceptional ability.
4. The society recognizes a difference between themselves and the hero; the hero is given a special status.
5. The society does not completely accept the hero.
6. There is a conflict of interests between the villains and the society.
7. The villains are stronger than the society; the society is weak.
8. There is a strong friendship or respect between the hero and a villain.
9. The villains threaten the society.
10. The hero avoids involvement in the conflict.
11. The villains endanger a friend of the hero.
12. The hero fights the villains.
13. The hero defeats the villains.
14. The society is safe.
15. The society accepts the hero.
16. The hero loses or gives up his special status.

These sixteen functions describe the narrative structure of the classical Western, which presents a dramatic model of communication and action between characters who represent different types of people inherent in our conceptualization of society. The characters who symbolize these social types are the heroes, the villains, and the society. We can make explicit the conceptual or classificatory meanings of these characters by revealing the oppositional structure of the Western myth; we must understand how the different characters are different, what their recurring or defining points of conflict and opposition are.

The code, in which these basic social concepts are represented by the characters, will vary from plot to plot; in the classical plot, probably because it is the prototype, the characters are vivid and their meanings clear. Just as there are three distinct sets of characters, there are also three basic oppositions, each differentiating between at least two of the characters, plus a fourth opposition that is less important structurally and will be treated separately. Perhaps the most important opposition is that separating the hero from the society, the opposition between those who are outside society and those who are inside society. This inside/outside contrast is fairly rigorous in its typing of the hero and the society, but it is rather relaxed in its treatment of the villains, who are, as we shall see, sometimes inside and sometimes outside. A second opposition is that between good and bad, a dichotomy that separates the society and the hero from the villains. Third, there is the clear distinction between the strong and the weak, which distinguishes the hero and the villains from the society. The fourth opposition primarily contrasts the hero with everybody else and is perhaps the typically American aspect of the Western – the opposition between wilderness and civilization; the opposition is similar to the inside/outside contrast, but not identical. The villains may be outside of society but are always seen as part of civilization.

[. . .]

The inside/outside opposition is coded at one level, in *Shane* as in most classical Westerns, through the contrast of wandering, unsettled life with domestic, established life. The film begins as Shane rides out of the mountains and across the valley in scenes that are crosscut with views of the Starrett farm, its garden, fences, cows; smoke is rising from the chimney as Joey plays, Marion cooks, and Starrett cuts down a tree. Shane rides up to the farm and immediately tells Starrett, 'I didn't expect to see any fences around here.' Then, a minute or two later, 'It's been a long time since I've seen a Jersey cow.' Shane is alone – he has no family, no friends, and no ties. When he is having dinner with the Starretts, using 'the good plates, an extra fork', Starrett says, 'I wouldn't ask you where you're bound,' and Shane replies, 'One place or another, someplace I've never been.' Then, as though to make the point absolutely clear, Starrett comments, 'Well, I know one thing. The only way they'll get me out of here is in a pine box. . . . We've got our roots down here. . . . It's the first real home we've ever had.'

This kind of coding can be observed throughout the film. The other farmers also have families, children, possessions; and they seem to distrust Shane for this reason – he's got nothing to lose; he doesn't fit in their world. At the end of the film, Shane rides back into the mountains alone. The same opposition is coded at other levels – Shane has no last name; he grows nervous and jumpy at ordinary domestic sounds, a playing child or a wandering calf; he wears buckskins, clothing that identifies him with the wilds and is worn by no one else in the film. When he first appears in buckskins, Starrett distrusts him, and afterward Shane changes into farming clothes, symbolically attempting to join society; but when he again dons his buckskins, Starrett immediately starts a fight with him, indicating again their basic difference.

The Riker brothers and Wilson are somewhat indeterminate on this opposition, yet clearly more inside than outside. They obviously do not share the values of the farmers; but if we agree to leave values for the good/bad opposition, then these villains are mostly inside society. The Rikers are ranchers – settled, with large amounts of land and cattle, and with important social responsibilities (an army contract, many hired hands, and so on). Rufus Riker, the owner and leader, is old and grizzled; he was fighting Indians when Starrett was a child. There is in *Shane* a sort of mini-opposition between the old society and the new society; but for our purposes the Rikers, old or new, are more identied with society than not. Wilson, like Shane, is a wandering gunfighter and thus could also be identified as completely outside the society. That he is not serves to reinforce the split between Shane and the society. Wilson is from Cheyenne, which, together with his last name, gives him more of a background and a home than the hero has; he comes to town wearing a black hat, a black, buttoned-down vest, a striped shirt, and black armbands, looking exactly like a gambler from the city who is out of place in the wilds of the isolated valley.

[. . .]

In the classical Western, the good/bad opposition repeats some of the social imagery of the inside/outside dichotomy; but since it is aimed more specifically at the difference between the society and the villains, it is more explicitly concerned with values. The opposition of good versus bad does not depend entirely upon a difference of values; the existence of a second coding of the distinction between good and bad will become important in the analysis of the professional plot, when the difference in values has virtually disappeared. But the explicit coding of good and bad is between the social, progressive values of the members of society versus the selfish, money values of the villains. The decent citizens are committed to taming the land, raising families, and bringing churches, schools, business, and law to the West, a commitment repeated in virtually every classical Western. The villains, however, are committed to personal gain by any means and at any cost, usually at the cost of progress, decency, and law. In *Shane*, the conflict is not between ranching and farming but between community progress and individual exploitation of the land. This is most clearly stated in a discussion that takes place after the burial of Torrey, the farmer killed by Wilson. Two of the farmers, Howells and Lewis, have given up and are about to leave the valley. When Starrett tells them they should stay, Howells asks 'What for?'

STARRETT: Because we can have a regular settlement here. We can have a town and churches and a school.
LEWIS: Graveyards.
STARRETT: I don't know, but you . . . you've just got to, that's all.
SHANE: Know what he wants you to stay for? Something that means more to you than anything else – your families, your wives and kids, like you, Lewis, with your girls, Shipstead with his boys. They've got a right to stay here and grow up and be happy, and it's up to you people to have nerve enough to not give it up.
STARRETT: That's right. We can't give up this valley and we ain't going to do it. This is farming country, a place where people can come and bring up their

families. Who is Ruff Riker or anyone else to run us away from our own homes? He only wants to grow his beef and what we want to grow up is families, to grow 'em good and grow 'em up strong, the way they was meant to be grown. God didn't make all this country just for one man like Riker.

LEWIS: He's got it though, and that's what counts.

This states the conflict clearly: – the farmers want community, Riker wants domination and money.

[. . .]

The second coding of the good/bad opposition is more subtle and perhaps even more important than that of social as opposed to selfish values. This coding, which differentiates those people who are kind and pleasant to others from those people who are not, separates the villains from the society, and it makes it possible for the hero, who is not obviously committed to churches and schools, to be considered as good. When Shane first rides up to the Starrett farm, he is friendly and pleasant to Starrett; he goes out of his way to speak kindly to the boy; and later, he compliments Marion on 'an elegant dinner'. On many other occasions – at the farmers' meeting, at the dance, at the store – Shane is seen to be friendly and nice. Similarly, the farmers and their wives never quarrel, say nice things to each other, and are often seen visiting one another and making small talk. The villains are never nice or friendly to anyone. They don't quarrel among themselves, but they are always complaining, bragging, threatening, or insulting someone. They seem to have and need no friends, they never relax, and they never give or receive human comfort. Wilson, in particular, only speaks to be sinister; his fixed, evil smile makes him a caricature of inhumanity.

This nice/not nice coding is true throughout the classical Western. Western villains, it seems, can only be cruel, unpleasant, or sly, never friendly and charming. Once in a while, as in *Bend of the River* or *Vera Cruz*, the villain starts out friendly and nice, but this always proves to be deceit and manipulation, not real kindness. Usually, the villains begin and end mean and nasty [. . .] in the classical Western, no villains are sympathetic and no heroes or members of society are unsympathetic, a fact that is due to this nice/not nice coding of the good/bad opposition. This coding is not derived from the social values versus selfish values distinction but is simply added to it, making it possible for the hero to be on the good side of an opposition even after the distinction in values has been lost.

A third opposition, between the strong and the weak, contrasts both the hero and the villains with the society. The hero is a gunfighter; he possesses some special ability that makes him capable of defending himself. Similarly, the villains are strong, in numbers as well as in fighting ability. The society is remarkably weak. They seldom carry guns and have no fighting skill. Though they are usually numerous, they never combine into a fighting group to defend their homes and families. To make their weakness as convincing as possible, the social group rarely contains young, healthy men; typically, the settlers or citizens consist of women, children, and elderly, middle-aged, plump or comic men.

The farmers in *Shane* are unusually young and healthy, but they are virtually helpless in the face of violence. They continually complain that the only law is three days' ride away. When one of their neighbors decides to leave after having his crops ruined, his fences cut, his animals shot, and his family scared to death, their only response is to wish him luck and have a picnic. Later, when another neighbor has been openly murdered by Wilson, their only thought is to get out as fast as possible. Shane tells them they should have nerve enough to fight for the valley, but they never get that nerve. Starrett convinces them to stay after they show a little anger at Riker's burning one of the abandoned farms, yet their disarray and weakness is shown in the ensuing discussion:

HOWELLS:	What's to keep Riker from setting fire to my place?
JOHNSON	Just stay on your own ground.
HOWELLS	Yeah, and you'll be Torrey there [the buried man].
STARRETT	Now don't you forget there's a law in this country against...
HOWELLS	The law's three days' ride from here.
SHIPSTEAD.	You know that, Joe.
STARRETT	Just give me a little time.
HOWELLS	Who's going to do the fighting with Riker? He's got us on the run and he knows it.
STARRETT	(desperate) Now you men... just hang on, that's all.
HOWELLS	(angry) That's it, just hang on.
STARRETT·	I promise you something's going to be done about it.
SHIPSTEAD	But just what, Joe?
STARRETT·	You leave that to me. I've made up my mind I'm going to have this out with Riker.
MARION	You're taking on too much, Joe.

Of all the farmers, only Starrett shows some nerve. It is just assumed that he's going to do their fighting; no one offers to help him. But, as Marion says, he's taking on too much. This is made clear when Riker and his men first ride up to his farm. Starrett, together with his wife and child, stands with his son's gun – which turns out to be unloaded – defending his cabin. Morgan, Riker's brother, grins and asks sarcastically if Starrett's expecting trouble. At this, Starrett grimaces, looks embarrassed, drops his eyes, and lowers his gun. Then, just as Riker is telling the farmer that he could gun-blast him off his land right now, Shane appears beside Starrett wearing a gun. Now, in his steely-eyed presence, the Rikers are confused and unsure. They ride off, leaving only threats. At the end of the film, as Starrett prepares to ride to town to kill Riker, Shane – once again in buckskins and wearing a gun stops him, saying, 'Maybe you're a match for Riker, maybe not. But you're no match for Wilson.'

Shane, Wilson, and the Rikers are clearly strong. Shane is typed early in the film as a gunfighter by his quickness to draw at any unexpected sound. He beats up Chris and then holds his own against an entire saloonful of cowboys; later, he demonstrates his speed and accuracy with a gun during Joey's shooting lesson; and finally, he rides alone to town to fight for the farmers. The Rikers are strong because they have the numbers, fighting background, and Wilson, a hired gunfighter whom even the farmers have heard of and who, Shane tells us twice, is 'fast, fast on the draw'. In one interesting scene, Wilson and Shane study each other in the moonlight, saying nothing but seeming to circle one another like equally skilled foes preparing for the kill.

[...]

The fourth basic opposition of the Western myth is that between the wilderness and civilization. The difference between this opposition and the inside society/outside society distinction will become clear if by society we mean having roots, an occupation, and responsibilities, while by civilization we mean a concern with the money, tools, and products of American culture. The Indians become an easy test, for, as in *Broken Arrow*, they would typically be inside society (their own) but outside of civilization. The wilderness/civilization contrast is not as central as the other oppositions, and it is sometimes, though rarely, only vaguely present or missing altogether. But it is important because it serves to separate the hero from every other character. The hero is the only character who is both good and strong, and this fourth opposition explains how he alone can be this way. It is because he is associated with the wilderness, while all other characters – good or bad, weak or strong, inside or outside society – are associated with civilization. This identification with the wilderness can be established in various ways, through purely visual imagery or an explanation of his background – his life as a trapper or association with the Indians – or through the dramatization of his knowledge of the land and wildlife; the minimal requirement for the hero is that he belongs to the West and has no association with the East, with education and culture. The East is always associated with weakness, cowardice, selfishness, or arrogance. The Western hero is felt to be good and strong because he is involved with the pure and noble wilderness, not with the contaminating civilization of the East. Large-scale, interesting Westerns, such as *The Big Country*, have been financial disasters perhaps because they have made the error (with respect to the myth) of making the hero an eastern dude.

The east–west polarity in *Shane* is tacit, since no one is from the East, and Shane's identification with the wilderness is entirely visual. As the film opens, he is seen riding down from the mountains and then as a tiny speck against the immense wilderness of the valley. Again, at the end of the film, he rides directly into the rugged, snow-capped Teton Mountains, even though that is obviously not the way to leave the valley, so that once more he is visualized as at one with the vast wilderness. In fact, he is the only character ever filmed alone against the spectacular mountains, just as he is the only character to wear buckskins, a clothing style that clearly associates him with the wilderness. The Teton Mountains are used visually in *Shane* to reinforce an association of the wilderness with strength and goodness;

this is done by never letting the mountains be seen at the same time as the villains and by always using the same mountains as background when Shane is with the farmers. This device is carried to such lengths that, when Shane and Starrett go to town from the farm, they go down the road that faces the mountains; but when the Rikers and Wilson come from the same town to the same farm, they arrive from the opposite direction, thus avoiding being seen against the mountains. In one moonlight scene, the snow-capped tips of the Tetons glow like a halo directly over the heads of the three Starretts and Shane. In another instance, when the farmers, the Rikers, or Wilson arrive in the town, the mountains are not seen; the town is filmed from the wrong angle or the saloon is simply seen in close-up, filling the screen. But the two times when Shane goes to town alone – particularly the last time, when he goes to destroy the villains – the town is filmed with the mountains towering over the saloon, as though they were about to crush and devour it. In this way Shane is strongly identified with the wilderness, while the others are associated with such artifacts of civilization as farms, buckboards, saloons, and stores.

[...]

These four oppositions – inside society/outside society, good/bad, strong/weak, and wilderness/civilization – comprise the basic classifications of people in the Western myth.

13 □ *Jules Verne: The Faulty Narrative*

Pierre Macherey

A The Point of Departure: The Ideological Project

It seems not only possible but necessary to begin from the work itself, rather than at a distance or simply by moving through it. It is even inevitable that we must begin where the work itself begins: at the point of departure which it has chosen, its project, or even its intentions, which are able to be read all through it like a programme. This is also what is called its *title*.

Firstly, then, a general and explicit theme against which the work is continuously defined: the internal transformation of the social order by a process which is history itself, but which has now (and here arises the theme of modernity) come to predominate: the conquest of nature by industry. This is an easily identifiable ideological theme:

> Verne belongs to the progressive line of the bourgeoisie: his work proclaims that man is capable of everything, that even the most distant world is an object within his reach, and that property is only after all a dialectical moment in the general subjection of nature. (Barthes, *Mythologies*, trans. Annette Lavers, London, Cape, 1972)

[...]

Man's domination of nature, the *subject* of all Verne's work, though sometimes in a disguised form, is presented as a conquest, as a movement – the propagation of the presence of man in the whole of nature, which is also a transformation of nature itself. Nature is invested by man: this is Verne's *elementary* obsession (elementary because it is conscious and deliberate). A total conquest is possible; man penetrates nature only because he is in total harmony with it. The great novelty is that this movement, like a voyage, has an ending, and that this ending can be seen

From Macherey, P., *A Theory of Literary Production*, Routledge & Kegan Paul, London, 1978, pp. 165–240.

and described: the future bathes in the present, the future is completely contained in the present.

[...]

At this primary level, at the level of the project, elaborated as far as the general means of its realisation (a literary *genre*: the imaginary narrative) but not the real implements of its fabrication (it is at this moment of generality, of totality, that criticism usually concludes), at this level, then, we have: (1) *a subject*, one that implies a total vision of the world, an ideology (seemingly complete), a subject which even depends on the vision and the ideology in so far as it is a summary of both; (2) the general shape of a representation: the book will be a narrative, it will belong to the literature of fantasy.

We now need more detail of the subject; we need to identify *spontaneously* and provisionally its essential thematic objects. This specificity is located entirely within the kind of coherence that has already been described; it does not involve any movement beyond the generality and totality of the established project.

Conquest, movement and transformation will be expressed in three major themes: the voyage, scientific invention. and colonisation. The three are actually equivalent: the scientist is in fact a traveller and a coloniser; all combinations are obviously possible. The most general title of the work is 'the voyage'; the protagonist is the scientist, not necessarily the inventor but perhaps simply the practitioner, the one who brings the objects of science to life (for Verne science has its reality only in the material objects that it produces); it might be the engineer, or even the patron (as in *Carpathian Castle* and *Twenty Thousand Leagues Under the Sea*). Verne acknowledges no gap between the theory and the practice of science; there is simply a constant flow from the one into the other. The theme of colonisation is less explicit, less frequently emphasised, as though it had to be kept out of sight; but the scientist is a conqueror, an appropriator, one who moves into the unknown as the expression of his power.

[...]

Reciprocally, the traveller-scholar-colonist will also be an adventurer, and thus he acquires a real form, a character, a social specificity. [...] Thus we have seen established a subject specified in individualised representations, the determination of a certain form of writing with its specific episodes, its psychological types, and even its ethics – all of which is both borrowed and bound together in the coherence of a genre: a total narrative *form*. But here deduction has its ending: we must move to a different level of analysis in order to find new *means*.

But, it must be emphasised once again, this remains at a level of generality: the project has crystallised in a typical intention, but also, most significantly, in other concrete forms: a publisher's contract, an audience, a plan of publication, collaborators, publicity, illustrations. This level is the practical, the conscious point of departure of the enterprise: it will suffice for the beginnings of a description of the work. But it is not self-sufficient.

In fact:

1. It is a question of an ideological representation, linked to the general conditions for an ideology. This ideology expresses equally the state of society as a form of social consciousness (whence the subject-programme); a state of literature or of writing – the form of the narrative, the typical characters; and even the situation of the writer, in so far as this representation reflects the ideology of the profession: an audience, a publisher, amongst others. This representation is *imported* into Verne's specific project: the ideological programme (the conquest of nature, the social position of science) enters literature and it will express itself there, but it does not have the freedom of the city, because it is not, initially, constituted as a fiction. As it is, it certainly cannot become literature; it must first undergo a few alterations, submit to a secondary elaboration which will transform it into a literary object. Verne's contract with the firm of Hetzel commits him to producing regularly novels 'of a new type'; in a letter to his father Verne specified that this means 'the science novel'. Verne is clearly aware of what he is doing: joining a new form and a new content in a new work. For this purpose, the project must create and employ new means (other than a programme), means which meet the requirements of the real *practice* of literary production. These means will not necessarily be borrowed from the same areas of ideology; they will probably need to be sought elsewhere.

2. The transition from the ideological project to the written work can only be accomplished within a practice which begins from determinate conditions. At this moment of the analysis it would be tempting to say that Verne has *everything necessary* for the writing of his books; but in fact he has nothing at all and must seek out other means: those true *themes* of his work – in their individuality, in the specificity of the writing of a page – which, unlike the ideological subject, cannot be immediately representative of a generality. For us these themes define another level of description, corresponding to the time of production, which can be called *figuration*. Naturally it remains to be seen whether this second level sustains and continues the first level, or whether it puts it into question; and then whether, at this new level, it is self-sufficient.

B The Realisation of This Project: Its Figuration, and the Symbology of This Figuration

The Signs

The journey through science and through nature, which is the historical process of the future within the present, by means of the language of the fiction, has to *figure* man's total mastery over nature. Figuration is something rather more than representation, since it is a question of devising, or at least collecting, the visible signs in which this important adventure can be read: the reading of these signs will give a certain representation of the project but it is necessary first to discover the signs.

[. . .]

A sign denotes itself as such by its obsessional character: its efficacy derives from its various repetitions. The signs thus form a veritable series, a series inevitably limited. Most frequently and conspicuously we find the following: the centre (of the earth), the straight line, the document in code, the volcano, the sea, the trail (of a previous voyage – this is another form of code); and we even find 'psychological' signs: haste, the fixed idea. (Obviously there is only an apparent psychology, in so far as we are dealing with signs necessarily symbolic and allusive: the psychology is there for other reasons; if it can seem schematic, it should also not be taken seriously.)

[. . .]

The voyage is a conquest because it manages to draw a straight line over the world [. . .]. The theme of the line is accordingly linked to that of the cipher: the secret of regularity is buried in a mutilated disguised document which must be interpreted, and the reason for movement depends on the multiplicity of possible interpretations (which each correspond to a region of the world). [. . .] The adventure is finished when the line is completely traced: the cipher only delivers its last secret at the moment when the world is contained entirely within the limits of a dominant principle – limits which are like the pole of all interpretations, and which are also enclosed within a circuit.

[. . .]

The traveller draws his inevitably straight line across the irregularity of nature in order to reform it: in this his enterprise is an allegory of scientific work. Dedicated entirely to this rigour, the traveller is himself metamorphosed into the instrument of its production.

[. . .]

Verne's work is simply a long reverie or meditation on the theme of the straight line – which represents the articulation of nature on industry, and industry upon nature, which is *narrated* as a narrative of exploration. [. . .] Adventures all the more rigorous in that they are uncertain, in that one never knows what point of the journey one is at, whether the cipher will render its secret, whether rectitude can be preserved to the end.

[. . .]

This is the moment to examine the importance for Verne of the geographical map, which is a real object, but is also poetic in so far as it entirely retrieves nature. By means of a map the journey is a conquest of the same sort as a scientific adventure.

It re-creates nature, in so far as it imposes its own norms upon it. The inventory is a form of organisation, and thus of invention.

[. . .]

The chaotic richness of nature is only a temporary obstacle, for it denotes the presence of an immense *reserve* which man will be able to exploit. Moreover, the straightness of the line can only be appreciated, acknowledged, at the moment when the line is completely drawn: meanwhile it seems very fragile[.]

[. . .]

All the other symbolic images which are the true heroes of the adventure – the Pole, the Centre – are merely the diverse representations of this line in its conclusive rectitude, of this central point which will render the world to itself, definitely[.]

[. . .]

One can thus show – and the preceding analyses were merely examples, not a complete inventory – that the general themes crystallise in specific images, objects, natural places, or even psychological attitudes. (Two of these attitudes, typical, figurative, and not simply anecdotal, are especially important: the *fixed idea* (Lindenbrock, Hatteras, Fogg . . .), which functions as the equivalent of the central image (the centre, the volcano, straightness); and *speed* (Lindenbrock), an important theme which will be taken up later: it is obviously significant that the adventurer is in such a hurry.) These are individual themes which are symbolic images. This is the level at which we find the true work [*oeuvre*] of Jules Verne, the product of his creation, at least in the literalness of its content; this is what he has *made*, this is what distinguishes his work from all other written works, and which establishes the final object of all the possible readings: these are the themes which have sustained the curiosity of many generations of readers, given substance to their imagination of the great programme of the conquest of nature. We would ask how far these images have been produced by Verne himself – but if he has not made them, at least he has brought them together and organised them into a system – how far he has taken them from the fund of images which the long history of the narrative of the fantastic placed at his disposal, that reserve from which the language of fiction has been progressively elaborated: that general history which has never been written, except perhaps at certain points, that is to say, frequently on its reverse side. The general project had to be embodied in images which were not original, which were sought in another domain, a domain which is not that of ideological projects but that of language in its reality. This was the only way to have established the continuity of a narrative, which groups the images in the logic of a series, and even into a totality of narratives. This can be called the stage of *figuration*, to distinguish it from that of *representation* (statement of the ideological project, transposition of this project into a general narrative form).

However, the identification of striking images is not enough to explain the *inscription* of the subject. At this moment of the analysis, one could think that the work in its real diversity had been produced by a simple deduction from the initial project, and that accordingly it could be studied at this level as an independent reality: independently of the works themselves, and of that 'beyond' through which they exist. The reservoir of images seems to establish a closed and self-sufficient totality. But it is not enough to bring the images together, to group them in an analytic unity, which as a pure disorder would be unreadable, and which would also inevitably be incomplete.

We must give the narrative a formal unity corresponding to the content which it has discovered, which directs and organises it. Once again we encounter the problem of the coherence between the form of the narrative and its thematic content, though this time at the level of the unfolding of the narrative. We shall see that this form is systematic, in the same way that the special images were enclosed within the limits of a determinate inventory. We must now study the movement of the fable.

The Fable

The problem will be the same, displaced from the objects to the form which organises and animates them: given an ideological programme (to describe in advance man's total mastery of nature), how to find the means of expression, that is to say, the form of the narrative which will make it possible to translate it? It must be said immediately that this form will only be artificially separate from the content which surrounds it, initially because we are concerned with an adventure story; that is to say, one in which the episodes, the encounters, give (or try to give) impetus to the narrative; accordingly we must not hesitate to talk once again about thematic objects which, strangely, will give the exposition its *angles*, if not its outline.

One of these thematic objects, which has been little discussed until now, and which is only an element of the image of straightness, will become important: the image of the trace or landmark. The journey goes forward because it is the progressive deciphering of a familiar-distant totality; the succession of possible ciphers is the occasion of so many repetitions; it is the reason for its progress. One after the other, Hatteras overtakes the ruins of the expeditions which have gone before him to the Pole, and the identification of these traces is an important moment in his progress, which stage by stage impels him to the final goal which he alone will attain: the open sea at the Pole, the northern Arcadia, the central volcano.

In the same way (and this example will be decisive) Lindenbrock and his nephew Axel move towards the centre only because they possess a coded message, and because they are able to recognise its reflection all along their route: for them it is the visible safe sign of *the closure of the line*. The two examples are analogous and yet inverse: Hatteras progresses through the failures of others, and also, for those who go with him, 'from indiscretion to indiscretion'; Lindenbrock, on the other hand, walks in the footsteps of a previous hero, *who has arrived*, who has even returned, and who, like Hatteras and Nemo, was himself marked out for success, among those who reach the goal, who close the line: Arne Saknussen. The journey through the crust of the earth is a new figuration of *mobilis in mobili* (right down to the identification of the explorer with the natural setting: Axel's dream). But here the guide is no longer a living presence, as was Nemo: he must be discovered and followed. Saknussen is the Nemo of another time: he is equally an outlaw, an alchemist burnt at the stake, rejected by his contemporaries, and thus projected towards the future, the only one able to attain the centre. The conqueror is always an exceptional being. Hatteras goes mad, Nemo is a political rebel, Saknussen is a convict, and Robur is definitively hounded from *our* world. Humanity can only follow the same road if it discovers their traces, if it is loyal to their absent presence which is disguised in the form of a cipher to be translated. After them, or even with them, there cannot be an exploration in the strict sense of the word, but only discovery, retrieval of a knowledge already complete, and which can also be definitively lost (Robur).

The journey, in all its progressive stages, is disclosed as having ineluctably happened before. This explains the theme of haste – a theme which is emphatically not a rigmarole of imitative psychology: with Verne the picturesque is always there for some other reason. Lindenbrock is the man who, in his garden, pulls the leaves to make them grow more quickly: beyond the comic portrait of an eccentric scholar there is that destiny of the explorer, always in a hurry because he is always late.

Finally, someone has gone more quickly than he, has *anticipated* him. And this 'someone' is in the last analysis not even the wretched hero (who would thus be marked for success), but is nature itself, which is always in advance, and which might simply be caught up with; this, for Verne, is the significance of the activity of the scholar. One must hurry, one must violate time: as with Phileas Fogg's eighty days. To explore is to follow, that is to say, to cover once again, under new conditions, a road already actually travelled. To explore, through this systematic form of the narrative of exploration, is to retrace time, to anticipate: to recover a little of lost time.

For the first time we encounter this aberrant and important phenomenon in the work of Jules Verne: anticipation is expressed only in the form of a regression or a retrospection. The relation between the past and the present is reflected in the real relation between the present and the past. The conquest is only possible because it has already been accomplished: the fiction of progress is only the attenuated reflection of a past adventure which is almost effaced. The advance, in its literal form, is like a return. And this is why it does not matter greatly that it is interrupted by a failure: Lindenbrock will only reach the antechambers of the centre; the mere sight of the first corridors (which have already been thoroughly explored) suffices to deny him access; at the end, the eruption of the central volcano completely closes the gateway to adventure, cuts the line at its beginning. In the same way, Nemo, in his death, effaces all the signs of his adventure by returning with all the products of his work to the chaos of nature. In the same way, Robur is finally lost in the sky. In the same way, Hatteras forgets how to even communicate his secret to others. Finally, anticipation does not follow a process of acquisition which shows in a flash what *will be lost*, obliterates all trace of what has been.

Accordingly, something absolutely extraordinary has happened; the succession of thematic images, in the systematic form of a narrative of exploration, produces an avant-garde meaning (the project, which is to write the future) with its real formation: a return, a regression. The future can only be told in images in the shape of yesterday. [...] We see that in this sense the future resembles that which has already been seen.

Anticipation will be this search for origins. Thus, the structure of the fable is always related to a very simple model: a journey in the footsteps of the other, and in fact it is the history of a return.

Various conclusions can be drawn from this analysis:

1. The fable which shapes the narrative does not correspond to the initial project until that project has been subjected to a reversal: the future projects itself in the form of the-past-definitively-surpassed (the symbolic death of the father). Verne wants to represent a forward movement, but in fact figures a movement backwards.

2. However, this form is filled by the special thematic figures (without any discord appearing between them) to the extent that it could seem artificial to study them separately. So that the level of figuration is as coherent as that of the general representation: the actual discord between the subject and its elaboration is no more reflected in this second level than in the first. The moment of figuration, in so far as it is an autonomous moment, is as homogeneous as the moment of representation.

The analytical description leads us to a paradoxical result: it enables us to make the distinction between two levels – *representation* and *figuration*; the discord which has appeared between these two levels shows that the distinction was not artificial. However, such an analysis is inadequate, because it leaves these two levels – which might be called elements, aspects, points of view or elements of the exposition – side by side, like stable elements, or at least apparently so, each measurable in relation to its own legality. Two coherent and *incompatible* realities are thus revealed: the method employed thus far gives us no insight into their coexistence, or even their simultaneity, within a single work, which yet exists (this is the least that one could say). This discord does not denote a failure but a success: this is why it demands explanation.

Rather than a contradiction between terms at the same level, we perceive a real incompatibility between the representation of the project and its figuration. Does this incompatibility signal a weakness in the work of Jules Verne? Must we say that Verne has not found the words through which he could have said what he had to say? (Which, *a priori*, is not the same as what he wanted to say: the fact that such a discontinuity should be possible gives the problem its meaning.) One could even go further, and say, for example, that the actual coherence between the thematic images and the structure of the fable is illusory, and that it conceals an antagonism: that is to say, that the 'form' betrays the content; the plot imposes on the themes a mistaken meaning which the themes do not necessarily display; in this case, some other organisation of the signs was possible which would have guaranteed both a new coherence and loyalty to the initial project. Did the crystallisation of the given project into an image necessarily produce an inversion of the intended ideological line? We can see the answer which is hiding behind this question: a reactionary distortion of the work was inevitable; it corresponds to the actual movement of Verne's project, and it serves finally to characterise the ideological situation which was the ultimate condition of its realisation. This contradiction between the form and the content in Verne's work would be the reflection, term for term, of the contradiction in the ideological project. Accordingly, it will be said that the composition of the work was not only inevitable but also fatal.

But it is too tempting to decompose Verne's work in this way, and to show that his great project is distorted: this is how one reaches the point of showing that the persistent themes of the narrative are organised according to a rigorous system which perfectly describes the closure, an example of the contradictory character of the bourgeois project of liberation.

This is the short cut taken by Barthes when he insists on the flagrant contradiction between Verne's project and the imagery which he offers: this is an easy definition of bourgeois reverie, out of breath and looking for a place to rest, which must be distinguished from poetic reverie which constructs a pure movement and which arises from the Drunken Boat rather than directing it. This is the kind of criticism which the preceding description seems to lead to: a criticism which, to be coherent, has to base itself on a series of identifications which are naturally implicit. The falsely polemical enterprise of a *mythology* is always based upon a reduction of the general to the particular: the world is like a house, and the house is like a ship, and thus the work of Jules Verne. This progression can be followed, in either direction according to need; Verne's work embodies the bourgeois ideal of progress, but it is also a real picture of confinement, whence its failure, or at least the contradictory aspects of the enterprise. The explanation is grounded in the most mechanistic of materialisms: in order to affirm a contradiction it postulates a systematic coherence of all the levels and decrees their rigorous connection. These distinctions are made the better to confuse us; he complains of no longer finding the coincidences he had initially posited. The rationalism of equivalences is only a methodological instrument which serves to flush out, like game birds, failures and contradictions; and this chasing after witches is called demystification.

It must be stated precisely that the point of greatest resistance of this method, which is also its charm, is that nothing which is said by this means is false; but the analysis is always incomplete; this is in fact its basic condition, since the incompleteness will be given as the solution to the problem posed by the work. Accordingly, there is failure and contradiction: and it is not enough to produce them, they must be explained, and this is what Barthes does, by appealing to the historical situation of the writer. This situation not only endows him with a dated programme, but at the same time it gives him all the contradictions of an epoch and its dominant ideology, which are then transposed into the work as they are.

(At the very least this is surprising, since Barthes elsewhere criticises all historical interpretations of the literary work. (See the last section of *Sur Racine* on the transhistorical essence of literature.) Must it be said that his thinking has developed?

It is more probable that he believes historical interpretations to be justified when he is dealing with a work which is not a classic, cannot be perfect, and is therefore not truly literary. Verne is not Racine (and who would complain?), and for what does not deserve to be called a work, everything is permitted, as it would not be for others. However, Verne's work exists as much as, and even more than, that of Racine, and if it deserves an appropriate explanation it does not admit of the skeleton-key interpretations which have too often devolved upon it. It even deserves this explanation all the more in that it is closer to the centre of its age: we have seen that it is perfectly *representative* – there is no doubt of this. This kind of study will perhaps disclose the secret of a work completely involved in history, which makes no pretence of escaping history – the desire to write a novel of a new type in order to narrate a new object should not be considered such a pretence – a work which does not seek any of the disguises of eternity, and this is not necessarily a weakness.)

Also it seems useless and even very dangerous to speak of *contradiction*: at the point which the description has reached, the contradiction could not be located. There can only be discovered a contradiction at the level of representation through a projection of the contradiction of the figures. In fact there is no such thing as an ideological contradiction: the inexact character of an ideology *excludes* contradiction (see the final section of Chapter 19, 'Lenin, Critic of Tolstoy'). At the source of ideology we find an attempt at *reconciliation*: also, by definition, ideology is in its way coherent, a coherence which is indefinite if not imprecise, which is not sustained by any real deduction. In this case, the discord is not *in* ideology but in its relation with that which limits it. An ideology can be *put into contradiction*: it is futile to denounce the presence of a contradiction in ideology. Also, the ideological project given to Jules Verne constitutes a level of representation which is relatively homogeneous and consistent, linked internally by a kind of analogical rigour: the *flaw* is not to be sought in the project. Similarly, the inventory of images and their insertion into the chosen fable is in itself perfectly consistent. Verne begins with an ideology of science which he makes into a mythology of science: both the ideology and the mythology are irreproachable in their authority. It is the path which leads from the one to the other which must be questioned: it is in this *in between*, which, as we shall see, has its marked place in the work, that a decisive encounter occurs. In the passage from the level of representation to that of figuration, ideology undergoes a complete *modification* – as though, in a critical reversal of the gaze, it were no longer seen from within but from the outside: not from its illusory and absent centre (an ideology is centred at all its points, that is to say, perfectly *credible* because its centre is excluded), not from its centre then, but from the limits which hold it in check and impose upon it a certain shape by preventing it from being a different ideology or something other than ideology.

What is particularly interesting in the work of Verne is that in one moment at least it encounters this obstacle, which is ultimately the condition of the *reality* of the ideological project, and that it manages to treat it as such, as an obstacle. It is obviously unable to overcome the obstacle by its own means: as soon as this limitation is grasped, as though by an unconscious movement of resolution, the book begins to walk alone, to move in an unforeseen direction. It is not a question of a true resolution: the conflict remains intact, at the end of an almost autonomous development which only enlarges the gap which separates the work in its true production from the conditions of its appearance.

In fact, between the contradictory situation of bourgeois ideology at the beginning of the Third Republic and the difficulties experienced in an analysis of the work of Jules Verne there is a large difference, which could not have escaped Verne himself, otherwise he would not perhaps have deserved the title of 'author'. Certain of the contradictions which characterise his epoch, he knew, not thoroughly, of course, but better perhaps than Barthes: he has reflected them, he is even aware of having made them the true subject of his work, which is thus not as unified as one would like to think, nor as naïve. If Verne has *felt* the contradictions of his time – and we shall see that this is in fact the case – and if he nevertheless wanted to give an uncritical picture of this time (and this is not true, at least for political criticism) and the picture is actually defective, this is because there is a dislocation [*décalage*] between the ensemble of the historical contradictions and the defect proper to his work, a dislocation which must be considered as the true centre of his work. In this case, it is not enough to say that Jules Verne is a bourgeois of the early Third Republic with all that this implies (business, scientism, as well as all that makes a bourgeois revolution). We know that a writer never reflects mechanically or rigorously the ideology which he represents, even if his sole intention is to represent it: perhaps because no ideology is sufficiently consistent to survive the test of figuration. And otherwise, his work would not be read. The writer always reveals or writes from a certain *position* (which is not simply a subjective viewpoint) in relation to this ideological climate: he constructs a specific image of ideology which is not exactly identical with ideology as it is given, whether it betrays it, whether it puts it in question, or whether it modifies it. This is what must finally be taken into account in order to know what the work is made of. And the author does not always need to say what he is making.

[. . .]

Indeed, in his work Verne systematically elaborated this conflict proper to a new situation which elaborates the future in forms already outdated. Thus he attempts to resolve the question of the relation of the bourgeoisie to its own past, to its history, and manages to clarify at least certain *limits* of a historical situation (by testing its dominant ideology). For in his work there exists a privileged thematic object in which one could read the ultimate conditions of a problematic of production. This motif is privileged because it joins exactly, in its real presence, form and content (sign and fable): it is both a particular theme and the origin of a plot, in so far as it *shows* on a 'unique object' the links in an ideological series, which will take the form of a narrative, which will shape the fable. Let us say, in anticipation, that it is in this unfolding of the narrative that we will discover the discord which had until now appeared between the two different levels of the account. This apparently simple narrative is in fact the confrontation, the encounter of two opposed and even irreconcilable narratives: the narrative no longer progresses by following the episodes of an adventure, except on the surface; its movement is that which impels an ideological problematic. This theme is that of the island. Rather than an image it is now a matter of a *revealing theme*, which sustains in its materiality a complete ideological series. We cannot confidently say that all the images which have been studied thus far are expressive in this manner for the simple reason that they are not in themselves expressive; the recurring question is whether these images could show *something else* within some other organisation of the work.

But this question is meaningless in relation to Verne's favourite theme. This theme is complete – not an image for a meaning which transcends it. That is to say, it is absolutely *objective*: it presents in one moment the totality of its possibilities. When it is put to work, as it will be in the experimental novel *The Mysterious Island*, it undergoes a variation which returns it to its point of departure, but not a mutation. It could thus be said that at this third level of the formulation we arrive at the junction of the symbolic and the real (that reality which the work defines, obviously), in so far as the vehicle of the meaning alludes solely to this meaning, and is accordingly not open to any *commentary*. One could study thoroughly the regression or the discord which is the token of the narrative through this revealing and profoundly expressive theme: completely, that is to say, at a stroke; one could then answer the question of whether the inversion of the fable, the return to origins, has not definitively contaminated the object of the narrative. Now we can see clearly what could be called, though without its usual pejorative implications, that defect which is not a lack but which constitutes the work itself. Note that the term 'defect' is preferable to that of 'contradiction': it acknowledges that what is not said could not be said.

It is fruitless to be wondering what role is played by creation in the production of a literary work: this mythological representation, the residue of all the possible theologies, is contradicted by the fact that the work is preceded by an ideological project, a project which is always excessive, which engulfs [*dépasse*] the conscious intentions of the individual author; there is also all that 'material variety', the repertoire of images and fables, without which nothing could be done, and which would not exist if it had to be invented afresh each time. The way in which the conditions of its possibility *precede* the work (a fact which is so obvious but which centuries of criticism have ignored) systematically censures in advance any psychology of inspiration, even if this psychology is expressed in a theory of an intellectual will, to produce novel beauty. Against these metaphysical and supernatural representations must be advanced a coherent conception of the business of the writer, which is not the same as the business of writing. (It is absolutely not a question of describing a literary or artistic work as pure technique.) This work is possible only because it answers a historical requirement, a certain necessity of working at a given moment under particular conditions.

Accordingly the work is inevitably limited by the conditions of its appearance, limited in a way that has surprising consequences. But this idea cannot be formulated in such a simple way. It suggests a certain ambiguity: does the work arrive to fill up a frame which is already there, is it *not* really produced, but summoned from without?

Thus this criticism of the idea of creation, in the absolute sense of the word, seems to deprive the work of both originality and specificity (spontaneity is not in question, for this critical concept is without interest). Between the conditions of the appearance of the work and this actual appearance there will be an identity or repetition. Verne's work is so important because it enables us to demonstrate that there is a dislocation between these two moments. The work exists only because it is not exactly what it could have been, what it ought to have been: it arises not from the simple linkages of a mechanical production which would lead progressively from the outside to the internal reality; on the contrary, it is born of the obscure realisation which is certainly not conscious from the beginning – of *the impossibility of the work's filling the ideological frame for which it should have been made*. This is where we can locate the personal intervention of the author in the work of literary production, a work which begins collectively (in so far as it invokes a society or a tradition, though if we stop at this determination we are merely dealing with a problem of communication), but which ends as an individual stand in the immense debate of real works and ideological imperatives; this is when the problematic of expression or of revelation intervenes. Verne pursued this process to its very end, since, as we can see in at least one of his novels, he took this incompatibility which defines a historical situation as his very subject. Interestingly, he does not attempt a resolution of the difficulty, a conclusion to the debate, an obliteration of the incompatibility; in fact, he poses the problem, but does not offer a solution; the discord forms the very structure of the novel which concludes with the statement of discord. And thus the fundamental question of the situation of the writer, although objectively treated, since it gives the narrative its true plot, remains so objective that one could never know if the author had really perceived it, or whether it intruded without his knowledge as a fundamental theme, a theme so unworkable that it escaped from his direct grasp: an irreducible, unchangeable image which cannot be conjured away by being given a 'history'. Paradoxically, it is in this that Verne is a true *author*: because perhaps without having needed to intervene, he knew how to acquiesce in this decisive interrogation, which placed in question the very work in which it appeared. Obviously the critic has no need to *unmake* Verne's work: it furnishes the principle of its own decomposition.

C The Revealing Theme

[. . .]

Mobilis in mobili: this, as we know, is Nemo's call-sign; it is also the basic maxim for a historical reverie about destiny. Through it we can penetrate easily to the general principle which Verne wanted to illustrate. It abruptly discloses all the ideological complications which are the necessary condition for the novel as Verne conceived it: like the still vague perception of a historical event, it involves the notion that science is the essential instrument of a transformation of nature. *Mobilis in mobili* – this is the position of science, and thus the position of man in his relation to nature; this is Axel, who rediscovers a unity with the original sea while bathing near the centre of the earth. Science is in nature, the future is in the present, just as the *Nautilus* is in its element, where the real can no longer be distinguished from the symbolic. The unknown bathes in the known: it is precisely this intimate liaison, this conjunction which is also a conjuncture (that of the modern itself), this adequation, which best characterises Verne's work, *from within*. It tells us what he has done; it is the very heart of his project. It could well serve as its general title.

But it is most important that this same idea can serve to designate the insufficiencies or, rather, the limits of the work; it instigates a revelation of the confusion which obscures the relation between science and nature, and it discloses the impossible work which is the inevitable and illusory complement of the realised work. The principle of an imaginary fidelity to the future is itself inevitably fictive: this fidelity announces itself in a contradiction, in the words of infidelity. Voyages and encounters are both merely returnings and rediscoveries.

Thus what we are obliged to call *the reverse of the work* begins to take shape: the conditions of its possibility which enable us to read it against the grain of its intended meaning.

Similarly, the imagined identity between science and nature is not an absolute identification, because it is elaborated within that indeterminate space between reality and fiction, in that interval which betrays the obsolescence of all forms of antipication. As we have just seen, Verne seems to have reached one of the limits of the aesthetic consciousness, to have travelled to the very frontier of his own knowledge, in so far as he took upon himself the task of this revelation. [. . .] It was never Verne's intention to argue *a* belief in the power of science, nor was it his intention to argue against such a belief. That was not his theme. Not a complacent representation, then, but an interrogation of the *image of science*. Obviously Verne's work must be grasped in relation to the notion of progress and industry, but these notions are not the centre or direct content of that work. Verne's problem is this: How is it possible to figure that *ideological project which is the self-consciousness of an industrial society*? Through this singular problematic he successfully reveals the true meaning of this historical project. Far from devising a poetic celebration of the scientist-expert, making him into a solitary exile, he wishes to demonstrate the distance between this kind of representation and the reality of human labour. Verne's originality is to have made this distance apparent *within* this representation.

For this reason it is not enough to say that Verne is the representative of a particular ideological moment or of a certain social class, unless we first question the notion of representation itself. There is a too ready tendency to interpret the idea of representation in a retrospective sense: a work, once it is finished, would be representative *because it had been made* – that would be the dubious reward for this accomplishment, just as an elected candidate becomes (by definition) a representative. But, before the work is finished, before the votes are cast, is there or is there not representation? In any case, it is there that we must seek out the roots, the meaning of all representativity: in the conditions for the emergence of the work, for example, conditions which do not necessarily belong to the movement of the work. The problem of representation must be posed at the moment when the work takes form [*se fait*], for it is this decisive moment which articulates both what the author intended to or had to represent and what he in fact represents. Thus the purpose of Verne's work is not to translate or illustrate an idea or programme, but to realise the *combination* of the thematic figures and the fable. The interest of Verne's work resides in the discovery of an object which indicates this very combination: the island, the juncture of the thematic figure with the events, of a certain plot-form which derives from the collision of two possible narratives which also symbolise two forms of fiction. This makes the island irreducibly different from all the other thematic figures.

An attempt to represent is not to be confused with a gesture of assimilation: an individual represents a social class and its ideology in so far as he situates himself in relation to this ideological 'climate'; otherwise, in the case of the writer, he would write nothing. The novel is only a *work* in so far as it is an apt contribution, in so far as it admits innovation in relation to the 'spirit' [*esprit*] on which it depends. ('Spirit', 'climate': both unsatisfactory expressions in that they attempt to define the indefinite, though let us not attribute any mystical value to this 'indefinite', impoverished as it is.)

Firstly, it is impossible for a specific work to reproduce the totality of an ideology: a partial apprehension is all that is possible; thus there is a choice, a choice which is significant in so far as it is more or less representative. The contradictions which inhabit the work cannot be the same, term for term, as those contradictions upon which the work depends, even if we should discover these same contradictions in the life of the author [. . .] The work can be described as the reflection of these real contradictions, in so far as it is an authentic *production* rather than a reproduction. And finally, an ideology is only *made* from the totality of these productions, or at least it is only made *from* them. Ideology is not, prior to the work, like a system which can be reproduced: it is resumed, elaborated by the work; it has no independent value.

The *act* of the writer is fundamental: he realises a particular crystallisation, a restructuration, and even a structuration of the data upon which he works: all that which was no more than a collective foreboding, project, aspiration, *precipitates* abruptly in an image which rapidly becomes familiar, becomes the real itself, the flesh of these projects. Verne's work furnishes a unique example of this process; it endows the ideological with a new form but also, more important, a visible form. This visible form is not shadowed by any ideal reality, any invisible form, but it does display the signs of its modification, without there being any substance there to support it. The work exists on the reverse side [*envers*] of what it would like to be, the reverse of itself.

[. . .]

Does this mean that the validity of the ideological project is challenged – or even challenges itself – at the very moment of its realisation? Does contradiction break forth in the passage from a form of consciousness to a form of writing? Emphatically, if there really is a contradiction, if contradiction is to mean anything at all, it is not *there* that it emerges or takes place. Jules Verne the bourgeois, and the bourgeoisie of Jules Verne, duly takes one step forward and three steps back. But this procrastination involves two realms: on this side of the book, in the historical relation which links the works in a specific sequence; and beyond the book, in the play of historical relations without which there would be no book. Within the book something else is happening.

[. . .]

It must not be thought that this has defined a necessary form of the writer's work, the general progression, as though determined in advance, of all literary projects, wherever they are situated in the history of works. But the book which we have just been engaged with could only appear in this form. For the appeal from book to book, culminating in the victory of antique representation, ultimately signifies the dependence of the present upon the past, of the contemporary upon the history *which constitutes it*. The flaws in Verne's project are the index of this dependence. The conquering bourgeoisie, whose fictional potential image Verne wanted to draw, was not a traveller from nowhere: the new man, as Verne manages actually and positively to describe him, is not a solitary, the conqueror of an absolute, the appropriator of virgin nature, but simply the master of a certain number of relations. His most essential feature is that he has *companions*; he is accompanied not only by other men but also by that which both gives meaning to his project and simultaneously presents the first challenge to it: all that history in which they are ineluctably involved. And this involvement is not only lived, directly perceived as the consequence of a conscious choice; it is a conflict, a trauma, burdened with secret repressions. This bourgeoisie which cannot abolish its history feels inarticulately that it is permanently bound to that history, that it will be history's consummation, that it will never be unburdened, and that this inertia which hinders its intention is also the necessary condition for any enterprise (as it is for the written expression of the project of transformation). It is this viscosity of history which only anchors decisions to their true meaning after passing through the acknowledgment of a necessary delay.

The new world is not so new that the world – as it has been described so meticulously and desultorily by classical political economy and even by classical literature, but with what compromises, what myopia! – can appear once and for all obsolete; in other words, as merely an object-lesson in the old-fashioned. The society which Verne's 'represents' has not yet cast off the fetters which checked the old mercantile society within the circle of a certain historical condition, described, in other respects, scientifically; and thus it is the prisoner of its old dreams. The bourgeoisie has its revolution behind it: it cannot be revived by any kind of technical progress. Consequently bourgeois ideology has become incapable of thinking and representing the future.

This is more or less what happens: Jules Verne wants to represent, to translate, an imperative which is profoundly ideological, that notion of labour and conquest which is at the centre of his work. In relation to the historical reality which it recuperates, this ideal is contradictory; real labour is alienated, perfect conquest is inevitably constrained by the conditions of former colonisation. These are the real limits of bourgeois ideology: but this ideology is emphatically not internally contradictory; for that would presuppose that it gave a complete description of reality, that it ceased to be an ideology, whereas it is precisely its insufficiencies, its incompleteness, which guarantee its flawed coherence. The interest of Verne's work lies in the fact that, through the unity of its project – a unity borrowed from a certain ideological coherence, or incoherence – and by the means which inform this project (or fail in this enterprise), by specifically literary means, it reveals the *limits*, and to some extent the *conditions* of this ideological coherence, which is necessarily built upon a discord in the historical reality, and upon a discord between this reality and its *dominant* representation.

The literary failure of Jules Verne, the fragility of that enterprise which is not his alone, this is what forms the matter of his books: the demonstration of a fundamental *historical defect*, whose most simple historical expression calls itself the *class struggle*. Accordingly it is no coincidence that all Verne's images of reconciliation open out on to the description of a conflict. Today and tomorrow, *mobilis in mobili* – for the novel this involves two things at once: and yet they are not the same thing. An attentive reading will prove this.

Like Balzac, then, though using very different forms, Verne encounters or rather witnesses within his work the encounter of the figures which he has created – figures which determine the real within the limits of the work – and the ideological project which he perhaps wished simply to illustrate. We have seen that there is a conflict between these two instances: the presence and the style of Nemo completely transform the enterprise of the aspiring colonists. Not that the objects of the adventure have been destroyed or replaced, but, crucially, their meaning has changed. Nature is not what one took it for; between that basic reality and human actions there is not only the mediation of labour and science, but also the entire screen of historical myths, factitiously constituted but none the less real, since facticity is its *raison d'être*. The Mysterious Island tells the story of just that test of its power which men make. It is indeed the myth which *emerges* with Nemo, and with it all the burden of history, that reticence and that inhibition which make it interminable. Nemo is the exact type of the hero who was thought to have vanished, whereas that disappearance was both the sign and the guarantee of the modern itself.

Nemo is Crusoe, a tragic, condemned Crusoe who does not progress, because he is already an anachronism. He is the recurring fiction. He is that ancestor: the bourgeois future. In this way the notion of mechanical progress is admitted to its role as an ideological representation, to its *place* as a great bourgeois rite, typical of a certain moment in the history of the bourgeoisie. Nemo is the fatal resurgence, the resurrection, not of the son but of the father.

What characterises Verne's novels is that by their structure they encounter this antagonism as an obstacle: and thus the enterprise of a demystification of the book is illusory, or rather it belongs to the makers of mythologies, because the book is itself this demystification. Everything happens as though Verne knew the ideological situation of the epoch whose aspirations he wanted to represent, by giving them the material incarnation of a book. But there is no such thing as an implicit knowledge: the book is not a simple reflection of the contradictions of its time, nor is it a deliberated description of the project of a social class at a given moment. It represents a form of final *perception* of reality, and this is what defines the nature of the book – this rather than the nature of art, for it is not saying much to say that Verne is an artist (it has merely a polemical value and is indeed indisputable, since it comes down to saying that he is no less an artist than others). On the other hand, there is some purpose in showing that Verne is a genuine writer. It is a perception rather than a knowledge in the true sense (a theoretical knowledge), rather than a mechanical (unconscious) reproduction of reality. It is an effort to express its profound nature, to illuminate its recesses, through the arrangement of animated figures and the unfolding of a chosen fable.

Verne's flaw, his defect, relates not to a *historical project* but to a *historical statute*. And this difference is crucial: this is not to offer yet another new 'interpretation' of Verne's work, another translation, another commentary; on the contrary, it is an explanation of the discords which connect the work to itself. These discords are not finally the direct reflection of an ideological contradiction, but the symptom of a historical opposition. What may seem no more than a simple literary allusion, the digression via Robinson Crusoe, enables us to reveal a real situation, better than any other form of consciousness (except, of course, a genuine theoretical elaboration, but that is no longer a question of consciousness in the strict sense of the word). In its way, so simple and curiously veiled, perspicacious and deceptive, the book finally shows us – though it may not be in the manner stated – what is proposed to enunciate: the history of its moment.

14 □ *Ideology and Ideological State Apparatuses*

Louis Althusser

[...]

The State Ideological Apparatuses

What are the Ideological State Apparatuses (ISAs)?

They must not be confused with the (repressive) State apparatus. Remember that in Marxist theory, the State Apparatus (SA) contains: the Government, the Administration, the Army, the Police, the Courts, the Prisons, etc., which constitute what I shall in future call the Repressive State Apparatus. Repressive suggests that the State Apparatus in question 'functions by violence' – at least ultimately (since repression, e.g. administrative repression, may take non-physical forms).

I shall call Ideological State Apparatuses a certain number of realities which present themselves to the immediate observer in the form of distinct and specialized institutions. I propose an empirical list of these which will obviously have to be examined in detail, tested, corrected and reorganized. With all the reservations implied by this requirement, we can for the moment regard the following institutions as Ideological State Apparatuses (the order in which I have listed them has no particular significance):

- the religious ISA (the system of the different Churches);
- the educational ISA (the system of the different public and private 'Schools');
- the family ISA;[1]
- the legal ISA;[2]
- the political ISA (the political system, including the different Parties);
- the trade-union ISA;

From Althusser, L., *Lenin and Philosophy*, Monthly Review Press, New York, 1971, pp. 142–6, 162–77.

- the communications ISA (press, radio and television, etc.);
- the cultural ISA (Literature, the Arts, sports, etc.).

I have said that the ISAs must not be confused with the (Repressive) State Apparatus. What constitutes the difference?

As a first moment, it is clear that while there is *one* (Repressive) State Apparatus, there is a *plurality* of Ideological State Apparatuses. Even presupposing that it exists, the unity that constitutes this plurality of ISAs as a body is not immediately visible.

As a second moment, it is clear that whereas the – unified – (Repressive) State Apparatus belongs entirely to the *public* domain, much the larger part of the Ideological State Apparatuses (in their apparent dispersion) are part, on the contrary, of the private domain. Churches, Parties, Trade Unions, families, some schools, most newspapers, cultural ventures, etc., etc., are private.

We can ignore the first observation for the moment. But someone is bound to question the second, asking me by what right I regard as Ideological *State* Apparatuses, institutions which for the most part do not possess public status, but are quite simply *private* institutions. As a conscious Marxist, Gramsci already forestalled this objection in one sentence. The distinction between the public and the private is a distinction internal to bourgeois law, and valid in the (subordinate) domains in which bourgeois law exercises its 'authority'. The domain of the State escapes it because the latter is 'above the law': the State, which is the State *of* the ruling class, is neither public nor private; on the contrary, it is the precondition for any distinction between public and private. The same thing can be said from the starting-point of our Ideological State Apparatuses. It is unimportant whether the institutions in which they are realized are 'public' or 'private'. What matters is how they function. Private institutions can perfectly well 'function' as Ideological State Apparatuses. A reasonably thorough analysis of any one of the ISAs proves it.

But now for what is essential. What distinguishes the ISAs from the (Repressive) State Apparatus is the following basic difference: the Repressive State Apparatus functions 'by violence', whereas the Ideological State Apparatuses *function 'by ideology'*.

I can clarify matters by correcting this distinction. I shall say rather that every State Apparatus, whether Repressive or Ideological, 'functions' both by violence and by ideology, but with one very important distinction which makes it imperative not to confuse the Ideological State Apparatuses with the (Repressive) State Apparatus.

This is the fact that the (Repressive) State Apparatus functions massively and predominantly *by repression* (including physical repression), while functioning secondarily by ideology. (There is no such thing as a purely repressive apparatus.) For example, the Army and the Police also function by ideology both to ensure their own cohesion and reproduction, and in the 'values' they propound externally.

In the same way, but inversely, it is essential to say that for their part the Ideological State Apparatuses function massively and predominantly *by ideology*, but they also function secondarily by repression, even if ultimately, but only ultimately, this is very attentuated and concealed, even symbolic. (There is no such thing as a purely ideological apparatus.) Thus Schools and Churches use suitable methods of punishment, expulsion, selection, etc., to 'discipline' not only their shepherds, but also their flocks. The same is true of the Family. . . . The same is true of the cultural IS Apparatus (censorship, among other things), etc.

Is it necessary to add that this determination of the double 'functioning' (predominantly, secondarily) by repression and by ideology, according to whether it is a matter of the (Repressive) State Apparatus or the Ideological State Apparatuses, makes it clear that very subtle explicit or tacit combinations may be woven from the interplay of the (Repressive) State Apparatus and the Ideological State Apparatuses? Everyday life provides us with innumerable examples of this, but they must be studied in detail if we are to go further than this mere observation.

Nevertheless, this remark leads us towards an understanding of what constitutes the unity of the apparently disparate body of the ISAs. If the ISAs 'function' massively and predominantly by ideology, what unifies their diversity is precisely this functioning, in so far as the ideology by which they function is always in fact unified, despite its diversity and its contradictions, *beneath the ruling ideology*, which is the ideology of 'the ruling class'. Given the fact that the 'ruling class' in principle holds State power (openly or more often by means of alliances between classes or class fractions), and therefore has at its disposal the (Repressive) State Apparatus, we can accept the fact that this same ruling class is active in the Ideological State Apparatuses in so far as it is ultimately the ruling ideology which is realized in the Ideological State Apparatuses, precisely in its contraditions. Of course, it is a quite different thing to act by laws and decrees in the (Repressive) State Apparatus and to 'act' through the intermediary of the ruling ideology in the Ideological State Apparatuses. We must go into the details of this difference – but it cannot mask the reality of a profound identity. To my knowledge, *no class can hold State power over a long period without at the same time exercising its hegemony over and in the Ideological State Apparatuses.*

[. . .]

Ideology is a 'Representation' of the Imaginary Relationship of Individuals to their Real Conditions of Existence

In order to approach my central thesis on the structure and functioning of ideology, I shall first present two theses, one negative, the other positive. The first concerns the object which is 'represented' in the imaginary form of ideology, the second concerns the materiality of ideology.

THESIS I: Ideology represents the imaginary relationship of individuals to their real conditions of existence.

We commonly call religious ideology, ethical ideology, legal ideology, political ideology, etc., so many 'world outlooks'. Of course, assuming that we do not live one of these ideologies as the truth (e.g. 'believe' in God, Duty, Justice, etc. . . .), we admit that the ideology we are discussing from a critical point of view, examining it as the ethnologist examines the myths of a 'primitive society', that these 'world outlooks' are largely imaginary, i.e. do not 'correspond to reality'.

However, while admitting that they do not correspond to reality, i.e. that they constitute an illusion, we admit that they do make allusion to reality, and that they need only be 'interpreted' to discover the reality of the world behind their imaginary representation of that world (ideology = *illusion/allusion*).

There are different types of interpretation, the most famous of which are the *mechanistic* type, current in the eighteenth century (God is the imaginary representation of the real King), and the *'hermeneutic'* interpretation, inaugurated by the earliest Church Fathers, and revived by Feuerbach and the theologico-philosophical school which descends from him, e.g. the theologian Barth (to Feuerbach, for example, God is the essence of real Man). The essential point is that on condition that we interpret the imaginary transposition (and inversion) of ideology we arrive at the conclusion that in ideology 'men represent their real conditions of existence to themselves in an imaginary form'.

Unfortunately, this interpretation leaves one small problem unsettled: why do men 'need' this imaginary transposition of their real conditions of existence in order to 'represent to themselves' their real conditions of existence?

The first answer (that of the eighteenth century) proposes a simple solution: Priests or Despots are responsible. They 'forged' the Beautiful Lies so that, in the belief that they were obeying God, men would in fact obey the Priests and Despots, who are usually in alliance in their imposture, the Priests acting in the interests of the Despots or vice versa, according to the political positions of the 'theoreticians' concerned. There is therefore a cause for the imaginary transposition of the real conditions of existence: that cause is the existence of a small number of cynical men who base their domination and exploitation of the 'people' on a falsified representation of the world which they have imagined in order to enslave other minds by dominating their imaginations.

The second answer (that of Feuerbach, taken over word for word by Marx in his Early Works) is more 'profound', i.e. just as false. It, too, seeks and finds a cause for the imaginary transposition and distortion of men's real conditions of existence, in short, for the alienation in the imaginary of the representation of men's conditions of existence. This cause is no longer Priests or Despots, nor their active imagination and the passive imagination of their victims. This cause is the material alienation which reigns in the conditions of existence of men themselves. This is how, in *The Jewish Question* and elsewhere, Marx defends the Feuerbachian idea that men make themselves an alienated (= imaginary) representation of their conditions of existence because these conditions of existence are themselves alienating (in the *1844 Manuscripts*: because these conditions are dominated by the essence of alienated society – '*alienated labour*').

All these interpretations thus take literally the thesis which they presuppose, and on which they depend, i.e. that what is reflected in the imaginary representation of the world found in an ideology is the conditions of existence of men, i.e. their real world.

Now I can return to a thesis which I have already advanced: it is not their real conditions of existence, their real world, that 'men' 'represent to themselves' in ideology, but above all it is their relation to those conditions of existence which is represented to them there. It is this relation which is at the centre of every ideological, i.e. imaginary, representation of the real world. It is this relation that contains the 'cause' which has to explain the imaginary distortion of the ideological representation of the real world. Or rather, to leave aside the language of causality it is necessary to advance the thesis that it is the *imaginary nature of this relation* which underlies all the imaginary distortion that we can observe (if we do not live in its truth) in all ideology.

To speak in a Marxist language, if it is true that the representation of the real conditions of existence of the individuals occupying the posts of agents of production, exploitation, repression, ideologization and scientific practice, does in the last analysis arise from the relations of production, and from relations deriving from the relations of production, we can say the following: all ideology represents in its necessarily imaginary distortion not the existing relations of production (and the other relations that derive from them), but above all the (imaginary) relationship of individuals to the relations of production and the relations that derive from them. What is represented in ideology is therefore not the system of the real relations which govern the existence of individuals, but the imaginary relation of those individuals to the real relations in which they live.

If this is the case, the question of the 'cause' of the imaginary distortion of the real relations in ideology disappears and must be replaced by a different question: why is the representation given to individuals of their (individual) relation to the social relations which govern their conditions of existence and their collective and individual life necessarily an imaginary relation? And what is the nature of this imaginariness? Posed in this way, the question explodes the solution by a 'clique',[3] by a group of individuals (Priests or Despots) who are the authors of the great ideological mystification, just as it explodes the solution by the alienated character of the real world. We shall see why later in my exposition. For the moment I shall go no further.

THESIS II: Ideology has a material existence.

I have already touched on this thesis by saying that the 'ideas' or 'representations', etc., which seem to make up ideology do not have an ideal [*idéale* or *idéelle*] or spiritual existence, but a material existence. I even suggested that the ideal [*idéale*, *idéelle*] and spiritual existence of 'ideas' arises exclusively in an ideology of the 'idea' and of ideology, and let me add, in an ideology of what seems to have 'founded' this conception since the emergence of the sciences, i.e. what the practicians of the sciences represent to themselves in their spontaneous ideology as 'ideas', true or false. Of course, presented in affirmative form, this thesis is unproven. I simply ask that the reader be favourably disposed towards it, say, in the name of materialism. A long series of arguments would be necessary to prove it.

This hypothetical thesis of the not spiritual but material existence of 'ideas' or other 'representations' is indeed necessary if we are to advance in our analysis of the nature of ideology. Or rather, it is merely useful to us in order the better to reveal what every at all serious analysis of any ideology will immediately and empirically show to every observer, however critical.

While discussing the Ideological State Apparatuses and their practices, I said that each of them was the realization of an ideology (the unity of these different regional ideologies – religious, ethical, legal, political, aesthetic, etc. – being assured by their subjection to the ruling ideology). I now return to this thesis: an ideology always exists in an apparatus, and its practice, or practices. This existence is material.

Of course, the material existence of the ideology in an apparatus and its practices does not have the same modality as the material existence of a paving-stone or a rifle. But, at the risk of being taken for a Neo-Aristotelian (NB: Marx had a very high regard for Aristotle), I shall say that 'matter is discussed in many senses', or rather that it exists in different modalities, all rooted in the last instance in 'physical' matter.

Having said this, let me move straight on and see what happens to the 'individuals' who live in ideology, i.e. in a determinate (religious, ethical, etc.) representation of the world whose imaginary distortion depends on their imaginary relation to their conditions of existence, in other words, in the last instance, to the relations of production and to class relations (ideology = an imaginary relation to real relations). I shall say that this imaginary relation is itself endowed with a material existence.

Now I observe the following.

An individual believes in God, or Duty, or Justice, etc. This belief derives (for everyone, i.e. for all those who live in an ideological representation of ideology, which reduces ideology to ideas endowed by definition with a spiritual existence) from the ideas of the individual concerned, i.e. from him as a subject with a consciousness which contains the ideas of his belief. In this way, i.e. by means of the absolutely ideological 'conceptual' device [*dispositif*] thus set up (a subject endowed with a consciousness in which he freely forms or freely recognizes ideas in which he believes), the (material) attitude of the subject concerned naturally follows.

The individual in question behaves in such and such a way, adopts such and such a practical attitude, and, what is more, participates in certain regular practices which are those of the ideological apparatus on which 'depend' the ideas which he has in all consciousness freely chosen as a subject. If he believes in God, he goes to Church to attend Mass, kneels, prays, confesses, does penance (once it was material in the ordinary sense of the term) and naturally repents, and so on. If he believes in Duty, he will have the corresponding attitudes, inscribed in ritual practices 'according to the correct principles'. If he believes in Justice, he will submit unconditionally to the rules of the Law, and may even protest when they are violated, sign petitions, take part in a demonstration, etc.

Throughout this schema we observe that the ideological representation of ideology is itself forced to recognize that every 'subject' endowed with a 'consciousness' and believing in the 'ideas' that his 'consciousness' inspires in him and freely accepts, must '*act* according to his ideas', must therefore inscribe his own ideas as a free subject in the actions of his material practice. If he does not do so, 'that is wicked'.

Indeed, if he does not do what he ought to do as a function of what he believes, it is because he does something else, which, still as a function of the same idealist scheme, implies that he has other ideas in his head as well as those he proclaims, and that he acts according to these other ideas, as a man who is either 'inconsistent' ('no one is willingly evil') or cynical, or perverse.

In every case, the ideology of ideology thus recognizes, despite its imaginary distortion, that the 'ideas' of a human subject exist in his actions, or ought to exist in his actions, and if that is not the case, it lends him other ideas corresponding to the actions (however perverse) that he does perform. This ideology talks of actions: I shall talk of actions inserted into *practices*. *And* I shall point out that these practices are governed by the *rituals* in which these practices are inscribed, within the *material existence of an ideological apparatus*, be it only a small part of that apparatus: a small Mass in a small church, a funeral, a minor match at a sports club, a school day, a political party meeting, etc.

Besides, we are indebted to Pascal's defensive 'dialectic' for the wonderful formula which will enable us to invert the order of the notional schema of ideology. Pascal says, more or less: 'Kneel down, move your lips in prayer, and you will believe.' He thus scandalously inverts the order of things, bringing, like Christ, not peace but strife, and in addition something hardly Christian (for woe to him who brings scandal into the world!) – scandal itself. A fortunate scandal which makes him stick with Jansenist defiance to a language that directly names the reality.

I will be allowed to leave Pascal to the arguments of his ideological struggle with the religious Ideological State Apparatus of his day. And I shall be expected to use a more directly Marxist vocabulary, if that is possible, for we are advancing in still poorly explored domains.

I shall therefore say that, where only a single subject (such and such an individual) is concerned, the existence of the ideas of his belief is material in that *his ideas are his material actions inserted into material practices governed by material rituals which are themselves defined by the material ideological apparatus from which derive the ideas of that subject*. Naturally, the four inscriptions of the adjective 'material' in my proposition must be affected by different modalities: the materialities of a displacement for going to Mass, of kneeling down, of the gesture of the sign of the cross, or of the *mea culpa*, of a sentence, of a prayer, of an act of contrition, of a penitence, of a gaze, of a handshake, of an external verbal discourse or an 'internal' verbal discourse (consciousness), are not one and the same materiality. I shall leave on one side the problem of a theory of the differences between the modalities of materiality.

It remains that in this inverted presentation of things, we are not dealing with an 'inversion' at all, since it is clear that certain notions have purely and simply disappeared from our presentation, whereas others on the contrary survive, and new terms appear.

Disappeared: the term *ideas*.

Survive: the terms *subject, consciousness, belief, actions*.

Appear: the terms *practices, rituals, ideological apparatus*.

It is therefore not an inversion or overturning (except in the sense in which one might say a government or a class is overturned), but a reshuffle (of a non-ministerial type), a rather strange reshuffle, since we obtain the following result.

Ideas have disappeared as such (in so far as they are endowed with an ideal or spiritual existence), to the precise extent that it has emerged that their existence is inscribed in the actions of practices governed by rituals defined in the last instance by an ideological apparatus. It therefore appears that the subject acts in so far as he is acted by the following system (set out in the order of its real determination): ideology existing in a material ideological apparatus, prescribing material practices governed by a material ritual, which practices exist in the material actions of a subject acting in all consciousness according to his belief.

But this very presentation reveals that we have retained the following notions: subject, consciousness, belief, actions. From this series I shall immediately extract the decisive central term on which everything else depends: the notion of the *subject*.

And I shall immediately set down two conjoint theses:

1. there is no practice except by and in an ideology;
2. there is no ideology except by the subject and for subjects.

I can now come to my central thesis.

Ideology Interpellates Individuals as Subjects

This thesis is simply a matter of making my last proposition explicit: there is no ideology except by the subject and for subjects. Meaning, there is no ideology except for concrete subjects, and this destination for ideology is only made possible by the subject: meaning, *by the category of the subject* and its functioning.

By this I mean that, even if it only appears under this name (the subject) with the rise of bourgeois ideology, above all with the rise of legal ideology,[4] the category of the subject (which may function under other names: e.g., as the soul in Plato, as God, etc.) is the constitutive category of all ideology, whatever its determination (regional or class) and whatever its historical date – since ideology has no history.

I say: the category of the subject is constitutive of all ideology, but at the same time and immediately I add that *the category of the subject is only constitutive of all ideology in so far as all ideology has the function (which defines it) of 'constituting' concrete individuals as subjects*. In the interaction of this double constitution exists the functioning of all ideology, ideology being nothing but its functioning in the material forms of existence of that functioning.

In order to grasp what follows, it is essential to realize that both he who is writing these lines and the reader who reads them are themselves subjects, and therefore ideological subjects (a tautological proposition), i.e. that the author and the reader of these lines both live 'spontaneously' or 'naturally' in ideology in the sense in which I have said that 'man is an ideological animal by nature'.

That the author, in so far as he writes the lines of a discourse which claims to be scientific, is completely absent as a 'subject' from 'his' scientific discourse (for all scientific discourse is by definition a subject-less discourse, there is no 'Subject of science' except in an ideology of science) is a different question which I shall leave on one side for the moment.

As St Paul admirably put it, it is in the 'Logos', meaning in ideology, that we 'live, move and have our being'. It follows that, for you and for me, the category of the subject is a primary 'obviousness' (obviousnesses are always primary): it is clear that you and I are subjects (free, ethical, etc. . . .). Like all obviousnesses, including those that make a word 'name a thing' or 'have a meaning' (therefore including the obviousness of the 'transparency' of language), the 'obviousness' that you and I are subjects – and that that does not cause any problems – is an ideological effect, the elementary ideological effect.[5] It is indeed a peculiarity of ideology that it imposes (without appearing to do so, since these are 'obviousnesses') obviousnesses as obviousnesses, which we cannot *fail to recognize* and before which we have the inevitable and natural reaction of crying out (aloud or in the 'still, small voice of conscience'): 'That's obvious! That's right! That's true!'

At work in this reaction is the ideological *recognition* function which is one of the two functions of ideology as such (its inverse being the function of *misrecognition* – *méconnaissance*).

To take a highly 'concrete' example, we all have friends who, when they knock on our door and we ask, through the door, the question 'Who's there?', answer (since 'it's obvious') 'It's me'. And we recognize that 'it is him', or 'her'. We open the door, and 'it's true, it really was she who was there'. To take another example, when we recognize somebody of our (previous) acquaintance [*(re)-connaissance*] in the street, we show him that we have recognized him (and have recognized that he has recognized us) by saying to him 'Hello, my friend', and shaking his hand (a material ritual practice of ideological recognition in everyday life – in France, at least; elsewhere, there are other rituals).

In this preliminary remark and these concrete illustrations, I only wish to point out that you and I are *always-already* subjects, and as such constantly practise the rituals of ideological recognition, which guarantee for us that we are indeed concrete, individual, distinguishable and (naturally) irreplaceable subjects. The writing I am currently executing and the reading you are currently[6] performing are also in this respect rituals of ideological recognition, including the 'obviousness' with which the 'truth' or 'error' of my reflections may impose itself on you.

But to recognize that we are subjects and that we function in the practical rituals of the most elementary everyday life (the handshake, the fact of calling you by your name, the fact of knowing, even if I do not know what it is, that you 'have' a name of your own, which means that you are recognized as a unique subject, etc.) – this recognition only gives us the 'consciousness' of our incessant (eternal) practice of ideological recognition – its consciousness, i.e. its *recognition* – but in no sense does it give us the (scientific) *knowledge* of the mechanism of this recognition. Now it is this knowledge that we have to reach, if you will, while speaking in ideology, and from within ideology we have to outline a discourse which tries to break with ideology, in order to dare to be the beginning of a scientific (i.e. subjectless) discourse on ideology.

Thus in order to represent why the category of the 'subject' is constitutive of ideology, which only exists by constituting concrete subjects as subjects, I shall employ a special mode of exposition: 'concrete' enough to be recognized, but abstract enough to be thinkable and thought, giving rise to a knowledge.

As a first formulation I shall say: *all ideology hails or interpellates concrete individuals as concrete subjects*, by the functioning of the category of the subject.

This is a proposition which entails that we distinguish for the moment between concrete individuals on the one hand and concrete subjects on the other, although at this level concrete subjects only exist in so far as they are supported by a concrete individual.

I shall then suggest that ideology 'acts' or 'functions' in such a way that it 'recruits' subjects among the individuals (it recruits them all), or 'transforms' the individuals into subjects (it transforms them all) by that very precise operation which I have called *interpellation* or hailing, and which can be imagined along the lines of the most commonplace everyday police (or other) hailing: 'Hey, you there!'[7]

Assuming that the theoretical scene I have imagined takes place in the street, the hailed individual will turn round. By this mere one-hundred-and-eighty-degree physical conversion, he becomes a *subject*. Why? Because he has recognized that the hail was 'really' addressed to him, and that 'it was *really him* who was hailed' (and not someone else). Experience shows that the practical telecommunication of hailing is such that they hardly ever miss their man: verbal call or whistle, the one hailed always recognizes that it is really him who is being hailed. And yet it is a strange phenomenon, and one which cannot be explained solely by 'guilt feelings', despite the large numbers who 'have something on their consciences'.

Naturally for the convenience and clarity of my little theoretical theatre I have had to present things in the form of a sequence, with a before and an after, and thus in the form of a temporal succession. There are individuals walking along. Somewhere (usually behind them) the hail rings out: 'Hey, you there!' One individual (nine times out of ten it is the right one) turns round, believing/suspecting/knowing that it is for him, i.e. recognizing that 'it really is he' who is meant by the hailing. But in reality these things happen without any succession. The existence of ideology and the hailing or interpellation of individuals as subjects are one and the same thing.

I might add: what thus seems to take place outside ideology (to be precise, in the street), in reality takes place in ideology. What really takes place in ideology seems therefore to take place outside it. That is why those who are in ideology believe themselves by definition outside ideology: one of the effects of ideology is the practical *denegation* of the ideological character of ideology by ideology: ideology never says, 'I am ideological'. It is necessary to be outside ideology, i.e. in scientific knowledge, to be able to say: I am in ideology (a quite exceptional case) or (the general case): I was in ideology. As is well known, the accusation of being in ideology only applies to others, never to oneself (unless one is really a Spinozist or a Marxist, which, in this matter, is to be exactly the same thing). Which amounts to saying that ideology *has no outside* (for itself), but at the same time *that it is nothing but outside* (for science and reality).

Spinoza explained this completely two centuries before Marx, who practised it but without explaining it in detail. But let us leave this point, although it is heavy with consequences, consequences which are not just theoretical, but also directly political, since, for example, the whole theory of criticism and self-criticism, the golden rule of the Marxist–Leninist practice of the class struggle, depends on it.

Thus ideology hails or interpellates individuals as subjects. As ideology is eternal, I must now suppress the temporal form in which I have presented the functioning of ideology, and say: ideology has always-already interpellated individuals as subjects, which amounts to making it clear that individuals are always-already interpellated by ideology as subjects, which necessarily leads us to one last proposition: *individuals are always-already subjects*. Hence individuals are 'abstract' with respect to the subjects which they always-already are. This proposition might seem paradoxical.

That an individual is always-already a subject, even before he is born, is nevertheless the plain reality, accessible to everyone and not a paradox at all. Freud shows that individuals are always 'abstract' with respect to the subjects they always-already are, simply by noting the ideological ritual that surrounds the expectation of a 'birth', that 'happy event'. Everyone knows how much and in what way an unborn child is expected. Which amounts to saying, very prosaically, if we agree to drop the 'sentiments', i.e. the forms of family ideology (paternal/maternal/conjugal/fraternal) in which the unborn child is expected: it is certain in advance that it will bear its Father's Name, and will therefore have an identity and be irreplaceable. Before its birth, the child is therefore always-already a subject, appointed as a subject in and by the specific familial ideological configuration in which it is 'expected' once it has been conceived. I hardly need add that this familial ideological configuration is, in its uniqueness, highly structured, and that it is in this implacable and more or less 'pathological' (presupposing that any meaning can be assigned to that term) structure that the former subject-to-be will have to 'find' 'its' place, i.e. 'become' the sexual subject (boy or girl) which it already is in advance. It is clear that this ideological constraint and pre-appointment, and all the rituals of rearing and then education in the family, have some relationship with what Freud studied in the forms of the pre-genital and genital 'stages' of sexuality, i.e. in the 'grip' of what Freud registered by its effects as being the unconscious. But let us leave this point, too, on one side.

Notes

1. The family obviously has other 'functions' than that of an ISA. It intervenes in the reproduction of labour-power. In different modes of production it is the unit of production and/or the unit of consumption.
2. The 'Law' belongs both to the (Repressive) State Apparatus and to the system of the ISAs.
3. I use this very modern term deliberately. For even in Communist circles, unfortunately, it is a commonplace to 'explain' some political deviation (left or right opportunism) by the action of a 'clique'.
4. Which borrowed the legal category of 'subject in law' to make an ideological notion: man is by nature a subject.
5. Linguists and those who appeal to linguistics for various purposes often run up against difficulties which arise because they ignore the action of the ideological effects in all discourses – including even scientific discourses.
6. NB: this double 'currently' is one more proof of the fact that ideology is 'eternal', since these two 'currentlys' are separated by an indefinite interval; I am writing these lines on 6 April 1969; you may read them at any subsequent time.
7. Hailing as an everyday practice subject to a precise ritual takes a quite 'special' form in the policeman's practice of 'hailing' which concerns the hailing of 'suspects'.

15 □ *Method*

Michel Foucault

Hence the objective is to analyze a certain form of knowledge regarding sex, not in terms of repression or law, but in terms of power. But the word *power* is apt to lead to a number of misunderstandings – misunderstandings with respect to its nature, its form, and its unity. By power, I do not mean 'Power' as a group of institutions and mechanisms that ensure the subservience of the citizens of a given state. By power, I do not mean, either, a mode of subjugation which, in contrast to violence, has the form of the rule. Finally, I do not have in mind a general system of domination exerted by one group over another, a system whose effects, through successive derivations, pervade the entire social body. The analysis, made in terms of power, must not assume that the sovereignty of the state, the form of the law, or the overall unity of a domination are given at the outset; rather, these are only the terminal forms power takes. It seems to me that power must be understood in the first instance as the multiplicity of force relations immanent in the sphere in which they operate and which constitute their own organization; as the process which, through ceaseless struggles and confrontations, transforms, strengthens, or reverses them; as the support which these force relations find in one another, thus forming a chain or a system, or on the contrary, the disjunctions and contradictions which isolate them from one another; and lastly, as the strategies in which they take effect, whose general design or institutional crystallization is embodied in the state apparatus, in the formulation of the law, in the various social hegemonies. Power's condition of possibility, or in any case the viewpoint which permits one to understand its exercise, even in its more 'peripheral' effects, and which also makes it possible to use its mechanisms as a grid of intelligibility of the social order, must not be sought in the primary existence of a central point, in a unique source of sovereignty from which secondary and descendent forms would emanate; it is the moving substrate of force relations which, by virtue of their inequality, constantly engender states of power, but the latter are always local and unstable. The

From Foucault, M., *The History of Sexuality*, vol. 1, Penguin, Harmondsworth, 1981, pp. 92–102.

omnipresence of power: not because it has the privilege of consolidating everything under its invincible unity, but because it is produced from one moment to the next, at every point, or rather in every relation from one point to another. Power is everywhere; not because it embraces everything, but because it comes from everywhere. And 'Power', in so far as it is permanent, repetitious, inert, and self-reproducing, is simply the overall effect that emerges from all these mobilities, the concatenation that rests on each of them and seeks in turn to arrest their movement. One needs to be nominalistic, no doubt: power is not an institution, and not a structure; neither is it a certain strength we are endowed with; it is the name that one attributes to a complex strategical situation in a particular society.

Should we turn the expression around, then, and say that politics is war pursued by other means? If we still wish to maintain a separation between war and politics, perhaps we should postulate rather that this multiplicity of force relations can be coded – in part but never totally – either in the form of 'war', or in the form of 'politics'; this would imply two different strategies (but the one always liable to switch into the other) for integrating these unbalanced, heterogeneous, unstable, and tense force relations.

Continuing this line of discussion, we can advance a certain number of propositions:

- Power is not something that is acquired, seized, or shared, something that one holds on to or allows to slip away; power is exercised from innumerable points, in the interplay of nonegalitarian and mobile relations.
- Relations of power are not in a position of exteriority with respect to other types of relationships (economic processes, knowledge relationships, sexual relations), but are immanent in the latter; they are the immediate effects of the divisions, inequalities, and disequilibriums which occur in the latter, and conversely they are the internal conditions of these differentiations; relations of power are not in superstructural positions, with merely a role of prohibition or accompaniment; they have a directly productive role, wherever they come into play.
- Power comes from below; that is, there is no binary and all-encompassing opposition between rulers and ruled at the root of power relations, and serving as a general matrix – no such duality extending from the top down and reacting on more and more limited groups to the very depths of the social body. One must suppose rather that the manifold relationships of force that take shape and come into play in the machinery of production, in families, limited groups, and institutions, are the basis for wide-ranging effects of cleavage that run through the social body as a whole. These then form a general line of force that traverses the local oppositions and links them together; to be sure, they also bring about redistribution, realignments, homogenizations, serial arrangements, and convergences of the force relations. Major dominations are the hegemonic effects that are sustained by all these confrontations.
- Power relations are both intentional and nonsubjective. If in fact they are intelligible, this is not because they are the effect of another instance that 'explains'

them, but rather because they are imbued, through and through, with calculation: there is no power that is exercised without a series of aims and objectives. But this does not mean that it results from the choice or decision of an individual subject; let us not look for the headquarters that presides over its rationality; neither the caste which governs, nor the groups which control the state apparatus, nor those who make the most important economic decisions direct the entire network of power that functions in a society (and makes *it* function); the rationality of power is characterized by tactics that are often quite explicit at the restricted level where they are inscribed (the local cynicism of power), tactics which, becoming connected to one another, attracting and propagating one another, but finding their base of support and their condition elsewhere, end by forming comprehensive systems: the logic is perfectly clear, the aims are decipherable, and yet it is often the case that no one is there to have invented them, and few who can be said to have formulated them: an implicit characteristic of the great anonymous, almost unspoken strategies which coordinate the loquacious tactics whose 'inventors' or decision-makers are often without hypocrisy.

● Where there is power, there is resistance, and yet, or rather consequently, this resistance is never in a position of exteriority in relation to power. Should it be said that one is always 'inside' power, there is no 'escaping' it, there is no absolute outside where it is concerned, because one is subject to the law in any case? Or that, history being the ruse of reason, power is the ruse of history, always emerging the winner? This would be to misunderstand the strictly relational character of power relationships. Their existence depends on a multiplicity of points of resistance: these play the role of adversary, target, support, or handle in power relations. These points of resistance are present everywhere in the power network. Hence there is no single locus of great Refusal, no soul of revolt, source of all rebellions, or pure law of the revolutionary. Instead there is a plurality of resistances, each of them a special case: resistances that are possible, necessary, improbable; others that are spontaneous, savage, solitary, concerted, rampant, or violent; still others that are quick to compromise, interested, or sacrificial; by definition, they can only exist in the strategic field of power relations. But this does not mean that they are only a reaction or rebound, forming with respect to the basic domination an underside that is in the end always passive, doomed to perpetual defeat. Resistances do not derive from a few heterogeneous principles; but neither are they a lure or a promise that is of necessity betrayed. They are the odd term in relations of power; they are inscribed in the latter as an irreducible opposite. Hence they too are distributed in irregular fashion: the points, knots, or focuses of resistance are spread over time and space at varying densities, at times mobilizing groups or individuals in a definitive way, inflaming certain points of the body, certain moments in life, certain types of behavior. Are there no great radical ruptures, massive binary divisions, then? Occasionally, yes. But more often one is dealing with mobile and transitory points of resistance, producing cleavages in a society that shift about, fracturing unities and effecting regroupings, furrowing across individuals themselves, cutting them up and remolding them, marking off irreducible regions in them, in their bodies and minds. Just as the network of power relations ends by forming a dense web that passes through apparatuses and institutions, without being exactly localized in them, so too the swarm of points of resistance traverses social stratifications and individual unities. And it is doubtless the strategic codification of these points of resistance that makes a revolution possible, somewhat similar to the way in which the state relies on the institutional integration of power relationships.

It is in this sphere of force relations that we must try to analyze the mechanisms of power. In this way we will escape from the system of Law-and-Sovereign which has captivated political thought for such a long time. And if it is true that Machiavelli was among the few – and this no doubt was the scandal of his 'cynicism' – who conceived the power of the Prince in terms of force relationships, perhaps we need to go one step further, do without the persona of the Prince, and decipher power mechanisms on the basis of a strategy that is immanent in force relationships.

To return to sex and the discourses of truth that have taken charge of it, the question that we must address, then, is not: Given a specific state structure, how and why is it that power needs to establish a knowledge of sex? Neither is the question: What overall domination was served by the concern, evidenced since the eighteenth century, to produce true discourses on sex? Nor is it: What law presided over both the regularity of sexual behavior and the conformity of what was said about it? It is rather: In a specific type of discourse on sex, in a specific form of extortion of truth, appearing historically and in specific places (around the child's body, apropos of women's sex, in connection with practices restricting births, and so on), what were the most immediate, the most local power relations at work? How did they make possible these kinds of discourses, and conversely, how were these discourses used to support power relations? How was the action of these power relations modified by their very exercise, entailing a strengthening of some terms and a weakening of others, with effects of resistance and counterinvestments, so that there has never existed one type of stable subjugation, given once and for all? How were these power relations linked to one another according to the logic of a great strategy, which in retrospect takes on the aspect of a unitary and voluntarist politics of sex? In general terms: rather than referring all the infinitesimal violences that are exerted on sex, all the anxious gazes that are directed at it, and all the hiding places whose discovery is made into an impossible task, to the unique form of a great Power, we must immerse the expanding production of discourses on sex in the field of multiple and mobile power relations.

Which leads us to advance, in a preliminary way, four rules to follow. But these are not intended as methodological imperatives; at most they are cautionary prescriptions.

1 Rule of Immanence

One must not suppose that there exists a certain sphere of sexuality that would be the legitimate concern of a free and disinterested scientific inquiry were it not the object of mechanisms of prohibition brought to bear by the economic or ideological requirement of power. If sexuality was constituted as an area of investigation, this was only because relations of power had established it as a possible object; and conversely, if power was able to take it as a target, this was because techniques of knowledge and procedures of discourse were capable of investing it. Between techniques of knowledge and strategies of power, there is no exteriority, even if they have specific roles and are linked together on the basis of their difference. We will start, therefore, from what might be called 'local centers' of power-knowledge: for example, the relations that obtain between penitents and confessors, or the faithful and their directors of conscience. Here, guided by the theme of the 'flesh' that must be mastered, different forms of discourse – self-examination, questionings, admissions, interpretations, interviews – were the vehicle of a kind of incessant back-and-forth movement of forms of subjugations and schemas of knowledge. Similarly, the body of the child, under surveillance, surrounded in his cradle, his bed, or his room by an entire watch-crew of parents, nurses, servants, educators, and doctors, all attentive to the least manifestations of his sex, has constituted, particularly since the eighteenth century, another 'local center' of power-knowledge.

2 Rules of Continual Variations

We must not look for who has the power in the order of sexuality (men, adults, parents, doctors) and who is deprived of it (women, adolescents, children, patients); nor for who has the right to know and who is forced to remain ignorant. We must seek rather the pattern of the modifications which the relationships of force imply by the very nature of their process. The 'distributions of power' and the 'appropriations of knowledge' never represent only instantaneous slices taken from processes involving, for example, a cumulative reinforcement of the strongest factor, or a reversal of relationship, or again, a simultaneous increase of two terms. Relations of power-knowledge are not static forms of distribution, they are 'matrices of transformations'. The nineteenth-century grouping made up of the father, the mother, the educator, and the doctor, around the child and his sex, was subjected to constant modifications, continual shifts. One of the more spectacular results of the latter was a strange reversal: whereas to begin with the child's sexuality had been problematized within the relationship established between doctor and parents (in the form of advice, or recommendations to keep the child under observation, or warnings of future dangers), ultimately it was in the relationship of the psychiatrist to the child that the sexuality of adults themselves was called into question.

3 Rule of Double Conditioning

No 'local center', no 'pattern of transformation' could function if, through a series of sequences, it did not eventually enter into an overall strategy. And inversely, no strategy could achieve comprehensive effects if did not gain support from precise and tenuous relations serving, not as its point of application or final outcome, but as its prop and anchor point. There is no discontinuity between them, as if one were dealing with two different levels (one microscopic and the other macroscopic); but neither is there homogeneity (as if the one were only the enlarged projection or the miniaturization of the other); rather, one must conceive of the double conditioning of a strategy by the specificity of possible tactics, and of tactics by the strategic envelope that makes them work. Thus the father in the family is not the 'representative' of the sovereign or the state; and the latter are not projections of the father on a different scale. The family does not duplicate society, just as society does not imitate the family. But the family organization, precisely to the extent that it was insular and heteromorphous with respect to the other power mechanisms, was used to support the great 'maneuvers' employed for the Malthusian control of the birthrate, for the populationist incitements, for the medicalization of sex and the psychiatrization of its nongenital forms.

4 Rule of the Tactical Polyvalence of Discourses

What is said about sex must not be analyzed simply as the surface of projection of these power mechanisms. Indeed, it is in discourse that power and knowledge are joined together. And for this very reason, we must conceive discourse as a series of discontinuous segments whose tactical function is neither uniform nor stable. To be more precise, we must not imagine a world of discourse divided between accepted discourse and excluded discourse, or between the dominant discourse and the dominated one; but as a multiplicity of discursive elements that can come into play in various strategies. It is this distribution that we must reconstruct, with the things said and those concealed, the enunciations required and those forbidden, that it comprises; with the variants and different effects – according to who is speaking, his position of power, the institutional context in which he happens to be situated – that it implies; and with the shifts and reutilizations of identical formulas for contrary objectives that it also includes. Discourses are not once and for all subservient to power or raised up against it, any more than silences are. We must make allowance for the complex and unstable process whereby discourse can be both an instrument and an effect of power, but also a hindrance, a stumbling-block, a point of resistance and a starting point for an opposing strategy. Discourse transmits and produces power; it reinforces it, but also undermines and exposes it, renders it fragile and makes it possible to thwart it. In like manner, silence and secrecy are a shelter for power, anchoring its prohibitions; but they also loosen its holds and provide for relatively obscure areas of tolerance. Consider for example the history of what was once 'the' great sin against nature. The extreme discretion of the texts dealing with sodomy – that utterly confused category – and the nearly universal reticence in talking about it made possible a twofold operation: on the one hand, there was an extreme severity (punishment by fire was meted out well into the eighteenth century, without there being any substantial protest expressed before the middle of the century), and on the other hand, a tolerance that must have been widespread (which one can deduce indirectly from the infrequency of judicial sentences, and which one glimpses more directly through certain statements concerning societies of men that were thought to exist in the army or in the courts). There is no question that the appearance in nineteenth-century psychiatry, jurisprudence, and literature of a whole series of discourses on the species and subspecies of homosexuality, inversion, pederasty, and 'psychic hermaphrodism' made possible a strong advance of social controls into this area of 'perversity'; but it also made possible the formation of a 'reverse' discourse: homosexuality began to speak in its own behalf, to demand that its legitimacy or 'naturality' be acknowledged, often in the same vocabulary, using the same categories by which it was medically disqualified. There is not, on the one side, a discourse of power, and opposite it, another discourse that runs counter to it. Discourses are tactical elements or blocks operating in the field of force relations; there can exist different and even contradictory discourses within the same strategy; they can, on the contrary, circulate without changing their form from one strategy to another, opposing strategy. We must not expect the discourses on sex to tell us, above all, what strategy they derive from, or what moral divisions they accompany, or what ideology – dominant or dominated – they represent; rather we must question them on the two levels of their tactical productivity (what reciprocal effects of power and knowledge they ensure) and their strategical integration (what conjunction and what force relationship make their utilization necessary in a given episode of the various confrontations that occur).

In short, it is a question of orienting ourselves to a conception of power which replaces the privilege of the law with the viewpoint of the objective, the privilege of prohibition with the viewpoint of tactical efficacy, the privilege of sovereignty with the analysis of a multiple and mobile field of force relations, wherein far-reaching, but never completely stable, effects of domination are produced. The strategical model, rather than the model based on law. And this, not out of a speculative choice or theoretical preference, but because in fact it is one of the essential traits of Western societies that the force relationships which for a long time had found expression in war, in every form of warfare, gradually became invested in the order of political power.

16 □ *Feminism & the Principles of Poststructuralism*

Chris Weedon

[...]

Poststructuralist Theory

The term 'poststructuralist' is, like all language, plural. It does not have one fixed meaning but is generally applied to a range of theoretical positions developed in and from the work of Derrida (1973, 1976), Lacan (1977), Kristeva (1981, 1984, 1986), Althusser (1971) and Foucault (1978, 1979a and b, 1981, 1986). The work which these theories inform varies considerably. It includes, for example, the apparently 'apolitical' deconstructive criticism practised by American literary critics in which they are concerned with the 'free play' of meaning in literary texts, the radical-feminist rewriting of the meanings of gender and language in the work of some French feminist writers and the detailed historical analysis of discourse and power in the work of Foucault. The differences between forms of poststructuralism are important. Not all forms are necessarily productive for feminism. In the course of this book, an attempt is made to distinguish between types of poststructuralism and to focus on the particular poststructuralist theories which seem most useful. In doing this I am producing a specific version of poststructuralism which I call 'feminist poststructuralism'. I do so not because I wish to discredit feminist work which uses other forms of poststructuralism, for example, the deconstructive work of Gayatri Spivak,[1] but in order to articulate for the reader a particular position and method which I hold to be useful for feminist practice. In this context, a theory is useful if it is able to address the questions of how social power is exercised and how social relations of gender, class and race might be transformed. This implies a concern with history, absent from many poststructuralist perspectives but central to the work of Michel Foucault.

From Weedon, C., *Feminist Practice and Poststructuralist Theory*, Blackwell, Oxford, 1987, pp. 19–27, 32–42.

While different forms of poststructuralism vary both in their practice and in their political implications, they share certain fundamental assumptions about language, meaning and subjectivity. There will be questions which feminists wish to ask which are not compatible with these assumptions, which do not fit into a poststructuralist perspective but require other discursive frameworks. This is the case with many of the concerns of liberal and radical feminism. The least that a feminist poststructuralism can do is explain the assumptions underlying the questions asked and answered by other forms of feminist theory, making their political assumptions explicit. Poststructuralism can also indicate the types of discourse from which particular feminist questions come and locate them both socially and institutionally. Most important of all, it can explain the implications for feminism of these other discourses.

In the rest of this chapter, a brief account is given of the key features of poststructuralist theory. While some attention is paid to differences between forms of poststructuralism, the main emphasis is on producing a form of poststructuralism which can meet feminist needs. This chapter is an initial introduction to the theory which is explored, expanded and clarified in the rest of the book. The theoretical material involved is not easy, but I hope that by the end of the book the reader will have been offered a useful understanding of the relationship between poststructuralist theory and feminist practice.

Language

For poststructuralist theory the common factor in the analysis of social organization, social meanings, power and individual consciousness is *language*. Language is the place where actual and possible forms of social organization and their likely social and political consequences are defined and contested. Yet it is also the place where our sense of ourselves, our subjectivity, is *constructed*. The assumption that subjectivity is constructed implies that it is not innate, not genetically determined, but socially produced. Subjectivity is produced in a whole range of discursive practices – economic, social and political – the meanings of which are a constant site of struggle over power. Language is not the expression of unique individuality; it constructs the individual's subjectivity in ways which are socially specific. Moreover, for poststructuralism, subjectivity is neither unified nor fixed. Unlike humanism, which implies a conscious, knowing, unified, rational subject, poststructuralism theorizes subjectivity as a site of disunity and conflict, central to the process of political change and to preserving the status quo. For example, in the events on the picket lines during the 1984–5 miners' strike in Britain, the fundamental conflict of interests involved led to a situation in which the actions of trade unionists, politicians and the police were given radically different meanings by various interest groups. These different meanings, which revolved around questions of legality and morality, produced conflicting subject positions for the individuals involved. The miners were simultaneously criminal thugs and ordinary decent men, anxious to protect their livelihoods and communities; the police were both upholders of the law and agents of class interest from which all vestiges of morality and decency had disappeared. The need to rescue a coherent subjectivity from this battle over the meaning of the strike led to a hardening of positions between striking and working miners, the police and the politicians which precluded any shift in power relations through the realignment of interests.

Like all theories, poststructuralism makes certain assumptions about language, subjectivity, knowledge and truth. Its founding insight, taken from the structuralist linguistics of Ferdinand de Saussure, is that language, far from reflecting an already given social reality, constitutes social reality for us. Neither social reality nor the 'natural' world has fixed intrinsic meanings which language reflects or expresses. Different languages and different discourses within the same language divide up the world and give it meaning in different ways which cannot be reduced to one another through translation or by an appeal to universally shared concepts reflecting a fixed reality. For example, the meanings of femininity and masculinity vary from culture to culture and language to language. They even vary between discourses within a particular language, between different feminist discourses, for instance, and are subject to historical change, from Victorian values to the suffrage movement, for example.

All forms of poststructuralism assume that meaning is constituted within language and is not guaranteed by the subject which speaks it. In this sense all poststructuralism is post-Saussurean. While there can be no essential qualities of femininity or masculinity, given for all times and reflected in language and the social relations which language structures, different forms of poststructuralism theorize the production of meaning in different ways. Psychoanalytic forms of poststructuralism look to a fixed psychosexual order; reconstruction looks to the relationship between different texts; and Foucauldian theory, which is arguably of most interest to feminists, looks to historically specific discursive relations and social practices. While each of these approaches is explained in the course of this book, the main focus is on the latter approach.

In this theory the meaning of gender is both socially produced and variable between different forms of discourse. Pornography and much advertising, for example, offer us models of femininity in which a particular version of female sexuality is paramount. It is a form of femininity in which women direct themselves totally to the satisfaction of the male gaze, male fantasies and male desires and gain an arguably masochistic pleasure in doing so. This contrasts with other versions of femininity, which stress women's asexuality, exalting either virginity or mother-hood, and which call for different sorts of masochistic feminine behaviour.

An understanding of Saussure's theory of the 'sign' is fundamental to all poststructuralism. It is Saussure's insistence on a pre-given fixed structuring of language, prior to its realization in speech or writing, which earns his linguistics the title 'structural'. Saussure theorized language as an abstract system, consisting of chains of signs. Each sign is made up of a *signifier* (sound or written image) and a *signified* (meaning). The two components of the sign are related to each other in an arbitrary way and there is therefore no natural connection between the sound image and the concept it identifies. The meaning of signs is not intrinsic but relational. Each sign derives its meaning from its difference from all the other signs in the language chain. It is not anything intrinsic to the signifier 'whore', for example, that gives it its meaning, but rather its difference from other signifiers of womanhood such as 'virgin' and 'mother'.

Poststructuralism, while building on Saussure's theory, radically modifies and transforms some of its important aspects. It takes from Saussure the principle that meaning is produced within language rather than reflected by language, and that individual signs do not have intrinsic meaning but acquire meaning through the language chain and their difference within it from other signs. These principles are important because they make language truly social and a site of political struggle. If we take the example of 'woman', Saussure's theory implies that the meaning of 'woman', or the qualities identified as womanly, are not fixed by a natural world and reflected in the term 'woman', but socially produced within language, plural and subject to change. Yet, to satisfy feminist interests, we need to move beyond Saussure's theory of an abstract system of language. To gain the full benefit of Saussure's theory of meaning, we need to view language as a system always existing in historically specific discourses. Once language is understood in terms of competing discourses, competing ways of giving meaning to the world, which imply differences in the organization of social power, then language becomes an important site of political struggle. [. . .]

The poststructuralist move beyond Saussure involves a critique of the fixing of meaning in the Saussurean sign through the arbitrary coming together of the signifiers and signifieds to form *positive* terms. Saussure attempts to locate meaning in the language system itself but then sees it as single, as 'fixed':

> A linguistic system is a series of differences of sound combined with differences of ideas, but the pairing of a certain number of acoustical signs with as many cuts made from the mass of thought engenders a system of values, and this system serves as the effective link between the phonic and the psychological elements within each sign. Although both the signified and the signifier are purely differential and negative when considered separately, their combination is a positive fact. (Saussure, 1974, p. 120)

The problem with this theory is that it does not account for the plurality of meaning or changes in meaning. It cannot account for why the signifier 'woman' can have many conflicting meanings which change over time. For Saussure, signs are fixed as positive facts which are the product of the conventions of a 'speech community' (1974, p. 14). Language does not originate from individual, intentional subjects and the individual's relation to language is 'largely unconscious' (1974, p. 72). Yet the language which the individual acquires consists of fixed meanings which are the result of an already existing social contract to which individual speakers are subject. The poststructuralist answer to the problems of the plurality of meaning and change is to question the location of social meaning in fixed signs. It speaks instead of signifiers in which the signified is never fixed once and for all, but is constantly *deferred*.

It is in the work of Jacques Derrida that this critique of the Saussurean sign is made most clearly.[2] Derrida questions Saussure's *logocentrism* in which signs have an already fixed meaning recognized by the self-consciousness of the rational speaking subject. Derrida moves from the Saussurean focus on speech to a concern with writing and textuality and replaces the fixed signifieds of Saussure's chains of signs with a concept of *différance* in which meaning is produced via the dual strategies of difference and deferral. For Derrida there can be no fixed signifieds (concepts), and signifiers (sound or written images), which have identity only in their difference from one another, are subject to an endless process of deferral. The effect of representation, in which meaning is apparently fixed, is but a temporary retrospective fixing. Signifiers are always located in a discursive context and the temporary fixing of meaning in a specific reading of a signifier depends on this discursive context. The meaning of the signifier 'woman' varies from ideal to victim to object of sexual desire, according to its context. Consequently, it is always open to challenge and redefinition with shifts in its discursive context. What it means at any particular moment depends on the discursive relations within which it is located, and it is open to constant rereading and reinterpretation. Deconstruction theorizes the discursive context as the relationship of difference between written texts, and while insisting that non-discursive forces are important, does not spell out the social power relations within which texts are located. However, a feminist poststructuralism must pay full attention to the social and institutional context of textuality in order to address the power relations of everyday life. Social meanings are produced within social institutions and practices in which individuals, who are shaped by these institutions, are agents of change, rather than its authors, change which may either serve hegemonic interests or challenge existing power relations.

Language, in the form of an historically specific range of ways of giving meaning to social reality, offers us various discursive positions, including modes of femininity and masculinity, through which we can consciously live our lives. A glance at women's magazines, for example, reveals a range of often competing subject positions offered to women readers, from career woman to romantic heroine, from successful wife and mother to irresistible sexual object. These different positions which magazines construct in their various features, advertising and fiction are part of the battle to determine the day-to-day practices of family life, education, work and leisure. How women understand the sexual division of labour, for example, whether in the home or in paid work, is crucial to its maintenance or transformation. Discourses of femininity and masculinity bear centrally on this understanding and it is in this sense that language in the form of various discourses is, in Louis Althusser's terms, the place in which we represent to ourselves our 'lived relation' to our material conditions of existence (Althusser, 1971).[3]

How we live our lives as conscious thinking subjects, and how we give meaning to the material social relations under which we live and which structure our every-day lives, depends on the range and social power of existing discourses, our access to them and the political strength of the interests which they represent. For example, there are currently several conflicting accounts of the sexual division of labour which inform different common-sense assumptions about women's subjectivity and social role. These include versions which see it as natural because biologically determined, as, for example, in sociobiology and behaviourist psychology, and theories which see it as a socially produced structure, as in much sociological theory. Marxists understand it to be an effect of capitalism, while socialist feminists see it as intrinsic to the capitalist mode of production but not reducible to it. Alternatively, radical feminism sees the sexual division of labour as an effect of patriarchy, the causes of which tend to be located in the nature or structure of masculinity.

Each of these accounts is competing for the meaning of a plural signifier, the sexual division of labour, in ways which imply not only different social and political consequences for women, but also the different forms of feminine subjectivity which are the precondition for meaningful action. Biologically based theory, for example, and the common-sense positions which it informs, offer women forms of fixed subjectivity which render the status quo natural and marginalize attempts to change it as unnatural. Conversely, in radical-feminist biologism, the status quo is rejected as an unnatural, patriarchal distortion of the truly female, in favour of a separate women's culture based in women's biological nature, but defined in different, more positive ways.

[. . .]

Subjectivity

The terms *subject* and *subjectivity* are central to poststructuralist theory and they mark a crucial break with humanist conceptions of the individual which are still central to Western philosophy and political and social organization. 'Subjectivity' is used to refer to the conscious and unconscious thoughts and emotions of the individual, her sense of herself and her ways of understanding her relation to the world. Humanist discourses presuppose an essence at the heart of the individual which is unique, fixed and coherent and which makes her what she *is*. The nature of this essence varies between different forms of humanist discourse. It may be the unified rational consciousness of liberal political philosophy, the essence of womanhood at the heart of much radical-feminist discourse or the true human nature, alienated by capitalism, which is the focus of humanist Marxism. Against this irreducible humanist essence of subjectivity, poststructuralism proposes a subjectivity which is precarious, contradictory and in process, constantly being reconstituted in discourse each time we think or speak.

The political significance of decentring the subject and abandoning the belief in essential subjectivity is that it opens up subjectivity to change. In making our subjectivity the product of the society and culture within which we live, feminist poststructuralism insists that forms of subjectivity are produced historically and change with shifts in the wide range of discursive fields which constitute them. However, feminist poststructuralism goes further than this to insist that the individual is always the site of conflicting forms of subjectivity. As we acquire language, we learn to give voice – meaning – to our experience and to understand it according to particular ways of thinking, particular discourses, which pre-date our entry into language. These ways of thinking constitute our consciousness, and the positions with which we identify structure our sense of ourselves, our subjectivity. Having grown up within a particular system of meanings and values, which may well be contradictory, we may find ourselves resisting alternatives. Or, as we move out of familiar circles, through education or politics, for example, we may be exposed to alternative ways of constituting the meaning of our experience which seem to address our interests more directly. For many women this is the meaning of the practice of consciousness-raising developed by the Women's Liberation Movement. The collective discussion of personal problems and conflicts, often previously understood as the result of personal inadequacies and neuroses, leads to a recognition that what have been experienced as personal failings are socially produced conflicts and contradictions shared by many women in similar social positions. This process of discovery can lead to a rewriting of personal experience in terms which give it social, changeable causes.

The inadequacies widely felt by the new mother, for example, who is inserted in a discourse of motherhood in which she is exposed to childcare demands structured by the social relations of the patriarchal nuclear family, may leave her feeling an unnatural or bad parent. As mother she is supposed to meet all the child's needs single-handed, to care for and stimulate the child's physical, emotional and mental development and to feel fulfilled in doing so. The recognition that feelings of inadequacy or failure are common among women in similar positions, that the current organization of child care is the result, not of nature, but of social and historical developments in the organization of work and procreation, and that contemporary definitions of woman as mother conflict with other subject positions which we are encouraged to assume, offers the frustrated mother a new subject position from which to make sense of her situation, a position which makes her the subject rather than the cause of the contraditions which she is living. As the subject of a range of conflicting discourses, she is *subjected* to their contradictions at great emotional cost.

Poststructuralist feminist theory suggests that experience has no inherent essential meaning. It may be given meaning in language through a range of discursive systems of meaning, which are often contradictory and constitute conflicting versions of social reality, which in turn serve conflicting interests. This range of discourses and their material supports in social institutions and practices is integral to the maintenance and contestation of forms of social power, since social reality has no meaning except in language.

Yet language, in the form of socially and historically specific discourses, cannot have any social and political effectivity except in and through the actions of the individuals who become its bearers by taking up the forms of subjectivity and the meanings and values which it proposes and acting upon them. The individual is both the site for a range of possible forms of subjectivity and, at any particular moment of thought or speech, a subject, subjected to the regime of meaning of a particular discourse and enabled to act accordingly. The position of subject from which language is articulated, from which speech acts, thoughts or writing appear to originate, is integral to the structure of language and, by extension, to the structure of conscious subjectivity which it constitutes. Language and the range of subject positions which it offers always exists in historically specific discourses which inhere in social institutions and practices and can be organized analytically in discursive fields.

Language as Discourse

Social structures and processes are organized through institutions and practices such as the law, the political system, the church, the family, the education system and the media, each of which is located in and structured by a particular *discursive field*. The concept of a discursive field was produced by the French theorist Michel Foucault as part of an attempt to understand the relationship between language, social institutions, subjectivity and power. Discursive fields consist of competing ways of giving meaning to the world and of organizing social institutions and processes. They offer the individual a range of modes of subjectivity. Within a discursive field, for instance, that of the law or the family, not all discourses will carry equal weight or power. Some will account for and justify the appropriateness of the status quo. Others will give rise to challenge to existing practices from within or will contest the very basis of current organization and the selective interests which it represents. Such discourses are likely to be marginal to existing practice and dismissed by the hegemonic system of meanings and practices as irrelevant or bad.

In the field of legal discourse in Britain today, for example, the legal apparatuses are not homogeneous in their views on the best way of organizing the system of trial, punishment, compensation and the rehabilitation of offenders. While there are dominant forms of legal practice, informed by particular values and interests, the discourses which justify or contest this practice are manifold. Some professionals and social groups are currently pressing for stronger custodial sentences, others for short, sharp shocks or for capital punishment. In opposition to this there are groups and individuals who champion greater use of community service and fines rather than prison. Certain types of crime, for example against the state, the police and property, are defined as worse than others and the hierarchization of crimes will vary between legal discourses and from interest group to interest group.

Yet in any society, one set of legal discourses is dominant and it reflects particular values and class, gender and racial interests. Current legal practice in rape cases in Britain, for example, which claims to represent 'natural justice', can be read as serving the interests of men in reproducing and legitimizing dominant forms of femininity and masculinity. What is in question here is the meaning of the 'natural' in 'natural justice'. Examining and sentencing practices in the courts often endorse a view of rape as a natural extension of an active male sexuality in the face of female 'provocation'. In the view of some judges, this may take the form of going out alone at night, wearing a mini-skirt or being a prostitute.

The values and interests which constitute norms of provocation in the eyes of judges and the police are not specific to the legal apparatuses. They have to be understood in the context of widely held beliefs about female sexuality and women's proper place and lifestyle which cross a whole range of discursive fields from the family, education and employment to the representation of women in the media. These are beliefs in which individuals have vested interests. Dominant discourses of female sexuality, which define it as naturally passive, together with dominant social definitions of women's place as first and foremost in the home, can be found in social policy, medicine, education, the media and the church and elsewhere. The conclusions widely drawn from such assumptions include the belief that women who are not sexually passive or virginally modest in their self-presentation are 'asking for it' and that a woman who goes out after dark should be accompanied by a man – father, brother, husband, boyfriend – who is responsible for her welfare. A common response to the threat of rape, especially on university campuses, is to tell women to stay in after dark. What is at issue is the meaning of the ways in which women dress or how we live. In some rape cases to go out unaccompanied has been interpreted as yet another sign of sexual availability, a provocation to male sexuality. This is itself socially constructed as an ever-present, powerful thrust of sexual drives, which society, and women in particular, must hold in check by not offering 'unreasonable' provocation. Attempts by feminist lawyers and women's pressure groups to change meanings, for example the assumptions about femininity which inform dominant legal practice, constitute a part of the legal discursive field which challenges and seeks to transform the hegemonic discourse from a position of relative powerlessness. The implications of this challenge are extremely important, both for rape victims and for all women.

The differences between competing views of justice within the field of legal discourse are articulated in language and in the material organization of state institutions which control the meaning of justice, punishment, compensation and rehabilitation. Institutions such as the courts, prisons and the probation service define justice in ways which serve particular values and interests. Yet the meaning and political significance of the organization of legal institutions and processes are themselves a site of struggle. They will vary according to the discursive position from which they are interpreted. While agents of the official organs of the state and the legislature may seek to explain and justify the system in terms of a discourse of law and order based on shared 'traditional' values and specific notions of what constitutes crime, others may see the system in radically different terms. It can be seen, for example, as repressive towards particular subordinated interest groups like women or blacks, and the discourses developed to represent these interests will seek among other things to redefine what constitutes crime by taking into account patriarchy and racism, and the social deprivations which they uphold. The redefinition of crimes can have important implications for the forms of subjectivity available to the 'criminal'. She may become a freedom fighter where she was a terrorist or, for example, in the case of attacks on sex shops, a champion of women's interests in the campaign against violence against women, rather than the perpetrator of criminal damage. The meaning of the existing structure of social institutions, as much as the structures themselves and the subject positions which they offer their subjects, is a site of political struggle waged mainly, though not exclusively, in *language*.

Where women are concerned this can be seen very clearly in conflicting definitions of the true or desirable nature and function of the family and more specifically what it means to be a wife and mother. Two examples will help illustrate this point. In conservative discourse the family is the natural basic unit of the social order, meeting individual emotional, sexual and practical needs, and it is primarily responsible for the reproduction and socialization of children. Power relations in the family, in which men usually have more power than women and women more power than children, are seen as part of a God-given natural order which guarantees the sexual division of labour within the family. The naturalness of women's responsibility for domestic labour and childcare is balanced by the naturalness of men's involvement in the worlds of work and politics. Both partners are equal in worth but different. The organization of society in family units guarantees the reproduction of social values and skills in differential class and gender terms. To be a wife and mother is seen as women's primary role and the source of full self-realization. The natural structure of femininity will ensure that women can achieve fulfilment through these tasks.

Women's magazines are addressed to the question of how women might best negotiate their familial roles. Relationships with men and children, concerns of family life more generally and the skills needed for a successful career in domesticity are central to the features, fiction, advertising and advice columns which constitute the dominant message of the magazines. Yet it is on the problem pages that the values underpinning the magazines as a whole become most explicit. The type of advice given to women on marital problems, in particular, urges women to make the best of the oppressive structures of family life. As wives and mothers, we are encouraged to accommodate ourselves to families as the expense of our own feelings and the quality of our lives. Examples of this can be found in the advice columns of all popular women's magazines.

While it would be most effective to let examples of readers' letters and the replies to them speak for themselves, the magazines do not allow the quotation of published letters. The discussion of the example which follows refers to one such real letter from a woman, whom I shall call Penny, whose husband has abused her for years in the context of a relationship where he has all the economic power. The letter describes long years of physical and mental cruelty by the husband which end in the woman's nervous breakdown. Penny describes how a recent change in her husband and an end to domestic violence has left her with feelings of contempt for him together with a desire to break away from a marriage which offers her no emotional satisfaction. She is restrained from doing so by the material constraints of marriage – she has nowhere else to go.

The reply to this letter urges Penny to make the best of her marriage and to work to improve its quality. The agony columnist regrets not the state of the marriage but her correspondent's attitude to it, suggesting it is a pity that after having stayed with her husband when he was 'mean, a bully and a drinker', she should now feel so hostile towards him. The reply argues that contempt inspires contemptibility rather than the other way round and suggests ways in which Penny might improve the quality of her relationship with her husband through demonstrations of affection which the correspondent has stressed she does not feel. Both the letter and the reply assume that language is transparent and expresses a singular reality of experience to which the reader, too, is offered access. The answer to Penny's appeal for advice reinforces the patriarchal values of family life.

The reply exemplifies the way in which conservative discourses fail to take issue with the power relations, particularly the economic ones both within the family and in society at large which keep women trapped. Instead it reproduces and legitimizes these relations by placing the responsibility to improve family relations on Penny, even suggesting that her wrong attitudes are responsible for the current state of relations between Penny and her husband. It offers her only one legitimate subject position, that of a long-suffering patient Griselda. There is no sense of the relationship as an enactment of patriarchal familial oppression and no question of self-determination for the woman involved.

In contrast, radical- and socialist-feminist discourses theorize the family as the instrument *par excellence* of the oppression of women through male control of female sexuality and procreative powers and their control of economic power. The family is seen as the major social instrument which ties women to heterosexual monogamy and constitutes their sexuality masochistically in the interests of the satisfaction of male desire. Instead of it being natural for women to defer constantly to the interests of men and children, feminism sees such behaviour as a result of forms of oppression exercised through the legally, economically and ideologically defined structures of the family and through the internalization of a masochistic form of femininity. Masochistic femininity is also acquired through the family, which encourages women to seek satisfaction in constantly deferring to men and to men's definitions of what they should be. It helps make women psychologically accepting of the material structures of their oppression. Yet the reality of the family as a social institution defined and materially supported by the law, the tax system, the welfare system, education, the media, the churches and a range of other social institutions, together with the lack of a real alternative to the patriarchal nuclear family, means that it is very difficult for women to opt out of family life. New subject positions, imaginable in theory or in feminist futurist novels like *Woman on the Edge of Time* (Piercy, 1979), in which sexual divisions of labour and of personal qualities have been dissolved, require new sets of material relations for their realization. Alternative feminist discourses of 'family' life as found, for example, in the last chapter of *The Anti-social Family* (Barrett and McIntosh, 1982), and the new forms of social organization which they imply, are still marginal and powerless in the social hierarchy of those Western societies which they seek to transform.

Feminist poststructuralism, then, is a mode of knowledge production which uses poststructuralist theories of language, subjectivity, social processes and institutions to understand existing power relations and to identify areas and strategies for change. Through a concept of *discourse*, which is seen as a structuring principle of society, in social institutions, modes of thought and individual subjectivity, feminist poststructuralism is able, in detailed, historically specific analysis, to explain the working of power on behalf of specific interests and to analyse the opportunities for resistance to it. It is a theory which decentres the rational, self-present subject of humanism, seeing subjectivity and consciousness, as socially produced in language, as a site of struggle and potential change. Language is not transparent, as in humanist discourse, it is not expressive and does not label a 'real' world. Meanings do not exist prior to their articulation in language and language is not an abstract system, but is always socially and historically located in discourses. Discourses represent political interests and in consequence are constantly vying for status and power. The site of this battle for power is the subjectivity of the individual and it is a battle in which the individual is an active but not sovereign protagonist.

At the level of the individual, this theory is able to offer an explanation of where our experience comes from, why it is contradictory or incoherent and why and how it can change. It offers a way of understanding the importance of subjective motivation and the illusion of full subjectivity necessary for individuals to act in the world. It can also account for the political limitations of change at the level of subjective consciousness stressing the importance of the material relations and practices which constitute individuals as embodied subjects with particular but not inevitable forms of conscious and unconscious motivation and desires which are themselves the effect of the social institutions and processes which structure society. It is for these reasons that this particular form of poststructuralism is a productive theory for feminism.

Feminism, in all its forms, and poststructuralism share a concern with subjectivity. The recent feminist movement began with the politics of the personal, challenging the unified, apparently ungendered individual of liberalism and suggesting that, in its gender blindness, liberal humanism masks structures of male privilege and domination. Poststructuralism, too, has been anxious to deconstruct the liberal-humanist subject in order to theorize how meanings are produced, how they are effective, why they conflict and how they change.

Notes

1. See, for example Gayatri Spivak's essay 'Three women's texts' in *Critical Enquiry*, 12 (1), pp. 243–61.
2. For a comprehensive and clear introduction to deconstruction, see *On Deconstruction* (Culler, 1983).

3. Althusser was writing here of ideology rather than discourse, but for poststructuralist theory the two terms become merged since, unlike much Marxist theory, poststructuralism has no concept of science as 'true' knowledge separate from ideology. It speaks rather of different forms of discourse with their own regularities, institutional locations, conditions of production and degrees of power within the social formation of which science is only one.

References

Althusser, L. (1971) *Lenin and Philosophy and Other Essays*, London: New Left Books.

Barrett, M. (1980) *Women's Oppression Today*, London: Verso.

Barrett, M. and McIntosh, M. (1982) *The Anti-social Family*, London: Verso.

Culler, J. (1983) *On Deconstruction*, London: Routledge & Kegan Paul.

Derrida, J. (1976) *Speech and Phenomenon*, Evanston: North-western University Press.

Derrida, J. (1973) *Of Grammatology*, Baltimore: Johns Hopkins University Press.

Foucault, M. (1978) *I, Pierre Rivière*, Harmondsworth: Peregrine.

Foucault, M. (1979a) *Discipline and Punish*, Harmondsworth: Penguin.

Foucault, M. (1979b) 'What is an author?', *Screen*, 20 (1), pp. 13–33.

Foucault, M. (1981) *The History of Sexuality, Volume One, An Introduction*, Harmondsworth: Pelican.

Foucault, M. (1986) *The History of Sexuality, Volume Two, The Use of Pleasure*, Harmondsworth: Viking.

Kristeva, J. (1981) 'Women's time', *Signs*, 7 (1), Chicago: University of Chicago Press.

Kristeva, J. (1984) *Revolution in Poetic Language*, New York: Columbia University Press.

Kristeva, J. (1986) *The Kristeva Reader* (ed. T. Moi), Oxford: Blackwell.

Lancan, J. (1977) *Ecrits*, London: Tavistock.

Piercy, M. (1979) *Woman on the Edge of Time*, London: The Women's Press.

Saussure, F. de (1974) *A Course in General Linguistics*, London: Fontana.

PART FOUR

Marxism

Introduction

To be fully understood, the Marxist approach to popular culture has to be situated within Marxism's wider concerns. Marxism is always more than a form of cultural analysis; it is a body of political theory with the purpose of changing the world. This does not mean that other approaches to popular culture are apolitical. On the contrary, Marxism insists, as Fredric Jameson puts it, that 'the political perspective ... [is] the absolute horizon of all reading and all interpretation'.[1] If the insistence on politics is one defining feature of the Marxist approach to popular culture, another is the insistence that the texts and practices of culture must be analysed and understood in their historical conditions of production (and in some versions, the changing conditions of their consumption and reception). What makes the Marxist approach different from other 'historical' approaches to popular culture is the Marxist conception of history. The clearest statement of this conception is contained in *Preface and Introduction to a Contribution to the Critique of Political Economy* (Reading 18). Marx argues that each significant 'stage' in history is constructed around a particular 'mode of production'. Each mode of production brings into being different ways to produce the necessaries of life, but also produces different social relationships between the different classes, and different social institutions (including cultural ones). Fundamental to this analysis is the claim that the way in which a society produces its means of existence (its particular mode of production) ultimately determines the political, social and cultural shape of the society and its possible future development. After Marx's death, Frederick Engels, his friend and collaborator, found himself, in a series of letters, having to explain many of the subtleties of Marxism to younger Marxists, who, in their revolutionary enthusiasm, threatened to reduce it to a simple form of economic determinism. Reading 19 is an edited version of perhaps the most famous of these letters.

In *The German Ideology* (Reading 17), Marx and Engels claim that the dominant class, on the basis of its control of the means of production, is virtually guaranteed to have control over the means of intellectual production. This, however, does not mean that the ideas of the dominant class will simply be imposed on subordinate classes. As Marx and Engels explain, a dominant class is 'compelled ... to represent its interests as the common interest of all the members of society ... to give its ideas the form of universality, and represent them as the only rational, universally valid ones'. The uncertainty of this project makes ideological struggle almost inevitable. As Marx points out (Reading 18), it is in the 'ideological forms' (legal, political, cultural, etc.) that men and women 'become conscious of ... conflict and fight it out'.

Using the analytical tools of 'classical' Marxism (the Marxism of Marx and Engels), how should we approach popular culture? First, in order to understand and explain a cultural text or practice, we must locate it in its moment of production, analysing the historical conditions which produced it. This does not mean that we 'reduce' the cultural text or practice to the economic conditions of its existence. For example, an analysis of the development of stage melodrama in the nineteenth century would have to pay attention to more than the economic conditions of its existence. Nevertheless, an account which failed to address the historical conditions which produced, shaped and sustained the new audience for theatre would not be a full analysis of stage melodrama. An approach informed by 'classical' Marxism would insist that ultimately, however indirectly, there is, nevertheless, a real and fundamental relationship between the emergence of stage melodrama and changes that had taken place in the capitalist mode of production.

The Frankfurt School's work on popular culture is mainly associated with the writings of Theodor Adorno, Walter Benjamin, Max Horkheimer, Leo Lowenthal and Herbert Marcuse. The term 'culture industry' was coined by Adorno and Horkheimer to describe the processes and products of mass culture. Mass culture, they claim, is uniform, predictable, and to the trained ear or eye, transparent. Unfortunately, for most people it is culture. The culture industry produces culture which the 'masses'[2] consume unthinkingly and are thus confirmed as unthinking. It is a culture which produces satisfaction in the here and now, depoliticising the working class, limiting its horizon to political and economic goals that can be achieved within the oppressive and exploitative framework of capitalist society. The culture industry manipulates and indoctrinates. 'Authentic' culture is different, a utopian space keeping alive the desire for a better world beyond the confines of the present. It embodies both a critique of today and the promise of tomorrow. It is a realm we can enter in order to renew ourselves for struggles in the world of the everyday. But even 'authentic' culture is threatened by the culture industry, as it draws it more and more into the realm of production for profit.

Adorno's essay 'On Popular Music' (Reading 20) is a representative example of the Frankfurt School approach to popular culture. In this essay, Adorno makes three specific claims about popular music: first, that popular music is standardised ('pseudo-individualisation' is used by the music industry to suggest otherwise); second, that it promotes passive consumption; and third, that popular music operates as 'social cement'. Even when we acknowledge that the essay was published in 1941, and therefore cannot be criticised for failing to take into account the complexities of recent popular music and popular music culture (his approach does not even allow the suspicion of the possibility of change), it is still not easy to accept Adorno's position. Does 'pseudo-individualisation' really explain differences between popular songs? Was the consumption of popular music ever as passive as Adorno claims? It is certainly difficult to maintain this position with regard to contemporary popular music. It has been estimated that about 80 per cent of records released actually lose money.[3] This does not sound like the operations of an all-powerful culture industry; more like an industry trying desperately to sell records to a critical and discriminating public. Finally, does popular music operate as social cement? Certainly, subcultural use of music (and it could be argued that all music consumption is, in effect, subcultural) suggests otherwise.

In the early 1970s, Louis Althusser's poststructuralist rereading of Marx had an enormous influence on cultural studies. By the late 1970s, however, the influence of Althusserianism had begun to wane. Paradoxically, the challenge came from the writings of a man who had died while Althusser himself was still a student: the Italian Marxist Antonio Gramsci. The change begins with the translation into English of *Selections from Prison Notebooks* in 1971 (see Reading 21). The key concept in the cultural studies reading of Gramsci is undoubtedly 'hegemony'. Since the mid-1970s it has been (and continued to be up until the fairly recent challenge of postmodernism) the central concept in cultural studies. In basic terms, this concept is used to refer to a situation in which a dominant class does not simply 'rule' a society, but actively 'leads' it through the exercise of moral and intellectual leadership. Ernesto Laclau explains it thus,

> A class is hegemonic not so much to the extent that it is able to impose a uniform conception of the world on the rest of society, but to the extent that it can articulate different visions of the world in such a way that their potential antagonism is neutralized.[4]

Tony Bennett's essay (Reading 22) provides an excellent introduction to the importance of Gramsci's concept to the study of popular culture. My account of West Coast rock's opposition to Amerika's[5] war in Vietnam (Reading 23) and Christine Gledhill's superb outline of a feminist approach to popular film (Reading 24) are examples of work which, in different ways, rely on Gramsci's concept of hegemony to organise its approach to popular culture.

In recent years there has been a growing interest in Mikhail Bakhtin's work on carnival.[6] His work has been deployed to explain what is seen as the carnivalesque aspect of contemporary popular culture. Reading 25 presents in outline form Bakhtin's understanding of the actual carnivals which dominated European popular culture throughout the Middle Ages.[7]

Notes

1. Fredric Jameson, *The Political Unconscious*, London: Methuen, 1981, p. 17.
2. It is perhaps worth noting Raymond Williams's observation, 'There are in fact no masses; there are only ways of seeing *other people* as masses' (my italics), *Culture and Society*, Harmondsworth: Penguin, 1963, p. 289.
3. See Simon Frith, *Sound Effects*, London: Constable, 1983, p. 17.
4. Ernesto Laclau, *Politics and Ideology in Marxist Theory*, London: Verso, p. 161.
5. Amerika with a 'k' instead of the customary 'c' was the preferred spelling of the American counterculture. It was intended to signify America as a Kafkaesque nightmare.
6. See, for example, Peter Stallybrass and Allon White, *The Politics and Poetics of Transgression*, Ithaca, NY: Cornell University Press, 1988; John Fiske, *Television Culture*, London: Routledge, 1987; John Fiske, *Understanding Popular Culture*, London: Unwin Hyman, 1989; John Docker, *Postmodernism and Popular Culture*, Cambridge: Cambridge University Press, 1994.
7. For a more detailed discussion of carnival and the carnivalesque, see Mikhail Bakhtin, *Rabelais and His World*, Bloomington: Indiana University Press, 1984.

17 □ *Ruling Class and Ruling Ideas*

Karl Marx and Frederick Engels

[...]

The ideas of the ruling class are in every epoch the ruling ideas, i.e. the class which is the ruling *material* force of society, is at the same time its ruling *intellectual* force. The class which has the means of material production at its disposal, has control at the same time over the means of mental production, so that thereby, generally speaking, the ideas of those who lack the means of mental production are subject to it. The ruling ideas are nothing more than the ideal expression of the dominant material relationships, the dominant material relationships grasped as ideas; hence of the relationships which make the one class the ruling one, therefore, the ideas of its dominance. The individuals composing the ruling class possess among other things consciousness, and therefore think. In so far, therefore, as they rule as a class and determine the extent and compass of an epoch, it is self-evident that they do this in its whole range, hence among other things rule also as thinkers, as producers of ideas, and regulate the production and distribution of the ideas of their age: thus their ideas are the ruling ideas of the epoch.

[...]

The division of labour [...] manifests itself also in the ruling class as the division of mental and material labour, so that inside this class one part appears as the thinkers of the class (its active, conceptive ideologists, who make the perfecting of the illusion of the class about itself their chief source of livelihood), while the others' attitude to these ideas and illusions is more passive and receptive, because they are in reality the active members of this class and have less time to make up illusions and ideas about themselves. Within this class this cleavage can even develop into a certain opposition and hostility between the two parts, which, however, in the case of a practical collision, in which the class itself is endangered, automatically comes

From Marx, K. and Engels, F. *The German Ideology*, Lawrence & Wishart, London, 1970, pp. 64–6.

to nothing, in which case there also vanishes the semblance that the ruling ideas were not the ideas of the ruling class and had a power distinct from the power of this class.

[...]

If now in considering the course of history we detach the ideas of the ruling class from the ruling class itself and attribute to them an independent existence, if we confine ourselves to saying that these or those ideas were dominant at a given time, without bothering ourselves about the conditions of production and the producers of these ideas, if we thus ignore the individuals and world conditions which are the source of the ideas, we can say, for instance, that during the time that the aristocracy was dominant, the concepts honour, loyalty, etc., were dominant, during the dominance of the bourgeoisie the concepts freedom, equality, etc. The ruling class itself on the whole imagines this to be so. This conception of history, which is common to all historians, particularly since the eighteenth century, will necessarily come up against the phenomenon that increasingly abstract ideas hold sway, i.e. ideas which increasingly take on the form of universality. For each new class which puts itself in the place of one ruling before it, is compelled, merely in order to carry through its aim, to represent its interest as the common interest of all the members of society, that is, expressed in ideal form: it has to give its ideas the form of universality, and represent them as the only rational, universally valid ones.

18 □ Base and Superstructure

Karl Marx

[...]

The general conclusion at which I arrived and which, once reached, became the guiding principle of my studies can be summarized as follows. In the social production of their existence, men enter into definite, necessary relations, which are independent of their will, namely, relations of production corresponding to a determinate stage of development of their material forces of production. The totality of these relations of production constitutes the economic structure of society, the real foundation on which there arises a legal and political superstructure and to which there correspond definite forms of social consciousness. The mode of production of material life conditions the social, political and intellectual life-process in general. It is not the consciousness of men that determines their being, but on the contrary it is their social being that determines their consciousness. At a certain stage of their development, the material productive forces of society come into conflict with the existing relations of production or – what is merely a legal expression for the same thing – with the property relations within the framework of which they have hitherto operated. From forms of development of the productive forces these relations turn into their fetters. At that point an era of social revolution begins. With the change in the economic foundation the whole immense superstructure is more slowly or more rapidly transformed. In considering such transformations it is always necessary to distinguish between the material transformation of the economic conditions of production, which can be determined with the precision of natural science, and the legal, political, religious, artistic or philosophic, in short, ideological forms in which men become conscious of this conflict and fight it out.

From Marx, K., *Preface and Introduction to A Critique of Political Economy*, Foreign Languages Press, Peking, 1976, pp. 3–5.

19 □ *Letter to Joseph Bloch*

Frederick Engels

London, September 21 [–22] 1890

According to the materialist conception of history, the *ultimately* determining element in history is the production and reproduction of real life. Neither Marx nor I have ever asserted more than this. Therefore if somebody twists this into saying that the economic factor is the *only* determining one, he is transforming that proposition into a meaningless, abstract, absurd phrase. The economic situation is the basis, but the various components of the superstructure – political form of the class struggle and its consequences, such as: constitutions drawn up by the victorious class after a successful battle, etc., juridical forms, and even the reflections of all these actual struggles in the minds of the participants, political, juristic, philosophical theories, religious views and their further development into systems of dogmas – also exercise their influence upon the course of the historical struggles and in many cases determine their *form* in particular. There is an interaction of all these elements in which, amid all the endless number of accidents (i.e. of things and events whose inner interconnection is so remote or so impossible to prove that we can regard it as non-existent and can neglect it) the economic movement is finally bound to assert itself. Otherwise the application of the theory to any period of history one chose would be easier than the solution of a simple equation of the first degree.

We make our history ourselves, but first of all, under very definite assumptions and conditions. Among these the economic ones are ultimately decisive. But the political ones, etc., and indeed even the traditions which haunt human minds also play a part, although not the decisive one. The Prussian state also arose and developed from historical, ultimately economic, causes. But one could scarcely maintain without being pedantic that among the many small states of North Germany, Brandenburg was specifically determined by economic necessity to

From Marx, K. and Engels, F., *Selected Letters*, Foreign Languages Press, Peking, 1977, pp. 75–8.

become the great power embodying the economic, linguistic and, after the Reformation, also the religious differences between North and South, and not by any other elements as well (above all by its entanglement with Poland, deriving from its possession of Prussia, and thus with international political relations – which were in fact also decisive in the establishment of the dynastic power of Austria). Without making oneself ridiculous it would be a difficult thing to explain in terms of economics the existence of every small state in Germany, past and present, or the origin of the High German consonant permutations which widened the geographic wall of partition formed by the mountains from the Sudetic range to the Taunus, making a regular division across all of Germany.

In the second place, however, history is made in such a way that the final result always arises from conflicts between individual wills, of which each in turn has been made what it is by a variety of particular conditions of life. Thus, there are innumerable crisscrossing forces, an infinite series of parallelograms of forces which give rise to one resultant – the historical event. This may again in turn be regarded as the product of a power which works as a whole *unconsciously* and without volition. For that which each individual wills is obstructed by everyone else, and what emerges is something that no one wanted. Thus history, up to the present, has proceeded in the manner of a natural process and is essentially subject to the same laws of motion. But from the fact that the wills of individuals – each of whom desires what he is impelled to by his physical constitution and external, in the final analysis economic, circumstances (either his own personal circumstances or those of society in general) – do not believe what they want, but are merged into an aggregate mean, common resultant, it must not be concluded that their value is equal to zero. On the contrary, each contributes to the resultant and is to this extent included in it.

I would furthermore ask you to study this theory from the original sources and not at second hand; it is really much easier. Marx hardly ever wrote anything in which it did not play a part. But especially *The Eighteenth Brumaire of Louis Bonaparte* is a very excellent example of its application. There are also many allusions to it in *Capital*. I may also refer you to my writings: *Herr Eugen Dühring's Revolution in Science*[*] and *Ludwig Feuerbach and the End of Classical German Philosophy*, in which I have given the most detailed account of historical materialism which, as far as I know, exists.

Marx and I are ourselves partly to blame for the fact that the younger people sometimes lay more stress on the economic side than is due to it. We had to emphasize the main principle over and against our adversaries, who denied it. We had not always the time, the place or the opportunity to let the other factors involved in the interaction be duly considered. But when it came to presenting an era of history, i.e. to making a practical application, it was a different matter and there no error could be permitted. Unfortunately, however, it happens all too often that people think they have fully understood a new theory and can apply it without

[*] [Published in English as *Anti-Dühring*.]

further ado from the very moment they have mastered its main principles, and even those not always correctly. And I cannot exempt many of the more recent 'Marxists' from this reproach, since some of the most amazing stuff has been produced among them, as well. . . .

20 □ On Popular Music

Theodor W. Adorno

The Musical Material

The Two Spheres of Music

Popular music, which produces the stimuli we are here invesigating, is usually characterized by its difference from serious music. This difference is generally taken for granted and is looked upon as a difference of levels considered so well defined that most people regard the values within them as totally independent of one another. We deem it necessary, however, first of all to translate these so-called levels into more precise terms, musical as well as social, which not only delimit them unequivocally but throw light upon the whole setting of the two musical spheres as well.

One possible method of achieving this clarification would be a historical analysis of the division as it occurred in music production and of the roots of the two main spheres. Since, however, the present study is concerned with the actual function of popular music in its present status, it is more advisable to follow the line of characterization of the phenomenon itself as it is given today than to trace it back to its origins. This is the more justified as the division into the two spheres of music took place in Europe long before American popular music arose. American music from its inception accepted the division as something pre-given, and therefore the historical background of the division applies to it only indirectly. Hence we seek, first of all, an insight into the fundamental characteristics of popular music in the broadest sense.

A clear judgment concerning the relation of serious music to popular music can be arrived at only by strict attention to the fundamental characteristic of popular music: standardization.[1] The whole structure of popular music is standardized, even where the attempt is made to circumvent standardization. Standardization

From Easthope, A. and McGowan, K. (eds), *A Critical and Cultural Theory Reader*, Open University Press, Milton Keynes, 1992, pp. 301–14.

extends from the most general features to the most specific ones. Best known is the rule that the chorus consists of thirty-two bars and that the range is limited to one octave and one note. The general types of hits are also standardized: not only the dance types, the rigidity of whose pattern is understood, but also the 'characters' such as mother songs, home songs, nonsense or 'novelty' songs, pseudo-nursery rhymes, laments for a lost girl. Most important of all, the harmonic cornerstones of each hit – the beginning and the end of each part – must beat out the standard scheme. This scheme emphasizes the most primitive harmonic facts no matter what has harmonically intervened. Complications have no consequences. This inexorable device guarantees that regardless of what aberrations occur, the hit will lead back to the same familiar experience, and nothing fundamentally novel will be introduced.

The details themselves are standardized no less than the form, and a whole terminology exists for them such as break, blue chords, dirty notes. Their standardization, however, is somewhat different from that of the framework. It is not overt like the latter but hidden behind a veneer of individual 'effects' whose prescriptions are handled as the experts' secret, however open this secret may be to musicians generally. This contrasting character of the standardization of the whole and part provides a rough, preliminary setting for the effect upon the listener.

The primary effect of this relation between the framework and the detail is that the listener becomes prone to evince stronger reactions to the part than to the whole. His grasp of the whole does not lie in the living experience of this one concrete piece of music he has followed. The whole is pre-given and pre-accepted, even before the actual experience of the music starts: therefore, it is not likely to influence, to any great extent, the reaction to the details, except to give them varying degrees of emphasis. Details which occupy musically strategic positions in the framework – the beginning of the chorus or its reentrance after the bridge – have a better chance for recognition and favourable reception than details not so situated, for instance, middle bars of the bridge. But this situational nexus never interferes with the scheme itself. To this limited situational extent the detail depends upon the whole. But no stress is ever placed upon the whole as a musical event, nor does the structure of the whole ever depend upon the details.

Serious music, for comparative purposes, may be thus characterized: Every detail derives its musical sense from the concrete totality of the piece which, in turn, consists of the life relationship of the details and never of a mere enforcement of a musical scheme. For example, in the introduction of the first movement of Beethoven's Seventh Symphony the second theme (in C-major) gets its true meaning only from the context. Only through the whole does it acquire its particular lyrical and expressive quality – that is, a whole built up of its very contrast with the *cantus firmus* like character of the first theme. Taken in isolation the second theme would be disrobed to insignificance. Another example may be found in the beginning of the recapitulation over the pedal point of the first movement of Beethoven's 'Appassionata'. By following the preceding outburst it achieves the utmost dramatic momentum. By omitting the exposition and development and starting with this repetition, all is lost.

Nothing corresponding to this can happen in popular music. It would not affect the musical sense if any detail were taken out of the context; the listener can supply the 'framework' automatically, since it is a mere musical automatism itself. The beginning of the chorus is replaceable by the beginning of innumerable other choruses. The interrelationship among the elements or the relationship of the elements to the whole would be unaffected. In Beethoven, position is important only in a living relation between a concrete totality and its concrete parts. In popular music, position is absolute. Every detail is substitutable; it serves its function only as a cog in a machine.

The mere establishment of this difference is not yet sufficient. It is possible to object that the far-reaching standard schemes and types of popular music are bound up with dance, and therefore are also applicable to dance derivatives in serious music, for example, the minuetto and scherzo of the classical Viennese School. It may be maintained either that this part of serious music is also to be comprehended in terms of detail rather than of whole, or that if the whole still is perceivable in the dance types in serious music despite recurrence of the types, there is no reason why it should not be perceivable in modern popular music.

The following consideration provides an answer to both objections by showing the radical differences even where serious music employs dance types. According to current formalistic views the scherzo of Beethoven's Fifth Symphony can be regarded as a highly stylized minuetto. What Beethoven takes from the traditional minuetto scheme in this scherzo is the idea of outspoken contrast between a minor minuetto, a major trio, and repetition of the minor minuetto; and also certain other characteristics such as the emphatic three-fourths rhythm often accentuated on the first fourth and, by and large, dancelike symmetry in the sequence of bars and periods. But the specific form-idea of this movement as a concrete totality transvaluates the devices borrowed from the minuetto scheme. The whole movement is conceived as an introduction to the finale in order to create tremendous tension, not only by its threatening, foreboding expression but even more by the very way in which its formal development is handled.

The classical minuetto scheme required first the appearance of the main theme, then the introduction of a second part which may lead to more distant tonal regions – formalistically similar, to be sure, to the 'bridge' of today's popular music – and finally the recurrence of the original part. All this occurs in Beethoven. He takes up the idea of thematic dualism within the scherzo part. But he forces what was, in the conventional minuetto, a mute and meaningless game rule to speak with meaning. He achieves complete consistency between the formal structure and its specific content, that is to say, the elaboration of its themes. The whole scherzo part of this scherzo (that is to say, what occurs before the entrance of the deep strings in C-major that marks the beginning of the trio) consists of the dualism of two themes, the creeping figure in the strings and the 'objective', stonelike answer of the wind instruments. This dualism is not developed in a schematic way so that first the phrase of the strings is elaborated, then the answer of the winds, and then the string theme is mechanically repeated. After the first occurrence of the second theme in the horns, the two essential elements are alternately interconnected in the manner of a dialogue, and the end of the scherzo part is actually marked, not by the first but by the second theme, which has overwhelmed the first musical phrase.

Furthermore, the repetition of the scherzo after the two is scored so differently that it sounds like a mere shadow of the scherzo and assumes that haunting character which vanishes only with the affirmative entry of the Finale theme. The whole device has been made dynamic. Not only the themes, but the musical form itself have been subjected to tension: the same tension which is already manifest within the twofold structure of the first theme that consists, as it were, of question and reply, and then even more manifest within the context between the two main themes. The whole scheme has become subject to the inherent demands of this particular movement.

To sum up the difference: in Beethoven and in good serious music in general – we are not concerned here with bad serious music which may be as rigid and mechanical as popular music – the detail virtually contains the whole and leads to the exposition of the whole, while, at the same time, it is produced out of the conception of the whole. In popular music the relationship is fortuitous. The detail has no bearing on a whole, which appears as an extraneous framework. Thus, the whole is never altered by the individual event and therefore remains, as it were, aloof, imperturbable, and unnoticed throughout the piece. At the same time, the detail is mutilated by a device which it can never influence and alter, so that the detail remains inconsequential. A musical detail which is not permitted to develop becomes a caricature of its own potentialities.

Standardization

The previous discussion shows that the difference between popular and serious music can be grasped in more precise terms than those referring to musical levels such as 'lowbrow and highbrow', 'simple and complex', 'naïve and sophisticated'. For example, the difference between the spheres cannot be adequately expressed in terms of complexity and simplicity. All works of the earlier Viennese classicism are, without exception, rhythmically simpler than stock arrangements of jazz. Melodically, the wide intervals of a good many hits such as 'Deep Purple' or 'Sunrise Serenade' are more difficult to follow *per se* than most melodies of, for example, Haydn, which consist mainly of circumscriptions of tonic triads and second steps. Harmonically, the supply of chords of the so-called classics is invariably more limited than that of any current Tin Pan Alley composer who draws from Debussy, Ravel, and even later sources. Standardization and nonstandardization are the key contrasting terms for the difference.

Structural Standardization Aims at Standard Reactions. Listening to popular music is manipulated not only by its promoters but, as it were, by the inherent nature of this music itself, into a system of response mechanisms wholly antagonistic to the ideal of individuality in a free, liberal society. This has nothing to do with simplicity and complexity. In serious music, each musical element, even the simplest one, is 'itself', and the more highly organized the work is, the less possibility there is of substitution among the details. In hit music, however, the structure underlying the piece is abstract, existing independent of the specific course of the music. This is basic to the illusion that certain complex harmonies are more easily understandable in popular music than the same harmonies in serious music. For the complicated in popular music never functions as 'itself' but only as a disguise or embellishment behind which the scheme can always be perceived. In jazz the amateur listener is capable of replacing complicated rhythmical or harmonic formulas by the schematic ones which they represent and which they still suggest, however adventurous they appear. The ear deals with the difficulties of hit music by achieving slight substitutions derived from the knowledge of the patterns. The listener, when faced with the complicated, actually hears only the simple which it represents and perceives the complicated only as a parodistic distortion of the simple.

No such mechanical substitution by stereotyped patterns is possible in serious music. Here even the simplest event necessitates an effort to grasp it immediately instead of summarizing it vaguely according to institutionalized prescriptions capable of producing only institutionalized effects. Otherwise the music is not 'understood'. Popular music, however, is composed in such a way that the process of translation of the unique into the norm is already planned and, to a certain extent, achieved within the composition itself.

The composition hears for the listener. This is how popular music divests the listener of his spontaneity and promotes conditioned reflexes. Not only does it now require his effort to follow its concrete stream; it actually gives him models under which anything concrete still remaining may be subsumed. The schematic buildup dictates the way in which he must listen while, at the same time, it makes any effort in listening unnecessary. Popular music is 'pre-digested' in a way strongly resembling the fad of 'digests' of printed material. It is this structure of contemporary popular music which, in the last analysis, accounts for those changes of listening habits which we shall later discuss.

So far standardisation of popular music has been considered in structural terms – that is, as an inherent quality without explicit reference to the process of production or to the underlying causes for standardization. Though all industrial mass production necessarily eventuates in standardization, the production of popular music can be called 'industrial' only in its promotion and distribution, whereas the act of producing a song-hit still remains in a handicraft stage. The production of popular music is highly centralized in its economic organization, but still 'individualistic' in its social mode of production. The division of labor among the composer, harmonizer, and arranger is not industrial but rather pretends industrialization, in order to look more up to date, whereas it has actually adapted industrial methods for the technique of its promotion. It would not increase the costs of production if the various composers of hit tunes did not follow certain standard patterns. Therefore, we must look for other reasons for structural standardization – very different reasons from those which account for the standardization of motor cars and breakfast foods.

Imitation offers a lead for coming to grips with the basic reasons for it. The musical standards of popular music were originally developed by a competitive process. As one particular song scored a great success, hundreds of others sprang up imitating the successful one. The most successful hits, types, and 'ratios' between elements were imitated, and the process culminated in the crystallization of standards. Under centralized conditions such as exist today these standards have become 'frozen'.[2] That is, they have been taken over by cartelized agencies, the final results of a competitive process, and rigidly enforced upon material to be promoted. Noncompliance with the rules of the game became the basis for exclusion. The original patterns that are now standardized evolved in a more or less competitive way. Large-scale economic concentration institutionalized the standardization, and made it imperative. As a result, innovations by rugged individualists have been outlawed. The standard patterns have become invested with the immunity of bigness – 'the King can do no wrong'. This also accounts for revivals in popular music. They do now have the outworn character of standardized products manufactured after a given pattern. The breath of free competition is still alive within them. On the other hand, the famous old hits which are revived set the patterns which have become standardized. They are the golden age of the game rules.

This 'freezing' of standards is socially enforced upon the agencies themselves. Popular music must simultaneously meet two demands. One is for stimuli that provoke the listener's attention. The other is for the material to fall within the category of what the musically untrained listener would call 'natural' music: that is, the sum total of all the conventions and material formulas in music to which he is accustomed and which he regards as the inherent, simple language of music itself, no matter how late the development might be which produced this natural language. This natural language for the American listener stems from his earliest musical experiences, the nursery rhymes, the hymns he sings in Sunday school, the little tunes he whistles on his way home from school. All these are vastly more important in the formation of musical language than his ability to distinguish the beginning of Brahms's Third Symphony from that of his Second. Official musical culture is, to a large extent, a mere superstructure of this underlying musical language, namely, the major and minor tonalities and all the tonal relationships they imply. But these tonal relationships of the primitive musical language set barriers to whatever does not conform to them. Extravagances are tolerated only in so far as they can be recast into this so-called natural language.

In terms of consumer demand, the standardization of popular music is only the expression of this dual desideratum imposed upon it by the musical frame of mind of the public – that it be 'stimulatory' by deviating in some way from the established 'natural', and that it maintain the supremacy of the natural against such deviations.

The attitude of the audiences toward the natural language is reinforced by standardized production, which institutionalizes desiderata which originally might have come from the public.

Pseudo-individualization

The paradox in the desiderata – stimulatory and natural – accounts for the dual character of standardization itself. Stylization of the ever identical framework is only one aspect of standardization. Concentration and control in our culture hide themselves in their very manifestation. Unhidden they would provoke resistance. Therefore the illusion and, to a certain extent, even the reality of individual achievement must be maintained. The maintenance of it is grounded in material reality itself, for while administrative control over life processes is concentrated, ownership is still diffuse.

In the sphere of luxury production, to which popular music belongs and in which no necessities of life are immediately involved, while, at the same time, the residues of individualism are most alive where in the form of ideological categories such as taste and free choice, it is imperative to hide standardization. The 'backwardness' of musical mass production, the fact that it is still on a handicraft level and not literally an industrial one, conforms perfectly to that necessity which is essential from the viewpoint of cultural big business. If the individual handicraft elements of popular music were abolished altogether, a synthetic means of hiding standardization would have to be evolved. Its elements are even now in existence.

The necessary correlate of musical standardization is *pseudo-individualization*. By pseudo-individualization we mean endowing cultural mass production with the halo of free choice or open market on the basis of standardization itself. Standardization of song hits keeps the customers in line by doing their listening for them, as it were. Pseudo-individualization, for its part, keeps them in line by making them forget that what they listen to is already listened to for them, or 'pre-digested'.

The most drastic example of standardization of presumably individualized features is to be found in so-called improvisations. Even though jazz musicians still improvise in practice, their improvisations have become so 'normalized' as to enable a whole terminology to be developed to express the standard devices of individualization: a terminology which in turn is ballyhooed by jazz publicity agents to foster the myth of pioneer artisanship and at the same time flatter the fans by apparently allowing them to peep behind the curtain and get the inside story. This pseudo-individualization is prescribed by the standardization of the framework. The latter is so rigid that the freedom it allows for any sort of improvisation is severely delimited. Improvisations – passages where spontaneous action of individuals is permitted ('Swing it boys') – are confined within the walls of the harmonic and metric scheme. In a great many cases, such as the 'break' of pre-swing jazz, the musical function of the improvised detail is determined completely by the scheme: the break can be nothing other than a disguised cadence. Here, very few possibilities for actual improvisation remain, due to the necessity of merely melodically circumscribing the same underlying harmonic functions. Since these possibilities were very quickly exhausted, stereotyping of improvisatory details speedily occurred. Thus, standardization of the norm enhances in a purely technical way standardization of its own deviation – pseudo-individualization.

This subservience of improvisation to standardization explains two main socio-psychological qualities of popular music. One is the fact that the detail remains openly connected with the underlying scheme so that the listener always feels on safe ground. The choice in individual alterations is so small that the perpetual recurrence of the same variations is a reassuring signpost of the identical behind them. The other is the function of 'substitution' – the improvisatory features forbid their being grasped as musical events in themselves. They can be received only as embellishments. It is a well-known fact that in daring jazz arrangements worried notes, dirty notes, in other words, false notes, play a conspicuous role. They are apperceived as exciting stimuli only because they are corrected by the ear to the right note. This, however, is only an extreme instance of what happens less conspicuously in all individualization in popular music. Any harmonic boldness, any chord which does no fall strictly within the simplest harmonic scheme, demands being apperceived as 'false', that is, as a stimulus which carries with it the unambiguous prescription to substitute for it the right detail, or rather the naked scheme. Understanding popular music means obeying such commands for listening. Popular music commands its own listening habits.

There is another type of individualization claimed in terms of kinds of popular music and differences in name bands. The types of popular music are carefully differentiated in production. The listener is presumed to be able to choose between them. The most widely recognized differentiations are those between swing and sweet and such name bands as Benny Goodman and Guy Lombardo. The listener is quickly able to distinguish the types of music and even the performing band, this in spite of the fundamental identity of the material and the great similarity of the presentations apart from their emphasized distinguishing trademarks. This labelling technique, as regards type of music and band, is pseudo-individualization, but of a sociological kind outside the realm of strict musical technology. It provides trademarks of identification for differentiating between the actually undifferentiated.

Popular music becomes a muliple-choice questionnaire. There are two main types and their derivatives from which to choose. The listener is encouraged by the inexorable presence of these types psychologically to cross out what he dislikes and check what he likes. The limitation inherent in this choice and the clear-cut alternative it entails provoke like–dislike patterns of behavior. This mechanical dichotomy breaks down indifference; it is imperative to favor sweet or swing if one wishes to continue to listen to popular music.

Theory about the Listener

Popular Music and 'Leisure Time'

In order to understand why this whole *type* of music (i.e. popular music in general) maintains its hold on the masses, some considerations of a general kind may be appropriate.

The frame of mind to which popular music originally appealed, on which it feeds, and which it perpetually reinforces, is simultaneously one of distraction and inattention. Listeners are distracted from the demands of reality by entertainment which does not demand attention either.

The notion of distraction can be properly understood only within its social setting and not in self-subsistent terms of individual psychology. Distraction is bound to the present mode of production, to the rationalized and mechanized process of labor to which, directly or indirectly, masses are subject. This mode of production, which engenders fears and anxiety about unemployment, loss of income, war, has its 'nonproductive' correlate in entertainment; that is, relaxation which does not involve the effort of concentration at all. People want to have fun. A fully concentrated and conscious experience of art is possible only to those whose lives do not put such a strain on them that in their spare time they want relief from both boredom and effort simultaneously. The whole sphere of cheap commercial entertainment reflects this dual desire. It induces relaxation because it is patterned and pre-digested. Its being patterned and predigested serves within the psychological household of the masses to spare them the effort of that participation (even in listening or observation) without which there can be no receptivity to art. On the other hand, the stimuli they provide permit an escape from the boredom of mechanized labor.

The promoters of commercialized entertainment exonerate themselves by referring to the fact that they are giving the masses what they want. This is an ideology appropriate to commercial purposes: the less the mass discriminates, the greater the possibility of selling cultural commodities indiscriminately. Yet this ideology of vested interest cannot be dismissed so easily. It is not possible completely to deny that mass consciousness can be molded by the operative agencies only because the masses 'want this stuff'.

But why do they want this stuff? In our present society the masses themselves are kneaded by the same mode of production as the arti-craft material foisted upon them. The customers of musical entertainment are themselves objects or, indeed, products of the same mechanisms which determine the production of popular music. Their spare time serves only to reproduce their working capacity. It is a means instead of an end. The power of the process of production extends over the time intervals which on the surface appear to be 'free'. They want standardized goods and pseudo-individualization, because their leisure is an escape from work and at the same time is molded after those psychological attitudes to which their workaday world exclusively habituates them. Popular music is for the masses a perpetual busman's holiday. Thus, there is justification for speaking of a preestablished harmony today between production and consumption of popular music. The people clamor for what they are going to get anyhow.

To escape boredom and avoid effort are incompatible – hence the reproduction of the very attitude from which escape is sought. To be sure, the way in which they must work on the assembly line, in the factory, or at office machines denies people any novelty. They seek novelty, but the strain and boredom associated with actual work lead to avoidance of effort in that leisure time which offers the only chance for really new experience. As a substitute, they crave a stimulant. Popular music comes to offer it. Its stimulations are met with the inability to vest effort in the ever-identical. This means boredom again. It is a circle which makes escape impossible. The impossibility of escape causes the widespread attitude of inattention toward popular music. The moment of recognition is that of effortless sensation. The sudden attention attached to this moment burns itself out *instanter* and relegates the listener to a realm of inattention and distraction. On the one hand, the domain of production and plugging presupposes distraction and, on the other, produces it.

In this situation the industry faces an insoluble problem. It must arouse attention by means of ever-new products, but this attention spells their doom. If no attention is given to the song, it cannot be sold; if attention is paid to it, there is always the possibility that people will no longer accept it, because they know it too well. This partly accounts for the constantly renewed effort to sweep the market with new products, to hound them to their graves; then to repeat the infanticidal maneuver again and again.

On the other hand, distraction is not only a presupposition but also a product of popular music. The tunes themselves lull the listener to inattention. They tell him not to worry, for he will not miss anything.[3]

The Social Cement

It is safe to assume that music listened to with a general inattention which is only interrupted by sudden flashes of recognition is not followed as a sequence of experiences that have a clear-cut meaning of their own, grasped in each instant and related to all the precedent and subsequent moments. One may go so far as to suggest that most listeners of popular music do not understand music as a language in itself. If they did it would be vastly difficult to explain how they could tolerate the incessant supply of largely undifferentiated material. What, then, does music mean to them? The answer is that the language that is music is transformed by objective processes into a language which they think is their own – into a language which serves as a receptacle for their institutionalized wants. The less music is a language *sui generis* to them, the more does it become established as such a receptacle. The autonomy of music is replaced by a mere socio-psychological function. Music today is largely a social cement. And the meaning listeners attribute to a material, the inherent logic of which is inaccessible to them, is above all a means by which they achieve some psychical adjustment to the mechanisms of present-day life. This 'adjustment' materializes in two different ways, corresponding to two major socio-psychological types of mass behavior toward music in general and popular music in particular, the 'rhythmically obedient' type and the 'emotional' type.

Individuals of the rhythmically obedient type are mainly found among the youth – the so-called radio generation. They are most susceptible to a process of masochistic adjustment to authoritarian collectivism. The type is not restricted to any one political attitude. The adjustment to anthropophagous collectivism is found as often among left-wing political groups as among right-wing groups. Indeed, both overlap: repression and crowd-mindedness overtake the followers of both trends. The psychologies tend to meet despite the surface distinctions in political attitudes.

This comes to the fore in popular music which appears to be aloof from political partisanship. It may be noted that a moderate leftist theater production such as *Pins and Needles* uses ordinary jazz as its musical medium, and that a Communist youth organization adapted the melody of 'Alexander's Ragtime Band' to its own lyrics. Those who ask for a song of social significance ask for it through a medium which deprives it of social significance. The uses of inexorable popular musical media is repressive *per se*. Such inconsistencies indicate that political conviction and socio-psychological structure by no means coincide.

This obedient type is the rhythmical type, the word 'rhythmical' being used in its everyday sense. Any musical experience of this type is based upon the underlying, unabating time unit of the music – its 'beat'. To play rhythmically means, to these people, to play in such a way that even if pseudo-individualizations – counter-accents and other 'differentiations' – occur, the relation to the ground meter is preserved. To be musical means to them to be capable of following given rhythmical patterns without being disturbed by 'individualizing' aberrations, and to fit even the syncopations into the basic time units. This is the way in which their response to music immediately expresses their desire to obey. However, as the standardized meter of dance music and of marching suggests the coordinated battalions of a mechanical collectivity, obedience to this rhythm by overcoming the responding individuals leads them to conceive of themselves as agglutinized with the untold millions of the meek who must be similarly overcome. Thus do the obedient inherit the earth.

Yet, if one looks at the serious compositions which correspond to this category of mass listening, one finds one very characteristic feature: that of disillusion. All these composers. among them Stravinsky and Hindemith, have expressed an 'antiromantic' feeling. They aimed at musical adaptation to reality – a reality understood by them in terms of the 'machine age'. The renunciation of dreaming by these composers is an index that listeners are ready to replace dreaming by adjustment to raw reality, that they reap new pleasure from their acceptance of the unpleasant. They are disillusioned about any possibility of realizing their own dreams in the world in which they live, and consequently adapt themselves to this world. They take what is called a realistic attitude and attempt to harvest consolation by identifying themselves with the external social forces which they think constitute the 'machine age'. Yet the very disillusion upon which their co-ordination is based is there to mar their pleasure. The cult of the machine which is represented by unabating jazz beats involves a self-renunciation that cannot but take root in the form of a fluctuating uneasiness somewhere in the personality of the obedient. For the machine is an end in itself only under given social conditions – where men are appendages of the machines on which they work. The adaptation to machine music necessarily implies a renunciation of one's own human feelings and at the same time a fetishism of the machine such that its instrumental character becomes obscured thereby.

As to the other, the 'emotional' type, there is some justification for linking it with a type of movie spectator. The kinship is with the poor shop girl who derives gratification by identification with Ginger Rogers, who, with her beautiful legs and unsullied character, marries the boss. Wish fulfillment is considered the guiding principle in the social psychology of moving pictures and similarly in the pleasure obtained from emotional, erotic music. This explanation, however, is only superficially appropriate.

Hollywood and Tin Pan Alley may be dream factories. But they do not merely supply categorical wish fulfillment for the girl behind the counter. She does not immediately identify herself with Ginger Rogers marrying. What does occur may be expressed as follows: when the audience at a sentimental film or sentimental music become aware of the overwhelming possibility of happiness, they dare to confess to themselves what the whole order of contemporary life ordinarily forbids them to admit, namely, that they actually have no part in happiness. What is supposed to be wish fulfillment is only the scant liberation that occurs with the realization that at last one need not deny oneself the happiness of knowing that one is unhappy and that one could be happy. The experience of the shop girl is related to that of the old woman who weeps at the wedding services of others, blissfully becoming aware of the wretchedness of her own life. Not even the most gullible individuals believe that eventually everyone will win the sweepstakes. The actual function of sentimental music lies rather in the temporary release given to the awareness that one has missed fulfillment.

The emotional listener listens to everything in terms of late romanticism and of the musical commodities derived from it which are already fashioned to fit the needs of emotional listening. They consume music in order to be allowed to weep. They are taken in by the musical expression of frustration rather than by that of happiness. The influence of the standard Slavic melancholy typified by Tchaikovsky and Dvořák is by far greater than that of the most 'fulfilled' moments of Mozart or of the young Beethoven. The so-called releasing element of music is simply the opportunity to feel something. But the actual content of this emotion can only be frustration. Emotional music has become the image of the mother who says, 'Come and weep, my child.' It is catharsis for the masses, but catharsis which keeps them all the more firmly in line. One who weeps does not resist any more than one who marches. Music that permits its listeners the confession of their unhappiness reconciles them, by means of this 'release', to their social dependence.

Notes

1. The basic importance of standardization has not altogether escaped the attention of current literature on popular music. 'The chief difference between a popular song and a standard, or serious, song like "Mandalay", "Sylvia", or "Trees", is that the melody and the lyric of a popular number are constructed within a definite pattern or structural form, whereas the poem, or lyric, of a standard number has no structural confinements, and the music is free to interpret the meaning and feeling of the words without following a set pattern or form. Putting it another way, the popular song is "custom built", while the standard song allows the composer freer play of imagination and interpretation.' Abner Silver and Robert Bruce, *How to Write and Sell a Song Hit* (New York, 1939), p. 2. The authors fail, however, to realize the external superimposed, commercial character of those patterns which aims at canalized reactions or, in the language of the regular announcement of one particular radio program, at 'easy listening'. They confuse the mechanical patterns with highly organized, strict art forms: 'Certainly there are few more stringent verse forms in poetry than the sonnet, and yet the greatest poets of all time have woven undying beauty within its small and limited frame. A composer has just as much opportunity for exhibiting his talent and genius in popular songs as in more serious music' (pp. 2–3). Thus the standard pattern of popular music appears to them virtually on the same level as the law of a fugue. It is this contamination which makes the insight into the basic standardization of popular music sterile. It ought to be added that what Silver and Bruce call a 'standard song' is just the opposite of what we mean by a standardized popular song.
2. See Max Horkheimer, *Zeitschrift für Sozialforschung 8* (1939), p. 115.
3. The attitude of distraction is not a completely universal one. Particularly youngsters who invest popular music with their own feelings are not yet completely blunted to all its effects. The whole problem of age levels with regard to popular music, however, is beyond the scope of the present study. Demographic problems, too, must remain out of consideration.

21 □ Hegemony, Intellectuals and the State

Antonio Gramsci

I Hegemony

(a) The methodological criterion on which our own study must be based is the following: that the supremacy of a social group manifests itself in two ways, as 'domination' and as 'intellectual and moral leadership'. A social group dominates antagonistic groups, which it tends to 'liquidate', or to subjugate perhaps even by armed force; it leads kindred and allied groups. A social group can, and indeed must, already exercise 'leadership' before winning governmental power (this indeed is one of the principal conditions for the winning of such power); it subsequently becomes dominant when it exercises power, but even if it holds it firmly in its grasp, it must continue to 'lead' as well (pp. 57–8).

(b) [A] class is dominant in two ways, i.e. 'leading' and 'dominant'. It leads the classes which are its allies, and dominates those which are its enemies. Therefore, even before attaining power a class can (and must) 'lead'; when it is in power it becomes dominant, but continues to 'lead' as well...there can and must be a 'political hegemony' even before the attainment of governmental power, and one should not count solely on the power and material force which such a position gives in order to exercise political leadership or hegemony (p. 57)

(c) The 'normal' exercise of hegemony on the now classical terrain of the parliamentary regime is characterised by the combination of force and consent, which balance each other reciprocally, without force predominating excessively over consent. Indeed, the attempt is always made to ensure that force will appear to be based on the consent of the majority, expressed by the so-called organs of public opinion – newspapers and associations – which, therefore, in certain situations, are artificially multiplied (p. 80).

From Gramsci, A., *Selection from Prison Notebooks* (trans. Quintin Hoare and Geoffrey Nowell-Smith), Lawrence & Wishart, London, 1971.

(d) Undoubtedly the fact of hegemony presupposes that account be taken of the interests and the tendencies of the groups over which hegemony is to be exercised, and that a certain compromise equilibrium should be formed – in other words, that the leading group should make sacrifices of an economic corporate kind. But there is also no doubt that such sacrifices and such a compromise cannot touch the essential; for though hegemony is ethical-political, it must also be economic, must necessarily be based on the decisive nucleus of economic activity (p. 161).

(e) A subsequent moment is the relation of political forces; in other words, an evaluation of the degree of homogeneity, self-awareness, and organisation attained by the various social classes. This moment can in its turn be analysed and differentiated into various levels, corresponding to the various moments of collective political consciousness, as they have manifested themselves in history up till now. The first and most elementary of these is the economic-corporate level: a tradesman feels *obliged* to stand by another tradesman, a manufacturer by another manufacturer, etc., but the tradesman does not yet feel solidarity with the manufacturer; in other words, the members of the professional group are conscious of its unity and homogeneity, and of the need to organise it, but in the case of the wider social group this is not yet so. A second moment is that in which consciousness is reached of the solidarity of interests among all the members of a social class – but still in the purely economic field. Already at this juncture the problem of the State is posed – but only in terms of winning politico-juridical equality with the ruling groups: the right is claimed to participate in legislation and administration, even to reform these – but within the existing fundamental structures. A third moment is that in which one becomes aware that one's own corporate interests, in their present and future development, transcend the corporate limits of the purely economic class, and can and must become the interests of other subordinate groups too. This is the most purely political phase, and marks the decisive passage from the structure to the sphere of the complex superstructures; it is the phase in which previously germinated ideologies become 'party', come into confrontation and conflict, until only one of them, or at least a single combination of them, tends to prevail, to gain the upper hand, to propagate itself throughout society – bringing about not only unison of economic and political aims, but also intellectual and moral unity, posing all the questions around which the struggle rages not on a corporate but on a 'universal' plane, and thus creating the hegemony of a fundamental social group over a series of subordinate groups. It is true that the State is seen as the organ of one particular group, destined to create favourable conditions for the latter's maximum expansion. But the development and expansion of the particular group are conceived of, and presented, as being the motor force of a universal expansion, of a development of all the 'national' energies. In other words, the dominant group is coordinated concretely with the general interests of the subordinate groups, and the life of the State is conceived of as a continuous process of formation and superseding of unstable equilibria (on the juridical plane) between the interests of the fundamental group and those of the subordinate groups – equilibria in which the interests of the dominant group prevail, but only up to a certain point, i.e. stopping short of narrowly corporate economic interest (pp. 181–2).

(f) Every relationship of 'hegemony' is necessarily an educational relationship and occurs not only within a nation, between the various forces of which the nation is composed, but in the international and worldwide field, between complexes of national and continental civilisations (p. 350)

2 Intellectuals

(a) Every social group, coming into existence on the original terrain of an essential function in the world of economic production, creates together with itself, organically, one or more strata of intellectuals which give it homogeneity and an awareness of its own function not only in the economic but also in the social and political fields. The capitalist entrepreneur creates alongside himself the industrial technician, the specialist in political economy, the organisers of a new culture, of a new legal system, etc. [. . .]

If not all entrepreneurs, at least an elite amongst them must have the capacity to be an organiser of society in general, including all its complex organism of services, right up to the state organism, because of the need to create the conditions most favourable to the expansion of their own class; or at the least they must possess the capacity to choose the deputies (specialised employees) to whom to entrust this activity of organising the general system of relationships external to the business itself. It can be observed that the 'organic' intellectuals which every new class creates alongside itself and elaborates in the course of its development are for the most part 'specialisations' of partial aspects of the primitive activity of the new social type which the new class has brought into prominence (p. 5).

(b) What are the 'maximum' limits of acceptance of the term 'intellectual'? Can one find a unitary criterion to characterise equally all the diverse and disparate activities of intellectuals and to distinguish these at the same time and in an essential way from the activities of other social groupings? The most widespread error of method seems to me that of having looked for this criterion of distinction in the intrinsic nature of intellectual activities, rather than in the ensemble of the system of relations in which these activities (and therefore the intellectual groups who personify them) have their place within the general complex of social relations. Indeed, the worker or proletarian, for example, is not specifically characterised by his manual or instrumental work, but by performing this work in specific conditions and in specific social relations (apart from the consideration that purely physical labour does not exist [. . .]: in any physical work, even the most degraded and mechanical, there exists a minimum of technical qualification, that is, a minimum of creative intellectual activity). And we have already observed that the entrepreneur, by virtue of his very function, must have to some degree a certain number of qualifications of an intellectual nature although his part in society is determined not by these, but by the general social relations which specifically characterise the position of the entrepreneur within industry.

All men are intellectuals, one could therefore say: but not all men have in society the function of intellectuals.

When one distinguishes between intellectuals and non-intellectuals, one is referring in reality only to the immediate social function of the professional category of the intellectuals, that is, one has in mind the direction in which their specific professional activity is weighted, whether towards intellectual elaboration or towards muscular-nervous effort. This means that, although one can speak of intellectuals, one cannot speak of non-intellectuals, because non-intellectuals do not exist. But even the relationship between efforts of intellectual-cerebral elaboration and muscular-nervous effort is not always the same, so that there are varying degrees of specific intellectual activity. There is no human activity from which every form of intellectual participation can be excluded: *Homo faber* cannot be separated from *Homo sapiens*. Each man, finally, outside his professional activity, carries on some form of intellectual activity, that is, he is a 'philosopher', an artist, a man of taste, he participates in a particular conception of the world, has a conscious line of moral conduct, and therefore contributes to sustain a conception of the world or to modify it, that is, to bring into being new modes of thought (pp. 8–9).

(c) Thus there are historically formed specialised categories for the exercise of the intellectual function. They are formed in connection with all social groups, but especially in connection with the more important, and they undergo more extensive and complex elaboration in connection with the dominant social group. One of the most important characteristics of any group that is developing towards dominance is its struggle to assimilate and to conquer 'ideologically' the traditional intellectuals, but this assimilation and conquest is made quicker and more efficacious the more the group in question succeeds in simultaneously elaborating its own organic intellectuals.

The enormous development of activity and organisation of education in the broad sense in the societies that emerged from the medieval world is an index of the importance assumed in the modern world by intellectual functions and categories. Parallel with the attempt to deepen and to broaden the 'intellectuality' of each individual, there has also been an attempt to multiply and narrow the various specialisations. This can be seen from educational institutions at all levels, up to and including the organisms that exist to promote so-called 'high culture' in all fields of science and technology (p. 10).

(d) What we can do, for the moment, is to fix two major superstructural 'levels': the one that can be called 'civil society', that is the ensemble of organisms commonly called 'private', and that of 'political society' or 'the State'. These two levels correspond on the one hand to the functions of 'hegemony' which the dominant group exercises throughout society and on the other hand to that of 'direct domination' or command exercised through the State and 'juridical' government. The functions in question are precisely organisational and connective. The intellectuals are the dominant group's 'deputies' exercising the subaltern functions of social hegemony and political government. These comprise:

1. The 'spontaneous' consent given by the great masses of the population to the general direction imposed on social life by the dominant fundamental group; this consent is 'historically' caused by the prestige (and consequent confidence) which the dominant group enjoys because of its position and function in the world of production.
2. The apparatus of state coercive power which 'legally' enforces discipline on those groups who do not 'consent' either actively or passively. This apparatus is, however, constituted for the whole of society in anticipation of moments of crisis of command and direction when spontaneous consent has failed (p. 12).

(e) France offers the example of an accomplished form of harmonious development of the energies of the nation and of the intellectual categories in particular. When in 1789 a new social grouping makes its political appearance on the historical stage, it is already completely equipped for all its social functions and can therefore struggle for total domination of the nation. It does not have to make any essential compromises with the old classes but instead can subordinate them to its own ends. The first intellectual cells of the new type are born along with their first economic counterparts. [. . .] This massive intellectual construction explains the function of culture in France in the eighteenth and nineteenth centuries. [. . .]

In England the development is very different from France. The new social grouping that grew up on the basis of modern industrialism shows a remarkable economic-corporate development but advances only gropingly in the intellectual-political field. There is a very extensive category of organic intellectuals – those, that is, who come into existence on the same industrial terrain as the economic group – but in the higher sphere we find that the old land-owning class preserves its position of virtual monopoly. It loses its economic supremacy but maintains for a long time a politic-intellectual supremacy and is assimilated as 'traditional intellectuals' and as directive group by the new group in power. The old land-owning aristocracy is joined to the industrialists by a kind of suture which is precisely that which in other countries unites the traditional intellectuals with the new dominant classes (p. 18)

3 The State

(a) In my opinion, the most reasonable and concrete thing that can be said about the ethical State, the cultural State, is this: every State is ethical inasmuch as one of its most important functions is to raise the great mass of the population to a particular cultural and moral level, a level (or type) which corresponds to the needs of the productive forces for development, and hence to the interests of the ruling classes. The school as a positive educative function, and the courts as a repressive and negative educative function, are the most important State activities in this sense: but, in reality, a multitude of other so-called private initiatives and activities tend to the same end – initiatives and activities which form the apparatus of the political and cultural hegemony of the ruling classes (p. 258).

(b) Government with the consent of the governed – but with this consent organised, and not generic and vague as it is expressed in the instant of elections. The State does have and request consent, but it also 'educates' this consent, by means of the political and syndical associations; these, however, are private organisms, left to the private initiative of the ruling class (p. 259).

(c) The previous ruling classes were essentially conservative in the sense that they did not tend to construct an organic passage from the other classes into their own, i.e. to enlarge their class sphere 'technically' and ideologically: their conception was that of a closed caste. The bourgeois class poses itself as an organism in continuous movement, capable of absorbing the entire society, assimilating it to its own cultural and economic level. The entire function of the State has been transformed; the State has become an 'educator', etc. (p. 260).

(d) We are still on the terrain of the identification of State and government – an identification which is precisely a representation of the economic-corporate form, in other words, of the confusion between civil society and political society. For it should be remarked that the general notion of State includes elements which need to be referred back to the notion of civil society (in the sense that one might say that State = political society + civil society, in other words, hegemony protected by the armour of coercion). In a doctrine of the State which conceives the latter as tendentially capable of withering away and of being subsumed into regulated society, the argument is a fundamental one. It is possible to imagine the coercive element of the State withering away by degrees, as ever more conspicuous elements of regulated society (or ethical State or civil society) make their appearance (pp. 262–3).

(e) Educative and formative role of the State. Its aim is always that of creating new and higher types of civilisation; of adapting the 'civilisation' and the morality of the broadest popular masses to the necessities of the continuous development of the economic apparatus of production; hence of evolving even physically new types of humanity (p. 242).

(f) In reality, the State must be conceived of as an 'educator', inasmuch as it tends precisely to create a new type or level of civilisation. Because one is acting essentially on economic forces, reorganising and developing the apparatus of economic production, creating a new structure, the conclusion must not be drawn that superstructural factors should be left to themselves, to develop spontaneously, to a haphazard and sporadic germination. The State, in this field, too, is an instrument of 'rationalisation', of acceleration [. . .]. It operates according to a plan, urges, incites, solicits, and 'punishes'; for, once the conditions are created in which a certain way of life is 'possible', then 'criminal action or omission' must have a punitive sanction, with moral implications, and not merely be judged generically as 'dangerous'. The Law is the repressive and negative aspect of the entire positive, civilising activity undertaken by the State. The 'prize-giving' activities of individuals and groups, etc., must also be incorporated in the conception of the Law; praiseworthy and meritorious activity is rewarded, just as criminal actions are punished (and punished in original ways, bringing in 'public opinion' as a form of sanction) (p. 247).

(g) [T]he State is the entire complex of practical and theoretical activities with which the ruling class not only justifies and maintains its dominance, but manages to win the active consent of those over whom it rules[.] (p. 244).

22 □ *Popular Culture and the 'turn to Gramsci'*

Tony Bennett

Why study popular culture? It's tempting to answer: why not? To do so, however, would merely be to lend hostage to fortune, for many reasons have been advanced as to why popular culture should not, or at least need not, be studied – on the grounds that it is too slight and ephemeral to be worthy of any sustained inquiry, for example – and, for the greater part of this century, such arguments have largely carried the day. Moreover, even where they have not prevailed, the grounds upon which the study of popular culture has been justified have been mainly negative: to expose its morally corrupting influences and aesthetic poverty, for example, or, in Marxist approaches, to reveal its role as a purveyor of dominant ideology. In the context of such assumptions, to study popular culture has also meant to adopt a position against and opposed to it, to view it as in need of replacement by a culture of another kind, usually 'high culture' – the view not only of reformist critics, such as F. R. Leavis, but, oddly enough, equally influential in Marxist circles too, especially in the work of Theodor Adorno, Herbert Marcuse and the other members of the Frankfurt School.

It is one of the quirks of history that these arguments, which once nowhere had quite so much sedimented cultural weight as in Britain, have been overturned perhaps more decisively in Britain than anywhere else over the course of the last twenty to thirty years. The study of cinema, popular music, sport, youth subcultures and of much else besides has now developed to the point where these are well-established fields of inquiry, with considerably developed bodies of theory and highly elaborated methodologies, in which debate is no longer stalked by the ghost of Leavis – or by the gloomy prognostications of the Frankfurt School, for that matter. Equally important, significant advances have been made in theorising the sphere of popular culture as a whole. The term had previously been used quite loosely to refer to a miscellaneous collection of cultural forms and practices having little in common beyond the fact of their exclusion from the accepted canon of 'high

From Bennett, T., Mercer, C. and Woollacott, J. (eds), *Popular Culture and Social Relations*, Open University Press, Milton Keynes, 1986, pp. xi–xix.

culture'. In more recent debates, by contrast, the many and diverse practices which
are typically grouped under the heading of popular culture are more usually
regarded as being systematically interconnected by virtue of the parts they play in
relation to broader social and political processes, particularly those bearing on the
production of consent to the prevailing social order in both its patriarchal and
capitalist dimensions. These theoretical developments, finally, have been accompanied by a sureness of political purpose as the study of popular culture has been
defined as a site of *positive* political engagement by both socialists and feminists in
their concern to identify both those aspects of popular culture which serve to secure
consent to existing social arrangements as well as those which, in embodying alternative values, supply a source of opposition to those arrangements.

Having said this, many problems, of both theory and politics, remain. Albeit in
different ways, the essays collected in this anthology seek to consolidate the
advances of recent years by engaging with these problems and outlining the
directions in which their resolution might most productively be sought. In particular, they reflect an attempt to confront and go beyond the terms in which problems
in the field were posed in the late 1970s. Debates in the area, at that time, were often
deadlocked around the polar opposites of structuralism and culturalism represented,
respectively, as the 'imported' and 'home-grown' varieties of cultural studies.[1] In
the perspective of structuralism, popular culture was often regarded as an 'ideological machine' which dictated the thoughts of the people just as rigidly and with
the same law-like regularity as, in Saussure's conspectus – which provided the
originating paradigm for structuralism – the system of *langue* dictated the events of
parole. Focusing particularly on the analysis of textual forms, structuralist analysis
was concerned to reveal the ways in which textual structures might be said to
organise reading or spectating practices, often with scant regard to the conditions
regulating either the production or the reception of those textual forms.[2]
Culturalism, by contrast, was often uncritically romantic in its celebration of
popular culture as expressing the authentic interests and values of subordinate social
groups and classes. This conception, moreover, resulted in an essentialist view of
culture: that is, as the embodiment of specific class or gender essences. In the logic
of this approach, as Roszika Parker and Griselda Pollock put it, many feminists were
led to look for an authentically female culture as if this could 'exist isolated like some
deep frozen essence in the freezer of male culture',[3] just as many socialists
rummaged through popular culture in search of the authentic voice of the working
class, as if this could exist in some pure form, preserved and nurtured in a recess
immune to the socially preponderant forms of cultural production in a capitalist
society.[4]

These theoretical divergences were accentuated by their association with different
disciplinary perspectives, structuralism being most strongly present in the study of
cinema, television and popular writings while culturalism tended to predominate
within history and sociology, particularly in studies concerned with working-class
'lived cultures' or 'ways of life'. Given this division of the field – a division that was
sometimes provocatively and needlessly deepened, particularly by E. P. Thompson's

The Poverty of Theory,[5] – there seemed little alternative but to pay one's money and take one's choice. Worse, it seemed as though, depending on one's area of interest, one was constrained to be either a structuralist or a culturalist – the former if one studied cinema, television or popular writing, and the latter if one's interests were in sport, say, or youth subcultures. It was almost as if the cultural sphere were divided into two hermetically separate regions, each exhibiting a different logic. While this was unsatisfactory, it was equally clear that the two traditions could not be forced into a shotgun marriage either. The only way out of this impasse, therefore, seemed to be to shift the debate on to a new terrain which would displace the structuralist–culturalist opposition, a project which inclined many working in the field at the time to draw increasingly on the writings of Antonio Gramsci, particularly those on the subject of hegemony.[6]

This is not the place for a detailed exposition of the whys and wherefores of this strategy, or for an appraisal of its productivity. These are matters the reader will be in a better position to assess having read the essays collected here since, with few exceptions, Gramsci's work, especially when viewed in the light of recent developments in discourse theory,[7] provides the organising framework within which the studies are located. However, some brief remarks are in order so as to give some general sense of the new kinds of emphasis which the 'turn to Gramsci' has helped to inaugurate.

Put in the most general terms, the critical spirit of Gramsci's work, totally shunning the intolerable condescension of the mass culture critic while simultaneously avoiding any tendency toward a celebratory populism, both avoids and disqualifies the bipolar alternatives of structuralism and culturalism. However, this is less a question of style or of Gramsci's mode of address – although these are important considerations in Gramsci's writing – than one of theory. In Gramsci's conspectus, popular culture is viewed neither as the site of the people's cultural deformation nor as that of their cultural self-affirmation or, in any simple Thompsonian sense, of their own self-making; rather, it is viewed as a force field of relations shaped, precisely, by these contradictory pressures and tendencies – a perspective which enables a significant reformulation of both the theoretical and the political issues at stake in the study of popular culture.

Politically speaking, both the structuralist and culturalist paradigms subscribe to a rather similar conception of the structure and organisation of the cultural and ideological spheres viewed in relation to the antagonistic economic and political relationships between social classes. Although importantly different in other respects, both paradigms regard the sphere of cultural and ideological practices as being governed by a dominant ideology, essentially and monolithically bourgeois in its characteristics, which, albeit with varying degrees of success, is imposed from without, as an alien force, on the subordinate classes. Viewed from this perspective, the main differences between the two perspectives are largely nominal or ones of orientation. In structuralism, 'popular culture', 'mass culture' and 'dominant ideology' are usually equated through a series of sliding definitions. In consequence, the chief political task assigned to the study of popular culture is that of reading through popular cultural forms and practices to reveal the obfuscating mechanisms of the dominant ideology at work within them, thus arming the reader against the occurrence of similar mechanisms in related practices. In culturalism, by contrast, popular culture, in being equated with the 'autochthonous' culture of subordinate classes, is explicitly distinguished from and opposed to dominant ideology in the form of mass culture. Where this conception prevails, analysis is dominated by a positive political hermeneutic: that of, having found the people's authentic voice, interpreting its meaning and amplifying its cultural volume. To be sure, the consequences of these contrasting orientations are by no means negligible. In spite of these, however, the two approaches share conception of the cultural and ideological field as being divided between two opposing cultural and ideological camps – bourgeois and working class – locked in a zero-sum game in which one side gains only at the expense of the other and in which the ultimate objective is the liquidation of one by the other so that the victor might then stand in the place of the vanquished.

For Gramsci too, of course, cultural and ideological practices are to be understood and assessed in terms of their functioning within the antagonistic relations between the bourgeoisie and the working class as the two fundamental classes of capitalist society. Indeed, Gramsci's insistence that these antagonistic class relations form the ultimately determining horizon within which cultural and ideological analysis must be located constitutes the outer limit to the programme of theoretical revision he inaugurated in relation to classical Marxist theories of ideology.[8] Where Gramsci departed from the earlier Marxist tradition was in arguing that the cultural and ideological relations between ruling and subordinate classes in capitalist societies consist less in the *domination* of the latter by the former than in the struggle for *hegemony* – that is, for moral, cultural, intellectual and, thereby, political leadership over the whole of society – between the ruling class and, as the principal subordinate class, the working class.

This substitution of the concept of hegemony for that of domination is not, as some commentators have suggested, merely terminological; it brings in tow an entirely different conception of the means by which cultural and ideological struggles are conducted.[9] Whereas, according to the dominant ideology thesis, bourgeois culture and ideology seek to take the place of working-class culture and ideology and thus to become directly operative in framing working-class experience, Gramsci argues that the bourgeoisie can become a hegemonic, leading class only to the degree that bourgeois ideology is able to accommodate, to find some space for, opposing class cultures and values. A bourgeois hegemony is secured not via the obliteration of working-class culture, but via its *articulation to* bourgeois culture and ideology so that, in being associated with and expressed in the forms of the latter, its political affiliations are altered in the process.

As a consequence of its accommodating elements of opposing class cultures, 'bourgeois culture' ceases to be purely or entirely bourgeois. It becomes, instead, a mobile combination of cultural and ideological elements derived from different class locations which are, but only provisionally and for the duration of a specific historical conjuncture, affiliated to bourgeois values, interests and objectives. By the same token, of course, the members of subordinate classes never encounter or are oppressed by a dominant ideology in some pure or class essentialist form; bourgeois ideology is encountered only in the compromised forms it must take in order to provide some accommodation for opposing class values. As Robert Gray remarks, if the Gramscian concept of hegemony refers to the processes through which the ruling class seeks to negotiate opposing class cultures on to a cultural and ideological terrain which wins for it a position of leadership, it is also true that what is thereby consented to is a *negotiated version* of ruling-class culture and ideology:

> Class hegemony is a dynamic and shifting relationship of social subordination, which operates in two directions. Certain aspects of the behaviour and consciousness of the subordinate classes may reproduce a version of the values of the ruling class. But in the process value systems are modified, through their necessary adaptation to diverse conditions of existence; the subordinate classes thus follow a 'negotiated version' of ruling-class values. On the other hand, structures of ideological hegemony transform and incorporate dissident values, so as effectively to prevent the working through of their full implications.[10]

Although an over-rapid and somewhat abstract summary of a complex body of theory, the main point is, perhaps, clear enough: that the spheres of culture and ideology cannot be conceived as being divided into two hermetically separate and entirely opposing class cultures and ideologies. The effect of this is to disqualify the bipolar options of the structuralist and culturalist perspectives on popular culture, viewed either as the carrier of an undiluted bourgeois ideology or as the site of the people's authentic culture and potential self-awakening, as unmitigated villain or unsullied hero. To the contrary, to the degree that it is implicated in the struggle for hegemony – and, for Gramsci, the part played by the most taken-for-granted, sedimented cultural aspects of everyday life are crucially implicated in the processes whereby hegemony is fought for, won, lost, resisted – the field of popular culture is structured by the attempt of the ruling class to win hegemony and by the forms of opposition to this endeavour. As such, it consists not simply of an imposed mass culture that is coincident with dominant ideology, nor simply of spontaneously oppositional cultures, but is rather an area of negotiation between the two within which – in different particular types of popular culture – dominant, subordinate and oppositional cultural and ideological values and elements are 'mixed' in different permutations.

In sum, then, the 'turn to Gramsci' has been influential in both disputing the assumption that cultural forms can be assigned an essential class-belongingness and contesting a simply 'bourgeois versus working class' conception of the organisation of the cultural and ideological relationships. These reorientations have resulted in two decisive shifts of political emphasis within the study of popular culture. First, they have produced a perspective, within Marxism, from which it is possible to analyse popular culture without adopting a position that is either opposed to it or uncritically for it. The forms of political assessment of cultural practices which the theory of hegemony calls for are much more conjunctural and pliable than that. A cultural practice does not carry its politics with it, as if written upon its brow for ever and a day; rather, its political functioning depends on the network of social and ideological relations in which it is inscribed as a consequence of the ways in which, in a particular conjuncture, it is articulated to other practices. In brief, in suggesting that the political and ideological articulations of cultural practices are *movable* – that a practice which is articulated to bourgeois values today may be disconnected from those values and connected to socialist ones tomorrow – the theory of hegemony opens up the field of popular culture as one of enormous political possibilities. It is thus, for example, that in many recent debates, the call has been made that nationalism, and the forms in which it is constructed and celebrated, should be given a socialist articulation rather than be dismissed as essentially and irredeemably bourgeois.[11]

Equally important, the Gramscian critique of class essentialist conceptions of culture and ideology and the associated principles of class reductionism enables due account to be taken of the relative separation of different regions of cultural struggle (class, race, gender) as well as of the complex and changing ways in which these may be overlapped on to one another in different historical circumstances. Apart from being an important advance on classical Marxism, this has also served as an important check on the Foucauldian tendency to view power and the struggle against it as equally diffuse and unrelated. Most important, though, it has offered a framework within which the relations between the cultural politics of socialist movements and those of, say, feminist or national liberation struggles can be productively debated without their respective specifications threatening either to engulf or be engulfed by the others.

This is not to suggest that Gramsci's writings contain the seeds of an answer to all problems in the field of popular culture analysis. There are specific and detailed technical and theoretical problems peculiar to television and film analysis, popular music, the study of lived cultures and the field of popular writings which no amount of general theorising might resolve. Likewise, questions concerning the relations between culture and class, culture and gender and culture and nation remain vexed and complex, requiring separate and detailed attention if progress is to be made. The value of the Gramscian theory of hegemony is that of providing an integrating framework within which both sets of issues might be addressed and worked through in relation to each other. By the same token, of course, it is liable to the criticism that it is too accommodating and expansive a framework, over-totalising in its analytical claims and ambit. The charge has certainly been made often enough, and it seems one likely to be pressed with increased vigour, particularly in the area of cultural studies.

For the moment, however, Gramsci's work constitutes a critical point of engagement for anyone interested in popular culture; certainly, it has been the most important single influence conditioning the organisation of this anthology and its main orientations. Viewed collectively, the various essays collected here examine a range of popular cultural forms and practices in the context of the varying social relations – principally those of class, gender and nation – which constitute the interacting fields of struggle within which such forms and practices are operative and have effects.

[. . .]

It's perhaps worth adding, in conclusion, that this collection avoids, and deliberately so, any attempt at apologetics. There are countless books which seek to justify, even dignify, the study of popular culture by claiming that popular culture is just as complex, as richly rewarding, historically exciting, and so on, as 'high culture'. It is not that the argument is wrong but that the constant *making* of it merely confirms the existing hierarchy of the arts in accepting the claim that 'high culture' constitutes a pre-given standard to which popular culture must measure up or be found wanting. Brecht gently satirised the logic of such comparisons in his story 'A Question of Taste'. A German, dining with a group of French artists and intellectuals who guy their visitor for the German penchant for idealist philosophies in contrast to the almost gastronomic materialism of the French, hesitates before praising the meal:

> The joint was excellent, a work of art. I was on the brink of saying so but feared they would ask me straight away if I could name one single German work of art that deserved to be called a joint of roast beef. Better stick to politics . . .[12]

Quite so.

Notes

1. While the term 'structuralism' has a more general currency, the concept of culturalism and the structuralism/culturalism polarity are mainly attributable to the collective work of the Centre for Contemporary Cultural Studies at the University of Birmingham. For the classic statement of this position, see S. Hall, 'Cultural studies: two paradigms', *Media, Culture and Society*, vol. 2, no. 1, 1980 (shortened version in T. Bennett *et al.* (eds), *Culture, Ideology and Social Process*, Batsford, London, 1981).
2. The heyday of structuralism, in this respect, is probably best represented by Umberto Eco's *The Role of the Reader*, Hutchinson, London, 1981 (first published in Italian in 1979). In addition to providing rigorous structuralist analyses of the ideological encoding of a range of popular texts (*Superman*, the James Bond novels, etc.), Eco's approach to the processes of reading is one in which such processes are conceived as entirely regulated by textual structures. For critical discussions of this aspect of Eco's work, see chapter 6 of T. de Lauretis, *Alice Doesn't: Feminism, Semiotics, Cinema*, Macmillan, London, 1984; and chapter 3 of T. Bennett and J. Woollacott, *Bond and Beyond: The political career of a popular hero*, Macmillan, London, 1986.
3. R. Parker and G. Pollock, *Old Mistresses: Women, art and ideology*, Pantheon Books, New York, 1982, p. 136.
4. The most pronounced recent example of this approach is David Harker's *One for the Money: Politics and popular song*, Hutchinson, London, 1980.

5. E. P. Thompson, *The Poverty of Theory, and Other Essays*, Merlin Press, London, 1978.

6. See, especially, A. Gramsci, *Selections from the Prison Notebooks*, Lawrence & Wishart, London, 1971. The more recent translation and publication of Gramsci's writings on culture and politics seems likely to strengthen the Gramscian influence on contemporary cultural theory; see A. Gramsci, *Selections from Cultural Writings*, Lawrence & Wishart, London, 1985.

7. For the most influential readings of Gramsci of this type, see E. Laclau, *Politics and Ideology in Marxist Theory*, New Left Books, London, 1977; and C. Mouffe, 'Hegemony and ideology in Gramsci', in C. Mouffe (ed.), *Gramsci and Marxist Theory*, Routledge & Kegan Paul, London, 1979.

8. There have, however, been a number of attempts recently to go beyond these 'outer limits', although whether the resulting formulations are meaningfully described as Marxist is debatable. See, for example, E. Laclau, 'Transformations of advanced industrial societies and the theory of the subject', in S. Hanninen and L. Paldán (eds), *Rethinking Ideology: A Marxist debate*, International General/IMMAC, New York, 1983.

9. The failure to appreciate this is one of the most conspicuous shortcomings of N. Abercrombie, S. Hill and B. S. Turner, *The Dominant Ideology Thesis*, George Allen & Unwin, London, 1980.

10. R. Gray, *The Labour Aristocracy in Victorian Edinburgh*, Clarendon Press, Oxford, 1976, p. 6.

11. See, for example, R. Gray, 'Left holding the flag', *Marxism Today*, vol. 25, no. 11, 1982.

12. B. Brecht, *Collected Short Stories*, Methuen, London, 1983, p. 185.

23 □ Rockin'
Hegemony: West Coast
Rock and Amerika's
War in Vietnam

John Storey

[...]

The West Coast Counterculture

> In Berkeley I found a culture in which rock and politics, music
> and the Movement, pleasure and action were inextricably
> linked.[1]

The West Coast counterculture was a social movement consisting of a variety of
predominantly middle-class cultural groupings – hippies, yippies, freaks, heads,
flower children, student radicals, etc. – who between 1965 and 1970 attempted to
establish a non-competitive, non-belligerent 'alternative' society.

It was a culture which came together on demonstrations, at love-ins, on marches
and, perhaps, most of all, at rock festivals. Despite its fluidity, it is possible to
distinguish between those who preferred the peace sign to the clenched fist, and
spoke about Amerika's war in Vietnam in terms of moral outrage, rather than as
a bloody example of American imperialism. The border separating the two groups
was often extremely fluid. Individuals often straddled both, or drifted from one side
to the other. At other times the differences became very marked. After the 'Spring
Mobilization to End the War in Vietnam' march in San Francisco, 15 April 1967,

From Louvre, A. and Walsh, J. (eds), *Tell Me Lies About Vietnam*, Open University Press,
Milton Keynes, 1988, pp. 181–97.

Country Joe McDonald of Country Joe and The Fish made the telling remark: 'Man, I learned one thing that afternoon. There's more than one revolution.'[2] Bands like Country Joe and The Fish, Jefferson Airplane, The Doors and the Byrds drifted from one side to the other. In the words of Iain Chambers, they 'vibrated between the harsh edges of American politics and the Utopian gestures of an alternative America'.[3] One has to be careful not to press this distinction too far. Too often this apparent rejection of politics has been misconstrued. What was usually being rejected was the conventional political structures and channels of American society. For example, before Crosby, Stills, Nash and Young played to the '15 November Moratorium Day' rally at San Francisco in 1969, Stephen Stills announced to the crowd: 'Politics is bullshit. Richard Nixon is bullshit. Spiro Agnew is bullshit. Our music *isn't* bullshit.'[4] Stills is not saying he is apolitical, only that he rejects conventional politics. He could hardly mean otherwise, the Moratorium being clearly a political event.

The counterculture developed around the colleges and universities of the West Coast. Student numbers had doubled between 1960 and 1966. The total student population was, by the mid-1960s, around six million. 'Students were so numerous', according to Abe Peck, 'that they seemed to constitute a new social class'.[5] This is in fact the argument Theodore Roszak makes in *The Making of a Counter Culture*:

> Just as the dark satanic mills of early industrialization concentrated labor and helped create the class-consciousness of the proletariat, so the university campus, where up to thirty thousand students may be gathered, has served to crystallize the group identity of the young – with the important effect of mingling freshmen of seventeen and eighteen with graduate students well away in their twenties.[6]

It is easy to dismiss the counterculture's 'revolution' as petty-bourgeois: idealist principles, Utopian visions, yet another example of a subversive Bohemian variant of bourgeois individualism.[7] While some of this is clearly recognizable, is the counterculture so easily dismissed? A great deal, for example, can be said for the general force of its Utopian politics. Its solutions may indeed have been inadequate, but it did highlight *real* problems, and help sustain *real* opposition to a *real* war.

The counterculture was certainly not beyond criticism: if it is true, as Antonio Gramsci insisted, that ruling groups cannot wholly and absolutely absorb and incorporate subordinate groups into the dominant order, it is also true that subordinate groups cannot drop out of the dominant order. Despite its claims to being an 'alternative' society the counterculture remained firmly sited in capitalist America, subjected to its rules and regulations. Certainly, at times, the connection seemed near to breaking point. But the tension soon eased, the profits flowed and the counterculture withered.

West Coast Rock: Resistance

> Rock music must not be seen apart from the movement among
> young people to reshape their lives. . . . As such it is a
> profoundly *political* form of music, one that opts for a
> different form of social organization, one that lets people love
> rather than makes them go to war.[8]

West Coast rock was the product of men and women who had started out as folk
musicians. Around 1965, following the example of Bob Dylan, they electrified their
instruments.[9] The Byrds had formed in 1964, but it was only with their recording
of Dylan's 'Mr Tambourine Man' in 1965 that they began to exist as anything other
than a collection of folk musicians. Country Joe and The Fish, The Doors, the Great
Society, Jefferson Airplane, and the Warlocks (who changed their name to The
Grateful Dead in 1966) all emerged in 1965. Early the following year, they were
joined by Buffalo Springfield and Big Brother and The Holding Company. In 1968,
as the West Coast counterculture crumbled, its first and last 'supergroup' was
formed, Crosby, Stills and Nash, becoming in 1969 Crosby, Stills, Nash and Young.

West Coast rock's folk heritage was never simply a question of music, more a way
of looking at the world and the significance of music in it. A general sense that music
was politics by other means was carried over from the folk circuit. This can be
clearly heard for example in Country Joe McDonald's 'I-Feel-Like-I'm-Fixin'-To-Die
Rag', undoubtedly the best anti-war song produced by the counterculture. Using
irony and hyperbole, the war effort is presented as a distorted extension of the
American Dream. The result is a song which holds up to ridicule the ugly triumvirate
of capitalism, imperialism and war.

Another influence, carried over from folk music, was the belief that they belonged
to an alternative community rather than an entertainment industry. For the political
folk singers music had been a means of class mobilization, of organization, the muse
of solidarity. For the counterculture it was the central and unique mode of political
and cultural expression. Put simply, the culture was built around the music. It was
the means by which it discovered and reproduced itself. Rather than mass meetings
and rallies, its organizing events were festivals and dances. Its 'coming out' party
took place at the 'A Tribute to Doctor Strange' dance held in San Francisco on 16
October 1965. Significantly, the same day marked the first big West Coast
demonstration against Amerika's war in Vietnam, the Berkeley Vietnam Day
Committee march to the navy installation at Oakland. The Doctor Strange dance
featured Jefferson Airplane, the march was 'entertained' by the band that was soon
to become Country Joe and The Fish, The Instant Action Jug Band. Luria Castell,
one of the organizers of the Doctor Strange dance, told Ralph Gleason, music critic
with the *San Francisco Chronicle*, 'Music is the most beautiful way to communicate,
it's the way we're going to change things.'[10] Gleason, who attended the dance,
described it as 'a hippie happening, which signified the linkage of the political and
social hip movements'.[11]

West Coast rock addressed its audience as members, or potential members, of an 'alternative' society. Part of the sense of belonging involved an attitude to the Vietnam War. Without exception all the major musicians of the counterculture performed material opposing the war in Vietnam. The prevalence of this anti-war feeling was such that in the context of the counterculture all songs were in a sense against the war. What I mean is this: the fact that Country Joe and The Fish, for example, performed songs against the war was enough to make all their songs seem implicitly against the war.

Opposition to the war was the central articulating principle of the counterculture. (I use articulate here in its double sense, meaning both to express and to make connections.) Music expressed the attitudes and values of the counterculture, while at the same time constituting and reproducing its values. Beneath a variety of slogans – 'Make Love, Not War' being, perhaps, the most famous – it engaged in a counter-hegemonic struggle over the meaning of the war. West Coast rock provided *counter-explanations* of the war and the draft. It helped set limits on the ability of *Johnson–Nixon Amerika* to sustain its war in Vietnam. At its most powerful its Utopian politics produced a cultural practice in which the present could be judged from the perspective of an alternative future. 'Unknown Soldier', for example, by The Doors is a song very much in this Utopian mode. The song fades to the sound of celebratory bells and a jubilant voice proclaiming that 'The war is over'. This is classic education of desire: the depiction of an imagined situation in order to produce the desire for such a situation in actuality.[12]

The fact that the West Coast musicians were, in the main, of the same class, age and race (white, middle-class and under 25) as their audience reinforced their links to the counterculture. As Paul Kanter put it, referring both to Jefferson Airplane and the wider counterculture: 'We're middle-class kids. We're spoiled and we're selfish and some of that hangs over. That's the way you grow up.'[13] Despite, or perhaps as a consequence of, its class origins,[14] the counterculture attempted to overturn commercial pop's ideal of music as a private one-to-one experience. It insisted instead that music should be a collective event. Its favourite pronoun was 'we', its favourite adverb 'together'. Perhaps the band which most epitomized this spirit was Jefferson Airplane. Songs such as 'Volunteers' and 'We Can Be Together' perfectly illustrate this ideal.

West Coast rock advocated and articulated a culture in which the distance between producer and consumer was minimal. After the Doctor Strange dance, Paul Kantner made the following remark: 'It was like a party. The audience often far overshadowed any of the bands, and the distance between the two was not that great. Grace used to say that the stage was just the least crowded place to stand'.[15] This is a view shared by Ralph Gleason. On the Golden Gate free festivals: 'At the Free Fairs you could see people like the Jefferson Airplane wandering around, just members of the crowd like anyone else, enjoying themselves. For the first time to my knowledge, an emerging mass entertainment style insisted that its leading figures were human beings.'[16] And on the Doctor Strange dance: 'That night you couldn't tell the bands from the people. It was obvious that the bands represented the community itself.'[17] Jim Morrison of The Doors expressed the relationship thus: 'A Doors concert is a public meeting called by us for a special kind of dramatic discussion and entertainment.... When we perform, we're participating in the creation of a world, and we celebrate that creation with the audience.'[18] As I have already indicated, the West Coast bands regarded their songs as ideological ambassadors, winning the world to the ways of the counterculture. As Grace Slick told Ralph Gleason, 'Music makes it easier to get your ideas across...being anti-war, music is a pleasant way of getting your ideas across.'[19] The musicians' assumption of this role, and the audiences' acceptance that they were in fact playing such a role, gives the bands a striking resemblance to Gramsci's concept of the organic intellectual.[20] Because we are in the main speaking of bands rather than individuals, we must modify Gramsci's concept and speak of *collective* organic intellectuals. A good example of how this worked in practice can be heard in Buffalo Springfield's 'For What It's Worth', a song inspired by an early clash between the police and the counterculture: the breaking up of a peaceful anti-war demonstration in Los Angeles. The song does not simply narrate events, but offers a warning about the possible cost of commitment to the counterculture for example:

> There's something happenin' here
> What it is ain't exactly clear
> There's a man with a gun over there
> Tellin' me I've got to beware
> I think it's time we STOP, children
> What's that sound?
> Everybody look what's goin' down.

Another example is 'Draft Morning' by the Byrds. The song interrogates the 'draft' both lyrically and musically. It poses the question: 'Why should it happen?' within a musical structure which plays the cacophony of war against the peace and tranquillity of a West Coast morning.

Other examples could be cited. But to repeat my argument, the point I am making is this: opposition to the war was genuine as articulated by the major West Coast bands at the centre of the counterculture. They were not following fashions and fads, but functioning as collective organic intellectuals, articulating one of the culture's chief organizing principles; Amerika's war in Vietnam was wrong and, therefore, involvement should be opposed and resisted.

West Coast Rock: Incorporation

West Coast rock was a music which had developed from the 'bottom' up, and not a music imposed from the 'top' down. But like all popular cultural initiatives under capitalism, it faced three possible futures: marginalization, disappearance, or incorporation into the system's profit-making concerns. Countercultural rock's future was incorporation. By 1968, Michael Phillips, the vice-president of the Bank of California, was claiming that all the indications were that rock was destined to become the fourth most important industry in San Francisco. What had started as a celebration of 'flowers that grow so incredibly high'[21] was being highjacked by those who 'Cultivate their flows to be/ Nothing more than something/ They invest in.'[22]

As I said earlier, the counterculture regarded its rock musicians as part of the community. To remain representative of the community they had to remain *part* of the community. It followed from this that involvement with the music industry was greeted with great suspicion (at least initially) by audience and artists alike. Commercial success threatened to break the links with the community. The problem was this: in order to make records musicians, however alternative, have to engage with capitalism in the form of the private ownership of the industry. If you want to continue making records you have to continue making profits. Your audience is no longer the community, but the marketplace. Moreover, musicians have no control over the use of profits, a fact that shocked Keith Richard of the Rolling Stones:

> We found out, and it wasn't for years that we did, that all the bread we made for Decca was going into making black boxes that go into American Air Force bombers to bomb fucking North Vietnam. They took the bread we made for them and put it into the radar section of their business. When we found that out, it blew our minds. That was it. Goddam, you find out you've helped kill God knows how many thousands of people without even knowing it.[23]

Such revelations pointed to a basic contradiction at the heart of the counterculture's music. On the one hand, it could inspire people to resist the draft and organize against the war, while on the other, it made profits which could be used to support the war effort.

While Jefferson Airplane sang 'All your private property/ Is target for your enemy/ And your enemy/ Is *We*' RCA made money. In other words, the proliferation of Jefferson Airplane's anti-capitalist politics increased the profits of their capitalist record company. This is a clear example of the process Gramsci called hegemony: the way dominant groups in society negotiate oppositional voices on to a terrain which secures for the dominant groups a continued position of leadership.[24] West Coast rock was not denied expression, but its expression was *articulated* in the economic interests of the capitalist music industry. It was a paradox record companies were more than happy to live with. By 1968 they had well and truly caught up with the spirit of the counterculture and had started marketing its music under slogans such as 'The revolutionaries are on Columbia,/ The man can't bust our music (Columbia),/ It's happening on Capital,/ Psychedelia – the sound of the NOW generation (MGM).' This kind of language even penetrated the 'business' side of the industry. The 1968 ABC distributors conference was held under the snappy slogan 'Turn On To Profit Power'. And they certainly did – profits flowed. Between 1965 and 1970, US record sales increased from $862 million to $1660 million.[25]

The changing nature of the counterculture's rock festivals provides another telling narrative of its incorporation and defusion. The first festivals took place between 1965 and 1967. They were free open-air concerts held in Golden Gate Park, San Francisco, with attendance ranging from 10,000 to 15,000 people. The Human Be-In, held on 14 January 1967, attracted 20,000 people. Besides inspiring Jefferson Airplane to write 'Won't You Try/Saturday Afternoon', and the Byrds to write 'Tribal Gathering', the event also inspired the Monterey Pop Festival (16–18 June 1967), the first 'commercial' countercultural festival of any note. The festival was intended as a countercultural happening, a display not just of its music, but its values. It was billed as 'Three days of music, love and flowers'. The intended tone was struck by David Crosby, then of the Byrds, who spoke against Amerika's war in Vietnam and in praise of the wonders of LSD. What it became, however, was a showcase for the A&R men (they usually were men); a marketplace for the purchase of profit-making talent. On the bill were Country Joe and The Fish, The Byrds, Big Brother and The Holding Company, Jefferson Airplane, Jimi Hendrix, etc. They played for expenses only, the profits supposedly going to finance free clinics and ghetto music programmes. A total of 175,000 attended, $500,000 was raised but, apparently, and unfortunately, the money went astray.[26]

Two years later, on 15 August 1969, Woodstock happened. Only 50,000 were expected, but 500,000 turned up. Woodstock is usually regarded as the greatest achievement of the counterculture. It was a new beginning. Not a festival, but a *nation*. All this optimism is present in Joni Mitchell's song 'Woodstock', recorded by Crosby, Stills, Nash and Young in 1970: 'I dreamed I saw the bomber death planes/ Riding shotgun in the sky/ Turning into butterflies/ Above our nation.'

The optimism soon faded. If Woodstock was the beginning of anything it was the beginning of the realization that the 'political' wing of the counterculture was now very much the junior partner in the movement. This knowledge had, perhaps, already been grasped after the events in Chicago the year before. It is surely significant that the yippies managed to attract only 10,000 to lobby the 'Demokratic Death Convention', while the organizers of Woodstock attracted 500,000. This point was compounded when Abbie Hoffman, while trying to make an appeal on behalf of the imprisoned White Panther John Sinclair, was knocked from the stage by Pete Townsend of the Who. Where Hoffman failed, others had some success. Country Joe McDonald got the audience to join him in a 'fuck-the-war' chant. Not satisfied with this, midway through his solo performance of 'I-Feel-Like-I'm-Fixin'-To-Die Rag', he appealed for more commitment from the crowd: 'Listen, people, I don't know how you expect to ever stop the war if you can't sing any better than that. There's about 300,000 of you fuckers out there. I want you to start singing. Come on!'

Besides revealing the divisions within the culture, the festival again showed the extent to which the counterculture was open to commercialization. While those on stage celebrated the size of the counterculture's community, the record companies celebrated the size of the rock market. Monterey had been viewed by the industry as a showcase for new talent. Woodstock was a successful exercise in market research.

Liberation News Service called Woodstock 'a victory for the businessmen who make a profit by exploiting youth culture'.[27] Bill Graham, ex-manager of Jefferson Airplane, made a similar comment: 'The real thing that Woodstock accomplished was that it told people that rock was big business.'[28]

If the revelations about Woodstock were not exactly the end of the counterculture, December 1969 seemed very much like it. On 1 December the draft lottery was introduced.[29] According to Abe Peck, this had immediate results: 'Many of those who'd protested because the war wasn't worth *their* lives now held numbers keyed to their birthdates that were high enough to keep them civilians, and many now said goodbye to the Movement.'[30] Worse was to follow: the first eight days of December witnessed the indictment of Charles Manson and his 'family' in Los Angeles for murder. The charges were heard amidst, to quote San Francisco's 'underground' paper *Good Times*, 'a public frenzy of hate and fear not only against Manson but also against communes and longhairs in general'.[31] *Rolling Stone* even felt obliged to pose the question: 'Is Manson a hippie?'[32]

The event, however, which perhaps hurt the counterculture the most happened on 6 December at the Altamont Speedway, outside San Francisco. While the Rolling Stones performed, Meredith Hunter, an 18-year-old black youth, was stabbed and beaten to death less than twenty feet from where Mick Jagger was dancing and singing. Hunter had sixteen stab wounds and various head abrasions, resulting from kicks. Earlier the same day, Hell's Angels had attacked another black youth. Marty Balin of Jefferson Airplane had gone to his assistance, only to be beaten unconscious.

With the counterculture in disarray, many who had dropped out of Amerika now considered dropping back in. The dilemma is dramatized in David Crosby's wonderful mixture of humour and paranoia 'Almost Cut My Hair'. In Crosby's song, loyalty to the counterculture overcomes the temptation to cut and run.

Coercion, the other side of the consent-winning strategies of hegemony, further limited options as the new decade began. On 4 May 1970 four students demonstrating at Kent State University against Nixon's further escalation of the war into Cambodia were shot dead by National Guardsmen. Other demonstrators were met with similar violence. Twelve students at the State University of New York were wounded by shotgun blasts. Nine students at the University of New Mexico were bayonetted. Two students were killed and twelve others wounded at Jackson State University. Nixon's response was to call anti-war students 'these bums, you know, blowing up campuses'.[33] Crosby, Stills, Nash and Young's response was the Neil Young song 'Ohio'.[34] It begins: 'Tin Soldiers and Nixon comin'/ We're finally on our own/ This summer I hear the drumming/ Four dead in Ohio.'

West Coast rock acted as both a symbol and a focal point of the counterculture's opposition to *Amerika*'s war in Vietnam. Of course the music alone could not stop the war; West Coast rock's achievement was to help to hold together a culture which made the making of war in Vietnam that much more difficult to justify in America.

Legacies

The collapse of the West Coast counterculture following the incorporation of its music, and the ending of the war, brought about an inevitable decrease in music relating to the conflict.

In the 1980s, two contradictory impulses have led to something of a revival: (i) the new political climate making Vietnam something of which to be 'proud', rather than 'ashamed'; and (ii) the view that US policy in Central America is laying the basis for a new Vietnam.

The new political climate has undoubtedly created an audience for the music of the Vietnam veterans. Men such as Michael Martin and Tim Holiday, who got back from Vietnam only to go back there every night, 'Torn between the need to remember/ And the good reasons to forget'.[35] Such music is beginning to be heard after the silences and historical amnesia of the past decade. The process has undoubtedly been helped by the success of Bruce Springsteen's 'Born in the USA'. Bob Dylan has also broken his silence on the war. On *Empire Burlesque* (1985), 'Clean Cut Kid' tells of the difficulties faced by the returning veteran.

What is interesting about Springsteen's work on the war is how it is for him a means of talking about the present. 'Born in the USA' is as much a song about working under US capitalism as it is a song about the problems of a Vietnam veteran. On a promotional video for his recent cover version of Edwin Starr's 'War' (1986), Springsteen again mobilizes the war to talk about contemporary America. This time the focus is on American involvement in Nicaragua. The video opens with a shot of a father and son watching a TV news report of the fighting in Vietnam. As Springsteen begins to introduce the song, we see a montage of shots linking what happened in Vietnam with what is happening in Nicaragua today. Springsteen's voice provides a commentary on the images:

> If you grew up in the sixties, you grew up with war on TV every night, a war that your friends were involved in. . . . I wanna do this song tonight for all the young people out there. . . . The next time they're going to be looking at you, and you're going to need a lot of information to know what you're going to want to do. Because in 1985, blind faith in your leaders or in anything will get you killed. What I'm talking about here is *War* . . .

Springsteen then does a very powerful 'live' version of Starr's classic anti-war song. As the music fades we see again the room in which father and son watched the news report from Vietnam; the reports are still coming, only now the father watches alone. Springsteen's song and video offers a counter-explanation of events in Central America. When he says to his audience 'You're going to need a lot of information', we hear an echo of the politics and practices of the West Coast counterculture. The situation is of course very different. Not just a different war, but a different audience – a market, rather than an 'alternative' community. Moreover, Springsteen is expressing his personal political concerns (not, of course, unshared), rather than articulating the views of an active and organized collectivity.

Notes

1. Simon Frith, *Sound Effects: Youth, leisure, and the politics of rock*, London: Constable, 1983, p. 4.
2. Quoted in Abe Peck, *Uncovering The Sixties: The life and times of the Underground press*, New York: Pantheon Books, 1985, p. 61.
3. Iain Chambers, *Urban Rhythms: Pop music and popular culture*, London: Macmillan, 1985, p. 94.
4. Quoted in Serge R. Denisoff, *Sing a Song of Social Significance*, Ohio: Bowling Green University Press, 1972, p. 157.
5. *Uncovering the Sixties: The life and times of the Underground press*, p. 20. In addition to this, for most of the 1960s, 50 per cent of the population was under 25 years of age. The counterculture thus had a very large constituency to which to appeal.
6. Theodore Roszak, *The Making of a Counter Culture*, London: Faber & Faber, 1971. p. 28.
7. See Richard Middleton and John Muncie, 'Pop culture, pop music and post-war youth: countercultures', in *Popular*, Culture Block 5, Unit 20, Milton Keynes: Open University Press, 1981, p. 88.
8. Jonathan Eisen (ed.), *The Age of Rock: Sounds of the American cultural revolution*, New York: Vintage Books, 1969, p. xiv.
9. Dylan material was the starting point for most of the West Coast musicians who electrified their instruments in the mid-1960s. His own anti-war songs – 'Masters of War', 'A Hard Rain's A-Gonna Fall', 'With God on our Side' and 'Blowin' in the Wind' – undoubtedly encouraged the counterculture's own attitude. It is difficult to exaggerate Dylan's influence.
10. Quoted in Ralph Gleason, *The Jefferson Airplane and the San Francisco Sound*, New York: Ballantine Books, 1969, p. 3.
11. *Ibid.*, p. 6.
12. The Doors' Utopian politics did not lose sight of the horrors of the present: 'Unknown Soldier' was promoted with a film of Morrison spewing blood.
13. Quoted in *The Jefferson Airplane and the San Francisco Sound*, p. 131.
14. The Utopian Marxist William Morris understood this possibility more than most. Commenting on his own privileged background, he wrote: 'I daresay that you will find some of my visions strange enough. One reason which will make some of you think them strange is a sad and shameful one. I have always belonged to the well-to-do classes and was born into luxury, so that necessarily I ask much more of the future than many of you do.' Quoted in Perry Anderson, *Arguments Within English Marxism*, London: Verso, 1980, p. 163.
15. Quoted in Gene Sculatti and Davin Seay, *San Francisco Nights: The psychedelic music trip, 1965–1968*, London: Sidgwick & Jackson, 1985, p. 48.

16. *The Jefferson Airplane and the San Francisco Sound*, p. 38.

17. *Ibid.*, p. 9.

18. Quoted in Lee Baxandall (ed.), *Radical Perspectives in the Arts*, Harmondsworth: Penguin, 1972, p. 386.

19. *The Jefferson Airplane and the San Francisco Sound*, p. 159.

20. According to Gramsci, social groups always produce their own organic intellectuals, men and women whose function is to provide 'leadership of a cultural and general ideological nature'. See Antonio Gramsci, *Selections from Prison Notebooks*, London: Lawrence & Wishart, 1971, p. 150.

21. John Lennon's 'Lucy in the Sky with Diamonds' on The Beatles' *Sergeant Pepper's Lonely Hearts Club Band*.

22. 'Its Alright, Ma (I'm Only Bleeding)'. This is the published version in Bob Dylan's *Writings and Drawings*, London: Panther, 1974, and not the one performed on *Bringing It All Back Home*.

23. Quoted in Dave Harker, *One For the Money: Politics and popular song*, London: Hutchinson, 1980, p. 103.

24. There is a vast amount of literature on Gramsci's key concept. Tony Bennett *et al.* (eds), *Culture, Ideology and Social Process* (Milton Keynes: Open University Press, 1981), provides a good introduction. See also Tony Bennett, 'Introduction: popular culture and "the return to Gramsci"', in *Popular Culure and Social Relations* (ed. Tony Bennett *et al.*) Milton Keynes: Open University Press, 1986 and Chapter 23 above.

25. See *One For the Money: Politics and popular song*, p. 223.

26. The Grateful Dead saw the festival as a 'sell out' of the counterculture's values. They refused to attend, and instead played for free outside the event.

27. Quoted in Jon Weiner, *Come Together: John Lennon in his time*, London: Faber & Faber, 1985, p. 103.

28. *Ibid.*, p. 104.

29. The Congressional Quarterly Almanac explained the new system thus: 'Under the new induction system the period of prime draft eligibility is reduced from seven to one year. A registrant's period of maximum eligibility begins on his nineteenth birthday and ends on his twentieth. Men not drafted during these twelve months are assigned a lower priority and would be called up only in an emergency.'

30. *Uncovering the Sixties: The life and times of the Underground press*, p. 200.

31. *Ibid.*, p. 227.

32. *Ibid.*

33. Quoted in *Come Together: John Lennon in his time*, p. 135.

34. 'Ohio' was released within twenty-four hours of the killings. Neil Young now introduces it in concerts as 'an old folk song'.

35. My knowledge of Martin and Holiday's work derives from two demo tapes sent to the EVAC project by Lydia Fish, State University College, Buffalo.

24 ☐ *Pleasurable Negotiations*

Christine Gledhill

This essay takes as its starting-point the recent renewal of feminist interest in mainstream popular culture. Whereas the ideological analysis of the late 1970s and early 1980s, influenced by poststructuralism and cine-psychoanalysis, had rejected mainstream cinema for its production of patriarchal/bourgeois spectatorship and simultaneous repression of femininity, other approaches, developing in parallel, and sometimes in opposition to, psychoanalytic theories argued for socioculturally differentiated modes of meaning production and reading.[1] Feminist analysis has focused in particular on forms directed at women. While feminist literary criticism recovers women's fiction – both Victorian and contemporary, written by women and/or for women – feminist work on film and television has particularly explored the woman's film, melodrama and soap opera.[2] A frequent aim of this enterprise, which relates commonly derided popular forms to the conditions of their consumption in the lives of sociohistorically constituted audiences, is to elucidate women's cultural forms, and thereby to challenge the male canon of cultural worth. In this respect, feminist analysis of the woman's film and soap opera is beginning to counter more negative cine-psychoanalytic views of female spectatorship.

Cine-psychoanalysis and Feminism

The theoretical convergence of psychoanalysis and cinema has been problematic for feminism in that it has been theorized largely from the perspective of masculinity and its constructions. Notions of cinematic voyeurism and fetishism serve as norms for the analysis of classic narrative cinema, and early cine-psychoanalysis found it difficult to theorize the feminine as anything other than 'lack', 'absence', 'otherness'. Underpinning these concepts lay the homology uncovered between certain features of cinematic spectatorship and textual organization, and the Oedipal psycho-linguistic scenario theorized by Jacques Lacan in which the child simultaneously

From Pribram, D. (ed.), *Female Spectators*, Verso, London, 1988, pp. 64–89.

acquires identity, language and the Unconscious.[3] In this structure, the child's perception of sexual difference as the maternal figure's castration and the consequent repression of this perception are linked to the similarly hidden role of phonological and linguistic difference in the operation of language and production of meaning (it is the difference between 't' and 'd' that enables the formation of different words, and the difference between 'sheep' and 'mutton' that enables meaning to arise from such linguistic forms). This homology between the psychic and the linguistic, it is argued, enables the (male) child both to enter the symbolic order and to master language. It also, however, results in the repression of femininity. Thus the patriarchal subject is constructed as a unified, consistent, but illusory identity – a 'self' whose words appear to give it control of a world to which it is central. (In this respect, the identity of the patriarchal subject coalesces with the centrality of the 'individual' in bourgeois ideology.) Underlying these constructs there exists another reality – language and subjectivity as processes that produce each other, ever in flux, and based in linguistic and psychic 'difference'. Self, speech and meaning can never coincide with each other and fail to provide more than the illusion of mastery. For both bourgeois and patriarchal subjects, 'difference' – gender, sex, class, race, age, and so on – is alienated as 'otherness' and repressed. The repressed threatens to return, however, through the processes of the 'Unconscious'.

According to cine-psychoanalysis, classic narrative cinema reproduces such psycholinguistic and ideological structures, offering the surface illusion of unity, plenitude and identity as compensation for the underlying realities of separation and difference.[4] The subject of mainstream narrative is the patriarchal, bourgeois individual: that unified, centred point from which the world is organized and given meaning. Narrative organization hierarchizes the different aesthetic and ideological discourses which intersect in the processes of the text, to produce a unifying, authoritative voice or viewpoint. This is the position – constructed outside the processes of contradiction, difference and meaning production – which the spectator must occupy in order to participate in the pleasures and meaning of the text.

Since in this argument narrative organization is patriarchal, the spectator constructed by the text is masculine. Pleasure is largely organized to flatter or console the patriarchal ego and its Unconscious. Simultaneous sublimation and repression of femininity is literally re-enacted in the way plot and camera place the female figure in situations of fetishistic idealization or voyeuristic punishment. This has led to the argument that female representations do not represent women at all, but are figures cut to the measure of the patriarchal Unconscious. In particular the 'look' of the camera – mediated through the 'gaze' of a generally male hero – has been identified as male.[5] While these arguments have attracted feminists for their power to explain the alternate misogyny and idealization of cinema's female representations, they offer largely negative accounts of female spectatorship, suggesting colonized, alienated or masochistic positions of identification. Moreover, given the absorption of class struggle within patriarchal narrative structures – the textual spectator is a trans-class construct – this perspective has difficulty in dealing with the female image or spectator in terms of class difference.

While the theoretical gap between textual and social subject may seem unproblematic when considering male spectatorship – perhaps because the account of
the male spectator fits our experience of the social subject – this distinction is crucial
for feminist criticism, with its investment in cultural and political change for women
in society. The psycholinguistic location of the feminine in the repressed semiotic
processes of signification leads to the advocacy of the 'feminine' avant-garde or the
'deconstructive' text as a means of countering the patriarchal mainstream. Such
works, it is argued, counteract the power of the classic narrative text to reduce the
play of semiotic and sexual difference to the 'fixed position' and 'identity' of the
patriarchal subject. The avant-garde or deconstructive text foregrounds the means
of its construction, refuses stable points of identification, puts 'the subject into
process' and invites the spectator into a play with language, form and identity. The
more politically tendentious work literally 'deconstructs' the text, taking it apart to
expose the mechanisms of mainstream narrative.[6] However, such procedures do
not, in my view, avoid the problems of positioning. While the political avant-garde
audience deconstructs the pleasures and identities offered by the mainstream text,
it participates in the comforting identity of critic or *cognoscente*, positioned in the
sphere of 'the ideologically correct', and the 'radical' – a position which is defined
by its difference from the ideological mystification attributed to the audiences of the
mass media. This suggests that the political problem is not positioning as such, but
which positions are put on offer, or audiences enter into.

Recent initiatives in feminist film theory – drawing on the work of feminist
psychoanalysts and social psychologists such as Luce Irigary, Julia Kristeva, Nancy
Chodorow and Dorothy Dinnerstein – have made possible considerable revisions to
the cine-psychoanalytic construction of the classic narrative text, facilitating
attempts to take account of the 'female spectator'.[7] However, as Annette Kuhn
points out, this work draws on theoretically divergent analytical approaches.
'Female spectatorship' elides conceptually distinct notions: the 'feminine spectator',
constructed by the text, and the female audience, constructed by the sociohistorical
categories of gender, class, race, and so on.[8] The question now confronting
feminist theory is how to conceive their relationship.

One approach to the problem of their elision is to question the identification of
mainstream narrative structures with patriarchal/bourgeois ideology on which it is
based. For while avant-garde practices may produce a spectator 'fixed' in the avant-
garde, recent work suggests that the textual possibilities of resistant or deconstructive reading exist in the processes of the mainstream text. To pursue this
avenue, however, we require a theory of texts which can also accommodate the
historical existence of social audiences. For 'femininity' is not simply an abstract
textual position; and what women's history tells us about femininity lived as a
socioculturally, as well as a psychically differentiated, category must have
consequences for our understanding of the formation of feminine subjectivity, of the
feminine textual spectator and the viewing/reading of female audiences. Work on
women's cultural forms, female audiences and female spectatorship poses this
problem in acute form.

Culture as Negotiation

Arguments which support the notion of a specific, sociohistorically constructed female cultural space come from diverse intellectual contexts and traditions and do not yet form a coherent theory. A range of concepts have been drawn on, including subcultural reading, cultural competence, decoding position, and so on. A notion frequently deployed in various contexts is that of 'negotiation'.[9] It is the purpose of this piece to suggest that this concept might take a central place in rethinking the relations between media products, ideologies and audiences – perhaps bridging the gap between textual and social subject. The value of this notion lies in its avoidance of an overly deterministic view of cultural production, whether economistic (the media product reflects dominant economic interests outside the text), or cine-psychoanalytic (the text constructs spectators through the psycholinguistic mechanisms of the patriarchal Unconscious). For the term 'negotiation' implies the holding together of opposite sides in an ongoing process of give-and-take. As a model of meaning production, negotiation conceives cultural exchange as the intersection of processes of production and reception, in which overlapping but non-matching determinations operate. Meaning is neither imposed, nor passively imbibed, but arises out of a struggle or negotiation between competing frames of reference, motivation and experience. This can be analysed at three different levels: institutions, texts and audiences – although distinctions between levels are ones of emphasis, rather than of rigid separation.

A theory of 'negotiation' as a tool for analysing meaning production would draw on a number of tenets of neo-Marxism, semiotics and psychoanalysis, while at the same time challenging the textual determinism and formalism of these approaches in the ideological analyses of the 1970s. In place of 'dominant ideology' – with its suggestion either of conspiratorial imposition or of unconscious interpellation – the concept of 'hegemony', as developed by Antonio Gramsci, underpins the model of negotiation.[10] According to Gramsci, since ideological power in bourgeois society is as much a matter of persuasion as of force, it is never secured once and for all, but has continually to be re-established in a constant to and fro between contesting groups. 'Hegemony' describes the ever shifting, ever negotiating play of ideological, social and political forces through which power is maintained and contested. The culture industries of bourgeois democracy can be conceptualized in a similar way: ideologies are not simply imposed – although this possibility always remains an institutional option through mechanisms such as censorship – but are subject to continuous (re-)negotiation.

Institutional Negotiations

The economics and ideologies of the 'free market' produce a contradictory situation which lays capitalist production open to the necessity of negotiation. Terry Lovell argues that the search for new markets requires new products, exchanged for a range of ever-extending use-values.[11] But these values vary according to particular groups of users and contexts of use. Even consumer products such as cars or washing-machines, which might seem predictable and amenable to ideological control (through advertising, for instance), may have unforeseen social and cultural uses for specific social groups.[12] If this is true of consumer products, then the use-values of media texts (which lie in a complex of pleasures and meanings operating at different levels – aesthetic, emotional, ideological, intellectual) are far less easily predicted and controlled. Thus the use-value to a particular group of a profitable (in the short term) media product may be in contradiction with the ideologies which in the long term maintain capitalism. An obvious example of this is the publishing industry, for certain branches of which Marxist and feminist books make profitable commodities.

Negotiation at the point of production is not, however, simply a matter of potential contradiction between the needs of the media industries and user groups. Within media institutions, the professional and aesthetic practices of 'creative' personnel operate within different frameworks from, and often in conflict with, the economic or ideological purposes of companies and shareholders. Such conflict is, indeed, part of the ideology of creativity itself. Aesthetic practice includes, as well as formal and generic traditions, codes of professional and technical performance, of cultural value and, moreover, must satisfy the pressure towards contemporary renewal and innovation. These traditions, codes and pressures produce their own conflicts which media professionals must attempt to solve.

An example of the kind of negotiation provoked by the inherent contradictoriness of the media industries is offered in Julie D'Acci's chronicle of struggles over the American television series *Cagney and Lacey* between CBS network executives and their advertisers, its independent writing/producing team (two women friends, plus a husband) and sections of the American women's movement.[13] According to D'Acci, the series would not have originated without the public spread of ideas circulated by the women's movement – with which the producing trio identified and which could be called on in times of trouble to support the programme. What made the series saleable was not its incipient 'feminism', but the innovation of a female buddy pairing in the cop show – an idea inspired by Molly Haskell's critique of the 1960s–1970s male buddy movie for its displacement of good female roles.[14] The series, however, despite successful ratings and an Emmy award, had been under frequent threat of cancellation from CBS, in large part, D'Acci argues, because of the problematic definitions of 'woman' and female sexuality that it invokes, particularly in relation to the unmarried Christine Cagney, whose fierce independence and intense relation to another woman have led to three changes of actress in an effort to bring the series under control and reduce the charge of lesbianism – something such strategies have singularly failed to do.

Textual Negotiations

The example of *Cagney and Lacey* suggests how the product itself becomes a site of textual negotiation. Contradictory pressures towards programming that is both recognizably familiar (that conforms to tradition, to formal or generic convention) and also innovative and realistic (offering a twist on, or modernizing, traditional genres) leads to complex technical, formal and ideological negotiations in mainstream media texts. For example, the decision by the makers of *Cagney and Lacey* to put a female buddy pair inside a cop series, as well as using gender reversal to breathe new life into an established genre, immediately raises aesthetic and ideological problems. Conflicting codes of recognition are demanded by the different generic motifs and stereotypes drawn into the series: the cop show, the buddy relationship, the woman's film, the independent heroine. Moreover, the female 'buddy' relationship can be 'realistically' constructed only by drawing on the subcultural codes of women's social intercourse and culture. Inside a soap opera, such codes are taken for granted. Inside a police series, however, they have a range of consequences for both genre and ideology. When female protagonists have to operate in a fictional world organized by male authority and criminality, gender conflict is inevitable. But the series could not evoke such gender conflict with any credibility if it did not acknowledge discourses about sexism already made public by the women's movement in America. Such discourses in their turn become an inevitable source of drama and ideological explanation. The plotting of *Cagney and Lacey* is itself made out of a negotiation, or series of negotiations, around definitions of gender roles and sexuality, definitions of heterosexual relations and female friendships, as well as around the nature of the law and policing.

Crucial to such a conception of the text are the semiotic notions of textual production, work and process. According to this perspective, meanings are not fixed entities to be deployed at the will of a communicator, but products of textual interactions shaped by a range of economic, aesthetic and ideological factors that often operate unconsciously, are unpredictable and difficult to control.

Reception as Negotiation

To the institutional and aesthetic vagaries of production is added the frequent diminution of textual control at the third level of media analysis – reception. The viewing or reading situation affects the meanings and pleasures of a work by introducing into the cultural exchange a range of determinations, potentially resistant or contradictory, arising from the differential social and cultural constitution of readers or viewers – by class, gender, race, age, personal history, and so on. This is potentially the most radical moment of negotiation, because the most variable and unpredictable. Moreover, we are not dealing with solitary viewers or readers. Ien Ang and Janice Radway, writing respectively on soap opera viewing and romance reading, discuss viewing and reading as a social practice, which differs between groups and historical periods and shapes the meanings which audiences derive from cultural products. This line of argument points beyond textual analysis, to the field of anthropological and ethnographic work with 'real' audiences.[15]

A frequent aim of this research is to rescue the female subcultural activity, resistance and pleasure that may be embedded in popular, mainstream culture. However, to start from the perspective of audiences and their putative pleasures is not without problems of its own. Such an approach is open to charges of relativism – in other words, there is no point to ideological analysis because meaning is so dependent on variable contexts. Or it may be accused of populism – a media product cannot be critiqued if audiences demonstrably enjoy it.[16] Counter-readings of popular texts often get caught up in arguments about whether particular films or television programmes are 'progressive' or 'subversive'. And concern with the pleasures or identifications of actual audiences seem to ignore the long-term task of overthrowing dominant structures, within which resistant or emergent voices struggle on unequal terms. In any case, it is often argued, capitalism cannot ignore the potential market represented by groups emerging into new public self-identity and its processes invariably turn alternative life-styles and identities into commodities, through which they are subtly modified and thereby recuperated for the status quo. Thus the media appropriate images and ideas circulating within the women's movement to supply a necessary aura of novelty and contemporaneity. In this process, bourgeois society adapts to new pressures, while at the same time bringing them under control.[17] To such criticisms, cine-psychoanalysis adds the argument that approaches from the perspective of the audience ignore the role of language and the Unconscious in the construction of subjectivity, assuming that external socioeconomic or cultural determinations provide material for the class or gender consciousness of otherwise free-thinking subjects.

To characterize cultural exchange between text and reader as one of negotiation, however, does not necessitate a return to an economistic view of language and cultural form as transparent instruments of subjective expression. The concept of negotiation allows space to the play of unconscious processes in cultural forms, but refuses them an undue determination. For if ideologies operate on an unconscious level through the forms of language, the role of the 'other' in these processes is not passively suffered. The everyday working of argument and misunderstanding – in which contesting parties are positioned by, and struggle to resist, the unarticulated, 'unconscious' meanings running through their opponents' words, tones and gestures – demonstrates the extent to which 'otherness' may be negotiated. In this process, such constraints may become available to conscious understanding. A similar struggle can be posited of cultural exchange. Language and cultural forms are sites in which different subjectivities struggle to impose or challenge, to confirm, negotiate or displace, definitions and identities. In this respect, the figure of woman, the look of the camera, the gestures and signs of human interaction, are not given over once and for all to a particular ideology – unconscious or otherwise. They are cultural signs and therefore sites of struggle; struggle between male and female voices, between class voices, ethnic voices, and so on.

Negotiation and Cultural Analysis

The value of 'negotiation', then, as an analytical concept is that it allows space to the subjectivities, identities and pleasures of audiences. While acknowledging the cine-psychoanalytic critique of the notion 'selfhood' – of 'fixed' and centred identity – the concept of negotiation stops short at the dissolution of identity suggested by avant-garde aesthetics. For if arguments about the non-identity of self and language, words and meaning, desire and its objects challenge bourgeois notions of the centrality and stability of the ego and the transparency of language, the political consequence is not to abandon the search for identity. As has been frequently noted, social out-groups seeking to identify themselves against dominant representations – the working class, women, blacks, gays – need clearly articulated, recognizable and self-respecting self-images. To adopt a political position is of necessity to assume for the moment a consistent and answerable identity. The object of attack should not be identity as such but its dominant construction as total, non-contradictory and unchanging. We need representations that take account of identities – representations that work with a degree of fluidity and contradiction – and we need to forge different identities – ones that help us to make productive use of the contradictions of our lives. This means entering socioeconomic, cultural and linguistic struggle to define and establish them in the media, which function as centres for the production and circulation of identity.

However, knowledge of the instability of identity, its continual process of construction and reconstruction, warns the cultural critic not to look for final and achieved models of representation. Paradoxically, cine-psychoanalytic arguments about ideological effects, in their dependence on the centrality of language acquisition to the formation of subjectivity, make the text a moment of 'fixation' in the process of cultural exchange. Too frequently, cine-psychoanalytic analyses suggest that to read a mainstream text, to 'submit' to its pleasures, is to take a single position from which it can be read or enjoyed – that of the textual (patriarchal) subject, bound into ideological submission. However, such analysis relies on a complete reading, on tracing the play of narrative processes through to narrative closure, which it is assumed conclusively ties up any ambiguity or enigmatic 'false' trails generated by the processes of the text. Such textual analysis depends on total consumption of the cultural product and merges with the economistic critique of the spectator as passive consumer. Janice Radway, in her work on romance reading, has pointed to the 'culinary fallacy' in the notion of viewer as consumer – one who, meeting with the media product as a discrete object, swallows it whole, an already textually processed package of the same order as a television dinner. It seems highly improbable that cultural experiences are 'consumed' in quite this totalistic way. The notion of 'process' suggests flux, discontinuities, digressions, rather than fixed positions. It suggests that a range of positions of identification may exist within any text; and that, within the social situation of their viewing, audiences may shift subject positions as they interact with the text. Such processes – far from being confined to the 'high art' or political avant-garde work – are also a crucial source of cultural and formal regeneration, without which the culture industries would dry up.

The complete reading – from narrative disruption, to enigma development, to resolution – that arises from repeated viewings and close analysis is the product of the critical profession and does not replicate the 'raw' reading/viewing of audiences. The notion that the last word of the text is also the final memory of the audience – a notion frequently critiqued from Molly Haskell's account of classic romantic comedy onwards – derives more from the exigencies of the critical essay than from the *experience* of films, which has no such neat boundaries. It is this haphazard, unsystematic viewing experience, and its aftermath, that the cultural analyst must investigate if she/he wants to determine the political *effects* of textual ideologies. The text alone does not provide sufficient evidence for conclusions on such questions, but requires the researches of the anthropologist or ethnographer.

Negotiation and Textual Criticism

This returns me to a final question concerning the role of textual criticism in cultural analysis[.] [. . .] To limit the textual critic's authority in the analysis of ideological effects need not [. . .] lead to critical relativism, passivity, nor even unemployment – even if it does mean that textual analysis cannot alone determine the progressiveness or otherwise of a particular work. Semioticians argue that while the majority of cultural products are polysemic, they are not open to any and every interpretation. Aesthetic constraints intersect with the institutional in conscious or unconscious effort to contain or to open out the possibilities of negotiation. By studying the history and forms of aesthetic practices, codes and traditions as they operate within institutions, by studying narrative forms and genres, or the interpretative frameworks and viewing habits suggested by ethnographic research, the textual critic analyses the *conditions and possibilities of reading*.

Approached from this perspective, the cultural 'work' of the text concerns the generation of different readings; readings which challenge each other, provoke social negotiation of meanings, definitions and identities. Cultural history demonstrates that changes in context can render previous 'dominant' readings outmoded, enabling texts to be restructured in preference for alternative readings. For example, film criticism in the 1960s struggled to win 'commercial' Hollywood cinema for 'art', a project rejected by the ideological concerns of the 1970s as 'bourgeois humanism'. While some films disappeared from view (for instance, Fred Zinneman's social problem Western, *High Noon*) others were saved by a re-evaluation and rereading of their textual operations (John Ford's *Young Mr Lincoln*), and yet others were 'discovered' for the critical canon (for instance, Douglas Sirk's family melodrama *Written on the Wind*).[18] In this respect criticism represents the professionalization of meaning production. The critic, attuned by training to the semiotic and social possibilities of texts, produces sophisticated, specialist readings. To the critical enterprise, ethnographic work contributes knowledge of the network of cultural relations and interactions in which texts are caught and which help shape their possibilities, suggesting what they are capable of generating for different social audiences. But the critical act is not finished with the 'reading' or 'evaluation' of a text. It generates new cycles of meaning production and negotiation – journalistic features, 'letters to the editor', classroom lectures, critical responses, changes in distribution or publication policy, more critical activity, and so on. In this way traditions are broken and remade. Thus critical activity itself participates in social negotiation of meaning, definition, identity. The circulation of the mainstream Hollywood film *Coma* into the orbit of feminist debates about cinema offers a good example of this interchange between general and specialized critical discourses.[19]

Feminist Film Analysis

A problem for feminist analysis is that it enters critical negotiation from a specific political position, often beginning with the aim of distinguishing 'progressive' from 'reactionary' texts. Yet, as we have seen, any attempt to fix meaning is illusory. Moreover, the feminist project seeks to open up definitions and identities, not to diminish them. While the attempt to define the ideological status of texts may stimulate debate, such judgements also threaten to foreclose prematurely on critical and textual negotiation. It is necessary, then, for feminist criticism to perform a dual operation. In the first instance, the critic uses textual and contextual analysis to determine the conditions and possibilities of gendered readings. The critic opens up the negotiations of the text in order to animate the contradictions in play. But the feminist critic is also interested in some readings more than others. She enters into the polemics of negotiation, exploiting textual contradiction to put into circulation readings that draw the text into a female and/or feminist orbit. For example, *Coma* (Michael Crichton, 1977) was conceived, publicized and discussed critically as a futuristic thriller exploiting public concern about organ transplants. But the film also makes the central investigative protagonist a woman doctor. This produces a series of textual negotiations which are both ideologically interesting to feminists and a considerable source of the film's generic pleasure. [. . .]

Conditions and Possibilities of Textual Negotiation

A major issue for the analysis of textual negotiations is how 'textual' and 'social' subjects intersect in a cultural product; how the aesthetic and fictional practices engaged by a particular text meet and negotiate with extra-textual social practices; and, more specifically, how we can distinguish the patriarchal *symbol* of 'woman' from those discourses which speak from and to the historical sociocultural experience of 'women'.

It is my argument that a considerable source of textual negotiation lies in the use by many mainstream film and television genres of both melodramatic and realist modes.[20] This dual constitution enables a text to work both on a symbolic, 'imaginary' level, internal to fictional production, and on a 'realist' level, referring to the sociohistorical world outside the text. Thus two aesthetic projects may coexist in the same work. Popular culture draws on a melodramatic framework to provide archetypal and atavistic symbolic enactments; for the focus of melodrama is a moral order constructed out of the conflict of Manichaean, polar opposites – a struggle between good and evil, personified in the conflicts of villain, heroine and hero. At the same time such conflicts have power only on the premiss of a recognizable, socially constructed world; the pressure towards realism and contemporaneity means that a popular text must also conform to ever-shifting criteria of relevance and credibility.

If, however, melodramatic conflicts still have imaginative resonance in twentieth-century culture, melodrama as a category is rejected for its association with a discarded Victorianism – for its simplistically polarized personifications of good and evil and 'feminized' sentimentalism. In order, therefore, to find credible articulations of such conflict, which will re-solicit the recognition of continually shifting audiences, current melodramatic forms draw on those contemporary discourses which apportion responsibility, guilt and innocence in 'modern' terms – psychoanalysis, for example, marriage guidance, medical ethics, politics, even feminism. The modern popular drama, then, exists as a negotiation between the terms of melodrama's Manichaean moral frameworks and conflicts and those contemporary discourses which will ground the drama in a recognizable verisimilitude. These conditions of aesthetic existence ensure the continuing renewal of popular forms, the generation of renewed use-values that will bring audiences back to the screen.

Gender representation is at the heart of such cultural negotiation. For during a period of active feminism, of social legislation for greater sexual equality and corresponding shifts in gender roles, gender and sexual definitions themselves become the focus of intense cultural negotiation. Central to such negotiation is the figure of woman, which has long served as a powerful and ambivalent patriarchal symbol, heavily overdetermined as expression of the male psyche. But while film theory suggests how narrative, visual and melodramatic pleasures are organized round this symbol, feminist cultural history also shows that the figure of woman cannot be fixed in her function as patriarchal value. The 'image of woman' has also been a site of gendered discourse, drawn from the specific sociocultural experiences of women and shared by women, which negotiates a space within, and sometimes resists, patriarchal domination. At the same time new definitions of gender and sexuality circulated by the women's movement contest the value and meaning of the female image, struggling for different, female recognitions and identifications. When popular cultural forms, operating within a melodramatic framework, attempt to engage contemporary discourses about women or draw on women's cultural forms in order to renew their gender verisimilitude and solicit the recognition of a female audience, the negotiation between 'woman' as patriarchal symbol and woman as generator of women's discourse is intensified. While melodrama orchestrates gender conflicts on a highly symbolic level to produce the clash of identities that will adumbrate its moral universe, the codes of women's discourse work in a more direct and articulate register to produce realist and gendered recognitions. [...]

Notes

1. For example, cultural studies in England, and reader-response theory in the United States, have explored the cultural processes and textual procedures that make differential readings possible.
2. For examples of feminist analysis of women's fiction, see: Nina Baym, *Woman's Fiction: A guide to novels by and about women in America, 1920–1970*, Ithaca, NY: Cornell University Press, 1978; Janice A. Radway, *Reading the Romance: Women, patriarchy, and popular literature*, London: Verso, 1987; Jane Tompkins, *Sensational Designs: The cultural work of American fiction, 1790–1860s*, Oxford: Oxford University Press, 1985. For feminist work on the woman's film, melodrama and soap opera, see: Tania Modleski, *Loving with a Vengeance*, Hamden, Connecticut: The Shoe String Press, 1982; Charlotte Brunsdon, 'Crossroads: notes on soap opera', in E. Ann Kaplan (ed.), *Regarding Television: Critical approaches – an anthology*, Los Angeles: American Film Institute, 1983; Dorothy Hobson, *Crossroads: The drama of a soap opera*, London: Methuen, 1982; Ien Ang, *Watching Dallas*, London: Methuen, 1985; Maria LaPlace, 'Producing and consuming the woman's film: discursive struggle in *Now, Voyager*', and Linda Williams, '"Something else besides a mother": *Stella Dallas* and the maternal melodrama', both in Christine Gledhill (ed.), *Home Is Where the Heart Is*, London: British Film Institute, 1987.
3. For an account of Lacanian psychoanalysis, see Steve Burniston, Frank Mort and Christine Weedon, 'Psychoanalysis and the cultural acquisition of sexuality and subjectivity', in Women's Studies Group, Centre for Contemporary Cultural Studies, University of Birmingham (ed.), *Women Take Issue*, London: Hutchinson, 1978.
4. The psychoanalytic underpinnings of classic narrative cinema were first signalled in a special issue of *Screen*, vol. 14 no. 1/2 (Spring/Summer 1973), dealing with semiotics and cinema, and were developed by Colin MacCabe in 'The politics of separation', and by Stephen Heath in 'Lessons from Brecht', both in *Screen*, vol. 15, no. 2 (Summer 1974). *Screen*, vol. 16, no. 2, translated Christian Metz's 'The imaginary signifier' in a special issue on psychoanalysis and the cinema.
5. Claire Johnston's 'Women's cinema as counter-cinema', *Screen* Pamphlet, no. 2, September 1972, is an early and influential exposition of this view. Laura Mulvey's 'Visual pleasure and narrative cinema' in *Screen*, vol. 16, no. 3 (Autumn 1975) provided an influential development of feminist cine-psychoanalysis. Annette Kuhn's book *Women's Pictures: Feminism and cinema*, London: Routledge & Kegan Paul, 1982, offers succinct and critical introduction to this work; and Ann Kaplan's *Women and Film: Both sides of the camera*, New York: Methuen, 1983, a distinctive development of it, dealing in particular with the notion of the 'male gaze' in classic narrative cinema. See also my 'Recent developments in feminist film criticism', in Mary Ann Doane, Patricia Mellencamp and Linda Williams (eds), *Re-Vision: Essays in feminist film criticism*, Frederick, Maryland: University Publications of America, in association with the American Film Institute, 1984, for an account of feminist engagement with psycho-analysis.

6. See Annette Kuhn, *Women's Pictures*.

7. For example, Tania Modleski, 'Never to be thirty-six years old: *Rebecca* as female oedipal drama', *Wide Angle*, vol. 5, no. 1 (1982); and Linda Williams, '"Something else besides a mother": *Stella Dallas* and the maternal melodrama'; and Tania Modleski, 'Time and desire in the woman's film', in Gledhill.

8. Annette Kuhn, 'Women's genres: melodrama, soap opera and theory', *Screen*, vol. 25, no. 1 (1984), reprinted in Gledhill.

9. For example, Stuart Hall, 'Encoding/decoding', in Hall *et al.* (eds), *Culture, Media, Language*, London: Hutchinson, 1980; David Morley, *The Nationwide Audience*, London: British Film Institute Television Monograph II, 1980; Richard Dyer, *Stars*, London: British Film Institute, 1980.

10. See Antonio Gramsci, *Selections from the Prison Notebooks*, (ed. and trans. Quintin Hoare and Geoffrey Nowell-Smith), London: Lawrence & Wishart, 1971. For discussion and application of the notion of hegemony to cultural products, see Terry Lovell, 'Ideology and Coronation Street', in Richard Dyer *et al.*, *Coronation Street*, London: British Film Institute Television Monograph 13, 1981; and Geoff Hurd, 'Notes on hegemony, the war and cinema', in *National Fictions: World War Two in British films and television*, London: British Film Institute, 1985.

11. See Terry Lovell, *Pictures of Reality: Aesthetics, politics and pleasure*, London: British Film Institute, 1980, pp. 56–63. She defines the 'use-value' of a commodity as 'the ability of the commodity to satisfy some human want', which, according to Marx, 'may spring from the stomach or from the fancy'. 'The use-value of a commodity is realised only when it is consumed, or used' (p. 57).

12. See Maria LaPlace, 'Producing and consuming the woman's film: discursive struggle in *Now, Voyager*', in Gledhill, for a discussion of the contradictions of consumerism for women.

13. Julie D'Acci, 'The case of *Cagney and Lacey*', in Helen Baehr and Gillian Dyer (eds), *Boxed In: Women and television*, London: Pandora, 1987.

14. Molly Haskell, *From Reverence to Rape: The treatment of women in the movies*, Harmondsworth: Penguin, 1979.

15. Ien Ang, *Watching Dallas*, London: Methuen, 1985; and Janice Radway, *Reading the Romance: Women, patriarchy and popular literature*, London: Verso, 1987.

16. See, for example, Judith Williamson, 'The problems of being popular', *New Socialist*, September 1986.

17. For examples of fully developed textual analysis of the 'recuperative' strategies of mainstream cinema, see Peter Steven (ed.), *Jump Cut: Hollywood, politics and counter-cinema*, New York: Praeger, 1985.

18. For a translation of the seminal analysis of *Young Mr. Lincoln* by the editors of *Cahiers du Cinéma*, see *Screen*, vol. 13, no. 3 (Autumn 1972), reprinted in Bill Nichols (ed.) *Movies and Methods*, Berkeley: University of California Press, 1976. For work on Douglas Sirk, see Jon Halliday (ed.), *Sirk on Sirk*, London: Secker & Warburg/British Film Institute, 1971; a special issue of *Screen*, vol. 12, no. 2 (Summer 1971); and Laura Mulvey and Jon Halliday (eds), *Douglas Sirk*, Edinburgh: Edinburgh Film Festival, 1972.

19. See, for example, Elizabeth Cowie's account of press coverage of *Coma* in 'The popular film as a progressive text – a discussion of *Coma* Part 1', *m/f*, no. 3, 1979. Part 2 of this article appeared in *m/f*. no. 4, 1980. *Coma* was discussed by Christine Geraghty under

the heading 'Three women's films' in *Movie*, nos 27/28, Winter/Spring 1980–81, an article which is reprinted in Charlotte Brunsdon (ed.), *Films for Women*, London: British Film Institute, 1986, as is also an extract from Part 1 of Elizabeth Cowie's piece. The film frequently appears in film study courses dealing with feminism and cinema.

20. See 'The melodramatic field: an investigation', in Gledhill.

25 □ Carnival and the Carnivalesque

Mikhail Bakhtin

The problem of *carnival* (in the sense of the sum total of all diverse festivities, rituals and forms of a carnival type) – its essence, its deep roots in the primordial order and the primordial thinking of man, its development under conditions of class society, its extraordinary life force and its undying fascination – is one of the most complex and most interesting problems in the history of culture. We cannot, of course, do justice to it here. What interests us here is essentially only the problem of carnivalization, that is, the determining influence of carnival on literature and more precisely on literary genre.

Carnival itself (we repeat in the sense of a sum total of all diverse festivities of the carnival type) is not, of course, a literary phenomenon. It is *syncretic pageantry* of a ritualistic sort. As a form it is very complex and varied, giving rise, on a general carnivalistic base, to diverse variants and nuances depending upon the epoch, the people, the individual festivity. Carnival has worked out an entire language of symbolic concretely sensuous forms – from large and complex mass actions to individual carnivalistic gestures. This language, in a differentiated and even (as in any language) articulate way, gave expression to a unified (but complex) carnival sense of the world, permeating all its forms. This language cannot be translated in any full or adequate way into a verbal language, and much less into a language of abstract concepts, but it is amenable to a certain transposition into a language of artistic images that has something in common with its concretely sensuous nature; that is, it can be transposed into the language of literature. We are calling this transposition of carnival into the language of literature the carnivalization of literature. From the vantage point of this transposition, we will isolate and examine individual aspects and characteristic features of carnival.

Carnival is a pageant without footlights and without a division into performers and spectators. In carnival everyone is an active participant, everyone communes in the carnival act. Carnival is not contemplated and, strictly speaking, not even performed; its participants *live* in it, they live by its laws as long as those laws are in effect; that is, they live a *carnivalistic life*. Because carnivalistic life is life drawn out of its *usual* rut, it is to some extent 'life turned inside out', 'the reverse side of the world' ('*monde à l'envers*').

The laws, prohibitions, and restrictions that determine the structure and order of ordinary, that is noncarnival, life are suspended during carnival: what is suspended first of all is hierarchical structure and all the forms of terror, reverence, piety, and etiquette connected with it – that is, everything resulting from socio-hierarchical inequality or any other form of inequality among people (including age). All *distance* between people is suspended, and a special carnival category goes into effect: *free and familiar contact among people*. This is a very important aspect of a carnival sense of the world. People who in life are separated by impenetrable hierarchical barriers enter into free familiar contact on the carnival square. The category of familiar contact is also responsible for the special way mass actions are organized, and for free carnival gesticulation, and for the outspoken carnivalistic word.

Carnival is the place for working out in a concretely sensuous, half-real and half-play-acted form, a *new mode of interrelationship between individuals*, counterposed to the all-powerful socio-hierarchical relationships of noncarnival life. The behavior, gesture, and discourse of a person are freed from the authority of all hierarchical positions (social estate, rank, age, property) defining them totally in noncarnival life, and thus from the vantage point of noncarnival life become eccentric and inappropriate. *Eccentricity* is a special category of the carnival sense of the world, organically connected with the category of familiar contact; it permits – in concretely sensuous form – the latent sides of human nature to reveal and express themselves.

Linked with familiarization is a third category of the carnival sense of the world: *carnivalistic mésalliances*. A free and familiar attitude spreads over everything: over all values, thoughts, phenomena, and things. All things that were once self-enclosed, disunified, distanced from one another by a noncarnivalistic hierarchical worldview are drawn into carnivalistic contacts and combinations. Carnival brings together, unifies, weds, and combines the sacred with the profane, the lofty with the low, the great with the insignificant, the wise with the stupid.

Connected with this is yet a fourth carnivalistic category, *profanation*: carnivalistic blasphemies, a whole system of carnivalistic debasings and bringings down to earth, carnivalistic obscenities linked with the reproductive power of the earth and the body, carnivalistic parodies on sacred texts and sayings, etc.

These carnivalistic categories are not *abstract thoughts* about equality and freedom, the interrelatedness of all things or the unity of opposites. No, these are concretely sensuous ritual-pageant 'thoughts' experienced and played out in the form of life itself, 'thoughts' that had coalesced and survived for thousands of years among the broadest masses of European mankind. This is why they were able to exercise such an immense *formal, genre-shaping* influence on literature.

These carnival categories, and above all the category of free familiarization of man and the world, were over thousands of years transposed into literature, particularly into the dialogic line of development in novelistic prose. Familiarization facilitated the destruction of epic and tragic distance and the transfer of all represented material to a zone of familiar contact; it was reflected significantly in the organization of plot and plot situations, it determined that special familiarity of the author's position with regard to his characters (impossible in the higher genres); it introduced the logic of mésalliances and profanatory debasings; finally, it exercised a powerful transforming influence on the very verbal style of literature. All this already shows up quite clearly in the menippea. We shall return to this later, but first we must touch upon several other aspects of carnival, most importantly *carnivalistic* acts.

The primary carnivalistic act is the *mock crowning and subsequent decrowning of the carnival king*. This ritual is encountered in one form or another in all festivities of the carnival type: in the most elaborately worked out forms – the saturnalia, the European carnival and festival of tools (in the latter, mock priests, bishops or popes, depending on the rank of the church, were chosen in place of a king); in a less elaborated form, all other festivities of this type, right down to festival banquets with their election of short-lived kings and queens of the festival.

Under this ritual act of decrowning a king lies the very core of the carnival sense of the world – *the pathos of shifts and changes, of death and renewal.* Carnival is the festival off all-annihilating and all-renewing time. Thus might one express the basic concept of carnival. But we emphasize again: this is not an abstract thought but a living sense of the world, expressed in the concretely sensuous forms (either experienced or play-acted) of the ritual act.

Crowning/decrowning is a dualistic ambivalent ritual, expressing the inevitability and at the same time the creative power of the shift-and-renewal, the *joyful relativity* of all structure and order, of all authority and all (hierarchical) position. Crowning already contains the idea of immanent decrowning: it is ambivalent from the very start. And he who is crowned is the antipode of a real king, a slave or a jester; this act, as it were, opens and sanctifies the inside-out world of carnival. In the ritual of crowning all aspects of the actual ceremony – the symbols of authority that are handed over to the newly crowned king and the clothing in which he is dressed – all become ambivalent and acquire a veneer of joyful relativity; they become almost stage props (although these are ritual stage props); their symbolic meaning becomes two-leveled (as real symbols of power, that is in the noncarnival world, they are single-leveled, absolute, heavy, and monolithically serious). From the very beginning, a decrowning glimmers through the crowning. And all carnivalistic symbols are of such a sort they always include within themselves a perspective of negation (death) or vice versa. Birth is fraught with death, and death with new birth.

The ritual of decrowning completes, as it were, the coronation and is inseparable from it (I repeat this is a dualistic ritual). And through it, a new crowning already glimmers. Carnival celebrates the shift itself, the very process of replaceability, and not the precise item that is replaced. Carnival is, so to speak, functional and not substantive. It absolutizes nothing, but rather proclaims the joyful relativity of everything. The ceremonial of the ritual of decrowning is conterposed to the ritual of crowning: regal vestments are stripped off the decrowned king, his crown is removed, the other symbols of authority are taken away, he is ridiculed and beaten. All the symbolic aspects of this ceremonial of decrowning acquire a second and positive level of meaning – it is not naked, absolute negation and destruction (absolute negation, like absolute affirmation, is unknown to carnival). Moreover, precisely in this ritual of decrowning does there emerge with special clarity the carnival pathos of shifts and renewals, the image of constructive death. Thus the ritual of decrowning has been the ritual most often transposed into literature. But, we repeat, crowning and decrowning are inseparable, they are dualistic and pass one into the other; in any absolute dissociation they would completely lose their carnivalistic sense.

The carnivalistic act of crowning/decrowning is, of course, permeated with carnival categories (with the logic of the carnival world): free and familiar contact (this is very clearly manifest in decrowning), carnivalistic mésalliances (slave-king), profanation (playing with the symbols of higher authority), and so on.

We shall not dwell here on the details of the crowning-decrowning ritual (although they are very interesting), nor on its diverse variations from epoch to epoch and in the various festivities of the carnival type. Nor shall we analyze the various accessary rituals of carnival, for example, disguise – that is, carnivalistic shifts of clothing and of positions and destinies in life; nor carnival mystifications, bloodless carnival wars, verbal agons[1] and cursing matches, exchanges of gifts (abundance as an aspect of carnivalistic utopia), and so on. These rituals too were transposed into literature, imparting symbolic depth and ambivalence to the corresponding plots and plot situations, imparting a joyful relativity, carnival levity and rapidity of change.

But of course an extraordinarily great influence on literary-artistic thinking was exercised by the ritual of crowning/decrowning. This ritual determined a special *decrowning type* of structure for artistic images and whole works, one in which the decrowning was essentially ambivalent and two-leveled. If carnivalistic ambivalence should happen to be extinguished in these images of decrowning, they degenerated into a purely negative *exposé* of a moral or socio-political sort, they became single-leveled, lost their artistic character, and were transformed into naked journalism.

We must consider again in more detail the ambivalent nature of carnival images. All the images of carnival are dualistic; they unite within themselves both poles of change and crisis: birth and death (the image of pregnant death), blessing and curse (benedictory carnival curses which call simultaneously for death and rebirth), praise and abuse, youth and old age, top and bottom, face and backside, stupidity and wisdom. Very characteristic for carnival thinking is paired images, chosen for their contrast (high/low, fat/thin, etc.) or for their similarity (doubles/twins). Also characteristic is the utilization of things in reverse: putting clothes on inside out (or wrong side out), trousers on the head, dishes in place of headgear, the use of household utensils as weapons, and so forth. This is a special instance of the carnival category of *eccentricity*, the violation of the usual and the generally accepted, life drawn out of its usual rut.

Deeply ambivalent also is the image of *fire* in carnival. It is a fire that simultaneously destroys and renews the world. In European carnivals there was almost always a special structure (usually a vehicle adorned with all possible sorts of gaudy carnival trash) called 'hell', and at the close of carnival this 'hell' was triumphantly set on fire (sometimes this carnival 'hell' was ambivalently linked with a horn of plenty). Characteristic is the ritual of 'moccoli' in Roman carnival: each participant in the carnival carried a lighted candle ('a candle stub'), and each tried to put out another's candle with the cry 'Sia ammazzato!' ('Death to thee!'). In his famous description of Roman carnival (in Italienische Reise)[2] Goethe, striving to uncover the deeper meaning behind carnival images, relates a profoundly symbolic little scene: during 'moccoli' a boy puts out his father's candle with the cheerful carnival cry: 'Sia ammazzato il Signore Padre!' [that is, 'death to thee, Signor Father!']

Deeply ambivalent also is carnival *laughter* itself. Genetically it is linked with the most ancient forms of ritual laughter. Ritual laughter was always directed toward something higher: the sun (the highest god), other gods, the highest earthly authority were put to shame and ridiculed to force them to *renew themselves*. All forms of ritual laughter were linked with death and rebirth, with the reproductive act, with symbols of the reproductive force. Ritual laughter was a reaction to *crises* in the life of the sun (solstices), crises in the life of a deity, in the life of the world and of man (funeral laughter). In it, ridicule was fused with rejoicing.

This ancient ritualistic practice of directing laughter toward something higher (a deity or authority) defined the privileges of laughter in antiquity and in the Middle Ages. Much was permitted in the form of laughter that was impermissible in serious form. In the Middle Ages, under cover of the legitimized license of laughter, 'parodia sacra' became possible – that is, parody of sacred texts and rituals.

Carnivalistic laughter likewise is directed toward something higher – toward a shift of authorities and truths, a shift of world orders. Laughter embraces both poles of change, it deals with the very process of change, with *crisis* itself. Combined in the act of carnival laughter are death and rebirth, negation (a smirk) and affirmation (rejoicing laughter). This is a profoundly universal laughter, a laughter that contains a whole outlook on the world. Such is the specific quality of ambivalent carnival laughter.

In connection with laughter we shall touch upon one more question – the carnivalistic nature of *parody*. Parody, as we have already noted, is an integral element in Menippean satire and in all carnivalized genres in general. To the pure genres (epic, tragedy) parody is organically alien; to the carnivalized genres it is, on the contrary, organically inherent. In antiquity, parody was inseparably linked to a carnival sense of the world. Parodying is the creation of a *decrowning double*; it is that same 'world turned inside out'. For this reason parody is ambivalent. Antiquity parodied essentially everything: the satyr drama, for example, was originally the parodic and laughing aspect of the tragic trilogy that preceded it. Parody here was not, of course, a naked rejection of the parodied object. Everything has its parody that is, its laughing aspect, for everything is reborn and renewed through death. In Rome, parody was an obligatory aspect of funeral as well as of triumphant laughter (both were of course rituals of the carnivalistic type). In carnival, parodying was employed very widely, in diverse forms and degrees: various images (for example, carnival pairs of various sorts) parodied one another variously and from various points of view; it was like an entire system of crooked mirrors elongating, diminishing, distorting in various directions and to various degrees.

Parodying doubles have become a rather common phenomenon in carnivalized literature. They find especially vivid expression in Dostoevsky – almost every one of the leading heroes of his novels has several doubles who parody him in various ways: for Raskolnikov there are Svidrigailov, Luzhin, and Lebeziatnikov; for Stavrogin – Peter Verkhovensky, Shatov, and Kirillov; for Ivan Karamazov – Smerdyakov, the devil, Rakitin. In each of them (that is, in each of the doubles) the hero dies (that is, is negated) in order to be renewed (that is, in order to be purified and to rise above himself).

In the narrowly formal literary parody of modern times, the connection with a carnival sense of the world is almost entirely broken. But in the parodies of the Renaissance (in Erasmus, Rabelais, and others) the carnival fire still burned: parody was ambivalent and sensed its bond with death/renewal. Thus could be born in the bosom of parody one of the greatest and at the same time most carnivalistic novels of world literature: Cervantes' *Don Quixote*. Here is how Dostoevsky assessed that novel: 'There is nothing in the world more profound and powerful than this work. It is the ultimate and greatest word yet uttered by human thought, it is the most bitter irony that a man could express, and if the world should end and people were asked there, somewhere, "Well, did you understand your life on earth and what conclusions have you drawn from it?" a person could silently point to Don Quixote: "Here is my conclusion about life, can you judge me for it?"'[3]

It is characteristic that Dostoevsky structures his evaluation of *Don Quixote* in the form of a typical 'threshold dialogue'.

To conclude our analysis of carnival (from the vantage point of carnivalized literature), a few words about the carnival square.

The main arena for carnival acts was the square and the streets adjoining it. To be sure, carnival also invaded the home; in essence it was limited in time only and not in space; carnival knows neither stage nor footlights. But the central arena could only be the square, for by its very idea carnival *belongs to the whole people*, it is *universal, everyone* must participate in its familiar contact. The public square was the symbol of communal performance. The carnival square – the square of carnival acts – acquired an additional symbolic overtone that broadened and deepened it. In carnivalized literature the square, as a setting for the action of the plot, becomes two-leveled and ambivalent: it is as if there glimmered through the actual square the carnival square of free familiar contact and communal performances of crowning and decrowning. Other places of action as well (provided they are realistically motivated by the plot, of course) can, if they become meeting- and contact-points for heterogeneous people – streets, taverns, roads, bathhouses, docks of ships, and so on – take on this additional carnival-square significance (for all the naturalistic qualities of the representation, the universal symbol-system of carnival is in no danger of naturalism).

Festivities of the carnival type occupied an enormous place in the life of the broadest masses of the people in ancient times – in Greek and even more in Roman life, where the central (but not the sole) festival of the carnival type was the *saturnalia*. These festivals had no less (and perhaps, even more) significance in medieval Europe and during the Renaissance, where they were in part a direct living continuation of Roman saturnalia. In the realm of carnivalistic folk culture there was no break in tradition between antiquity and the Middle Ages. In all epochs of their development, festivities of the carnival type have exercised an enormous influence – as yet insufficiently appreciated and researched – on the development of culture as a whole, including literature, several of whose genres and movements have undergone a particularly intense *carnivalization*. In the ancient period, early Attic comedy and the entire realm of the serio-comical were subjected to a particularly powerful carnivalization. In Rome, the many diverse varieties of satire and epigram were linked, and were designed to be linked, with the saturnalia; they were either written for saturnalia, or at least were created under cover of that legitimized carnival license enjoyed by the festival.

In the Middle Ages the vast comic and parodic literature in vernacular languages and in Latin was, one way or another, connected with festivals of the carnival type – with carnival proper, with the 'Festival of Fools', with free 'paschal laughter' (*risus paschalis*), and so forth. Essentially every church holiday in the Middle Ages had its carnivalistic side, the side facing the public square (especially those holidays like Corpus Christi). Many national festivities, such as the bullfight, for example, were of a clearly expressed carnivalistic character. A carnival atmosphere reigned during the days of a fair, on the festival of the harvesting of grapes, on the performance days of miracle plays, mystery plays, *soties*[4] and so forth; the entire theatrical life of the Middle Ages was carnivalistic. The large cities of the late Middle Ages (such cities as Rome, Naples, Venice, Paris, Lyon, Nuremberg, Cologne) lived a full carnival life on the average of three months out of the year (and sometimes more). It could be said (with certain reservations, of course) that a person of the Middle Ages lived, as it were, *two lives*: one was the *official* life, monolithically serious and gloomy, subjugated to a strict hierarchical order, full of terror, dogmatism, reverence, and piety; the other was the *life of the carnival square*, free and unrestricted, full of ambivalent laughter, blasphemy, the profanation of everything sacred, full of debasing and obscenities, familiar contact with everyone and everything. Both these lives were legitimate, but separated by strict temporal boundaries.

Without taking into account the alternation and mutual estrangement of these two systems of life and thought (the official and the carnivalistic), one cannot understand correctly the peculiar nature of medieval man's cultural consciousness, and cannot make sense of many phenomena in medieval literature – such as, for example, the 'parodia sacra'.[5]

This epoch also witnessed the carnivalization of the *speech life* of European peoples: whole layers of language, the so-called *familiar speech of the public square*, were permeated with a carnival sense of the world; there came into being an enormous fund of unrestrained carnivalistic gesticulations. The familiar speech of all European peoples is to this day filled with relics of carnival, especially speech of abuse and ridicule; the symbol-system of carnival also fills the abusive, ridiculing gesticulations of today.

During the Renaissance, one could say that the primordial elements of carnival swept away many barriers and invaded many realms of official life and worldview. Most importantly, they took possession of all the genres of high literature and transformed them fundamentally. There occurred a deep and almost total carnivalization of all artistic literature. The carnival sense of the world, with its categories, its carnival laughter, its symbol-system of carnival acts of crowning/decrowning, of shifts and disguises, carnival ambivalence and all the overtones of the unrestrained carnival word – familiar, cynically frank, eccentric, eulogistic-abusive and so on – penetrated deeply into almost all genres of artistic literature. On the basis of this carnival sense of the world, the complex forms of the Renaissance worldview came into being. Even antiquity, as assimilated by the humanists of the epoch, was to a certain extent refracted throught the prism of the carnival sense of the world. The Renaissance is the high point of carnival life.[6] Thereafter begins its decline.

Beginning with the seventeenth century, folk-carnival life is on the wane: it almost loses touch with communal performance, its specific weight in the life of people is sharply reduced, its forms are impoverished, made petty and less complex. As early as the Renaissance a *festive court masquerade* culture begins to develop, having absorbed into itself a whole series of carnivalistic forms and symbols (mostly of an externally decorative sort). Later there begins to develop a broader line of festivities and entertainments (no longer limited to the court) which we might call the *masquerade line* of development; it preserved in itself a bit of the license and some faint reflections of the carnival sense of the world. Many carnival forms were completely cut off from their folk base and left the public square to enter this chamber masquerade line, which exists even today. Many ancient forms of carnival were preserved and continue to live and renew themselves in the *farcical* comic antics of the public square, and also in the *circus*. Certain elements of carnival are also preserved in the life of the theater and spectacle in modern times. It is characteristic that the subculture of the theater has even retained something of carnivalistic license, the carnivalistic sense of the world, the fascination of carnival; this was very well illustrated by Goethe in *Wilhelm Meisters Lehrjahre*, and for our time by Nemirovich-Danchenko in his memoirs.[7] Something of the carnival atmosphere is retained, under certain conditions, among

the so-called bohemians, but here in most cases we are dealing with the degrad-
ation and trivialization of the carnival sense of the world (there is, for example,
not a grain of that carnival spirit of communal performance).

Alongside these later branchings from the basic carnival trunk – branchings that
had emaciated the trunk – there continued and still continues to exist a public-
square carnival in the proper sense, as well as other festivities of the carnivalistic
type, but they have lost their former significance and their former wealth of forms
and symbols.

As a consequence, there occurred a deterioration and dissipation of carnival and
the carnival sense of the world; it lost that authentic sense of a communal
performance on the public square. And thus a change also occurred in the nature
of the carnivalization of literature. Until the second half of the seventeenth century,
people were *direct participants* in carnivalistic acts and in a carnival sense of the
world; they still *lived* in carnival, that is, carnival was one of the forms of life
itself. Therefore carnivalization was experienced as something unmediated (several
genres in fact directly serviced carnival). *The source of carnivalization was carnival
itself.* In addition, carnivalization had genre-shaping significance; that is, it
determined not only the content but also the very generic foundations of a work.
From the second half of the seventeenth century on, carnival almost completely
ceases to be a direct source of carnivalization, ceding its place to the influence of
already carnivalized literature; in this way carnivalization becomes a purely literary
tradition. Carnival elements in this literature – already cut off from their direct
source, carnival – change their appearance somewhat and are reconceptualized.

It is of course true that carnival in the proper sense as well as other festivities of
the carnival type (bullfights, for example), the masquerade line, farcical street
antics, and other forms of carnivalistic folklore continue to exercise a certain direct
influence on literature even to this day. But in the majority of cases this influence is
limited to the content of works and does not touch their generic foundation; that
is, it is deprived of any genre-shaping power.

Notes

1. Agon: in Greek, 'contest'. An agon is that part of a Greek drama in which two
   protagonists, each aided by half of the chorus, engaged in verbal conflict.
2. J. W. Goethe, *Italian Journey*, trans. W. H. Auden and Elizabeth Mayer, London:
   Collins, 1962. See Part Three (January 1788),'The Roman Carnival', and especially the
   section 'Moccoli', pp. 467–9.
3. The comment on Quixote occurs in *The Diary of a Writer*, 1876, March, Ch. II, 1: 'Don
   Carlos and Sir Watkin. Again, Symptoms of "the Beginning of the End," p. 260.
4. *Soties*: French satirical farces of the medieval period, in which actors (in fool's costume)
   ridiculed social manners and political events.
5. Two lives – the official and the carnivalistic – also existed in the ancient world, but there
   was never such a sharp break between them (especially in Greece).
6. My work *Rabelais and the Folk Culture of the Middle Ages and the Renaissance* (1940),

at the present time [1963] being prepared for publication, is devoted to the carnivalistic folk culture of the Middle Ages and the Renaissance. It provides a special bibliography on the question. [Bakhtin's book on Rabelais, submitted as a doctoral dissertation in 1940, was not published until 1965. It exists in English as Mikhail Bakhtin, *Rabelais and His World*, trans. Hélène Iswolsky, Cambridge, MA: MIT Press, 1968.]

7. See, in English, Vladimir Ivanovich Nemirovich-Danchenko, *My Life in the Russian Theatre*, trans. John Cournos, Boston: Little, Brown & Co., 1936.

PART FIVE

Feminism

Introduction

Feminism, like Marxism, is always more than a body of academic texts and practices; it is also, and fundamentally so, a political movement, concerned with women's oppression and the ways and means to empower women. Feminist work in cultural studies has made an enormous contribution to the study of popular culture. More than any other approach, it is feminism which has made the final break with the assumption explicit in the 'culture and civilisation' tradition (but implicit elsewhere) that the study of popular culture is always the study (from a 'respectable' distance) of the culture of 'other people'. Rosalind Coward's *Female Desire*, for example, does not approach women's pleasure in popular culture as an 'outsider.... a stranger.... The pleasures I describe are often my pleasures.... I don't approach these things as a distant critic but as someone examining myself, examining my own life under a microscope.'[1] This is a discourse about 'our' culture.

Ien Ang's *Watching Dallas* (Reading 26), an analysis of the American prime-time soap *Dallas*, organised around the forty-two letters she received in response to an advertisement in a Dutch women's magazine, is also concerned with female pleasure. Again, like Coward, she writes as 'an intellectual and a feminist', but also as someone who has 'always particularly liked watching soap operas like *Dallas*'. As she explains: 'The admission of the reality of this pleasure [her own] ... formed the starting point for this study – I wanted in the first place to understand this pleasure, without having to pass judgement on whether *Dallas* is good or bad.'

Ang identifies what she calls 'the ideology of mass culture'. According to this ideology soap operas, like other examples of popular culture, are commodities produced by the capitalist culture industries with only two aims in mind: ideological subjection and the accumulation of profit. Ang, quite rightly, sees this as a distorted and one-sided version of Marx's analysis of capitalist commodity production, allowing 'exchange value' completely to mask 'use value' (see Terry Lovell, Reading 44). Against this, she insists, as would have Marx, that it is not possible to read off how a product might be consumed from the means by which it was produced. Christine Geraghty (Reading 30) provides an excellent account of the 'Utopian possibilities' of prime-time soap opera.

The focus of Janice Radway's *Reading the Romance* is the 'ordinary woman' as romance reader. The book investigates the reading practices of a group of forty-two women (mostly married with children) who regularly read romances. Through a series of individual questionnaires, open-ended group discussions, face-to-face interviews, informal discussions, and observations, Radway constructed a model of actual romance reading. She discovered why the women read, how they read, why they read romance fiction, and how they discriminate between 'ideal' and 'failed' romances. Radway's conclusions on the cultural significance of romance reading, as she readily acknowledges, are contradictory. On the one hand, if the focus is the text, romance reading seems like a surrender to patriarchy; while on the other, if the focus is the act, romance reading appears to be an oppositional activity. It is this tension, between the meaning of 'the act' and the meaning of 'the text', that must be analysed, if we are to understand the full meaning of romance reading. Reading 28 is Radway's introduction to the British edition of her book, in which she presents a critical retrospective on her work in the context of an alignment with British cultural studies.

Yvonne Tasker's analysis of feminist crime writing (Reading 31) focuses both on the crime fiction itself and on the feminist critical response to it. Like Ang (Readings 26 and 48), she is concerned about interventions into popular culture which treat it and its consumers as objects to be fought over and won for an alternative cultural practice, an alternative politics. The problem, as she sees it, is that 'The desire for a feminist popular culture is in part a guilty one, associated as it is with indulgence and escapism.' Jacqueline Bobo's essay '*The Color Purple*: Black Women as Cultural Readers' (Reading 29) is a study based on a group interview with selected black women viewers of the film. Her purpose is to examine the way in which black women create meaning(s) from the film version of Alice Walker's novel and use 'the reconstructed meaning to empower themselves and their social group'. She locates the responses of the black women interviewed in a wider 'community of heightened consciousness ... in the process of creating new self-images and forming a force for change'.

The final two readings collected here in this section, by Lane F. Rakow (Reading 27) and Morag Shiach (Reading 32) provide excellent overviews (and differently focused from my own) of the development of feminist approaches to popular culture.

Notes

1. Rosalind Coward, *Female Desire: Women's sexuality today*, London: Paladin, 1984, p. 14.

26 □ Dallas *and the Ideology of Mass Culture*

Ien Ang

[...]

The Ideology of Mass Culture

Dallas is not only widely watched, but also widely discussed: a lot is said and written about the programme. These public discourses about *Dallas* provide a framework within which answers can be given to questions such as: what must I think about such a television serial? What arguments can I use to make my opinion plausible? How must I react to people who hold a different opinion? Not all existing discourses, however, are equally capable of formulating satisfactory answers to such questions. Some discourses are more prestigious than others, they sound more logical or convincing, and are more successful in determining the social image of TV programmes like *Dallas*.

In many European countries nowadays there is an official aversion to American television series: they are regarded as a threat to one's own, national culture and as an undermining of high-principled cultural values in general.[1] Against this ideological background, professional intellectuals (television critics, social scientists, politicians) put a lot of energy into creating a consistent and elaborated 'theory' on American television series – a theory which provides a 'scientific' cloak for the aversion. A representative and revealing formulation of this theory comes from the sociology of mass communications:

> The most important characteristic of a TV series is that the film content is dependent on its economic marketability. Aiming at a very broad market means that the content must be reduced to universally consumable motifs. This applies in particular to American series which in the United States serve as 'commercial' packaging. ... The commercial character of the TV series hinders the introduction of concrete social and

From Ang, I., *Watching Dallas*, Methuen, London, 1985, pp. 86–116.

political attitudes, because they might provoke controversies in various groups. . . . The film is given a 'universal appeal' character; it deals with familiar, broadly institutionalized ingredients. The necessary ingredients of a successful series include romantic love . . . simple patterns of good and evil and the building-up of suspense, climax and relief. . . . This reduction to the normal human aspects of existence means that the content is recognizable for a wider audience, but it offers a stereotypical and schematized image of reality. . . . In this regard TV series succeed in fulfilling primarily economic functions, and thus in reproducing a bourgeois ideology, without losing their attraction for different sectors of the audience.[2]

As a description of the working method of the commercial, American television industry this account certainly offers some adequate insights, although one might wonder whether such a direct connection exists between the economic conditions under which TV series are produced and their aesthetic and narrative structures. Such crude economic determinism is often criticized in media studies circles. Nevertheless, the core of this theory tends to be accepted as correct. What interests us here, however, is not the correctness or adequacy of the theory itself, but the way in which some of its elements carry over into the way in which American TV series are evaluated. A theory fulfils an ideological function if it fulfils an *emotional* function in people's heads, to which the assertions contained in the theory are subordinated. As Terry Eagleton puts it, 'what *is* important to recognize is that the cognitive structure of an ideological discourse is subordinated to its emotive structure – that such cognitions or miscognitions as it contains are on the whole articulated according to the demands . . . of the emotive "intentionality" it embodies.'[3]

Emotionally, then, the above-described theory on American TV series leads to their total rejection and condemnation. They become 'bad objects'. These then are the contours of what I would like to call the 'ideology of mass culture'. In this ideology some cultural forms – mostly very popular cultural products and practices cast in an American mould – are *tout court* labelled 'bad mass culture'. 'Mass culture' is a denigrating term, which arouses definitely negative associations.[4] In opposition to 'bad mass culture' implicitly or explicitly something like 'good culture' is set up. One letter-writer expresses this dichotomization of 'bad' and 'good' culture very clearly:

> In *Dallas* no attention at all is paid to any realistic problems in this world, the problems of ordinary people, whereas even in America social equality is a long way off. . . . I mean, I'd rather read a good book or watch a programme like *Koot en Bie* [a high-brow Dutch satirical programme]. (Letter 31)

So dominant is this ideology of mass culture where the judging of American TV series is concerned that the chairman of the Dutch Broadcasting Foundation, Eric Jurgens, can say without any hesitation: 'The Dutch broadcasting organizations *of course* don't exist primarily to broadcast Dallas. . . . *No one* can maintain that these American series are of a high standard as regards content. They are at most cleverly made.'[5] The ideology of mass culture takes on here the status of Absolute Truth. Judgement is passed, no doubts allowed.

The emotional attraction of the ideology of mass culture, however, is not confined to the select circle of professional intellectuals. As we have seen, the letter-writers who dislike *Dallas* also all too easily reach for its categories. Apparently the ideology of mass culture has such a monopoly on the judging of a phenomenon like *Dallas* that it supplies ready-made conceptions, as it were, which sound self-evident and can be used without any strain or hesitation. The dominance of the ideology of mass culture apparently even extends to the common sense of everyday thinking: for ordinary people too it appears to offer a credible framework of interpretation for judging cultural forms like *Dallas*.

It therefore looks as though the letter-writers who hate *Dallas* have adopted the ideology of mass culture as a guideline for its rejection. Because of this the border between individual experience and social ideology tends to become blurred: the way in which these letter-writers watch *Dallas* is described in terms of the ideologically dominant status *Dallas* as 'mass culture'. The ideology of mass culture therefore not only offers a (negative) label for the programme itself, but also serves as a mould for the way in which a large number of haters of *Dallas* account for their displeasure. To put it briefly, their reasoning boils down to this: '*Dallas* is obviously bad because it's mass culture, and that's why I dislike it.' And so the ideology of mass culture fulfils a comforting and reassuring role: it makes a search for more detailed and personal explanations superfluous, because it provides a finished explanatory model that convinces, sounds logical and radiates legitimacy.

Hating *Dallas* need not, however, necessarily coincide with subscribing to the ideology of mass culture. Other factors may be responsible, or the fact that one is not attracted to the television serial itself. The letters from those who dislike it, however, are so structured by the schemas of this ideology that they offer us little insight into the way in which they watch the programme, which meanings they attach to it, etc. Hence, despite the confidence of their expressed opinions, it remains even more puzzling why some letter-writers don't like *Dallas* than why its fans do.

[. . .]

Loving *Dallas*

But what about those who 'really' like *Dallas*? How do they relate to the ideology of mass culture?

Ideologies not only organize the ideas and images people make of reality, they also enable people to form an image of themselves and thus to occupy a position in the world. Through ideologies people acquire an identity, they become subjects with their own convictions, their own will, their own preferences. So, an individual living in the ideology of mass culture may qualify him- or herself as, for example, 'a person of taste', 'a cultural expert' or 'someone who is not seduced by the cheap tricks of the commercial culture industry'. In addition to an image of oneself, however, an ideology also offers an image of others. Not only does one's own identity take on form in this way, but the ideology serves also to outline the identity of other people. As Göran Therborn puts it, 'in one's subjection to and qualification for a particular position, one becomes aware of the difference between oneself and others'.[6] Thus a dividing line is drawn by the ideology of mass culture between the 'person of taste', the 'cultural expert', etc., and those who, according to this ideology, are not such. Or to be more specific, between those who do recognize *Dallas* as 'bad mass culture' and those who do not.

One *Dallas*-hater thus tries to distance herself from those who like *Dallas*:

> I don't understand either why so many people watch it, as there are lots of people who find it a serious matter if they have to miss a week. At school you really notice it when you turn up on Wednesday morning then it's, 'Did you see *Dallas*, wasn't it fabulous?' Now and then I get really annoyed, because I find it just a waste of time watching it.... Then you hear them saying that they had tears in their eyes when something happened to someone in the film, and I just can't understand it. At home they usually turn it on too, but then I always go off to bed. (Letter 33)

She outlines the identity of the others, those who like *Dallas*, in a negative way, and with a particular degree of confidence: lovers of *Dallas* are almost declared idiots by this letter-writer! Roughly the same pattern, but in somewhat milder terms, emerges in the following extract: 'Reading through it [her own letter], it's a serial a normal person shouldn't watch, because you feel someone else's sorrow and difficulties. For me that's also the reason why so many people find the serial good' (Letter 38). The image of the others, of those who do not recognize *Dallas* as 'bad mass culture', can be summed up shortly but forcefully from the viewpoint of the ideology of mass culture: 'The aim is simply to rake in money, lots of money. And people try to do that by means of all these things – sex, beautiful people, wealth. *And you always have people who fall for it*' (Letter 35, my italics). The ideology of mass culture therefore definitely does not offer a flattering picture of those who like *Dallas*. They are presented as the opposite of 'persons of taste', 'cultural experts' or 'people who are not seduced by the cheap tricks of the commercial culture industry'. How do lovers of *Dallas* react to this? Do they know that this negative image of them exists and does it worry them at all?

In the small advertisement which the letter-writers replied to, I included the following clause: 'I like watching the TV serial *Dallas* but often get odd reactions to it.' It seems to me that the phrase 'odd reactions' is vague at the very least: from the context of the advertisement there is no way of knowing what I meant. Yet various lovers of *Dallas* go explicitly into this clause in their letters: the words 'odd reactions' seem sufficient to effect an 'Aha!' experience in some fans.

> I have the same 'problem' as you! When I let drop in front of my fellow students (political science) that I do my utmost to be able to watch *Dallas* on Tuesday evenings, they look incredulous. (Letter 19)

It always hits me too that people react 'oddly' when you say you like watching *Dallas*. I think everyone I know watches it but some of my friends get very worked up over this serial and even go on about the dangerous effects on the average TV viewer. I really don't know what I should think of this. (Letter 22)

These extracts lead one to suspect that the rules and judgements of the ideology of mass culture are not unknown to *Dallas* fans. What is more, they too seem to respond to this ideology. But they tend to do so in a completely different way from those who hate *Dallas* or who love it ironically. 'Really' loving *Dallas* (without irony) would seem to involve a strained attitude toward the norms of the ideology of mass culture. And it is this strained relationship which the fans have to try to resolve.

In contrast to the haters and ironic lovers, who, as we have seen, express their attitude to the ideology of mass culture in a rather uniform and unconflicting way, the 'real' fans use very divergent strategies to come to terms with its norms. One strategy is to take over and internalize the judgements of the ideology of mass culture itself:

I just wanted to react to your advertisement concerning *Dallas*. I myself enjoy *Dallas* and the tears roll down when something tragic happens in it (in nearly every episode, that is). In my circle too people react dismissively to it, they find it a typical commercial programme far beneath their standards. I find you can relax best with a programme like this, although you just have to keep your eye on the kind of influence such a programme can have, it is role-confirming, 'class-confirming', etc., etc. And it's useful too if you think what kind of cheap sentiment really does get to you. (Letter 14)

There is a remarkable about-face in this letter. Instead of stating why she likes *Dallas* so much (which was the question I had put in my advertisement), the letter-writer confines herself to reiterating a reasoning which derives from the ideology of mass culture in answer to the 'dismissive reactions' of her milieu. She doesn't adopt an independent attitude towards this ideology but merely takes over its morals. But whom is she addressing with these morals? Herself? Me (she knows from my advertisement that I like watching *Dallas*)? All *Dallas* fans? It is as though she wants to defend the fact that she enjoys *Dallas* by showing that she is in fact aware of its 'dangers' and 'tricks'; aware, in other words, that *Dallas* is 'bad mass culture'. A similar reasoning can be read in the following letter extract:

In fact it's a flight from reality. I myself am a realistic person and I know that reality is different. Sometimes too I really enjoy having a good old cry with them. And why not? In this way my other bottled-up emotions find an outlet. (Letter 5)

In other words: watching *Dallas* is all right if you know that it is not realistic and therefore 'bad'.

But a protective strategy can also be employed by actually challenging the ideology of mass culture.

> I am replying to your advertisement as I would like to speak my mind about *Dallas*.
> I've noticed too that you get funny reactions when you like watching *Dallas* (and I like
> watching it). Many people find it worthless or without substance. But I think it does
> have substance. Just think of the saying: 'Money can't buy happiness', you can certainly
> trace that in *Dallas*. (Letter 13)

But what has been said here against the ideology of mass culture remains caught
within the categories of that ideology. Against the opinion 'no substance' (= 'bad')
is placed the alternative opinion 'does have substance' (= 'good'); the category
'substance' (and thus the difference 'good/bad') is therefore upheld. This letter-writer
'negotiates' as it were within the discursive space created by the ideology of mass
culture, she does not situate herself outside it and does not speak from an opposing
ideological position.

But why do these *Dallas* lovers feel the need to defend themselves against the
ideology of mass culture? They obviously feel under attack. Obviously they can't get
round its norms and judgements, but must stand out against them in order to be able
to like *Dallas* and not to have to disavow that pleasure. But it is never pleasant to
be manoeuvred into a defensive position: it shows weakness. To have to defend
oneself is nearly always coupled with a feeling of unease.

> You are right in saying that you often get these strange reactions. Such as 'So you like
> watching cheap mass entertainment, eh?' Yes, I watch it and I'm not ashamed of it. But
> I do try to defend my motivation tooth and nail. (Letter 7)

'Tooth and nail'; the pent-up intensity of this expression reveals the strong desire
of this letter-writer to defend herself and to justify herself, in spite of her contention
that she 'is not ashamed of it'.

And another letter-writer says:

> Oh well, I'm one of those people who sit in front of the box every Tuesday for the
> *Dallas* programme, actually to my own amazement. . . . I must honestly confess that I
> do like watching the serial now. By 'confess' I mean this: at first I felt a bit guilty about
> the fact that I had gone mad on such a cheap serial without any morals. Now I look
> at it rather differently. (Letter 11)

'To my own amazement', she writes; in other words 'I hadn't thought it possible'.
Her feeling of guilt arises precisely because she has not escaped the power of
conviction of the ideology of mass culture, from the branding of *Dallas* as a 'cheap
serial without any morals'.

Finally, yet another defence mechanism against the ideology of mass culture is
possible. That is, strangely enough, irony again. But in this case irony is not
integrated so unproblematically in the experience of watching *Dallas* as in the case
of the ironic fans we encountered earlier. On the contrary, here irony is an
expression of a conflicting viewing experience. One letter-writer has put this
psychological conflict clearly into words. In her account there is an uncomfortable

mixture of 'really' liking *Dallas* and an ironic viewing attitude:

> Just like you often get odd reactions when I say that at the moment *Dallas* is my favourite TV programme. . . . I get carried along intensely with what is happening on TV. I find most figures in the serial horrible, except Miss Ellie. The worst thing I find is how they treat one another. I also find them particularly ugly. Jock because he doesn't have an aesthetically justifiable head, Pamela because she has to seem so smart, I find that 'common'. I can't stand it that everyone [in the serial] finds her sexy when she looks like Dolly Parton with those breasts. Sue Ellen is really pathetic, she looks marvellously ravaged by all that drink. J.R. needs no explanation. He keeps my interest because I always have the feeling that one day that wooden mask is going to drop. Bobby I find just a stupid drip, I always call him 'Aqualung' (his former role in a series). They are a sad lot, so honest, stinking rich, they want to seem perfect but (fortunately for us!) none of them is perfect (even Miss Ellie has breast cancer, and that cowboy Ray, whom I've really fallen for, is always running into trouble). (Letter 23)

The distance from the *Dallas* characters is great for this letter-writer – witness the annihilating judgement that she passes so ironically on them. Nevertheless her account is imbued with a kind of intimacy which betrays a great involvement in the serial ('I get carried along intensely' . . . 'I can't stand it' . . . 'I am interested in him' . . . 'whom I've really fallen for'). The detached irony on the one hand and the intimate involvement on the other appear difficult to reconcile. So it emerges from further on in her letter that irony gains the upper hand when watching *Dallas* is a social occasion:

> I notice that I use *Dallas* as a peg for thinking about what I find good and bad in my relations with others. I notice this in particular *when I'm watching with a group of people* because then we usually can't keep our mouths shut; we shout disgraceful! and bastard! and bitch! (sorry, but emotions really run high!). We also sometimes try to get an idea of how the Ewings are all doing. Sue Ellen has postnatal depression and that's why she is so against her baby. Pamela is actually very nice and suffers because of Sue Ellen's jealousy. J.R. is just a big scaredy-cat, you can see that from that uncertain little laugh of his. (Letter 23, my italics)

The ironic commentaries are presented here as a *social* practice. This is confirmed by the sudden transition from the use of 'I' to 'we' in this extract. Is it perhaps true to say that the need to emphasize an ironic attitude to viewing, thereby creating a distance from *Dallas*, is aroused in this letter-writer by the social control emanating from an ideological climate in which 'really' liking the programme is almost taboo? In any case intimacy returns further on in the letter as soon as she is talking again in terms of 'I'. And the irony then disappears into the background.

> Actually they are all a bit stupid. And oversensational. Affected and genuinely American (money-appearance-relationship-maniacs – family and nation! etc.). I know all this very well. And yet. . . . The Ewings go through a lot more than I do. They seem to have a richer emotional life. Everyone knows them in Dallas. Sometimes they run

into trouble, but they have a beautiful house and anything else they might want. I find it pleasant to watch. I do realize their ideals of beauty. I look at how their hair is done. I'm very impressed by their brilliant dialogues. Why can't I ever think what to say in a crisis? (Letter 23)

Real love and irony – both determine the way in which this letter-writer relates to *Dallas*. It is clear that they are difficult to reconcile: real love involves identification, whereas irony creates distance. This ambivalent attitude to *Dallas* seems to stem from the fact that on the one hand she accepts the correctness of the ideology of mass culture (at least in a social context), but on the other hand 'really' likes *Dallas* – which is against the rules of this ideology. The irony lies here then in the 'social surface'; it functions, in contrast to the ironizing lovers, for whom irony is interwoven with the way in which they experience pleasure in *Dallas*, as a sort of screen for 'real' love. In other words, irony is here a defence mechanism with which this letter-writer tries to fulfil the social norms set by the ideology of mass culture, while secretly she 'really' likes *Dallas*.

We can draw two conclusions from these examples. First, the fans quoted seem spontaneously, of their own free will, to take the ideology of mass culture into account: they come into contact with it and cannot apparently avoid it. Its norms and prescriptions exert pressure on them, so that they feel the necessity to defend themselves against it. Second, it emerges from their letters that they use a very wide variety of defence strategies: one tries simply to internalize the ideology of mass culture, another tries to negotiate within its discursive framework, and yet another uses surface irony. And so it would appear that there is not one obvious defence strategy *Dallas* fans can use, that there is no clear-cut ideological alternative which can be employed against the ideology of mass culture – at least no alternative that offsets the latter in power of conviction and coherence. And so the letter-writers take refuge in various discursive strategies, none of which, however, is as well worked out and systematic as the discourses of the ideology of mass culture. Fragmentary as they are, these strategies are therefore much more liable to contradictions. In short, these fans do not seem to be able to take up an effective ideological position – an identity – from which they can say in a positive way and independently of the ideology of mass culture: 'I like *Dallas* because...'.

But this weak position the fans are in, this lack of a positive ideological basis for legitimizing their love of *Dallas*, has tiresome consequences. Whereas those who hate the programme can present their 'opponents' as, for example, 'cultural barbarians', 'people with no taste' or 'people who let themselves be led astray by the tricks of the commercial culture industry' (thus implying that they themselves are *not*), the fans do not have such favourable representation to hand. They are not in a position to hit back by forming in their turn an equally negative image of those who dislike *Dallas*; they can only offer resistance to the negative identities that *others* ascribe to them.

According to Therborn, such a psychologically problematic situation is characteristic for subject positions which get the worst of it ideologically. From an ideologically dominant subject position it is possible to stigmatize 'the others', as it were. For the victims of this dominant ideology, however, no such reassuring position is available: they find themselves in a position which, 'while also involving a perception and calculation of the differences between ego and alter, tends towards resistance to the Other rather than towards forming him or her. This difference is inscribed in the asymmetry of domination'.[7] This situation can have disastrous consequences for *Dallas* fans who feel pushed into a corner by the ideology of mass culture. They can easily be reduced to silence because they can literally find no words to defend themselves. The ground is cut from under them. As one of the letter-writers says: 'I personally find it terrible when I hear people saying they don't like *Dallas*' (Letter 2). As finding it 'terrible' is her only word of defence – apparently nothing else occurred to her – isn't that a form of capitulation?

Popular Culture, Populism and the Ideology of Mass Culture

But the power of the ideology of mass culture is certainly not absolute. Indeed, it is precisely the markedly 'theoretical', discursive nature of this ideology that reveals the limits of its power. Its influence will be mainly restricted to people's opinions and rational consciousness, to the discourses people use when *talking* about culture. These opinions and rationalizations need not, however, necessarily prescribe people's cultural *practices*. It could even be that the dominance of the normative discourses of the ideology of mass culture – as it is expressed in all sorts of social institutions such as education and cultural criticism – has in fact a counter-productive effect on people's practical cultural preferences so that, not through ignorance or lack of knowledge, but out of self-respect they refuse to subject themselves to the prescriptions of the ideology of mass culture or to let their preferences be determined by it.[8] The populist position offers a direct justification for such a refusal, because it rejects altogether any paternalistic distinction between 'good' and 'bad' and dismisses any feeling of guilt or shame over a particular taste. There exists then a cynical dialectic between the intellectual dominance of the ideology of mass culture and the 'spontaneous', practical attraction of the populist ideology. The stricter the standards of the ideology of mass culture are, the more they will be felt as oppressive and the more attractive the populist position will become. This position offers the possibility, contrary to the morals of the ideology of mass culture, of following one's own preferences and enjoying one's own taste.

The commercial culture industry has understood this well. It employs the populist ideology for its own ends by reinforcing the cultural eclecticism underlying it and propagating the idea that indeed there's no accounting for taste, that in other words no objective aesthetic judgements are possible. It sells its products by propagating the idea that everyone has the right to his or her own taste and has the freedom to enjoy pleasure in his or her own way. Perhaps it's not so surprising that the most striking description of the commercial application of the populist position was recently given by Frankie Goes To Hollywood: 'One of the main jobs of the advertisers . . . is not so much to sell the product as to give moral permission to have fun without guilt.'[9]

But the populist ideology is applicable not only for the aims and interests of the commercial culture industry. It also links up with what Bourdieu has called the popular 'aesthetic':[10] an aesthetic which is the exact opposite of the bourgeois aesthetic disposition in which an art object is judged according to extremely formal, universalized criteria which are totally devoid of subjective passions and pleasures. In the popular 'aesthetic', on the other hand, no 'judgements of Solomon' are passed on the quality of cultural artifacts. This aesthetic is of an essentially pluralist and conditional nature because it is based on the premise that the significance of a cultural object can differ from person to person and from situation to situation. It is based on an affirmation of the continuity of cultural forms and daily life, and on a deep-rooted desire for participation, and on emotional involvement. In other words, what matters for the popular aesthetic is the recognition of pleasure, and that pleasure is a personal thing. According to Bourdieu the popular aesthetic is deeply anchored in common sense, in the way in which cultural forms in everyday life are approached by ordinary people.

Pleasure, however, is *the* category that is ignored in the ideology of mass culture. In its discourses pleasure seems to be non-existent. Instead it makes things like responsibility, critical distance or aesthetic purity central – moral categories that make pleasure an irrelevant and illegitimate criterion. In this way the ideology of mass culture places itself totally outside the framework of the popular aesthetic, of the way in which popular cultural practices take shape in the routines of daily life. Thus it remains both literally and figuratively caught in the ivory towers of 'theory'.

Notes

1. For a more general view of the negative reception by European intellectuals of the rise of American popular culture after the Second World War, see D. Hebdige, 'Towards a cartography of taste, 1935–1962', *Block*, no. 4, 1981, pp. 39–56.
2. J. Bardoel, J. Bierhoff, B. Manschot, P. Vasterman, *Marges in de media*, Baarn; Het Wereldvenster, 1975, pp. 58–9.
3. T. Eagleton, 'Ideology, fiction, narrative', *Social Text*, no. 2, 1979, p. 64.
4. For an evaluation of mass culture theories, see A. Swingewood, *The Myth of Mass Culture*, Basingstoke: Macmillan, 1977.
5. In *De Volkskrant*, 14 November 1981 (my italics).
6. G. Therborn, *The Ideology of Power and the Power of Ideology*, London: Verso, 1980, p. 27.
7. *Ibid.*, p. 28.
8. Compare Bourdieu, 'The aristocracy of culture', *Media, Culture and Society*, vol. 2, no. 3, 1980, pp. 243–4.
9. Frankie Goes To Hollywood, *Welcome to the Pleasure Dome*, Island, 1984.
10. Bourdieu, 'The aristocracy of culture', p. 237.

27 □ *Feminist Approaches to Popular Culture: Giving Patriarchy its Due*

Lana F. Rakow

What are commonly referred to in communication as the 'popular culture debates' are troubling from a feminist perspective for two reasons: first, the canon of debaters includes no women; second, the debates' analyses of social power do not focus on patriarchal society, thus excluding feminist theoretical analysis. Yet feminist approaches to popular culture do constitute a serious social analysis and an important theoretical agenda. The four approaches described here – the images and representations approach, the recovery and reappraisal approach, the reception and experience approach, and the cultural theory approach argue that popular culture plays a role in patriarchal society and that theoretical analysis of this role warrants a major position in the ongoing debates.

Introduction

Following a long history of literature arising out of the humanities and social sciences taking positions on the value and functions of British and US popular culture, a second body of literature has arisen to define, categorize, critique, and extend those positions. It is these two bodies of literature that together can be said to constitute what are so often referred to as the 'popular culture debates'. The first provided the raw material which has been selected, interpreted, and constituted by the second into a historical canon, a tradition of positions about the quality and changing nature of culture, the rise of the mass media, and the political implications of capitalist-industrialization. Over time, the two have come to overlap, as early interpreters of the debate recede into the past and are themselves accorded positions within it.

How these positions should be sorted out, into gross or fine categories, has not been uniformly agreed upon. Stuart Hall and Paddy Whannel (1965), for example, have cited four approaches: they see taken respectively by Providers, Traditionalists, Progressives, and Radicals. Providers and Progressives view popular culture with more optimism because they support the present society. Traditionalists and Radicals reject the present order, but the first do so on the basis of the values that it is replacing, the second on the basis of the values it frustrates (pp. 364–5). Tom Kando (1975) has divided the debates into two positions: 'those who feel that mass culture and popular culture are bad culture, and those who do not' (p.438). He divides those positions into subcategories: elitist, conservative, radical, and marxist arguments against popular culture; liberal and radical arguments in favor of popular culture. C. W. E. Bigsby (1976) has described the debates as consisting of two major divisions reflecting two extreme ideologies, expressing in their positions on popular culture epiphantic and apocalyptic fears and hopes about the direction of society. Patrick Brantlinger (1983) has classified those on the left and the right who argue against popular culture as sharing a mythology of 'negative classicism', a mythology defended by Marshall McLuhan and his disciples and by cultural pluralists.

While the categorizations of these writers vary, their summaries share assumptions that underlie most analyses of the 'popular culture debates'. First, they assume a canon of debaters: Matthew Arnold, T. S. Eliot, F. R. Leavis, the Frankfurt School (Theodor Adorno, Max Horkheimer, and Herbert Marcuse), Leo Lowenthal, Daniel Bell, Herbert Gans, Dwight Macdonald, Edward Shils, Richard Hoggart, and Raymond Williams, to identify a few. Second, they share, explicitly or implicitly, Bigsby's insight that 'the politics of popular culture … conceal a more basic concern with the nature of the individual and his [sic] society' (Bigsby, 1976, p. 5). They assume, at most, three possible social structures, over which the struggle is then conducted: mass society, class society, and pluralist society. That is, the categories of social power are defined along lines given in advance.

The popular culture debates as currently constituted are troubling from a feminist perspective for two reasons, suggested by these underlying assumptions. First, the canon of debaters contains no women. Though Hannah Arendt and Q. D. Leavis are occasionally accorded the status of minor figures, Arendt has usually been overshadowed by members of the Frankfurt School and Leavis has usually been overshadowed by her husband, F. R. Leavis. Regardless of their status, however, neither offered positions substantially different from the male figures in the canon. Second, the competing analysis of social power (which the debates are presumed to be about) do not include patriarchal society, excluding a feminist analysis of popular culture at the level of theory rather than artifact.[1] By assuming that a stratified society can sufficiently be described in terms of relations between elite and mass, ruling class and working class, dominant culture and subcultures, they obscure other social categories, such as that of men and women.

The first problem, the exclusion of women from theoretical discourse, is typical of received academic histories. Susan Sniader Lanser and Evelyn Torton Beck

(1979) have pointed this out as it relates to the tradition of literary criticism:

> It is useful to remind ourselves that in a patriarchal society, the idea of woman as thinker or theoretician is seen virtually as a contradiction in terms. While the term *woman writer* is clear evidence of the society's basic conception of the artist as male, our comfort with the phrase does suggest some recognition of women as creators ... [P]atriarchal culture has grudgingly learned to tolerate the woman artist, yet it continues to resist, denigrate, and mistrust woman as critic, theory-builder, or judge ... the term *woman critic* sounds like an awkward, faulty construction, not corresponding to any veritable reality. (Lanser and Beck, 1979, p. 79)

Lanser and Beck's comments suggest that before we assume that no women have historically made significant theoretical contributions that bear on the subject of popular culture, we should look to see who else has been excluded from the canon of debaters. We need not look far. Charlotte Perkins Gilman's 1911 book, *The Man-Made World or Our Androcentric Culture*, is a feminist analysis of culture that stands apart from the positions usually included within the popular culture debates. Gilman argued that men have monopolized, managed, and masculinized human activities, excluding women from many spheres of creativity and from many forms of amusement and leisure activities. Fiction, she said, 'has not given any true picture of woman's life, very little of human life, and a disproportionate section of man's life' (p. 102). Games and sports 'are essentially masculine, and as such [are] alien to women' (p. 109). Rather than critiquing a mass, class, or pluralist society, she critiqued a patriarchal one, or as she called it, an androcentric one, where two sets of cultural activities exist, one for men and one for women, both dictated by men.

Beatrice Forbes-Robertson Hale, in her 1914 book *What Women Want: An interpretation of the feminist movement*, posed a similar critique of men's control over culture:

> Women have often been taunted with lack of the creative and reasoning faculties. But until the present age the number of women possessing opportunities to develop these has been so small in proportion to men as to make any comparison insidious. Only now are the faculties of women emerging from obscurity. Through all time women as a class have been silent; now a proportion becomes articulate. During the years of their silence Man the Romancer has spoken for them, clothing them with the garments of his own Fantasy. So well has his fancy wrought that sometimes women have even believed it fact, though more often their acquiescence has been superficial .... He forgets, too, that his fantasy clothed but one creature – 'Woman' – a chimera of his own brain, and that what he is at last witnessing is the rise of women, individually and collectively, an infinite variety of conscious persons bound together by the single need of self-development. When as many women as men are free to express themselves, there will remain but one great struggle on earth, the struggle of all the dispossessed, men and women alike, for their inheritance. (Hale, 1914, pp. 6–7)

These passages illustrate that taking up the standpoint of women within a patriarchal society has presented feminists with a very different perspective on the question of popular culture. They raise questions about women's opportunities for creativity and how these may have changed historically, how women's creativity has been evaluated, how women have been silenced, how women have made meaning of their lives with the myths and activities accorded to them by men, and how men have made meaning of their lives at the expense of women. While the history of feminist approaches to popular culture remains to be written, these examples from Gilman and Hale suggest that the canon that has come to constitute and set the terms of the 'popular culture debates' is in need of critique and revision. Feminism is a challenge to the very power relations that have determined the ground over which the discussion can be waged.

While the history of feminist approaches to popular culture remains to be recovered and constructed, we can look to feminist work within the past twenty years, during the resurgence of the feminist movement, to gain an understanding of contemporary feminist positions about popular culture. We need not wait for a new history to begin the process of examining and interpreting what feminists have been saying about women's relationship to popular culture and to begin according these positions the status of history within ongoing academic debates.[2]

Though contemporary feminists have taken a diversity of approaches to popular culture, they have shared two major assumptions. The first is that women have a particular relationship to popular culture that is different from men's. They have pointed out that women have played central roles as consumers of certain popular culture products, that they are a central subject matter of popular culture for both men and women, and that, in some cases and in some time periods, they have been significant creators and producers of popular culture. The second assumption is that understanding how popular culture functions both for women and for a patriarchal culture is important if women are to gain control over their own identities and change both social mythologies and social relations. Feminism, as a critique of existing social relations, assumes that change is not only desirable but necessary. What kind of change and how it will be accomplished is, however, not as readily agreed upon.

To enter into an analysis of popular culture from a feminist position is a complicated task because, to paraphrase Bigsby, it involves a basic concern with the individual and her relation to society. The scope of this task is apparent from Katherine Fishburn's annotated bibliography (1982), a reference guide to works about women's images in popular culture that encompasses far-ranging feminist research. In order to give some form and coherence to feminist work on popular culture, I will present here a selection of contemporary work grouped roughly into four approaches: the Images and Representations Approach, the Recovery and Reappraisal Approach, the Reception and Experience Approach, and the Cultural Theory Approach. The works discussed under each category share some essential elements; however, the categories do overlap and are not intended to be exclusive.

The Images and Representations Approach

Since Betty Friedan (1963) pointed out the disparity between the messages of popular culture and the experiences and growing despair of real women, feminists within and outside of academia have devoted considerable attention to the characteristics of women's images in popular culture. This approach was the entree of contemporary feminists into discussions of popular culture, and signaled a departure from the traditional academic debates in that the critique often originated from non-academic, middle class women, the very group that was the intended audience of much popular culture.

As Fishburn points out (1982, p. 3), women's most significant relationship to popular culture has been in providing its major images, so the amount of attention devoted by feminists to images should not be surprising. The work in this area has looked for answers to several related questions: (1) what kind of images are present and what do those images reveal about women's position in the culture? (2) whose images are they and whom do they serve? (3) what are the consequences of those images? and (4) how do such images have meaning?

Friedan looked at images in women's magazines in particular, comparing fictional heroines prior to and following World War II. The message in post-World War II magazines had become what Friedan named the 'feminine mystique', the fulfillment of femininity through women's roles as housewives as women's highest value and only commitment. Frieden explored the consequences of those messages for women by conducting extensive interviews with eighty women; she discovered a schizophrenic split between what they believed should be a fulfilling role in life and the actual isolation and despair they felt about their own lives. While the images may have been detrimental to women, they did nevertheless serve a function. 'Why is it never said', Friedan observed, 'that the really crucial function, the really important role that women serve as housewives, is to buy more things for the house' (p. 206).

Some of the work on images that followed Friedan's came from women within the mass media industries who focused on the fact that popular culture images are for the most part men's images of women. Through class action suits some drew the connection between the discriminatory employment conditions in the industries and the decision-making processes that created those images. A collection of critiques by women working within the media appeared in 1974, compiled by the Media Women's Association (Strainchamps, 1974). One woman complained: 'The editorial message driven home by the *Ladies' Home Journal* to date is that women are meant to be totally passive, ever-suffering, second-class citizens whose greatest fulfillment in life is having their collective psyche divined by the out-of-touch men, the editors and advertisers, who determine the content of this magazine' (p. 46).

Other feminists looked at the longer historical tradition of women's images. As Fishburn points out, the myth that there is a quintessentially American woman has remained constant, but the myth changes (1982, p. 4). Carol Wald (1975) collected visual images of women in popular culture items through a period of eighty years: trading cards, postage stamps, pin-ups. Kathryn Weibel (1977) looked at images since the nineteenth century of women in fiction, television, movies, women's magazines and magazine advertising, and fashion. She concluded that popular culture has consistently portrayed [white] American women as 'housewifely, passive, wholesome, and pretty' (p. ix). She draws a connection between the type of images presented and whether they are created by men or women:

> It's true that over the years many women have created and consumed the traditional passive, domestic female images with relish. But it also seems true that the greater the control women have exerted over popular culture images, the less passive and domestic they have been and the more reflective of women's work and commitments outside the home. Conversely, the greater the influence of men over a particular medium at a particular time, the more traditional and outdated the images have been. (p. 244)

Women of color have had additional critiques to make of women's images in popular culture. Jill Lewis and Gloria Joseph (*Common Differences*, 1981) note that, in advertising, Black women must 'become White', pose, dress, and make themselves up like White women, before they can compete and gain status and security by having a man: 'The concept of beauty for women is based on White male values – the values of those who are empowered to make the rules' (p. 159). bell hooks examines the negative images of Black womanhood in the mass media, especially television:

> Negative images of black women in television and film are not simply impressed upon the psyches of white males, they affect all Americans. Black mothers and fathers constantly complain that television lowers the self-confidence and self-esteem of black girls. Even on television commercials the black female child is rarely visible – largely because sexist-racist Americans tend to see the black male as the representative of the black race. (hooks, 1981, p. 66)

The negative stereotypes and invisibility of Asian American, Native American, Black, and Chicana women have been pointed out by the writers in Cherrie Moraga and Gloria Anzaldúa's edited book, *This Bridge Called My Back: Writings by radical women of color* (1981).

Mainstream social science communication researchers became interested in women's relationship to popular culture during the 1970s. Given this research tradition's historical emphasis on audience effects research and its increasing interest in the relationship between content and effects during the time period, it is not surprising that it would enter the discussion from this approach. The *Journal of Communication* devoted its Spring 1974 issue to nine reports focusing on media content and women's roles, signaling a legitimization of the subject area. *Hearth and Home: Images of women in the mass media* (Tuchman, Daniels, and Benet (eds)), published in 1978, is an often-cited collection of quantitative content analyses and other empirical studies on the content of effects of television, magazines, and newspapers. Gaye Tuchman (p. 5) characterized the mass media's treatment of women as 'symbolic annihilation', in that women are underrepresented and trivialized by the media.

Public policy and media industry involvement have been most likely to arise out of this approach to popular culture. The US Commission on Civil Rights, for example, prepared a report in 1977, updated in 1979, that summarized social science research on the portrayal of women and minorities in television and on employment problems, making recommendations to the Federal Communications Commission. The advertising industry issued a report in 1975 recommending changes in the portrayal of women in advertising (National Advertising Review Board, 1975).

The usefulness of the concept of 'images' and the assumptions that underlie it has become a subject for discussion among feminists, leading some to suggest new ways of conceptualizing media content, as discourse, myth, fantasy, or representation, and attending to the fourth question suggested above, how images have meaning. Noreene Janus' critique ('Research on sex-roles in the mass media' in *The Insurgent Sociologist*, 1977) pointed out that 'images' research, usually conducted by US liberal feminists, implicitly assumes that sexism can be eradicated within the present economic system, reaffirming the very framework that creates those images. Elizabeth Cowie (1977) and Griselda Pollock (1977) have both argued that the concept of 'images of women' should be replaced with the notion of woman as a signifier in ideological discourses. Images have meanings because they exist in other discourses as well. Gaye Tuchman (1979) suggested that concepts of images should be replaced with frame analyses or concepts of myth, since images can never be veridical accounts of reality. Rosalind Coward (1982) has argued that sexist codes that specify how an image can be read, not specific images per se, are the problem for feminist critics.

Feminist psychoanalysis, particularly as developed in film theory, has also suggested that content can be examined differently from the implied position of viewer, with women seen as functioning (in Classical Hollywood movies, at least) as a construction of male fantasy. Such feminist psychoanalytic film theory work as Laura Mulvey's 'Visual pleasure and narrative cinema' (1975), E. Ann Kaplan's *Women and Film: Both sides of the camera* (1983), and Janet Walker's review article, 'The problem of sexual difference and identity' (1984) represent a different kind of discussion of the representation of women, while sharing the basic focus on content with others in this approach.

The Recovery and Reappraisal Approach

While examining, cataloging, and criticizing images of women may have been the earliest of the contemporary feminist approaches to popular culture and a major one for both members of the women's movement and mainstream social science researchers, another approach came on its heels from the humanities – art, literature, and social history. Feminists approaching popular culture from this directions have been interested in these questions: (1) given a male-dominated culture, how have women managed to express themselves? (2) why has women's creativity been overlooked, undervalued or ignored? (3) how do men's and women's creativity differ? (4) what are women's stories and myths?

Rather than suggesting that changing women's portrayal within popular culture content will solve the problem, feminists in this approach are more likely to place a positive value on women's culture as something distinct from men's culture, something that should be recovered and encouraged. Rather than focusing on men's images of women, they focus on women's images of themselves and women's stories about their own experiences.

The recovery process has included searching for the lost voices of women and constructing a matriarchal creative heritage. Often those voices have been found outside the dominant culture; other times they have been found in popular culture reaching a female audience. Alison Adburgham (1972) uncovered a long and rich history of women writers in Great Britain in a time period particularly hostile to such a role.

> This book should be regarded as rescue work. It salvages pre-Victorian periodicals from the limbo of forgotten publications, and exhumes from long undisturbed sources a curious collection of women who, at a time when it was considered humiliating for a gentlewoman to earn money, contrived to support themselves by writing, editing or publishing ... sometimes even supporting husbands and children as well. (Adburgham, 1972, p. 9)

This social history corrects myths and fills gaps about women's history as writers and publishers and their connection to popular culture as producers as well as consumers. It begins with Aphra Behn, author of seventeen 'licentious' plays, who died in 1689, travels through numerous periodicals written for and by women, including a popular one dedicated to mathematical puzzles, and ends with the beginning of the Victorian era. During this time, female literacy rose and light fiction became popular with women in all classes. Most women writers, however, were scorned by the male intellectual elite because of their 'low-brow' appeal.

Another work that attempts to reconstruct a lost history of women's relationship to popular culture as producers and as consumers is Ann Douglas' history of nineteenth century American culture (Douglas, 1977). Douglas has argued that there is an intimate connection between Victorian culture and modern mass culture. Her thesis is that in the nineteenth century middle-class Protestant women and the disaffected male clergy took over 'culture' as their special province, changing the literary scene with their preoccupation with sentimentalism and establishing the anti-intellectualism still prevalent today. Sympathetic to their motives and necessities for doing so, she argues that the clergy and middle class women had lost their practical function in the new economic order, so they used 'cultural' as their vehicle for exercising power.

The novel in particular has been retrieved and re-evaluated by feminists as one available and popular forum in which women, white women in particular, could speak to other women. Josephine Donovan ('The Silence is Broken', 1980) has noted that prior to the nineteenth century women were denied access to Latin rhetorical training and hence to the symbolic tools to create public art: 'Only when the Latin influence had weakened, when serious prose was being written in the vernaculars, and in a nontraditional form, and only after the rhetoric of the home and of the forum had once again merged, could women hope to have equal access to the means of literary creation' (p. 216). The novel, as a new form with no classical models or rules one needed to know in order to write it and with its capacity to deal with the details of everyday life in a 'plain' rather than 'high' style, was particularly suited for adoption by women as a legitimated form of literary expression. Madonne Miner (1984) has suggested that novels popular with women readers today share a common, white, middle class 'women's story' that can be traced to its nineteenth century predeccesors, suggesting a matrilineal literary tradition.

The literary and artistic tradition of Black women has survived even in the face of a history of denials of access to its creation, as Gloria T. Hull and Barbara Smith (1982) have explained:

> As a major result of the historical realities which brought us enslaved to this continent, we have kept separated in every way possible from recognized intellectual work. Our legacy as chattel, as sexual slaves as well as forced laborers, would adequately explain why most Black women are, to this day, far away from the centers of academic power and why Black women's studies has just begun to surface in the latter part of the 1970s. What our multilayered oppression does not explain are the ways in which we have created and maintained our own intellectual traditions as Black women, without either the recognition or the support of white-male society. (p. xviii)

Black women, Barbara Smith has pointed out (in 'Toward a black feminist criticism', 1982), have a literary tradition paralleling that of Black men and white women, but its themes, styles, and aesthetics reflect their particular political, social, and economic experiences that make it very different from white-male literary convention.

Feminist critics have been particularly prone to criticizing the formalist tradition that divorces a cultural product from its historically situated context and to challenging the notion that criticism is an objective practice that can claim universal judgments. Janet Wolff (1981), for example, works from the premise that '[a]rt is a social product', historically and culturally situated, not the creation of 'genius' transcending time and society (p. 1). This starting point requires an understanding of how social institutions affect '*who* becomes an artist, *how* they become an artist, how they are able to *practice* their art, and how they can ensure that their work is produced, performed, and *made available* to a public' (p. 40), as well as the ways in which value is ascribed to various forms and genres by certain groups.

Lillian Robinson (1978) has noted that stripping art and literature of their historical meaning and transporting them to the realm of universals denies all but the dominant white elite their full historical identity, and it is no accident that they do. Popular culture and 'high' culture, she argues, carry an ideology which serves certain segments of society. Feminist criticism provides a better way to understand our experiences as historical beings, especially those who because of race, class, or gender, have learned to view themselves as the 'other' in cultural practices.

Tania Modleski (1982) has pointed out the double critical standard that male critics have applied to women's popular culture – novels and soap operas – as compared to their aggrandizement of popular male genres. She has suggested that criticism of female culture cannot simply 'plug into' categories used in studies of male popular culture. The disdain with which both men and women critics have tended to view women's popular culture has prevented them from seeing how it speaks to the real problems and tensions in women's lives (p. 14).

The category called here the Recovery and Reappraisal Approach most directly challenges traditional notions of high and low art, folk art, and popular culture. It calls not for adding women artists to a literary or artistic canon but for a re-evaluation of the criteria that establish canons and determine the artistic and social merit of creative expressions. It calls for challenges to the social, political, and economic structures that discourage women from their own creativity and myth-making. It suggests that popular culture has both served women's creativity and expression and excluded it in complex ways, providing some means for women to articulate their experiences, despite the disdain of critics, and yet in other ways barring women from active creativity in myth-making and story telling, providing women with male myths, drowning out their own cultural heritage and what they have had to say about their own lives.

The Reception and Experience Approach

This feminist approach to popular culture focuses on readers and viewers of cultural products, their experiences and perceptions. It has taken an appreciative view of women and their interactions with cultural products within their particular social situations and frames of understanding. This approach can be traced back to Betty Friedan's interviews with women, the means by which she discovered the discrepancy between popular culture messages and women's feelings about their own lives. It is implicit in much early activism, as women who were the intended audiences for popular culture expressed their outrage over images of women in television programming and advertising. More recently, feminist scholarship has focused on those cultural forms that are popular with women to understand how those forms function for women and for patriarchy. This approach would seem to hold a particular appeal to feminists because it captures a basic commitment of most feminists: to provide women the means of speaking about their own understanding of their lives and their experiences. As Dorothy Smith has reminded us, 'The distinctive and deep significance of consciousness raising at an earlier period of the women's movement was precisely this process of opening up what was personal, idiosyncratic, and inchoate and discovering with others how this was shared, was objectively part of women's oppression, finding ways of speaking of it and ways of speaking it politically' ('A sociology for women', 1979, p. 144).

A number of feminists have commented upon the need for and value of this approach. Michèle Mattelart, for example, has made this comment:

> [T]here are a great many studies of media power structures, national and international, and a great many too of the content of media messages, but very few on the manner in which the 'dominated' groups and individuals read and respond to them, or oppose to them a specific manner of, precisely, appropriation, and resist them ... in the name of some project of their own. (Mattelart, 1982, p. 141)

Referring to the popularity of the melodramatic serial, she pointed out that the question of taste and pleasure produced by these products cannot be ignored. In the case of this particular fictional genre, she has suggested that its popularity may depend on its correspondence to the psychic structure of female subjective time.

Angela McRobbie, following a reading of the ideology operating in the British teen magazine *Jackie*, pointed out how popular the magazine is with teen girls, based on sales figures, yet cautioned: 'Of course this does not mean that its readers swallow its axioms unquestioningly. And indeed until we have a clearer idea of just how girls "read" *Jackie* and encounter its ideological force, our analysis remains one-sided' (McRobbie, 1982, p. 283).

Dorothy Hobson's analysis of soap operas (1982) is an attempt to understand the popularity of the British series *Crossroads* from the standpoint of its viewers. She studied viewers in their homes as they watched the program, observing how the program fit into the structure of their home roles. Hobson challenges the usual critical judgments that viewers watch to escape. She found that viewers watched because of their involvement over time with particular characters and because they were interested in resolutions to problems they recognized as shared by other women in the program and in real life. She concluded:

> They [the viewers] do not sit there watching and taking it all in without any mental activity or creativity. It seems that they expect to contribute to the production which they are watching and bring their own knowledge to augment the text. Stories which seem almost too fantastic for an everyday serial are transformed through a sympathetic audience reading whereby they strip the storyline to the idea behind it and construct an understanding of the skeleton that is left. (p. 136)

Janice Radway's ethnographic study of a group of romance readers (1984) is a similar project in understanding the popularity or this genre And how it functions for women within the context of their own lives. The readers she studied saw their act of reading as a minor act of independence that allowed them to assert their need for time and space away from the demands made on them in their roles as primary family caretakers. The readers did not view the heroines of the romances they preferred as weak and passive but as independent and assertive. The heroines were seen as victorious because the hero came to acknowledge the primacy of the female world of love and human relations over the public world of fame and success. Radway has suggested that romance novels may be seen as an exploration of the meaning of patriarchy for women. They provide readers a minor resistance to patriarchy, a moment where patriarchy is imagined as transformed, while at the same time restoring women to their role within it as it currently exists.

Approaching popular culture from the standpoint of women's experiences with cultural forms presents feminists with a central tension in feminism. That is, it presents feminists with the challenge of respecting other women's understanding of their own lives, though that understanding may be different from a feminists reading of their situation. It also, however, presents feminists with a central objective of feminism, the opportunity for activism and change as feminists come to better understand how other women function within patriarchy. Dorothy Smith (1979) has identified the ruptures between women's experiences and the social forms of expression available to talk about them. Women's encounters with popular culture may be an important site where those ruptures can be made visible and available for critique and development.

The Cultural Theory Approach

While any feminist approach to popular culture contains at the least an implicit critique of the social structure and the organization of social relations, there is a body of feminist theory that focuses on the organization and production of culture in general.[3] Rather than looking at the content or uses of popular culture, as the previous categories did, this feminist approach requires us to stand back from popular culture to see the larger set of social and economic arrangements that produce culture and to see their implications for women's position and experience.

One theme that runs through much of feminist cultural theory is that men and women live in two different spheres and have two different cultural experiences. Elizabeth Janeway (1971) has related women's subordinate position in society to social myths that have restricted women's access to the public world by confining them to the private sphere. Despite the fact that separate spheres have existed since ancient times, Janeway has argued that this is socially determined, not innate or inevitable. The goal should be not two, but one, androgynous culture: 'One might describe these changes as the tendency for woman's place and role to expand and take over man's world: To feminize it, as the first women's movement aimed to do' (p. 305). Jessie Bernard (1981), however, has described these two separate spheres as inevitable. Bernard's solution to a female world that is currently in a state of 'cultural siege' (pp. 458-9) is not to attempt to create an androgynous society but to change the quality of those two worlds: 'Sometimes discussed by feminists are the pros and cons of separatism as a deliberate policy. Actually, the separatism is there, whether it is deliberately sought or rejected on ideological principles. The basic issue is not whether to encourage it but how best to use it' (p. 11). Women need to recover their own culture to assume control over the definition of their own world, according to Bernard.

Mary Daly (1978) has made separatism a goal to counteract the deleterious effects of male culture: 'Women's minds have been mutilated and muted ... women become eager for acceptance as docile tokens mouthing male texts, employing technology for male ends, accepting male fabrications as the true texture of reality. Patriarchy has stolen our cosmos and returned it in the form of *Cosmopolitan* magazine and cosmetics' (p. 5). Feminists should instead continue their subversive acts of creating women's own culture, 'creating new forms of writing, singing, celebrating, cerebrating, searching' (p. xv).

Angela McRobbie's critique of youth culture and subculture sociological analysis ('Settling accounts with subcultures: a feminist critique', 1980) takes a different categorization of cultures and challenges the radical celebrative analyses of subcultures that see them as subversive and oppositional to dominant cultures. Not only are boys' subcultures often cruelly anti-woman and exploitative of girls, girls' subcultures do not often contain the same possibilities for resistance and rebellion.

Another area of theorizing has been in understanding how women function symbolically in male culture. Sherry Ortner ('Is female to male as nature is to culture?', 1974) described women's symbolic role in male culture as existing in different societies in three positions in relation to culture and nature: (1) in a middle position between culture and nature, lower than man and culture but higher than nature; (2) as a mediating element in the relationship between culture and nature necessitating restrictions on women's functions so that role can be performed; (3) in an ambiguous position, with polarized and contradictory meanings, where women may on occasion be aligned with culture. These symbolic positions of women become institutionalized in a culture, requiring a change in institutions along with cultural symbolism for a change in women's position to occur. Elizabeth Cowie (1978) has challenged Claude Lévi-Strauss' analysis of kinship and communication based on the exchange of women. Cowie has argued that in order for women to have value within a system of exchange, that valuation must have existed prior to the exchange system. Culture cannot then be reduced to the exchange system as its essence, since it must exist prior to it for hierarchical social values to be established. Those social values are produced and reproduced in cultural practices such as image-producing systems.

Dorothy Smith (1978) has focused on how women are excluded from the communicative work of society because of the development of an 'ideological apparatus':

> ... women have largely been excluded from the work of producing the forms of thought and the images and symbols in which thought is expressed and ordered.

> There is a circle effect. Men attend to and treat as significant only what men say. The circle of men whose writing and talk was significant to each other extends backwards in time as far as our records reach. What men were doing was relevant to men, was written by men about men for men. Men listened and listen to what one another said. (Smith, 1978, p. 281)

This silencing of women and making them and their experiences invisible is a common theme in feminist theory. Smith here has made it particularly relevant to the question of who has access to the means of cultural expression and production.

British Marxist feminists have been dealing with the question of, as phrased by Michèle Barrett, 'what is the relationship between women's oppression and the general features of a mode of production?' (Barrett, 1980, p. 97). Barrett has come at the question from the standpoint of the ideology of gender, produced and reproduced in cultural practice. She has identified three elements in the process of the construction of an ideology of gender: production, consumption, and representation. About production she has pointed out that the conditions under which men and women produce literature are materially different, using Virginia Woolf's analysis from *A Room of One's Own*. About consumption she has noted there has been a failure to develop a theory of reading, so that an account of consumption and reception of texts from the point of view of the ideology of gender is not yet possible. She has suggested that representation of gender can be profitably thought about in terms of stereotyping in content, compensation (presenting imagery and ideas that elevate the moral value of femininity), collusion (attempts to manipulate women's consent to their subordination as well as women's consent to oppression) and recuperation (negating and diffusing challenges to the dominant meaning of gender).

Feminist cultural theory, as these selections from feminist writings suggest, locates popular culture within a broader context of women's relationships to the means of symbolic production and expression and within a larger struggle to understand and change social relations and organization.

Summary

What has been presented here is a broad and incomplete outline of feminist approaches to popular culture. Yet even this sampling of feminist work demonstrates the breadth of areas that are being examined and the diversity of starting points and proposed solutions. It should by now be apparent that a feminist analysis of popular culture does not just mean critiquing a cultural product – whether it be a romance novel, an advertisement, or a musical hit – as sexist or nonsexist. Feminists approaching popular culture proceed from a variety of theoretical positions that carry with them a deeper social analysis and political agenda. The academic 'popular culture debates', as they continue to be fought over theories of society and the role of popular culture, should pause to hear what feminists are saying. Feminists are saying that popular culture plays a role in patriarchal society and that theoretical analysis of this role warrants a major position in ongoing discussions.

Notes

1. While I am aware of the discussion within feminism, particularly by Marxist feminists, about the use of the term 'patriarchy' and the desire by some to restrict its use to a particular historic time period characterized by the literal 'rule of the father' or to reserve it for describing 'patriarchal relations' between men and women (see Michèle Barrett, 1980), I prefer the widespread feminist practice of using the term broadly, here referring to societies characterizable by the figurative 'rule of the father'. I hope my discussion in this essay illustrates the value of placing such a term next to other theories of society.
2. It seems appropriate here to take up Barbara Smith's challenge (in 'Toward a black feminist criticism', 1982, p. 162) that white women should acknowledge who and what are being left out of their own research and writing. While I have attempted to be self-aware of my own position as a white woman approaching this topic, I realize that my work here cannot fully address the perspectives women of color bring to the subject. This work, then, should be seen as partial and exploratory, and the beginning of what I hope might become a larger collaborative project by many women in constructing and asserting feminist theories of popular culture.
3. A body of related and relevant feminist work could more generally be called social theory because it deals with the organization of social life – the division of labor and production and reproduction, concepts of the public and the private, the role of the family, and the role of the state and other institutions of control. However, that work will not be considered here in the interest of remaining closer to the subject matter of popular culture.

References

Adburgham, Alison, *Women in Print: Writing women and women's magazines from the restoration to the accession of Victoria*, London: George Allen and Unwin, 1972.

Barrett, Michèle, *Women's Oppression Today: Problems in Marxist feminist analysis*, London: Verso Editions and NLB, 1980.

Bernard, Jessie, *The Female World*, New York: The Free Press, 1981.

Bigsby, C. W. E, 'The politics of popular culture', in C. W. E. Bigsby (ed.) *Approaches to Popular Culture,* Bowling Green, OH: Bowling Green University Popular Press, 3–25. Reprinted from *Cultures: An international review,* 1, 1976, 2.

Brantlinger, Patrick, *Bread and Circuses: Theories of mass culture as social decay*, Ithaca and London: Cornell University Press, 1983.

Coward, Rosalind, 'Sexual violence and sexuality', *Feminist Review,* 11, 1982, 9–22.

Cowie, Elizabeth, 'Women, representation and the image', *Screen Education,* 23, 1982, 15–23.

Cowie, Elizabeth, 'Woman as sign', *m/f,* 1, 1978, 49–63.

Daly, Mary, *Gyn/Ecology: The metaethics of radical feminism*, Boston: Beacon Press, 1978.

Donovan, Josephine, 'The silence is broken', in Sally McConnell-Ginet, Ruth Borker and Nelly Furman (eds) *Women and Language in Literature and Society*, New York: Praeger Publishers, 1980.

Douglas, Ann. *The Feminization of American Culture*, New York: Alfred A. Knopf, 1977.

Fishburn, Katherine, *Women in Popular Culture*, Westport, CT: Greenwood Press, 1982.

Friedan, Betty, *The Feminine Mystique*, New York: Norton & Co., Inc., 1963.

Gilman, Charlotte Perkins, *The Man-Made World or Our Androcentric Culture*, New York: Charlton Company, 1911. Reprinted by Johnson Reprint Corporation, New York and London, 1971.

Hale, Beatrice Forbes-Robertson, *What Women Want: An interpretation of the feminist movement*, New York: Frederick A. Stokes Co., 1914.

Hall, Stuart and Whannel, Paddy, *The Popular Arts*, New York: Pantheon Books, 1965.

Hobson, Dorothy, *Crossroads: The drama of a soap opera*, London: Methuen, 1982.

hooks, bell, *Ain't I a Woman: Black women and feminism*, Boston: South End Press, 1981.

Hull, Gloria T. and Smith, Barbara, 'The politics of Black women's studies', introduction to Gloria T. Hull, Patricia Bell Scott, and Barbara Smith (eds) *All the Women are White, All the Blacks are Men, but Some of Us Are Brave: Black women's studies*, New York: The Feminist Press, 1982.

Janeway, Elizabeth, *Man's World, Woman's Place: A study in social mythology*, New York: William Morrow & Co, 1971.

Janus, Noreene, 'Research on sex-roles in the mass media: toward a critical approach', *Insurgent Sociologist*, VII, 1977, 19–32.

Kando, Tom, 'Popular culture and its sociology: two controversies', *Journal of Popular Culture*, IX, 1975, 438–55.

Kaplan, E. Ann, *Women and Film: Both sides of the camera*, New York: Methuen, 1983.

Lanser, Susan Sniader and Beck, Evelyn Torton, '[Why] are there no great women critics?: And what difference does it make?' in Julia A. Sherman and Evelyn Torton Beck (eds) *The Prism of Sex: Essays in the sociology of knowledge*, Madison, WI: University of Wisconsin Press, 1979.

Lewis, Jill and Joseph, Gloria I., *Common Differences: Conflicts in black and white feminist perspectives*, Garden City, NY: Anchor Books, 1981.

Mattelart, Michèle, 'Women and the cultural industries', *Media, Culture and Society*, 4, 1982, 133–51. Translated by Keith Reader.

McRobbie, Angela, 'Settling accounts with subcultures: a feminist critique', *Screen Edition*, 34, 1982, 37–49.

McRobbie, Angela, 'Jackie: an ideology of adolescent feminity', in Bernard Waites, Tony Bennett and Graham Martin (eds) *Popular Culture: Past and present*, London: Croom Helm, 1982.

Miner, Madonne M., *Insatiable Appetites: Twentieth-century American women's bestsellers*, Westport, CT: Greenwood Press, 1984.

Modleski, Tania, *Loving with a Vengeance: Mass-produced fantasies for women*, Hamden, CT: Archon Books, 1982.

Moraga, Cherrie and Anzaldúa, Gloria (eds), *This Bridge Called My Back: Writings by radical women of colour*, Watertown, MA: Persephone Press, 1981.

Mulvey, Laura, 'Visual pleasure and narrative cinema', *Screen*, 16, 1975, 6–18.

National Advertising Review Board, *Advertising and Women: A report of advertising portraying or directed to women*, New York: National Advertising Review Board, 1975.

Ortner, Sherry B., 'Is female to male as nature is to culture?' in Michelle Zimbalist Rosaldo and Louise Lamphere (eds) *Woman, Culture, and Society*, Stanford, CA: Stanford University Press, 1974.

Pollock, Griselda, 'What's wrong with images of women?' *Screen Education*, 24, 1977, 25–33.

Radway, Janice A., *Reading the Romance: Women, patriarchy, and popular literature*, Chapel Hill and London: University of North Carolina Press, 1984.

Robinson, Lillian, *Sex, Class, and Culture*, Bloomington: Indiana University Press, 1978.

Smith, Barbara, 'Toward a black feminist criticism', in Gloria T. Hull, Patricia Bell Scott and Barbara Smith (eds) *All the Women an White, All the Blacks are Men, But Some of Us are Brave*, Old Westbury, NY: The Feminist Press, 1982.

Smith, Dorothy E., 'A peculiar eclipsing: women's exclusion from man's culture', *Women's Studies International Quarterly*, 1, 1978, 281–95.

Smith, Dorothy E., 'A sociology for women', in Julia A. Sherman and Evelyn Torton Beck (eds) *The Prism of Sex: Essays in the sociology of knowledge*, Madison, Wl: University of Wisconsin Press, 1979.

Strainchamps, Ethel (ed.), *Rooms with No View: A woman's guide to the man's world of the media*, New York: Harper and Row, 1974.

Tuchman, Gaye, Daniels, Arlene Kaplan, and Benet, James (eds), *Hearth and Home: Images of women in the mass media*, New York: Oxford University Press, 1978.

United States Commission on Civil Rights, *Window Dressing on the Set: Women and minorities in Television*, Washington, DC, August 1979.

United States Commission on Civil Rights, *Window Dressing on the Set: An update*, Washington, DC, January 1979.

Wald, Carol, *Myth America: Picturing women 1865–1945*, New York: Pantheon Books, 1975.

Walker, Janet, 'Psychoanalysis and feminist film theory: the problem of sexual difference and identity', *Wide Angle*, 6, 1984, 16–23.

Weibel, Kathryn, *Mirror, Mirror: Images of women reflected in popular culture*, New York: Garden City, 1977.

Wolff, Janet, *The Social Production of Art*, London: Macmillan, 1981.

28 □ *Reading* Reading the Romance

Janice Radway

It seems especially fitting that a book about the *particular* nature of the relationship between audiences and texts, which was itself initially conceived for and addressed to a specific community of readers, should require a new introduction precisely at the moment that it is to be offered to a new and different set of readers situated in another social context. Indeed, in reading *Reading the Romance* for the first time since the manuscript was completed, in preparation for offering it to a British audience, I have been struck by how much the book's argument is a product of my own intellectual history and that of the community I intended and hoped to address. As a consequence, these new remarks will constitute something of an apologia for the book's limitations and an effort to secure a particular reading in the British context.[1] I want to situate and explain the polemic of *Reading the Romance* because I suspect that the book's early theoretical claim to be doing something new will seem odd to a British audience, which will also particularly note the absence of certain references and concepts. Despite those absences, however, *Reading the Romance* does take up specific questions that have preoccupied British feminists and cultural studies scholars for some time. Thus I would like to highlight those questions, consider how and why they were posed as they were in *Reading the Romance*, and explore their similarity to and differences from the questions posed by British scholars working on subcultures and the culture of women and girls. Finally, I would like to say something about the political implications of *Reading the Romance* as I now understand them, because they have been articulated more clearly for me by my continuing engagement with the work of British feminists and cultural studies scholars.

British readers of *Reading the Romance* will note immediately that the book's theoretical argument is directed generally to American Studies scholars working in the United States (although this latter qualification is not stated specifically) and more particularly to those who take literature as their primary object of concern. The resulting preoccupation with the question of what a literary text can be taken as

From Radway, J., *Reading the Romance*, Verso, London, 1987, pp. 1–18.

evidence for may seem a peculiar and oblique focus for a book that has largely been read as a contribution to feminist scholarship or as a contribution to discussions within communications theory about the status of the reader and the nature of mass cultural consumption.[2] This latter fact simply demonstrates, however, that whatever her intentions no writer can foresee or prescribe the way her book will develop, be taken up, or read. Neither can she predict how it will transform her, I might add, a subject to which I will return. Still, I think it will be helpful to know something about the immediate personal and intellectual situation which served as the polemical ground and orienting context for the writing of *Reading the Romance* because I think it goes a long way toward explaining why the book was eventually hijacked by its own theory and subject and, *en route* to its intended destination, gradually found itself directed to another.

As much as the theoretical argument of chapter one is the product of an intellectual quarrel, so too is it the product of an institutional and political one as well. It was born of the fact that I had been hired in 1977 by the American Civilization Department at the University of Pennsylvania, which has been known within the American Studies community in the United States for its particular challenge to an earlier American Studies orthodoxy. That orthoxody, formed in the late 1940s and early 1950s, developed as part of the reaction to the hegemony of New Criticism in American English Departments. Disturbed by the extreme preoccupation with formalist criticism in an historical context that seemed to cry out for a consideration once again of what constituted 'the American', certain students of the national literature began to reassert the validity of an enterprise that would reunite the classic American literary texts with the historical context within which they were conceived. Resulting largely in an alliance between literary scholars and intellectual historians, the impulse led to the creation of American Studies programs and departments which, whatever their differences with more traditional English departments, at least still assumed that the most reliable and complex record of the American past could be found in the country's 'greatest' works of art.[3]

In opposition to such claims, however, the American Civilization Department at Pennsylvania began to elaborate a critique of the assumption that works selected on the basis of their aesthetic achievement would necessarily be representative of the large sections of the population that had never read such books. Writing within the framework prescribed by the social sciences and preoccupied therefore with questions of evidentiary validity and statistical representivity, my future colleagues (who were not, for the most part, literary critics) argued that while 'elite' literature might be taken as evidence for the beliefs of a particular section of the American population, assertions based upon it could not easily be extrapolated to wholly different classes or ethnic groups. They argued that if accurate statements were to be made about more 'ordinary' Americans, the popular literature produced for and consumed by large numbers ought to become the primary focus of culturally oriented scholarship.[4]

I was hired, then, because much of my graduate work had been preoccupied with popular literature of one sort or another. That work had been directed by Russel

Nye, one of the first serious scholars of American popular culture in the United States.[5] Although Nye was himself trained as an historian, he worked within the English Department at Michigan State University. Therefore, under his tutelage, its American Studies program articulated the need for the study of popular culture even though it remained theoretically more traditional than that at Pennsylvania. The methods of analysis it taught were still primarily those of formal analysis and textual exegesis. Thus I went to Pennsylvania as a student of popular culture but also as a literary critic. *Reading the Romance* clearly demonstrates that provenance in the conversations it chooses to join.

By the time I arrived in the department, my colleagues had turned away somewhat from statistical models for the study of society and behavior and had elaborated instead a complex rationale for the use of ethnographic methods in the effort to make sense of American culture. Drawing on anthropology rather than sociology, they argued that cultural investigation must always take account of spatial and temporal specificity. Thus they moved from what Stuart Hall and others have called the 'literary-moral' definition of culture to an anthropological one, defining it as the whole way of life of a historically and temporally situated people.[6] The department's essential graduate seminars were structured as ethnographies of particular communities which were studied synchronically and in depth. Interestingly enough, these were initiated at almost the same time investigators at the Birmingham Centre for Contemporary Cultural Studies, prompted by arguments made by Raymond Williams, E. P. Thompson, Hall, and others, were turning to ethnographic methods in their effort to study the necessary 'struggle, tension, and conflict' between subcultures or different ways of life.[7] Because this latter move originated within the well-developed Marxist tradition in Britain, even the earliest work at the Centre made an effort to consider the nature of the relationship between ethnographic investigation of behavior and cultural meaning and ideological analysis of the structures of determination.[8] Although the turn to ethnography in American Studies was prompted by a concern with the relationship (if not the struggle) between subgroups within a complex society and by an interest in the relationship between behavior and 'belief systems', the relative weakness of the Marxist tradition in the USA meant that most of the early work did not explicitly engage debates over ideology or the place of specifically cultural production in securing the domination of one group over another.

In any case, the ethnographic turn began to have relevance for me when I simultaneously began to engage with the theoretical work developing within the literary critical community on the reader and semiotic conceptions of the literary text. I grappled with this work as a result of discussions carried on within the Penn Semiotics Seminar which was heavily influenced by Dell Hymes, Erving Goffman, and Barbara Herrnstein Smith, among others. Thus, even as I was attempting to respond to my departmental colleagues' questions about what a literary text could be taken as evidence for, I was being gradually convinced by the theoretical arguments about the social and hence variable nature of semiotic processes. If one could talk of the necessity for ethnographies of speaking, I saw no reason why one shouldn't also assume that as speech varied across space and over time, so, too, reading must as well. If this was true and one could discover how actual communities actually read particular texts, I thought I saw a way to answer my colleagues' questions about the evidentiary status of literature. If reading varied spatially and temporally and one did wish to use literature in an effort to reconstruct culture, it would be necessary to connect particular texts with the communities that produced and consumed them and to make some effort to specify how the individuals involved actually constructed those texts as meaningful semiotic structures. Hence my conclusion that what American Studies needed were ethnographies of reading.

Reading the Romance was therefore conceived in response to a set of theoretical questions about literary texts. As a consequence, it was designed initially to see whether it was possible to investigate reading empirically so as to make 'accurate' statements about the historical and cultural meaning of literary production and consumption. The decision to move beyond the various concepts of the inscribed, ideal, or model reader and to work with actual subjects in history was thus a product of the difficult questions that had been put to me by colleagues trained in the social science tradition and in culture theory. The resulting empiricism of *Reading the Romance*, embodied most obviously in its claim that empirically based ethnographies of reading should replace *all* intuitively conducted interpretation in cultural study, precisely because such empiricism would guarantee a more *accurate* description of what a book meant to a given audience, was thus a function of my situation within the American Studies intellectual community as it carried on the familiar debate about the relative merits of 'scientific' as opposed to 'literary' methods in cultural study.[9]

The book that resulted did not ultimately sustain its initial project, however, because the activity of actually 'doing ethnography' produced many surprises, not the least of which was the realization that even ethnographic description of the 'native's' point of view must be an interpretation or, in words adapted from Clifford Geertz, my own construction of my informants' construction of what they were up to in reading romances. This, of course, will not be news to anyone familiar with the anthropological method or with the ethnographic work of the CCCS, but it was something I only really discovered in the course of attempting to write the ethnography. I tried to acknowledge this point in the introduction to the American edition which, like so many others, was substantially revised after all the other chapters were completed. I attempted to do this by proclaiming openly my feminism and by acknowledging that it had affected the way I evaluated or reacted to my subject's self-understanding. However, I now think that my initial preoccupation with the empiricist claims of social science prevented me from recognizing fully that even what I took to be simple descriptions of my interviewee's self-understandings were produced through an internal organization of data and thus mediated by my own conceptual constructs and ways of seeing the world.[10]

I would therefore now want to agree with Angela McRobbie when she states flatly that 'representations are interpretations'.[11] As she goes on to say, they can never be pure mirror images of some objective reality but exist always as the result of 'a whole set of selective devices, such as highlighting, editing, cutting, transcribing and inflecting'. Consequently, I no longer feel that ethnographies of reading should *replace* textual interpretation completely because of their greater adequacy to the task of revealing an objective cultural reality. Rather, I think they should become an essential and necessary component of a multiply focused approach that attempts to do justice to the ways historical subjects understood and partially control their own behavior while recognizing at the same time that such behavior and self-understanding are limited if not in crucial ways complexly determined by the social formation within which those subjects find themselves.

In practice, if not perhaps in theory, I think *Reading the Romance* actually does make an effort to do this in large part because my attempts to deal with literary production and consumption as complex social processes were affected by my first serious engagement with Marxist literary theory. That engagement had been prompted initially by Jerry Palmer's suggestion and I might want to read Terry Eagleton's *Criticism and Ideology*.[12] This initiated the pursuit of a trail of bibliographic references through the Marxist literature on ideology, an intellectual move that was reinforced by my ongoing reading in feminist literature as I began to grapple with the social situation of the women who were sharing their perceptions with me. The question of determination was thus posed for me by my attention to the material and social context within which romance reading generally occurs.

I had first taken up the subject of romances in graduate school as part of my dissertation on the differences between 'popular' and 'elite' literature.[13] Searching for a way to trace the variable use of generic conventions across these evaluative categories, I chose the gothic romance because my participation in a feminist consciousness-raising group had made me curious about feminist scholarly writing and I saw the study of the romance as a way to engage with this literature. Thus I hoped to bring together my feminist 'personal' life with my supposedly non-gendered academic work which, until that point, had not focused on women. This decision set in motion a slow, imperfect, often painful process of transformation which only really gathered impetus in the actual writing on *Reading the Romance* some six to seven years later, when the difficulties of accounting for the complexities of actual romance reading produced a more intense and personal engagement with feminist theory and its analysis of women's situation. That engagement was fostered by the romance readers' eloquence about their own lives. Even as I began to see myself in their accounts of themselves and thus to admit my identification with them, feminist writers helped me to analyze women's situation and to begin to trace its various determinants. Thus, another of the major surprises produced by doing ethnographic work was my own growing politicization. This politicization had not proceeded very far, however, at the time I began writing, and that fact, along with my preoccupation with the methodological questions about how to conduct the cultural study of literature, caused me to misread earlier feminist work on the romance, resulting in a blindness to the continuity between my own arguments and those of scholars such as Tania Modleski and Ann Barr Snitow.[14]

As a consequence, the way the study was formulated and carried out was largely a function of my first theoretical concerns, concerns that I formulated at the outset within the terms of literary critical debates. Since I was assuming from the start with reader theorist Stanley Fish that textual interpretations are constructed by interpretive communities using specific interpretive strategies, I sought to contrast the then-current interpretation of romances produced by trained literary critics with that produced by fans of the genre.[15] Thus, in going into the field. I still conceived of reading in a limited fashion *an interpretation* and saw the project largely as one focusing on the differential interpretation of texts. It was only when the Smithton women repeatedly answered my questions about the meaning of romances by talking about the meaning of romance *reading* as a social event in a familial context that the study began to interact with work being carried on in Britain.

What is so striking to me now is the way in which the romance readers themselves and their articulation of their concerns pushed me into a consideration of many of the same issues then preoccupying Paul Willis, David Morley, Charlotte Brunsdon, Angela McRobbie, Dorothy Hobson and many others.[16] Indeed, it was the women readers' construction of the act of romance reading as a 'declaration of independence' that surprised me into the realization that the meaning of their media-use was multiply determined and internally contradictory and that to get at its complexity it would be helpful to distinguish analytically between the significance of the *event* of reading and the meaning of the *text* constructed as its consequence. Although I did not then formulate it in so many words, this notion of the event of reading directed me towards a series of questions about the uses 'to which a particular text is put, its function within a particular conjuncture, in particular institutional spaces, and in relation to particular audiences'.[17] What the book gradually became, then, was less an account of the way romances as texts were interpreted than of the way romance reading as a form of behavior operated as a complex intervention in the ongoing social life of actual social subjects, women who saw themselves first as wives and mothers.

As a consequence, *Reading the Romance* bears striking similarities to Dorothy Hobson's *Crossroads*, to the work on the TV program 'Nationwide' by David Morley and Charlotte Brunsdon, and to Angela McRobbie's work on the culture of working-class girls. Although the central problematic of the book is not formulated in the languages they employ, nor is their work cited specifically, *Reading the Romance* shares their preoccupation with questions about the degree of freedom audiences demonstrate in their interaction with media messages and their interest in the way such cultural forms are embedded in the social life of their users. The theoretical position taken up to the book is quite close to Dorothy Hobson's conclusion that 'there is no overall intrinsic message or meaning in the work', and that 'it comes alive and communicates when the viewers add their own interpretation and understanding to the programme'.[18] Indeed, because I agreed at the outset with Stanley Fish's claim that textual features are not an essential structure upon which an interpretation is hung but rather produced *through* the interpretive process. I think the theoretical position of *Reading the Romance* is also close to Hobson's additional observation that 'there can be as many interpretations of a programme [or text] as the individual viewers bring to it'.[19] However, the book argues additionally that whatever the theoretical possibility of an infinite number of readings, in fact, there are patterns or regularities to what viewers and readers bring to texts and media messages in large part because they acquire specific cultural competencies as a consequence of their particular social location. Similar readings are produced, I argue, because similarly located readers learn a similar set of reading strategies and interpretive codes which they bring to bear upon the texts they encounter.

Reading the Romance turns to Fish's notion of 'interpretive communities' to theorize these regularities and then attempts to determine whether the Smithton women operate on romances as an interpretive community that is somehow different from the community of trained literary scholars. However, because Fish developed the notion of the interpretive community only to account for varying modes of literary criticism within the academy, that is, to account for the differing interpretations produced by Freudian, Jungian, mythic, or Marxist critics, the concept is insufficiently theorized to deal with the complexities of social groups or to explain how, when, and why they are constituted precisely *as* interpretive communities. Thus it cannot do justice to the nature of the connection between social location and the complex process of interpretation. It is inadequate finally to the task of explaining determination.

The question of determination and regularities became immediately relevant to the research, however, because the group I examined was relatively homogeneous. Not only did the women give remarkably similar answers to my questions about romances, but they referred constantly and *voluntarily* to the connection between their reading and their daily social situation as wives and mothers. I thus theorized the correlation between their patterned answers and their similar social location by resorting to the explanatory constructs of feminist theory, to the notion of 'patriarchal marriage' in particular. Not only have I used the concept to account for the social situation within which their reading occurs and thus employed it to make sense of their reading as an intervention within that situation, but I have also projected it back in time as a social form and, with the help of the psychoanalytic theories of Nancy Chodorow, used it to explain the construction of desire responsible for their location and their partial dissatisfaction with it, which itself leads ultimately in repetitive romance reading.

While I now feel this reification of patriarchal marriage was helped in generating detailed knowledge about the ways in which romances engage these women, I also think it permitted me to avoid certain crucial theoretical questions about the precise mechanisms of determination. Had I designed the study comparatively, perhaps some of the issues David Morley has raised in his critical postscript to *The 'Nationwide' Audience* might have come more prominently to the fore.[20] He points there in particular to the inadequacies he sees in his own earlier discussion of the determinations upon meaning produced by the effectivity of the traditional sociological/structural variables – age, sex, race and class. Many of the problems Morley identifies in his work with respect to this problem are also present in mine. Whereas he notes his excessive concentration on the single variable of class and the rather simple way in which the concept itself was constructed, so I might point in my own study to the exclusive preoccupation with gender and to the use of a rather rigid notion of patriarchy. Indeed, I would now want to organize an ethnography of romance reading comparatively in order to make some effort to ascertain how other sociological variables like age, class location, education and race intersect with gender to produce varying, even conflicting engagements with the romance form. It might also be interesting to study similarly situated women who are non-romance readers in an effort to locate the absence (or perhaps the addition) of certain discursive competencies which render the romance incomprehensible, uninteresting, or irrelevant.

Whatever the sociological weaknesses of *Reading the Romance*, I continue to feel that the particular method (or aggregate of methods) employed there to map the complexities of the romance's 'purchase' on this small group of women can serve as a starting point for further discussion and perhaps for future analysis. I think this true, in part, because the understanding of reading that is worked out in the course of the discussion is close to the very useful generic or discursive model Morley has recommended in place of the earlier encoding–decoding formulation. I don't mean simply to imply here that *Reading the Romance* does what Morley calls for, although there are some striking similarities between what he recommends and the set of procedures the Smithton women's observations eventually pushed me toward. Rather, I want to suggest that his thoughtful comments in the postscript can usefully be employed to identify some of the other insufficiently theorized steps in my own analysis and thus might be used to extend and to improve it.

Having identified what he takes to be the principal sociological problems with his earlier work on the 'Nationwide' audience, Morley suggests that audience research might be more successful if it turned to a genre-based theory of interpretation and interaction instead of to a simple encoding–decoding model. Such a theory, he observes, might more adequately theorize the process of reading as a complex and interrelated series of actions which involves questions of relevance/irrelevance and comprehension/incomprehension in addition to that of ideological agreement. A theory in which genre is conceived as a set of rules for the production of meaning, operable through both writing and reading, might therefore be able to explain why certain sets of texts are especially interesting to particular groups of people (and not to others) because it would direct one's attention to the question of how and where a given set of generic rules had been created, learned, and used. This genre framework would focus attention on interdiscursive formations, that is, on questions about the kinds of cultural competencies that are learned as a consequence of certain social formations and how those are activated and perpetuated within and through multiple, related genres or discourses. Thus, just as one might want to ask what sorts of social grammars prepare working-class kids to understand Kung-fu movies and to find them interesting, so one might also want to ask what competencies prepare certain women to recognize romances as relevant to their experience and as potential routes to pleasure.

Although *Reading the Romance* does not use Morley's terms, it does work toward a kind of genre theory as he conceives it. To begin with, it attempts to understand how the Smithton women's social and material situation prepares them to find the act of reading attractive and even necessary. Secondly, through detailed questioning of the women about their own definition of romance and their criteria for distinguishing between ideal and failed versions of the genre, the study attempt to characterize the struggle of the particular narrative the women have chosen to engage because they find it especially enjoyable. Finally, through its use of psychoanalytic theory, the book attempts to explain how and why such a structured 'story' might be experienced as pleasurable by those women as a consequence of their socialization within a particular family unit. I would like to elaborate briefly on each of these movements in *Reading the Romance* in order to prepare the reader for what she or he will find in the subsequent pages and point to issues which would repay further exploration.

Most of the first half of *Reading the Romance* is devoted to a discussion of the social and material situation within which romance reading occurs. Thus I initially survey the collection of social forces resulting in the mass production of romances in the 1970s and 1980s, which are marketed in ways particularly appropriate to women, that is, through mail order and at commercial outlets largely frequented by them.[21] Although the move is analogous to Dorothy Hobson's detailed effort to explore the production of *Crossroads*, I have not gone so far as to investigate the professional ideologies informing the writing and editing of romances as she has done with the soap opera. The text does, however, recognize the importance of the romance writing community even to readers, because the Smithton women made it absolutely clear that they understood themselves to be reading particular and individual authors, whose special marks of style they could recount in detail, rather than identical, factory-produced commodities. Despite the mediations of the publishing industry, romance reading was seen by the women as a way of participating in a large, exclusively female community. Were I conducting this study today, I would want to compare the meaning and significance of the romance as it is inserted in the day-to-day existence of both writers and readers, for such a move might demonstrate the problems inherent in a simple reading off of cultural meaning or ideology from a single text.[22]

Turning from the particular processes impinging on production which create the conditions of possibility for regular romance purchases, *Reading the Romance* then attempts a parallel look at the conditions organizing women's private lives which likewise contribute to the possibility of regular romance reading. It is in this context that I distinguish analytically between the event of reading and the text encountered through the process. I found it necessary to do so, the reader will discover, because the Smithton women so insistently and articulately explained that their reading was a way of temporarily refusing the demands associated with their social role as wives and mothers. As they observed, it functioned as a 'declaration of independence', as a way of securing privacy while at the same time providing companionship and conversation. In effect, what chapters two and three try to do as a result is to unpack the significance of the phrase 'escape' by taking it somewhat more literally than have most analysts of the media in order to specify the origin and character of the distance the women find it necessary to maintain between their 'ordinary' lives and their fantasies.[23] I have therefore tried to take seriously the dual implications of the word escape, that is, its reference to conditions left behind and its intentional projection of a utopian future.

It is this move, I think, that specifically relates *Reading the Romance* to Hobson's *Crossroads* work, to her work on housewives, and to McRobbie's work on the culture of working-class girls. Indeed, there are remarkable similarities to the way all of the women who contributed to these studies use traditionally female forms to resist their situation *as women* by enabling them to cope with the features of the situation that oppress them. Thus, just as the adolescent girls studied by McRobbie manipulate the culture of femininity to 'combat the class-based and oppressive features of the school', and the housewives in Hobson's study rely on radio and TV to address their extreme loneliness, so the romance readers of Smithton use their books to erect a barrier between themselves and their families in order to declare themselves temporarily off-limits to those who would mine them for emotional support and material care. What the reader will find in chapter three, then, is an effort to explore the myriad ways in which the simple act of taking up a book addresses the personal costs hidden within the social role of wife and mother. I try to make a case for seeing romance reading as a form of individual resistance to a situation predicted on the assumption that it is women alone who are responsible for the care and emotional nurturance of others. Romance reading buys time and privacy for women even as it addresses the corollary consequence of their situation, the physical exhaustion and emotional depletion brought about by the fact that no one within the patriarchal family is charged with *their* care. Given the Smithton women's high specific reference to such costs, I found it impossible to ignore their equally fervent insistence that romance reading creates a feeling of hope, provides emotional sustenance and produces a fully visceral sense of well-being.

It was the effort to account for the ability of romance reading to address the women's longing for emotional replenishment that subsequently directed my attention to the cultural conditions that had prepared the women to choose romances from among all the other books available to them. Thus I found myself wondering how, given the particular 'needs' the event of reading seemed to address for the Smithton women, the romance story itself figured in this conjuncture. I began to wonder what it was about the romance heroine's experience that fostered the readers' ability to see her story as interesting and accounted for their willingness to seek their own pleasure through hers precisely at the moment when they were most directly confronting their dissatisfaction with traditionally structured heterosexual relationships. What contribution did the narration of a romance make to their experience of pleasure? Why didn't the Smithton women choose to read detective stories, Westerns or bestsellers in their precious private moments?

In thus searching for a way to link a specific desire with a particularly chosen route to the fulfilment at that desire, I turned to psychoanalytic theory in general and to Nancy Chodorow's feminist revision of Freud in particular. Her work seemed relevant in this context because it insistently focused on the precise manner in which the social fact of parenting by women constitutes a female child with an ongoing need for the style of care associated originally with her primary parent, that is, with her mother. What I was trying to explain was the fact that the Smithton women apparently felt an intense need to be nurtured and cared for and that despite their universal claim to being happily married (a claim I did not doubt), that need was not being met adequately in their day-to-day existence. Romance reading, it appeared, addressed needs, desires, and wishes that a male partner could not. Chodorow's work looked useful precisely because it theorized an asymmetrical engendering process constituting women and men in profoundly mismatched ways. That work appeared additionally relevant when an investigation of the romances the Smithton women like best revealed that the heroines they most appreciated were virtually always provided with the kind of attention and care the Smithton women claimed to desire, and further, that the hero's ministrations were nearly always linked metaphorically with material concern and nurturance. Thus I found Chodorow's theories attractive because they could account for the ongoing search for the *mother* that I detected in the Smithton women's discussion of the act of romance reading and in their preferences for particular examples of the genre.

Chodorow's revisions of the psychoanalytic account of the family romance was interesting to me, in other words, because it postulated in women an ongoing, unfulfilled longing for the mother even after the oedipal turn to the father and heterosexuality had been negotiated. Although Chodorow's principal argument was that the triparite internal object configuration with which women are therefore endowed is addressed by a woman's subsequent turn to mothering and to her child (an argument that might be taken to imply that the constructed desire for the preoedipal mother may be met through particular social arrangements), it seemed to me that what the Smithton readers were saying about romance reading indicated that in fact not even the activity of mothering could satisfy that lack or desire for the mother, at least for some women.[24] I thought this might be true because so much of what the women consciously said and unconsciously revealed through their evaluative procedures pointed to the centrality of the fact that in ideal romances the hero is constructed androgynously. Although the women were clearly taken with his spectacularly masculine phallic power, in their voluntary comments and in their revealed preferences they emphasized equally that his capacity for tenderness and attentive concern was essential as well. Chodorow's theories seemed helpful because of their capacity to explain what I thought of as the twin objects of desire underlying romance reading, that is, the desire for the nurturance represented and promised by the preoedipal mother and for the power and autonomy associated with the oedipal father. Romance reading, it seemed to me, permitted the ritual retelling of the psychic process by which traditional heterosexuality was constructed for women, but it also seemed to exist as a protest against the fundamental inability of heterosexuality to satisfy the very desires with which it engendered women.[25]

Reading the Romance turns to Chodorow's revision of psychoanalytic theory in order to explain the construction of the particular desires that seem to be met by the *act* of romance reading. However, it additionally uses that theory to explore the psychological resonance of the romantic *narrative* itself for readers so constructed and engendered, a narrative which is itself precisely about the process by which female subjectivity is brought into being within the patriarchal family. Psycho-analysis is thus used also to explain why the story hails these readers, why they believe it possible to pursue their own pleasure by serving as witness to the romantic heroine's achievement of hers. What the psychoanalytically based interpretation reveals is the deep irony hidden in the fact that women who are experiencing the consequences of patriarchal marriage's failure to address their needs turn to a story which ritually recites the history of the process by which those needs are constituted. They do so, it appears, because the fantasy resolution of the tale ensures the heroine's achievement of the very pleasure the readers endlessly long for. In thus reading the story of a woman who is granted adult autonomy, a secure social position, and the completion produced by maternal nurturance, all in the person of the romantic hero, the Smithton women are repetitively asserting to be true what their still-unfilled desire demonstrates to be false, that is, that heterosexuality can create a fully coherent, fully satisfied, female subjectivity.[26]

In the end, *Reading the Romance* argues that romance reading is a profoundly conflicted activity centered upon a profoundly conflicted form. Thus the view of the romance developed here is similar to Valerie Walkerdine's account of girls' comics as a practice that channels psychic conflicts and contradictions in particular ways. It is also close to the view developed by Valerie Hey[27] as well as to that of Alison Light, who argues in her conclusion to her analysis of Daphne du Maurier's *Rebecca* that women's romance reading is 'as much a measure of their deep dissatisfaction with heterosexual options as of any desire to be fully identified with the submissive versions of femininity the texts endorse. Romance imagines peace, security and ease precisely because there is dissension, insecurity and difficulty.'[28] Light herself points to the crucial question raised by these fundamental ambiguities surrounding and infusing the act of romance reading, that is, to the crucial question of the ultimate effects the fantasy resolution has on the women who seek it out again and again. Does the romance's endless rediscovery of the virtues of a passive female sexuality merely stitch the reader ever more resolutely into the fabric of patriarchal culture? Or, alternatively, does the satisfaction a reader derives from the act of reading itself, an act she chooses, often in explicit defiance of others' opposition, lead to a new sense of strength and independence? *Reading the Romance* ends without managing to resolve these questions, asserting that an adequate answer will come only with time and with careful investigation of the developmental trajectory of the lives of adult romance readers. However much I would like to resolve the issue here, once and forever, I continue to believe that such a resolution is theoretically impossible simply because the practices of reading and writing romance continue and their effects, even now, are not fully realized.

Recent critical work on the romance that focuses on developments both within the genre and within the changing profession of romance writing itself suggests that the recontainment of protest and the channelling of desire staged by the form have not been perfect enough to thwart all change. Indeed, Ann Jones has shown in an analysis of recent Mills & Boon romances that the genre has found it increasingly necessary to engage specifically with feminism.[29] She demonstrates that the contradictions within the genre have been intensified by a tendency to consolidate certain feminist agendas for women in the character of a working, independent heroine even while disparaging the women's movement itself, usually through the speeches of the hero. This 'conflict between feminism as emergent ideology and romance as a residual genre,' contends Jones, produces three kinds of contradiction, including narrative discontinuity, irreconcilable settings, and inconsistency in realist dialogue.

I have found similar contradictions in recent American romances and have been struck by the urgency, indeed, by the near hysteria, with which romance authors assert that the newly active, more insistent female sexuality displayed in the genre is still most adequately fulfilled in an initimate, monogamous relationship characterized by love and permanence. Endless assertions of this claim are necessary because many of the more sexually explicit romances in lines such as Candlelight Ecstasy, Silhouette Desire, and Harlequin Temptation come very close to validating female desire and even to locating his origins within the woman herself. Many of the books in these lines, in fact, contain explicit depictions of premarital sexual relationships between hero and heroine and acknowledge that the heroine desires the hero as much as he does her and that she derives pleasure from the encounter. Yet in every case, these romances refuse finally to unravel the connection between female sexual desire and monogamous marriage. The stories therefore close off the vista they open up by virtue of their greater willingness to foreground the sexual fantasy at the heart of the genre. The editorial guidelines concerning the treatment of sex in Harlequin Temptations are illuminating in this context:

> Because this series mirrors the lives of comtemporary women, realistic descriptions of love scenes should be included, provided they are tastefully handled. Each book should sustain a high level of sexual tension throughout, balanced by a strong story line. Sensuous encounters should concentrate on passion and the emotional sensations aroused by kisses and caresses rather than the mechanics of sex. Of course, the couple have to be obviously in love, with emphasis put on all that being in love entails. They should definitely consummate their relationship before the end of the story, at whatever points fits naturally into the plot. The love scenes may be frequent, but not overwhelming, and should never be gratuitously included.

It seems clear that while the sexually explicit romance of the eighties may begin positively to valorize female sexuality and thus to question the equation of femininity with virtue and virginity, it must nevertheless continue to motivate sexual activity through love. It does so by retaining the notion of passion as the natural and inevitable expression of a prior *emotional* attachment, itself dependent on a natural, biologically based sexual difference. Thus, as Jones has suggested, 'critiques of the double standard are now admissible; the notion that sexuality is socially constructed, variable, re-inventable rather than instinctive is not'.[30] Consequently, even the most progressive of recent romances continue to bind female desire to a heterosexuality constructed as the only natural sexual alliance, and thus continue to prescribe partriarchal marriage as the ultimate route to the realization of a mature female subjectivity.

The recuperation is clearly important, but again I feel that we must not allow it to blind us to the fact that the romance *is* being changed and struggled over by the women who write it. Indeed, it is essential to note that in response to the creation of these sexually explicit romances, publishers have found it necessary to retain the more traditional 'sweet' romance and to create other new forms such as the 'evangelical', or 'inspirational' romance, as it is called, for women who still cannot incorporate a more explicit sexuality into the ideology of love. Thus while some romance writers are perfectly willing to identify themselves as feminists, as Catherine Kirkland has found in her study of a local chapter of the Romance Writers of America, other vociferously assert that the romance is in fact the proper response to the havoc wrought by feminism on gender relations.[31] Furthermore, it cannot be said with any certainty whether the writers who are trying to incorporate feminist demands into the genre have been moved to do so by their recognition of the contradictions within the form itself or by the pressures exerted by developments in the larger culture. What does seem clear, however, is that the struggle over the romance is itself part of the larger struggle for the right to define and to control female sexuality. Thus, it matters enormously what the cumulative effects of the act of romance reading are on actual readers. Unfortunately, those effects are extraordinarily difficult to trace.

That the problem might be even more complicated than we think is suggested by Kirkland's discovery that most of the women in the group of romance writers she studied had been avid readers *before* they tried their hand at romance writing. Some of those women suggested that they turned to writing in order to intensify the fantasy experience they associated with the act of romance reading. Others, however, did so out of newfound confidence, which they attributed to romance reading, and which led to a desire to provide pleasure for other women. Romance reading, it would seem, profoundly changes at least some women by moving them to act and to speak in a public forum. Prompted to purchase their own word processor, to convert the former sewing-room into a study, and to demand time, not now for pleasure but for their own work, such women clearly begin to challenge in a fundamental way the balance of power in the traditional family. Of course this does not happen to all romance readers, but we should not discount it as an insignificant phenomenon since the crossover rate from consumer to producer seems to be unusually high within this genre. Indeed, the romance boom could not continue to the extent it has were not thousands of women producing their own manuscripts and mailing them off regularly to Harlequin, Silhouette and Candlelight. Whether the satisfaction they derive from this activity ever prompts them to demand changes outside the privatized family environment is impossible to say, but I am not willing to rule out the possibility. Indeed, positive political strategies might be developed from the recognition that the practices of romance writing and reading continue, that they are fluid and actively being changed by both writers and readers, and that their final effects can neither be foreseen nor guaranteed in advance.

Such open-endedness, of course, immediately raises questions about specific modes of intervention, about how romance writers and readers, as well as feminist intellectuals, might contribute to the rewriting of the romance in an effort to articulate its founding fantasy to a more relevant politics. However, as many feminist theorists have acknowledged, to call for such a project from within the privileged space of the academy is highly problematic, since that call is almost inevitably grounded on a residual elitism which assumes that feminist intellectuals alone know what is best for all women. In this context, Angela McRobbie's admonition that academic feminists tend to 'underestimate the resources and capacities of "ordinary" women and girls . . . to participate in their own struggles as women but quite autonomously' is well taken.[32] What is needed, I have come to feel, is a recognition that romance writers and readers are themselves struggling with gender definitions and sexual politics *on their own terms* and that what they may need most from those of us struggling in other arenas is our support rather than our criticism or direction. To find a way to provide such support, however, or alternatively to learn from romance writers and readers, is not easy, for we lack the space and channels for integrating our practices with theirs. Our segregation by class, occupation, and race, once again, works against us.

I am drawn finally to McRobbie's brilliant suggestion that it might be our traditional restriction to the arena of personal relations and our resultant penchant for talk about them that will enable us to come together as women and to explore both our common cause and our divergent agendas.[33] What we perhaps need most, then, is a place and a vocabulary with which to carry on a conversation about the meaning of such personal relations and the seemingly endless renewal of their primacy through the genre of romance. If we could begin to talk to each other from within our culture's 'pink ghetto', we might indeed learn how 'to make talk walk'.[34] We might learn how to activate the critical power that even now lies buried in the romance as one of the few widely shared womanly commentaries on the contradictions and costs of patriarchy.

Notes

1. Although I am still somewhat uncomfortable with the voice I have adopted here, in part because I fear this sort of discussion can be read as simple personal display, I have finally

decided to use it because I agree with Angela McRobbie's argument in 'The politics of feminist research', *Feminist Review*, 12 (1982) that we must begin to acknowledge the ways in which our private, professional and intellectual lives intersect. Thus what I have tried to do is to indicate the ways in which my personal situation and insertion into already existing social institutions and theoretical conversations both served as the conditions of possibility for *Reading the Romance* and structured its limitations.

2. See, for instance, Sandra Gilbert's review in the *New York Times Book Review*, 30 December (1984).

3. For a comprehensive history of these debates, see Gene Wise, 'Paradigm dramas', *American Quarterly*, 31 (1979), pp. 293–337.

4. See, for instance, Murray Murphey, 'American civilization at Pennsylvania', *American Quarterly*, 22 (Summer 1970), pp. 489–502.

5. See, for instance, *The Unembarrassed Muse: The popular arts in America*, New York: The Dial Press, 1970.

6. Stuart Hall, 'Cultural studies and the centre: some problematics and problems', in *Culture, Media, Language: Working papers in cultural studies, 1972–79*, London: Hutchinson, 1980, p. 19. See also his 'Cultural studies: two paradigms', *Media, Culture and Society*, 2 (1980), pp. 52–72.

7. Apparently, no one in my department knew at that time of the work carried out at the Birmingham Centre. I also remained unaware of this research until after I had completed *Reading the Romance*. I cannot now recall exactly how I learned of British ethnographic studies of media use, but I would like to express my great gratitude to Patrick Hagopian and Elaine Collins, who directed my attention to many references, xeroxed chapters and articles in their possession not easily available in Philadelphia, and discussed all of it with me. Thanks also to Larry Grossberg for his more recent bibliographic help, criticism, and support.

8. I am thinking here of Paul Willis's early work, including his 'Notes on method' in *Culture, Media, Language* and his *Profane Culture* as well as of the work by the Women's Studies Group at Birmingham collected in *Women Take Issue: Aspects of women's subordination*, London: Hutchinson, 1978.

9. For a perspective discussion of the dangers inherent in conceptualizing empirical work as objectively scientific and interpretive work as subjectively humanist and therefore as categorical opposites, see Lawrence Grossberg, 'Critical theory and the politics of research', *Hass Communication Yearbook*, 6 (Forthcoming).

10. Paul Willis, 'Notes on method', p. 90.

11. Angela McRobbie, 'The politics of feminist research', p. 51.

12. See Palmer's *Thrillers: Genesis and structure of a popular genre*, London: Edward Arnold, 1978; Terry Eagleton, *Criticism and Ideology: A study in Marxist literary theory*, London: NLB, 1976.

13. *A Phenomenological Theory of Popular and Elite Literature*, Ph.D. Dissertation, Michigan State University, 1977.

14. See, for instance, my comments throughout the introduction to the American edition. However, I should not minimize the fact that significant differences in method and political perspective, particularly with respect to the audience for mass culture, continue to separate my approach and that taken by Modleski. See, for instance, her introduction to the recent *Studies in Entertainment: Critical approaches to mass culture*, Bloomington: University of Indiana, 1986, pp. ix–xix, where she specifically takes issue with the work

of the 'Birmingham School' and related approaches to the study of mass culture and charges that work with being celebratory rather than critical.

15. See his *Is There a Text in This Class?: The authority of interpretive communities*, Cambridge, MA: Harvard University Press, 1980.

16. See the aforementioned titles by Willis and David Morley and Charlotte Brundson, *Everyday Television: Nationwide*, London: British Film Institute (1978); David Morley, *The 'Nationwide' Audience*, London: British Film Institute (1980); Angela McRobbie, 'Working class girls and the culture of femininity', in *Women Take Issue*, pp. 96–108; 'Settling accounts with subcultures: a feminist critique', *Screen*, 34 (Spring, 1980), pp. 39–49; and 'Jackie: an ideology of adolescent femininity', in *Popular Culture: past and present*, ed. Bernard Waites et al., London (1982), pp. 263–83; Dorothy Hobson, 'Housewives: isolation as oppression', in *Women Take Issue*, pp. 79–95; and *Crossroads. The drama of a soap opera*, London: Methuen (1982).

17. David Morley, *The 'Nationwide' Audience*, p. 18.

18. Dorothy Hobson, *Crossroads*, p. 170.

19. *Ibid.*

20. David Morley, 'The 'Nationwide' Audience – a critical postscript', *Screen Education*, 39 (Summer, 1981), pp. 3–14.

21. I should perhaps note here that this boom was initiated in the USA by the Canadian firm of Harlequin Enterprises, which began its rise to prominence in mass market publishing by reprinting the romances of Mills & Boon in the 1950s and 1960s. The genre took off in the USA when Harlequin began to issue romance written by American women and when other firms simultaneously introduced explicit sex into the genre. The Smithton women did not confine themselves to a single kind of romance but read widely in the genre and appreciated many different variations.

22. On this point, see Grossberg's discussion in 'Critical theory and the politics of research', *Mass Communications Yearbook*, 6 (Forthcoming, 1987).

23. The tendency to deplore the 'escapist' nature of popular fantasy seems much less pronounced in British work than in American. See, for instance, Valerie Walkerdine's sensitive discussion of the nature of fantasy escape for girls in 'Some day my prince will come: young girls and the preparation for adolescent sexuality', in *Gender and Genderation*, ed. Angela McRobbie and Mica Nava, London: Macmillan (1984), pp. 162–84.

24. The British reader will no doubt note that this did not lead me to reconsider Chodorow's work and its relation to object-relations theory. Walkerdine's comments in 'Some day my prince will come' (pp. 178–81) have since suggested to me that the revision romance reading caused me to produce in Chodorow's theory may be of more significance than I had thought. It may not be the case that mothering fails to work only for some (aberrant) women, but in fact that the struggle over gender identity is never resolved as she suggests, following Freud, Lacan, and Rose.

25. For a somewhat different use of Chodorow that also connects romance reading to the search for preoedipal merging, see Angela Mile's fascinating unpublished article 'Confessions of a Harlequin reader: romance and the fantasy of male mothering'.

26. Cora Kaplan has recently advanced an argument which suggests that readers do not identify only with the romantic heroine but in fact identify in multiple and wandering fashion with the seducer, the seduced and the process of seduction itself. See '*The Thorn Birds*: fiction, fantasy, femininity', in *Sea Changes: Feminism and culture* (London:

Verso, 1986), pp. 117–46. Although I found little evidence of this kind of multiple identification in the group I interviewed (at least at a conscious level). I have been told by many romance writers that the act of writing a romance is especially enjoyable because it gives them the opportunity to imagine themselves as the hero. It is also interesting to note that several American publishers of romances have recently permitted writers to experiment with the writing of a romance entirely from the hero's point of view. Thus it might be possible that this sort of multiple identification actually varied from reader to reader and therefore can be increased by cultural or personal changes.

27. Valerie Hey, 'The necessity of romance', University of Kent at Canterbury, Women's Studies Occasional Papers, no. 3, 1983.
28. Alison Light, '"Returning to Manderley" – romance fiction, female sexuality and class', *Feminist Review*, 16 (April, 1984), pp. 7–25.
29. Ann Rosalind Jones, 'Mills & Boon meets feminism', in *The Progress of Romance: The politics of popular fiction*, ed. Jean Radford, London: Routledge & Kegan Paul (1986), pp. 195–220.
30. Ann Jones, 'Mills & Boon meets feminism', p. 210.
31. Catherine Kirkland, *For the Love of it: Women writers and the popular romance*, Ph.D. diss., University of Pennsylvania, 1984.
32. Angela McRobbie, 'The politics of feminist research', p. 53.
33. *Ibid.*, p. 57.
34. The phrases are Catherine Kirkland's and Angela McRobbie's respectively.

29 □ The Color Purple: *Black Women as Cultural Readers*

Jacqueline Bobo

[...]

My aim is to examine the way in which a specific audience creates meaning from a mainstream text and uses the reconstructed meaning to empower themselves and their social group. This analysis will show how Black women as audience members and cultural consumers have connected up with what has been characterized as the 'renaissance of Black women writers'.[1] The predominant element of this movement is the creation and maintenance of images of Black women that are based upon Black women's constructions, history and real-life experiences.

As part of a larger study I am doing on *The Color Purple* I conducted a group interview with selected Black women viewers of the film.[2] Statements from members of the group focused on how moved they were by the fact that Celie eventually triumphs in the film. One woman talked about the variety of emotions she experienced: 'I had different feelings all the way through the film, because first I was very angry, and then I started to feel so sad I wanted to cry because of the way Celie was being treated. It just upset me the way she was being treated and the way she was so totally dominated. But gradually, as time went on, she began to realize that she could do something for herself, that she could start moving and progressing, that she could start reasoning and thinking things out for herself.' Another woman stated that she was proud of Celie for her growth: 'The lady was a strong lady, like I am. And she hung in there and she overcame.'

One of the women in the group talked about the scene where Shug tells Celie that she has a beautiful smile and that she should stop covering up her face. This woman said that she could relate to that part because it made Celie's transformation in the film so much more powerful. At first, she said, everybody who loved Celie [Shug and Nettie], and everyone that Celie loved, kept telling her to put her hand down. The woman then pointed out 'that last time Celie put her hand down nobody told her to put her hand down. She had started coming into her own. So when she

From Pribram, D. (ed.), *Female Spectators*, Verso, London, 1988, pp. 93–109.

grabbed that knife she was ready to use it.' This comment refers to the scene in the film at the dinner table, when Celie and Shug are about to leave for Memphis. Mister begins to chastise Celie, telling her that she will be back. He says, 'You ugly, you skinny, you shaped funny and you scared to open your mouth to people.' Celie sits there quietly and takes Mister's verbal abuse. Then she asks him, 'Any more letters come?' She is talking about Nettie's letters from Africa that Mister has been hiding from Celie and that Celie and Shug had recently found. Mister replies, 'Could be, could be not.' Celie jumps up at that point, grabs the knife, and sticks it to Mister's throat.

The woman who found this scene significant continued: 'But had she not got to that point, built up to that point [of feeling herself worthwhile], she could have grabbed the knife and turned it the other way for all that it mattered to her. She wouldn't have been any worse off. But she say herself getting better. So when she grabbed that knife she was getting ready to use it and it wasn't on herself.'

Other comments from the women were expressions of outrage at criticisms made against the film. The women were especially disturbed by vicious attacks against Alice Walker and against Black women critics and scholars who were publicly defending the film. One of the women in the interview session commented that she was surprised that there was such controversy over the film: 'I had such a positive feeling about it, I couldn't imagine someone saying that they didn't like it.' Another said that she was shocked at the outcry from some Black men: 'I didn't look at it as being stereotypically Black or all Black men are this way' (referring to the portrayal of the character Mister).

[. . .]

I have found that on the whole Black women have discovered something progressive and useful in the film. It is crucial to understand how this is possible when viewing a work made according to the encoding of dominant ideology. Black women's responses to *The Color Purple* loom as an extreme contrast to those of many other viewers. Not only is the difference in reception noteworthy, but Black women's responses confront and challenge a prevalent method of media audience analysis which insists that viewers of mainstream works have no control or influence over a cultural product. Recent developments in media audience analysis demonstrate that there is a complex process of negotiation whereby specific members of a culture construct meaning from a mainstream text that is different from the meanings others would produce. These different readings are based, in part, on viewers' various histories and experiences.

Oppositional Readings

The encoding–decoding model is useful for understanding how a cultural product can evoke such different viewer reactions. The model was developed by the University of Birmingham Centre for Contemporary Cultural Studies, under the direction of Stuart Hall, in an attempt to synthesize various perspectives on media audience analysis and to incorporate theory from sociology and cultural studies. This model is concerned with an understanding of the communication process as it operates in a specific cultural context. It analyses ideological and cultural power and the way in which meaning is produced in that context. The researchers at the Centre felt that media analysts should not look simply at the meaning of a text but should also investigate the social and cultural framework in which communication takes place.[3]

From political sociology, the encoding–decoding model was drawn from the work of Frank Parkin, who developed a theory of meaning systems.[4] This theory delineates three potential responses to a media message: dominant, negotiated or oppositional. A dominant (or preferred) reading of a text accepts the content of the cultural product without question. A negotiated reading questions parts of the content of the text but does not question the dominant ideology which underlies the production of the text. An oppositional response to a cultural product is one in which the recipient of the text understands that the system that produced the text is one with which she/he is fundamentally at odds.[5]

A viewer of a film (reader of a text) comes to the moment of engagement with the work with a knowledge of the world and a knowledge of other texts, or media products. What this means is that when a person comes to view a film, she/he does not leave her/his histories, whether social, cultural, economic, racial, or sexual, at the door. An audience member from a marginalized group (people of colour, women, the poor, and so on) has an oppositional stance as they participate in mainstream media. The motivation for this counter-reception is that we understand that mainstream media has never rendered our segment of the population faithfully. We have as evidence our years of watching films and television programmes and reading plays and books. Out of habit, as readers of mainstream texts, we have learned to ferret out the beneficial and put up blinders against the rest.

From this wary viewing standpoint, a subversive reading of a text can occur. This alternative reading comes from something in the work that strikes the viewer as amiss, that appears 'strange'. Behind the idea of subversion lies a reader-oriented notion of 'making strange'.[6] When things appear strange to the viewer, she/he may then bring other viewpoints to bear on the watching of the film and may see things other than what the film-makers intended. The viewer, that is, will read 'against the grain' of the film.

Producers of mainstream media products are not aligned in a conspiracy against an audience. When they construct a work they draw on their own background, experience and social and cultural milieu. They are therefore under 'ideological pressure' to reproduce the familiar.[7] When Steven Spielberg made *The Color Purple* he did not intend to make a film that would be in the mould of previous films that were directed by a successful white director and had an all-Black or mostly Black cast.

[. . .]

Black Women's Response

Given the similarities of *The Color Purple* to past films that have portrayed Black people negatively, Black women's positive reaction to the film seems inconceivable. However, their stated comments and published reports prove that Black women not only like the film but have formed a strong attachment to it. The film is significant in their lives.

John Fiske provides a useful explanation of what is meant by the term 'the subject' in cultural analysis. 'The subject' is different from the individual. The individual is the biological being produced by nature; the 'subject' is a social and theoretical construction that is used to designate individuals as they become significant in a political or theoretical sense. When considering a text – a cultural product – the subject is defined as the political being who is affected by the ideological construction of the text.[8]

Black women, as subjects for the text, *The Color Purple*, have a different history and consequently a different perspective from other viewers of the film. This became evident in the controversy surrounding the film, and in the critical comments from some Black males about what they perceived as the detrimental depiction of Black men. In contrast to this view, Black women have demonstrated that they found something useful and positive in the film. Barbara Christian relates that the most frequent statement from Black women has been: 'Finally, somebody says something about us.'[9] This sense of identification with what was in the film would provide an impetus for Black women to form an engagement with the film. This engagement could have been either positive or negative. That it was favourable indicates something about the way in which Black women have constructed meaning from this text.

It would be too easy, I think, to categorize Black women's reaction to the film as an example of 'false consciousness'; to consider Black women as cultural dupes in the path of a media barrage who cannot figure out when a media product portrays them and their race in a negative manner. Black women are aware, along with others, of the oppression and harm that come from a negative media history. But Black women are also aware that their specific experience, as Black people, as women, in a rigid class/caste state, has never been adequately dealt with in mainstream media.

One of the Black women that I interviewed talked about this cultural past and how it affected her reaction to *The Color Purple*: 'When I went to the movie, I thought, here I am, I grew up looking at Elvis Presley kissing on all these white girls. I grew up listening to "Tammy, Tammy, Tammy". [She sings the song that Debbie Reynolds sang in the movie of the same name.] And it wasn't that I had anything projected before me on the screen to really give me something that I could grow up to be like. Or even wanted to be. Because I knew I wasn't Goldilocks, you know, and I had heard those stories all my life. So when I got to the movie, the first thing I say was "God, this is good acting." And I liked that. I felt a lot of pride in my Black brothers and sisters. . . . By the end of the movie I was totally emotionally drained. . . . The emotional things were all in the book, but the movie just took every one of my emotions. . . . Towards the end, when she looks up and sees her sister Nettie . . . I had gotten so emotionally high at that point . . . when she saw her sister, when she started to call her name and to recognize who she was, the hairs on my neck started to stick up. I had never had a movie do that to me before.'

The concept 'interpellation' sheds light on the process by which Black women were able to form a positive engagement with *The Color Purple*. Interpellation is the way in which the subject is hailed by the text; it is the method by which ideological discourses constitute subjects and draw them into the text/subject relationship. John Fiske describes 'hailing' as similar to hailing a cab. The viewer is hailed by a particular work; if she/he gives a co-operative response to the beckoning, then not only are they constructed as a subject, but the text then becomes a text, in the sense that the subject begins to construct meaning from the work and is constructed by the work.[10]

The moment of the encounter of the text and the subject is known as the 'interdiscourse'. David Morley explains this concept, developed by Michel Pêcheux, as the space, the specific moment when subjects bring their histories to bear on meaning production in a text.[11] Within this interdiscursive space, cultural competencies come into play. A cultural competency is the repertoire of discursive strategies, the range of knowledge, that a viewer brings to the act of watching a film and creating meaning from a work. As has been stated before, the meanings of a text will be constructed differently depending on the various backgrounds of the viewers. The viewers' position in the social structure determines, in part, what sets of discourses or interpretive strategies they will bring to their encounter with the text. A specific cultural competency will set some of the boundaries to meaning construction.

The cultural competency perspective has allowed media researchers to understand how elements in a viewer's background play a determining role in the way in which she/he interprets a text. Stuart Hall, David Morley and others utilize the theories of Dell Hymes, Basil Bernstein and Pierre Bourdieu for an understanding of the ways in which a social structure distributes different forms of cultural decoding strategies throughout the different sections of the media audience. These understandings are not the same for everyone in the audience because they are shaped by the individual's history, both media and cultural, and by the individual's social affiliations such as race, class, gender, and so on.[12]

As I see it, there can be two aspects to a cultural competency, or the store of understandings that a marginalized viewer brings to interpreting a cultural product. One is a positive response where the viewer constructs something useful from the work by negotiating her/his response, and/or gives a subversive reading to the work. The other is a negative response in which the viewer rejects the work. Both types of oppositional readings are prompted by the store of negative images that have come from prior mainstream media experience: in the case of *The Color Purple*, from Black people's negative history in Hollywood films.

A positive engagement with a work could come from an intertextual cultural experience. This is true, I think, with the way in which Black women constructed meaning from *The Color Purple*. Creative works by Black women are proliferating now. This intense level of productivity is not accidental nor coincidental. It stems from a desire on the part of Black women to construct works more in keeping with their experiences, their history, and with the daily lives of other Black women. And Black women, as cultural consumers, are receptive to these works. The intertextual cultural knowledge is forming Black women's store of decoding strategies for films that are about them. This is the cultural competency that Black women brought to their favourable readings of *The Color Purple*.

Black Women's Writing Tradition: Community and Articulation

The historical moment in which the film *The Color Purple* was produced and received is what one Black feminist scholar has categorized the 'renaissance of Black women writers' of the 1970s and 1980s. Within this renaissance the central concern of the writers has been the personal lives and collective histories of Black women. The writers are reconstructing a heritage that has either been distorted or ignored. In this reconstruction, Black women are both audience and subject.[13]

A major difference in the current period of writing from that of the well-known Harlem Renaissance of the 1920s, the protest literature of the 1940s and the Black activist literature of the 1960s, is that Black women writers are getting more exposure and recognition today, and the target of their works is different. In the earlier periods of Black writing, male writers were given dominant exposure and the audience to whom they addressed their works was white. The writers believed that because Black people's oppression was the direct result of white racism, exposing this fact to white people would result in change. By contrast, for Black women writers within the last forty years, the Black community has been the major focus of their work.

Hortense J. Spillers writes that the community of Black women writing is a vivid new fact of national life. Spillers includes in this community not only the writers but Black women critics, scholars, and audience members. This community, which Spillers labels a community of 'cultural workers', is fashioning its own tradition. Its writers and its readers are, she writes, creating their works against the established canons and are excavating a legacy that is more appropriate to their lives. Spillers argues compellingly that traditions are made, not born. Traditions do not arise spontaneously out of nature, but are created social events. She insists that traditions exist not only because there are writers there to make them, but also because there is a 'strategic audience of heightened consciousness prepared to read and interpret the works as such'.[14]

Spillers adds that traditions need to be maintained by an audience if they are to survive, and she argues that this is currently happening. She writes that 'we are called upon to witness' the formation of a new social order of Black women as a community conscious of itself. This is not a random association of writers creating in isolation or readers consuming the works in a vacuum. According to Spillers, the group views itself as a community and is aware that it is creating new symbolic values and a new sense of empowerment for itself and the members of the group.

Stuart Hall has defined the principle of 'articulation', developed by Ernesto Laclau, to explain how individuals within a particular society at a specific historical moment wrest control away from the dominant forces in a culture and attain authority over their lives for themselves and for others within their social group. The way in which an articulation is accomplished, and its significance, has bearing on this examination of the film *The Color Purple*. An articulation is defined as the form of a connection, a linkage, that can establish a unity among different elements within a culture, under certain conditions.[15] In the case of a cultural product such as the film *The Color Purple*, the unity that is formed links a discourse (the film) and a specific social group (Black women or, more precisely, what Spillers has defined as the Black women's writing community). Such unity is flexible, but not for all time. It must constantly be strengthened. The strength of the unity formed between a discourse and a social alliance comes from the use to which the group puts the discourse, or the cultural product. In the case of *The Color Purple*, the film has been used to give new meaning to the lives of Black women.

Articulation, as it is normally defined, can have two meanings: 'joining up' in the sense of the limbs of a body or an anatomical structure, or 'giving expression to'.[16] Hall disagrees with the use of articulation to mean 'giving expression to' because it implies that a social group shares an expressive unity, which Hall believes it does not. An articulation results from a coming together of separate discourses under certain specific conditions and at specific times. The use of articulation to mean 'giving expression to' implies that the two elements that are linked are the same, but for Hall they are not. The unity formed 'is not that of an identity where one structure perfectly reproduces or recapitulates' the other. The social group and the signifying text are not the same. An articulation occurs because a social alliance forms it, in a political act which makes the group a cohesive one for a time, as long as it goes on acting for a political purpose.

When an articulation arises, old ideologies are disrupted and a cultural transformation is accomplished. The cultural transformation is not something totally new, nor does it have an unbroken line of continuity with the past. It is always in a process of becoming. But at a particular moment the reality of the cultural transformation becomes apparent. The group that is the catalyst for it recognizes that a change is occurring and that they are in the midst of a cultural transition. The formal elements of the transformation are then recognized and consolidated.

The Black women's writing tradition laid a foundation for the way in which Black women formed an articulation through which they interpreted the film *The Color Purple*. The boundaries of the tradition are set from 1850 onward. Although Black women were socially and politically active from the beginning of their enforced presence in the 'new world', their writings, speeches, and lectures, their 'public voice', as Hazel Carby describes it, was not being recorded and preserved. Carby makes the critical point, however, that Black women's voices were being heard.[17] The public voice of nineteenth-century Black women activists resounds now in the creative works of Black women in the 1970s and the 1980s, thus giving contemporary texts all the elements of a tradition.

[. . .]

Black women's positive response to the film *The Color Purple* is not coincidental, nor is it insignificant. It is in keeping with the recent emergence of a body of critical works about the heritage of Black women writers, the recent appearance of other novels by Black women written in the same vein as *The Color Purple* and, very importantly, the fact that there is a knowledgeable core of Black women readers of both literary and filmic texts. This community of heightened consciousness is in the process of creating new self-images and forming a force for change.

Notes

1. Mary Helen Washington, 'Book review of Barbara Christian's *Black Women Novelists*', *Signs Journal of Women in Culture and Society*, vol. 8, no. 1 (August 1982), p. 182.
2. I am at present writing a dissertation on Black women's response to the film *The Color Purple*. As part of this study I conducted what will be an ethnography of reading with selected Black women viewers of the film in December 1987 in California. All references to women interviewed come from this study. For a discussion of the issues of readers' response to texts in media audience analysis, see Ellen Seiter *et al.*, 'Don't treat us like we're so stupid and naive: towards an ethnography of soap opera viewers', in *Rethinking Television Audiences*, in Ellen Seiter (ed.), Chapel Hill: University of North Carolina Press, forthcoming. See also Seiter's use of Umberto Eco's open/closed text distinction to examine the role of the woman reader. Seiter uses Eco's narrative theory to argue for the possibility of 'alternative' readings unintended by their producers in 'Eco's TV guide: the soaps', *Tabloid*, no. 6 (1981), pp. 36–43.
3. David Morley, 'Changing paradigms in audience studies', in *Rethinking Television Audiences*, Ellen Seiter (ed.), Chapel Hill: University of North Carolina Press, forthcoming.
4. David Morley, 'Changing paradigms', p. 4.
5. Lawrence Grossberg, 'Strategies of Marxist cultural interpretation', *Critical Studies in Mass Communication*, no. 1 (1984), p. 404.
6. Christine Gledhill explains the idea of 'making strange' in two articles: 'Developments in feminist film criticism', in *Re-Vision: Essays in feminist film criticism*, Mary Ann Doane, Patricia Mellencamp and Linda Williams (eds), Frederick, MD: University Publications of America, in association with the American Film Institute, 1984; and 'Klute I: a contemporary film noir and feminist criticism', in *Women in Film Noir*, E. Ann Kaplan (ed.), London: British Film Institute, 1984.
7. Lawrence Grossberg, p. 403.
8. John Fiske, 'British cultural studies and television', *Channels of Discourse: Television*

and contemporary criticism, Robert C. Allen (ed.), Chapel Hill: University of North Carolina Press, 1987, p. 258.

9. Barbara Christian, University of Oregon, 20 May 1986.

10. John Fiske, 'British cultural studies and television', p. 258.

11. David Morley, 'Texts, readers, subjects', in *Culture, Media, Language*, Stuart Hall, Dorothy Hobson, Andrew Lowe and Paul Willis (eds), London: Hutchinson, 1980, p. 164.

12. David Morley, 'Changing paradigms in audience studies', p. 4.

13. Barbara Christian, Seminar: 'Black women's literature and the canon', University of Oregon, 7 December 1987.

14. Hortense J. Spillers, 'Cross-currents, discontinuities: Black women's fiction', *Conjuring: Black women, fiction, and literary tradition*, Marjorie Pryse and Hortense J. Spillers (eds), Bloomington: Indiana University Press, 1985, p. 250.

15. Stuart Hall discusses the principle of 'articulation' in two articles: 'Race, articulation and societies structured in dominance', in *Sociological Theories: Race and colonialism*, UNESCO, 1980, pp. 305–45. Also, Lawrence Grossberg (ed.), 'On postmodernism and articulation: an interview with Stuart Hall', *Journal of Communication Inquiry*, vol. 10, no. 2, Summer 1986, p. 45–60.

   I explore the principle of 'articulation' further in the larger study that I am doing on Black women's response to *The Color Purple*. I see the articulation between Black women as audience, the Black women's writing community and Black women's collective response to the film as constituting a social force that will affect other areas in Black people's lives: politically, economically and socially.

16. Hall, 'Race, articulation and societies structured in dominance', p. 28.

17. Hazel V. Carby, *Restructuring Womanhood: The emergence of the Afro-American woman novelist*, New York: Oxford University Press, 1987. Other critical works that examine the Black women's writing tradition are: *The Black Woman* (1970), by Toni Cade; *Black-Eyed Susans* (1975) and *Midnight Birds* (1980), by Mary Helen Washington; *Black Women Writers at Work* (1983), Claudia Tate (ed.); *Black Women Writers* (1984), by Mari Evens; *Invented Lives* (1987), by Mary Helen Washington; and *Specifying* (1987), by Susan Willis.

30 □ Soap Opera and Utopia

Christine Geraghty

Placing prime time soap opera within the complex discourse of women's fiction is problematic. [. . .] [B]oth the romance and the woman's film have their own internal conventions and their relationship with their audience has only begun to be explored. In addition prime time soaps, unlike their daytime equivalents, have never been conceived of as entirely or even predominantly for women in the same way as the romance and the woman's film have, and in the 1980s, [. . .], the pressures to change have moved them even further from exclusive categorisation as women's fiction.

Nevertheless, the soap operas I have been discussing [. . .] do have much in common with their equivalents in the other media, enough to make a comparison of their similarities and differences a fruitful task. Even this brief survey has shown areas of common ground between the romance, the woman's film and these prime time soaps. In each genre, the emphasis is on the central woman protagonist(s) whom the reader is invited to support and whose reasons for action are understood by the audience, although not necessarily by the male characters. In all three, there is a division between the public and the private sphere, male and female spaces respectively, and the woman's pre-eminence in the narrative is based on her understanding and control of the emotional arena. If she is threatened or defeated, it is because this commitment proves inadequate in the public world and her skills go unrecognised or are discarded. Within the three genres, physical action tends not to be the motivating force in the narrative; instead the emphasis is on the building up and maintenance of relationships in which the verbal expression of feeling or indeed the withholding of such expression is crucial to the resolution.

In addition, I would argue that all three genres seek to enable their readers to imagine an ideal world in which values traditionally associated with women are given space and expression and in which there is some model of the way in which relationships, particularly those between men and women, could be differently organised on women's terms. The emphasis on fantasy and escapism in women's

From Geraghty, C., *Women and Soap Opera*, Polity Press, Cambridge, 1991, pp. 116–250.

fiction is linked with the way in which it explores these issues through the creation of utopias, in which the values associated with the personal sphere are dominant, or of dystopias, in which the consequences of ignoring such values are laid bare. This double-edged escapism is so central to women's fiction that it is worth pursuing further and examining more closely the ideal world which is so tantalisingly offered. In doing so, I want to move away from the psychoanalytical model used almost exclusively by US feminist critics and instead to map the contours of soap opera and subsequently some elements of women's fiction across the utopian framework offered by Richard Dyer in his influential work on the values of entertainment.

Dyer, in his article 'Entertainment and utopia', provides a model which enables us to look at the function of the urge to escape and to explain why it remains such a persistent characteristic not just of entertainment, as Dyer argues, but more specifically of women's fiction. Dyer proposes that entertainment functions by offering

> the image of 'something better' to escape into, or something that we want deeply that our day-to-day lives don't provide. Alternatives, hopes, wishes – these are the stuff of utopia, the sense that things could be better, that something other than what is can be imagined and may be realised.[1]

Dyer stresses that what entertainment offers is not a representation of what an ideal world might be like but what it would feel like; 'the utopianism is contained in the feeling it embodies. It presents, head-on as it were, what utopia would feel like rather than how it would be organised.'[2]

Dyer categorises the experience offered by entertainment into five 'utopian solutions' and suggests that they are related to specific inadequacies in society. Thus the experience of scarcity and the unequal distribution of wealth is set against the utopian satisfaction of abundance and material equality; exhaustion, 'work as a grind, alienated labour, pressures of urban life', is contrasted with the expression of energy in which work and play are united; dreariness and monotony are set against the utopian solution of intensity with its emphasis on excitement and drama in individuals' lives; a feeling of manipulation, an inability to get beneath the surface, is contrasted with the utopian concept of transparency, of 'open, spontaneous, honest communications and relationships'; and, finally, the experience of fragmentation, 'job mobility, rehousing and development... legislation against collective action', is set against the utopian feeling of belonging to a community which is underpinned by communal interests and collective activity.[3] Entertainment thus offers the experience of a different world, one which is escapist precisely because it is based on the inadequacies experienced in day-to-day life. Dyer does not argue that the full possibilities of this search for a utopian solution are exploited in the musicals he analyses but suggests that 'this possibility is always latent in them'[4] and that the utopian sensibility represented in entertainment needs to be understood if change is to be both achieved and enjoyed.

The utopian possibilities offered by the prime time soaps under discussion here are not uniformly present in all the programmes. The application of Dyer's model demonstrates that soaps offer a spectrum of pleasure which allows for a different emphasis within individual programmes and ensures that gaps in, for instance, the British soaps are filled by their US counterparts. Different functions are fulfilled by different programmes and it is only when we look at the range of soaps that we can understand that the utopian promise is offered by the soap opera genre taken as a whole. Table 31.1 shows the area of overlap as well as the differences, and a more detailed examination of how the five categories can be applied will enable us to delineate more accurately the utopian worlds of the soaps.

Energy in British and US prime time soaps is expressed formally through the pace at which the plots are developed and used up and through a narrative structure which allows the overlapping stories to succeed each other with scarcely a pause for breath. *EastEnders* in particular moves with rapidity, cutting from story to story in quick bursts of action. One half-hour episode in March 1988 had thirty scenes, some of which dealt with more than one storyline; in one story a major character, Mags, conceived the idea of leaving the Square at the beginning of the episode and effected the move at the end of it. Events in *Dallas* and *Dynasty* have a similar urgency in their storylines and a capacity to change pace within an episode. Since daytime soaps have been characterised by their slowness of pace it is worth noting the way in which all the prime time soaps discussed here are marked by the capacity to move very quickly in and out of storylines to effect rapid changes in characters and to develop a situation swiftly through a number of short scenes.

Energy it also expressed through character, and indeed, characterisation is important in particularising each of the abstract qualities outlined in Dyer's definitions. The difference in the way in which the US and British programmes characterise energy is quite distinct. In the US prime time soaps, energy is expressed largely through the male characters or through the female characters who are operating in the public sphere. It is marked by an emphasis on the dynamics of business, on the willingness to gamble on a risky hunch and experience swift changes in fortune. Since many of the business operations are deliberately opaque the emphasis is on the activity itself rather than its purpose. J. R. is the character most readily associated with this kind of energy but Alexis and Blake are also examples of the way in which energy is expressed through the business side. In pointing to these examples, it is noticeable that energy is a concept most readily associated with the 'evil' character, making attractive those like J. R. and Alexis who cannot be trusted and bringing out the ruthless characteristics in Blake. Energy is thus a characteristic which appeals to the viewer as an expression of how it feels to act vigorously and to affect events, but it is also understood that it can be readily misdirected if it is not allied with one of the other categories.

Energy in the British soaps, however, tends to be associated with women characters and is expressed not through business but through active engagement with the public life of the community. It can be seen most clearly in the strong women characters in *Coronation Street* and *EastEnders* with their quick repartee, capacity for organisation and determination not to be overlooked. Bet Lynch, never

Table 31.1 Utopian possibilities in women's fiction

	Energy	Abundance	Intensity	Transparency	Community
British soaps	strong women characters, quick repartee, pace of plot	—	emotions strongly expressed at key moments, Angie/Den, Sheila/Bobby	*sincerity of key characters:* Deirdre Barlow, Kathy Beale, Sheila Grant, *True Love:* Deirdre/Ken Chris/Frank	characters offer support, friendship, gossip outside programme
US soaps	strong male characters, business activity, pace of plot	glamorous settings, clothes, luxurious objects food, etc.	emotions strongly expressed at key moments, Sue Ellen's madness	*sincerity of key characters:* Bobby, Pamela, Miss Ellie, Krystle *True Love:* Blake/Krystle Bobby/Pamela	asserted within family, rarely achieved, reltionship with audience
Romance	stong male character	provided at end by hero	story works towards moment when hero speak of love	story works towards moment when true love is revealed	community not important
Gothic woman's film	strong male character	wealthy male, luxurious trappings, big house	emotion sought by heroine, withheld by hero	sincerity of heroine, opacity of hero	community presented ambiguously
'Heroine's text' woman's film	strong female character as heroine	heroine works for it, for herself or her children	heroine's expression of love for child, work or man	sincerity of heroine, misunderstood by man	woman initially outside community, may fight her way in

lost for a word behind the bar at The Rover's, resilient in her private affairs and with a brave face in public, exemplifies this concept in the British soaps. As in the US soaps, it is the activity which is important rather than the actual events but this expression of energy, like that of the US prime time soaps, has a dark underside when it can be experienced as bossiness and self-importance and is resented by the other characters. There seems also to be a difficulty here in relation to how women express energy through activity, which we shall return to at the end of this section.

The category of abundance is also handled differently across the programmes, being more readily identifiable in the US soaps than in the British programmes. In the US programmes, poverty is eliminated by the simple tactic of ignoring it and the audience is invited to enjoy the spectacle of abundance through the emphasis on sensuous luxury. This is particularly the case in *Dynasty*, where the costumes and setting seem chosen more for their look and feel than for their appropriateness to the plot. The women's dresses are silk, satin and velvet, fabrics with a sheen which connotes sensuality. The settings overflow with luxurious items, ranging from fresh flowers in every corner to expensive paintings on every wall. Basic necessities are transformed into luxuries by their endless availability. Food and drink appear magically in their most expensive form – champagne flows literally like water or like tea in the British soaps. Hotel suites are used as homes as if a holiday treat were a commonplace means of getting a roof over one's head. Land is bought and sold as if in a supermarket. Transport is summoned up and private jets whisk characters across the United States as if they were crossing town. However unhappy the characters, they have at their disposal the abundant fruits of Western capitalism. It is interesting, indeed, that abundance is impartially available and, unlike energy, is not made problematic by its association with the 'evil' characters. Both Krystle and Alexis, deliberately contrasted in other respects, enjoy the ease of abundance and the sensuousness of material fulfilment.

It is precisely this endless consumerism which so scandalises the critics of *Dallas* and *Dynasty*, and there is indeed a shocking irony in the way in which *Dallas* is watched worldwide by those who are themselves the victims of the predatory activities of US big business. But to criticise the viewers is to underestimate the phenomenon and the utopian basis of its appeal. What *Dallas* and *Dynasty* offer is the feeling of what it would be like to have all material needs met, to conquer scarcity and enjoy abundance. Critics may call it greed, but greed and selfishness have their roots in scarcity, the knowledge that there may not be enough to go round. With a world where everything is on offer, the viewer is safe merely to enjoy, without the fear that anything will run out. Hans Magnus Enzensberger's words apply with particular aptness to the US soaps:

> Consumption as spectacle contains the promise that want will disappear. The deceptive, brutal and obscene features of this festival derive from the fact that there can be no question of a real fulfilment of its promise . . . trickery on such a scale is only conceivable if it is based on mass need. . . . Consumption as spectacle is – in parody form – the anticipation of a utopian situation.[5]

If abundance is the category most vividly and extravagantly figured in the US prime time soaps, community is by and large the prerogative of the British programmes. Enough has been said [. . .] to indicate how crucially the sense of a community underpins the British soaps. As we have seen, the experience of community is offered to the audience most explicitly in the rituals which mark major events in *Coronation Street* or *EastEnders*. But it is present in the more everyday exchanges in which the role of each individual in the community is understood and valued. It is the women characters who embody the function of community in the form of the matriarchs who hold the community together. It is clear that the ideal community only functions if women are in control: they bring isolated and disparate individuals into the community/family; they organise its rituals; they transmit its values and spin the web of gossip through which it is continually renewed. In the British soaps, a sense of community remains the ideal to which the characters and the audience are invited to aspire. Unlike abundance, however, which fits into strongly articulated ideas of the individual consumer, a sense of community has become more difficult to express in the 1980s. It runs against the prevailing emphasis on the pursuit of individual success and entrepreneurial enterprise and both *Brookside* and *EastEnders* have questioned the more unproblematic version of community presented in *Coronation Street*. Nevertheless, it may be that one of the most important and hard-fought functions of British soaps in the eighties has been to keep the ideal of the community as a utopian possibility at a time when the tide in political thought was firmly running the other way.

But community is not simply present in the soaps themselves, it is also experienced in the interaction between the programmes and their audience. Soaps offer a common currency to viewers which permits the enjoyment to be shared between those who do not watch the programmes together. This effect of uniting disparate audiences goes well beyond television's capacity to provide the subject of conversation the morning after. The pleasures of soaps are so much bound up with speculation and analysis that they demand that viewers share the experience. The narrative strategies outlined in this book are dependent on the audience's capacity to predict and evaluate the characters' actions so that there is a common participation in the problems being portrayed and the variety of solutions on offer. While soaps are viewed in the home, alone or in the 'family circle', they can be discussed by friends, acquaintances and strangers in a variety of situations – at work, in pubs or bars, at bus stops or on trains. Like conversations about sport, which are probably the male equivalent, such conversations demand a shared knowledge of the history of the subject and offer a mutual pleasure in the pooling of information on significant details and the disagreement over questions of interpretation. Unlike sport, discussion of soap operas also involves sharing ideas on personal relationships and emotional dilemmas. There is some evidence that families use soaps as a way of raising awkward issues and easing discussion of them.[6] Such a process can also be seen in conversations at work where soaps provide a common basis for conversation for those who share an intimacy based on proximity rather than choice. In such situations, soaps can be used to establish a common perspective or negotiate difficult situations in a way which would not have been possible had the fictional crises occurred in real life. They enable attitudes to be tested out within the safe haven of a fictional world. Such a process offers the feeling of community, through the experience of shared pleasure, even when viewing soaps like *Dallas* and *Dynasty* in which the concept itself is scarcely represented.

If energy, abundance and community are handled rather differently in the British and US prime time soaps, intensity and transparency are the two categories where the similarities can be most clearly seen. Soaps certainly offer moments of intensity when emotion is expressed, as Dyer puts it, 'directly, fully, unambiguously'.[7] Such moments may occur between characters when feelings of love, or indeed anger and hatred, are expressed without the characters stopping to think or fearing the consequences. What is valued is this capacity for expression, even if the outcome is not always a happy one. Characters who live life full-bloodedly are essential to soaps and provide a source of much of the drama. But intensity is also a feature of the relationship between the audience and these characters so that the full emotional intensity is often expressed directly to the audience when the character is alone. This relationship with the audience is particularly marked in the treatment of women stars such as Sue Ellen in *Dallas*, Elsie Tanner in *Coronation Street* or Angie Watts in *EastEnders*. The mask that they put on for other characters, particularly their husbands, is dropped and the full extent of their grief and anger is revealed. Thus while Sue Ellen and Angie often behave deviously and hide their true feelings from the other characters, they still fulfil the function of intensity by expressing emotion 'authentically' to the audience. Elsie Tanner and Bet Lynch similarly keep a brave face in public but the audience shares with them their private moments of grief and despair. The audience knows these characters more intimately and more directly than the others and this may help to explain why these particular characters become the 'incandescent star performers'[8] of the soaps and are a source of particular interest and pleasure.

Transparency is closely linked to intensity in that it too can be recognised through the way in which emotions are represented in the programmes. In this category, however, it is the nature of the emotion which is at stake rather than the way it is experienced. Transparency emphasises the utopian possibilities of being open and honest in emotions without being hurt and Dyer associates it with the conventions of 'true love'. In soaps, it is associated with the idyllic marriages of, for example, Blake and Krystle and Bobby and Pamela. Despite ups and downs, these marriages are seen as ideal because neither partner lies or deceives the other and they represent a partnership which is based on mutual support and trust. As we shall see, there is a strong element of romance fiction here and examples are easier to find in the US soaps, which incline more to fantasy. More modest British examples might be Sally and Kevin and Ken and Deirdre in *Coronation Street* (until the crisis of Ken's departure) or Chrissie and Frank in *Brookside*, whose marriages are founded on common sense, frankness and affection which carries them through day-to-day difficulties and major upsets.

Transparency, like the other categories, is associated with particular characters and creates its own kind of stars who not merely are deemed to be sincere in relation to other characters but can also be trusted by the audience. Bobby Ewing is the clearest example of a male star consistently associated with sincerity. He is J. R.'s opposite and expresses their antithesis in terms of his commitment to the truth: 'J. R. lives by the two things I hate most – secrecy and lying.' Bobby has sometimes deviated from this commitment, particularly in his battle with J. R. over control of the company. It was significant that, in this storyline, Bobby displayed qualities associated with the category of energy and promptly threatened the utopian relationship between himself and Pam. In the main, it is the women characters who are marked by the ability to see and speak out honestly and consistently. In the US prime time soaps, Pam and Krystle are associated not merely with moral values but also with the capacity to speak out when necessary in defence of the truth. Deirdre Barlow has a similar function in *Coronation Street*, and Kathy Beale in *EastEnders* can be trusted by the audience to divine what is right and to hold firmly to that position.

We can see then that within the soap spectrum the whole range of utopian possibilities are on offer but that they differ in the weighting accorded to each of them in the individual programmes. A hierarchy is thus established whereby certain functions are essential to the utopian world delineated by these soaps while others offer more peripheral pleasures. All of the soaps under discussion here are characterised by the intensity and openness with which emotional lives are laid bare and great value is placed on the capacity to express feeling vividly and directly. On the other hand, there is a clear difference in the way in which the US and British soaps articulate the concepts of community and abundance, and this split in functions accords with the aesthetic and thematic differences we have identified [. . .]. Thus, the emphasis in US soaps on the possibilities of abundance chimes with the values of light entertainment – stars, spectacle, decor – outlined [. . .]. In their British counterparts, however, a tradition of realism finds it less easy to accommodate the illusion of all material wants fulfilled but is able to draw on an ideology of community which offers an equally utopian promise of individual needs met by a communal response.

A study of the way in which these soap operas present the possibility of an ideal world also reveals that the concepts offered by Dyer for its analysis are not gender neutral. Intensity and transparency, the functions most crucially concerned with the ideal experience of personal emotions, are present and central to all these programmes and are, with the exception of Bobby Ewing (a deliberate contrast to his macho brother), associated with key women characters. Community too in British soaps is linked with women characters who are the most successful in providing the nurturing strength on which a successful community is based. Abundance in US prime time soaps is also refracted through gender; it tends to be provided by the men for the women to enjoy and display. When a woman claims it for herself, as Alexis does so wholeheartedly, it becomes a sign that she is taking on the masculine role. The provision of abundance. as opposed to the sensuous enjoyment of it, is thus linked with the concept of energy, the category least amenable to female co-option. The association of men with the 'capacity to act vigorously'[9] goes deep and the public sphere in which this action is best expressed in soaps is difficult ground for the women characters. Energy, then, is linked with masculine behaviour, either openly through male characters like J. R. or women like Alexis who take on male values in the business world or less overtly with bossy women in the British soaps who try to impose their own wishes on others rather than enable communal energies to be expressed. Either way, unless it is softened by being linked with one of the other more 'female' categories, energy is likely to be associated with cruelty and lack of emotional integrity.

Notes

1. Richard Dyer, 'Entertainment and utopia', in Rick Altman (ed.), *Genre: The musical: A reader* (London: Routledge & Kegan Paul, 1981), p. 177.
2. *Ibid.*
3. *Ibid.*, pp. 183–4.
4. *Ibid.*, p. 189.
5. Hans Magnus Enzensberger, 'Constituents of a theory of the media', in *Dreams of the Absolute* (London: Radius, 1988), pp. 36–7.
6. Jane Root, *Open the Box* (London: Comedia, 1986), p. 40.
7. Dyer, 'Entertainment and Utopia', p. 180.
8. *Ibid.*
9. *Ibid.*

31 □ *Feminist Crime Writing: The Politics of Genre*

Yvonne Tasker

[...]

Enthusiasm for new feminist crime writing is perhaps precisely to do with the provision of an alternative space, a space in which to situate a radical culture for feminism, or at least the hopes for one. These works are hailed quite specifically for their radical potential, for their ability both to subvert a genre that is both masculine and reactionary, and to provide 'strong positive heroines' that offer themselves as figures of identification for the radical reader. Feminist crime writing answers a desire for texts 'which are radical in themselves and for their readers, and which are produced in a space outside of the mainstream. While the 'mainstream' thriller has been evaluated (if not totally dismissed) as 'masculine' and 'reactionary', the genre can be inhabited, subverted from within, that is, invested with new meanings specific to feminism. Significantly this struggle for meaning, which is necessarily the feature of a feminist cultural practice, is sited in the field of the popular, or a version of it. Mainstream and feminist crime writings are produced and consumed in radically different institutional contexts. This difference, however, does not present a problem to be avoided but is fundamental to the project of a feminist crime writing which self-consciously declares itself to be part of a feminist culture. Thus my discussion focuses on not only feminist thrillers as a particular subgenre but the ways in which these works have been discussed critically as valuable for feminism and for feminist culture. Such critical comments suggest the possibility of an appropriation of popular forms for a feminist/radical culture.

This move, towards the appropriation of the popular, is far from unprecedented within feminist criticism and cultural production. The late 1970s and the 1980s have seen a boom in academic feminist criticism of forms like romance fiction, criticism which stresses the diverse uses which readers make of such texts, as well as the pleasures that are to be found in such seemingly 'dubious' sites. In part this

From Tasker, Y., *Feminist Crime Writing: The politics of genre*, Pavic, Sheffield, 1991, pp. 1–34.

can be seen as a response to a critical double standard in popular cultural analyses, whereby those forms perceived as 'for women' remained on the cultural trash heap at the same time as forms broadly seen to be 'for men' became objects of study within the academy. But we can also see in this move a very important feminist desire not to dismiss or reject those women who read romance, an awareness that such a rejection might represent little more than an attempt to be equal to male-defined cultural standards. Rather, in the way that Elaine Showalter had suggested in *A Literature of Their Own*, that women had a literary tradition all along, it was 'becoming clear' that they had also had a popular culture all of their own. Such a critical impulse, representing as it does the desire to engage with the actual practices and pleasures of women readers, needs to be held on to.

There are problems involved in this process of appropriation, though. Both the thriller, and traditions of crime writing more generally, have been criticised by left and feminist critics not just as a result of the 'position of women' (though this has remained part of the attack) but also at the level of formal politics. Whilst detective novels and thrillers involve the disruption of order, the individual hero, it is claimed, ultimately solves all problems as the world is restored, and the reader with it, to the cosy equilibrium of late capitalist patriarchy. 'It is often accepted as axiomatic', points out Ann Constable 'that the detective novel is an inherently reactionary genre'. Qualifying her arguments for the possibilities of a feminist crime writing, she asserts that:

> any novel based on a straightforward application of the formula crime/investigation/ solution/resolution of social order must be part of the literature of reassurance, and the classic English detective novel has typically asserted values that are overwhelmingly authoritarian and conservative. (1985, p. 12)

Such criticism is relatively familiar and involves more than the desire for a radical culture which actively refuses the kinds of resolution described. A more general suspicion of all formulaic material, reassuring in its repetitiveness, can be seen to inform such critical views. Within the parameters of genre study, accounts of crime writing typically address two areas of concern: firstly, the mapping of the develop-ment, structure and workings of a genre, and secondly, questions of literary value and greatness. The identification of basic, repeated structures as well as classic texts and great writers (Chandler, Hammett, Higgins, Leonard) function to construct a narrative of the genre, to make sense out of a vast amount of material. Questions of value, as is implicit above, are equally important to feminist accounts. In the case of the classic genre study individual works are of interest as a literary form, 'worthy of merit'; in the case of popular cultural analyses works are deemed 'interesting' as cultural artifacts in a related but nonetheless different sense. While in traditional criticism the achievement of narrative resolution represents a failure to produce great art, a failure to step outside the formula, in radical accounts it represents a return to order, a failure to transgress at a deeper level. For it is often experimentation which is seen as the essential guarantor of the status of a work.

After all, what is good is playing with the form, doing new things with conventions, subverting them. By the same criteria those texts which 'simply', 'merely', 'do nothing more than' attempt to 'rehash', 'repeat' a 'jaded formula', are obviously bad.

[...]

The Politics of Popular Forms

If traditions of crime writing have consistently been perceived negatively by both the left and feminism – described as both masculine and reactionary – the claims made for this new body of work, and the premises upon which they are built, are significant: i.e. that it is possible to redeem this popular, though reactionary, form for something else, a more progressive political project. An interesting set of moves are in operation here. It was those models which sought to move away from the figure of the passive consumer which began to consider the popular in a more positive light, indeed, to produce the popular as potentially radical. Yet at the same time there has also been a contradictory attempt to claim that terrain of pliant readers for a radical culture. For if people like reading thrillers, but the politics of the form are bad, then it follows that it is both possible and necessary to appropriate their appeal for a new political project. The role of the reader in this process is unclear: are we simply left to be passively positioned by 'progressive' ways of thinking rather than reactionary ones? And if we are, then what is at stake in this for feminism?

What role is given to popular forms in this model? This can be partly understood with reference to Ann Rosalind Jones's argument, put forward in the context of her discussion of the potential that romance fiction holds out for feminism. Jones suggests a strategy of 'stealing into mass markets via temporary literary camouflage' (in Radford, 1986, p. 215). such a strategy holds out the possibility of somehow 'converting' the reader without them knowing. The implications of this lead us to the models associated with a language of subversion, of struggle over meaning, but also the stealth and disguise of guerrilla warfare. Here the tactics of a siege mentality give way to the strategy of the Trojan Horse. Within this strategy the figure of the active reader is displaced, since it no longer has a function. The notion of a struggle over meaning in the popular is transformed into a struggle between factions over the popular. Popular culture and the reader are positioned in this struggle as objects to be fought over, or as a site to be occupied.

[...]

Investigating the Other

[...]

The texts of feminist crime writing are informed by a strong tradition of autobiographical writing within feminist and women's fiction. Within this the first person narration and the diary form have come to have a special significance, offering a route into the persona through a narrative of self-discovery. The first person narration of Mary Wings's *She Came Too Late* borrows as much from this tradition as from the distinctive style of hard-boiled fiction which is explicitly referenced. The female protagonist's journey to self-discovery is a typical feature of women's fiction, as the heroine progresses from ignorance to a knowledge of self and a position of strength. Since the politicising of the personal was central to the women's movement of the early 1970s, the investigation of the self forms a privileged narrative within feminist discourses.

The heroines of feminist crime writing are often on the margins of society as a result of their political commitments, rather than their ambiguous status in relation to the institutions of authority. As in O'Rourkes's *Jumping the Cracks*, for example, the main concern is with relationships – personal relationships (Rats and Helen), power relations (men and women), social relations (rich and poor) – rather than with detection. Through the work of description such relationships are outlined and explored in the feminist thriller. Such a pattern clearly emerges in *Sisters of the Road* with its focus on the relationship between middle-class Pam and teenage prostitute Trish, whose liking for junk food and blockbusting novels signals her as an 'undeveloped' personality. Pam learns from social workers, friends and from herself. The personal is centre stage: an area, as noted, with significant resonances for feminism. The book's author, Barbara Wilson, has suggested that the works of Raymond Chandler suffer because we don't know anything about Marlowe's personal life. For Wilson the priorities of such fiction are all wrong. The 'human heart' needs to be centred over the investigation of a specific crime.

This desire to make the personal central to crime fiction arises not only from a feminist input, but from the difficulties associated with placing the figure of 'woman' in the role of investigator. The position of ambiguity that the hero often occupies in detective fictions, the problematising of his status, cannot be simply or easily translated into a comparable portrayal of the figure of the heroine. The heroine already carries radically different connotations, so that it becomes problematic to present her as 'psychotic', unbalanced or morally dubious. Certainly this is the case within the frame of reference set up by a self-consciously feminist project, which necessarily brings with it the legacy of a commitment to presenting positive images of women. These difficulties are only accentuated in the attempt to place a feminist figure (as most of the heroines announce themselves to be) at the centre of such fictions. For the feminist thriller, published by a feminist press, the figure of the feminist is not one whose status is (or can be) uncertain. This context allows an understanding of the particular stress which has come to fall on an exploration of the self and the significant positioning of the feminist investigator as an amateur (Forrest's Kate Delafield, a detective with the LAPD, is an interesting exception). The amateur is located outside the established institutions of law enforcement.

[. . .]

The Pleasures of the Popular

[...]

The desire for a feminist popular culture is in part a guilty one, associated as it is with indulgence and escapism. Such negative associations pervade feminist commentary on TV and invade the texts of many feminist thrillers themselves. From this unease stems a need for reassurance. In this context, the language of Rose Collis's praise for the feminist thriller carries as additional burden of meaning. Collis speaks of her search for 'her kind of heroine' now at an end, a search which had taken her to 'countless clandestine rendezvous with persons of dubious character and motive'. Such encounters are now over. In contrast, there are few 'dubious' motives in the feminist thriller: villains are villains and victims are victims.

A counterpoint to these strategies is provided by the work of other feminist thriller writers. Mary Wings's *She Came Too Late* (1986) addresses a lesbian and feminist audience without labouring to carve out a space for teaching feminist theory. Wings has said that she 'wanted to write about women who fucked and drank and detected their way through exciting stories'. In this the books work to provide an alternative space for the reader without being a slave to notions of the 'correct'. Yet popular culture often seems to figure for feminism, as Trish does for Pam in *Sisters of the Road*. The search for an object invested with a sexualised promise, an object which, once found, must be rewritten. What remains unspoken, then, both in the critical enthusiasm for the genre and in the texts themselves, in a thinly disguised contempt for (or perhaps a fear of?) popular forms. This ambivalent feeling is marked by a guilty enjoyment. In terms of what is at stake in a feminist engagement with the popular, feminist works masquerading as popular fictions (all for the cause) seem to fit the bill precisely. However, they only 'seem to', since this obsessive search for the perfect object is not one that can end.

References

Collis, R. (1987) 'My kind of heroine', *New Socialist*.
Constable, A. (1985) 'Crime for social change', *Red Letters*, 18.
Radford, J. (ed.) (1986) *The Progress of Romance*, London: Routledge & Kegan Paul.
Wilson, B. (1987) *Sisters of the Road*, London: The Women's Press.

32 □ Feminism and Popular Culture

Morag Shiach

This paper will consider the ways in which feminist critics have intervened in, and reworked, the study of 'popular culture'. The institutionalisation of 'cultural studies' over the last twenty years has opened up a new space for the consideration of cultural hierarchies and for the analysis of the social construction of subjectivity, both areas of recurring theoretical and practical concern for feminist critics. The challenge to the literary canon represented by the introduction of film and media studies has echoed feminist reworkings of literary history to include works by women authors: both developments tending to foreground the selectivity of the canon, and to stretch the curriculum to a point which usefully demonstrates the impossibility of 'comprehensiveness'. Both have also served to undermine the obviousness of concepts of 'the literary', choosing instead to engage with a range of cultural texts and practices in order to uncover the complexity of class or gender formation.

Despite these shared concerns and methodologies, however, the intersection of 'feminism' and 'popular culture' has never been anything other than troubled. To some extent, this is hardly surprising, since the two terms are not parallel: one designates a political space, the other an object of study. Yet 'popular culture' has always, implicitly, been more than another area of study. The term carries within it a series of debates about political legitimacy, class identity, and cultural value, which inform the theoretical framework and the methodological procedures of cultural studies. My contention is that it is the very inescapability of these associations that is the problem for 'feminism'. 'Popular culture' as an institutional space, and as a political concept, embodies definitions of class identity, historical change and political struggle which are often blind to the questions of feminism.

In order to understand the terms in which feminist critics have been able to engage with the 'popular', it is necessary first of all to reflect on the constitution of 'cultural studies' as a discipline: to see the political and educational priorities and assumptions that determined its formation. To some extent this history is by now

From *Critical Quarterly*, vol. 33, 1991, pp. 37–45.

familiar: cultural studies has been a very self-conscious discipline, which has reflected on the legitimacy of its paternity (Williams and Hoggart, Marx and Gramsci, Lacan and Barthes) with a surprising degree of regularity. The implications of such histories for feminist cultural critics have, however, been less fully explored.[1]

In beginning to think about 'feminism and popular culture', then, we have to start with the history of cultural studies as a discipline. What are the sources of the critical languages of cultural studies, and what aspects of cultural production or consumption do these languages privilege, or exclude?

There are in fact two relatively distinct ideological and institutional sources for British cultural studies. The first, and probably the most formative, lies in the historical and ethnographic rescuing of working-class culture, found in the early work of Richard Hoggart, Raymond Williams, or E. P. Thompson. The second emerged through the rescuing of film, television and popular fiction from the realm of 'mass culture' by the mobilisation of French psychoanalytic and textual theory. The first of these has proved relatively resistant to feminist criticism, the second perhaps disconcertingly open.

Raymond Williams's *Culture and Society* was published in 1958. In it, Williams set out to trace the developing meanings of 'culture' within British social thought and literary criticism. He argued that 'culture' functioned throughout the nineteenth century as a term which could focus the developing critique of the industrialisation of British society. Thus, social theorists, from different political positions, used the concept of 'culture' as a space in which they could locate values such as 'organicism', 'authenticity' and 'humanism'. Williams takes issue throughout *Culture and Society* with the increasing specialisation of the notion of culture, its narrowing down to the point of becoming a shorthand term for a small number of literary and artistic texts. He insists that if culture is the space of meaning, creativity and humanism, it is also in an important sense 'ordinary', and argues for an understanding of 'culture' not as a series of texts, but rather as 'the way of life as a whole' of any particular social or national group.

The overwhelming importance of this text was its politicisation of the meanings surrounding 'culture', its insistence that cultural hierarchies both embodied and transformed social and historical struggles. The form in which this argument was developed, however, cut across its transformative capacity in important ways. Williams's argument was with, and also to some extent within, the literary canon; his techniques of reading were still recognisably Leavisite. These two facts constrained the texts that were studied in *Culture and Society*, producing an alternative reading of an already constituted textual history, rather than challenging the exclusions or priorities of such a history.

The dependence of this history on a version of the literary canon and on techniques of literary analysis raises particular problems for feminist critics. Such problems relate not simply to the selectivity of the canon, but much more broadly to the naturalisation of gender identities, or of the social institution of the family, which emerges from historians' encounters with this version of nineteenth-century history. Julia Swindells and Lisa Jardine have analysed the centrality of the 'literary' to Left thought in the sixties, insisting that:

> The argument tends inexorably towards the 'literary', towards a particular version of class-consciousness (the authorized account), at the very moment at which it is clearest that key assumptions there are profoundly damaging to any attempt to narrate women in relation to the Labour movement.[2]

The extent to which literary images and narratives have shaped the production of cultural histories is perhaps even clearer when we examine Hoggart's *The Uses of Literacy*. In this text, Hoggart begins by trying to uncover the meanings and values inherent in many of the rituals and practices of working-class life: an ethnographic focus, shaped by the notion of 'participant observation' that is to inform many studies produced by the Birmingham Centre for Contemporary Cultural Studies. Hoggart looks back to working-class communities of the 1920s and 1930s and, instead of a manipulated mass or an ignorant mob, he finds a complex pattern of cultural commitments and beliefs.

Hoggart's methodology is derived both from sociology and from literary studies, and combines a careful description of behaviour, housing, and dress with an assessment of the moral and social values they embody. He describes the spatial organisation of the working-class community, particularly its domestic interiors, the sense of identity and resistance implicit in the contrast between 'them' and 'us', and the cultural meaning of the popular press, of club singing or of leisure excursions. He thus sets the agenda of family, political resistance, and class-specific use of leisure time which is to dominate subsequent analyses of popular culture.

This version of the people's culture does, however, have its limitations and blind spots. Hoggart identifies this thirties social formation, particularly its organisation of the domestic, with an essentially unchanging tradition. He suggests a complete enclosure and intactness which seem to have little relation to the cultural hierarchies and the economic and political conflicts of this period. Also, more worryingly, his huge emotional investment in the stability of the working-class home seems to naturalise his intensely novelistic descriptions of domestic life. When he writes:

> the iron thumps on the table, the dog scratches and yawns or the cat miaows to be let out; the son, drying himself on the family towel near the fire, whistles, or rustles the communal letter from his brother in the army which has been lying on the mantelpiece behind the photo of his sister's wedding ...[3]

we are invited to identify with the sense of ease and community, but not to ask who is wielding the iron.

Having set up the 1920s and 1930s as a golden age of popular culture, Hoggart proceeds to analyse the dangers he sees as implicit in the culture of the late 1950s, which he describes as 'the newer mass art'. This culture he sees as debased, parasitic and dangerous, a threat to critical thought and class identity. He thus creates a paradigm common to many theorists of popular culture: having set up a golden age of continuity, rootedness, authenticity, and tradition, based round the family, he can see his contemporary world only in terms of rootlessness, decline, and superficiality.

This drift towards a sense of powerlessness was challenged by the argument of E. P. Thompson's *The Making of the English Working Class*, another 'formative' text for cultural studies. Thompson set out to dispute versions of history which saw the working class as helpless victims of historical change, and argued instead that 'the working class was present at its own history'. In examining religious beliefs, radical publishing, and the clubs and societies which supported the radical cause, Thompson aimed to demonstrate that working-class people participated in history, struggling to shape it, rather than being subjected to it.

Thompson's book led to an explosion of studies of popular culture by social historians, who hoped to rediscover through the organisation of leisure time and the daily forms and practices of working-class life a different version of nineteenth-century society, and a different model of political struggle and of social change.[4] Popular culture was seen as the place where resistance to the Industrial Revolution might have been articulated, and where alternative values and beliefs might have been formed.

Historians committed to the rescuing of popular history, to the rediscovery and analysis of popular culture, thus brought to their study a clear agenda. They privileged those cultural forms which seemed to be an expression of resistance and class identity. Such forms were often both public and communal: sport, religion, or ritualised forms of political protest. They were also frequently either seasonal or regional. As such, they could be understood as points of resistance to the imposition of the work discipline necessary to capital-intensive, centralised, industrial production.

This political agenda constrained the cultural forms that seemed worthy of study, and effectively marginalised many of the cultural forms and practices of nineteenth-century women. We know, of course, that women were present and active in campaigns for literacy, in selling the radical press, in editing and contributing to radical journals. Yet an article like David Vincent's 'Reading in the working-class home', despite its location in the domestic sphere, can produce women only as distraction. The working-class reader, we are told, 'needed time from the demands of his family', and was consequently reliant on the public, and often the all-male, resources of the Mechanics' Institute.[5] So, in terms of self-improvement, the model is of politically conscious man, struggling to free himself from distracting women.

In relation to popular fiction and the growth of the periodical press, women are even more awkwardly placed by the priorities of cultural historians. Both Chartists and trade unionists in the nineteenth century viewed popular fiction with suspicion, and treated it as depoliticising, debased, and trivial. They saw it as 'sensual gratification', as impure, as addictive. This suspicion and marginalisation are reproduced in the work of recent cultural critics, who talk of nineteenth-century periodicals as containing political writing 'for working men of the metropolis', but also 'an ample provision of fiction and anecdote for the mental regalement of their wives and the rising generation'.[6]

In relation to 'popular culture', what we have inherited, then, is not just the cultural hierarchies of the nineteenth century, but distinctive ways of theorising them, which select cultural forms that exclude or marginalise women, and describe them as representative of the 'typical working-class condition'. Such spaces of resistance and class identity are then set against the weakening of popular taste implicit in the sensual, 'namby-pamby' distraction of popular fiction or song.

This set of emphases was certainly to structure the work of the Birmingham Centre for Contemporary Cultural Studies, whose analyses of popular culture as a site of resistance were to shape the institutional and pedagogical understandings of 'popular culture' in the 1970s. A text like *Resistance Through Rituals* (1976) embodies many of the most important theoretical models and methodologies developed at the Centre. Its ethnographic studies of Teds, mods, skinheads, or Rastas were undertaken in the context of an analysis of class and hegemony derived from the work of Gramsci. In each case, the interest was in seeing the ways in which subcultural groups negotiated a space in relation to the dominant culture, which allowed for the articulation of oppositional class identities. Thus the skinhead mob 'may be viewed as an attempt to retrieve the disappearing sense of community with its emphasis on mutual assistance in moments of need'.[7] The choice of significant subcultures, those that were both visible and disruptive, however, led to the effective exclusion of the cultural practices and political identities of working-class girls. This point was raised within the text by Angela McRobbie and Jenny Garber, but they were unable to move, within the available theoretical framework, beyond the articulation of absence, and a general assertion that the inclusion of girls would necessarily inflect the whole analysis.[8]

This sense of exclusion, for both the cultural practices of working-class girls and the research priorities of feminist critics, led to the production of another text by the Centre in 1978, *Women Take Issue*. In this volume, women working at the Centre tried to find ways of challenging the gender blindness of previous studies. Their starting point was the belief that working-class girls 'are both saved by and locked within the culture of femininity'.[9] This led them to a consideration of psychoanalytic theories of the construction of a gendered subjectivity, and to an analysis of the importance of 'femininity' as an organising category within political identities. Thus they looked at the isolated economic and cultural role of the housewife, at relations of reproduction, and at the ideology of romance fiction.

Women Take Issue represented a crucial step in the consideration of gender in relation to class and to cultural production and consumption. However, it also represented an important shift of methodological and theoretical terrain. Ideas of resistance, of class identity, gave way to a focus on reproduction, on consumption, and on the problematic of 'femininity'. The move is understandable: women were absent from models of collective and public cultural expression. Yet it also leaves the prevailing models intact. After all, other texts produced by the Centre did not foreground 'masculinity', they simply assumed it. In finding a space where women could be both visible and theorised, the space of consumption and of 'femininity', there was a risk of simply reinforcing the gendered exclusivity of dominant models of class identity and of resistance.

Such a move towards the politics of consumption is also clear in the work of Tania Modleski, whose *Loving with a Vengeance* (1982) represented a sustained analysis of the subjective and social meanings of 'mass-produced fantasies for women'. Modleski analysed three cultural forms, romance fiction, Gothic novels, and television soap opera, arguing that each was both overwhelmingly consumed by women, and notably absent from theorisations of popular culture.

Modleski's work does not emerge from the context of Marxist historiography which shaped the approach of the Birmingham Centre for Contemporary Cultural Studies. Rather, her argument is part of the widespread rejection of cultural pessimism – the critique of the concept, associated with the Frankfurt School, of mass culture as manipulative and debased, which transformed cultural studies in the US in the 1980s. Thus, in looking at soap opera or romance fiction, she refuses to see such texts as either escapism or ideological manipulation. Instead, she argues that 'their enormous and continuing popularity suggests that they speak to very real problems and tensions in women's lives'.[10]

Modleski examines both the form and the content of popular culture as consumed by women. Thus, in relation to soap opera, she identifies repetition, deferral and incompleteness as characteristic of the genre, and sees such strategies not as failure, but as a positive departure from the seamless closure that characterises most popular fictions. Further, she argues that such deferral and incompleteness speak in particular ways to women, since they mirror the experience of unfocused repetition characteristic of domestic labour:

> The formal properties of daytime television thus accord closely with the rhythms of women's work in the home. Individual soap operas as well as the flow of various programmes and commercials tend to make repetition, interruption, and distraction pleasurable. (p. 102)

Soap opera is also important, according to Modleski, because it allows for the representation of strong and transgressive women. The fact that these women are always punished, and always contained within the home, does not, she insists, detract from the importance of their articulation of anger, ambition, and contempt for those who try to control them. The same sort of argument has been made about the older, relatively independent, and sexually active working-class women found in *Coronation Street*.[11]

Modleski's argument changes somewhat in her analysis of romance fiction. Again, she refuses to see it as ideological manipulation. Instead, she argues that, for women, reading romance fiction is a way of exploring the contradictions in their own lives between cultural representations of femininity and the family, and their own experiences of domestic labour in the home. The very impossibility of becoming a romantic heroine, experienced in each reading of a romantic novel, is,

Modleski argues, a way of negotiating identity as a tension between aspiration and reality.

This rediscovery of romance fiction as a place of contradictory, and of political, meanings is echoed in the work of Alison Light. Light argues, in relation to *Rebecca*, that the genre does offer the possibility of resistance, and suggests that although it is difficult to see the experience of reading romance fiction as progressive, it can perhaps at least be understood as transgressive.[12] Light's argument here is particularly interesting because it seems to represent some sort of synthesis of the two trends within cultural studies: focusing on consumption, but also engaging with the political possibilities of resistance.

Thus it seems that, for feminist critics, all roads within cultural studies lead to consumption, pleasure and femininity, with only brief detours via hegemony, production, and class. Modleski is certainly aware of this tendency, and seems at first to reject the inevitability of such dichotomies: 'countless critics... persist in equating femininity, consumption and reading on the one hand and masculinity, production and writing on the other'.[13] She challenges this theoretical division, and the consequent privileging of metaphors of 'production' in cultural analysis. However, despite a call for the reconstruction of such oppositions, Modleski is finally constrained by them. Her methodological and her theoretical commitment is to a feminist critique that will 'search out the radical potential of the subordinate terms' (p. 42).

Within the field of cultural studies, then, the attempt to develop a feminist critique has driven women increasingly towards questions of pleasure and consumption, and away from those of history and production. Within this space important studies have been produced, and theoretical and methodological attention has been paid to texts which had been dismissed as trivial, distracting, and irrelevant. The identification of the ways in which class identities are inflected by the negotiation with 'femininity', or of the capacity of women to establish productive, or at least transgressive, relations with cultural commodities, represent significant theoretical and political advances. My anxiety, however, is that this emphasis on consumption, on pleasure, on femininity, can make it impossible for feminist critics to develop a sustained critique of the dominant paradigms of cultural studies, which offer universality, productivity, politics, and struggle. It therefore tends to marginalise feminist critique within the discipline of cultural studies, and to reinforce those unhelpful dichotomies which place men in history and women in the home.

This critical placing of women, and of feminist critique, so resolutely within the domains of pleasure and of consumption has more profound limitations, however, which can be identified through a reading of a study such as Andrew Ross's *No Respect: Intellectuals and popular culture* (1989). Basically, Ross claims the spheres of consumption and of pleasure for a politics of postmodern masculinity. His study is a fascinating engagement with the history of intellectual intervention within the domain of popular culture: 'the historically fractious relationship between intellectuals and popular culture'.[14] Its theoretical and methodological debt to the ethnographic and historical aspect of cultural studies is clearly signalled, with chapter titles such as 'Uses of Camp', both invoking and negating Hoggart's text.

Ross seeks to distance himself from what he sees as the imaginary, or perhaps the anachronistic, ease of languages of class and of resistance, instead 'taking the messy part of consumption at the cost of a neat, critical analysis of production' (p. 8). This move towards consumption does not, however, lead Ross to a consideration of the cultural or political identities of women, but rather to 'the history of redefining masculinity in response to feminist initiatives' (p. 158). Thus the space of feminist critique is fractured. Consumption, pleasure and 'messiness' can no longer be seen as linked to the experience of femininity. Ross takes them over for 'the liberator body' and 'the creativity of consumption' (p. 11). Such embodied cultural practice does not, however, open up any easy space for feminist analysis: Ross insists that his aim is to establish 'a politics of sexuality that is relatively autonomous from categories of gender' (p. 177).

When Ross concludes his study with a consideration of 'The Popularity of Pornography', the stakes involved in this theoretical shift become clear. Ross attacks feminists who have argued against the proliferation of pornographic images, accusing them of self-righteous moralism which fails to register the importance of the 'liberator body', and evades the fact that 'female consumers [are] . . . acknowledged as the largest potential growth market for pornographic entertainment' (p. 171).

Of course, the status of such 'acknowledgement' must be open to question: whether political critique should proceed on the basis of marketing plans for particular cultural commodities is far from clear. Still, Ross's work does open up problems for the theoretical and methodological procedures of feminist cultural studies. It is surely no longer possible to assume that simply by moving ground, from production to consumption, a space will be found in which to articulate the political and cultural identities of women. Consumption, with its constructed identities and its 'messiness', cannot simply deliver a feminist politics. If feminist critics wish to challenge the paradigms and procedures of cultural studies, to find models and theories that will address the experience of women as both producers and consumers of cultural meanings, they must find ways to challenge the hierarchies and oppositions that have fractured the discipline of cultural studies. Thus abstractions of class and of pleasure will be challenged by attention to questions such as 'whose labour, whose consumption, and whose body?'

Notes

1. Leslie G. Roman and Linda K. Christian-Smiith have, however, discussed this question in the Introduction to Leslie G. Rolan *et al.*, *Becoming Feminine: The politics of popular culture* (Barcombe, East Sussex: The Falmer Press, 1988), pp. 1–34.
2. Julia Swindells and Lisa Jardine, *What's Left? Women in Culture and the Labour Movement* (London: Routledge, 1990), p. 3.
3. Richard Hoggart, *The Uses of Literacy* (Harmondsworth: Penguin, 1958), p. 22.

4. Examples include Eileen and Stephen Yeo (eds), *Popular Culture and Class Conflict 1590–1914: Explorations in the history of labour and leisure* (Brighton 1981), or John K. Walton and James Walvin (eds), *Leisure in Britain 1780–1939* (Manchester, 1983).

5. David Vincent, 'Reading in the Working-Class Home', in Walton and Walvin (eds), *Leisure in Britain*, pp. 207–26 (p. 219).

6. J. F. C. Harrison, *Learning and Living 1790–1960* (London, 1961), p. 30.

7. J. Clarke, 'The Skinheads and the Study of Youth Culture', Stencilled Occasional Paper, 23, Birmingham University Centre for Contemporary Cultural Studies (1973), p. 11.

8. A. McRobbie and J. Garber, 'Girls and Subcultures', in S. Hall and T. Jefferson (eds), *Resistance Through Rituals: Youth subcultures in post-war Britain* (London, 1976), pp. 209–22.

9. A. McRobbie, 'Working Class Girls and the Culture of Femininity', in Women's Studies Group, *Women Take Issue: Aspects of women's subordination* (London, 1978), pp. 96–108 (p. 108).

10. Tania Modleski, *Loving With a Vengeance: Mass-produced fantasies for women* (London, 1984), p. 14.

11. See Richard Dyer *et al.*, *Coronation Street* (London, 1981).

12. Alison Light '"Returning to Manderley" – Romance Fiction, Female Sexuality and Class', in Mary Eagleton (ed.), *Feminist Literary Theory: A reader* (Oxford, 1986), pp. 140–5.

13. Tania Modleski, 'Femininity as Mas(s)querade: A feminist approach to mass culture', in C. MacCabe (ed.), *High Theory/Low Culture: Analysing popular television and film* (Manchester, 1986), pp. 37–52 (p. 41).

14. Andrew Ross, *No Respect: intellectuals and popular culture* (London, 1989), p. 5.

PART SIX

Postmodernism

Introduction

The postmodern, according to Dick Hebdige (Reading 36), is a contemporary 'buzzword'. It has so many different meanings, in so many different debates and different discourses, that it is tempting to dismiss it and move on to something with more academic substance. But this is not Hebdige's approach. He argues – and I agree – that when a term has entered so many debates and discourses, it must be articulating something fundamental. Although the term has been in circulation since the 1870s, it is only in the late 1950s and early 1960s that we see the beginnings of what is now understood as postmodernism. In the work of the American cultural critic, Susan Sontag, we encounter the celebration of what she calls a 'new sensibility'. As she explains, 'One important consequence of the new sensibility [is] that the distinction between "high" and "low" culture seems less and less meaningful'.[1]

It is a sensibility in revolt against modernism now canonised as the official culture of the capitalist world order. No longer scandalous and bohemian, modernism had lost its ability to shock and disgust the bourgeoisie. Instead of outraging from the critical margins of bourgeois society, the work of Bertolt Brecht, T. S. Eliot, James Joyce, Virginia Woolf, Pablo Picasso, Igor Stravinsky, and others had not only lost the ability to shock and disturb, it had become central, classical, the canon.

The postmodern 'new sensibility' rejected the cultural elitism of modernism. Although modernism often 'quoted' popular culture, it was marked by a deep suspicion of all things popular. Its entry into the museum and the academy as official culture was undoubtedly made easier (despite its declared antagonism to bourgeois philistinism) by its appeal to, and homologous relationship with, the elitism of class society.

The response of the postmodern 'new sensibility' to modernism's canonisation was a re-evaluation of popular culture. The postmodernism of the 1960s was therefore in part a populist attack on the elitism of modernism. It signalled a refusal of what Andreas Huyssen calls 'the great divide ... [a] discourse which insists on the categorical distinction between high art and mass culture'. Moreover, according to Huyssen, 'To a large extent, it is by the distance we have travelled from this "great divide" between mass culture and modernism that we can measure our own cultural postmodernity.'[2]

The American and British pop art movement of the 1950s and the 1960s, with its rejection of the distinction between popular and high culture, is postmodernism's first cultural flowering. As pop art's first theorist, Lawrence Alloway, explains,

> The area of contact was mass produced urban culture: movies, advertising, science fiction, pop music. We felt none of the dislike of commercial culture standard among most intellectuals, but accepted it as a fact, discussed it in detail, and consumed it enthusiastically. One result of our discussions was to take Pop culture out of the realm of 'escapism', 'sheer entertainment', 'relaxation', and to treat it with the seriousness of art.[3]

Seen from this perspective, postmodernism first emerges out of a generational refusal of the categorical certainties of high modernism. The insistence on an absolute distinction between high and popular culture came to be regarded as the 'unhip' assumption of an older generation. This is particularly evident in the cultural politics of both the American counterculture and the British underground of the 1960s.

In the 1970s, when the discourse of postmodernism moved from mainly describing a set of cultural practices and an accompanying sensibility to become a description of a cultural condition (i.e. when it crossed from Britain and America to France), its tone grew less optimistic. In *The Postmodern Condition*, Jean-François Lyotard defines postmodernism as 'incredulity towards metanarratives'.[4] What he means by this is the supposed contemporary rejection of all overarching or totalising modes of thought that tell universalist stories ('metanarratives'): Marxism, Christianity, 'scientific progress', for example, which organise and justify the everyday practices of a plurality of different stories ('narratives'). According to Lyotard, metanarratives operate through strategies of inclusion and exclusion, marshalling and homogenising heterogeneity into ordered realms; always attempting to silence other voices, other discourses, in the name of universal principles and general goals.

Postmodernism is said to signal the collapse of all universalist metanarratives, with their privileged truth to tell, and to herald instead the increasing sound of a plurality of voices from the margins, with their insistence on difference, on cultural diversity, and on the claims of heterogeneity over homogeneity. Angela McRobbie claims that this has enfranchised a whole 'new generation of intellectuals (often black, female, or working class)'.[5] These voices from the margins, speaking from positions of difference, have challenged theoretically (and by their very presence in academia) the metanarrative of the categorical distinction between high and popular culture. This is the metanarrative that all postmodernists agree has collapsed: the Arnoldian distinction between high culture as 'culture' and the culture of everyone else as 'anarchy'. In this way, postmodernism is said to proclaim the end of Culture and the beginning of a plurality of cultures.

bell hooks (Reading 40) is '[c]critical of most writing on postmodernism [because] there is seldom any mention of black experience or writings by black people'. She is also 'suspicious of postmodern critiques of the "subject" when they surface at a historical moment when many subjugated people feel themselves coming to voice for the first time'. In spite of her reservations, she is committed to what she calls 'a postmodern oppositional sensibility'. As she maintains, 'It's exciting to think, write, talk about, and create art that reflects passionate engagement with popular culture, because this may very well be "the" central future location of resistance struggle, a meeting place where new and radical happenings can occur.'

Jean Baudrillard defines postmodernism as a world of 'simulations' and 'hyper-reality'. The capitalist democracies of the West have ceased to be economies based on the production of things and have become economies based on the production of images and information. These are societies of the 'simulacrum'. A simulacrum is an identical copy without an original (see Reading 33). In the realm of the postmodern, the distinction between simulation and the 'real' continually implodes; the real and the imaginary continually collapse into each other. The result is hyperrealism: the real and the simulated are experienced as without difference. These are societies in which men and women make offers of marriage to characters in soap operas; where television villains are confronted in the street and warned about the possible future consequences of their villainous behaviour; where television doctors, television lawyers and television detectives regularly receive requests for help and advice. Baudrillard gives the example of Disneyland as 'a perfect model of all the entangled orders of simulation'. He also cites the reporting of 'Watergate' as operating in much the same way. Reporting it as a scandal conceals the fact that it is a commonplace of American political life.

In two very influential essays, Fredric Jameson breaks with the positions of Lyotard and Baudrillard in that he insists that Marxism can explain postmoder-nism.[6] For Jameson, postmodernism is more than just a particular cultural style; it is above all 'the cultural dominant' of late or multinational capitalism. This is capitalism in its purest form, reaching the parts of the social formation that other stages of capitalism were unable to reach. According to Jameson, postmodernism is marked by pastiche, depthless intertextuality, and schizophrenia. It is a culture in which 'real' history is displaced by nostalgia. The result is a discontinuous flow of perpetual presents. His example is what he calls the 'nostalgia film'. Such films set out stylistically and atmospherically, and in terms of audience experience, to provide a sense of the past, even when the film is set in the future; for these are not historical films; history is always effaced by 'historicism', the 'random cannibaliz-ation' of past filmic styles and past experiences of viewing.

Elizabeth Wilson (Reading 38) applies Jameson's analysis to the world of fashion ('the most popular aesthetic practice of all', as she calls it). Although she is generous enough to describe his analysis as 'brilliant', she quickly begins to distance herself from it. For example, she doubts whether pastiche and the nostalgia mode are unique to postmodernism. She also believes that Jameson underplays the element of utopian protest in nostalgia. As she puts it, 'Utopianism has always been nostalgic and in a curious way backward looking'. In addition, where Jameson sees only the hypertrophy of styles destroying meaning, she sides with the postmodern optimists (Angela McRobbie, Iain Chambers, Andreas Huyssen,[7] for example) to argue for a pluralist politics of new possibilities. In the end, she wonders if Jameson's analysis might in fact represent 'a cultural myth of "our times"', extending to the present a stereotype after the fashion of 'the thirties' or 'the sixties', and so on.

Barbara Creed's essay (Reading 34) explores the connection between feminism and postmodernism. She is critical, for example, of Jameson's apparent indifference to questions of gender in the nostalgia film. She also wonders why he never questions the appeal of nostalgia. Moreover, she asks: 'Does this nostalgia take a different form for men and women?' The nostalgia film, with its 'intensely polarised gender roles', she believes, invokes a longing not for a lost historical past, but for an imaginary past – 'an order where gender identity was secure and appeared to validate the social contract established by the myth of romantic love'. Meaghan Morris (Reading 35) also considers the connection between feminism and postmodernism. She is critical of a paradoxical mode of thought which claims on the one hand that the debate on postmodernism would be unthinkable without the impact of feminist cultural politics, yet on the other that there has been little or no feminist input into this debate. Morris wonders if the best response is to 'adopt a complacent paranoia, and assume that the male pantheon of postmodernism is merely a twilight of the gods – the last ruse of the patriarchal university trying for power to fix the meaning and contain the damage, of its own decline'. But with less 'complacency', paranoid or otherwise, she wonders if women still have to ask whether men are reading their work?

In 'Popular Music and Postmodern Theory' (Reading 39), Andrew Goodwin argues that Jameson's distinction between modern and postmodern pop music does not make sense. Although Goodwin concludes that the concept of postmodernism has little to offer the student of pop music, his account of the (non-) relationship between music and concept is an exemplary analysis of pop music culture. Cornel West (Reading 37), however, does see a relationship between pop music and postmodernism. He cites 'rap' as *the* black postmodernist cultural practice. He speaks of rap's 'tremendous articulateness ... syncopated with the African drumbeat, the African funk, into an American postmodernist product'.

In the first part of his essay (Reading 36), Dick Hebdige presents an illuminating and authoritative overview of what is at stake in the debate on postmodernism. In the second half, he confronts postmodernism with the politics of Gramscian cultural studies. But he knows that these are not polar opposites; there is common ground between – common ground that connects – the two positions. Ultimately, however, it is with Marxism that he remains, but 'a Marxism more prone perhaps to listen, learn, adapt and to appreciate, for instance, that words like "emergency" and "struggle" don't just mean fight, conflict, war and death but birthing, the prospect of new life emerging: a struggle to the light ...'.[8]

Notes

1. Susan Sontag, *Against Interpretation*, New York: Deli, 1966, p. 302.
2. Andreas Huyssen, *After the Great Divide: Modernism, mass culture and postmodernism*, London: Macmillan, 1986, p. viii.
3. Quoted in John Storey, *An Introduction to Cultural Theory and Popular Culture*, second edition, Hemel Hempstead: Harvester Wheatsheaf, 1997, p. 172.
4. Jean-François Lyotard, *The Postmodern Condition*, Manchester: Manchester University Press, 1986, p. xxiv.
5. Angela McRobbie, *Postmodernism and Popular Culture*, London: Routledge, 1994, p. 23. See also, Kobena Mercer, *Welcome to the Jungle*, London: Routledge, 1994.
6. Fredric Jameson, 'Postmodernism, or the cultural logic of late capitalism', *New Left Review* 146, 1984, pp. 53–92; 'Postmodernism and consumer society', in *Postmodern Culture*, ed. Hal Foster, London: Pluto, 1985, pp. 111–25.
7. See notes 2 and 5 above, and Iain Chambers, *Popular Culture: The metropolitan experience*, London: Routledge, 1988.
8. Dick Hebdige's essay is also available in his *Hiding in the Light*, London: Routledge, 1988.

33 □ *The Precession of Simulacra*

Jean Baudrillard

The simulacrum is never that which conceals the truth – it is
the truth which conceals that there is none.
The simulacrum is true.

(Ecclesiastes)

If we were able to take as the finest allegory of simulation the Borges tale where the cartographers of the Empire draw up a map so detailed that it ends up exactly covering the territory (but where the decline of the Empire sees this map become frayed and finally ruined, a few shreds still discernible in the deserts – the metaphysical beauty of this ruined abstraction, bearing witness to an Imperial pride and rotting like a carcass, returning to the substance of the soil, rather as an ageing double ends up being confused with the real thing) – then this fable has come full circle for us, and now has nothing but the discreet charm of second-order simulacra.[1]

Abstraction today is no longer that of the map, the double, the mirror or the concept. Simulation is no longer that of a territory, a referential being or a substance. It is the generation by models of a real without origin or reality: a hyperreal. The territory no longer precedes the map, nor survives it. Henceforth, it is the map that precedes the territory – PRECESSION OF SIMULACRA – it is the map that engenders the territory, and if we were to revive the fable today, it would be the territory whose shreds are slowly rotting across the map. It is the real, and not the map, whose vestiges subsist here and there, in the deserts which are no longer those of the Empire, but our own. *The desert of the real itself.*

In fact, even inverted, the fable is useless. Perhaps only the allegory of the Empire remains. For it is with the same Imperialism that present-day simulators try to make the real, all the real, coincide with their simulation models. But it is no longer a

From Baudrillard, J., *Simulations*, Semiotext(e), New York, 1983, pp. 1–30.

question of either maps or territory. Something has disappeared: the sovereign difference between them that was the abstraction's charm. For it is the difference which forms the poetry of the map and the charm of the territory, the magic of the concept and the charm of the real. This representational imaginary, which both culminates in and is engulfed by the cartographer's mad project of an ideal coextensivity between the map and the territory, disappears with simulation – whose operation is nuclear and genetic, and no longer specular and discursive. With it goes all of metaphysics. No more mirror of being and appearances, of the real and its concept. No more imaginary coextensivity: rather, genetic miniaturisation is the dimension of simulation. The real is produced from miniaturised units, from matrices, memory banks and command models – and with these it can be reproduced an indefinite number of times. It no longer has to be rational, since it is no longer measured against some ideal or negative instance. It is nothing more than operational. In fact, since it is no longer enveloped by an imaginary, it is no longer real at all. It is a hyperreal, the product of an irradiating synthesis of combinatory models in a hyperspace without atmosphere.

In this passage to a space whose curvature is no longer that of the real, nor of truth, the age of simulation thus begins with a liquidation of all referentials – worse: by their artificial resurrection in systems of signs, a more ductile material than meaning, in that it lends itself to all systems of equivalence, all binary oppositions and all combinatory algebra. It is no longer a question of imitation, nor of reduplication, nor even of parody. It is rather a question of substituting signs of the real for the real itself, that is, an operation to deter every real process by its operational double, a metastable, programmatic, perfect descriptive machine which provides all the signs of the real and short-circuits all its vicissitudes. Never again will the real have to be produced – this is the vital function of the model in a system of death, or rather, of anticipated resurrection which no longer leaves any chance even in the event of death. A hyperreal henceforth sheltered from the imaginary, and from any distinction between the real and the imaginary, leaving room only for the orbital recurrence of models and the simulated generation of difference.

The Divine Irreference of Images

To dissimulate is to feign not to have what one has. To simulate is to feign to have what one hasn't. One implies a presence, the other an absence. But the matter is more complicated, since to simulate is not simply to feign: 'Someone who feigns an illness can simply go to bed and make believe he is ill. Some one who simulates an illness produces in himself some of the symptoms' (Littré). Thus, feigning or dissimulating leaves the reality principle intact: the difference is always clear, it is only masked; whereas simulation threatens the difference between 'true' and 'false', between 'real' and 'imaginary'. Since the simulator produces 'true' symptoms, is he ill or not? He cannot be treated objectively either as ill, or as not ill. Psychology and medicine stop at this point, before a thereafter undiscoverable truth of the illness. For if any symptom can be 'produced', and can no longer be accepted as a fact of nature, then every illness may be considered as simulatable and simulated, and medicine loses its meaning since it only knows how to treat 'true' illnesses by their objective causes. Psychosomatic evolves in a dubious way on the edge of the illness principle. As for psychoanalysis, it transfers the symptom from the organic to the unconscious order: once again, the latter is held to be true, more true than the former – but why should simulation stop at the portals of the unconscious? Why couldn't the 'work' of the unconscious be 'produced' in the same way as any other symptom in classical medicine? Dreams already are.

The alienist, of course, claims that 'for each form of the mental alienation there is a particular order in the succession of symptoms, of which the simulator is unaware and in the absence of which the alienist is unlikely to be deceived'. This (which dates from 1865) in order to save at all cost the truth principle, and to escape the spectre raised by simulation – namely that truth, reference and objective causes have ceased to exist. What can medicine do with something which floats on either side of illness, on either side of health, or with the reduplication of illness in a discourse that is no longer true or false? What can psychoanalysis do with the reduplication of the discourse of the unconscious in a discourse of simulation that can never be unmasked, since it isn't false either?[2]

What can the army do with simulators? Traditionally, following a direct principle of identification, it unmasks and punishes them. Today, it can reform an excellent simulator as though he were equivalent to a 'real' homosexual, heart-case or lunatic. Even military psychology retreats from the Cartesian clarities and hesitates to draw the distinction between true and false, between the 'produced' symptom and the authentic symptom. 'If he acts crazy so well, then he must be mad.' Nor is it mistaken: in the sense that all lunatics are simulators, and this lack of distinction is the worst form of subversion. Against it classical reason armed itself with all its categories. But it is this today which again outflanks them, submerging the truth principle.

Outside of medicine and the army, favored terrains of simulation, the affair goes back to religion and the simulacrum of divinity: 'I forbad any simulacrum in the temples because the divinity that breathes life into nature cannot be represented.' Indeed it can. But what becomes of the divinity when it reveals itself in icons, when it is multiplied in simulacra? Does it remain the supreme authority, simply incarnated in images as a visible theology? Or is it volatilized into simulacra which alone deploy their pomp and power of fascination – the visible machinery of icons being substituted for the pure and intelligible Idea of God? This is precisely what was feared by the Iconoclasts, whose millennial quarrel is still with us today.[3] Their rage to destroy images rose precisely because they sensed this omnipotence of simulacra, this facility they have of effacing God from the consciousness of men, and the overwhelming, destructive truth which they suggest: that ultimately there has never been any God, that only the simulacrum exists, indeed that God himself has only ever been his own simulacrum. Had they been able to believe that images only occulted or masked the Platonic Idea of God, there would have been no reason to destroy them. One can live with the idea of a distorted truth. But their metaphysical despair came from the idea that the images concealed nothing at all, and that in fact they were not images, such as the original model would have made them, but actually perfect simulacra forever radiant with their own fascination. But this death of the divine referential has to be exorcised at all cost.

It can be seen that the iconoclasts, who are often accused of despising and denying images, were in fact the ones who accorded them their actual worth, unlike the iconolators, who saw in them only reflections and were content to venerate God at one remove. But the converse can also be said, namely that the iconolaters were the most modern and adventurous minds, since underneath the idea of the apparition of God in the mirror of images, they already enacted his death and his disappearance in the epiphany of his representations (which they perhaps knew no longer represented anything, and that they were purely a game, but that this was precisely the greatest game – knowing also that it is dangerous to unmask images, since they dissimulate the fact that there is nothing behind them).

This was the approach of the Jesuits, who based their politics on the virtual disappearance of God and on the worldly and spectacular manipulation of consciences – the evanescence of God in the epiphany of power – the end of transcendence, which no longer serves as alibi for a strategy completely free of influences and signs. Behind the baroque of images hides the grey eminence of politics.

Thus perhaps at stake has always been the murderous capacity of images, murderers of the real, murderers of their own model as the Byzantine icons could murder the divine identity. To this murderous capacity is opposed the dialectical capacity of representations as a visible and intelligible mediation of the Real. All of Western faith and good faith was engaged in this wager on representation: that a sign could refer to the depth of meaning, that a sign could *exchange* for meaning and that something could guarantee this exchange – God, of course. But what if God himself can be simulated, that is to say, reduced to the signs which attest his existence? Then the whole system becomes weightless, it is no longer anything but a gigantic simulacrum – not unreal, but a simulacrum, never again exchanging for what is real, but exchanging in itself, in an uninterrupted circuit without reference or circumference.

So it is with simulation, in so far as it is opposed to representation. The latter starts from the principle that the sign and the real are equivalent (even if this equivalence is utopian, it is a fundamental axiom). Conversely, simulation starts from the *utopia* of this principle of equivalence, *from the radical negation of the sign as value*, from the sign as reversion and death sentence of every reference. Whereas representation tries to absorb simulation by interpreting it as false representation, simulation envelops the whole edifice of representation as itself a simulacrum.

This would be the successive phases of the image:

● it is the reflection of a basic reality;

- it masks and perverts a basic reality;
- it masks the *absence* of a basic reality;
- it bears no relation to any reality whatever: it is its own pure simulacrum.

In the first case, the image is a *good* appearance – the representation is of the order of sacrament. In the second, it is an *evil* appearance – of the order of malefice. In the third, it *plays at being* an appearance – it is of the order of sorcery. In the fourth, it is no longer in the order of appearance at all, but of simulation.

The transition from signs which dissimulate something to signs which dissimulate that there is nothing marks the decisive turning point. The first implies a theology of truth and secrecy (to which the notion of ideology still belongs). The second inaugurates an age of simulacra and stimulation, in which there is no longer any God to recognise his own, nor any last judgement to separate true from false, the real from its artificial resurrection, since everything is already dead and risen in advance.

When the real is no longer what it used to be, nostalgia assumes its full meaning. There is a proliferation of myths of origin and signs of reality; of second-hand truth, objectivity and authenticity. There is an escalation of the true, of the lived experience; a resurrection of the figurative where the object and substance have disappeared. And there is a panic-stricken production of the real and the referential, above and parallel to the panic of material production: this is how simulation appears in the phase that concerns us – a strategy of the real, neo-real and hyperreal whose universal double is a strategy of deterrence.

[. . .]

Hyperreal and Imaginary

Disneyland is a perfect model of all the entangled orders of simulation. To begin with it is a play of illusions and phantasms: Pirates, the Frontier, Future World, etc. This imaginary world is supposed to be what makes the operation successful. But what draws the crowds is undoubtedly much more the social microcosm, the miniaturised and *religious* revelling in real America, in its delights and drawbacks. You park outside, queue up inside, and are totally abandoned at the exit. In this imaginary world the only phantasmagoria is in the inherent warmth and affection of the crowd, and in that sufficiently excessive number of gadgets used there to specifically maintain the multitudinous effect. The contrast with the absolute solitude of the parking lot – a veritable concentration camp – is total. Or rather: inside, a whole range of gadgets magnetise the crowd into direct flows – outside, solitude is directed on to a single gadget: the automobile. By an extraordinary coincidence (one that undoubtedly belongs to the peculiar enchantment of this universe), this deep-frozen infantile world happens to have been conceived and realised by a man who is himself now cryogenised: Walt Disney, who awaits his resurrection at minus 180 degrees centigrade.

The objective profile of America, then, may be traced throughout Disneyland, even down to the morphology of individuals and the crowd. All its values are exalted here, in miniature and comic strip form. Embalmed and pacified. Whence the possibility of an ideological analysis of Disneyland (L. Marin does it well in *Utopies, jeux d'espaces*): digest of the American way of life, panegyric to American values, idealised transposition of a contradictory reality. To be sure. But this conceals something else, and that 'ideological' blanket exactly serves to cover over a *third-order simulation*: Disneyland is there to conceal the fact that it is the 'real' country, all of 'real' America, which *is* Disneyland (just as prisons are there to conceal the fact that it is the social in its entirety, in its banal omnipresence, which is carceral). Disneyland is presented as imaginary in order to make us believe that the rest is real, when in fact all of Los Angeles and the America surrounding it are no longer real, but of the order of the hyperreal and of simulation. It is no longer a question of a false representation of reality (ideology), but of concealing the fact that the real is no longer real, and thus of saving the reality principle.

The Disneyland imaginary is neither true nor false; it is a deterrence machine set up in order to rejuvenate in reverse the fiction of the real. Whence the debility, the infantile degeneration of this imaginary. It is meant to be an infantile world, in order to make us believe that the adults are elsewhere, in the 'real' world, and to conceal the fact that real childishness is everywhere, particularly amongst those adults who go there to act the child in order to foster illusions as to their real childishness.

Moreover, Disneyland is not the only one. Enchanted Village, Magic Mountain, Marine World: Los Angeles is encircled by these 'imaginary stations' which feed reality, reality-energy, to a town whose mystery is precisely that it is nothing more than a network of endless, unreal circulation – a town of fabulous proportions, but without space or dimensions. As much as electrical and nuclear power stations, as much as film studios, this town, which is nothing more than an immense script and a perpetual motion picture, needs this old imaginary made up of childhood signals and faked phantasm for its sympathetic nervous system.

Political Incantation

Watergate. Same scenario as Disneyland (an imaginary effect concealing that reality no more exists outside than inside the bounds of the artificial perimeter): though here it is a scandal effect concealing that there is no difference between the facts and their denunciation (identical methods are employed by the CIA and the *Washington Post* journalists). Same operation, though this time tending towards scandal as a means to regenerate a moral and political principle, towards the imaginary as a means to regenerate a reality principle in distress.

The denunciation of scandal always pays homage to the law. And Watergate above all succeeded in imposing the idea that Watergate *was* a scandal – in this sense it was an extraordinary operation of intoxication. The reinjection of a large dose of political morality on a global scale. It could be said along with Bourdieu that:

'The specific character of every relation of force is to dissimulate itself as such, and to acquire all its force only because it is so dissimulated', understood as follows: capital, which is immoral and unscrupulous, can only function behind a moral superstructure, and whoever regenerates this public morality (by indignation, denunciation, etc.) spontaneously furthers the order of capital, as did the *Washington Post* journalists.

But this is still only the formula of ideology, and when Bourdieu enunciates it he takes 'relation of force' to mean the *truth* of capitalist domination, and he *denounces* this relation of force as itself a *scandal* – he therefore occupies the same deterministic and moralistic position as the *Washington Post* journalists. He does the same job of purging and reviving moral order, an order of truth wherein the genuine symbolic violence of the social order is engendered, well beyond all relations of force, which are only its indifferent and shifting configuration in the moral and political consciousness of men.

All that capital asks of us is to receive it as rational or to combat it in the name of rationality, to receive it as moral or to combat it in the name of morality. For they are *identical*, meaning *they can be read another way*: before, the task was to dissimulate scandal; today, the task is to conceal the fact that there is none.

Watergate is not a scandal: this is what must be said at all costs, for this is what everyone is concerned to conceal, this dissimulation masking a strengthening of morality, a moral panic as we approach the primal (mise en) scene of capital: its instantaneous cruelty, its incomprehensible ferocity, its fundamental immorality – this is what is scandalous, unaccountable for in that system of moral and economic equivalence which remains the axiom of leftist thought, from Enlightenment theory to Communism. Capital doesn't give a damn about the idea of the contract which is imputed to it – it is a monstrous unprincipled undertaking, nothing more. Rather, it is 'enlightened' thought which seeks to control capital by imposing rules on it. And all that recrimination which replaced revolutionary thought today comes down to reproaching capital for not following the rules of the game. 'Power is unjust, its justice is a class justice, capital exploits us, etc.' – as if capital were linked by a contract to the society it rules. It is the left which holds out the mirror of equivalence, hoping that capital will fall for this phantasmagoria of the social contract and fulfill its obligation towards the whole of society (at the same time, no need for revolution: it is enough that capital accept the rational formula of exchange).

Capital in fact has never been linked by a contract to the society it dominates. It is a sorcery of the social relation, it is a *challenge to society* and should be responded to as such. It is not a scandal to be denounced according to moral and economic rationality, but a challenge to take up according to symbolic law.

Notes

1. Counterfeit and reproduction imply always an anguish, a disquieting foreignness: the uneasiness before the photograph, considered like a witches' trick – and more generally

before any technical apparatus, which is always an apparatus of reproduction, is related by Benjamin to the uneasiness before the mirror-image. There is already sorcery at work in the mirror. But how much more so when this image can be detached from the mirror and be transported, stocked, reproduced at will (cf. *The Student of Prague*, where the devil detaches talk image of the student from the mirror and harasses him to death by the intermediary of this image. All reproduction implies therefore a kind of black magic, from the fact of being seduced by one's own image in the water, like Narcissus, to being haunted by the double and, who knows, to the mortal turning back of this vast technical apparatus secreted today by man as his own image (the narcissistic mirage of technique, McLuhan) and that returns to him, cancelled and distorted – endless reproduction of himself and his power to the limits of the world. Reproduction is diabolical in its very essence; it makes something fundamental vacillate. This has hardly changed for us: simulation (that we describe here as the operation of the code) is still and always the place of a gigantic enterprise of manipulation, of control and of death, just like the imitative object (primitive statuette, image of photo) always had as objective an operation of black image.

2. There is furthermore in Monod's book a flagrant contradiction, which reflects the ambiguity of all current science. His discourse concerns the code, that is the third-order simulacra, but it does so still according to 'scientific' schemes of the second order – objectiveness, 'scientific' ethic of knowledge, science's principle of truth and transcendence. All things incompatible with the indeterminable models of the third order.

3. 'It's the feeble "definition" of TV which condemns its spectator to rearranging the few points retained into a kind of *abstract work*. He participates suddenly in the creation of a reality that was only just presented to him in dots: the television watcher is in the position of an individual who is asked to project his own fantasies on inkblots that are not supposed to represent anything.' TV as perpetual Rorschach test. And furthermore: 'The TV image requires each instant that we "close" the spaces in the mesh by a convulsive sensuous participation that is profoundly kinetic and tactile.'

34 □ *From Here to Modernity: Feminism and Postmodernism*

Barbara Creed

What is at stake in the debate surrounding a possible intersection between feminist theory and postmodern theory? The future of feminist theory itself: its directions theoretical bases, alignments? Is feminism a symptom or result of the postmodern condition or is feminism linked more directly to this crisis in theory? Alice Jardine and Craig Owens have explored the connections between feminism and postmodernism. A comparison of their work should prove helpful to the newcomer – myself included – who is attempting to negotiate what Owens rightly describes as a 'treacherous course' between the two.[1]

In 'The discourse of others: feminism and postmodernism', Owens argues that here is an 'apparent crossing of the feminist critique of patriarchy and the postmodernist critique of representation' (p. 59). Owens points out that his intention is not to propose a relationship of either 'antagonism or opposition' between the two (although at times he seems to do just this) but rather to explore this possible intersection in order to introduce the issue of sexual difference into the modernism/postmodernism debate', an issue of which this debate 'has until now been scandalously in-different' (p. 59) – a debatable point.

According to Owens there are many areas where feminism is not only 'compatible with, but also an instance of, postmodern thought' (p. 62): both feminism and postmodernism endorse Lyotard's argument that there is a crisis in the legitimising function of narrative, that the *grands récits* or Great Narratives of the West have lost credibility; both present a critique of representation, that 'system of power that authorizes certain representations while blocking, prohibiting or invalidating others' (p. 59); both agree that the 'representational systems of the West admit only one vision – that of the constitutive male subject' (p. 58); both present a critique of binarism, that is, thinking by means of oppositions; both insist on the importance of 'difference and incommensurability' (pp. 61–2); both seek to heal the breach between theory and practice and support an artistic strategy of 'simultaneous activity on multiple fronts' (p. 63); both critique the privileging of vision as the

From *Screen*, vol. 28, no. 2, 1987, pp. 47–67.

superior sense and as the guarantor of truth. The difference, it appears, is that where postmodernism, defined as a cultural theory, sees itself as engaging in a debate with modernism, feminism identifies patriarchal ideology as its 'other'. For instance, in relation to the issue of vision, feminism 'links the privileging of vision with sexual privilege' (p. 70), particularly in relation to the psychoanalytic theory of castration, whereas postmodernism situates the problem as one of 'modern aesthetics'. While there are some problems with Owens's argument, which I shall discuss below, I think he is correct to argue that there is a common ground shared by feminism and postmodernism.

[. . .]

The Collapse of the Master Narrative

[. . .] In *The Postmodern Condition*[2] Lyotard discusses in detail the question of knowledge and the problem of its legitimation in so-called advanced societies given what he sees as a collapse of the *grands récits* or Great Narratives, that is, narratives which have been used to legitimate the quest for knowledge and the importance of scientific research. There are two major forms of the legitimation narrative. In the first, the narrative of emancipation, the people are the subject of science. Here, it is argued that through scientific research man will eventually create a society free from poverty and injustice. According to this narrative legitimation, all research undertaken by members of the general scientific community is justified because it will eventually lead to an improvement in the lives of the people. In the second major narrative of legitimation, the speculative mind, the practice of philosophy, is the subject of science. Here, knowledge is sought for its own sake on the assumption that every small contribution will eventually lead to an advancement in the totality of knowledge.

According to Lyotard, neither of these two narratives can now be used to justify scientific research. This crisis of legitimation has been partly brought about by the breakdown in the belief that a unified totality of knowledge is possible and that if it were it would necessarily benefit humankind. Citing the way in which the techno-sciences can be said to have increased rather than alleviated disease, Lyotard critiques the very idea of progress:

> One can note a sort of decay in the confidence placed by the two last centres in the idea of progress. The idea of progress as possible, probable or necessary was rooted in the certainty that the development of the arts, technology, knowledge and liberty would be profitable to mankind as a whole.[3]

He points out that although there were disagreements, even wars, over the 'name of the subject' to be liberated, the contestants agreed that activities were 'legitimate' if they contributed to the eventual liberation of humankind. However:

> After two centuries, we are more sensitive to signs that signify the contrary. Neither economic nor political liberalism, nor the various Marxisms, emerge from the sanguinary last two centuries free from the suspicion of crimes against mankind.[4]

In *The Postmodern Condition*, Lyotard partly defines the postmodern as a condition in which the 'grand narrative has lost its credibility, regardless of what mode of unification it uses, regardless of whether it is a speculative narrative or a narrative of emancipation'.[5] He argues that we cannot hope to know the origin of this incredulity, all we can do is map its existence and its manifestations. Owens translates *grand récit* first as 'master narrative' and then as 'narratives of mastery, of man seeking his telos in the conquest of nature'.[6] He claims that not only the status of narrative is in question but also that of representation, specifically man's androcentric representation of the world in which he has constructed himself as 'subject'. Owens argues that here feminism and postmodernism share common ground – both present a critique of forms of narrative and representation which place man as subject. Owens points to the visual arts where, he argues, 'symptoms' of man's 'recent loss of mastery' are most apparent: the multiplicity of signs of mastery; a mourning of loss; images of phallic woman. While I think that Owens's comments are valid – there is a crossing of both the feminist and postmodern critiques of narrative and representation – I am not certain that Lyotard's *grand récit* is the same as Owens's 'narratives of mastery', nor am I convinced that the master narrative crisis is necessarily beneficial to women – a point that Meaghan Morris[7] raises in her work on Lyotard.

First, Lyotard is addressing narratives of legitimation and a crisis which is essentially a crisis in the status of knowledge – that is, a crisis in the ability to decide what is true and just, a crisis in the validity of the social contract between governments and the people. This crisis is not the same as the one pointed to by Owens at the outset of this article as 'a crisis of cultural authority', which he situates as a crisis in representation and narrative specifically in relation to the representation of man as 'subject' within the signifying practices of Western patriarchal societies. Owens's conceptualisation of this crisis, however, does represent the feminist position.

If Lyotard has pointed to the crisis of the master narrative in terms of 'legitimacy', Laura Mulvey's work on cinema has raised questions about a different kind of narrative crisis – one based in questions of sexual difference and brought about by the self-aggrandising structures of the unconscious of patriarchal society.[8] The feminist critique of *classic* narrative, with which it is mainly concerned, comes from a different theoretical basis and addresses itself to a different theoretical object, although both agree that there is a crisis of narrative which has shaken the credibility of the major institutions of the West. Whereas feminism would attempt to explain that crisis in terms of the workings of patriarchal ideology and the oppression of women and other minority groups, postmodernism looks to other possible causes

– particularly the West's reliance on ideologies which posit universal truths – Humanism, History, Religion, Progress, etc. While feminism would argue that the common ideological position of all these 'truths' is that they are patriarchal, postmodern theory – as I understand it – would be reluctant to isolate a single major determining factor.

Craig Owens argues that the postmodern debate has been 'scandalously in-different' to the issue of sexual difference; however, it would be more accurate to say that *some* writers have been indifferent. Jardine points out that although Lyotard does not take up the issue of the paternal signifier as a major theme in his discussion of the postmodern crisis in narrative, 'he makes it clear that the crisis is not sexually neutral'.

> He does this primarily through his descriptions of the only viable source and place he sees for legitimacy in postmodern culture: 'para-logic'. This kind of logic is dependent upon and valorizes the kinds of incomplete 'short stories' historically embedded, hidden, within so-called 'scientific' or 'objective' discourse: the kinds of short narratives that this discourse attempts to evacuate in order to shore up its 'Truths'. (p. 66)

Jardine explains that the elements of these short narratives constitute what Lyotard describes in another article as 'a feminine relation of ductility and ductibility, polymorphism . . . women are discovering something that could cause the greatest revolution in the West, something that (masculine) domination has never ceased to stifle: there is no signifier, or else the class above all classes is just one among many . . .' (p. 66). On the basis of such comments, which clearly raise the issue of sexual difference, Jardine claims that it is important to recognise 'that delegitim-ation, experienced as crisis, is the loss of the paternal fiction, the West's heritage and guarantee . . .' (p. 67). Unlike Owens, she does not reduce Lyotard's *grands récits* to 'narratives of mastery, of man seeking his telos in the conquest of nature', but rather analyses the nature of the crisis as an experience of 'the loss of the paternal signifier' – a different proposition altogether and one which provides us with a more helpful basis from which to discuss this crisis of narrative in relation to feminist theory, postmodernism and the cinema.

The 'Nostalgia' Film

I would like to relate this discussion to Fredric Jameson's argument about post-modernism and the nostalgia film. Jameson discusses this phenomenon without any reference to feminism or questions of sexual difference, apparently 'in-different' to these issues in a context where, I would have thought, they were crucial. Jameson argues that the changes currently taking place in post-industrial society have been registered in the postmodern fascination for the nostalgia film. He sees a 'desperate attempt to appropriate a missing past'[9] in films such as *American Graffiti, Rumble Fish, Chinatown, The Conformist, Body Heat*. He refers to 'the colonization' of our immediate past and argues that the preference for films which rely on quotation (of past versions, other remakes, the original novel, etc.) represents an attempt to construct '... "intertextuality" as a deliberate, built-in feature of the aesthetic effect, and as the operator of a new connotation of "pastness" and pseudo-historical depth, in which the history of aesthetic styles displaces "real" history'. Jameson sees this 'mesmerizing new aesthetic mode ... as an elaborated symptom of the waning of our historicity, of our lived possibility of experiencing history in some active way ...'.[10]

In an earlier article, Jameson discussed another category of films (*Star Wars, Raiders of the Lost Ark*) which, while not strictly historical, re-create cultural experiences in the form of pastiche as well as reawakening a sense of the past in the viewer. Jameson argues that for those who grew up in the 1930s to the 1950s one of the major cultural forms was the adventure serial, awash with 'alien villains, true American heroes, heroines in distress'. He argues that a film like *Star Wars*:

> ... reinvents this experience in the form of a pastiche: that is, there is no longer any point to a parody of such serials since they are long extinct. *Star Wars*, far from being a pointless satire of such now dead forms, satisfies a deep (might I even say repressed?) longing to experience them again: it is a complex object in which on some first level children and adolescents can take the adventure straight, while the adult public is able to gratify a deeper and more properly nostalgic desire to return to the older period and to live its strange old aesthetic artifacts through once again. This film is thus metonymically a historical or nostalgia film. . . . .[11]

What is most interesting about Jameson's otherwise incisive observations is that he does not analyse this longing for the 'past'. Exactly what is it that modern audiences wish to feel nostalgic about? Does this nostalgia take a different form for men and women? Since Jameson refers to two different forms of the nostalgia film – the period recreation and the adventure film – I shall discuss this question in relation to each.

The intensely polarised gender roles of the adventure serial, with its true heroes and distressed heroines, invoke a desire to relive a 'time' when gender roles were more clearly defined, stable, predictable. I am not arguing that this 'time' was the 1930s or the 1950s; it may be that audiences of those decades were also watching the serials in order to satisfy their desire to relive an imaginary order – an order where gender identity was secure and appeared to validate the social contract established by the myth of romantic love. Given the current crisis in gender roles, often cited as an instance of postmodernism and certainly represented in the cinema, and audience incredulity in the fact of cinematic derring-do, films like *Raiders of the Lost Ark* are required both to romanticise and parody the roles of hero and heroine. (I would also include *Crocodile Dundee* in this category.)

The problem with Jameson's argument is that he situates that 'older period' literarily in the past; he does not consider the possibility that all generations may have similar longings (although often tempered with cynicism), and that the cinema, along with other forms of popular culture, addresses these longings in different ways and through different filmic modes across the decades. It is difficult to see how Jameson could embark on such an analysis without considering the theoretical work already undertaken by feminism in this area in relation to questions of desire and the construction of sexual difference in the cinema.

Jameson's discussion of the history/nostalgia film also suffers from a similar lack. Given Lyotard's comments about the attempts of the patriarchal order to disguise the fact that 'there is no signifier', isn't it possible that the 'missing past' which lies at the heart of these films is that which once validated the paternal signifier? Significantly, at least three of the films quoted by Jameson, *Chinatown*, *The Conformist* and *Body Heat*, belong to the category of *film noir*, a genre which deliberately plays with the notion of the *femme fatale*, the phallic mother whose image constantly threatens to undermine the phallocentric order and turn son against father. In each of these remakes the male protagonist fails in his self-appointed task, largely because the patriarchal symbolic, the Law, has also failed – reduced already to the status of just one 'class' among many, to cite Lyotard again. In *Chinatown* (the title itself is used as a metaphor for corruption at all levels of city government), all characters – including the hero – have a 'past'. The possibility of incest, symbolically alluded to in the 1940s *noir* film, has become a reality in *Chinatown*; it signifies the complete failure of the symbolic order. In *The Conformist* the four symbolic fathers (Italo, Quadri, Mussolini and the hero's own 'mad' father) all signify the end of an order and a failure of 'truth' suggested by the myth of Plato's cave;[12] while *Body Heat* alludes continuously, through its references to earlier *films noirs*, to the failure of the paternal figure and the power of the phallic mother.

[...]

Conclusions

[...]

First, any attempt to assimilate feminism to postmodernism may well result in a confusion over terms, as revealed in the way in which Lyotard's notion of the grand narrative has been misleadingly reduced to 'master' narrative; such confusion only serves to undermine the specificities of the positions of both feminism and postmodernism. Second, as I have attempted to demonstrate, some theorists of the postmodern – such as Jameson – have been completely indifferent to feminism and its theorisation of the current crisis: this has resulted, in some instances, in an inadequate analysis of the postmodern film. Third, writers such as Owens, in his attempt to 'introduce' feminism into the postmodern debate, do so on terms which situate feminism as if it were a 'guest', the other brought in from the cold to join the 'host'. Owens never considers the possibility that feminist theory may not see itself as marginal to postmodernism and wish to join the club.

[...]

The title of this article was originally intended to designate the strategy of a feminism speaking from a position not identical to that which Jardine calls 'modernity' and others 'postmodernism'. I wanted to keep a tension, a space between the two. Having travelled a little way down the road, trying to negotiate Craig Owens's 'treacherous course', I am glad I did not try to unite them. Any attempt to speak from a 'place' is immediately rendered problematic by the fact that one of the positions central to postmodernism is that there are no places left from which to speak – there are no 'Truths', 'Beliefs', or 'Positions'. Yet this is in itself a position, and one now in danger of becoming a new orthodoxy. Even, perhaps, a master discourse? The paradox in which we feminists find ourselves is that while we regard patriarchal discourses as fictions, we nevertheless proceed as if our position, based on a belief in the oppression of women, were somewhat closer to the truth. Perhaps Lyotard is 'correct' [*sic*] to recommend at least the provisional abandonment of all 'Truths' in favour of the short narratives which the master discourses have attempted to suppress in order to validate their own positions. It would therefore be crucial that any theoretical discourse which emerges from the current crisis should not attempt to explain 'everything', to become a totalising theory, be it feminism *or* postmodernism.

Notes

1. Craig Owens, 'The discourse of others: feminists and postmodernism', in Hal Foster (ed.), *The Anti-Aesthetic: Essays on postmodern culture*, USA: Bay Press, 1983, p. 59. All page citations are included in the text.
2. Jean-François Lyotard, *The Postmodern Condition: A report on Knowledge*, Theory and History of Literature, vol. 10, Manchester University Press, 1984.
3. Jean-François Lyotard, 'Defining the postmodern', *Postmodernism*, ICA Documents 4, London, 1986, p. 6.
4. *Ibid.*, p. 6.
5. Jean-François Lyotard, *The Postmodern Condition*, p. 37.
6. Craig Owens, 'The discourse of others', p. 65.
7. Meaghan Morris, 'Postmodernity and Lyotard's sublime', *Art & Text*, 16, Summer 1984, p. 51.
8. Alice Jardine notes that feminist film theory, unlike many other feminist areas, has already addressed itself to postmodern theory (Alice Jardine, *Gynesis: Configurations of women and modernity*, Ithaca, NY and London: Cornell University Press, 1985), p. 75. See Laura Mulvey, 'Visual pleasure and narrative cinema', *Screen*, Autumn 1975, vol. 16, no. 3, pp. 6–18; and 'Afterthoughts on "Visual pleasure and narrative cinema"... inspired by *Duel in The Sun*', *Framework*, 15, 16/17, 1981, pp. 12–15.
9. Fredric Jameson, 'Postmodernism, or the cultural logic of late capitalism', *New Left Review*, no. 146, July–August, 1984, p. 66.
10. *Ibid.*, pp. 67, 68.
11. Fredric Jameson, 'Postmodernism and consumer society', in Hal Foster (ed.), *The Anti-Aesthetic*, p. 116.
12. See Luce Irigaray's *Speculum of the Other Woman*, Ithaca, NY, Cornell University Press, 1985, for a fascinating reinterpretation of Plato's myth of the cave.

35 □ Feminism, Reading, Postmodernism

Meaghan Morris

[...]

In a number of recent discussions of postmodernism, a sense of intrigue develops around a presumed absence – or withholding – of women's speech in relation to what has certainly become one of the boom discourses of the 1980s. Feminists in particular, in this intrigue, have had little or nothing to say about postmodernism. This very curious *doxa* emerges from texts by male critics referring primarily to each other commenting on the rarity of women's speech.

In 1983, in a text commenting on his own 'remarkable oversight' in ignoring the question of sexual difference in his previous critical practice, Craig Owens noted 'the fact that few women have engaged in the modernism/postmodernism debate'.[1] In an essay first published the following year, Andreas Huyssen – warmly agreeing with Owens that feminist work in art, literature and criticism has been 'a measure of the vitality and energy' of postmodern culture – none the less found it 'somewhat baffling that feminist criticism has so far largely stayed away from the post-modernism debate which is considered not to be pertinent to feminist concerns'.[2]

Both of these critics stressed the complexity and importance of a feminist contribution to what *they*, in turn, wished to describe as a 'postmodern' culture. Owens in particular was careful to disclaim any desire to efface the specificity of feminist critique, and to insist that his own project was to consider the implications of an *intersection* of feminism and postmodernism.

More recently, however, Jonathan Arac stated baldly in his Introduction to *Postmodernism and Politics*:

> ...*almost no women have figured in the debate*, even though many analysts include current feminism among the features of postmodernity. Nancy Fraser's important feminist critique of Habermas ('What's Critical') stands nearly alone (see also Kristeva), although Craig Owens and Andrew Ross have effectively situated feminist work by women in relation to postmodernism.[3]

From Morris, M., *The Pirate's Fiancée*, Verso, London, 1988, pp. 11–16.

In the bibliography which concludes Arac's Introduction, very few women do figure beside Fraser and Kristeva: five, to be precise, out of more than seventy individual and collaborative authorial entries. One of the five is Virginia Woolf. Another is Hannah Arendt.[4] Any bibliography, it is true, must be exclusive. This one is, when it comes to gender, *very* exclusive.

The interesting question, I think, is not whether feminists have or have not written about postmodernism, or whether they should have (for despite the 'baffled' expectation, the hope, perhaps, of eventual *fiançailles*, there is no suggestion here that feminism in any sense *needs* postmodernism as complement or supplement).[5] My question is rather under what conditions women's work *can* 'figure' currently in such a debate. There is general agreement between the male critics I've cited that 'feminist work *by women*' can figure when appropriately framed ('effectively situated') by what has mainly been, apparently, a man's discourse. But by what criteria does feminist work by women come to figure, or *not* to figure when it comes raw-edged, without a frame?

Common sense suggests that perhaps all that is meant by these remarks is that few women so far have written articles explicitly entitled 'Feminism and postmodernism'; or that few have written analyses focused on the standard (male) referents of present debate – Habermas, Lyotard, Rorty, Jameson, Huyssen, Foster, Owens, and so on. If we accept that this is true (or that many of the texts that fulfil these conditions are quite recent) then perhaps feminists have merely been busy doing other things. It would be hard to deny that in spite of its heavy (if lightly acknowledged) borrowings from feminist theory, its frequent celebrations of 'difference' and 'specificity', and its critiques of 'Enlightenment' paternalism, postmodernism as a publishing phenomenon has pulled off the peculiar feat of reconstituting an overwhelmingly male pantheon of proper names to function as ritual objects of academic exegesis and commentary. It would be easy to shrug away a presumed feminist noninvolvement with postmodernism as a wise avoidance by women of a singularly ponderous, phallo-centred conversation – and to point out with Michèle Le Doeuff that the position of faithful reader to the great male philosopher is one that women have good reason to approach with caution. Many feminist criticisms of theories of postmodernism have occurred, in fact, in passing, in the context of saying something else as well.

Yet the matter is not quite so simple. *If* it is true that few women have explicitly inscribed their work in relation to postmodernism (and I am skeptical of such claims, since they tend to present the limits and biases of our local reading habits as a satisfactory survey of the state of the world), it should also be true that only male writers who *do* inscribe their work then come to 'figure' in the debate.

Yet in Arac's bibliography, we find numerous figures whose contribution could only strictly be described as formative, enabling and/or indirect: Adorno and Horkheimer, Derrida, Heideger, Lacan, Foucault (not to mention Althusser, Perry Anderson, Lukács and Raymond Williams). Their work can only be part of a debate about postmodernism when 'effectively situated' in relation to it by subsequent commentary and citation. But a formative or indirect role in postmodernism has been willingly accorded, by men cited by Arac, to feminism. Why then, alongside the names of those men, do we not find references to (for example) the closely and critically associated work of Catherine Clément, Hélène Cixous, Luce Irigaray, Shoshana Felman, Jane Gallop, Sarah Kofman, Alice Jardine, Michèle Le Doeuff, Gayatri Chakravorty Spivak, or Jacqueline Rose?

One could continue this line of questioning. For example, it might be argued that the 'enabling' male figures have at least explicitly theorized 'modernity', and so provide the bases for thinking postmodernity. But then not only would my brief list of women recur with even greater insistence, but it would need immediate expansion: Janet Bergstrom, Mary Anne Doane, Elizabeth Grosz, Barbara Johnson, Donna Haraway, Teresa de Lauretis, Angela McRobbie, Patricia Mellencamp, Tania Modleski, Nancy K. Miller, Naomi Schor, Kaja Silverman, Judith Williamson ... (many of whom have had, in fact, quite a bit to say about postmodernism). Furthermore, if the 'politics' in the conjunction of *Postmodernism and Politics* authorizes the figuring under that rubric of the work of a Perry Anderson – then surely we might also expect to find listed works by Nancy Hartsock, Carole Pateman, Juliet Mitchell or Chantal Mouffe?

At this point, however, it becomes difficult to keep restricting my own enquiries to the names of (mostly white and Western) women. In the first and last sentence of his introductory text, Arac invokes 'the world' as the context of criticism. So why would a bibliography of 'postmodernism and *politics*' today still privilege only the great names of Western Marxism and their American academic heirs – at the expense of new theorizations of politics and culture by writers differently placed in histories of racism and colonialism? Rasheed Araeen, Homi K. Bhabha, Eduardo Galeano, Henry Louis Gates Jr, Geeta Kapur, Trinh T. Minh-ha, Nelly Richard.... After all, if postmodernism really has defined a useful sphere for political debate, it is because of the awareness it can foster that its 'world' is finally not so small, so clearly 'mapped'.

It is, as a Derridean might observe, all a matter of borderlines and frames. Any bibliography 'frames', as it defines, its field of representation. But the paradox of the frame does not prevent us from asking, in relation to any instance of framing, where and why a line is drawn. As John Frow has argued in *Marxism and Literary History*, the paradox of the frame is most useful precisely for framing a political project of working on 'the limits of reading'.

In reading the limits of Arac's bibliography, it becomes particularly difficult to determine the difference between an act of re-presenting a presupposed historical not-figuring of women in postmodernism debates, and an act of re-*producing* the not-figuring, not counting, of women's work, by 'simple' omission (writing it out of history, by writing its absence into history).

I have a similar difficulty with the more sensitive comments of Owens and Huyssen. Why do women artists and feminist theorists count *as* postmodernist (and as objects of commentary) for Owens, but not as 'engaging' in a debate? Doesn't this distinction return us precisely to that division between a (feminized) object-language and (masculine) metalanguage that feminist theory has taught us to question for its political function, rather than for its epistemological validity? How can Huyssen simply cite and confirm what Owens says, while conceding that crucial aspects of postmodernism now would be 'unthinkable'[6] without the impact of feminist thought?

After all, it is Huyssen himself who has stressed in his feminist reading of 'Mass culture as woman: modernism's other' that male authors' preoccupation with imaginary femininity 'can easily go hand in hand with the exclusion of real women from the literary enterprise'.[7] Following Huyssen, then, a 'male' postmodernism could be seen as renewing one of the inaugural gestures (in Lyotard's sense) of modernism: inscribing its 'bafflement' by an imaginary, 'absent', silent femininity, while erasing and silencing the work of real women in the history and practice of the theoretical enterprise.

Given the persistence of the figure of woman as mass culture (the irony of modernism), it is no accident that a debate about a presumed silence and absence of women has already taken place in relation to the work on popular culture that is in turn a component of postmodernism.[8] But the bafflement about women that besets both is also perhaps the latest version of the 'why have there been no great women artists (mathematicians, scientists...)?' conundrum – a badly posed question that assumes a negative response to a previous question, which remains, by default, unasked and unexamined.

How can this happen again? Again, there are some obvious responses that feminists might make. We could say that 'feminist theory' has come to function in academic publishing as a limiting category to a certain extent. It's now too easy to assume that if a text is labelled 'feminist' theory, then it can't properly 'count' or 'figure' as anything else ('woman's sphere', again). We could adopt a complacent paranoia, and assume that the male pantheon of postmodernism is merely a twilight of the gods – the last ruse of the patriarchal University trying for power to fix the meaning, and contain the damage, of its own decline. Or we could claim, probably with some justice if much brutality, that in spite of many rhetorical flourishes from men about their recognition and acceptance of feminism's 'contribution' to cultural and political theory, not very many men have really read extensively, or kept on reading, very many women's books and essays – particularly those published off the fast-track of prestige journals, or in strictly feminist contexts. The bottom line of any working bibliography is not, after all, a frame, but a practical prerequisite: you have to know it to use it.

The problem that interests me, however, is rather the difficulty that a feminist critic now faces in *saying* something about this – in trying to point out, let alone come to terms with, what seems to be a continued, repeated, basic *exclusion* of women's work from a highly invested field of intellectual and political endeavour. What woman writer wants to say, in 1987, that men still aren't reading feminist work?; that women are being 'left out again'?; thus running the risk of being suspected of talking about herself ('if she writes about women's experiences, especially the unpleasant ones, declare her hysterical or "confessional"').[9]

In addressing the myth of a postmodernism still waiting for its women we can find an example of a genre, as well as a discourse, which in its untransformed state leaves a woman no place from which to speak, or nothing to say. For by resorting to the device of listing 'excluded' women, women excluded for no obvious reason except that given by the discourse – their gender – I have positioned myself in a speech genre all too familiar in everyday life, as well as in pantomime, cartoons, and sitcoms: the woman's complaint, or *nagging*. One of the defining generic rules of 'nagging' is unsuccessful repetition of the same statements. It is unsuccessful, because it blocks change: nagging is a mode of repetition which fails to produce the desired effects of difference that might allow the complaint to end. In this it is quite close to what Anne Freadman, in her analysis of *Indiana*, calls the lament: a 'powerless text'. (A coventional comic scenario goes: she nags, he stops listening, nothing changes, she nags.) Yet there is always a change of sorts implied by repetition: in this case, her 'place' in speech becomes, if not strictly nonexistent, then insufferable – leaving frenzy or silence as the only places left to go. It is an awesome genre, and I am not sure, I confess, how to transform it.

A traditional method has always been for the nagger somehow to lose interest, and so learn to change her subject (and her addressee). One possibility in this context is to follow up Dana Polan's suggestion that postmodernism is a 'machine for producing discourse'.[10] Polan argues that as the input to this machine begins to determine what it is possible to say in its name, so it becomes increasing difficult to generate as output anything non-repetitive. Participants in a postmodernism debate are 'constrained' to refer back to previous input, and to take sides in familiar battles on a marked-out, well-trodden, terrain ('Habermas v. Lyotard', for example). The solution to feminist complaint might then be a simple one – switch position from nagger to nagged, then switch off.

But assuming a calculated deafness to discussion about postmodernism is not much of a solution for feminist women. To choose to *accept* a given constraint is not to challenge, overcome or transform anything. Besides, one of the fascinating paradoxes of the postmodernism machine is precisely how difficult it can be to switch it off (or switch off to it). Many of its best operators (Lyotard and Baudrillard, for example) have tried, and failed. As a discourse which runs on a 'paradoxical concern with its own lateness', as Andrew Ross points out (in one of the few essays relating feminism to postmodernism without attributing silence to women),[11] postmodernism has so far proved compatible with, rather than vulnerable to, vast quantities of input about its obsolescence or imminent breakdown.

A different response worth making would be, it seems to me, to make a generically feminist gesture of reclaiming women's work, and women's names, as a context *in* which debates about postmodernism might further be considered, developed, transformed (or abandoned). [. . .] feminism has acted as one of the enabling conditions of discourse *about* postmodernism; it is therefore appropriate to use feminist work to frame discussions of postmodernism, and not the other way around. To make this gesture of changing frames is to propose at least one alternative to nagging – and to wasting time waiting and watching for imaginary acts of piracy.

Notes

1. Craig Owens, 'Feminists and postmodernism', in Hal Foster, ed., *The Anti-Aesthetic: Essays on postmodern culture*, Washington 1983, p. 61.
2. Andreas Huyssen, *After the Great Divide: Modernism, mass culture, postmodernism*, Indiana, 1986, pp. 198–9.
3. Jonathan Arac, ed., *Postmodernism and Politics*, Manchester 1986, p. xi. (Emphasis mine.)
4. The others are Rosalind Coward (as co-author with John Ellis); Sally Hassan (as co-editor with Ihab Hassan); and Laura Kipnis, for one article.
5. For discussions of the problems of an intersection between feminism and postmodernism (and responses to Craig Owens's essay), see Barbara Creed, 'From here to modernity: feminism and postmodernism', *Screen*, vol. 28, no. 2, 1987, pp. 47–67 (see Chapter 36 of this volume), and Elspeth Probyn, 'Bodies and anti-bodies: feminism and the postmodern', *Cultural Studies*, vol. 1, no. 3, 1987, pp. 349–60.
6. *After the Great Divide*, p. 220.
7. *Ibid.*, p. 45.
8. See papers in Colin MacCabe, ed., *High Theory/Low Culture: Analyzing popular television and film*, Manchester 1986.
9. Joanna Russ, *How To Suppress Women's Writing*, London 1983, p. 66.
10. Dana Polan, 'Postmodernism as machine', paper to the Australian Screen Studies Association, Sydney, December 1986.
11. Andrew Ross, 'Viennese waltzes', *Enclitic*, vol. 8, nos 1–2, 1984, p. 76.

36 □ Postmodernism and 'The Other Side'

Dick Hebdige

The success of the term postmodernism – its currency and varied use within a range of critical and descriptive discourses both within the academy and outside in the broader streams of 'informed' cultural commentary – has generated its own problems. It becomes more and more difficult as the 1980s wear on to specify exactly what it is that 'postmodernism' is supposed to refer to as the term gets stretched in all directions across different debates, different disciplinary and discursive boundaries, as different factions seek to make it their own, using it to designate a plethora of incommensurable objects, tendencies, emergencies. When it becomes possible for people to describe as 'postmodern' the decor of a room, the design of a building, the diegesis of a film, the construction of a record, or a 'scratch' video, a TV commercial, or an arts documentary, or the 'intertextual' relations between them, the layout of a page in a fashion magazine or critical journal, an anti-teleological tendency within epistemology, the attack on the 'metaphysics of presence', a general attenuation of feeling, the collective chagrin and morbid projections of a post-War generation of Baby Boomers confronting disillusioned middle age, the 'predicament' of reflexivity, a group of rhetorical tropes, a prolifer-ation of surfaces, a new phase in commodity fetishism, a fascination for 'images', codes and styles, a process of cultural, political or existential fragmentation and/or crisis, the 'de-centring' of the subject, an 'incredulity towards metanarratives', the replacement of unitary power axes by a pluralism of power/discourse formations, the 'implosion of meaning', the collapse of cultural hierarchies, the dread engendered by the threat of nuclear self-destruction, the decline of the University, the functioning and effects of the new miniaturised technologies, broad societal and economic shifts into a 'media', 'consumer' or 'multinational' phase, a sense (depen-ding on whom you read) of 'placelessness' or the abandonment of placelessness ('critical regionalism') or (even) a generalised substitution of spatial for temporal co-ordinates – when it becomes possible to describe all those things as 'postmodern'

From *Journal of Communication Inquiry*, vol. 10, no. 2, 1986, pp. 78–97.

(or even simply, using a current abbreviation as 'post' or 'very post') then it's clear we are in the presence of a buzzword.

This is not a claim that because it is being used to designate so much the term is meaningless (though there is a danger that the kind of blurring of categories, objects, levels which goes on within certain kinds of 'postmodernist' writing will be used to license a lot of lazy thinking: many of the (contentious) orientations and assertions of the post are already becoming submerged as unexplicated, taken for granted 'truths' in some branches of contemporary critique). Rather I would prefer to believe, as Raymond Williams indicates in *Keywords*, that the more complexly and contradictorily nuanced a word is, the more likely it is to have formed the focus for historically significant debates, to have occupied a semantic ground in which something precious and important was felt to be embedded. I take, then, as my (possibly ingenuous) starting point that the degree of semantic complexity and overload surrounding the term 'postmodernism' at the moment signals that a significant number of people with conflicting interests and opinions feel that there is something sufficiently important at stake here to be worth struggling and arguing over.

[. . .]

Staking out the Posts

To say 'post' is to say 'past' – hence questions of periodisation are inevitably raised. There is, however, little agreement as to what it is we are alleged to have surpassed, when that passage is supposed to have occurred and what effects it is supposed to have had (see, for example, Perry Anderson's (1984) closely argued objections to Marshall Berman's (1982) (extremely loose and imprecise) periodisation of modernisation/modernism in *All That is Solid Melts into Air*). Michael Newman (1986) further problematises the apparently superseded term in postmodernism by pointing out that there are at least two artistic modernisms articulating different politico-aesthetic aspirations which remain broadly incompatible and non-synchronous. The first, which is ultimately derived from Kant, seeks to establish the absolute autonomy of art and finds its most extreme and dictatorial apologist in Clement Greenberg, the American critic who sought to 'purify' art of all 'non-essentials' by championing the cause of abstract expressionism – the style of painting most strictly confined to an exploration of the materials and two-dimensionality of paint on canvas. The second modernist tradition, which Newman (1986) traces back to Hegel, aspires to the heteronomous dissolution of art into life/political practice and leads through the surrealists, the constructivists, the futurists, etc., to performance artists and the conceptualists of the 1970s.

If the unity, the boundaries and the timing of modernism itself remains contentious issue, then *post*modernism seems to defy any kind of critical consensus. Not only do different writers define it differently, but a single writer can talk at different times about different 'posts'. Thus Jean-François Lyotard (1986a) has recently used the term postmodernism to refer to three separate tendencies: (i) a trend within architecture away from the Modern Movement's project 'of a last rebuilding of the whole space occupied by humanity', (ii) a decay in confidence in the idea of progress and modernisation ('there is a sort of sorrow in the Zeitgeist') and (iii) a recognition that it is no longer appropriate to employ the metaphor of the 'avant-garde' as if modern artists were soldiers fighting on the borders of knowledge and the visible, prefiguring in their art some kind of collective global future. J. G. Merquior (1986) (in a hostile critique of what he calls the 'post-modern ideology') offers a different triptych: (i) a style or mood of exhaustion of/dissatisfaction with modernism in art and literature, (ii) a trend in post-structuralist philosophy and (iii) a new cultural age in the West.

Furthermore the Post is differently inflected in different national contexts. It was, for instance, notable that *The Anti-Aesthetic* in the edition available in the United States arrived on the shelves beneath a suitably austere, baleful and more or less abstract (modernist?) lilac and black cover which echoed the Nietzschian tone of the title. However, when the same book was published in Britain it appeared as *Post Modern Culture* with a yellow cover consisting of a photograph of a postmodernist 'installation' incorporating cameras, speakers, etc., complete with comic book sound and light rays. The 'translation' of postmodernism as a set of discourses addressed in America to a demographically dispersed, university and gallery centred constituency for a similar though perhaps slightly more diverse, more geographically concentrated readership in Britain (where cultural pluralism, multiculturalism, the appeal or otherwise of 'Americana', the flattening out of aesthetic and moral standards, etc., are still 'hot' issues and where there is still – despite all the factional disputes and fragmentations of the last twenty years – a sizeable, organised Marxist Left) involved the negotiation of different cultural-semantic background expectancies.

National differences were further highlighted during the weekend symposium at the London ICA (Institute of Contemporary Arts) in 1985 when native speakers giving papers which stressed the enabling potentialities of the new 'user-friendly' communication technologies and the gradual deregulation of the airwaves, and which celebrated popular culture-as-postmodern-bricolage-and-play were confronted with the Gallic anti-populism of Lyotard, who declared a market preference for the fine arts, idealist aesthetics and the European avant-garde tradition, and demonstrated in comments made in response to the papers in the session on Popular Culture and Postmodernism a deep, abiding suspicion for the blandishments and commodified simplicities of 'mass culture' (Lyotard, 1986c).

To introduce a further nexus of distinctions, Hal Foster (1983), in his Preface to *The Anti-Aesthetic*, distinguishes between neo-conservative, anti-modernist and critical postmodernisms and points out that whereas some critics and practitioners seek to extend and revitalise the modernist project(s), others condemn modernist objectives and set out to remedy the imputed effects of modernism on family life, moral values, etc., whilst still others working in a spirit of ludic and/or critical pluralism endeavour to open up new discursive spaces and subject positions outside the confines of established practices, the art market and the modernist orthodoxy. In this latter 'critical' alternative (the one favoured by Foster) postmodernism is defined as a positive critical advance which fractures through negation (i) the petrified hegemony of an earlier corpus of 'radical aesthetic' strategies and proscriptions, and/or (ii) the pre-Freudian unitary subject which formed the hub of the 'progressive' wheel of modernisation and which functioned in the modern period as the regulated focus for a range of scientific, literary, legal, medical and bureaucratic discourses. In this positive 'anti-aesthetic', the critical postmodernists are said to challenge the validity of the kind of global, unilinear version of artistic and economic-technological development which a term like modernism implies and to concentrate instead on what gets left out, marginalised, repressed or buried underneath that term. The selective tradition is here seen in terms of exclusion and violence. As an initial counter-move, modernism is discarded by some critical post-modernists as a Eurocentric and phallocentric category which involves a systematic preference for certain forms and voices over others. What is recommended in its place is an inversion of the modernist hierarchy – a hierarchy which, since its inception in the eighteenth, nineteenth or early twentieth centuries (depending on your periodisation) consistently places the metropolitan centre over the 'under-developed' periphery, Western art forms over Third World ones, men's art over women's art or, alternatively, in less anatomical terms, 'masculine' or 'masculinist' forms, institutions and practices over 'feminine', 'feminist' or 'femineist' ones. Here the word 'postmodernism' is used to cover all those strategies which set out to dismantle the power of the white, male author as privileged source of meaning and value.

The Three Negations

[. . .]

There are, I think, three closely linked negations which bind the compound of postmodernism together and thereby serve to distinguish it in an approximate sort of way from other adjacent 'isms' (though the links between poststructuralism and postmodernism are in places so tight that absolute distinctions become difficult if not impossible). These founding negotiations, all of which involve – incidentally or otherwise – an attack on Marxism as a total explanatory system, can be traced back to two sources: on the one hand, historically to the blocked hopes and frustrated rhetoric of the late 1960s and the student revolts (what a friend once described to me as the 'repressed trauma of 1968'), and on the other, through the philosophical tradition to Nietzsche:

1 Against Totalisation

An antagonism to the 'generalising' aspirations of all those pre-Post-erous discourses which are associated with either the Enlightenment or the Western philosophical tradition – those discourses which set out to address a transcendental Subject, to define an essential human nature, to prescribe a global human density or to prescribe collective human goals. This abandonment of the universalist claims underwriting all previous (legitimate) forms of authority in the West involves more specifically a rejection of Hegelianism, Marxism, any philosophy of history (more 'developed' or 'linear' than, say, Nietzsche's doctrine of the Eternal Recurrence) and tends (incidentally?) towards the abandonment of all 'sociological' concepts, categories, modes of enquiry and methods, etc.

[. . .]

The move against universalist or value-free knowledge claims gathers momentum in the 1960s with the growth of phenomenology, but reaches its apogee in the late 1960s and 1970s under pressure from 'external' demands mediated through social and political movements, rather than from epistemological debates narrowly defined within the academy, i.e. in the late 1960s the challenge comes from the acid perspectivism of the drug culture, from the post-'68 politics of subjectivity and utterance (psychoanalysis, poststructuralism) and from the fusion of the personal and the political in feminism, etc.

[. . .]

From '68 we can date the widespread jettisoning of the belief amongst educated, 'radical' factions, not only in Marxist–Leninism but in any kind of power structure administered from a bureaucratically organised centre, and the suspicion of any kind of political programme formulated by an elite and disseminated through a hierarchical chain of command. The process of fragmentation and growing sensitivity to the micro-relations of power both facilitated and was facilitated by the articulation of new radical or revolutionary demands, and the formation of new collectivities, new subjectivities which could not be contained within the old paradigms, and which could be neither addressed by nor 'spoken' in the old critical, descriptive and expressive languages. Feminism, molecular and micro-politics, the autonomy movements, the counterculture, the politics of sexuality, the politics of utterance (who says what how to whom on whose behalf: the issue of the politics of power and discourse, the issue of discursive 'space') – all these 'movements' and 'tendencies' grew out of the cracks, the gaps and silences in the old 'radical' articulations. [. . .] All these fractures and the new forms which grew inside them can be understood in this context as responses to the 'crisis of representation' where the term 'representation' – understood both in its everyday sense of 'political representation' and in the structuralist sense of a distortive 'ideological' representation of a pre-existent real – is regarded as problematic. From this point on, all forms and processes of 'representation' are suspect. [. . .] All such representations were more or less complicit with, more or less oppositional to, the 'dominant ideology'. At the same time, the self-congratulatory rhetoric of political representation as a guarantor of individual and collective freedoms managed through the orderly routines and institutions of parliamentary democracy was rejected as a sham. This, of course, was nothing new: such an orientation forms the basis of a much older oppositional consensus. But more than that, for the disaffected factions who lived through the events of May '68 the idea of an individual or a political party representing, speaking for a social group, a class, a gender, a society, a collectivity, let alone for some general notion of History or Progress, was untenable. (What 'he' could ever speak adequately for 'her', could recognise 'her' needs, could represent 'her' interests?) What tended to happen after '68 is that these two senses of the term 'representation' were run together around and through the notion of discourse and language as *in themselves* productive of social relations, social and sexual inequalities, through the operations of identification, differentiation and subject positioning. In the closely related interrogation of and assault upon the idea of the (unitary) subject a similar ambiguity was there to be exploited: subject as in classical rhetoric and grammar, the subject of the sentence, the 'I' as in 'I did it my way', 'I changed the world', etc., the mythical 'I' implying as it does the self-conscious, self-present Cartesian subject capable of intentional, transparent communication and unmediated action on the world. On the other hand, there is the 'subjected subject': 'subject' as in subject to the crown, subjugated, owned by some Higher Power. In the gap between these two meanings we became subjects of ideology, subject to the Law of the Father in the Althusserian and Lacanian senses respectively: apparently free agents and yet at the same time subject to an authority which was at once symbolic and imaginary – not 'really' there but thoroughly real in its effects. The project of freeing the subject from subjection to the Subject was interpreted after '68 by a growing and increasingly influential intellectual contingent as being most effectively accomplished through the deflection of critical and activist energies away from abstractions like the State-as-source-and-repository-of-all-oppressive-powers towards particular, localised struggles and by directing attention to the play of power on the ground as it were in particular discursive formations.

But Paris represents just one '68. There were others – the '68, for instance, of Woodstock and the West Coast, of Haight-Ashbury, the Pranksters, the hippies, the Yippies, the Weatherman, the Panthers and the opposition to the war in Vietnam. The lunar desertscapes and dune buggies of Manson and the Angels: the space of acid: the libertarian imaginary of unlimited social and sexual licence, for unlimited existential risking. Here too the rights of pleasure, the play of desire and the silent 'discourse of the body' were being asserted against the puritanism and logocentricism of an earlier 'straighter' set of 'radical' demands and aspirations.

[...]

To end this section on a footnote, it is perhaps surprising, given the anti-generalist bias which informs and directs the manifold vectors of the Post, that thinkers such as Jean Baudrillard, Jean-François Lyotard and Fredric Jameson should retain such a panoptic focus in their work, writing often at an extremely high level of abstraction and generality of a 'postmodern condition', or 'predicament', a 'dominant cultural norm', etc.

2 Against Teleology

A scepticism regarding 'the idea of decidable origins/causes; this anti-teleological tendency is sometimes invoked explicitly against the precepts of historical materialism: 'mode of production', 'determination', etc. The doctrine of productive causality is here replaced by less mechanical, less unidirectional and expository accounts of process and transformation such as those available within the epistemological framework provided by, for instance, 'catastrophe theory' – to take one frequently cited example. [. . .] The anti-teleological tendency is potentially there in the Saussurean insistence on the arbitrary nature of the sign. It 'comes out' explicitly in the poststructuralist elevation of the signifier/withering away of the signified, and is most pronounced in Baudrillard's order of the simulacra where, in a parodic inversion of historical materialism, the model precedes and generates the real-seeming (which in the age of miniaturised communications is all that's left of the 'real'), where use value is completely absorbed into exchange value (in the form of sign-exchange value), where the old base–superstructure analogy is turned upside down so that value is seen to be generated in the production and exchange of insubstantials (information, image, 'communications', in speculation on, for example, the currency and commodity future markets) rather than from the expropriation of 'surplus value' through the direct exploitation of an industrial proletariat employed to produce three-dimensional goods in factories.

[. . .]

The rhetorical tropes which form the literary-artistic-critical means for effacing the traces of teleology are parody, simulation, pastiche and allegory (Newman, 1986). All these tropes tend to deny the primacy or originary power of the 'author' as sole source of meaning, remove the injunction placed upon the (romantic) artist to create substance out of nothing (i.e. to 'invent', be 'original') and confine the critic/artist instead to an endless 'reworking of the antecedent' in such a way that the purity of the text gives way to the promiscuity of the intertext and the distinction between originals and copies, hosts and parasites, 'creative' texts and 'critical' ones is eroded (i.e. with the development of meta-fiction and paracriticism). In parody, pastiche, allegory and simulation what tends to get celebrated is the *accretion* of texts and meanings, the *proliferation* of sources and readings rather than the isolation and deconstruction of the single text or utterance. None of these favoured tropes (parody, etc.) offers the artist a way of speaking from an 'authentic' (that is (After Barthes, Derrida and Foucault) imaginary) point of pure presence (romanticism). Nor do they offer the critic a way of uncovering the 'real' (intended) meaning or meanings buried in a text or a 'phenomenon' (hermeneutics).

In Jameson's autopsia, the idea of depthlessness as a marker of postmodernism, accompanied as it is by a rejection of the vocabulary of intellectual 'penetration' and the binary structures on which post-Socratic thought is reckoned to be based (e.g. reality v. appearance, real relations v. phenomenal forms, science v. false consciousness, consciousness v. the unconscious, inside v. outside, subject v. object, etc.), can be understood in this context as another step away from the old explanatory models and certainties. Derridean deconstruction and grammatology further destabilise such dualistic structures by disrupting the illusion of priority which tends to collect around one term in any binary opposition through the prepositional links which bind antinomies together (e.g. *behind* consciousness, the primary unconscious; *underneath* illusory phenomenal forms, the real relations; *beyond* subjective distortions, a world of stable objects, etc.). If the 'depth model' disappears, then so, too, does the intellectual as seer, the intellectual as informed but dispassionate observer/custodian of a 'field of enquiry' armed with 'penetrating insights' and 'authoritative overviews', enemy of sophistry, artifice and superficial detail. Once such oppositions dissolve, a lot of other things go too: there can be no more rectification of popular errors, no more trawling for hidden truths, no more going behind appearances or 'against the grain' of the visible and the obvious. [. . .] Instead what is left, to use another postmodernist key word, is a 'fascination' with mirrors, icons, surfaces. In those accounts of postmodernism produced by writers who retain a problematic, residual commitment to Marxian frames of reference, this ending of critical distance and the depth model is seen to be tied to (though not, presumably, determined by) a larger historical shift into a 'post-industrial', 'consumer', 'media', 'multinational' or 'monopoly' phase in the development of capitalism. After the prohibitions, the instrumental rationality, and the purposiveness of a production economy (and the complementary 'oppositions' and 'interruptions' of modernism), we get – or so the argument goes – the licensed promiscuity, the unconstrained imaginaries, the merger of subjects and objects, mainstreams and margins, the drift and the dreamwork which characterise life in the consumption economy of the Post. In an economy geared towards the spinning of endlessly accelerating spirals of desire, consumption allegedly imposes its own 'ecstatic' or pluralist (dis)order (Jameson's 'heterogeneity without norms'). Idolatry, the worship of Baal (commodity fetishism), replaces positivism and its doppelgänger, Marxism, the dominant epistemic faiths of the modern period. Adorno and Horkheimer's *Dialectic of Enlightenment* collapses as the combatative strategies of modernism – negation, estrangement, 'non-identity thinking' – which were supposed to work to reveal the arbitrariness/mutability of symbolic-social orders and to form the last line of defence for the 'authentic' and 'autonomous' values of a kingdom yet to come – are either rendered invalid (obsolete: no longer offering a purchase on the contemporary condition) or are absorbed as just another set of options on a horizontal plane of meaning and value where either everything means everything else (poststructuralist polysemy) or alternatively – what amounts to the same thing – everything means nothing whatsoever (Baudrillard's 'implosion of meaning'). Ultimately these two options achieve the same effect: the evacuation of an axis of power external to discourse itself: end of 'ideology', the cutting effect of Marxist critical practice. . .

[. . .]

Just as Marshall Berman proposes that modernisation (urbanisation, industrialisation, mechanisation) and modernism, the late answering wave of innovations in the arts, together articulated a third term, the experience of modernity itself; so the prophets of the Post are suggesting that postmodernisation (automation, microtechnologies, decline of manual labour and traditional work forms, consumerism, the rise of multinational media conglomerates, deregulation of the airwaves, etc.) together with postmodernism (bricolage, pastiche, allegory, the 'hyperspace' of the new architecture) are serving to articulate the experience of the Post. Whereas the experience of modernity represented an undecidable mix of anticipated freedoms and lost certainties incorporating both the terror of disintegrating social and moral bonds, of spatial and temporal horizons, and the prospect of an unprecedented mastery of nature, an emancipation from the very chains of natural scarcity – whereas, in other words, modernity was always a Janus-faced affair – the experience of *post*modernity is positively schizogenic: a grotesque attenuation – possibly monstrous, occasionally joyous – of our capacity to feel and to respond. Postmodernity is modernity without the hopes and dreams which made modernity bearable. It is a Hydra-headed, decentred condition in which we get dragged along from pillow to Post across a succession of reflecting surfaces drawn by the call of the wild signifier. The implication is that when time and progress stop, at the moment when the clocks wind down, we get wound up. In Nietzsche's dread eternal Now, as the world stops turning (stroke of noon, stroke of midnight), we start spinning around instead. That, at least, is the implication of the end of history argument: thus – Zarathustra-like – speak the prophets of the Post.

[. . .]

3 Against Utopia

Running parallel to the anti-teleological impulse, and in many ways, as is indicated above, serving as the inevitable complement to it, there is a strongly marked vein of scepticism concerning any collective destination, global framework of prediction, any claims to envisage, for instance, the 'ultimate mastery of nature', the 'rational control of social forms', a 'perfect state of being', 'end of all (oppressive) powers', etc. This anti-utopian theme is directed against all those programmes and solutions (most especially against Marxism and fascism) which have recourse to a bogus scientificity, which place a high premium on centralised planning/social engineering, and which tend to rely heavily for their implementation on the maintenance of strict party discipline, a conviction of ideological certitude, etc. The barbaric excesses (e.g. Auschwitz, the Gulag) which are said to occur *automatically* when people attempt to put such solutions and programmes into action are seen to be licensed by reference to what Lyotard (1984) calls the '*grands récits*' of the West: by the blind faith in progress, evolution, race struggle, class struggle, etc., which is itself a product of the deep metaphysical residue which lies at the root of Western thought and culture. In other words (and here there is an explicit link with the *nouvelles philosophes* of the 1970s) all Holy Wars require casualties and infidels, all utopias come wrapped in barbed wire. Many commentators have remarked upon both the banality and the irrefutability of these conclusions.

[. . .]

In that becomes in effect an explicit renunciation of Marxism (Lyotard was a founder member of the *Socialism or barbarism* group in the 1950s), Lyotard returns to Kant – especially to the *Critique of Judgement* – to reflect upon the origins of modern social thought, aesthetics and the relationship between the two. He sets out to examine the philosophical underpinning of the Enlightenment project which is defined as a twofold impetus towards universalisation (Reason) and social engineering (Revolution), both of which find support and legitimacy in the related doctrines of progress, social planning and historical 'necessity'. Much of Lyotard's (1986b) argument turns on an involved discussion of the distinction in Kant (following Burke) between the two orders of aesthetic experience: the beautiful and the sublime. Whereas the beautiful in Kant consists in all those views, objects, sounds from which we derive aesthetic pleasure but which can be framed, contained, harmoniously assimilated, the sublime is reserved for all those phenomena which exceed logical containment and which elicit a mixture of both pleasure and terror in the viewer (Burke mentions, for instance, the spectacle of a stormy sea or a volcano).

Lyotard argues that in so far as the various modernist literary and artistic avant-gardes attempt to 'present the unpresentable' (through abstraction, alienation, defamiliarisation, etc.) they remain firmly committed to an aesthetics of the sublime rather than the beautiful. For Lyotard, a properly avant-garde poem or canvas takes us to this sublime point where consciousness and being bang up against their own limitations in the prospect of absolute otherness – God or infinity – in the prospect, that is, of their disappearance in death and silence. That encounter compels the spectator's, the reader's and the artist's subjectivities to be predicated for as long as it lasts in an unlivable tense: the postmodern tense. Postmodernity is here defined as a condition that is also a contradiction in terms. Lyotard calls this timeless tense the future anterior: 'post' meaning 'after', 'modo' meaning 'now'. (What Lyotard calls 'postmodernity' is similar to Paul de Man's (1983) a(nti)historical definition of 'modernity' as the perpetual present tense within which human beings have always lived at all times and in all places, pinioned for ever between a disintegrating, irrecoverable, half-remembered past and an always uncertain future.) Lyotard insists on the validity and the viability of this avant-garde project of the sublime and seeks to promote those artistic practices which pose the issue of the unpresentable in a gesture which has to be incessantly forgotten and repeated. Using a term from psychoanalytic theory, Lyotard calls this process 'anamnesis': the re-encounter with a trauma or former experience of intensity through a process of recollection, utterance and invocation which involves not so much a recovery of the original experience as a recapitulation of it.

What might at first seem a quite arbitrary, unnecessarily abstruse and idiosyncratic detour through eighteenth-century German idealist aesthetics actually provides Lyotard with an opportunity to flesh out his central objections to Habermas's attempts to defend and build on the Enlightenment inheritance, to revive what Habermas regards as the prematurely arrested project of modernity.

For Lyotard uses the notion of the sublime as a kind of metaphor for the *absolute* nature of those limitations placed on what can be said, seen, shown, presented, demonstrated, put into play, put into practice, and implies that each encounter with the sublime in art provides us with the single salutary lesson that complexity, difficulty, opacity are always there in the same place: *beyond our grasp*. The inference here in the insistence on the palpability of human limitation is politically nuanced at those points when Lyotard talks about the disastrous consequences which have flowed from all attempts to implement the 'perfect (rational) system' or to create the 'perfect society' during what he calls the 'last two sanguinary centuries' (1986a, p. 6).

Habermas, publicly aligned with the Frankfurt tradition which he is concerned both to revise and to revive, has emphasised the emancipatory and utopian dimensions of art favouring an aesthetics of the beautiful. From this position, the fact that the harmonious integration of formal elements in an artwork gives us pleasure indicates that we are all drawn ineluctably by some internal logos (reason reflexively unfolding/folding back upon itself through the dispassionate contemplation of form), that we are, in other words, drawn towards the ideal resolution of conflict in the perfection of good form. Here our capacity both to produce and to appreciate the beautiful stands as a kind of 'promissory note' for the eventual emancipation of humanity. Lyotard, on the other hand, in a move which mirrors the deconstructive strategies exemplified by Derrida, takes the relatively subordinate, residual term, the 'sublime' in the binary coupling upon which 'modern' (i.e. Enlightenment) aesthetics is based (the Beautiful − (the sublime) where the sublime functions as that-which-is-aesthetic-but-not-beautiful) and privileges it to such an extent that the whole edifice of Enlightenment thought and achievement is (supposedly) threatened. For whereas the idea of the beautiful contains within it the promise of an ideal, as yet unrealised community (to say 'this is beautiful' is to assert the generalisability of aesthetic judgements and hence the possibility/ideal of consensus), the sublime, in contrast, atomises the community by confronting each individual with the prospect of his or her imminent and solitary demise. In Lyotard's words, with the sublime, 'everyone is alone when it comes to judging' (1986b, p. 11).

[. . .]

Gramsci and Articulation

[. . .]

[. . .] what distinguishes the Gramscian approach is the way in which it requires us to negotiate and engage with the multiple axes of both power and the popular, and to acknowledge the ways in which these two axes are 'mutually articulated' through a range of popul*ist* discourses which centre by and large precisely on those pre-Posterous 'modern' categories: the 'nation', 'roots', the 'national past', 'heritage', 'the rights of the individual' (variously) 'to life and liberty', 'to work', 'to own property', 'to expect a better future for his or her children', the right 'to *be* an individual': the 'right to choose'. To engage with the popular as constructed and as lived – to negotiate this bumpy and intractable terrain – we are forced at once to desert the perfection of a purely theoretical analysis, of a 'negative dialectic' (Adorno) in favour of a more 'sensuous (and strategic) logic' (Gramsci) – a logic attuned to the living textures of popular culture, to the ebb and flow of popular debate.

In this shift in the critical focus, the meaning of the phrase 'legitimation crisis' is inflected right away from problems of epistemology directly on to the political, as our attention is drawn to the *processes* whereby particular power blocs seek to impose their moral leadership on the masses and to legitimate their authority through the construction (rather than the realisation) of consensus. The Gramscian model demands that we grasp these processes not because we want to expose them or to understand them in the abstract but because we want to *use* them to *effectively* contest that authority and leadership by offering arguments and alternatives that are not only 'correct' ('right on') but convincing and convincingly presented, arguments that capture the popular imagination, that engage directly with the issues, problems, anxieties, dreams and hopes of real (i.e. actually existing) men and women: arguments, in other words, that take the popular (and hence the populace) seriously *on its own terms*.

At the same time, the Gramscian line is identified, at least in Britain, with a commitment to flexible strategies, to responsive, accountable power structures, with a commitment to decentralisation and local democracy. It is associated with a challenge to the workerism and masculinism of the old Labour Left, a move away from the dogmatism which can still plague the fringe parties, with a sensitivity to local and regional issues, with an alertness, too, to race and gender as well as class as significant axes of power. It is associated with a commitment to 'advance along multiple fronts', with the kinds of radical policy implemented by those progressive enclaves within the local State (e.g. sponsorship for feminist, gay rights, ethnic minority; citizens' rights; health care and support groups; Police Monitoring committees; small, alternative presses; alternative arts programmes; cheap public transport; expanded public information services and issue-oriented 'consciousness raising' (e.g. anti-nuclear power) publicity campaigns; popular festivals, etc.) – policies which so provoked the Thatcher administration that during the last parliamentary session they dismantled the system of local municipal government in the big urban centres run throughout the 1980s by Labour administrations (leaving London as the only major Western European capital without its own elected council).

The commitment on the one hand to local radicalism, to a menu of bold, experimental policies for the inner city and on the other, the critique of Thatcherite 'authoritarian populism' (Hall, 1980a) and the resolve to engage, for instance, on the traditional rightist ground of 'national-popular' discourses, represent perhaps the two dominant and potentially opposed tendencies which derive in part from debates amongst the British Left on the relatively recently translated work of Gramsci (1985). However, while the first tendency clearly resonates with many of the (more positive) themes of the Post ('68) debates, the stress on populism seems to run directly counter to the drift of the Post. For the popular exists solely in and through the problematic 'we' – the denigrated mode of address, the obsolescent shifter. This 'we' is the imaginary community which remains unspeakable within the Post – literally unspeakable in Baudrillard, who presents the myth of the masses as a 'black hole' drawing all meaning to its nonexistent centre (1983a). In Gramsci, of course, the 'we' is neither 'fatal' in the Baudrillardian sense, nor given, pre-existent, 'out here' in the pre-Post-erous sense. Instead it is itself the site of struggle. The 'we' in Gramsci has to be *made* and re-made, actively articulated in the double sense that Stuart Hall refers to in the interview: both 'spoken', 'uttered' and 'linked with', 'combined'. (It has to be at once 'positioned' *and* brought into being.) The term 'articulation' is thus a key bridging concept between two distinct paradigms or problematics. It bridges the 'structuralist' and the 'culturalist' paradigms which Hall (1980b) has identified and since the late 1960s sought to integrate in that it both acknowledges the constitutive role played by (ideological!) discourses in the shaping of (historical) subjectivities and at the same time it insists that there is somewhere outside 'discourse' (a world where groups and classes differentiated by conflicting interests, cultures, goals, aspirations; by the positions they occupy in various hierarchies, are working in and on dynamic (i.e. changing) power structures) – a world which has in turn *to be linked with*, shaped, acted upon, struggled over, intervened in: changed. In other words, the concept of 'articulation' itself articulates the two paradigms by linking together and expressing the double emphasis which characterises Gramscian cultural studies. It performs the same metonymic function, is as homologous to and as exemplary of Stuart Hall's project as *'différance'* is to Derrida's (where the term *différance* simultaneously connotes and itself *enacts* the double process of differing and deferring meaning which Derrida sees as language's essential operation). The reliance on the concept of articulation suggests that the 'social' in Gramsci is neither a 'beautiful' dream nor a dangerous abstraction, neither a contract made and re-made on the ground, as it were, by the members of a 'communicative community' in multiple face-to-face interactions which are 'context-dependent' (Habermas) nor an empirically nonexistent 'Idea in Reason' which bears no relation whatsoever to experience (Lyotard). It is instead a continually shifting, mediated relation between groups and classes, a structured field and a set of lived relations in which complex ideological formations composed of elements derived from diversive sources have to be actively combined, dismantled, bricolaged so that new politically effective alliances can be secured between different fractional groupings which can themselves no longer be returned to static, homogeneous classes. In other words, we can't collapse the social into speech act theory or subsume its contradictory dynamics underneath the impossible quest for universal validity claims. At the same time, rather than dispensing with the 'claim for simplicity' by equating it with barbarism, we might do better to begin by distinguishing a claim from a demand, and by acknowledging that a *demand* for simplicity exists, that such a demand has to be negotiated, that it is neither essentially noble nor barbaric, that it is, however, *complexly articulated* with different ideological fragments and social forces in the form of a range of competing populisms.

It would be foolish to present a polar opposition between the Gramscian line(s) and the (heterogeneous) Posts. There is too much shared historical and intellectual ground for such a partition to serve any valid purpose. It was, after all, the generation of Marxist intellectuals who lived through '68 and who took the events in Paris and the West Coast seriously who turned in the 1970s to Gramsci. In addition, there are clear cross-Channel links between the two sets of concerns and emphases, for instance, in the work of Michel Pêcheux (1982) on 'interdiscourse'. The retention of the old Marxist terms should not be allowed to obscure the extent to which many of these terms have been transformed – wrenched away from the 'scientific' mooring constructed in the Althusserian phase. What looks at first glance a lot like the old 'rationalist' dualism ('Left' v. 'Right', etc.); the old 'modernising' teleology ('progressive', 'reactionary', 'emergent', 'residual', etc.); a typically 'modernist' penchant for military metaphors ('dominant' and 'subaltern classes', etc.); an unreconstructed, 'modernist' epistemology ('ideology', for instance, rather than 'discourse') looks different closer to. From the perspectives heavily influenced by the Gramscian approach, nothing is anchored to the '*grands récits*', to master narratives, to stable (positive) identities, to fixed and certain meanings: all social and semantic relations are contestable and hence mutable: everything appears to be in flux: there are no predictable outcomes. Though classes still exist, there is no guaranteed dynamic to class struggle and no 'class belonging': there are no solid homes to return to, no places reserved in advance for the righteous. No one 'owns' an 'ideology' because ideologies are themselves in process: in a state of constant formation and re-formation. In the same way, the concept of hegemony remains distinct from the Frankfurt model of a 'total closure of discourse' (Marcuse) and from the ascription of total class domination which is implied in the Althusserian model of a contradictory social formation held in check eternally (at least until 'the last (ruptural) instance') by the work of the RSAs and the ISAs. Instead hegemony is a precarious, 'moving equilibrium' (Gramsci) achieved through the orchestration of conflicting and competing forces by more or less unstable, more or less temporary alliances of class fractions.

Within this model, there is no 'science' to be opposed to the monolith of ideology, only prescience: an alertness to possibility and emergence – that and the always imperfect, risky, undecidable 'science' of strategy. There are only competing ideolog*ies*, themselves unstable constellations liable to collapse at any moment into their component parts. These parts in turn can be recombined with other elements from other ideological formations to form fragile unities which in turn act to interpellate and bond together new imaginary communities, to forge fresh alliances between disparate social groups (see, for instance, Hall (1980a, 1985) and others (Jessop *et al.*, 1984), on 'national-popular' discourses).

But it would be equally foolish to deny that there are crucial differences between the two sets of orientations. A Marxism of whatever kind could never move back from or go beyond 'modernity' in the very general terms in which it is defined within the Post, which is not to say that Marxism is necessarily bound to a 'dynamic' and destructive model of technological 'advance' (see Bahro (1984) on the possibility of eco-Marxism: a union of 'greens' and 'reds'). However, it should be said that the kind of Marxism Stuart Hall proposes bears little or no relation to the caricatured, teleological *religion* of Marxism which – legitimately in my view – is pilloried by the Post. A Marxism without guarantees is a Marxism which has suffered a sea change. It is a Marxism which has 'gone under' in a succession of tempests that include the smoke and fire of 1968 and the shrinkage of imaginative horizons in the monetarist 'new realism' of the 1980s, and yet it is a Marxism that has survived, returning perhaps a little lighter on its feet (staggering at first), a Marxism more prone perhaps to listen, learn, adapt and to appreciate, for instance, that words like 'emergency' and 'struggle' don't just mean fight, conflict, war and death but birthing, the prospect of new life emerging: a struggling to the light.....

References

Anderson, P. (1984) 'Modernity and revolution', *New Left Review*, no. 144, pp. 96–113.

Appignanesi, L. and Bennington, G. (eds) (1986) *Postmodernism: ICA Documents 4*, London: Institute of Contemporary Arts.

Bahro, R. (1984) *From Red to Green*, London: New Left Books.

Barthes, R. (1977) *Image, Music, Text* (trans. S. Heath), New York: Hill & Wang.

Baudrillard, J. (1983a) *In the Shadow of the Silent Majorities*, New York: Semiotext(e).

Baudrillard, J. (1983b) *Simulations*, New York: Semiotext(e).

Baudrillard, J. (1983c) 'Ecstasy of communication', in H. Foster (ed.), *The Anti-Aesthetic*, pp. 126–34.

Berman, M. (1984) 'Signs in the street', *New Left Review*, no. 114.

Berman, M. (1982) *All That is Solid Melts into Air*, New York: Simon & Schuster.

De Man, P. (1983) *Blindness and Insight*, Minneapolis: University of Minnesota Press.

Derrida, J. (1980) *Writing and Differance* (trans. A. Bass), Chicago: University of Chicago Press.

Foster, H. (ed.) (1983) *The Anti-Aesthetic*, Port Townsend, WA: Bay Press.

Foucault, M. (1977) *Language, Counter-memory, Practice*, D. F. Bouchard (ed.), Ithaca, NY: Cornell University Press.

Gramsci, A. (1985) *Selections from Cultural Writings*, D. Forgacs and G. Nowell-Smith (eds) Cambridge, MA: Harvard University Press.

Hall, S. (1980a) 'Popular-democratic vs. authoritarian populism', in A. Hunt (ed.), *Marxism and Democracy*, London: Lawrence & Wishart, pp. 157–85.

Hall, S. (1980b) 'Cultural studies: two paradigms', *Media, Culture, and Society*, no. 2, pp. 57–72.

Hall, S. (1985) 'Authoritarian populism: a response to Jessop *et al.*', *New Left Review*, no. 151, pp. 115–124.

Jameson, F. (1984) 'Postmodernism, or the cultural logic of late capitalism', *New Left Review*, no. 146.

Jameson, F. (1983) 'Postmodernism and consumer society', in H. Foster (ed.), *The Anti-Aesthetic*, pp. 111–125.

Jessop, B. *et al.* (1984) 'Authoritarian populism, two nations, and Thatcherism', *New Left Review*, no. 147, pp. 32–60.

Lyotard, J.-F. (1986a) 'Defining the postmodern', in Appignanesi and Bennington (eds), *ICA Documents 4*, pp. 6–7.

Lyotard, J.-F. (1986b) 'Complexity and the sublime', in Appignanesi and Bennington (eds), *ICA Documents 4*, pp. 10–12.

Lyotard, J.-F. (1986c) 'Reflections on popular culture', in Appignanesi and Bennington (eds), *ICA Documents 4*, p. 58.

Lyotard, J.-F. (1984) *The Postmodern Condition: A report on knowledge* (trans. G. Bennington and B. Massumi), Minneapolis: University of Minnesota Press.

Merquior, J. G. (1986) 'Spider and bee: toward a critique of postmodern ideology', in Appignanesi and Bennington (eds), *ICA Documents 4*, pp. 16–18.

Newman, M. (1986) 'Revising modernism, representing postmodernism: critical discourse of the visual arts', in Appignanesi and Bennington (eds), *ICA Documents 4*, pp. 32–51.

37 □ Black
Postmodernist Practices

Cornel West

(interviewed by
Anders Stephanson)

[...]

Anders Stephanson: Features of what we associate with the concept of postmodernism have been part of American life for a long time: fragmentation, heterogeneity, surfaces without history. Is postmodernism in some sense really the codification of life in Los Angeles?

Cornel West: Only in one form and specifically at the level of middlebrow culture. The other side is the potentially oppositional aspect of the notion. Postmodernism ought never to be viewed as a homogeneous phenomenon, but rather as one in which political contestation is central. Even if we look at it principally as a form of Americanization of the world, it is clear that within the US there are various forms of ideological and political conflict going on.

AS: The black community, for example, is more 'contestational' than average America.

CW: The black political constituency still has some sense of the reality of the world, some sense of what is going on in the Third World. Look at the issues Jesse Jackson pressed in 1984 and now in 1988, and you find that they were issues normally reserved for the salons of leftist intellectuals. Bringing that on television had a great impact.

AS: Yet the black American condition, so to speak, is not an uplifting sight at the moment.

CW: Not at all. There is increasing class division and differentiation, creating on

From Ross, A. (ed), *Universal Abandon: The politics of postmodernism*, Minneapolis, University of Minnesota Press, 1988, pp. 276–81.

the one hand a significant black middle class, highly anxiety-ridden, insecure, willing to be co-opted and incorporated into the powers that be, concerned with racism to the degree that it poses constraints on upward social mobility; and, on the other, a vast and growing black underclass, an underclass that embodies a kind of *walking nihilism* of pervasive drug addiction, pervasive alcoholism, pervasive homocide, and an exponential rise in suicide. Now, because of the deindustrialization, we also have a devastated black industrial working class. We are talking here about tremendous hopelessness.

AS: Suicide has increased enormously?

CW: It has increased six times in the last decades for black males like myself who are between eighteen and thirty-five. This is unprecedented. Afro-Americans have always killed themselves less than other Americans, but this is no longer true.

AS: What does a black oppositional intellectual do in these generally dire circumstances?

CW: One falls back on those black institutions that have attempted to serve as resources for sustenance and survival, the black churches being one such institution, especially their progressive and prophetic wing. One tries to root oneself organically in these institutions so that one can speak to a black consistency, while maintaining a conversation with the most engaging political and postmodernist debates on the outside so that the insights they provide can be brought in.

AS: That explains why you are, among other things, a kind of lay preacher. It does not explain why you are a Christian.

CW: My own left Christianity is not simply instrumentalist. It is in part a response to those dimensions of life that have been flattened out, to the surfacelike character of a postmodern culture that refuses to speak to issues of despair, that refuses to speak to issues of the absurd. To that extent I still find Christian narratives and stories *empowering and enabling*.

AS: What does it mean to a black American to hear that, in Baudrillard's language, we are in a simulated space of hyperreality, that we have lost the real?

CW: I read that symptomatically. Baudrillard seems to be articulating a sense of what it is to be a French, middle-class intellectual, or perhaps what it is to be middle-class generally. Let me put it in terms of a formulation from Henry James that Fredric Jameson has appropriated: there is a reality *that one cannot not know*. The ragged edges of the Real, of *Necessity*, not being able to eat, not having shelter, not having health care, all this is something that one cannot not know. The black condition acknowledges that. It is so much more acutely felt because this is a society where a lot of people live a Teflon existence, where a lot of people have no sense of the ragged edges of necessity, of what it means to be impinged upon by structures of oppression. To be an upper-middle-class American is actually to live a life of unimaginable comfort, convenience, and luxury. Half of the black population is denied this, which is why they have a strong sense of reality.

AS: Does that make notions of postmodernism meaningless from a black perspective?

CW: It must be conceived very differently at least. Take Ishmael Reed, an exemplary postmodern writer. Despite his conservative politics, he cannot deny the black acknowledgement of the reality one cannot not know. In writing about black American history, for instance, he has to come to terms with the state-sponsored terrorism of lynching blacks and so on. This is inescapable in black postmodernist practices.

AS: How is one in fact to understand black postmodernist practices?

CW: To talk about black postmodernist practices is to go back to bebop music and see how it relates to literary expressions like Reed's and Charles Wright's. It is to go back, in other words, to the genius of Charlie Parker, John Coltrane, and Miles Davis. Bebop was, after all, a revolt against the middle-class 'jazz of the museum', against swing and white musicians like Benny Goodman, who had become hegemonic by colonizing a black art form. What Parker did, of course, was to Africanize jazz radically: to accent the polyrhythms, to combine these rhythms with unprecedented virtuosity on the sax. He said explicitly that his music was not produced to be accepted by white Americans. He would be suspicious if it were. This sense of revolt was to be part and parcel of the postmodern rebellion against the modernism of the museum.

AS: To me, bebop seems like a black cultural avant-garde that corresponds historically to abstract expressionism in painting – the last gasp of modernism – on which indeed it had come considerable influence.

CW: Certainly they emerge together, and people do tend to parallel them as though they were the same; but abstract expressionism was not a revolt in the way bebop was. In fact, it was an instance of modernism itself. Bebop also had much to do with fragmentation, with heterogeneity, with the articulation of difference and marginality, aspects of what we associate with postmodernism today.

AS: Aspects of the cultural dominant, yes; but these elements are also part of modernism. Surely one can still talk about Charlie Parker as a unified subject expressing inner *angst* or whatever, an archetypal characteristic of modernism.

CW: True, but think too of another basic feature of postmodernism, the breakdown of highbrow and pop culture. Parker would use whistling off the streets of common black life: 'Cherokee', for instance, was actually a song that black children used to sing when jumping rope or, as I did, playing marbles. Parker took that melody of the black masses and filtered it through his polyrhythms and technical virtuosity, turning it into a highbrow jazz feature that was not quite highbrow anymore. He was already calling into question the distinction between high and low culture, pulling from a bricolage, as it were, what was seemingly popular and relating it to what was then high. Yet I would not deny the modernist impulse, nor would I deny that they were resisting jazz as commodity very much like Joyce and Kafka resisted literary production as commodity. In that sense bebop straddles the fence.

AS: The ultimate problem, however, is whether it is actually useful to talk about someone like Charlie Parker in these terms.

CW: It is useful to the degree that it contests the prevailing image of him as a modernist. As you imply, on the other hand, there is a much deeper as to question [*sic*] whether these terms *modernism/postmodernism* relate to Afro-American cultural practices in any illuminating way at all. We are only at the beginning of that inquiry.

AS: Was there ever actually a mass black audience for bebop?

CW: Yes, Parker's was the sort of music black people danced to in the 1940s. Miles's 'cool' stage was also big in the 1950s with albums like *Kinda Blue*, though it went hand in hand with the popularity of Nat King Cole and Dinah Washington.

AS: What happened to this avant-garde black music when Motown and Aretha Franklin came along?

CW: It was made a fetish for the educated middle class, principally, but not solely, the white middle class. In absolute terms, its domain actually expanded because the black audience of middle-class origin also expanded. But the great dilemma of black musicians who try to preserve a tradition from mainstream domestication and dilution is in fact that they lose contact with the black masses. In this case, there was eventually a move toward 'fusion', jazz artists attempting to produce objects intended for broader black-and-white consumption.

AS: Miles Davis is the central figure of that avant-garde story.

CW: And he crossed over with the seminal record *Bitches Brew* in 1970, accenting his jazz origins while borrowing from James Brown's polyrhythms and Sly Stone's syncopation. *Bitches Brew* brought him a black mass audience that he had lost in the 1960s – certainly one that Coltrane had lost completely.

AS: Crossover artists, in the sense of having a racially mixed mass audience, are not very numerous today.

CW: No, but there are more than ever: Whitney Houston, Dionne Warwick, Lionel Richie, Diana Ross, and Anita Baker. Baker is a very different crossover artist because she is still deeply rooted in the black context. Michael Jackson and Prince are crossover in another sense: their music is less rooted in black musical traditions and much more open to white rock and so forth.

AS: In Prince's case it has to do with the fact that he is not entirely from a black background.

CW: Still, he grew up in a black foster home and a black Seventh Day Adventist church, but in Minneapolis, which is very different from growing up like Michael Jackson in a black part of Gary, Indiana. Minneapolis has always been a place of cultural cross-fertilization, of interracial marriages and relationships. The early Jackson Five, on the other hand, were thoroughly ensconced in a black tradition, and Michael began his career dancing like James Brown. Now, he is at the center of the black–white interface.

AS: Prince never really played 'black' music as one thinks of it. His music is 'fused' from the start.

CW: To be in a black context in Minneapolis is already to be in a situation of fusion, because the blacks themselves have much broader access to mainstream white culture in general. You get the same thing with other black stars who have come out of that place.

AS: Michael Jackson, by contrast, is now a packaged middle-American product.

CW: A nonoppositional instance of commodification in black skin that is becoming more and more like candy, more radical than McDonald's, but not by much. It is watered-down black music, but still with a lot of the aggressiveness and power of that tradition.

AS: Music is *the* black means of cultural expression, is it not?

CW: Music and preaching. Here, rap is unique because it combines the black preacher and the black music tradition, replacing the liturgical-ecclesiastical setting with the African polyrhythms of the street. A tremendous *articulateness* is syncopated with the African drumbeat, the African funk, into an American postmodernist product: there is no subject expressing originary anguish here but a fragmented subject, pulling from past and present, innovatively producing a heterogeneous product. The stylistic combination of the oral, the literate, and the musical is exemplary as well. Otherwise, it is part and parcel of the subversive energies of black underclass youth, energies that are forced to take a cultural mode of articulation because of the political lethargy of American society. The music of Grandmaster Flash and the Furious Five, Kurtis Blow, and Sugar Hill Gang has to take on a deeply political character because, again, they are in the reality that the black underclass *cannot not know*: the brutal side of American capital, the brutal side of American racism, the brutal side of sexism against black women.

AS: I always thought rap was too indigenous a black form of expression to make it in the general marketplace. Run/DMC has proven me wrong on this.

CW: Indeed. Run/DMC is as indigenous as you can get. Upper-middle-class white students at Yale consume a lot of Run/DMC.

AS: Yet the constitutive elements of rap seemed to me too fixed for it to become a permanent presence on the crossover scene: more anonymous and less easily assimilated into existing white concepts of melody and structure. This, too, is probably wrong.

CW: People said the same thing about Motown in 1961, the same thing about Aretha Franklin, who is about as organic as you can get. She is not as accepted by mainstream white society as the smoother and more diluted Warwick and Ross, but she *is* accepted. That, from the perspective of 1964–65, is unbelievable. The same thing could happen with rap music, since the boundaries are actually rather fluid. But it won't remain the same.

AS: Where will rap end up?

CW: Where most American postmodern products end up: highly packaged, regulated, distributed, circulated, and consumed.

38 □ *Fashion and Postmodernism*

Elizabeth Wilson

[...]

I turn now to look at what light fashion and postmodernism shed on each other. Today, there is a blurring between mainstream and countercultural fashions: all fashion has become 'stagey', self-conscious about its own status as a discourse, about its irrationality, about its message. The work of Jean Paul Gaultier, a Parisian designer who draws inspiration from punk and street clothes, is relevant here, for when the 'subversive' questionings of punk appear on the Paris catwalk itself, who is to say what is for real and what is parody? Gaultier's own pronouncements on his work add to this uncertainty, since he appears to mount an attack on what we think of as fashion: 'People who make mistakes or dress badly are the real stylists. My "You feel as though you've eaten too much" collection [clothes deliberately designed to look "too tight"] is taken from exactly those moments when you are mistaken or embarrassed',[1] while Carl Lagerfeld at Chanel has produced outfits that parody the original styles, and 'pudding' hats that parody the surrealist motifs of the 1930s. This cuts the ground from under our feet and recentres our perception of fashion. This is one aspect of the compulsory confusion of contemporary modes. Its eclecticism and oscillation is part of its 'postmodern-ness'. Its irony and cynical self-parody also seem very postmodern, its knowingness about its own performance. Thus the 'confusion' that so puzzled fashion writers in the 1970s, the apparent ending of the orderly evolution of one style out of another, is explicable once it is seen as part of postmodernism.

On the other hand, if we examine, from the point of view of fashion, some of the critiques of postmodernism, we may begin to have reservations about the arguments that are deployed. Fredric Jameson, for example, in his brilliant article 'Postmodernism, or the cultural logic of late capitalism', attempts to relate postmodernism to the economic and ideological developments of late capitalism, and treats postmodernism as a general contemporary sensibility. It is rather

From Boyne, R. and Rattansi, A. (eds), *Postmodernism and society*, Macmillan, London, 1990, pp. 222–36.

surprising, therefore, that he does not include fashion explicitly in his denunciation, which could certainly be applied very directly to it:

> modernist styles ... become postmodernist codes: and that the stupendous pro-
> liferation of social codes today into professional and disciplinary jargons, but also into
> the badges of affirmation of ethnic, gender, race, religious and class-fraction adhesion,
> is also a political phenomenon, the problem of micropolitics sufficiently demonstrates.
> If the ideas of a ruling class were once the dominant (or hegemonic) ideology of
> bourgeois society, the advanced capitalist countries today are now a field of stylistic and
> discursive heterogeneity without a norm.[2]

For as we saw, it has become a cliché of fashion journalism that the tyranny of fashion crumbled in the 1970s. No longer did Paris dictate a line every season, compelling women to lower and raise their hemlines and transform their silhouettes in obedience to some *haute couture* guru. From Jameson's perspective, this pluralism – or anarchy – would surely represent simply another instance of the *compulsory* confusion of styles, which, for him, exemplifies the postmodern, a sensibility in which all sense of development and history are lost, so that the jumble of stylistic mannerisms becomes as 'schizophrenic' as the consumer culture that spawns them. The era of *haute couture* dominance would then appear, retrospectively, as 'modernist': the great designers saw themselves as unique artists, and the evolution of fashion has its own internal aesthetic dynamic. This has now been lost – so the argument might go – and the promiscuity of contemporary modes is just part of the fragmentation and depersonalisation of postmodern times. In so far as fashion has relied heavily on 'retro chic' in recent years, this too fits into Jameson's description of the postmodern, since pastiche – 'parody without laughter', 'statue with blind eyeballs' – is, for him, a significant aspect of postmodern culture, or even its typical moment.

But although fashion fits so well into Jameson's postmodern dystopia, we are forced, when we investigate the use of pastiche and retro in fashion, to question whether Jameson is correct in placing 'nostalgia mode' and pastiche as so central not simply to contemporary art, film and architecture, but to a generalised postmodern panorama. Is retro so exclusively *de nos jours*? Fashion, in fact, has relied on pastiche and the recycling of styles throughout the industrial period. Christian Dior[3] believed that until designers such as Madame Vionnet introduced revolutionary techniques of cutting into fashion design in the early twentieth century, the shapes of garments changed only very slowly, and that the impression of change was created by the use of superficial decoration, stylistic motifs often rifled from the past. The Victorians incorporated all sorts of historical styles – the classical Greek and the medieval, for example – into their fashions. The Pre-Raphaelites, also in love with the medieval, harnessed the fashions of that remote period to their particular version of dress reform, but dress designers, too, looked to the past for inspiration. And in the Edwardian period Liberty catalogues advertised evening gowns in a variety of 'historical' styles: Egyptian, medieval, Elizabethan, Madame de Pompadour.

Even in the 1950s, which have now been invested with a seamlessly perfect style and ambience, the then reality was more complex. Fashion in the 1950s flirted more than once with – of all periods – the 1920s: Dior's sack dress of 1958, and Sandy Wilson's 1955 musical *The Boyfriend*, are two examples of how the 1950s interest in the modern and forward-looking turned quite naturally to the 1920s for images of emancipation and leisure. The enormous popularity of Nancy Mitford's novels about the 1920s, *The Pursuit of Love* and *Love in a Cold Climate*, is another example of 1950s nostalgia. (In the late 1960s, *The Boyfriend* was made into a film that was very much of *that* period, and which starred Twiggy, the most famous fashion model of the 1960s.) Again, the 1954 Diaghilev exhibition took London by storm; and it was in 1956 that Liberty relaunched their original Morris designs for fashion and furnishing fabrics – all these events anticipating recycled motifs we now think of as more characteristic of the 1970s. 'Our' fifties is already not 'the' fifties. Jameson finds a specific quality in contemporary re-creations of the past:

> [Nostalgia mode] was never a matter of some old-fashioned 'representation' of historical content, but approached the 'past' through stylistic connotation, conveying 'pastness' by the glossy qualities of the image, and '1930s-ness' or '1950s-ness' by the attributes of fashion (therein following the Barthes of *Mythologies*, who saw connotation as the purveying of imaginary and stereotypical idealities. 'Sinité', for example, as some Disney–EPCOT 'concept' of China).[4]

Jameson does not, however, make clear just what is the difference between an 'old-fashioned "representation" of historical content' and 'stylistic connotation'. We might enquire when one ceases to be and the other comes into existence. Are the operas of Verdi, for example, straightforward 'representations of historical content'? Walter Scott's novels would be another possible example. Indeed, Walter Scott appears to have invented a whole mythology of 'Scottishness' for the Royal Family, for whose benefit, on a visit to Scotland, tartans were reintroduced. The Lairds had forgotten the colours of their clan tartans, which had to be rediscovered, or indeed invented for the occasion. To take a more recent example, is the superficial pastiche of contemporary architecture *the same thing* as the loving re-creation of the early 1960s in *American Graffiti*, or the careful (if self-indulgent) evocations of the British Raj in *The Jewel in the Crown* and *Passage to India*?

Jameson uses the example of contemporary film to develop his argument against pastiche and retro style, arguing that recent 'nostalgia films' attempt the re-creation of that 'lost object of desire', the fifties (a kind of kitsch utopia). Yet he also questions whether the 'cannibalising historicism' of postmodern architecture *is* nostalgic, for it is, he argues, too affectless, too flat.

In fact, the re-creation of a sentimentalised past evoked through stereotype has been a pervasive feature of cinema for years. What of a whole string of French films from the 1940s: *Les Enfants du Paradis*, *Madame de*, *The Golden Marie* and many others; while Anne Hollander,[5] in her discussion of Hollywood costume films of the 1920s and 1930s, argues that despite an at times obsessive preoccupation with accuracy of period detail, the results were distinctively 'twenties' or 'thirties'. She tells us that although Oliver Messel, a specialist in sixteenth-century costume, was invited to California to advise on the designs for *Romeo and Juliet*, the star, Norma Shearer, preferred those of Adrian, the resident MGM designer. 'Flavour' and 'suggestion' were more important than historical accuracy, film and stage costume being primarily a series of signals whereby 'powdered hair' equals the eighteenth century, 'a puff' the Elizabethan period, and a 'Juliet cap' Renaissance Italy (even though this cap was invented for Theda Bara in 1916 and did not even exist in the *Quattrocento*). This evidence from the past that pastiche and nostalgia have been pervasive in popular culture throughout the twentieth century and indeed earlier appears to contradict Jameson's belief that 'nostalgia mode' is peculiarly a feature of his postmodern epoch.

Hal Foster argues that in the nineteenth-century use of styles from the past there was at least some sense of protest:

> What ... does this 'return' imply if not a flight from the present? Clearly, this was the thrust of eclectic historicism in nineteenth century art and architecture (especially British): a flight from the modern – in its romantic form, from the industrial present into a preindustrial past; in its neoclassical (academic) form from lived class conflict to the ideal realm of myth. But then this flight expressed a social protest, however dreamy; now it seems symptomatic of sheer *post histoire* escapism.[6]

But I would find it difficult to argue that there is any sense of 'social protest, however dreamy' in the majority of historical Hollywood confections of the 1930s.

During the years between the death of the tight-laced corset and the short skirts and boyish modes of the 1920s, the influence of the designer Paul Poiret was at its height. Then, as now, exotic motifs were 'in', and shapeless clothes, which often seemed exaggerated and eclectic, sent forth no clear message. Marcel Proust, walking in the Bois de Boulogne, longed for the elegant women of his youth, and could see no meaning in the fashions of 1912. Where once there had been the splendour of horse-drawn carriages, was now nothing 'but motor cars driven each by a moustached mechanic'. And:

> I wished to hold before my bodily eyes ... little women's hats so low crowned as to seem no more than garlands. All the hats now were immense, covered with all manner of fruits and flowers and birds. In place of the beautiful dresses in which Madame Swann walked like a queen, Graeco-Saxon tunics, pleated à la Tanagra, or sometimes in the Directoire style, accentuated Liberty chiffons sprinkled with flowers like wallpaper. ... And seeing all these new components of the spectacle, I had no longer a belief to infuse into them to give them consistency, unity and life; they passed before me in a desultory, haphazard, meaningless fashion, containing in themselves no beauty which my eye might have tried, in the old days, to recreate. They were just women,

in whose elegance I had no faith, and whose clothes seemed to me unimportant. But when a belief vanishes, there survives it – more and more vigorously so as to cloak the absence of the power, now lost to us, of imparting reality to new things – a fetishistic attachment to the old things which it did once animate, as if it was in them and not in ourselves that the divine spark resided, and as if our present incredulity had a contingent cause – the death of the gods.[7]

So a sense of the loss of meaning is already present in the high modernist *A la recherche du temps perdu*, and, set against Proust's insightful comments on the subjective quality of our aesthetic judgments, Jameson's lament for the loss of norms is revealed as a romantic longing for some past that is never made explicit. Is it modernism? Is it realism? Is it the orderliness of bourgeois society or the unrealised collective purpose of a socialism infused with functional aesthetic values? We do not know.

In the 1970s, Kennedy Fraser, then fashion correspondent to the *New York Times*, saw retro chic as merely another twist in the fashion cycle. In her awareness of the 'irony' of retro dressing she touches on Jameson's themes:

Clothes came to be worn and seen as an assemblage of thought – our paradoxes, as irony, whimsy, or deliberate disguise. Thrift shop dressing carried it all to its ultimate. We took to clothes for which we had spent little money, which didn't necessarily fit us, and which had belonged in the past to some dead stranger's life. Behind the bravado of what came to be known as 'style', there may have lurked a fear of being part of our time, of being locked into our own personalities, and of revealing too much about our own lives.

Above all, what ultimately characterised the fashion of the past decade was detachment.[8]

But Kaja Silverman takes issue with this view. For her, retro is a countercultural mode, a 'sartorial strategy which works to denaturalise its wearer's specular identity, and one which is fundamentally irreconcilable with fashion'. Far from destroying the past, 'it inserts its wearer into a complex network of cultural and historical references'.[9] She agrees with Kennedy Fraser that there is a 'masquerade' quality about it, but for her this has radical potential. Roland Barthes argued that fashion journalism strove to 'naturalise the arbitrary': each successive fashion was, for him, actually meaningless, the 'fashion system' alone giving it (spurious) meaning; whereas, for Kaja Silverman, countercultural dressing, at least, draws attention to its own work of representation, and it could be argued that it is therefore 'modernist' rather than 'postmodernist'.

Jameson castigates the nostalgia of postmodernism while Hal Foster notes the absence of utopian vision in postmodern art. Yet Western dress reveals how close together utopianism and nostalgia lie. Utopianism has always been nostalgic and in a curious way backward looking – a search for the lost happiness of a romanticised infancy in which contradiction and conflict did not exist. This utopian nostalgia is expressive of the wish to recall the lost – narcissistic – object of desire, the idealised image of Lacan's mirror stage,[10] in which the unstable infant body is magically 'fixed' in a never-to-be-realised perfection. The self you see in the mirror is a self made permanent, divested of its fragmentary, fleeting, changing quality.

The dress reform project was utopian in a different sense: the transcendence of the 'ugliness' and above all the *change* that is central to fashionable styles.[11] Literary utopias, such as the first, Thomas More's *Utopia*,[12] and that of William Morris in *News From Nowhere*,[13] have often been fashion-free – Thomas More's was written specifically as a critique of Tudor courtly consumerism in the period of early mercantile capitalism. Yet, paradoxically, fashion itself is also utopian in its attempt to fix the fleeting moment as final, always to present its every new manifestation as the final solution to the problem of what to wear.[14] Fashion tries to hold back, or rather to deny, change, decay and death. In this sense, fashion is consolatory, as Foucault argues that utopias also are.[15] (Julia Emberley[16] suggests that in contemporary fashion this utopian consolation is produced in a 'heterotopic' or 'heterogeneous' way – another way of accounting for or, rather, alluding to its eclecticism.)

Dress is like a 'mirror phase'. Denounced as narcissistic in the lay sense of self-regard, it places a line around the shifting, vulnerable and indeterminate contours of the body, acts as armour, as carapace. Dress, in this sense, is less Kennedy Fraser's 'masquerade', which puts an 'ironic distance' between the self and the costume/uniform/camouflage which it sports as mask or disguise, than the form in which the body actually manifests itself. The language in which we habitually speak of dress alludes to this notion of manifestation: we take a pride in our 'appearance'; we are seen by others as 'visions' of loveliness'; we look like 'a dream'. As Kaja Silverman puts it so well:

> Clothing and other kinds of ornamentation make the human body culturally visible . . . clothing draws the body so that it can be culturally seen, and articulates it in a meaningful form. . . . Clothing is a necessary condition of subjectivity . . . in articulating the body it simultaneously articulates the psyche.[17]

It is a 'vestimentary envelope' that holds body and ego together. Our finished 'appearance', therefore, is the end result (yet itself alterable and altering) of an often elaborate construction, both bodily and mental, of identity itself. The very concept of 'appearance' (after all, ghosts and visions 'appear' to the blessed and the cursed) suggests the ghostly aspect of apparel without a wearer, its 'uncanniness', and the ambiguity of the relationship between 'ourselves' and our clothes. Many attempts to theorise fashion have foundered on this ambiguity between 'appearance' and an assumed 'reality' behind it, dress reform being one of the most radical attempts to justify this separation of the two.

Within postmodernism, discourse theory seems to offer the possibility of an interpretation of fashion within the proliferation of discursive and social practices that centre on the human body. Here, the work of Michel Foucault, especially *Discipline and Punish*[18] and *The History of Sexuality*,[19] is important. For Foucault, modernity inaugurates a multitude of practices which act upon the body – to discipline it, to make it more apt, in a 'positive' sense to alter and adapt it to the modern world. This discursive universe does not repress but, on the contrary, actively produces the body: drilling, eurythmics, aerobics – and of course fashion and beauty culture – may all be seen as part of this disciplinary mode, and, like dieting, exercise and dance, they have become integral to twentieth-century life. For Foucault, the very inescapability of this discursive and regimentary universe appears as one aspect of the 'carceral' nature of modern society.

Fredric Jameson objects to this proliferation of practices for the opposite reason to Foucault. For Jameson, the hysteric overflow of possibilities, the hypertrophy of styles, destroys meaning.

What these and many writers on postmodernism do is themselves create an imprisoning universe. Although some writers, Angela McRobbie[20] and Andreas Huyssen,[21] for example, emphasise the optimistic possibilities of the postmodern, it is the dystopic vision of the postmodern world that usually wins out:

> In a postmodern culture typified by the disappearance of the Real and by the suffocation of natural contexts, fashion provides *aesthetic holograms* as moveable texts for the general economy of excess. . . . An entire postmodern scene . . . brought under the double sign of culture where, as Baudrillard has hinted, the secret of fashion is to introduce the *appearance* of radical novelty, while maintaining the *reality* of no substantial change. Or is it the opposite? Not fashion as a referent of the third (simulational) order of the real, but as itself the spectacular sign of a parasitical culture which, always anyway excessive, disaccumulative, and sacrificial, is drawn inexorably towards the ecstasy of catastrophe.[22]

This overblown passage is rather typical of writing about the postmodern, which, whatever the overt ethical or political position of the writer, often seems to exude a fascinated horror or gleeful immersion in the most decadent and even in the grimmest aspects of the 'postmodern' world. A feature, indeed, of the explosion of writing on postmodernism is its peculiarly hyperbolic tone. At one moment, postmodernism is seen as a totalising *Zeitgeist* in which we inhabit a seamless dystopia, Foucault's carceral society spread across the globe; at another, the disintegration of the postmodern is what is emphasised, and welcomed as offering cracks and fissures in a terroristic totality – and thereby the means of escape (although into what is not clear). And yet, behind this embrace of the new and what sometimes seems like an aesthetic idealisation of the ugly, lie some very old moral assumptions about hedonism, consumption and worldly enjoyment: that they are unworthy. Both those who denounce and those who claim to welcome the postmodern implicitly portray a world of selfishness, greed and narcissism, whether they rejoice in or denounce the consumerism at the heart of it all. If some writers reject Marx for his refusal of the utopian vision, they themselves seem to wallow in a *dystopia* of negation, while relying on a never explicitly stated set of conservative and often utilitarian assumptions. They inhabit a new zone of romanticism, in which there is a curious simultaneous denunciation and idealisation of pollution, consumerism, novelty, media bombardment, an aestheticisation of the excesses of the post-industrial landscape, 'B Movie' cities and junk in all its forms.

I have tried to show that, if we look at fashion, we find that some of the themes and hallmarks of what is today termed postmodernism have been around for a long, long time, so that it is doubtful whether a postmodern *Zeitgeist* or ethos does exist in the way in which writers such as Jameson and Baudrillard would have us believe. Their generalisations begin to seem to have more to do with the creation of a cultural myth about 'our times' which flattens out the contradictory, refractory reality nature of contemporary existence and seeks to create a stereotype of the present in the present. It has been a feature of postwar culture to create stereotypes of past decades – 'the twenties', 'the thirties', 'the fifties', 'the sixties' – but now this is extended into the fabric of the very moment in which the critic is living and writing. Perhaps this in itself simply demonstrates how 'postmodern' the present has become, involved even as it unfolds in a simulacrum of itself, in a collapse of 'reality' into 'image'.

Yet to examine the discourse of the cultural critics themselves is to become aware of their conservatism, not in any directly political sense, necessarily (although there is that too), but rather in the sense in which they remain anchored in the *project* of defining a *Zeitgeist* – a surely unpostmodern concept. Furthermore, there is the tendency to accept what amounts to a reflexionist notion of ideology – another Marxist sin. Both John Urry and Scott Lash, for example, in their detailed work on 'disorganised capitalism', assume that there is a general cultural parallel to economic transformations: that postmodernism is, as it were, the ideology of 'disorganised capitalism'; and they even assume a collective psyche typical of a given period. Fredric Jameson, perhaps metaphorically, speaks of schizophrenia, but Lash and Urry cite the supposed empirical decline of neuroses, typically conversion hysteria, which are said to have been replaced by personality disorders. They refer also to the work of Heinz Kohut on narcissism and to the sweeping generalisations of Christopher Lasch on the same subject, and to Bryan Turner's assertion of 'a shift in dominant psychopathologies from hysteria to narcissism and anorexia'.[23] But not only are the shifts determined in part by fashions in diagnosis (anorexia may be more common today simply because it is more recognised), it is also questionable whether there is any such thing as a periodised collective psyche. The attempt to align mental disorder, all cultural phenomena and the economy seems inescapably reductionist in writers some of whom have precisely rejected what they see as the reductionism of Marx.

In a balanced overview, Andreas Huyssen suggests that postmodernism:

> operates in a field of tension between tradition and innovation, conservation and renewal, mass culture and high art . . . a field of tension which can no longer be grasped in categories such as progress vs. reaction, Left vs. Right, present vs. past, modernism vs. realism, abstraction vs. representation, avant garde vs. Kitsch.[24]

For him, it is the fact that such categories have broken down which creates a crisis – of representation, among other things. And postmodernism is the representation of the crisis. He saves postmodernism from its own ambiguity by making it the site from which the Others – as opposed to the Western modernist male intellectual who believed he stood at the cutting edge of history – may find a site from which to speak: women, the non-Western world, the ecology movement. These movements can create a 'post modernism of resistance' as opposed to '"anything goes" postmodernism'. Translated to the field of fashion, this would seem to support alternative, countercultural fashions. Yet some would argue that postmodern eclecticism destroys any perspective from which a fashion could truly be defined as countercultural, precisely *because* 'anything goes'.

So far as women are concerned[25] – and fashion is still primarily associated with women – contemporary fashions arguably have liberator potential (whether or not this is realised). For in 'denaturalising the wearer's specular identity' contemporary fashion refuses the dichotomy nature/culture. Fashion in our epoch denaturalises the body and thus divests itself of all essentialism. This must be good news for women, since essentialism ideologies have been oppressive to them. Fashion often plays with, and playfully transgresses, gender boundaries, inverting stereotypes and making us aware of the masquerade of femininity. Hal Foster takes a different view of essentialism, arguing that it may now be more important to struggle against the notion of 'woman as artifice' than that of 'woman as Nature'.[26] But it would be more subversive to extend the notion of artifice to masculinity.

The postmodern disturbance of accepted meanings does not inevitably involve Jameson's 'schizophrenia'. The expression of dissidence, whether in artworks or in fashion, is obviously open to recuperation and does often represent a displacement of overtly political protest. Yet, as fashion increasingly extends its ambiguous sway over both sexes, it acts not to reinforce a Veblenesque set of meanings organised around 'woman as cultural display', nor does it necessarily contribute to the carceral society – also implicit in Veblen's picture of the capitalist world – in which everything is imposed from without. Rather, it creates a space in which the normative nature of social practices, always so intensely encoded in dress, may be questioned.

Fashion, as the most popular aesthetic practice of all, extends art into life and offers a medium across the social spectrum with which to experiment. In our anxiety about the environment and our new-found sensitivity to the destruction of nature, it is tempting to forget that urban life has always offered advantages that cannot be matched by rural existence. And fashion is an inescapable part of the urban scene. We are in danger, too, of creating a one-dimensional, oversimplified account of postmodernism that both loses its ambiguity and exaggerates its grip. Better than envisaging it as a total system, a nightmare of the mind would be to use it as an intuitive interpretative tool, one possible way of many in which we may investigate 'these new components of the spectacle'.

Notes and References

1. Quoted in Elizabeth Wilson (1985), *Adorned in Dreams: Fashion and modernity*, London: Virago, p. 10.
2. Fredric Jameson (1984), 'Postmodernism, or the cultural logic of late capitalism', *New Left Review*, number 146, July/August, p. 65.
3. Christian Dior (1957), *Dior by Dior*, London: Weidenfeld & Nicolson.
4. Jameson, 'Postmodernism', p. 67.
5. Anne Hollander (1975), *Seeing Through Clothes*, New York: Avon Books.
6. Hal Foster (1985), *Recordings: Art, spectacle, cultural politics*, Port Townsend, WA: Bay Press, pp. 122–3.
7. Marcel Proust (1981), *Remembrance of Things Past*, Volume I, London: Chatto & Windus, p. 460.
8. Kennedy Fraser (1985), *The Fashionable Mind: Reflections on fashion, 1970–1982*, Boston, MA: David R. Godine, p. 238.
9. Kaja Silverman (1986), 'Fragments of a fashionable discourse', in Tania Modleski (ed.). *Studies in Entertainment: Critical approaches to mass culture*, Bloomington and Indianapolis: Indiana University Press, p. 150.
10. Jacques Lacan (1949), 'The mirror stage as formative of the function of the I', in Lacan (1981), *Écrits: A selection*, London: Tavistock.
11. Stella Mary Newton (1974), *Health, Art and Reason: Dress reformers of the nineteenth century*, London: John Murray.
12. Thomas More (1965), *Complete Works*, Volume IV, New Haven, CT/London: Yale University Press.
13. William Morris (1980), *News From Nowhere and Selected Writings and Designs*, Harmondsworth: Penguin.
14. René König (1973), *The Restless Image*, London: Allen & Unwin.
15. Michel Foucault (1970), *The Order of Things*, London: Tavistock, p. xxiii.
16. Julia Emberley (1988), 'The fashion apparatus and the deconstruction of postmodern subjectivity', in Arthur Kroker and Marilouise Kroker (eds), *Body Invaders: Sexuality and the postmodern condition*, London: Macmillan.
17. Silverman, 'Fragments'.
18. Michel Foucault (1977), *Discipline and Punish*, Harmondsworth: Penguin.
19. Michel Foucault (1979), *The History of Sexuality: Volume I: An Introduction*, Harmondsworth: Penguin.
20. Angela McRobbie (1986), 'Postmodernism and popular culture', in Lisa Appignanesi (ed.), *ICA Documents 4*, London: ICA.
21. Andreas Huyssen (1984), 'Mapping the postmodern', *New German Critique*, no. 33.
22. Kroker and Kroker, *Body Invaders*, p. 45.
23. Scott Lash and John Urry (1987), *The End of Organised Capitalism*, Cambridge: Polity Press, Ch. 9.
24. Huyssen, 'Mapping the postmodern', p. 48.
25. For a further discussion on women and postmodernism, see Elizabeth Wilson (1988), 'Rewinding the video', in Wilson, *Hallucinations*, London: Radius/Century Hutchinson.
26. Foster, *Recordings*, p. 213, note 27, where he cites a feminist writer, Jane Weinstock, in defence of this view, which he qualifies by adding: 'I take this not as a call to any

essentialism as such but as the need, in "the post-natural world of late capitalism" (Jameson) in which patriarchal structures are continually recoded, to remove beyond the opposition nature/culture to a genuine order of difference.' This argument is unclear to me, since I do not understand what is meant by a 'genuine order of difference'. How is the genuine to be distinguished from the essential? It seems merely to substitute some sort of ethical in place of the biologically based definition.

39 □ *Popular Music and Postmodern Theory*

Andrew Goodwin

[...]

In Search of the Postmodern Text

Confronted by the divergent nature of postmodern accounts of culture, scholars have tended to work very ineffectively with the specific empirical demands of understanding popular music. The debate about postmodernism is certainly not notable for the precision of its definitions; as many commentators have observed, it is often unclear whether postmodernism is a cultural condition or new theoretical paradigm. There is also confusion around the question of whether postmodernism deploys irony, or a post-ironic discourse of 'blank parody'. And in the analysis of cultural capital, postmodernists have often confused *intertextuality* with the mere blurring of generic categories, and then gone on to read the collapse of aesthetic distinctions into these processes, as if they necessarily imply the latter, which they do not.

Some writers argue that rock music is postmodern by virtue of its eclecticism, through its foundations in interracial, intercultural and intertextual practices (e.g. McRobbie, 1986; Hebdige, 1988; Weinstein, 1989). Lipsitz (1986/7) provides the most fully empirical version of this position. His argument is acute and important, although in my opinion its references to postmodernism are largely redundant. Empirically, Lipsitz cannot be faulted for his observation that rock music is characterized by extraordinary eclecticism and intertextuality: specifically, his argument relates postmodern concepts to Mexican-American musics developed by musicians in East Los Angeles, including the internationally popular band Los Lobos. But, like all accounts which use eclecticism as their founding postmodern motif, it is hard to see what is being explained here. The logic that one typically finds is this: postmodernism employs eclecticism and intertextuality; rock music is eclectic

From *Cultural Studies*, vol. 5, no. 2, 1991, pp. 174–88.

and intertextual; *ergo*, rock music is postmodern. But what does this tell us about rock music or postmodernism, other than that they might explain each other? (In other words, postmodernism might as well be a parasite *description* of postwar pop, rather than an explanatory paradigm.)

If the textual specifics of pop's genres are merely redundant (if, in fact, one believes that rock, pop and contemporary music *tout court* are postmodern in some more general sense), then what is the point of analysing them? There is an urgent need to clarify the terms of this debate. Unsurprisingly, given the confusion of its terms, the identification of postmodern texts has ranged across an extraordinarily divergent, and incoherent, profusion of textual instances: John Cage, Steve Reich, Laurie Anderson, Philip Glass, Brian Eno, Talking Heads, Prince, punk rock, Madonna, Bruce Springsteen, the British 'New Pop' (Thompson Twins, Scritti Politti, Duran Duran, Thomas Dolby, etc.), Sigue Sigue Sputnik, rap, hip-hop, Los Lobos, and World Beat music have all been cited as quintessentially postmodern.

This *eclecticism of theory* is extremely unhelpful. It stems in part from an initial confusion of two debates, which postmodern theory fails to distinguish. Firstly, there is a debate within 'serious' avant-garde circles about the trajectory of modernist music in the age of Philip Glass, Steve Reich and Terry Riley (see, for a brief and accessible account, Jones, 1987). Secondly, there are debates within popular music about pastiche and authenticity. 'Modernism' means something quite different within each of these two fields, for in the first area it has been the dominant aesthetic strategy, while in the latter it remains – within different genres – everything from utterly marginal to coexistent with older, realist forms. Hence the term 'postmodern' not only describes different musical (and extra-musical) strategies, it also relates quite differently to the field of cultural power, and to the possession of cultural and economic capital in each area.

This confusion is obvious in an early formative attempt to understand rock music in postmodern terms – Fredric Jameson's (1984) deployment of rock and roll in the initial moment of bringing postmodernism into the cultural studies academy (a position which has recently been restated without revision in Jameson, 1988).[1] Commenting on Jameson's analysis of architecture, Mike Davis has recently written that 'Jameson's postmodernism tends to homogenize the details of the contemporary landscape, to subsume under a master concept too many contradictory phenomena which, though undoubtedly visible in the same chronological moment, are none the less separated in their true temporalities' (Davis, 1988: 80). The same can be said of Jameson's analysis of music, which offers a reading of rock history that places The Beatles and The Rolling Stones, on the one hand, as examples of 'high modernism' and The Clash, Talking Heads and the Gang of Four, on the other, as 'postmodern'. What this broad classification of music elides, however, is the necessity of identifying musical differences within the two historical moments which suggest more specific, if still crude, parameters of rock 'realism' (The Clash) and rock 'modernism' (Talking Heads, Gang of Four), and of rock 'authenticity' (The Stones) versus pop artifice (The Beatles).

Historically, the music of The Beatles and The Rolling Stones articulated the social and political currents of the 1960s counterculture. The Clash and The Gang of Four (the latter being explicitly Marxist in orientation) addressed political questions from a standpoint associated with the emergence of punk rock – a quite different countercultural form which eschewed the love and peace message of The Beatles or the nihilistic hedonism of The Stones in favour of blunt left-wing critiques of life in Britain in the late 1970s.

Looked at from the point of view of aesthetic form, The Beatles and The Rolling Stones need to be differentiated: if the development of modernism is at issue here, the increasingly artificial (up until the last, posthumous 1970 LP *Let It Be*) of The Beatles is modernist (self-conscious, ironic, knowingly artificial), in contrast with the 'authentic' rough-edged blues inflections of The Stones and their lyrical themes of sexuality and violence. The Beatles, it might be argued, typified a notion of musical 'progress', where The Rolling Stones (with the exception of their Beatles-influenced album *Their Satanic Majesties Request*) simply repeated a rhythm and blues formula which typifies a form of rock realism (e.g. in both the social content of their lyrics, and in the transparent, unselfconscious nature of the music itself). That The Stones have mined this groove almost unrelentingly is apparent in the critical responses and marketing strategies which framed their 1989 LP *Steel Wheels* – an album that was reviewed and discussed in terms of its 'truth' to an older rhythm and blues aesthetic. (Paul McCartney, in contrast, spent 1989 and 1990 on tour with a band who play extracts from The Beatles' inaugural art-rock album *Sgt Pepper*.)

When we move on to the music of the late 1970s there is another very clear distinction to be made between realist and modernist musics. The Clash are, in this context (and in many other ways), the Rolling Stones of the punk era with their 'realist' raw sound, their incorporation of 'black' musical genres (R&B for The Stones, reggae for The Clash), and in the effort to be transparent in their musical and lyrical communication with the audience. Talking Heads[2] and the Gang of Four are explicitly modernist in orientation – offering such classic modernist techniques as ambiguity, self-reflexivity, use of shock effects and reconstructions of song structure and tonal rationality.

Jameson's first efforts to grapple with rock music from within an account of the postmodern condition remain, then, empirically quite unconvincing – a criticism that has often been made of the *detail* of the textual illustration deployed in what must now be considered the founding essays of a Marxist postmodernism. But while later efforts to work with this theory in relation to popular music are certainly better informed about the music, there is a noticeable shift in orientation, away from Jameson's concern with the relation between social formation and aesthetic form, in favour of an emphasis upon cultural capital and the apparent dismantling of distinctions between art and mass culture.

But Is It Art?

In recent debates about postmodernism, it is often quite casually assumed that we are now living in an era where distinctions between art and mass culture have collapsed. Popular music is sometimes used to establish this argument, and in postmodern writing on pop the elision of high art and pop culture is usually taken for granted. A central problem in these accounts, as I will show, is the conceptual tension that exists between postmodernism's insistence on eclecticism in contemporary culture, and its focus on the apparent conflation of art and mass culture.

Much of this work suffers from two debilitating limitations. Firstly, it often misreads the argument about cultural capital as though the presence or absence of particular aesthetic discourses could be discerned through the identification of timeless historical features, instead of undertaking a conjunctural analysis of the mobilizing categories of cultural power. As Andrew Ross has reminded us, via Bourdieu: 'Cultural power does not inhere in the contents of categories of taste. On the contrary it is exercised through the capacity to draw the line between and around categories of taste; it is the power to define where each relational category begins and ends, and the power to determine what it contains at any one time' (Ross, 1989: 61). Within the field of contemporary popular music, the processes of selection, exclusion, celebration and denigration are used by critics, fans and the musicians themselves in ways that continue to sustain the operation of forms of cultural capital. In particular there remains a tendency to identify as 'serious' those acts who subvert and undermine the conventions of the pop song, often in ways that are classically modernist. This process operates *within* generic categories as well as across the whole field of pop, so that art/pop distinctions can be made (and are made, by fans and critics), respectively, in mainstream pop (Pet Shop Boys/New Kids On the Block), soul (Prince/Michael Jackson), rock (Sonic Youth/U2), heavy metal (Metallica/Def Leppard), and rap (Public Enemy/MC Hammer). The briefest of conversations with almost any fan of one of the above acts would confirm that arguments about art versus trash remain rampant within today's pop.

Secondly, postmodern theory establishes its categories too easily, by defining discourses of art and mass culture through the use of extremely limited terms of reference. A standard strategy is the presentation of two bi-polar opposites which are held to signify art, on the one hand, and mass culture, on the other. The writer will then show how they have increasingly converged, thus magically bringing the truth of postmodernism to light. What is usually missing are all the various genres of pop music which lie *outside* the binary opposition, and which may run counter to the analysis.

Jon Stratton's (1989) account of three key moments in rock history and their relation to aesthetic categories pays much closer attention to musical meanings and is more historically specific in its arguments than Jameson's early typology. Yet it, too, contains a curious flaw. Stratton identifies a convergence of popular and high cultural discourses in rock's third 'moment', *circa* 1975–9, when a 'postmodern' aesthetic (Stratton's description) of minimalism in form, combined with excessive effect, straddles both popular culture (the punk rock of The Sex Pistols, for instance) and the art-music of Brian Eno, Laurie Anderson and Philip Glass. This makes sound musicological sense, but its usefulness is diminished by the sociological realities of pop consumption. Eno, Anderson, and Glass *are* consumed as high art, with the exception of Eno's work with the pop group Roxy Music (and even there he was portrayed as the freakish, arty boffin, to Brian Ferry's populist neo-Sinatra) and Anderson's freakish 1983 hit single 'O Superman'. For many pop fans, Eno is known as someone who helps to produce the rock group U2 (and perhaps Talking Heads), not as an avant-garde or postmodern composer. In that area his work is closely associated with art-rock; so much so that a recent musicological account of Eno places his solo work firmly in a tradition of 'progressive rock' (Tamm, 1989) – a category which should be (as I will demonstrate later) anathema to postmodernism. Musicologically, Stratton's account is persuasive; sociologically it demonstrates the limits of text analysis (however well-grounded historically) when confronted with the actual practices of pop consumption.

What the postmodernists frequently miss in their accounts of popular music is the continuing presence of the categories of the popular and the artistic. There are, in a sense, two Brian Enos: Eno the avant-garde musician and Eno the popular record producer – and the audience for both Enos is probably infinitesimal. Scholars accustomed to listening to Laurie Anderson, Philip Glass and even Talking Heads run the danger of greatly overestimating their impact in pop culture, and – most importantly – the crucial elements of cultural capital that attach to them.

It seems to me almost redundant to have to point out the sociological specifics that place, say, Philip Glass in the category of art-pop, but in this context it seems important to spell out the details: Glass does not produce music which is recognizably like a pop song; lyrics, where they are used, deviate from the conventional modes of address of pop[3] and the structural and (poly)rhythmic content of his pieces deviates from rock convention. For instance, while much has been made of the superficial resemblance between the music of Philip Glass and rock through their shared emphasis on *repetition*, this misses the point that Glass's music takes this technique to extremes that are rarely deployed in pop. Because he defies the recognized forms of rock and pop music, Philip Glass albums are usually found in record stores under headings such as 'Classical', 'Jazz' and (a telling insult) 'New Age'. His concerts take place in halls associated with classical and modern music performances, rather than rock clubs or stadia. In solo performance, the staging of his music reflects the 'serious' conventions of the venue (e.g. the absence of dramatic use of lighting, stage set or visual effects). When the Philip Glass Ensemble performs its operatic works, the staging is highly visual – but the conventions are those of the art-rock 'concept' performance (Pink Floyd, Genesis, etc.), not a rock and roll show. Glass (1987: 3–26) himself makes the influence of modernist artists like Beckett, Brecht, Pinter and Godard quite explicit here – influences that are also very clearly at work in the performances of Laurie Anderson.[4] The behavior of the audience is in either case reverential and distanced, listening attentively to the music, rather than moving, cheering or singing along.[5] Artists like Glass, Eno and Laurie Anderson in fact occupy a space within contemporary pop that reproduces the position of progressive rock and art-rock in the 1960s and 1970s. It is music for college students and middle-class graduates who have the cultural capital to decode the significance of its heightened use of repetition, its minimalism, and its shifting of attention away from the pop star and towards multimedia contextualization. The music may share an abstract principle with rock and roll (a basis in the use of repetitive structures), but its sound and staging hardly resemble that world at all.

I want now to develop these criticisms by making two points, which operate at discrete levels. First, empirically speaking, each of the different attempts to substantiate the legitimacy of postmodern theory operates by bracketing out vast areas of contemporary pop that contradict the theory. Secondly, and more fundamentally, each of these approaches establishes the category of postmodernism by setting up binary oppositions from within extremely limited (and quite divergent) fields of reference. Categories of the postmodern which are constructed around oppositions such as punk/pop, authenticity/artifice, rock/New Pop, modernist rock/postmodern pop and so forth each leave out too much – indeed, the *absences* are precisely what allows each account to seem coherent. (This problem in its turn derives partially from the fact that analysts have tended to focus on just one or two aspects of the debate about postmodernism, thus generating entirely different, and sometimes contradictory, positions using the same conceptual field. The problem, in other words, is that the conceptual field is itself unstable.)

A way out of this confusion is suggested, in my view, by Susan McClary's (1989) careful analysis of avant-garde and postmodern musics. McClary's definition of the postmodern is tight and focused, centring on art-music which abandons the 'difficulty' of high modernism (e.g. Schoenberg) in favor of popular, pleasurable devices such as tonality, melody and simpler rhythms. It thus represents an account of the postmodern which (reasonably, if unusually) relates that category to modernism itself. For McClary, the quintessential postmodern composers are Philip Glass, Steve Reich and Laurie Anderson. Her account offers a definition of postmodern music which has the merit of being clearly argued and coherent. However, in revealing the limited appeal of postmodern music (none of these artists are mass sellers) amongst audiences for 'serious' music, McClary's arguments undermine a central tenet of postmodern theory – the notion of a convergence of art and mass culture.

The confusion arises because postmodern theory has mixed up two different issues – the identification of eclecticism (which pervades rock and pop) and the collapse of distinctions based on cultural capital (which remain pervasive, especially *within* the field of rock music, as Frith and Horne (1987) have shown). When this mistake is laid over the misapprehension that modernism operates in the field of pop music just as it does in 'serious' modern music, the result is conceptual chaos. Whatever its inroads in the visual codes of television (Brechtian devices in prime-time programming, modernist jump cuts in soap-powder commercials, etc.), the much neglected *aural* codes of music are a different matter. While modernist techniques are accepted by the gatekeepers of high culture, in the marketplace of commerce the sounds of dissonance are not so welcome. Today's rap music, like punk rock before it, encounters extraordinary difficulty in gaining airplay and media exposure precisely because its *sounds*, as much as its sentiments, are not conducive to a commercial environment. The music is, in classic modernist tradition, *disruptive*. It would be interesting to consider further the reasons for this disjuncture between visual and aural modernism in the marketplace. For my purpose here, I simply wish to note the pertinence of Georgina Born's comments:

> It is odd and significant that music is so often cited as the success story of postmodern reintegration.... Effectively, these cultural theorists collude in asserting that the postmodern *rapprochement* has been achieved.... It is not only by ignoring the hegemonic 'other' of powerful, contemporary high culture, and failing to deconstruct its rhetoric of *rapprochement*, that writers have arrived at their optimistic and utopian postmodern perspectives. The assertion that modern music culture is moving beyond the modernist/populist divide to achieve a postmodern synthesis or reintegration must be based on empirical study ... rather than making facile assertions, it is necessary to analyse real socio-economic and aesthetic differences that exist. (1987: 70)

This seems to me to be the problem, for instance, with Lawrence Levine's (1988) tendency to see the collapse of cultural categories in the work of The Kronos Quartet (a San Francisco act who have worked with Philip Glass, and whose repertoire includes string quartet arrangements of Jimi Hendrix songs) as an example, along with numerous instances where jazz has been incorporated into high cultural institutions. It might be possible to cite The Kronos Quartet as postmodern, but as with Philip Glass, they clearly have very little to do with popular culture as it is actually lived by fans of rock and pop. And the argument about jazz was countered in the late 1970s by Roger Taylor (1978), in an essay written against what he saw as the incorporation of a radical musical form via its integration into the category of 'Art'.

There is a parallel with Taylor's account of jazz within rock music itself. It is noticeable, for instance, that postmodern accounts do not, as they might be tempted to do, invoke the development of art-rock following the 1967 release of The Beatles' LP *Sgt Pepper*, or the subsequent flowering of 'progressive rock', which had both modernist (Velvet Underground, Henry Cow, Soft Machine, Hatfield and the North) and neoclassical (Emerson, Lake & Palmer, Genesis, Pink Floyd, Yes) aspirations. There is evidence for an art/mass culture fusion in a variety of elements here: the specific use of texts from high culture (beginning with Procul Harum's appropriation of Bach's Suite No. 3 in D major in 'A Whiter Shade Of Pale' and continuing with pieces such as Emerson, Lake & Palmer's versions of Aaron Copland's 'Hoedown', Ravel's 'Bolero' – which in structure significantly parallels the later work of Philip Glass – and Mussorgsky's *Pictures from An Exhibition*); neoclassical performances featuring rock bands with symphony orchestras (Deep Purple, Rick Wakeman); the use of poetry and prose rendered outside the context of a rock lyric (Henry Cow, Rick Wakeman, David Bowie's use of 'cut-ups');

attempts to expand the pop song to twenty-minute pieces, sometimes linked across more than one side of an album (e.g. Yes's *Tales from Topographic Oceans*, Jethro Tull's *Thick as a Brick*) – a trend which reached a peak in ELP's pretentiously titled double album *Works*; the rejection of the gestures of rock performance, in favor of a neo-operatic 'acting out' of the songs (David Bowie, Genesis) or 'serious' strategies, such as having the lead guitarist seated on a stool (King Crimson, Genesis); performances in neo-classical settings (Pink Floyd's album/movie *Live At Pompeii*); and instances of rock musicians citing and using classical and modern symphonic works to 'educate' the rock audience – employing an extract from Stravinsky's *Firebird Suite*, for instance, as an introductory theme to a rock concert (e.g. *Yessongs*).

These instances are not generally cited, of course, because they work against a central premise of postmodernism. Art-music in the pop context confirms the vague notion of eclecticism, and buttresses superficial descriptions of intertextuality, while it *undermines* the postmodern thesis of cultural fusion, in its explicit effort to preserve a bourgeois notion of Art in opposition to mainstream, 'commercial' rock and pop. The genre of progressive rock is clearly a declining (albeit a persistent) one, but my example is none the less instructive, since it is a discourse which persists. Following the emergence of punk rock (which had its own art wing, typified by bands like Devo, Talking Heads, Cabaret Voltaire, 23 Skidoo and Wire), a number of New Wave bands have effectively replaced the progressive rock acts as favorites amongst students and college-educated consumers (Hüsker Du, New Order, The Sugarcubes, The Replacements, Public Image Limited). This is particularly so in the United States, where the most important ideological component of punk rock (a progressive sweeping away of the rock establishment) has had very little lasting effect. Three of the acts mentioned above toured North America in 1989 under a 'Monsters of *Art*' rubric – a slogan which marks itself out from the 'Monsters of Rock' label used to promote heavy metal bands. (As I will show in the final section of this paper, that particular definition of art-rock is almost coterminous with one understanding of the term 'postmodern rock'.)

Indeed, the progressive rock/postmodern rock connection is, as I write, about to be institutionalized in British broadcasting, in a forthcoming program on the BBC's art-music service, Radio 3:

PROG ROCK

Radio 3 chiefs have agreed to roll over Beethoven to make way for a new programme which will bring rock to the classical station. The BBC's hitherto conservative network have enlisted the help of two young(ish) rocking fellows to boost their listenership on a new show *Mixing It*.

From next month you can tune in to a meaty musical stew which includes Peter Gabriel, Laurie Anderson, Brian Eno, Philip Glass and the godfather of minimalism, Steve Reich. (*New Musical Express*, 29 September 1990)

Far from constituting a crossover phenomenon, yesterday's prog rockers, like today's postmodernists, explicitly marked themselves out from the field of 'pop' in rejection of the structural form of the pop song, their use of complex, dissonant forms of tonality, and in the absence of lyrical themes centred on romance, escape or 'the street'. Progressive rock bands aspired to a cultural capital of Art, and anyone who doubts that Steve Reich still does this should read his program notes, which unambiguously locate the music within institutional contexts of serious music, and which describe the music itself with a reverence which is, to my rock fan's sensibility, rather comic:

> Sextet for four percussionists and two keyboard players, is scored for three marimbas, two vibraphones, two bass drums, crotales, sticks, tam-tam, two pianos and two synthesisers.
> The work is in five movements played without pause. The relationship of the five movements is that of an arch form A-B-C-B-A. The first and last movements are fast, the second and fourth moderate, and the third, slow. Changes of tempo are made abruptly at the beginning of new movements by metric modulation to either get slower or faster.... The harmonies used are largely dominant chords with added tones creating a somewhat darker, chromatic, and more varied harmonic language than in my earlier works.[6]

My point is *not* that this description of the music intrinsically establishes Reich's work as art-music. Pop and rock can also be described in these ways; and they frequently are, in musician's magazines like *Guitar Player*, and in the occasional forays made by 'serious' critics into pop (see, for example, Mellers, 1973). My point is rather that this critical discourse illustrates a manner of promoting the music and assumes a mode of listening both of which are the antithesis of popular music.

Another way of arguing for Reich as a postmodernist is in his use of Third World musics. Weinstein (1989), among others, has implied that the phenomenon of World Beat music is postmodern by virtue of its generic conflation. (As I have already suggested, if this is true, then the whole of rock music must also be postmodern.) A problem here, for the art-pop fusion argument, is that African percussion techniques played in a Western concert hall (Reich's 1971 composition *Drumming*, for instance) where the audience is immobile and the performers enact the music with the gestures and costume of the 'serious' musician can no longer be heard as 'popular' or 'folk' music. (Furthermore, it seems to me it might also be objected that Reich's use of Third World folk music is, in the concert hall environment in which it is usually performed, no more postmodern than is, for instance, Haydn's use of European folk.)

More pertinently, there persists a modernist strand in pop music which continues to draw on masculinist traditions of noise, *music concrète* and Futurism, in both the sounds and the (sometimes neo-fascist or proto-Soviet) iconography used to promote the music. This music has thus taken up the modernist strand of progressive rock; a fact that is made biographically concrete in the career of drummer Chris Cutler, who played with art-rock acts Henry Cow and The Art Bears in the 1970s, and who now performs with one of punk's original art-groups, Pere Ubu. The continuity is apparent in this comment from rock musician Billy Bragg, concerning the transparent connection between Russian constructivism and British electro-pop: 'If Mayakovsky had been alive today he'd have been in Depeche Mode.'[7] Here I would cite the 'industrial' bands like Nitzer Ebb, Front 242, Laibach and Ministry, and avant-garde rock noise-makers like Sonic Youth (who defy pop codes in part by using a variety of unconventional guitar tunings) as the most obvious examples. There is also the use of politicized *bricolage* and dissonance in American rap music (mobilized around images of drugs, gangs and crime), and a heavy metal/thrash metal wing articulating this same discourse (but with a different iconography – horror and Satanism). Crucially, many of these acts display an unrelenting hostility to mass culture, especially television (Beatnigs, Negativland, Wire, Metallica, Megadeth, Public Enemy, NWA, Ice-T). Their perceived authenticity derives in no small measure from their antipathy to popular culture, and this remains a crucial nuance of contemporary pop that postmodern critics consistently overlook.

The music of Public Enemy, for instance (*It Takes a Nation of Millions to Hold Us Back*, *Fear of a Black Planet*), can be seen as postmodern in its use of a modernist dissonance within the framework of mass popularity (via CBS Records). But the debate about rap (which is so often cited as a postmodern musical form, because of the pervasive intertextuality implied by its use of 'sampling') routinely overlooks the continuing presence of an art/mass culture discourse located in resistance to it; i.e. the continuing arguments (which precisely reproduce debates about rock and roll in the 1950s, and punk rock in the 1970s) about whether or not rap 'really' is *music*. These debates can be followed in arenas as diverse as conversations between rock and rap fans, published rock criticism, music-business institutions such as the Grammy awards, and in the arts pages of the elite press. If postmodernist critics paid the slightest attention to these accounts of popular music they would know that the battle against bourgeois notions of culture is waged, every day, by acts like Public Enemy, whose 'postmodernism' (if it is such) exists in a totally different environment from the music of Philip Glass *et al.*, and where the struggle for *modernism* (let alone *post*modernism) cannot yet be taken for granted.

Just as social divisions persist and underlie the construction of supposedly postmodern buildings (Davis, 1988; Jacoby, 1987: 169–72), so they are also replicated in the marketplace for contemporary music. Postmodern music, whether defined tightly as a form which develops in opposition to the difficulty of the avant-garde (McClary's usage, which in my view remains the only meaningful sense in which postmodern *texts* can be identified, since it is the only approach which shows how music might be related to a dominant modernism), or more loosely as an intertextual movement in more mainstream pop, often erases itself on the terrain of cultural capital. The abolition of the art/mass culture distinction is not apparent in either instance, for postmodern pop remains in most cases either an explicitly high cultural form, or a pop form constructed in at least partial opposition to 'inauthentic' popular culture (TV, advertising, mainstream pop).

Coda: Hyper-marketing Postmodernism

It is not possible to provide a neat 'conclusion' to this discussion. Since I maintain that the premises of postmodern theory are incoherent and that its aesthetic is a grab-bag of interesting observations which do not necessarily belong together, it follows that conclusions about the nature of postmodern music will depend on which part of the postmodern condition we choose to stress. Arguments about *aesthetic form* produce one way of looking at pop music. The concept of *cultural capital* produces quite different results. The relationship between the two is extremely complex. Looked at from the point of view of tonality or narrative structure, it can be argued quite convincingly that modernism persists as an art-rock form within pop, amongst those acts who defy the description of popular music set out in Adorno's classic (1941) article. (Indeed, one good reason for arguing for the continued distinction between pop music and art-rock lies in the fact that the 'postmodern' artists precisely subvert the conventions of pop that Adorno described so well, but failed to understand.) If, however, the focus were on *timbre*, then the noise of rock music (especially in the use of distorted electric guitar sounds) would be modernist in a much more general sense,[8] and the relation between aesthetic form and cultural capital would have to be thought through differently. The notion of *pastiche*, on the other hand, would generate entirely different conclusions – it might form a basis for seeing postmodernism in contemporary acts as diverse as Prince, Transvision Vamp and The Mekons, where it *does* seem that 'blank parody' is an accurate term for the self-referential deployment of 'found' music.

Unless we are committed to demonstrating the coherence or explanatory purpose of postmodern theory (which I am not), there is no need to construct rational order from these confusions. In order to grapple adequately with these issues, we need both a better theory of pop music (which would include, for example, some investigation of the relation between *timbre* and modernism) and more empirical work on today's pop audience. 'More work needs to be done' is, however, a boring conclusion, even where it is true. I will finish instead by noting one of the most bizarre developments in the brief history of media and cultural studies, in which abstruse French theory has 'trickled down' into the popular consciousness, via the cultural industries, so that the word 'postmodern' reached record stores, magazines and television programs just a few years after it entered the academy: proponents of postmodernism will no doubt feel that this phenomenon is itself hugely postmodern.

As if to confuse the debate further still, the music industry has now pitched in with its own effort to define the terms of our debate, with the emergence (around 1988) of the new category of 'postmodern rock'. MTV was a pioneer in this trend, labelling its 'alternative' rock program *Post Modern MTV*, in August 1988. Record companies then began to adopt the term, using it to promote records by Thrashing Doves, Pere Ubu and Peter Case. Pop stars like Elvis Costello and Bono (of U2) began to use the term in media interviews. Across these usages, from French theorist Jean Baudrillard (the subject of 1988 articles in both *The Face* and *Rolling Stone*[9]) to the musings of a Christian rock vocalist, there is of course little coherence.

Talking to students about the term 'postmodern rock', I have been able to discover three distinct usages. For some consumers it seems to correspond roughly with categories like 'art-rock', 'indie pop' or 'college radio' music – that is to say, acts who define themselves as existing outside the mainstream of the charts, and whose music is supposed to be taken more seriously than the supposedly disposable sounds of pop. (This interpretation buttresses my argument above, of course, since it implies the conventional division between rock and pop, with the former having artistic pretensions not deemed appropriate for the latter.) This seems to be the understanding employed in the music industry itself. For instance, in the 1989 MTV *Video Music Awards* program, host Arsenio Hall framed college-radio favorites The Cure thus: 'They're nominees for one of our next categories. That is, postmodern video. In other words, the best video by a performer or a group that's brought an alternative music [*sic*]'.[10] This understanding of postmodernity has also leaked into the music press. The Los Angeles-based magazine *Hits* now publishes a 'Post Modern' chart and airplay listing (Jane's Addiction, Living Colour, Bob Mould, Sonic Youth, World Party, Depeche Mode), a 'PoMo Picks' review section (Prefab Sprout, Los Lobos, An Emotional Fish, The Cure) and a 'Post Toasted' gossip column! Interviewed in *Hits*, Arista Records Senior Vice-President of Sales and Distribution Rick Bleiweiss offers his definition of a Post-Modern act: 'Post Modern or alternative are wide-ranging terms. The acts I'm talking about are Urban Dance Squad, Kris McKay, the Church.... We're treating Jimmy Ryser in a similar manner. While you couldn't call him alternative like some of the groups I've mentioned, the plan is the same.'[11]

A second definition takes a more literal approach, defining the category in relation to 'modern rock' – a catch-all category used by radio stations in the United States (such as KITS in San Francisco) to promote 1980s music, including the straightforward rock of bands like U2, but with special emphasis on the electro-pop of acts like Erasure and Depeche Mode. Postmodern music, here, refers to those acts who, chronologically speaking, come after 'Modern Rock'. This common-sense usage is not routine in the industry, but it is interesting, since it suggests that the Modern Rock acts have now become established as a genre not unlike 'Classic Rock', in some markets at least, which will generate its own 'alternative'.

Thirdly, postmodern rock can be defined as that music which follows punk, evacuating its articulation of political resistance. Groups like The Smiths, The Cure and New Order can thus be understood as a postmodern response to the 'defeat' of punk and the parallel rise of Thatcherism and Reaganism,[12] which is thus seen to 'explain' what has sometimes half-jokingly been described as this music's 'miserablism'. 'Industrial' music might also fit this pattern. The exact antithesis of what Herbert Marcuse (1968) called 'affirmative culture', this music might constitute a form of postmodern resistance.

The debate about postmodernism in popular music has thus become newly complex in a unique way: since the postmodern is now a sales category/musical genre, in addition to being a theory, cultural condition and artistic practice, further analysis of its relation to music will have to take account of this epistemological feedback loop. But in the dominant usage established by the music industry itself (the first of the three listed above), the term constructs 'postmodern rock' just as I have suggested – as a synonym for 'art-rock'. The debate about postmodernism as it relates to cultural capital therefore continues to chip away at its own conceptual foundations.

Notes

1. Jameson (1979) suggest a different parallel between pop and postmodernism, when he locates pop music as a 'simulacrum', in which there is no 'original' textual moment.
2. A strictly modernist reading is given of the David Byrne (of Talking Heads) movie *True Stories*, for instance, when it is read as a social parody, a satirical comment on alienation in a post-industrial society (see Coulson, 1987).
3. Even on *Songs From Liquid Days* (CBS Records, 1986), where Philip Glass collaborates with rock songwriters like David Byrne and Suzanne Vega, the musical setting typically undercuts any connection that the words might have forged with pop culture. Fusing the work of Laurie Anderson and the Kronos Quartet with a performance by Linda Ronstadt (on 'Forgetting') is something of a postmodern landmark – but how many Ronstadt fans will have heard it, let alone *understood* it?
4. A cursory glance at Laurie Anderson's performance video *Home of the Brave* will confirm the presence of alienated, episodic modes of presentation.
5. I am obliged to note, however, that at a Philip Glass concert in Berkeley's Zellerbach Hall in June 1989, two members of the audience were seen playing 'air piano'!
6. These notes are taken from a program for a concert given at Berkeley's Zellerbach Hall, 3 March 1990.
7. Billy Bragg, quoted in *New Musical Express*, 23/30 December 1989.
8. I am grateful to Paul Kendall for pointing this out to me. However, pop and rock remain so conventional, and – I would argue – realist/naturalist in form, through elements such as tonality, narrative musical development and song structure, that to elevate timbre to such a position of prominence surely fails to engage with the way that contemporary music is actually heard by its audiences.
9. See, for instance, the interview with Jean Baudrillard in *The Face* (vol. 2, no. 4, January 1989); and the issue of *Rolling Stone* (18 May 1989) in which he is listed as that summer's 'Hot Philosopher King'.
10. *Music Video Awards*, MTV, September 1989. The winners in the postmodern music video category were another 'alternative' rock act, REM (for the clip 'Orange Crush'). The following year, the winning clip was from Sinead O'Connor ('Nothing Compares 2 U – a cover of a Prince song), the other contenders being Depeche Mode, Red Hot Chili Peppers and Tears for Fears.
11. See *Hits*, vol. 5, no. 209, 17 September 1990. I am grateful to Keith Negus for bringing this material to my attention.
12. I am grateful to Andrew Pogue for an explanation of this use of the term.

References

Adorno, T. (1941) 'On popular music', *Studies in Philosophy and Social Science* no. 9. Reprinted in Frith and Goodwin (1990).

Appignanesi, L. (ed.) (1986) *Postmodernism: ICA Documents 4*, London: Institute of Contemporary Arts.

Born, G. (1987) 'On modern music: shock, pop and synthesis', *New Formations*, no. 2, Summer.

Coulson, C. (1987) 'Start making sense'. *New Republic*, 23 March.

Davis, M. (1988) 'Urban renaissance and the spirit of postmodernism', *New Left Review*, no. 151, May–June 1985. Reprinted in Kaplan (1988).

Frith, S. and Goodwin, A. (eds) (1990) *On Record: Rock, pop and the written word*, New York: Pantheon; London: Routledge.

Frith, S. and Horne, H. (1987) *Art Into Pop*, London: Methuen.

Glass, P. (1987) *Music by Philip Glass*, New York: Harper & Row.

Hebdige, D. (1988) *Hiding in the Light: On images and things*, London: Comedia/Routledge.

Jacoby, R. (1987) *The Last Intellectuals: American culture in the age of academe*, New York: Basic Books.

Jameson, F. (1979) 'Reification and Utopia in mass culture', *Social Text*, no. 1, Winter.

Jameson, F. (1984) 'The politics of theory: ideological positions in the postmodernism debate', *New German Critique*, no. 33, Fall.

Jameson, F. (1988) 'Postmodernism and consumer society', in Kaplan (1988).

Jones, R. (1987) 'Introduction' to Glass (1987).

Kaplan, A. (ed.) (1988) *Postmodernism and its Discontents: Theories, practices*, London: Verso.

Levine, L. (1988) *Highbrow/Lowbrow: The emergence of cultural hierarchy in America*, Berkeley: University of California Press.

Lipsitz, G. (1986/7), 'Cruising around the historical bloc: postmodernism and popular music in east Los Angeles', *Cultural Critique*, no. 5, Winter. Reprinted in *Time Passages: Collective memory and American popular culture*, Minneapolis: University of Minnesota Press (1990).

Marcuse, H. (1968) *Negations*, London: Allen & Unwin.

McClary, S. (1989) 'Terminal prestige: the case of avant-garde music composition', *Cultural Critique*, no. 12, Spring.

McRobbie, A. (1986) 'Postmodernism and popular culture', in Appignanesi (1986).

Mellers W. (1973) *Twilight of the Gods: The Beatles in retrospect*, London: Faber & Faber.

Ross, A. (1989) *No Respect: Intellectuals and popular culture*, New York: Routledge.

Stratton, J. (1989) 'Beyond art: postmodernism and the case of popular music', *Theory, Culture & Society*, vol. 6, no. 1, February.

Tamm, E. (1989) *Brian Eno: His music and the vertical color of sound*, Winchester, MA: Faber & Faber.

Taylor, R. (1978) *Art, An Enemy of the People*, Brighton, Sussex: Harvester.

Weinstein, D. (1989) 'The Amnesty International concert tour: transnationalism as cultural commodity', *Public Culture* (Bulletin for the Project of Transnational Cultural Studies), vol. 1, no. 2, Spring.

40 □ *Postmodern Blackness*

bell hooks

Postmodernist discourses are often exclusionary, even as they call attention to, appropriate even, the experience of 'difference' and 'Otherness' to provide oppositional political meaning, legitimacy, and immediacy when they are accused of lacking concrete relevance. Very few African-American intellectuals have talked or written about postmodernism. At a dinner party I talked about trying to grapple with the significance of postmodernism for contemporary black experience. It was one of those social gatherings where only one other black person was present. The setting quickly became a field of contestation. I was told by the other black person that I was wasting my time, that 'this stuff does not relate in any way to what's happening with black people'. Speaking in the presence of a group of white onlookers, staring at us as though this encounter were staged for their benefit, we engaged in a passionate discussion about black experience. Apparently, no one sympathized with my insistence that racism is perpetuated when blackness is associated solely with concrete gut level experience conceived as either opposing or having no connection to abstract thinking and the production of critical theory. The idea that there is no meaningful connection between black experience and critical thinking about aesthetics or culture must be continually interrogated.

My defense of postmodernism and its relevance to black folks sounded good, but I worried that I lacked conviction, largely because I approach the subject cautiously and with suspicion.

Disturbed not so much by the 'sense' of postmodernism but by the conventional language used when it is written or talked about and by those who speak it, I find myself on the outside of the discourse looking in. As a discursive practice it is dominated primarily by the voices of white male intellectuals and/or academic elites who speak to and about one another with coded familiarity. Reading and studying their writing to understand postmodernism in its multiple manifestations, I appreciate it but feel little inclination to ally myself with the academic hierarchy and exclusivity pervasive in the movement today.

Critical of most writing on postmodernism, I perhaps am more conscious of the way in which the focus on 'Otherness and difference' that is often alluded to in these works seems to have little concrete impact as an analysis or standpoint that might change the nature and direction of postmodernist theory. Since much of this theory has been constructed in reaction to and against high modernism, there is seldom any mention of black experience or writings by black people in this work, specifically black women (though in more recent work one may see a reference to Cornel West, the black male scholar who has most engaged postmodernist discourse). Even if an aspect of black culture is the subject of postmodern critical writing, the works cited will usually be those of black men. A work that comes immediately to mind is Andrew Ross's chapter 'Hip, and the long front of color' in *No Respect: Intellectuals and popular culture*; while it is an interesting reading, it constructs black culture as though black women have had no role in black cultural production. At the end of Meaghan Morris' discussion of postmodernism in her collection of essays *The Pirate's Fiancée: Feminism and postmodernism*, she provides a bibliography of works by women, identifying them as important contributions to a discourse on postmodernism that offer new insight as well as challenging male theoretical hegemony. Even though many of the works do not directly address postmodernism, they address similar concerns. There are no references to works by black women.

The failure to recognize a critical black presence in the culture and in most scholarship and writing on postmodernism compels a black reader, particularly a black female reader, to interrogate her interest in a subject where those who discuss and write about it seem not to know black women exist or even to consider the possibility that we might be somewhere writing or saying something that should be listened to, or producing art that should be seen, heard, approached with intellectual seriousness. This is especially the case with works that go on and on about the way in which postmodernist discourse has opened up a theoretical terrain where 'difference' and 'Otherness' can be considered legitimate issues in the academy. Confronting both the absence of recognition of black female presence that much postmodernist theory re-inscribes and the resistance on the part of most black folks to hearing about real connection between postmodernism and black experience, I enter a discourse, a practice, where there may be no ready audience for my words, no clear listener, uncertain then, that my voice can or will be heard.

During the sixties, the black power movement was influenced by perspectives that could easily be labeled modernist. Certainly many of the ways black folks addressed issues of identity conformed to a modernist universalizing agenda. There was little critique of patriarchy as a master narrative among black militants. Despite the fact that black power ideology reflected a modernist sensibility, these elements were soon rendered irrelevant as militant protest was stifled by a powerful, repressive postmodern state. The period directly after the black power movement was a time when major news magazines carried articles with cocky headlines like 'Whatever Happened to Black America?' This response was an ironic reply to the aggressive, unmet demand by decentered, marginalized black subjects who had at least momentarily successfully demanded a hearing, who had made it possible for black liberation to be on the national political agenda. In the wake of the black power movement, after so many rebels were slaughtered and lost, many of these voices were silenced by a repressive state; others became inarticulate. It has become necessary to find new avenues to transmit the messages of black liberation struggle, new ways to talk about racism and other politics of domination. Radical postmodernist practice, most powerfully conceptualized as a 'politics of difference', should incorporate the voices of displaced, marginalized, exploited, and oppressed black people. It is sadly ironic that the contemporary discourse which talks the most about heterogeneity, the decentered subject, declaring break-throughs that allow recognition of Otherness, still directs its critical voice primarily to a specialized audience that shares a common language rooted in the very master narratives it claims to challenge. If radical postmodernist thinking is to have a transformative impact, then a critical break with the notion of 'authority' as 'mastery over' must not simply be a rhetorical device. It must be reflected in habits of being, including styles of writing as well as chosen subject matter. Third world nationals, elites, and white critics who passively absorb white supremacist think-ing, and therefore never notice or look at black people on the streets or at their jobs, who render us invisible with their gaze in all areas of daily life, are not likely to produce liberatory theory that will challenge racist domination, or promote a breakdown in traditional ways of seeing and thinking about reality, ways of constructing aesthetic theory and practice. From a different standpoint, Robert Storr makes a similar critique in the global issue of *Art in America* when he asserts:

> To be sure, much postmodernist critical inquiry has centered precisely on the issues of 'difference' and 'Otherness'. On the purely theoretical plane the exploration of these concepts has produced some important results, but in the absence of any sustained research into what artists of color and others outside the mainstream might be up to, such discussions become rootless instead of radical. Endless second guessing about the latent imperialism of intruding upon other cultures only compounded matters, preventing or excusing these theorists from investigating what black, Hispanic, Asian and Native American artists were actually doing.

Without adequate concrete knowledge of and contact with the non-white 'Other', white theorists may move in discursive theoretical directions that are threatening and potentially disruptive of that critical practice which would support radical liberation struggle.

The postmodern critique of 'identity', though relevant for renewed black liberation struggle, is often posed in ways that are problematic. Given a pervasive politic of white supremacy which seeks to prevent the formation of radical black subjectivity, we cannot cavalierly dismiss a concern with identity politics. Any critic exploring the radical potential of postmodernism as it relates to racial difference and racial domination would need to consider the implications of a critique of identity for oppressed groups. Many of us are struggling to find new strategies of resistance. We must engage decolonization as a critical practice if we are to have meaningful chances of survival even as we must simultaneously cope with the loss of political grounding which made radical activism more possible. I am thinking here about the postmodernist critique of essentialism as it pertains to the construction of 'identity' as one example.

Postmodern theory that is not seeking to simply appropriate the experience of 'Otherness' to enhance the discourse or to be radically chic should not separate the 'politics of difference' from the politics of racism. To take racism seriously one must consider the plight of underclass people of color, a vast majority of whom are black. For African-Americans our collective condition prior to the advent of postmodernism and perhaps more tragically expressed under current postmodern conditions has been and is characterized by continued displacement, profound alienation, and despair. Writing about blacks and postmodernism, Cornel West describes our collective plight:

> There is increasing class division and differentiation, creating on the one hand a significant black middle-class, highly anxiety-ridden, insecure, willing to be co-opted and incorporated into the powers that be, concerned with racism to the degree that it poses constraints on upward social mobility; and, on the other, a vast and growing black underclass, an underclass that embodies a kind of walking nihilism of pervasive drug addiction, pervasive alcoholism, pervasive homicide, and an exponential rise in suicide. Now because of the deindustrialization, we also have a devastated black industrial working class, we are talking here about tremendous hopelessness.

This hopelessness creates longing for insight and strategies for change that can renew spirits and reconstruct grounds for collective black liberation struggle. The overall impact of postmodernism is that many other groups now share with black folks a sense of deep alienation, despair, uncertainty, loss of a sense of grounding even if it is not informed by shared circumstance. Radical postmodernism calls attention to those shared sensibilities which cross the boundaries of class, gender, race, etc., that could be fertile ground for the construction of empathy-ties that would promote recognition of common commitments, and serve as a base for solidarity and coalition.

Yearning is the word that best describes a common psychological state shared by many of us, cutting across boundaries of race, class, gender, and sexual practice. Specifically, in relation to the postmodernist deconstruction of 'master' narratives, the yearning that wells in the hearts and minds of those whom such narratives have silenced is the longing for critical voice. It is no accident that 'rap' has usurped the primary position of rhythm and blues music among young black folks as the most desired sound or that it began as a form of 'testimony' for the underclass. It has enabled underclass black youth to develop a critical voice, as a group of young black men told me, a 'common literacy'. Rap projects a critical voice, explaining, demanding, urging. Working with this insight in his essay 'Putting the pop back into postmodernism', Lawrence Grossberg comments:

> The postmodern sensibility appropriates practices as boasts that announce their own – and consequently our own – existence, like a rap song boasting of the imaginary

(or real – it makes no difference) accomplishments of the rapper. They offer forms of empowerment not only in the face of nihilism but precisely through the forms of nihilism itself: an empowering nihilism, a moment of positivity through the production and structuring of affective relations.

Considering that it is as subject one comes to voice, then the postmodernist focus on the critique of identity appears at first glance to threaten and close down the possibility that this discourse and practice will allow those who have suffered the crippling effects of colonization and domination to gain or regain a hearing. Even if this sense of threat and the fear it evokes are based on a misunderstanding of the postmodernist political project, they nevertheless shape responses. It never surprises me when black folks respond to the critique of essentialism, especially when it denies the validity of identity politics by saying, 'Yeah, it's easy to give up identity, when you got one'. Should we not be suspicious of postmodern critiques of the 'subject' when they surface at a historical moment when many subjugated people feel themselves coming to voice for the first time. Though an apt and oftentimes appropriate comeback, it does not really intervene in the discourse in a way that alters and transforms.

Criticisms of directions in postmodern thinking should not obscure insights it may offer that open up our understanding of African-American experience. The critique of essentialism encouraged by postmodernist thought is useful for African-Americans concerned with reformulating outmoded notions of identity. We have too long had imposed upon us from both the outside and the inside a narrow, constricting notion of blackness. Postmodern critiques of essentialism which challenge notions of universality and static over-determined identity within mass culture and mass consciousness can open up new possibilities for the construction of self and the assertion of agency.

Employing a critique of essentialism allows African-Americans to acknowledge the way in which class mobility has altered collective black experience so that racism does not necessarily have the same impact on our lives. Such a critique allows us to affirm multiple black identities, varied black experience. It also challenges colonial imperialist paradigms of black identity which represent blackness one-dimensionally in ways that reinforce and sustain white supremacy. This discourse created the idea of the 'primitive' and promoted the notion of an 'authentic' experience, seeing as 'natural' those expressions of black life which conformed to a pre-existing pattern or stereotype. Abandoning essentialist notions would be a serious challenge to racism. Contemporary African-American resistance struggle must be rooted in a process of decolonization that continually opposes re-inscribing notions of 'authentic' black identity. This critique should not be made synonymous with a dismissal of the struggle of oppressed and exploited peoples to make ourselves subjects. Nor should it deny that in certain circumstances this experience affords us a privileged critical location from which to speak. This is not a re-inscription of modernist master narratives of authority which privilege some voices by denying voice to others. Part of our struggle for radical black subjectivity is the quest to find ways to construct self and identity that are oppositional and liberatory. The unwillingness to critique essentialism on the part of many African-Americans is rooted in the fear that it will cause folks to lose sight of the specific history and experience of African-Americans and the unique sensibilities and culture that arise from that experience. An adequate response to this concern is to critique essentialism while emphasizing the significance of 'the authority of experience'. There is a radical difference between a repudiation of the idea that there is a black ·'essence' and recognition of the way black identity has been specifically constituted in the experience of exile and struggle.

When black folks critique essentialism, we are empowered to recognize multiple experiences of black identity that are the lived conditions which make diverse cultural productions possible. When this diversity is ignored, it is easy to see black folks as falling into two categories: nationalist or assimilationist, black-identified or white-identified. Coming to terms with the impact of postmodernism for black experience, particularly as it changes our sense of identity, means that we must and can rearticulate the basis for collective bonding. Given the various crises facing African-Americans (economic, spiritual, escalating racial violence, etc.), we are compelled by circumstance to reassess our relationship to popular culture and resistance struggle. Many of us are as reluctant to face this task as many non-black postmodern thinkers who focus theoretically on the issue of 'difference' are to confront the issue of race and racism.

Music is the cultural product created by African-Americans that has most attracted postmodern theorists. It is rarely acknowledged that there is far greater censorship and restriction of other forms of cultural production by black folks – literary, critical writing, etc. Attempts on the part of editors and publishing houses to control and manipulate the representation of black culture, as well as the desire to promote the creation of products that will attract the widest audience, limit in a crippling and stifling way the kind of work many black folks feel we can do and still receive recognition. Using myself as an example, that creative writing I do which I consider to be most reflective of a postmodern oppositional sensibility, work that is abstract, fragmented, non-linear narrative, is constantly rejected by editors and publishers. It does not conform to the type of writing they think black women should be doing or the type of writing they believe will sell. Certainly I do not think I am the only black person engaged in forms of cultural production, especially experimental ones, who is constrained by the lack of an audience for certain kinds of work. It is important for postmodern thinkers and theorists to constitute themselves as an audience for such work. To do this they must assert power and privilege within the space of critical writing to open up the field so that it will be more inclusive. To change the exclusionary practice of postmodern critical discourse is to enact a postmodernism of resistance. Part of this intervention entails black intellectual participation in the discourse.

In his essay 'Postmodernism and black America', Cornel West suggests that black intellectuals 'are marginal – usually languishing at the interface of Black and white cultures or thoroughly ensconced in Euro-American settings'. He cannot see this group as potential producers of radical postmodernist thought. While I generally agree with this assessment, black intellectuals must proceed with the understanding that we are not condemned to the margins. The way we work and what we do can determine whether or not what we produce will be meaningful to a wider audience, one that includes all classes of black people. West suggests that black intellectuals lack 'any organic link with most of Black life' and that this 'diminishes their value to Black resistance'. This statement bears traces of essentialism. Perhaps we need to focus more on those black intellectuals, however rare our presence, who do not feel this lack and whose work is primarily directed towards the enhancement of black critical consciousness and the strengthening of our collective capacity to engage in meaningful resistance struggle. Theoretical ideas and critical thinking need not be transmitted solely in written work or solely in the academy. While I work in a predominantly white institution, I remain intimately and passionately engaged with black community. It's not like I'm going to talk about writing and thinking about postmodernism with other academics and/or intellectuals and not discuss these ideas with underclass non-academic black folks who are family, friends, and comrades. Since I have not broken the ties that bind me to underclass poor black community, I have seen that knowledge, especially that which enhances daily life and strengthens our capacity to survive, can be shared. It means that critics, writers, and academics have to give the same critical attention to nurturing and cultivating our ties to black community that we give to writing articles, teaching, and lecturing. Here again I am really talking about cultivating habits of being that reinforce awareness that knowledge can be disseminated and shared on a number of fronts. The extent to which knowledge is made available, accessible, etc. depends on the nature of one's political commitments.

Postmodern culture with its decentered subject can be the space where ties are severed or it can provide the occasion for new and varied forms of bonding. To some extent, ruptures, surfaces, contextuality, and a host of other happenings create gaps that make space for oppositional practices which no longer require intellectuals to be confined by narrow separate spheres with no meaningful connection to the world of the everyday. Much postmodern engagement with culture emerges from the yearning to do intellectual work that connects with habits of being, forms of artistic expression, and aesthetics that inform the daily life of writers and scholars as well as a mass population. On the terrain of culture, one can participate in critical dialogue with the uneducated poor, the black underclass who are thinking about aesthetics. One can talk about what we are seeing, thinking, or listening to; a space is there for critical exchange. It's exciting to think, write, talk about, and create art that reflects passionate engagement with popular culture, because this may very well be 'the' central future location of resistance struggle, a meeting place where new and radical happenings can occur.

References

Grossberg, Lawrence, 'Putting the pop back in postmodernism', *Universal Abandon*, ed.
  Andrew Ross, Minneapolis: University of Minnesota Press, 1988.
Morris, Meaghan, *The Pirate's Fiancée*, London: Verso, 1980.
Ross, Andrew, *No Respect: Intellectuals and Popular Culture*, New York: Routledge, 1989.
Storr, Robert, *Art in America*, New York: Abbeville Press, 1986.
West, Cornel, *Post Analytic Philosophy*, New York: Columbia University Press, 1985.
West, Cornel, *Prophetic Fragments*, Trenton: Africa World Press, 1988.
Whitman, Walt, *Leaves of Grass*, New York: Book League of America, 1942.

PART SEVEN

The Politics of the Popular

Introduction

This section collects together a number of readings which, in different ways, address the question of a politics of the popular. The extract from Pierre Bourdieu's *Distinction* (Reading 41) offers an introduction to his thesis that distinctions of 'culture' (whether understood as text, practice or way of living) are a significant aspect of the struggle between dominant and subordinate groups in society. Throughout the course of the book he shows how arbitrary tastes and arbitrary ways of living are continually transmuted into legitimate taste and *the* legitimate way of life. Bourdieu writes that the 'illusion of "natural distinction" is ultimately based on the power of the dominant to impose, by their very existence, a definition of excellence which [is] nothing other than their own way of existing'. For Bourdieu, taste is a profoundly ideological discourse: it functions as a marker of 'class' (using the term in the double sense to mean both socio-economic category and a particular level of quality). The consumption of culture is 'predisposed, consciously and deliberately or not, to fulfil a social function of legitimating social difference'. Bourdieu's purpose is not to prove the self-evident – that different classes have different lifestyles, different tastes in culture – but to interrogate the processes by which the making of cultural distinctions secures and legitimates forms of power and control rooted in economic inequalities. He is interested not so much in the actual differences as in how these differences are used by the dominant class as a means of social reproduction.

Stuart Hall makes a similar argument in 'Notes on Deconstructing "the Popular"' (Reading 42). Hall maintains that the field of culture is always a site of ideological struggle. Part of this struggle takes the form of a vigilant policing of the boundaries between dominant and popular culture. Hall maintains that the difference between dominant and popular is a matter of 'form' rather than 'content'. What must be policed is the categories – the categorical differences. The content of these categories can change, and does change; it is the distinction between them and, more importantly, the distinction between their occupants (for these are, ultimately, 'social' rather than 'cultural' categories) which is of crucial importance and must be policed at all cost.

Paul DiMaggio's work gives these claims a historical explanation. In Reading 43 he demonstrates how 'the distinction between high and popular culture, in its American version, emerged in the period between 1850 and 1900 out of the efforts of urban elites to build organizational forms that, first, isolated high culture and, second, differentiated it from popular culture'.

In another argument influenced by Bourdieu, the Norwegian cultural critic Jostein Gripsrud (Reading 49) rejects the 'postmodern' claim that 'the distinction between high and low culture is "in fact" outmoded and only kept alive in reactionary rhetoric'. Academics who make this claim, he contends, are acting ideologically: 'Our ability to take part in both high and low culture's codes and practices is a class privilege; it does not mean that the socially operative distinctions between the two spheres have ceased to exist.'

Bourdieu's influence can also be seen in the work of Paul Willis (Reading 50). Willis develops Bourdieu's theory of the 'ideology of natural taste' to argue that dominant culture attempts to locate the majority of the population as 'uncultured': to interpellate them 'as ignorant, insensitive and without the finer sensibilities of those who really "appreciate"'. The ideology of natural taste operates by a disavowal of the role of education (both formal and informal): 'to know without having learnt'. What is the result of education is 'naturalised' as a gift of nature. The effect of the ideology is to make 'culture' appear as nature – as cultivated nature: 'I am *naturally* better than you'. This produces a situation in which people who make culture in their everyday lives see themselves as uncultured. Against the logic of this ideology, Willis argues the case for what he calls 'grounded aesthetics', the process through which ordinary people make cultural sense of the world.

Bourdieu's influence is also evident in the work of John Fiske. In Reading 47 he maintains that the cultural commodities produced by the culture industries, from which popular culture is made, circulate in two simultaneous economies: 'the financial' and 'the cultural'. 'The workings of the financial economy', according to Fiske, 'cannot account adequately for all cultural factors, but it still needs to be taken into account in any investigation.... But the cultural commodity cannot be adequately described in financial terms only: the circulation that is crucial to its popularity occurs in the parallel economy – the cultural.' The financial economy is primarily concerned with exchange value, whereas the cultural is primarily focused on use – 'meanings, pleasures, and social identities'. Although they are separate, there is continual interaction between the two economies.

Fiske's work also acknowledges the influence of Michel de Certeau. Reading 45 is a slightly edited version of de Certeau's 'Introduction' to *The Practice of Everyday Life*. De Certeau's aim is to unpack the term consumer, to reveal the activity which lies within the act of consumption: what he calls 'secondary production'. Consumption 'is devious, it is dispersed, but it insinuates itself everywhere, silently and almost invisibly, because it does not manifest itself through its own products, but rather through its ways of using the products imposed by a dominant economic order'. For de Certeau, the cultural field is a site of continual conflict (silent and almost invisible) between the 'strategy' of cultural imposition (production) and the 'tactics' of cultural use (consumption). The cultural critic must be alert to 'the difference or similarity between ... production ... and ... secondary production hidden in the process of ... utilization'.

The readings by Ien Ang (Reading 48), Michael Schudson (Reading 46), Duncan Webster (Reading 51), and the extract from Jim McGuigan's *Cultural Populism* (Reading 53) all represent particular positions in and accounts of a debate that could be called: 'pessimists v. populists'. The extract from Terry Lovell's very influential *Pictures of Reality* (Reading 44), can also be placed (if before the event) as part of the debate. Each of these readings is on one side or the other of the debate. Some are quite explicit about where they stand; others have to be claimed for one side or the other. The division (to include all the readings in this section) might be presented thus: on the side of the 'pessimists': McGuigan, Schudson; on the side of the 'populists': Willis, Fiske, Ang, de Certeau, Webster; Bourdieu, Hall and Lovell have been claimed by both sides. The balance is rather lopsided, but it does more or less represent the current state of play in the study of popular culture in cultural studies. The focus of the debate is what McGuigan describes as 'an uncritical populist drift in the study of popular culture'. In Reading 53, he focuses on the recent work of Fiske, presented here as a typical example of 'cultural populism'. From the opposite side of the debate, Ang criticises Janice Radway's *Reading the Romance* for establishing an absolute distinction between feminism and romance reading. Ang sees this as 'political moralism, propelled by a desire to make "them" more like "us"'. The readings by Webster (Reading 51) and Schudson (Reading 46) are overviews of the debate from 'positions' within it. Schudson, in a rather agonised account, welcomes what he calls the 'new validation of popular culture' within academia, but is concerned 'that the new study of popular culture now offers a serious challenge to the identity of the modern university'. The crisis for Schudson is one of valuation. In brief, what does studying popular culture do to the study of 'high' or 'elite' culture? He finds himself 'caught' between a belief that the university should be a 'moral educator' and the difficulties of 'defining the basis of moral education'. Webster is much more sanguine. He presents an overview in which the crisis is really a debate between pessimists and optimists, advocates of critical distance and populist celebrators of the popular. Like Ang (Reading 48), Webster sees pleasure as 'the blindspot of much past Marxist and feminist analysis'. He welcomes its introduction into much recent analysis, but thinks it has not gone far enough. It is not enough to celebrate pleasure as 'empowering the consumer'; we must also address the pleasure and the power (usually invisible) of the intellectual gaze.

Simon Frith (Reading 52) refuses to be placed on either side of the binary opposition. He is critical of Fiske's account of popular discrimination. Although he accepts that the culture industries are unable to predict or manipulate popular taste, he rejects the view 'that a market failure is by definition unpopular or that a market success has by definition a popular audience'. He also rejects the populism inherent in such arguments, especially its unthinking dismissal of value judgements, arguing that 'what needs challenging is not the notion of the superior, but the claim that it is the exclusive property of the "high"'.

The debate between 'populists' and 'pessimists' has also reactivated an earlier antagonism between cultural studies and the political economy of culture approach. Nicholas Garnham (Reading 54) and Lawrence Grossberg (Reading 55) present an excellent overview of the main issues at stake.

41 □ *Distinction & The Aristocracy of Culture*

Pierre Bourdieu

Distinction

There is an economy of cultural goods, but it has a specific logic. Sociology endeavours to establish the conditions in which the consumers of cultural goods, and their taste for them, are produced, and at the same time to describe the different ways of appropriating such of these objects as are regarded at a particular moment as works of art, and the social conditions of the constitution of the mode of appropriation that is considered legitimate. But one cannot fully understand cultural practices unless 'culture', in the restricted, normative sense of ordinary usage, is brought back into 'culture' in the anthropological sense, and the elaborated taste for the most refined objects is reconnected with the elementary taste for the flavours of food.

Whereas the ideology of charisma regards taste in legitimate culture as a gift of nature, scientific observation shows that cultural needs are the product of upbringing and education: surveys establish that all cultural practices (museum visits, concert-going, reading, etc.) and preferences in literature, painting or music, are closely linked to educational level (measured by qualifications or length of schooling) and secondarily to social origin.[1] The relative weight of home background and of formal education (the effectiveness and duration of which are closely dependent on social origin) varies according to the extent to which the different cultural practices are recognized and taught by the educational system, and the influence of social origin is strongest – other things being equal – in 'extra-curricular' and avant-garde culture. To the socially recognized hierarchy of the arts, and within each of them, of genres, schools or periods, corresponds a social hierarchy of the consumers. This predisposes tastes to function as markers of 'class'. The manner in which culture has been acquired lives on in the manner of using it: the importance attached to manners can be understood once it is seen that it is these

From Bourdieu, P., *Distinctions: A social critique of the judgement of taste*, Routledge, London, 1984, pp. 1–7, 28–33.

imponderables of practice which distinguish the different – and ranked – modes of culture acquisition, early or late, domestic or scholastic, and the classes of individuals which they characterize (such as 'pedants' and *mondains*). Culture also has its titles of nobility – awarded by the educational system – and its pedigrees, measured by seniority in admission to the nobility.

The definition of cultural nobility is the stake in a struggle which has gone on unceasingly, from the seventeenth century to the present day, between groups differing in their ideas of culture and of the legitimate relation to culture and to works of art, and therefore differing in the conditions of acquisition of which these dispositions are the product.[2] Even in the classroom, the dominant definition of the legitimate way of appropriating culture and works of art favours those who have had early access to legitimate culture, in a cultured household, outside of scholastic disciplines, since even within the educational system it devalues scholarly knowledge and interpretation as 'scholastic' or even 'pedantic' in favour of direct experience and simple delight.

The logic of what is sometimes called, in typically 'pedantic' language, the 'reading' of a work of art, offers an objective basis for this opposition. Consumption is, in this case, a stage in a process of communication, that is, an act of deciphering, decoding, which presupposes practical or explicit mastery of a cipher or code. In a sense, one can say that the capacity to see (*voir*) is a function of the knowledge (*savoir*), or concepts, that is, the words, that are available to name visible things, and which are, as it were, programmes for perception. A work of art has meaning and interest only for someone who possesses the cultural competence, that is, the code, into which it is encoded. The conscious or unconscious implementation of explicit or implicit schemes of perception and appreciation which constitutes pictorial or musical culture is the hidden condition for recognizing the styles characteristic of a period, a school or an author, and, more generally, for the familiarity with the internal logic of works that aesthetic enjoyment presupposes. A beholder who lacks the specific code feels lost in a chaos of sounds and rhythms, colours and lines, without rhyme or reason. Not having learnt to adopt the adequate disposition, he stops short at what Erwin Panofsky calls the 'sensible properties', perceiving a skin as downy or lace-work as delicate, or at the emotional resonances aroused by these properties, referring to 'austere' colours or a 'joyful' melody. He cannot move from the 'primary stratum of the meaning we can grasp on the basis of our ordinary experience' to the 'stratum of secondary meanings', i.e. the 'level of the meaning of what is signified', unless he possesses the concepts which go beyond the sensible properties and which identify the specifically stylistic properties of the work.[3] Thus the encounter with a work of art is not 'love at first sight', as is generally supposed, and the act of empathy, *Einfühlung*, which is the art-lover's pleasure, presupposes an act of cognition, a decoding operation, which implies the implementation of a cognitive acquirement, a cultural code.[4]

This typically intellectualist theory of artistic perception directly contradicts the experience of the art-lovers closest to the legitimate definition; acquisition of legitimate culture by insensible familiarization within the family circle tends to

favour an enchanted experience of culture which implies forgetting the acquisition.[5] The 'eye' is a product of history reproduced by education. This is true of
the mode of artistic perception now accepted as legitimate, that is, the aesthetic
disposition, the capacity to consider in and for themselves, as form rather than
function, not only the work designated for such apprehension, i.e. legitimate
works of art, but everything in the world, including cultural objects which are not
yet consecrated – such as, at one time, primitive arts, or, nowadays, popular
photography or kitsch – and natural objects. The 'pure' gaze is a historical
invention linked to the emergence of an autonomous field of artistic production, that
is, a field capable of imposing its own norms on both the production and the
consumption of its products.[6] An art which, like all Post-Impressionist painting, is
the product of an artistic intention which asserts the primacy of the mode of
representation over the object of representation demands categorically an attention
to form which previous art only demanded conditionally.

The pure intention of the artist is that of a producer who aims to be autonomous,
that is, entirely the master of his product, who tends to reject not only the
'programmes' imposed *a priori* by scholars and scribes, but also – following the old
hierarchy of doing and saying – the interpretations superimposed *a posteriori* on his
work. The production of an 'open work', intrinsically and deliberately polysemic,
can thus be understood as the final stage in the conquest of artistic autonomy by
poets and, following in their footsteps, by painters, who had long been reliant on
writers and their work of 'showing' and 'illustrating'. To assert the autonomy of
production is to give primacy to that of which the artist is master, i.e. form, manner,
style, rather than the 'subject', the external referent, which involves subordination
to functions – even if only the most elementary one, that of representing, signifying,
saying something. It also means a refusal to recognize any necessity other than that
inscribed in the specific tradition of the artistic discipline in question: the shift from
an art which imitates nature to an art which imitates art, deriving from its own
history the exclusive source of its experiments and even of its breaks and tradition.
An art which ever increasingly contains reference to its own history demands to be
perceived historically; it asks to be referred not to an external referent, the
represented or designated 'reality', but to the universe of past and present works of
art. Like artistic production in that it is generated in a field, aesthetic perception is
necessarily historical, inasmuch as it is differential, relational, attentive to the
deviations (*écarts*) which make styles. Like the so-called naïve painter who,
operating outside the field and its specific traditions, remains external to the history
of the art, the 'naïve' spectator cannot attain a specific grasp of works of art which
only have meaning – or value – in relation to the specific history of an artistic
tradition. The aesthetic disposition demanded by the products of a highly
autonomous field of production is inseparable from a specific cultural competence.
This historical culture functions as a principle of pertinence which enables one to
identify, among the elements offered to the gaze, all the distinctive features and only
these, by referring them, consciously or unconsciously, to the universe of possible
alternatives. This mastery is, for the most part, acquired simply by contact with

works of art – that is, through an implicit learning analogous to that which makes it possible to recognize familiar faces without explicit rules or criteria – and it generally remains at a practical level; it is what makes it possible to identify styles, i.e. modes of expression characteristic of a period, a civilization or a school, without having to distinguish clearly, or state explicitly, the features which constitute their originality. Everything seems to suggest that even among professional valuers, the criteria which define the stylistic properties of the 'typical works' on which all their judgements are based usually remain implicit.

The pure gaze implies a break with the ordinary attitude towards the world, which, given the conditions in which it is performed, is also a social separation. Ortega y Gasset can be believed when he attributes to modern art a systematic refusal of all that is 'human', i.e. generic, common – as opposed to distinctive, or distinguished – namely, the passions, emotions and feelings which 'ordinary' people invest in their 'ordinary' lives. It is as if the 'popular aesthetic' (the quotation marks are there to indicate that this is an aesthetic 'in itself' not 'for itself') were based on the affirmation of the continuity between art and life, which implies the subordination of form to function. This is seen clearly in the case of the novel and especially the theatre, where the working-class audience refuses any sort of formal experimentation and all the effects which, by introducing a distance from the accepted conventions (as regards scenery, plot, etc.), tend to distance the spectator, preventing him from getting involved and fully identifying with the characters (I am thinking of Brechtian 'alienation' or the disruption of plot in the *nouveau roman*). In contrast to the detachment and disinterestedness which aesthetic theory regards as the only way of recognizing the work of art for what it is, i.e. autonomous, *selbständig*, the 'popular aesthetic' ignores or refuses the refusal of 'facile' involvement and 'vulgar' enjoyment, a refusal which is the basis of the taste for formal experiment. And popular judgements of paintings or photographs spring from an 'aesthetic' (in fact it is an ethos) which is the exact opposite of the Kantian aesthetic. Whereas, in order to grasp the specificity of the aesthetic judgement, Kant strove to distinguish that which pleases from that which gratifies and, more generally, to distinguish disinterestedness, the sole guarantor of the specifically aesthetic quality of contemplation, from the interest of reason which defines the Good, working-class people expect every image to explicitly perform a function, if only that of a sign, and their judgements make reference, often explicitly, to the norms of morality or agreeableness. Whether rejecting or praising, their appreciation always has an ethical basis.

Popular taste applies the schemes of the ethos, which pertain in the ordinary circumstances of life, to legitimate works of art, and so performs a systematic reduction of the things of art to the things of life. The very seriousness (or naïvety) which this taste invests in fictions and representations demonstrates *a contrario* that pure taste performs a suspension of 'naïve' involvement which is one dimension of a 'quasi-ludic' relationship with the necessities of the world. Intellectuals could be said to believe in the representation – literature, theatre, painting – more than in the things represented, whereas the people chiefly expect representations and the conventions which govern them to allow them to believe 'naïvely' in the things represented. The pure aesthetic is rooted in an ethic, or rather, an ethos of elective distance from the necessities of the natural and social world, which may take the form of moral agnosticism (visible when ethical transgression becomes an artistic *parti pris*) or of an aestheticism which presents the aesthetic disposition as a universally valid principle and takes the bourgeois denial of the social world to its limit. The detachment of the pure gaze cannot be dissociated from a general disposition towards the world which is the paradoxical product of conditioning by negative economic necessities – a life of ease – that tends to induce an active distance from necessity.

Although art obviously offers the greatest scope to the aesthetic disposition, there is no area of practice in which the aim of purifying, refining and sublimating primary needs and impulses cannot assert itself, no area in which the stylization of life, that is, the primacy of forms over function, of manner over matter, does not produce the same effects. And nothing is more distinctive, more distinguished, than the capacity to confer aesthetic status on objects that are banal or even 'common' (because the 'common' people make them their own, especially for aesthetic purposes), or the ability to apply the principles of a 'pure' aesthetic to the most everyday choices of everyday life, e.g. in cooking, clothing or decoration, completely reversing the popular disposition which annexes aesthetics to ethics.

In fact, through the economic and social conditions which they presuppose, the different ways of relating to realities and fictions, of believing in fictions and the realities they simulate, with more or less distance and detachment, are very closely linked to the different possible positions in social space and, consequently, bound up with the systems of dispositions (habitus) characteristic of the different classes and class fractions. Taste classifies, and it classifies the classifier. Social subjects, classified by their classifications, distinguish themselves by the distinctions they make, between the beautiful and the ugly, the distinguished and the vulgar, in which their position in the objective classifications is expressed or betrayed. And statistical analysis does indeed show that oppositions similar in structure to those found in cultural practices also appear in eating habits. The antithesis between quantity and quality, substance and form, corresponds to the opposition – linked to different distances from necessity – between the taste of necessity, which favours the most 'filling' and most economical foods, and the taste of liberty – or luxury – which shifts the emphasis to the manner (of presenting, serving, eating, etc.) and tends to use stylized forms to deny function.

The science of taste and of cultural consumption begins with a transgression that is in no way aesthetic: it has to abolish the sacred frontier which makes legitimate culture a separate universe, in order to discover the intelligible relations which unite apparently incommensurable 'choices', such as preferences in music and food, painting and sport, literature and hairstyle. This barbarous reintegration of aesthetic consumption into the world of ordinary consumption abolishes the opposition, which has been the basis of high aesthetics since Kant, between the 'taste of sense' and the 'taste of reflection', and between facile pleasure, pleasure reduced to a pleasure of the senses, and pure pleasure, pleasure purified of pleasure, which is predisposed to become a symbol of moral excellence and a measure of the capacity for sublimation which defines the truly human man. The culture which results from this magical division is sacred. Cultural consecration does indeed confer, on the objects, persons and situations it touches, a sort of ontological promotion akin to a transubstantiation. Proof enough of this is found in the two following quotations, which might almost have been written for the delight of the sociologist:

'What struck me most is this: nothing could be obscene on the stage of our premier theatre, and the ballerinas of the Opera, even as naked dancers, sylphs, sprites or Bacchae, retain an inviolable purity.'[7]

'There are obscene postures: the simulated intercourse which offends the eye. Clearly, it is impossible to approve, although the interpolation of such gestures in dance routines does give them a symbolic and aesthetic quality which is absent from the intimate scenes the cinema daily flaunts before its spectators' eyes. . . . As for the nude scene, what can one say, except that it is brief and theatrically not very effective? I will not say it is chaste or innocent, for nothing commercial can be so described. Let us say it is not shocking, and that the chief objection is that it serves as a box-office gimmick. . . . In *Hair*, the nakedness fails to be symbolic.'[8]

The denial of lower, coarse, vulgar, venal, servile – in a word, natural – enjoyment, which constitutes the sacred sphere of culture, implies an affirmation of the superiority of those who can be satisfied with the sublimated, refined, disinterested, gratuitous, distinguished pleasures forever closed to the profane. That is why art and cultural consumption are predisposed, consciously and deliberately or not, to fulfil a social function of legitimating social differences.

The Aristocracy of Culture

[. . .]

THE AESTHETIC DISPOSITION   Any legitimate work tends in fact to impose the norms of its own perception and tacitly defines as the only legitimate mode of perception the one which brings into play a certain disposition and a certain competence. Recognizing this fact does not mean constituting a particular mode of perception as an essence, thereby falling into the illusion which is the basis of recognition of artistic legitimacy. It does mean taking note of the fact that all agents, whether they like it or not, whether or not they have the means of conforming to them, find themselves objectively measured by those norms. At the same time it becomes possible to establish whether these dispositions and competences are gifts of nature, as the charismatic ideology of the relation to the work of art would have it, or products of learning, and to bring to light the hidden conditions of the miracle of the unequal class distribution of the capacity for inspired encounters with works of art and high culture in general.

Every essentialist analysis of the aesthetic disposition, the only socially accepted 'right' way of approaching the objects socially designated as works of art, that is, as both demanding and deserving to be approached with a specifically aesthetic intention capable of recognizing and constituting them as works of art, is bound to fail. Refusing to take account of the collective and individual genesis of this product of history which must be endlessly 're-produced' by education, it is unable to reconstruct its sole *raison d'être*, that is, the historical reason which underlies the arbitrary necessity of the institution. If the work of art is indeed, as Panofsky says, that which 'demands to be experienced aesthetically', and if any object natural or artificial, can be perceived aesthetically, how can one escape the conclusion that it is the aesthetic intention which 'makes the work of art', or, to transpose a formula of Saussure's, that it is the aesthetic point of view that creates the aesthetic object? To get out of this vicious circle, Panofsky has to endow the work of art with an 'intention', in the Scholastic sense. A purely 'practical' perception contradicts this objective intention, just as an aesthetic perception would in a sense be a practical negation of the objective intention of a signal, a red light, for example, which requires a 'practical' response: braking. Thus, within the class of worked-upon objects, themselves defined in opposition to natural objects, the class of art objects would be defined by the fact that it demands to be perceived aesthetically, i.e. in terms of form rather than function. But how can such a definition be made operational? Panofsky himself observes that it is virtually impossible to determine scientifically at what moment a worked-upon object becomes an art object, that is, at what moment form takes over from function: 'If I write to a friend to invite him to dinner, my letter is primarily a communication. But the more I shift the emphasis to the form of my script, the more nearly does it become a work of literature or poetry.'[9]

Does this mean that the demarcation line between the world of technical objects and the world of aesthetic objects depend on the 'intention' of the producer of those objects? In fact, this 'intention' is itself the product of the social norms and conventions which combine to define the always uncertain and historically changing frontier between simple technical objects and *objets d'art*: 'Classical tastes', Panofsky observes, 'demanded that private letters, legal speeches and the shields of heroes should be "artistic" . . . while modern taste demands that architecture and ash trays should be "functional".'[10]

But the apprehension and appreciation of the work also depend on the beholder's intention, which is itself a function of the conventional norms governing the relation to the work of art in a certain historical and social situation and also of the beholder's capacity to conform to those norms, i.e. his artistic training. To break out of this circle one only has to observe that the ideal of 'pure' perception of a work of art *qua* work of art is the product of the enunciation and systematization of the principles of specifically aesthetic legitimacy which accompany the constituting of a relatively autonomous artistic field. The aesthetic mode of perception in the 'pure' form which it has now assumed corresponds to a particular state of the mode of artistic production. An art which, like all Post-Impressionist painting, for example, is the product of an artistic intention which asserts the *absolute primacy of form over function*, of the mode of representation over the object represented, *categorically* demands a purely aesthetic disposition which earlier art demanded only conditionally. The demiurgic ambition of the artist, capable of applying to *any* object the pure intention of an artistic effort which is an end in itself, calls for unlimited receptiveness on the part of an aesthete capable of applying the specifically aesthetic intention to any object, whether or not it has been produced with aesthetic intention.

This demand is objectified in the art museum; there the aesthetic disposition becomes an institution. Nothing more totally manifests and achieves the autonomizing of aesthetic activity *vis-à-vis* extra-aesthetic interests or functions than the art museum's juxtaposition of works. Though originally subordinated to quite different or even incompatible functions (crucifix and fetish, Pietà and still life), these juxtaposed works tacitly demand attention to form rather than function, technique rather than theme, and, being constructed in styles that are mutually exclusive but all equally necessary, they are a practical challenge to the expectation of realistic representation as defined by the arbitrary canons of an everyday aesthetic, and so lead naturally from stylistic relativism to the neutralization of the very function of representation. Objects previously treated as collectors' curios or historical and ethnographic documents have achieved the status of works of art, thereby materializing the omnipotence of the aesthetic gaze and making it difficult to ignore the fact that – if it is not to be merely an arbitrary and therefore suspect affirmation of this absolute power – artistic contemplation now has to include a degree of erudition which is liable to damage the illusion of immediate illumination that is an essential element of pure pleasure.

PURE TASTE AND 'BARBAROUS' TASTE   In short, never perhaps has more been asked of the spectator, who is now required to 're-produce' the primary operation whereby the artist (with the complicity of his whole intellectual field) produced this new fetish.[11] But never perhaps has he been given so much in return. The naïve exhibitionism of 'conspicuous consumption', which seeks distinction in the crude display of ill-mastered luxury, is nothing compared to the unique capacity of the pure gaze, a quasi-creative power which sets the aesthete apart from the common herd by a radical difference which seems to be inscribed in 'persons'. One only has to read Ortega y Gasset to see the reinforcement the charismatic ideology derives from art, which is 'essentially unpopular, indeed, anti-popular', and from the 'curious sociological effect' it produces by dividing the public into two 'antagonistic castes', those who understand and those who do not. 'This implies', Ortega goes on, 'that some possess an organ of understanding which others have been denied; that these are two distinct varieties of the human species. The new art is not for everyone, like Romantic art, but destined for an especially gifted minority.' And he ascribes to the 'humiliation' and 'obscure sense of inferiority' inspired by 'this art of privilege, sensuous nobility, instinctive aristocracy', the irritation it arouses in the mass, 'unworthy of artistic sacraments':

> For a century and a half, the 'people', the mass, have claimed to be the whole of society. The music of Stravinsky or the plays of Pirandello have the sociological power of obliging them to see themselves as they are, as the 'common people', a mere ingredient among others in the social structure, the inert material of the historical process, a secondary factor in the spiritual cosmos. By contrast, the young art helps the 'best' to know and recognize one another in the greyness of the multitude and to learn their mission, which is to be few in number and to have to fight against the multitude.[12]

And to show that the self-legitimating imagination of the 'happy few' has no limits, one only has to quote a recent text by Suzanne Langer, who is presented as 'one of the world's most influential philosophers':

> In the past, the masses did not have access to art; music, painting, and even books, were pleasures reserved for the rich. It might have been supposed that the poor, the 'common people', would have enjoyed them equally, if they had had the chance. But now that everyone can read, go to museums, listen to great music, at least on the radio, the judgement of the masses about these things has become a reality and through this it has become clear that great art is not a direct sensuous pleasure. Otherwise, like cookies or cocktails, it would flatter uneducated taste as much as cultured taste.[13]

It should not be thought that the relationship of distinction (which may or may not imply the conscious intention of distinguishing oneself from common people) and is only an incidental component in the aesthetic disposition. The pure gaze implies a break with the ordinary attitude towards the world which, as such, is a social break. One can agree with Ortega y Gasset when he attributes to modern art – which merely takes to its extreme conclusions an intention implicit in art since the Renaissance – a systematic refusal of all that is 'human', by which he means the passions, emotions and feelings which *ordinary* people put into their *ordinary* existence, and consequently all the themes and objects capable of evoking them: 'People like a play when they are able to take an interest in the human destinies put before them', in which 'they participate as if they were real-life events.'[14] Rejecting the 'human' clearly means rejecting what is generic, i.e. *common*, 'easy' and immediately accessible, starting with everything that reduces the aesthetic animal to pure and simple animality, to palpable pleasure or sensual desire. The interest in the content of the representation which leads people to call 'beautiful' the representation of beautiful things, especially those which speak most immediately to the sense and the sensibility, is rejected in favour of the indifference and distance which refuse to subordinate judgement of the representation to the nature of the object repre-sented.[15] It can be seen that it is not so easy to describe the 'pure' gaze without also describing the naïve gaze which it defines itself against, and vice versa; and that there is no *neutral*, impartial, 'pure' description of either of these opposing visions (which does not mean that one has to subscribe to aesthetic relativism, when it is so obvious that the 'popular aesthetic' is defined in relation to 'high' aesthetics and that reference to legitimate art and its negative judgement on 'popular' taste never ceases to haunt the popular experience of beauty). Refusal or privation? It is as dangerous to attribute the coherence′ of a systematic aesthetic to the objectively aesthetic commitments of ordinary people as it is to adopt, albeit unconsciously, the strictly negative conception of ordinary vision which is the basis of every 'high' aesthetic.

Notes

1. Bourdieu *et al.*, *Un art moyen: essai sur les usages sociaux de la photographie* (Paris: Editions de Minuit, 1965); P. Bourdieu and A. Darbel, *L'Amour de l'art: les musées et leur public* (Paris: Editions de Minuit, 1966).
2. The word *disposition* seems particularly suited to express what is covered by the concept of habitus (defined as a system of dispositions) – used later in this chapter. It expresses first the *result of an organizing action*, with a meaning close to that of words such as structure; it also designates a way of being, a habitual state (especially of the body) and, in particular, a *predisposition, tendency, propensity* or *inclination*. [The semantic cluster of 'disposition' is rather wider in French than in English, but as this note – translated literally – shows, the equivalence is adequate. Translator.] P. Bourdieu, *Outline of a Theory of Practice* (Cambridge: Cambridge University Press, 1977), p. 214, n. 1.
3. E. Panofsky, 'Iconography and iconology: an introduction to the study of Renaissance art', in *Meaning in the Visual Arts* (New York: Doubleday, 1955), p. 28.
4. It will be seen that this internalized code called culture functions as cultural capital owing to the fact that, being unequally distributed, it secures profits of distinction.
5. The sense of familiarity in no way excludes the ethnocentric misunderstanding which results from applying the wrong code. Thus, Michael Baxandall's work in historical ethnology enables us to measure all that separates the perceptual schemes that now tend to be applied to *Quattrocento* paintings and those which their immediate addressees applied. The 'moral and spiritual eye' of *Quattrocento* man, that is, the set of cognitive and evaluative dispositions which were the basis of his perception of the world and his perception of pictorial representation of the world, differs radically from the 'pure' gaze (purified, first of all, of reference to economic value) with which the modern cultivated spectator looks at works of art. As the contracts show, the clients of Filippo Lippi, Domenico Ghirlandaio or Piero della Francesca were concerned to get 'value for money'. They approached works of art with the mercantile dispositions of a businessman who can calculate quantities and prices at a glance, and they applied some surprising criteria of appreciation, such as the expense of the colours, which sets gold and ultramarine at the top of the hierarchy. The artists, who shared this world-view, were led to include arithmetical and geometrical devices in their compositions so as to flatter this taste for measurement and calculation; and they tended to exhibit the technical virtuosity which, in this context, is the most visible evidence of the quantity and quality of the labour provided; M. Baxandall, *Painting and Experience in Fifteenth-Century Italy: A primer in the social history of pictorial style* (Oxford: Oxford University Press, 1972).
6. See P. Bourdieu, 'Le marché des biens symboliques', *L'Année Sociologique*, 22 (1973), 49–126; and 'Outline of a social theory of art perception', *International Social Science Journal*, 20 (Winter 1968), 589–612.

7. O. Merlin, 'Mlle. Thibon dans la vision de Marguerite', *Le Monde*, 9 December 1965.

8. F. Chenique, '*Hair* est-il immoral?', *Le Monde*, 28 January 1970.

9. E. Panofsky, *Meaning in the Visual Arts* (New York: Doubleday Anchor Books, 1955), p. 12.

10. *Ibid.*, p. 13.

11. For a more extensive analysis of the opposition between the specifically aesthetic disposition and the 'practical' disposition, and the collective and individual genesis of the 'pure' disposition which genesis-amnesia tends to constitute as 'natural', see P. Bourdieu, 'Disposition esthétique et compétence artistique', *Les Temps Modernes*, 295 (1971), 1345–78, and 'L'invention de la vie d'artiste', *Actes*, 2 (1975), 67–93. For an analysis of the aesthetic *illusio* and of the *collusio* which produces it, see P. Bourdieu, 'The production of belief', *Media, Culture and Society*, 2 (July 1980), 261–93.

12. J. Ortega y Gasset, 'La deshumanización del arte' (1925), in *Obras Completas* (Madrid: Revista de Occidente, 1966), III, 355–6.

13. S. K. Langer, 'On significance in music' in L. A. Jacobus (ed.), *Aesthetics and the Arts* (New York: McGraw-Hill, 1968), pp. 182–212; quotation on p. 183. (One recognizes the Kantian theme – endlessly reinvented even without any conscious reference to Kant – of the antinomy of pure pleasure and the pleasure of the senses, which is analysed in the Postscript.)

14. Ortega y Gasset, 'La deshumanización del arte', pp. 356–7.

15. The 'cultivated' spectator's concern with distinction is paralleled by the artist's concern (which grows with the autonomy of the field of production) to assert his autonomy *vis-à-vis* external demands (of which commissions are the most visible form) and to give priority to form, over which he has full control, rather than function, which leads him, through art for art's sake, i.e. art for artists, to an art of pure form.

42 □ Notes on Deconstructing 'the Popular'

Stuart Hall

First, I want to say something about periodisations in the study of popular culture. Difficult problems are posed here by periodisation – I don't offer it to you simply as a sort of gesture to the historians. Are the major breaks largely descriptive? Do they arise largely from within popular culture itself, or from factors which are outside of but impinge on it? With what other movements and periodisations is 'popular culture' most revealingly linked? Then I want to tell you some of the difficulties I have with the term 'popular'. I have almost as many problems with 'popular' as I have with 'culture'. When you put the two terms together the difficulties can be pretty horrendous.

Throughout the long transition into agrarian capitalism and then in the formation and development of industrial capitalism, there is a more or less continuous struggle over the culture of working people, the labouring classes and the poor. This fact must be the starting point for any study, both of the basis for, and of the transformations of, popular culture. The changing balance and relations of social forces throughout that history reveal themselves, time and again, in struggles over the forms of the culture, traditions and ways of life of the popular classes. Capital had a stake in the culture of the popular classes because the constitution of a whole new social order around capital required a more or less continuous, if intermittent, process of re-education, in the broadest sense. And one of the principal sites of resistance to the forms through which this 'reformation' of the people was pursued lay in popular tradition. That is why popular culture is linked, for so long, to questions of tradition, of traditional forms of life and why its 'traditionalism' has been so often misinterpreted as a product of a merely conservative impulse, backward-looking and anachronistic. Struggle and resistance – but also, of course, appropriation and *ex*-propriation. Time and again, what we are really looking at

From Samuel, R. (ed.), *People's History and Socialist Theory*, Routledge & Kegan Paul, London, 1981, pp. 227–40.

is the active destruction of particular ways of life, and their transformation into something new. 'Cultural change' is a polite euphemism for the process by which some cultural forms and practices are driven out of the centre of popular life, actively marginalised. Rather than simply 'falling into disuse' through the Long March to modernisation, things are actively pushed aside, so that something else can take their place. The magistrate and the evangelical police have, or ought to have, a more 'honoured' place in the history of popular culture than they have usually been accorded. Even more important than ban and proscription is that subtle and slippery customer – 'reform' (with all the positive and unambiguous overtones it carries today). One way or another, 'the people' are frequently the object of 'reform': often, for their own good, of course – 'in their best interests'. We understand struggle and resistance, nowadays, rather better than we do reform and transformation. Yet 'transformations' are at the heart of the study of popular culture. I mean the active work on existing traditions and activities, their active reworking, so that they come out a different way: they appear to 'persist' – yet, from one period to another, they come to stand in a different relation to the ways working people live and the ways they define their relations to each other, to 'the others' and to their conditions of life. Transformation is the key to the long and protracted process of the 'moralisation' of the labouring classes, and the 'demoralisation' of the poor, and the 're-education' of the people. Popular culture is neither, in a 'pure' sense, the popular traditions of resistance to these processes; nor is it the forms which are superimposed on and over them. It is the ground on which the transformations are worked.

In the study of popular culture, we should always start here: with the double stake in popular culture, the double movement of containment and resistance, which is always inevitably inside it.

The study of popular culture has tended to oscillate wildly between the two alternative poles of that dialectic – containment/resistance. We have had some striking and marvellous reversals. Think of the really major revolution in historical understanding which has followed as the history of 'polite society' and the Whig aristocracy in eighteenth-century England has been upturned by the addition of the history of the turbulent and ungovernable people. The popular traditions of the eighteenth-century labouring poor, the popular classes and the 'loose and disorderly sort' often, now, appear as virtually independent formations: tolerated in a state of permanently unstable equilibrium in relatively peaceful and prosperous times; subject to arbitrary excursions and expeditions in times of panic and crisis. Yet though formally these were the cultures of the people 'outside the walls', beyond political society and the triangle of power, they were never, in fact, outside of the larger field of social forces and cultural relations. They not only constantly pressed on 'society'; they were linked and connected with it, by a multitude of traditions and practices. Lines of 'alliance' as well as lines of cleavage. From these cultural bases, often far removed from the dispositions of law, power and authority, 'the people' threatened constantly to erupt; and, when they did so, they broke on to the stage of patronage and power with a threatening din and clamour – with fife and drum, cockade and effigy, proclamation and ritual – and, often, with a striking, popular, ritual discipline. Yet never quite overturning the delicate strands of paternalism, deference and terror within which they were constantly if insecurely constrained. In the following century, when the 'labouring' and the 'dangerous' classes lived without benefit of that fine distinction the reformers were so anxious to draw (this was a *cultural* distinction as well as a moral and economic one: and a great deal of legislation and regulation was devised to operate directly on it), some areas preserved for long periods a virtually impenetrable enclave character. It took virtually the whole length of the century before the representatives of 'law and order' – the new police – could acquire anything like a regular and customary foothold within them. Yet, at the same time, the penetration of the cultures of the labouring masses and the urban poor was deeper, more continuous – and more continuously 'educative' and reformatory – in that period than at any time since.

One of the main difficulties standing in the way of a proper periodisation of popular culture is the profound transformation in the culture of the popular classes which occurs between the 1880s and the 1920s. There are whole histories yet to be written about this period. But although there are probably many things not right about its detail, I do think Gareth Stedman Jones's article on the 'Re-making of the English working class' in this period has drawn our attention to something fundamental and qualitatively different and important about it. It was a period of deep structural change. The more we look at it, the more convinced we become that somewhere in this period lies the matrix of factors and problems from which *our* history – and our peculiar dilemmas – arise. Everything changes – not just a shift in the relations of forces but a reconstitution of the terrain of political struggle itself. It isn't just by chance that so many of the characteristic forms of what we now think of as 'traditional' popular culture either emerge from or emerge in their distinctive modern form, in that period. What has been done for the 1790s and for the 1840s, and is being done for the eighteenth century, now radically needs to be done for the period of what we might call the 'social imperialist' crisis.

The general point made earlier is true, without qualification, for this period, so far as popular culture is concerned. There is no separate, autonomous, 'authentic' layer of working-class culture to be found. Much of the most immediate forms of popular recreation, for example, are saturated by popular imperialism. Could we expect otherwise? How could we explain, and what would we *do* with the idea of, the culture of a dominated class which, despite its complex interior formations and differentiations, stood in a very particular relation to a major restructuring of capital; which itself stood in a peculiar relation to the rest of the world; a people bound by the most complex ties to a changing set of material relations and conditions; who managed somehow to construct 'a culture' which remained untouched by the most powerful dominant ideology – popular imperialism? Especially when that ideology – belying its name – was directed as much at them as it was at Britain's changing position in a world capitalist expansion?

Think, in relation to the question of popular imperialism, of the history and relations between the people and one of the major means of cultural expression: the press. To go back to displacement and superimposition – we can see clearly how the liberal middle-class press of the mid-nineteenth century was constructed on the back of the active destruction and marginalisation of the indigenous radical and working-class press. But, on top of that process, something qualitatively new occurs towards the end of the nineteenth century and the beginning of the twentieth century in this area: the active, mass insertion of a developed and mature working-class audience into a new kind of *popular*, commercial press. This has had profound cultural consequences: though it isn't in any narrow sense exclusively a 'cultural' question at all. It required the whole reorganisation of the capital basis and structure of the cultural industry; a harnessing of new forms of technology and of labour processes; the establishment of new types of distribution operating through the new cultural mass markets. But one of its effects was indeed a reconstituting of the cultural and political relations between the dominant and the dominated classes: a change intimately connected with that containment of popular democracy on which 'our democratic way of life' today appears to be so securely based. Its results are all too palpably with us still, today: a popular press, the more strident and virulent as it gradually shrinks; organised by capital 'for' the working classes; with, nevertheless, deep and influential roots in the culture and language of the 'underdog', of 'Us': with the power to represent the class to itself in its most traditionalist form. This is a slice of the history of 'popular culture' well worth unravelling.

Of course, one could not begin to do so without talking about many things which don't usually figure in the discussion of 'culture' at all. They have to do with the reconstruction of capital and the rise of the collectivism and the formation of a new kind of 'educative' state as much as with recreation, dance and popular song. As an area of serious historical work, the study of popular culture is like the study of labour history and its institutions. To declare an interest in it is to correct a major imbalance, to mark a significant oversight. But, in the end, it yields most when it is seen in relation to a more general, a wider history.

I select this period – the 1880s–1920s – because it is one of the real test cases for the revived interest in popular culture. Without in any way casting aspersions on the important historical work which has been done and remains to do on earlier periods, I do believe that many of the real difficulties (theoretical as well as empirical) will only be confronted when we begin to examine closely popular culture in a period which begins to resemble our own, which poses the same kind of interpretive problems as our own, and which is informed by our own sense of contemporary questions. I am dubious about that kind of interest in 'popular culture' which comes to a sudden and unexpected halt at roughly the same point as the decline of Chartism. It isn't by chance that very few of us are working in popular culture in the 1930s. I suspect there is something peculiarly awkward, especially for socialists, in the non-appearance of a militant radical mature culture of the working class in the 1930s when – to tell you the truth – most of us would have expected it to appear. From the viewpoint of a purely 'heroic' or 'autonomous' popular culture, the 1930s is a pretty barren period. This 'barrenness' – like the earlier unexpected richness and diversity – cannot be explained from *within* popular culture alone.

We have now to begin to speak not just about discontinuities and qualitative change, but about a very severe fracture, a deep rupture – especially in popular culture in the postwar period. Here it is a matter not only of a change in cultural relations between the classes, but of the changed relationship between the people and the concentration and expansion of the new cultural apparatuses. But could one seriously now set out to write the history of popular culture without taking into account the monopolisation of the cultural industries, on the back of a profound technological revolution (it goes without saying that no 'profound technological revolution' is ever in any sense 'purely' technical)? To write a history of the culture of the popular classes exclusively from inside those classes, without understanding the ways in which they are constantly held in relation with the institutions of dominant cultural production, is not to live in the twentieth century. The point is clear about the twentieth century. I believe it holds good for the nineteenth and eighteenth centuries as well.

So much for 'some problems of periodisation'.

Next, I want to say something about 'popular'. The term can have a number of different meanings: not all of them useful. Take the most common-sense meaning: the things which are said to be 'popular' because masses of people listen to them, buy them, read them, consume them, and seem to enjoy them to the full. This is the 'market' or commercial definition of the term: the one which brings socialists out in spots. It is quite rightly associated with the manipulation and debasement of the culture of the people. In one sense, it is the direct opposite of the way I have been using the word earlier. I have, though, two reservations about entirely dispensing with this meaning, unsatisfactory as it is.

First, if it is true that, in the twentieth century, vast numbers of people *do* consume and even indeed enjoy the cultural products of our modern cultural industry, then it follows that very substantial numbers of working people must be included within the audiences for such products. Now, if the forms and relationships on which participation in this sort of commercially provided 'culture' depend are purely manipulative and debased, then the people who consume and enjoy them must either be themselves debased by these activities or else living in a permanent state of 'false consciousness'. They must be 'cultural dopes' who can't tell that what they are being fed is an updated form of the opium of the people. That judgment may make us feel right, decent and self-satisfied about our denunciations of the agents of mass manipulation and deception – the capitalist cultural industries: but I don't know that it is a view which can survive for long as an adequate account of cultural relationships; and even less as a socialist perspective on the culture and nature of the working class. Ultimately, the notion of the people as a purely *passive*, outline force is a deeply unsocialist perspective.

Second, then: can we get around this problem without dropping the inevitable and necessary attention to the manipulative aspect of a great deal of commercial popular culture? There are a number of strategies for doing so, adopted by radical critics and theorists of popular culture, which, I think, are highly dubious. One is to counterpose to it another, whole, 'alternative' culture – the authentic 'popular culture'; and to suggest that the 'real' working class (whatever that is) isn't taken in by the commercial substitutes. This is a heroic alternative; but not a very convincing one. Basically what is wrong with it is that it neglects the absolutely essential relations of cultural power – of domination and subordination – which is an intrinsic feature of cultural relation. I want to assert on the contrary that there is no whole, authentic, autonomous 'popular culture' which lies outside the field of force of the relations of cultural power and domination. Second, it greatly underestimates the power of cultural implantation. This is a tricky point to make, for as soon as it *is* made, one opens oneself to the charge that one is subscribing to the thesis of cultural incorporation. The study of popular culture keeps shifting between these two, quite unacceptable, poles: pure 'autonomy' or total encapsulation.

Actually, I don't think it is necessary or right to subscribe to either. Since ordinary people are not cultural dopes, they are perfectly capable of recognising the way the realities of working-class life are reorganised, reconstructed and reshaped by the way they are represented (i.e. re-presented) in, say, *Coronation Street*. The cultural industries do have the power constantly to rework and reshape what they represent; and, by repetition and selection, to impose and implant such definitions of ourselves as fit more easily the descriptions of the dominant or preferred culture. That is what the concentration of cultural power – the means of culture-making in the heads of the few – actually means. These definitions don't have the power to occupy our minds; they don't function on us as if we are blank screens. But they do occupy and rework the interior contradictions of feeling and perception in the dominated classes; they *do* find or clear a space of recognition in those who respond to them. Cultural domination has real effects – even if these are neither all-powerful nor all-inclusive. If we were to argue that these imposed forms have no influence, it would be tantamount to arguing that the culture of the people can exist as a separate enclave, outside the distribution of cultural power and the relations of cultural force. I do not believe that. Rather, I think there is a continuous and necessarily uneven and unequal struggle, by the dominant culture, constantly to disorganise and reorganise popular culture; to enclose and confine its definitions and forms within a more inclusive range of dominant forms. There are points of resistance; there are also moments of supersession. This is the dialectic of cultural struggle. In our times, it goes on continuously, in the complex lines of resistance and acceptance, refusal and capitulation, which make the field of culture a sort of constant battlefield. A battlefield where no once-for-all victories are obtained but where there are always strategic positions to be won and lost.

This first definition, then, is not a useful one for our purposes; but it might force us to think more deeply about the complexity of cultural relations, about the reality of cultural power and about the nature of cultural implantation. If the forms of provided commercial popular culture are not purely manipulative, then it is because, alongside the false appeals, the foreshortenings, the trivialisation and short circuits, there are also elements of recognition and identification, something approaching a re-creation of recognisable experiences and attitudes, to which people are responding. The danger arises because we tend to think of cultural forms as whole and coherent: either wholly corrupt or wholly authentic. Whereas they are deeply contradictory; they play on contradictions, especially when they function in the domain of the 'popular'. The language of the *Daily Mirror* is neither a pure construction of Fleet Street 'newspeak' nor is it the language which its working class readers actually speak. It is a highly complex species of linguistic *ventriloquism* in which the debased brutalism of popular journalism is skillfully combined and intricate with some elements of the directness and vivid particularity of working-class language. It cannot get by without preserving some element of its roots in a real vernacular – in 'the popular'. It wouldn't get very far unless it were capable of reshaping popular elements into a species of canned and neutralised demotic populism.

The second definition of 'popular' is easier to live with. This is the descriptive one. Popular culture is all those things that 'the people' do or have done. This is close to an 'anthropological' definition of the term: the culture, mores, customs and folkways of 'the people'. What defines their 'distinctive way of life'. I have two difficulties with this definition, too.

First, I am suspicious of it precisely because it is too descriptive. This is putting it mildly. Actually, it is based on an infinitely expanding inventory. Virtually *anything* which 'the people' have ever done can fall into the list. Pigeon-fancying and stamp-collecting, flying ducks on the wall and garden gnomes. The problem is how to distinguish this infinite list, in any but a descriptive way, from what popular culture is *not*.

But the second difficulty is more important – and relates to a point made earlier. We can't simply collect into one category all the things which 'the people' do, without observing that the real analytic distinction arises, not from the list itself – an inert category of things and activities – but from the key opposition: the people/not of the people. That is to say, the structuring principle of 'the popular' in this sense is the tensions and oppositions between what belongs to the central domain of elite or dominant culture, and the culture of the 'periphery'. It is this opposition which constantly structures the domain of culture into the 'popular' and the 'non-popular'. But you cannot construct these oppositions in a purely descriptive way. For, from period to period, the *contents* of each category change. Popular forms become enhanced in cultural value, go up the cultural escalator – and find themselves on the opposite side. Others things cease to have high cultural value, and are appropriated into the popular, becoming transformed in the process. The structuring principle does not consist of the contents of each category – which, I insist, will alter from one period to another. Rather, it consists of the forces and relations which sustain the distinction, the difference: roughly, between what, at any time, counts as an elite cultural activity or form, and what does not. These categories remain, though the inventories change. What is more, a whole set of institutions and institutional processes are required to sustain each – and to continually mark the difference between them. The school and the education system is one such institution – distinguishing the valued part of the culture, the cultural heritage, the history to be transmitted, from the 'valueless' part. The literary and scholarly apparatus is another – marking off certain kinds of valued knowledge from others. The important fact, then, is not a mere descriptive inventory – which may have the negative effect of freezing popular culture into some timeless descriptive mould – but the relations of power which are constantly punctuating and dividing the domain of culture into its preferred and its residual categories.

So I settle for a third definition of 'popular', though it is a rather uneasy one. This looks, in any particular period, at those forms and activities which have their roots in the social and material conditions of particular classes; which have been embodied in popular traditions and practices. In this sense, it retains what is valuable in the descriptive definition. But it goes on to insist that what is essential to the definition of popular culture is the relations which define 'popular culture' in a continuing tension (relationship, influence and antagonism) to the dominant culture. It is a conception of culture which is polarised around this cultural dialectic. It treats the domain of cultural forms and activities as a constantly changing field. Then it looks at the relations which constantly structure this field into dominant and subordinate formations. It looks at the process by which these relations of dominance and subordination are articulated. It treats them as a process: the process by means of which some things are actively preferred so that others can be dethroned. It has at its centre the changing and uneven relations of force which define the field of culture – that is, the question of cultural struggle and its many forms. Its main focus of attention is the relation between culture and questions of hegemony.

What we have to be concerned with, in this definition, is not the question of the 'authenticity' or organic wholeness of popular culture. Actually, it recognises that almost *all* cultural forms will be contradictory in this sense, composed of antagonistic and unstable elements. The meaning of a cultural form and its place or position in the cultural field is *not* inscribed inside its form. Nor is its position fixed once and for ever. This year's radical symbol or slogan will be neutralised into next year's fashion; the year after, it will be the object of a profound cultural nostalgia. Today's rebel folksinger ends up, tomorrow, on the cover of the *Observer* colour magazine. The meaning of a cultural symbol is given in part by the social field into which it is incorporated, the practices with which it articulates and is made to resonate. What matters is *not* the intrinsic or historically fixed objects of culture, but the state of play in cultural relations: to put it bluntly and in an oversimplified form – what counts is the class struggle in and over culture.

Almost every fixed inventory will betray us. Is the novel a 'bourgeois' form? The answer can only be historically provisional: When? Which novels? For whom? Under what conditions?

What that very great Marxist theoretician of language who used the name Volosinov once said about the sign – the key element of all signifying practices –

is true of cultural forms:

> Class does not coincide with the sign community, i.e. with . . . the totality of users of the same sets of signs for ideological communication. Thus various different classes will use one and the same language. As a result, differently oriented accents intersect in every ideological sign. Sign becomes an arena of class struggle. . . . By and large it is thanks to this intersecting of accents that a sign maintains its vitality and dynamism and the capacity for further development. A sign that has been withdrawn from the pressure of the social struggle – which so to speak crosses beyond the pale of the social struggle – inevitably loses force, degenerating into an allegory and becoming the object not of live social intelligibility but of philosophical comprehension. . . . The ruling class strives to impart a supraclass, eternal character to the ideological sign, to extinguish or drive inward the struggle between social value judgements which occurs in it, to make the sign unaccentual. In actual fact, each living ideological sign has two faces, like Janus. Any current curse word can become a word of praise, any current truth must inevitably sound to many people as the greatest lie. This inner dialectic quality of the sign comes out fully in the open only in times of social crisis or revolutionary change.[1]

Cultural struggle, of course, takes many forms: incorporation, distortion, resistance, negotiation, recuperation. Raymond Williams has done us a great deal of service by outlining some of these processes, with his distinction between emergent, residual and incorporated moments. We need to expand and develop this rudimentary schema. The important thing is to look at it dynamically: as an historical process. Emergent forces reappear in ancient historical disguise; emergent forces, pointing to the future, lose their anticipatory power, and become merely backward-looking; today's cultural breaks can be recuperated as a support to tomorrow's dominant system of values and meanings. The struggle continues: but it is almost never in the same place, over the same meaning or value. It seems to me that the cultural process – cultural power – in our society depends, in the first instance, on this drawing of the line, always in each period in a different place, as to what is to be incorporated into 'the great tradition' and what is not. Educational and cultural institutions, along with the many positive things they do, also help to discipline and police this boundary.

This should make us think again about that tricky term in popular culture, 'tradition'. Tradition is a vital element in culture; but it has little to do with the mere persistence of old forms. It has much more to do with the way elements have been linked together or articulated. These arrangements in a national-popular culture have no fixed or inscribed position, and certainly no meaning which is carried along, so to speak, in the stream of historical tradition, unchanged. Not only can the elements of 'tradition' be rearranged, so that they articulate with different practices and positions, and take on a new meaning and relevance. It is also often the case that cultural struggle arises in its sharpest form just at the point where different, opposed traditions meet, intersect. They seek to detach a cultural form from its implantation in one tradition, and to give it a new cultural resonance or accent.

Traditions are not fixed for ever: certainly not in any universal position in relation to a single class. Cultures, conceived not as separate 'ways of life', but as 'ways of struggle', constantly intersect: the pertinent cultural struggles arise at the points of intersection. Think of the ways in the eighteenth century in which a certain language of legality, of constitutionalism and of 'rights' becomes a battleground, at the point of intersection between two divergent traditions: between the 'tradition' of gentry 'majesty and terror' and the traditions of popular justice. Gramsci, providing a tentative answer to his own question as to how a new 'collective will' arises, and a national-popular culture is transformed, observed that

> What matters is the criticism to which such an ideological complex is subjected by the first representatives of the new historical phase. This criticism makes possible a process of differentiation and change in the relative weight that the elements of old ideologies used to possess. What was previously secondary and subordinate, even incidental, is now taken to be primary – becomes the nucleus of a new ideological and theoretical complex. The old collective will dissolves into it contradictory elements since the subordinate ones develop socially.

This is the terrain of national-popular culture and tradition as a battlefield.

This provides us with a warning against those self-enclosed approaches to popular culture which, valuing 'tradition' for its own sake, and treating it in an ahistorical manner, analyse popular cultural forms as if they contained within themselves, from their moment of origin, some fixed and unchanging meaning or value. The relationship between historical position and aesthetic value is an important and difficult question in popular culture. But the attempt to develop some universal popular aesthetic, founded on the moment of origin of cultural forms and practices, is almost certainly profoundly mistaken. What could be more eclectic and random than that assemblage of dead symbols and bric-à-brac, ransacked from yesterday's dressing-up box, in which, just now, many young people have chosen to adorn themselves? These symbols and bits and pieces are profoundly ambiguous. A thousand lost cultural causes could be summoned up through them. Every now and then, amongst the other trinkets, we find that sign which, above all other signs, ought to be fixed – solidified – in its cultural meaning and connotation for ever: the swastika. And yet there it dangles, partly – but not entirely – cut loose from its profound cultural reference in twentieth-century history. What does it mean? What is it signifying? Its signification is rich, and richly ambiguous: certainly unstable. This terrifying sign may delimit a range of meanings, but it carries no guarantee of a single meaning within itself. The streets are full of kids who are not 'fascist' because they may wear a swastika on a chain. On the other hand, perhaps they *could* be. . . . What this sign means will ultimately, depend, in the politics of youth culture, less on the intrinsic cultural symbolism of the thing in itself, and more on the balance of forces between, say, the National Front and the Anti-Nazi League, between White Rock and the Two Tone Sound.

Not only is there no intrinsic guarantee within the cultural sign or form itself.

There is no guarantee that, because at one time it was linked with a pertinent struggle, it will always be the living expression of a class: so that every time you give it an airing it will 'speak the language of socialism'. If cultural expressions register for socialism, it is because they have been linked as the practices, the forms and organisation of a living struggle, which has succeeded in appropriating those symbols and giving them a socialist connotation. Culture is not already permanently inscribed with the conditions of a class before that struggle begins. The struggle consists in the success or failure to give 'the cultural' a socialist accent.

The term 'popular' has very complex relations to the term 'class'. We know this, but are often at pains to forget it. We speak of particular forms of working-class culture; but we use the more inclusive term 'popular culture' to refer to the general field of enquiry. It's perfectly clear that what I've been saying would make little sense without reference to a class perspective and to class struggle. But it is also clear that there is no one-to-one relationship between a class and a particular cultural form or practice. The terms 'class' and 'popular' are deeply related, but they are not absolutely interchangeable. The reason for that is obvious. There are no wholly separate 'cultures' paradigmatically attached, in a relation of historical fixity, to specific 'whole' classes – although there are clearly distinct and variable class-cultural formations. Class cultures tend to intersect and overlap in the same field of struggle. The term 'popular' indicates this somewhat displaced relationship of culture to classes. More accurately, it refers to that alliance of classes and forces which constitute the 'popular classes'. The culture of the oppressed, the excluded classes: this is the area to which the term 'popular' refers us. And the opposite side to that – the side with the cultural power to decide what belongs and what does not – is, by definition, not another 'whole' class, but that other alliance of classes, strata and social forces which constitute what is not 'the people' and not the 'popular classes': the culture of the power bloc.

The people versus the power bloc: this, rather than 'class-against-class', is the central line of contradiction around which the terrain of culture is polarised. Popular culture, especially, is organised around the contradiction: the popular forces versus the power bloc. This gives to the terrain of cultural struggle its own kind of specificity. But the term 'popular', and even more, the collective subject to which it must refer – 'the people' – is highly problematic. It is made problematic by, say, the ability of Mrs Thatcher to pronounce a sentence like 'We have to limit the power of the trade unions because that is what the people want.' That suggests to me that, just as there is no fixed content to the category of 'popular culture', so there is no fixed subject to attach to it – 'the people'. 'The people' are not always back there, where they have always been, their culture untouched, their liberties and their instincts intact, still struggling on against the Norman yoke or whatever: as if, if only we can 'discover' them and bring them back on stage, they will always stand up in the right, appointed place and be counted. The capacity to *constitute* classes and individuals as a popular force – that is the nature of political and cultural struggle: to *make* the divided classes and the separated peoples – divided and separated by culture as much as by other factors – *into* a popular-democratic cultural force.

We can be certain that other forces also have a stake in defining 'the people' as something else: 'the people' who need to be disciplined more, ruled better, more effectively policed, whose way of life needs to be protected from 'alien cultures', and so on. There is some part of both those alternatives inside each of us. Sometimes we can be constituted as a force against the power bloc: that is the historical opening in which it is possible to construct a culture which is genuinely popular. But, in our society, if we are not constituted like that, we will be constituted into its opposite: an effective populist force, saying 'Yes' to power. Popular culture is one of the sites where this struggle for and against a culture of the powerful is engaged: it is also the stake to be won or lost in that struggle. It is the arena of consent and resistance. It is partly where hegemony arises, and where it is secured. It is not a sphere where socialism, a socialist culture – already fully formed – might be simply 'expressed'. But it is one of the places where socialism might be constituted. That is why 'popular culture' matters. Otherwise, to tell you the truth, I don't give a damn about it.

Note

1. A. Volosinov, *Marxism and the Philosophy of Language*, New York, 1977.

43 □ Cultural Entrepreneurship in Nineteenth-Century Boston: The Creation of an Organizational Base for High Culture in American

Paul DiMaggio

Sociological and political discussions of culture have been predicated on a strong dichotomy between high culture – what goes on in museums, opera houses, symphony halls and theatres – and popular culture, of both the folk and commercial varieties. Such culture critics as Dwight Mcdonald (1957 and Reading 3) and Theodor Adorno (1941 and Reading 20) have based on this dichotomy thorough-going critiques of popular culture and the mass media. Defenders of popular culture (Lowenthal, 1961; Gans, 1974) have questioned the normative aspect of the critique of popular culture, but have, for the most part, accepted the basic categories. The distinction between high and popular culture has. been implicit, as well, in the discussion of public policy towards culture in both the United States and Great Britain (DiMaggio and Useem, 1978).

Yet high and popular culture can be defined neither by qualities inherent to the work of art, nor, as some have argued, by simple reference to the class character of their publics. The distinction between high and popular culture, in its American version, emerged in the period between 1850 and 1900 out of the efforts of urban elites to build organizational forms that, first, isolated high culture and, second, differentiated it from popular culture. Americans did not merely adopt available European models. Instead they groped their way to a workable distinction. Not until two distinct organizational forms – the private or semi-private, non-profit cultural institution and the commercial popular-culture industry – took shape did the high/popular-culture dichotomy emerge in its modern form. Once these organizational models developed, the first in the bosom of elite urban status communities, the second in the relative impersonality of emerging regional and national markets, they shaped the rôle that cultural institutions would play, the careers of artistes, the nature of the works created and performed, and the purposes and publics that cultural organizations would serve.

In this paper I will address only one side of this process of classification, the institutionalization of high culture and the creation of distinctly high-cultural organizations. While high culture could be defined only in opposition to popular culture, it is the process by which urban elites forged an institutional system embodying their ideas about the high arts that will engage us here. In order to grasp the extent to which the creation of modern high-cultural institutions was a task that involved elites as an organic group, we will focus on that process in one American city. Boston in the nineteenth century was the most active center of American culture; and its elite– the Boston Brahmins – constituted the most well defined status group of any of the urban upper classes of this period. For this reason the processes with which I am concerned appear here in particularly clear relief.[1]

When we look at Boston before 1850 we see a culture defined by the pulpit, the lectern and a collection of artistic efforts, amateurish by modern standards, in which effort rarely was made to distinguish between art and entertainment, or between culture and commerce. The arts in Boston were not self-conscious; they drew few boundaries. While intellectuals and ministers distinguished culture that elevated the spirit from that which debased it, there was relatively little agreement on what works or genres constituted which (see Hatch, 1962; Harris, 1966). Harvard's Pierian Sodality mixed popular songs with student compositions and works by European fine-arts composers. The Philharmonic Society played classical concerts, but also backed visiting popular vocalists. Throughout this period, most of Boston music was in the hands of commercial entrepreneurs. Gottlieb Graupner, the city's leading impresario in the 1830s, sold sheet music and instruments, published songs and promoted concerts at which religious, classical and popular tunes mingled freely. (One typical performance included a bit of Italian opera, a devotional song by Mrs Graupner, a piece by Verdi, 'Bluebell of Scotland' and 'The Origin of Common Nails', recited by Mr Bernard, a comedian.) The two exceptions, the Handel and Haydn Society and the Harvard Musical Association, founded in the 1840s and 1850s respectively, were associations of amateurs and professionals that appealed only to a relatively narrow segment of the elite.

The visual arts were also organized on a largely commercial basis in this era. In the 1840s, the American Art Union sold paintings by national lottery (Lynnes, 1953). These lotteries were succeeded, in Boston, New York and Philadelphia, by private galleries. Museums were modelled on Barnum's (Barnum, 1879; Harris, 1973): fine art was interspersed among such curiosities as bearded women and mutant animals, and popular entertainments were offered for the price of admission to a clientele that included working people as well as the upper middle class. Founded as a commercial venture in 1841, Moses Kemball's Boston Museum exhibited works by such painters as Sully and Peale alongside Chinese curiosities, stuffed animals, mermaids and dwarves. For the entrance fee visitors could also attend the Boston Museum Theatre, which presented works by Dickens and Shakespeare as well as performances by gymnasts and contortionists, and brought to Boston the leading players of the American and British stage (McGlinchee, 1940). The promiscuous combination of genres that later would be considered incompatible was not uncommon. As late as the 1880s, American circuses employed Shakespearian clowns who recited the bard's lines in full clown make-up (Fellows and Freeman, 1936).

By 1910, high and popular culture were encountered far less frequently in the same settings. The distinction towards which Boston's clerics and critics had groped 50 years before had emerged in institutional form. The Boston Symphony Orchestra was a permanent aggregation, wresting the favor of Boston's upper class decisively from the commercial and co-operative ensembles with which it first competed. The Museum of Fine Arts, founded in 1873, was at the center of the city's artistic life, its exhibitions complemented by those of Harvard and the eccentric Mrs Gardner. Music and art critics might disagree on the merits of individual conductors or painters; but they were united in an aesthetic ideology that distinguished sharply between the nobility of art and the vulgarity of mere entertainment. The distinction between true art, distributed by not-for-profit corporations managed by artistic professionals and governed closely by prosperous and influential trustees, and popular entertainment, sponsored by entrepreneurs and distributed via the market to whomever would buy it, had taken a form that has persisted to the present. So, too, had the social distinctions that would differentiate the publics for high and popular culture.

The sacralization of art, the definition of high culture and its opposite, popular culture and the institutionalization of this classification, was the work of men and women whom I refer to as *cultural capitalists*. I use the term in two senses to describe the capitalists (and the professionals whose wealth came from the participation of their families in the industrial ventures – textiles, railroads and mining – of the day) who founded the museums and the symphony orchestras that embodied and elaborated the high-cultural ideal. They were capitalists in the sense that their wealth came from the management of industrial enterprises from which they extracted a profit, and cultural capitalists in that they invested some of these profits in the foundation and maintenance of distinctly cultural enterprises. They also – and this is the second sense in which I use the term – were collectors of what Bourdieu has called 'cultural capital', knowledge and familiarity with styles and genres that are socially valued and that confer prestige upon those who have mastered them (Bourdieu and Passeron, 1977, 1979). It was the vision of the founders of the institutions that have become, in effect, the treasuries of cultural capital upon which their descendants have drawn that defined the nature of cultural capital in American society.[2]

To create an institutional high culture, Boston's upper class had to accomplish three concurrent, but analytically distinct, projects: entrepreneurship, classification and framing. By entrepreneurship, I mean the creation of an organizational form that members of the elite could control and govern. By classification, I refer to the erection of strong and clearly defined boundaries between art and entertainment, the definition of a high art that elites and segments of the middle class could appropriate as their own cultural property; and the acknowledgment of that classification's legitimacy by other classes and the state. Finally, I use the term framing to refer to the development of a new etiquette of appropriation, a new relationship between the audience and the work of art.[3]

The Predecessors: Organizational Models Before the Gilded Age

By the close of the Civil War, Boston was in many ways the hub of America's cultural life. But, as Martin Green (1966) has illustrated, the unity of the city's economic and cultural elite, the relative vibrancy of Harvard and the vitality of the communal cultural associations of the elite – the Handel and Haydn Society, the Athenaeum, the Dante Circle, the singing clubs – made Boston unique among America's cities. Godkin called Boston 'the one place in America where wealth and the knowledge of how to use it are apt to coincide' (ibid.: 41).

Yet at the close of the Civil War, Boston lacked the organizational arrangements that could sustain a public 'high culture' distinct and insulated from more popular forms. As we have seen, the boundaries between high art and mass art were poorly drawn; artists and performers had not yet segmented elite and popular markets. It is not that the wealthy were uninterested in art. Henry Lee Higginson, later head of the Lee, Higginson brokerage house and founder of the Boston Symphony Orchestra, could reminisce of his not atypical student days in Cambridge in the mid-1850s:

> we had been to the Italian opera, getting there seats for twenty-five cents in the upper gallery enjoying it highly. I had an inborn taste for music which was nourished by a few concerts in Boston and by the opera (Perry, 1921: 29).

His wife recollected

> There were private theatricals, sometimes in German, there was a German class, and there were readings which finished with a delightful social gathering in the evening. He [Higginson] belonged to a private singing club in Boston, and often went to James Savage's room in Holworthy, where there was much informal singing and music (ibid.: 81).

Many young Brahmins, like Higginson, spent time in Europe, studying art or music (e.g. Adams, 1928). And many more learned and played music in or around Boston (Whipple, n.d.), or attended public lectures on the arts.

Nor was there a lack of theories about the nature of good art. Although aesthetic philosophies blossomed after the high-culture institutions were established, even the mid-1850s nurtured aesthetic philosophers like Brook Farmer John S. Dwight, editor of *Dwight's Journal of Music*. Some Bostonians were aware of the latest developments in European music and acquainted with classical standards in the visual arts.

High culture (and by this I mean a strongly classified, consensually defined body of art distinct from 'popular' fare) failed to develop in Boston prior to the 1870s because the organizational models through which art was distributed were not equipped to define and sustain such a body and a view of art. Each of the three major models for organizing the distribution of aesthetic experience before 1870 – the for-profit firm, the co-operative enterprise and the communal association – was flawed in some important way.

The problems of the privately owned, for-profit firm are most obvious. As Weber (1968, vol. 2, sec. 9: 937) has argued, the market declassifies culture: presenters of cultural events mix genres and cross boundaries to reach out to larger audiences. The Boston Museum, founded in the 1840s, mixed fine art and sideshow oddities, Shakespeare and theatrical ephemerata. For-profit galleries exhibited art as spectacle: when James Jackson Jarves showed his fine collection of Italian primitives at Derby's Institute of Fine Arts in New York, 'the decor of this ... dazzlingly ornate commercial emporium ... caused much more favorable comment than Jarves' queer old pictures' (Burt, 1977: 57).

If anything, commerce was even less favorable to the insulation of high art in the performance media. Fine-art theatre in Boston never seems to have got off the ground. And the numerous commercial orchestras that either resided in or toured Boston during this period mixed fine-arts and light music indiscriminately. A memoir of the period recalls a concert of the Germania Society (one of the better orchestras of this type):

> One of the numbers was the 'Railway Gallop', – composer forgotten – during the playing of which a little mock steam-engine kept scooting about the floor of the hall, with black cotton wool smoke coming out of the funnel.

The same writer describes the memorable

> evening when a fantasia on themes from Wallace's 'Maritana' was played as a duet for mouth harmonica and the Great Organ; a combination, as the program informed us, 'never before attempted in the history of music!' (William F. Apthorp, quoted in Howe, 1914).

As with the visual arts, the commercial treatment of serious music tended to the extravagant rather than to the sacred. In 1869, an entrepreneur organized a Peace Jubilee to celebrate the end of the Civil War. A structure large enough to accommodate 30,000 people was built (at what would later be the first site of the Museum of Fine Arts) and 'star' instrumentalists and vocalists were contracted to perform along with an orchestra of 1000 and a chorus of 10,000. As a finale, the orchestra (which included 330 strings, 75 drums and 83 tubas) played the anvil chorus with accompaniment from a squadron of firemen beating anvils, and the firing of live cannon (Fisher, 1918: 45–6).

An alternative form of organization, embraced by some musical societies, was the workers' co-operative, in which each member had a vote, shared in the profits of the enterprise and elected a conductor from among their number.[4] The co-operative was vulnerable to market incentives. Perhaps more important, however, it was (also like its privately owned counterpart) unable to secure the complete allegiance of its members, who supported themselves by playing many different kinds of music in a wide range of settings. The early New York Philharmonic, for example, performed as a group only monthly. Members anticipated the concert

> as a pleasant relief from more remunerative occupational duties, and the rehearsal periods were cluttered up with routine business matters, from which members could absent themselves with relative impunity (Mueller, 1951: 41).

The lines dividing non-profit, co-operative, for-profit and public enterprise were not as strong in the nineteenth century as they would become in the twentieth. Civic-minded guarantors might hold stock in commercial ventures with no hope of gaining a profit (e.g. Symphony Hall at the end of the century). The goals of the charitable corporation were usually defined into its charter, but otherwise it legally resembled its for-profit counterpart. Even less clearly defined was what I call the voluntary association: closed associations of individuals (sometimes incorporated, sometimes not) to further the aims of the participating members, rather than of the community as a whole. For associations like the Handel and Haydn Society, which might give public concerts, or the Athenaeum, which took an active rôle in public affairs, privateness was relative. But, ultimately, each was a voluntary and exclusive instrument of its members.

Why were these communal associations ill-suited to serve as the organizational bases for high culture in Boston? Why could the Athenaeum, a private library, or the Boston Art Club, which sponsored contemporary art shows (Boston Art Club, 1878), not have developed continuous programs of public exhibitions? Could not the Handel and Haydn Society, the Harvard Musical Association (formed by Harvard graduates who wished to pursue after graduation musical interests developed in the College's Pierian Sodality) or one of the numerous singing circles have developed into a permanent orchestra? They faced no commercial temptations to study, exhibit or perform any but the highest art. (Indeed, the Harvard Musical Association's performances were so austere as to give rise to the proverb 'dull as a symphony concert' (Howe, 1914: 8).)

None of them, however, could, by the late nineteenth century, claim to speak for the community as a whole, even if they chose to. Each represented only a fraction (although, in the case of Athenaeum, a very large and potent fraction) of the elite; and, in the case of the musical associations and the Art Club, members of the middle class and artistic professionals were active as well. The culture of an elite status group must be monopolized, it must be legitimate and it must be sacralized. Boston's cultural capitalists would have to find a form able to achieve all these aims: a single organizational base for each art form; institutions that could claim to serve the community, even as they defined the community to include only the elite and the upper-middle classes; and enough social distance between artist and audience, between performer and public, to permit the mystification necessary to define a body of artistic work as sacred.

This they did in the period between 1870 and 1900. By the end of the century, in art and music (but not in theatre [see Twentieth Century Club, 1919; Poggi, 1968]), the differences between high- and popular-culture artists and performers were becoming distinct, as were the physical settings in which high and popular art were presented.

The form that the distribution of high culture would take was the non-profit corporation, governed by a self-perpetuating board of trustees who, eventually, would delegate most artistic decisions to professional artists or art historians (Zolberg, 1974, 1981). The charitable corporation was not designed to define a high culture that elites could monopolize; nor are non-profit organizations by their nature exclusive. But the non-profit corporation had five virtues that enabled it to play a key role in this instance. First, the corporation was a familiar and successful tool by which nineteenth-century elites organized their affairs (see Fredrickson, 1965; Story, 1980; Hall, forthcoming). In the economic realm it enabled them to raise capital for such profitable ventures as the Calumet and Hecla Mines, the western railroads and the telephone company. In the non-profit arena, it had been a useful instrument for elite communal governance at Harvard, the Massachusetts Central Hospital and a host of charitable institutions (Story, 1980). Second, by entrusting governance decisions to trustees who were committed either to providing financial support or to soliciting it from their peers, the non-profit form effectively (if not completely) insulated museums and orchestras from the pressures of the market. Third, by vesting control in a well integrated social and financial elite, the charitable corporation enabled its governors to rule without interference from the state or from other social classes. Fourth, those organizations whose trustees were able to enlist the support of the greater part of the elite could provide the stability needed for a necessarily lengthy process of defining art and developing ancillary institutions to insulate high-cultural from popular-cultural work, performance and careers. Finally, and less obviously, the goals of the charitable corporation, unlike those of the profit-seeking firm, are diffuse and ambiguous enough to accommodate a range of conflicting purposes and changing ends. The broad charters of Boston's major cultural organizations permitted their missions to be redefined with time, and enabled their governors to claim (and to believe) that they pursued communitarian goals even as they institutionalized a view and vision of art that made elite culture less and less accessible to the vast majority of Boston's citizens.

The Context of Cultural Capitalism

In almost every literate society, dominant status groups or classes eventually have developed their own styles of art and the institutional means of supporting them. It was predictable that this would happen in the United States, despite the absence of an hereditary aristocracy. It is more difficult, however, to explain the timing of this process. Dwight and others wished (but failed) to start a permanent professional symphony orchestra from at least the 1840s. The Athenaeum's proprietors tried to raise a public subscription to purchase the Jarves collection in the late 1850s, but they failed. What had changed?

Consider, first, the simple increase in scale and wealth between 1800 and 1870. At the time of the revolution, Boston's population was under 10,000. By 1800 it had risen to 25,000; by 1846 it was 120,000. By 1870, over a quarter of a million people lived in Boston (Lane, 1975). The increase in the size of the local cultural market facilitated a boom in theatre building in the 1830s (Nye, 1960: 264), a rise in the number and stability of book and music stores (Fisher, 1918: 30) and the growth of markets for theatre, music, opera, dancing and equestrian shows (Nye, 1960: 143). The growth of population was accompanied by an increase in wealth. Boston's first fortunes were mercantile, the fruits of the China trade, large by local, but small by national standards. In 1840, Boston had but a handful of millionaires. By 1890, after post-Civil War booms in railroads, mining, banking and communications, there were 400 (Jaher, 1968, 1972; Story, 1980). Even the physical scale of the city changed during this period: beginning in 1856, developers began filling in the waters of the Back Bay, creating a huge tract of publicly owned land partially devoted to civic and cultural buildings. As wealthy outlanders from Lawrence, Lynn and Lexington migrated to Beacon Hill and Cambridge, streetcars reduced the cost and the difficulty of travel to Boston from its suburbs (Warner, 1970). In short, Boston was larger, wealthier and more compact in 1870 than it had been 50 years before.

With growth came challenges to the stability of the community and to the cultural authority (Starr, forthcoming) of elites. Irish immigrants flowed into Boston from the 1840s to work in the city's industrial enterprises (Handlin, 1972; Thernstrom, 1972); industrial employment rôles doubled between 1845 and 1855 (Handlin, 1972). With industry and immigration came disease, pauperism, alcoholism, rising infant mortality and vice. The Catholic Irish were, by provenance and religion, outside the consensus that the Brahmins had established. By 1900, 30% of Boston's residents were foreign-born and 70% were of foreign parentage (Green, 1966: 102). By the close of the Civil War, Boston's immigrants were organizing to challenge the native elite in the political arena (Solomon, 1956).

If immigration and industrialization wrought traumatic changes in the city's social fabric, the political assault on Brahmin institutions by native populists proved even more frightening. The Know-Nothings who captured state government in the 1850s attacked the social exclusivity of Harvard College frontally, amending its charter and threatening state control over its governance, hiring and admissions policies (Story, 1980). Scalded by these attacks, Boston's leadership retreated from the public sector to found a system of non-profit organizations that permitted them to maintain some control over the community even as they lost their command of its political institutions.[5]

Story (1980) argues persuasively that this political challenge, and the wave of institution-building that followed it, transformed the Brahmins from an elite into a social class.[6] As a social class, the Brahmins built institutions (schools, almshouses and charitable societies) aimed at securing control over the city's social life (Huggins, 1971; Vogel, 1981). As a status group, they constructed organizations (clubs, prep schools and cultural institutions) to seal themselves off from their increasingly unruly environment. Thus Vernon Parrington's only partially accurate observation that 'The Brahmins conceived the great business of life to be the erection of barriers against the intrusion of the unpleasant' (quoted in Shiverick, 1970: 129). The creation of a network of private institutions that could define and monopolize high art was an essential part of this process of building cultural boundaries.

The Brahmin class, however, was neither large enough to constitute a public for large-scale arts organizations, nor was it content to keep its cultural achievements solely to itself. Alongside of, and complicating, the Brahmins' drive towards exclusivity was a conflicting desire, as they saw it, to educate the community. The growth of the middle class during this period – class that was economically and socially closer to the working class and thus in greater need of differentiating itself from it culturally – provided a natural clientele for Boston's inchoate high culture. While we have all too little information about the nature of the visitors to Boston's Museum or of the audiences for the Symphony, it seems certain from contemporary accounts (and sheer arithmetic) that many of them were middle class. The same impulse that created the markets for etiquette and instruction books in the mid-nineteenth century helped populate the galleries and concert halls of the century's last quarter (Nye, 1960; Douglas, 1978).

Cultural Entrepreneurship: The Museum of Fine Arts and the Boston Symphony Orchestra

The first step in the creation of a high culture was the centralization of artistic activities within institutions controlled by Boston's cultural capitalists. This was accomplished with the foundings of the Museum of Fine Arts and the Boston Symphony Orchestra. These institutions were to provide a framework, in the visual arts and music, respectively, for the definition of high art, for its segregation from popular forms and for the elaboration of an etiquette of appropriation.

Bostonians had sought to found a museum for some time before 1870. In 1858, the state legislature, dominated by factions unfriendly to Boston's elite, refused to provide Back Bay land for a similar venture (Harris, 1962: 548). The immediate impetus for the Museum, however, was a bequest by Colonel Timothy Bigelow Lawrence of an armor collection too large for the Athenaeum's small gallery to accommodate. Three years earlier the Athenaeum's Fine Arts Committee had suggested that the galleries be expanded, but nothing had been done. With the

Lawrence bequest, and his widow's offer to contribute a wing to a new gallery, the trustees voted that

> the present is a proper time for making an appeal to the public and especially to the friends of the Fine Arts, to raise the sum required to make available Mrs. Lawrence's proposed donation, and, if possible, to provide even larger means to carry out so noble a design in the confident hope that it may be attended with success ... (Whitehill, 1970: 6–8).

A new museum promised to solve problems for several of Boston's elite institutions: Harvard had a collection of prints for which it sought a fire-safe depository, and MIT and the American Social Science Association possessed collections of architectural casts too large for them to store conveniently. After a series of meetings between the Athenaeum trustees and other public and private decision makers, it was decided to raise money for a museum on a tract of land in the Back Bay. (The land, owned by the Boston Water Power Company, was made available through the intervention of Mathias Denman Ross, a local developer who was keenly aware of the effects of public and cultural buildings on the value of nearby real estate.) In 1870 the state legislature chartered the enterprise and, with the help of the Athenaeum, which sponsored exhibitions throughout this period, fund-raising began.[7]

The initial aspirations of the Museum founders were somewhat modest. The key figure in the founding was Charles Callahan Perkins, great-nephew of a China-trade magnate, kinsmen of the chairman of the Athenaeum's Fine Arts Committee and himself President of the Boston Art Club. Perkins wrote two books on Italian sculpture in the 1860s, championed arts education in Boston's public schools and served as head of the American Social Science Association's arts-education panel in 1869. (He had studied painting and sculpture in Europe for almost 10 years before concluding that he lacked the creativity to be a good artist.) Perkins, in a report to the ASSA had asserted 'the feasibility of establishing a regular Museum of Art at moderate expense', with primarily educational aims. Since Boston's collections had few originals, he recommended that the new collection consist of reproductions, primarily plaster casts of sculpture and architecture.

The breadth of response to the first appeal for funds for the museum is striking. Although the economy was not robust, $261,425 was collected for the building. Of this amount, the largest gift was $25,000, only two were larger than $5000 and all but $100,000 came from over 1000 gifts of less than $2000 from such sources as local newspapers, public school teachers and workers at a piano factory. (By contrast, when the Museum sought to raise $400,000 for new galleries and an endowment 15 years later, $218,000 of the initial $240,000 in contributions came from a mere 58 donors (Whitehill, 1970: 42).)

One reason for the breadth of early support was that the Museum, although in private hands, was to be a professedly communitarian and educational venture.

The Board of Trustees contained a large segment of the Brahmin class: All but one of the first 23 trustees were proprietors of the Athenaeum; 11 were members of the Saturday Club, while many others were members of the Somerset and St Botolph's clubs; most were graduates of Harvard and many were active in its affairs. The public nature of the Board was further emphasized by the inclusion on it of permanent and *ex-officio* appointments: from Harvard, MIT and Athenaeum; the Mayor, the Chairman of the Boston Public Library's board, the trustee of the Lowell Institute, the Secretary of the State Board of Education and the Superintendent of Boston's schools. The trustees dedicated the institution to education; one hoped that the breadth of the board's membership would ensure that the Museum's managers would be 'prevented from squandering their funds upon the private fancies of would-be connoisseurs'. Indeed, the articles of incorporation required that the Museum be open free of charge at least four times a month. The public responded by flooding the Museum on free weekend days in the early years (Harris, 1962: 48–52).

The centralization of the visual arts around a museum required only the provision of a building and an institution controlled by a board of civic-minded members of the elite. The Museum functioned on a relatively small budget in its early years, under the direction of Charles Greely Loring, a Harvard graduate and Civil War general, who had studied Egyptology when his physician sent him to the banks of the Nile. The Museum's founders, facing the need to raise substantial funds, organized both private and public support carefully, mobilizing a consensus in favor of their project from the onset.

By contrast, the Boston Symphony Orchestra was, for its first years at least, a one-man operation, forced to wrest hegemony over Boston's musical life from several contenders, each with its own coterie of elite support. That Henry Lee Higginson, a partner in the brokerage firm of Lee, Higginson, was able to do so was a consequence of the soundness of his organizational vision, the firmness of his commitment, and, equally important, his centrality to Boston's economic and social elite.

In a sense, Higginson began as a relative outsider. Although his father, founder of the family firm, made a fortune in shipping, Henry was the first of his line to matriculate at Harvard; and soon he dropped out (claiming poor vision), visiting Europe and returning to private tutelage in Cambridge. Upon completing his education, he studied music in Europe for several years, ultimately against the wishes of his father, as their tense and sometimes acrimonious correspondence suggests (Perry, 1921: 121–35). After an accident lamed his arm, he returned to the United States for good, fought in the Civil War, married a daughter of the Harvard scientist Louis Agassiz and, following a disastrous venture in southern farming and a lucrative investment in the Calumet and Hecla copper mines, finally joined his father's State Street firm.[8]

Higginson was a knowledgeable student of music, and a follower of the aesthetic doctrines of John S. Dwight. As early as 1840, Dwight had called for the founding of a permanent orchestra in Boston, 'This promises something', he wrote of an amateur performance.

> We could not but feel that the materials that evening collected might, if they could be kept together through the year, and induced to practice, form an orchestra worthy to execute the grand works of Haydn and Mozart .... To secure these ends might not a plan of this kind be realized? Let a few of our most accomplished and refined musicians institute a series of cheap instrumental concerts .... Let them engage to perform quartettes, etc., occasionally a symphony, by the best masters and no others. Let them repeat the best and most characteristic pieces enough to make them a study to the audiences (Howe, 1914: 4–5).

As we have seen, a number of ensembles attempted to realize Dwight's ambitions. But it was Higginson's organizational skills (and his money) that gave Boston the nation's first permanent, philanthropically supported and governed, full-season symphony orchestra. In achieving the dream of a large permanent orchestra devoted to fine-arts music, Higginson faced and overcame two challenges: first, establishing control over fine-arts music in Boston as a whole; and, second, enforcing internal discipline over the orchestra's members. Against him were arrayed the supporters of Boston's existing ensembles, principally the Philharmonia and the Harvard Musical Association, and the city's musicians, jealous of their personal and professional autonomy.

Higginson published his plans for the orchestra in a column, headed 'In the Interest of Good Music', that appeared in several of Boston's newspapers:

> Notwithstanding the development of musical taste in Boston, we have never yet possessed a full and permanent orchestra, offering the best music at low prices, such as may be found in all the large European cities .... The essential condition of such orchestras is their stability, whereas ours are necessarily shifting and uncertain, because we are dependent upon musicians whose work and time are largely pledged elsewhere. To obviate this difficulty the following plan is offered. It is an effort made simply in the interest of good music, and though individual in as much as it is independent of societies or clubs, it is in no way antagonistic to any previously existing musical organization (Howe, 1914: 41).

In this last sentence, Higginson treads on delicate ground. He goes on to praise, specifically, the Handel and Haydn Society and the Harvard Musical Association, the two musical societies with the closest Brahmin connections, while indicating implicitly that there will be no further need for the services of the latter. To launch this new enterprise, Higginson proposes to spend, annually, $20,000 of his own money until the orchestra becomes self-supporting.

Despite a measure of public incredulity, and some resentment at Higginson's choice of European conductor, George Henschel, over local candidates, the BSO opened in December 1881 to the enthusiastic response of the musical public. (The demand for tickets was great; lines formed outside the box office the evening before they went on sale.) The social complexion of the first night's audience is indicated by a report in a Boston newspaper that 'the spirit of the music so affected the audience that when the English national air was recognized in Weber's Festival Overture, the people arose en masse and remained standing until the close'. By employing local musicians and permitting them to play with the Philharmonic Society and the Harvard Musical Association (both of which, like the BSO, offered about 20 concerts that season), Higginson earned the gratitude of the city's music lovers.

The trouble began in February 1882, when the players received Higginson's terms for the following season. To continue to work for the Symphony, they would be required to make themselves available for rehearsals and performances from October through April, four days a week, and to play for no other conductor or musical association. (The Handel and Haydn Society, which had strong ties to the Athenaeum, was exempted from this prohibition.) The implications of the contract, which the players resisted unsuccessfully, were clear: Boston's other orchestras, lacking the salaries that Higginson's subsidies permitted, would be unable to compete for the services of Boston's musicians. (To make matters worse, a number of the city's journeymen musicians received no offers from Higginson at all.)

The response of the press, particularly of the Brahmin *Transcript*, suggests that loyalists of the other ensembles responded to Higginson's actions with outrage. The *Transcript* editorialized of Higginson

> He thus 'makes a corner' in orchestral players, and monopolizes these for his own concerts and those of the Handel and Haydn Society .... Mr. Higginson's gift becomes an imposition, it is something that we must receive, or else we look musical starvation in the face. It is as if a man should make a poor friend a present of several baskets of champagne and, at the same time, cut off his whole water supply.

A more populist newspaper complained that the 'monopoly of music' was 'an idea that could scarcely have emanated from any association except that of deluded wealth with arrant charlatanism'. Even *Music*, a New York publication originally friendly to Higginson's efforts, called his contract

> a direct stab at the older organizations and rival conductors of Boston. It means that one or two organizations may make efforts to place their concerts on the off days which Mr. Henschel has been pleased to allow them, but some must be left in the cold, orchestraless and forlorn .... The manner in which the proposal was made was also one that forbodes tyranny. Some of the oldest members of the Orchestra, men whose services to music in Boston have entitled them to deference and respect, were omitted altogether, and will be left out of the new organization. It was intimated strongly that in case the offer was rejected by the men, their places would be filled from the ranks of European orchestras (Howe, 1914: 67–9).

Higginson and his orchestra weathered the storm. Attendance stayed up and, within a year, his was the only orchestral association in Boston, co-existing peacefully with the smaller Handel and Haydn Society. In order to achieve the kind of ensemble he desired, however, Higginson had to ensure that his musicians would commit their time and their attention to the BSO alone, and accept his (and his agent's, the conductor's) authority as inviolate. Since, in the past, all musicians, whatever their affiliations, were freelancers upon whom no single obligation weighted supreme, accomplishing these aspirations required a fundamental change in the relationship between musicians and their employers.

In part, effecting this internal monopolization of attention was simply a matter of gaining an external monopoly of classical-music performance. With the surrender of the Philharmonic Society and the Harvard Musical Association, two major competitors for the working time of Boston's musicians disappeared. Nonetheless, while his musicians were now more dependent upon the BSO for their livelihoods, and thus more amenable to his demands, his control over the work force was still challenged by the availability of light-music or dance engagements, teaching commitments and the tradition of lax discipline to which the players were accustomed.

Throughout his life, Higginson fought to maintain control over the Orchestra's employees, and the issue of discipline was foremost in his mind from the beginning. In an early plan for the Orchestra, he suggested engaging a conductor and eight to ten exceptionally good younger musicians from outside Boston at a fixed salary, 'who would be ready at my call to play anywhere, and then to draw around them the best of our Boston musicians, thus refreshing and renewing the present orchestra, and getting more nearly possession of it ...' (Howe, 1914: 28). At that time, exclusive employment contracts were so rare that the more timid Henschel, after agreeing to serve as conductor, tried to convince Higginson to abandon his insistence on total commitment. 'I assure you', he wrote as the first orchestra was being assembled,

> that is the best thing we can do, and if you have any confidence in my judgement, pray drop all conditions in the contract except those relating to our own welfare. I mean now the conditions of discipline, etc. (Perry, 1921: 299).

Despite his frequent assertions that he yielded in all cases to his conductors' advice on orchestral matters, Higginson, as we have seen, insisted on exclusive contracts in the orchestra's second year, threatening to break any strike with the importation of European players. Although he won that battle, he nonetheless replaced the locals gradually, over the course of the next decade, with new men with few Boston ties, mostly European, of greater technical accomplishment, upon whose loyalty he could count (Howe, 1914: 121–3).

In this, Higginson was not merely following a European model. 'My contracts', he wrote an associate in 1888, 'are very stong, indeed much stronger than European contracts usually are ...' (Perry, 1921: 398). Characteristic of the orchestra contract was section 12:

> If said musician fails to play to the satisfaction of said Higginson, said Higginson may dismiss said musician from the Orchestra, paying his salary to the time of dismissal,

and shall not be liable to pay him any compensation or damages for such dismissal (Perry, 1921: 398).

Higginson was undeniably an autocrat. In later years he rejected the suggestions of friends to place the Orchestra under a board of trustees; and he used the threat of discontinuing his annual subventions as a bludgeon to forestall the unionization of the players. Yet Higginson accomplished what all orchestras would have to achieve if orchestral work was to be separated permanently from the playing of popular music and Dwight's dream of a permanent orchestra devoted to high-art music achieved: the creation of a musical work force, under exclusive contract, willing to accept without question the authority of the conductor.

The Brahmins as an Organization-Forming Class

The Museum of Fine Arts and the Boston Symphony Orchestra were both organizations embedded in a social class, formal organizations whose official structure was draped around the ongoing life of the group that governed, patronized, and staffed them.[9] They were not separate products of different segments of an elite; or of artists and critics who mobilized wealthy men to bankroll their causes. Rather they were the creations of a densely connected self-conscious social group intensely unified by multiple ties among its members based in kinship, commerce, club life and participation in a wide range of philanthropic associations. Indeed, if, as Stinchcombe (1965) has argued, there are 'organization-forming organizations' – organizations that spawn off other organizations in profusion – there are also organization-forming status groups and the Brahmins were one of these. This they could be not just because of their cultural or religious convictions (to which Green (1966), Baltzell (1979) and Hall (forthcoming) have called attention), but because they were integrated by their families' marriages, their Harvard educations, their joint business ventures, their memberships in a web of social clubs and their trusteeships of charitable and cultural organizations. This integration is exemplified in the associations of Higginson, and in the ties between the Museum and the Orchestra during the last 20 years of the nineteenth century.

It is likely that Higginson's keen instinct for brokerage – and the obligations he accrued as principal in one of Boston's two major houses – served him well in his efforts to establish the Orchestra. At first glance Higginson's achievement in creating America's first elite-governed permanent symphony orchestra in Boston appears to be the work of a rugged individualist. On closer inspection, we see that it was precisely Higginson's centrality to the Brahmin social structure that enabled him to succeed. Only a lone, centrally located entrepreneur could have done what Higginson did, because to do so ruffled so many feathers: a committee would have compromised with the supporters of other musical associations and with the patrons of the more established local musicians. Nonetheless, if Higginson's youthful marginality permitted the attempt, it was his eventual centrality that enabled him to succeed. His career illustrates the importance of kinship, commerce, clubs and philanthropy in Boston elite life. Ties in each of these areas reinforced those in the others; each facilitated the success of the Orchestra, and each brought him into close connection with the cultural capitalists active in the MFA and led, eventually, to his selection as a Museum trustee.

Higginson was born a cousin to some of the leading families in Boston: the Cabots, the Lowells, the Perkinses, the Morses, the Jacksons, the Channings and the Paines, among others (Perry, 1921: 14). (The first four of these families produced trustees of the Museum of Fine Arts during Higginson's lifetime. His kinsmen Frances W. Higginson was also a Museum trustee.) In Cambridge, he was close to Charles Lowell and, after his first European adventure, he studied with Samuel Eliot, a cousin of Harvard President Charles W. Eliot, and later a trustee of the Museum. During this period, he spent a great deal of time in the salon-like household of Louis Agassiz, befriending the scientist's son and marrying his daughter. So close did Henry remain to his Harvard classmates that, despite his withdrawal after freshman year, they permitted him to take part in their class's Commencement exercises.

When Henry went into business, he brought his family and college ties with him. A contemporary said of the Lee, Higginson firm, it 'owed in some measure to family alliances its well-advised connections with the best financial enterprises of the day' (Perry, 1921: 272). Indeed, Higginson's first successful speculation was his investment in the Calumet and Hecla mines, at the behest of his in-laws Agassiz and Shaw (the latter an early donor of paintings to the Museum). The family firm was instrumental in the development of the western railroads, through the efforts of cousin Charles Jackson Paine. In this enterprise, Higginson associated with John M. Forbes and with Charles H. Perkins (kinsmen of the MFA founder). Higginson was so intimate with the latter that he invested Perkins' money without consultation. Lee, Higginson made a fortune in the telephone company, and Higginson, in later years, was a director of General Electric. In some of these ventures, the firm co-operated with other Boston financiers. Higginson was on close terms with his competitors Kidder of Kidder, Peabody (the Museum's first treasurer) and Endicott, President of the New England Trust and Suffolk Savings (and the Museum's second treasurer). Gardiner Martin Lane was a partner in Lee, Higginson when he resigned his position to assume the Museum's presidency in 1907.

Higginson was also an active clubman, a member of the Tavern Club (and its President for twenty years), the Wednesday Evening Club, the Wintersnight, Friday Night and Officers Clubs, New York's Knicker-bocker Club and, from 1893, the Saturday Club. Among his Tavern Club colleagues were Harvard's Charles Eliot Norton (spiritual godfather of the Museum's aesthetes), William Dean Howells and Henry Lee. At the Friday Club he consorted with Howells, William James and Henry Adams. At the Saturday Club, his clubmates included the MFA's Thomas Cold Appleton and Martin Brimmer.

In the 1890s, Higginson's career in Boston philanthropy blossomed. (By now he was on the MFA's Board. Earlier, when the Museum's first President, Martin Brimmer, asked Charles Eliot Norton if Higginson should be invited, Norton wrote back that 'Higginson would be excellent, but he never attends meetings' (Harris, 1962: 551).) He lavished most of his attention (beyond that devoted to the Orchestra) on Harvard, which elected him a Fellow in 1893. He gave Harvard Soldiers Field and a new student union, was Treasurer of Radcliffe College, played a key rôle in the founding of the Graduate School of Business, patronized the medical school and gave anonymous gifts to deserving faculties.[10] Higginson's position as Fellow of Harvard placed him at the summit of Boston's institutional life and undoubtedly reinforced his contacts with the Museum's trustees and friends. His personal art collection, which included Turners, Corots and Rodins, encouraged such interactions as well. (In 1893, he donated a valuable Dutch master to the MFA.)

Thus was the Orchestra's founder embedded in the Brahmin community. When Lee, Higginson furnished an emergency loan of $17,000 to the Museum of Fine Arts in 1889, with little prospect of repayment, was this because he was on the Board; was it a consequence of Higginson's kinship ties with the Cabots, Perkinses or Lowells; his business alliances with Kidder or Endicott; his club friendship with Norton; Harvard ties to the Eliots? The range of possibilities renders the question trivial and illustrates how closely knit was Higginson's world.

In 1893, when Higginson demanded that Boston build him a new and suitable Symphony Hall, lest he abandon the Orchestra to bankruptcy and dissolution, the initial appeal for funds was signed by a broad cross section of the city's elite: his friends and kinsmen Agassiz, Lodge, Lowell, Lee and John Lowell Gardner; Harvard's Eliot, Norton, Longfellow, Shattuck and Parkman; Peabody of Kidder Peabody, to name a few. Present on the list were at least four of Higginson's fellow MFA trustees: the President (Martin Brimmer), the Treasurer (by now, John L. Gardner), Eliot and Norton.[11] The group raised over $400,000, a substantial stake in that financially troubled year.

Conclusions

The Museum of Fine Arts and the Boston Symphony Orchestra were creations of the Brahmins, and the Brahmins alone. As such, their origins are easier to understand than were British or Continental efforts in which aristocrats and bourgeoisie played complex and interrelated rôles (Wolff, 1982). The Brahmins were a status group, and as such they strove towards exclusivity, towards the definition of a prestigious culture that they could monopolize as their own. Yet they were also a social class, and they were concerned, as is any dominant social class, with establishing hegemony over those they dominated. Some Marxist students of culture have misinterpreted the cultural institutions as efforts to dictate taste or to inculcate the masses with the ideas of elites. Certainly, the cultural capitalists, consummate organizers and intelligent men and woman, were wise enough to understand the impossibility of socializing the masses in institutions from which they effectively were barred. Their concern with education, however, was not simply window-dressing or an effort at public relations. Higginson, for example, devoted much of his fortune to American universities and secondary schools. He once wrote a kinsmen, from whom he sought a donation of $100,000 for Harvard, 'Educate, and save ourselves and our families and our money from the mobs!' (Perry, 1921: 329). Moreover, a secret or thoroughly esoteric culture could not have served to legitimate the status of American elites; it would be necessary to share it, at least partially. The tension between monopolization and hegemony, between exclusivity and legitimation, was a constant counterpoint to the efforts at classification of American urban elites.

This explains, in part, the initial emphasis on education at the Museum of Fine Arts. Yet, from the first, the Museum managers sought to educate through distinguishing true from vulgar art – at first, cautiously, later with more confidence. In the years that followed they would place increased emphasis on the original art that became available to them, until they abandoned reproductions altogether and with them their emphasis on education. In a less dramatic way, the Orchestra, which began with an artistic mandate, would further classify the contents of its programs and frame the aesthetic experience in the years to come.

In structure, however, the Museum and the Orchestra were similar innovations. Each was private, controlled by members of the Brahmin class, and established on the corporate model, dependent on private philanthropy and relatively long-range financial planning; each was sparely staffed and relied for much of its management on elite volunteers; and each counted among its founders wealthy men with considerable scholarly or artistic credentials who were centrally located in Boston's elite social structure. The Museum was established under broad auspices for the education of the community as a whole; the Orchestra was created by one man in the service of art and of those in the community with the sophistication or motivation to appreciate it. Within 40 years, the logic of cultural capitalism would moderate sharply, if not eliminate, these historically grounded differences. The Symphony would come to resemble the Museum in charter and governance, and the Museum would abandon its broad social mission in favor of aestheticism and an elite clientele.

The creation of the MFA, the BSO and similar organizations throughout the United States created a base through which the ideal of high culture could be given institutional flesh. The alliance between class and culture that emerged was defined by, and thus inseparable from, its organizational mediation. As a consequence, the classification 'high culture/popular culture' is comprehensible only in its dual sense as characterizing both a ritual classification and the organizational systems that give that classification meaning.

Notes

1. The process, in other American cities, was to a large extent influenced by the Boston

model. A final, more mundane, consideration recommends Boston as the focus for this study. The work in this paper is still in an exploratory stage at which I am plundering history rather than writing it; the prolixity of nineteenth-century Boston's men and women of letters and the dedication and quality of her local historians makes Boston an ideal site for such an enterprise

2. In a third sense, 'cultural capital' might refer to the entrepreneurs of popular culture – the Barnums, the Keiths, the Shuberts and others – who turned culture into profits. While we will not consider this group at any length we must remember that it was in opposition to their activities that the former defined their own.

3. My debt to Bernstein (1975*a, b*) and to Mary Douglas (1966) is evident here. My use of the terms 'classification' and 'framing' is similar to Bernstein's

4. See Couch (1976*a, b*) and Mueller (1951: 37ff.) for more detailed descriptions of this form.

5. Shiverick (1970) notes the contrast between the founding of the public library in the 1850s and that of the private art museum 20 years later, both enterprises in which Athenaeum members were central.

6. I use the term 'class' to refer to a self-conscious elite united by bonds of economic interest, kinship and culture (see Thompson, 1966: 8; Story, 1980: xi).

7. This section relies heavily upon Walter Muir Whitehill's classic two-volume history of the Museum (1970) and, to a lesser extent, on Neil Harris' fine paper (1962) for its facts, albeit not for their interpretation.

8. In Henry Adams' words, 'Higginson, after a desperate struggle, was forced into State Street' (Adams, 1928: 210). In later years, Higginson told a relative that 'he never walked into 44 State Street without wanting to sit down on the doorstep and cry' (Perry, 1921: 135).

9. In James Thompson's terms, they were organizations whose resource dependencies all coincided. For their financial support, for their governance and for their clients, they looked to a class whose members were 'functionally interdependent and interact[ed] regularly with respect to religious, economic, recreational, and governmental matters' (Thompson, 1967: 27).

10. Higginson, whose vision extended beyond Boston, also gave generously to Princeton, Williams, the University of Virginia and Middlesex, and sent the Orchestra to play, at his expense, at Williams, Princeton and Yale.

11. Higginson's relationship with Gardner and his mildly scandalous wife Isabella Stewart Gardner, is revealing. When Isabella, a New Yorker, entered Boston society in the 1880s, she was accorded a frosty reception. According to Morris Carter, her biographer and the first Director of her collection, she won social acceptance by employing the BSO to entertain at one of her parties (Carter, 1925), an action that would have required Higginson's approval. After her palace opened (more or less) to the public in 1909, Higginson presented her with a book compiled by her admirers (Green, 1966: 112).

Acknowledgements

For advice and encouragement I am indebted to Randall Collins, David Karen, Michael Schudson, Ann Swidler and to the members of Professor Mary Douglas's

'Mass Media and Mythology' seminar at the New York University Institute for the Humanities, of Theda Skocpol's graduate research seminar at Harvard University and of Paul Hirsch's production-of-culture session at the 1980 Sociology and the Arts conference in Chicago. Research and institutional support from the Andrew W. Mellon Foundation and from Yale University's Program on Non-Profit Organizations is gratefully acknowledged.

REFERENCES

Adams, H., *The Education of Henry Adams: An Autobiography*, New York: Book League of America, 1928.

Adorno, T. W., 'On popular music', *Studies in Philosophy and Social Science*, vol. 9, no. 1 [in this volume as Reading 20], 1941.

Baltzell, E. D., *Puritan Boston and Quaker Philadelphia*, New York, Free Press, 1979.

Barnum, P. T., *Struggles and Triumphs; or Forty Years Recollections*, Buffalo, New York: The Courier Company, 1879.

Bernstein, B., 'On the classification and framing of educational knowledge', in *Class, Codes and Control*, vol. 3, London: Routledge and Kegan Paul, 1975a.

Bernstein, B., 'Ritual in education', in *Class, Codes and Control*, vol. 3, London: Routledge and Kegan Paul, 1975b.

Boston Art Club, *Constitution and By-Laws of the Boston Art Club, With a Sketch of its History*, Boston: E. H. Trulan, 1878.

Bourdieu, P. and Passeron, J.-C., *Reproduction in Education, Society and Culture*, Beverly Hills: Sage, 1977.

Bourdieu, P. and Passeron, J.-C., *The Inheritors: French students and their relation to culture*, Chicago: University of Chicago Press, 1979.

Burt, N., *Palaces for the People*, Boston: Little, Brown and Co., 1977.

Carter, M., *Isabella Stewart Gardner and Fenway Court*, Boston: Houghton Mifflin, 1925

Couch, S. R., 'Class, politics and symphony orchestras', *Society*, vol. 14, no. 1, 1976a.

Couch, S. R., The symphony orchestra in London and New York: some political considerations, presented at the Third Annual Conference on Social Theory and the Arts, Albany, New York, 1976b.

DiMaggio, P. and Useem, M., 'Cultural property and public policy: emerging tensions in government support for the arts', *Social Research*, vol. 45, Summer, 1978.

Douglas, A., *The Feminization of American Culture*, New York: Avon, 1978.

Douglas, M., *Purity and Danger: An analysis of pollution and taboo*, London: Routledge and Kegan Paul, 1966.

Fellows, D. W. and Freeman, A. A., *This Way to the Big Show: The life of Dexter Fellows*, New York: Viking Press, 1936.

Fisher, W. A., *Notes on Music in Old Boston*, Boston: Oliver Ditson, 1918.

Fredrickson, G. M., *The Inner Civil War: Northern intellectuals and the crisis of the union*, New York: Harper and Row, 1965.

Gans, H. J., *Popular Culture and High Culture*, New York: Basic Books, 1974.

Green, M., *The Problem of Boston*, New York: Norton, 1966.

Hall, P. D., *Institutions and the Making of American Culture*, Westport, Connecticut: Greenwood (forthcoming).

Handlin, O., *Boston's Immigrants, 1790-1880*, New York: Atheneum, 1972.

Harris, N., 'The Gilded Age rivisited: Boston and the museum movement', *American Quarterly*, vol. 14, Winter, 1962.

Harris, N., *The Artist in American Society: The formative years, 1790–1860*, New York: George Braziller, 1966.

Harris, N., *Humbug: The art of P. T. Barnum*, Boston: Little, Brown and Co., 1973.

Hatch, C., 'Music for America: a cultural controversy of the 1850s', *American Quarterly*, vol. 14, Winter, 1962.

Howe, M. A. D., *The Boston Symphony Orchestra: An historical Sketch*, Boston: Houghton Mifflin, 1914.

Huggins, N. J., *Protestants against Poverty: Boston's charities, 1870–1900*, Westport, CO: Greenwood, 1971.

Jaher, F. C., 'The Boston Brahmins in the age of industrial capitalism', in Jaher, F. C. (ed.), *The Age of Industrialism in America*, New York: Oxford University Press, 1968.

Jaher, F. C., 'Nineteenth-century elites in Boston and New York', *Journal of Social History*, vol. 6, Spring, 1972.

Lane, R., *Policing the City: Boston, 1822–85*, New York: Atheneum, 1975.

Lowenthal, L., *Literature, Popular Culture, and Society*, Englewood Cliffs: Prentice-Hall, 1961.

Lynnes, T., *The Tastemakers*, New York: Grosset and Dunlap, 1953.

McDonald, D., 'A theory of mass culture', in Rosenberg, B. and White, D. M. (eds), *Mass Culture: The popular arts in America*, Glencoe, IL: Free Press [in this volume as Reading 3], 1957.

McGlinchee, C., *The First Decade of the Boston Museum*, Boston: Bruce Humphries, 1940.

Mueller, J. H., *The American Symphony Orchestra: A social history of musical taste*, Bloomington: Indiana University Press, 1951.

Nye, R. B., *The Cultural Life of the New Nation, 1776–1830*, New York: Harper and Row, 1960.

Perry, B., *Life and Letters of Henry Lee Higginson*, Boston: Atlantic Monthly Press, 1921.

Poggi, J., *Theater in America: The impact of economic forces, 1870–1967*, Ithaca: Cornell University Press, 1968.

Ryan, K., *Old Boston Museum Days*, Boston: Little, Brown and Co., 1915.

Shiverick, N. C., 'The social reorganization of Boston', in Williams, A. W., *A Social History of the Greater Boston Clubs*, New York: Barre, 1970.

Solomon, B. M., *Ancestors and Immigrants*, New York: John Wiley, 1956.

Starr, P., *The Social Transfomation of American Medicine*, New York: Basic Books, 1983.

Stinchcombe, A. L., 'Social structure and organizations', in March, J. G. (ed.), *Handbook of Organizations*, Chicago: Rand McNally, 1965.

Story, R., *The Forging of an Aristocracy: Harvard and the Boston upper class, 1800–1870*, Middletown, CO: Wesleyan University Press, 1980.

Thernstrom, S., *Poverty and Progress: Social mobility in a nineteenth-century city*, New York: Atheneum, 1972.

Thompson, E. P., *The Making of the English Working Class*, New York: Random House, 1966.

Thompson, J. D., *Organizations in Action*, New York: McGraw-Hill, 1967.

Twentieth Century Club, *The Amusement Situation in Boston*, Boston, 1910.

Vogel, M., *The Invention of the Modern Hospital*, Chicago: University of Chicago Press, 1981.

Warner, S. B., *Streetcar Suburbs: The process of growth in Boston, 1870–1900*, New York: Atheneum, 1970

Weber, M., *Economy and Society*, 3 volumes, New York: Bedminster Press, 1968.

Whipple, G. M., *A Sketch of Musical Societies of Salem*, Salem, MA: Essex Institute (n.d.).

Whitehill, W. M., *Museum of Fine Arts, Boston: A centennial history*, Cambridge: Harvard University Press, 1970.

Wolff, J. 'The problem of ideology in the sociology of art: a case study of Manchester in the nineteenth century', *Media, Culture and Society*, vol. 4. no. 1, 1982.

Zolberg, V. L., 'The art institute of Chicago: the sociology of a cultural institution', Ph.D. Dissertation, Department of Sociology, University of Chicago, 1974.

Zolberg, V. L., 'Conflicting visions of American art museums', *Theory and Society*, vol. 10, January, 1981.

44 □ Cultural Production

Terry Lovell

[...]

ii Cultural Production and the Commodity Form

With the penetration of capital into cultural production, the product is transformed into a commodity. As such, cultural production shares features with *all* capitalist commodity production, and the most appropriate starting point for a Marxist analysis of cultural production might be Marx's own categories for the analysis of capitalist commodity production. These are *use-value, value, exchange-value, surplus-value*, and *commodity fetishism*. Commodities have a double existence, as repositories of use-value and of value. Use-value, the utility or usefulness of a commodity to its consumer, depends on the ability of the commodity to satisfy some human want. Marx's concept of what is not limited to material needs. He says that wants 'may spring from the stomach or from the fancy'. In most cases when the commodity is used, it is also used *up*. The use-value of a commodity is realised only when it is consumed, or used.

The *value* of a commodity depends not on its usefulness, but on the amount of socially necessary labour time which has been expended in its production. The value which a commodity has is realised only when the commodity is exchanged. The rate at which one commodity exchanges for another on the market is its *exchange-value*. This also depends on the amount of socially necessary labour time which each commodity embodies. Money is that commodity which is used as a measure of value and means of exchange.

Cultural artifacts are commodities of a peculiar kind, in part precisely because they satisfy wants which spring from the fancy, not the stomach, while Marx's own analysis was based on the latter kind of want satisfaction. They are unlike material wants, in that the commodities which satisfy them are not always used up when they

From Lovell, T., *Pictures of Reality*, British Film Institute, London, 1983, pp. 57–63.

are used to satisfy that want. Commodities which satisfy material wants vary, it is true, in the extent to which their use involves consumption, or using up. Houses last much longer than motor cars, which in turn are used up on a much longer time scale than, say, food. But in each case there is some relationship between the amount of use and the commodities wearing out. Cultural artifacts vary in the extent to which their usefulness in satisfying wants which 'spring from the fancy' is bound up with physical form. Such artifacts, such as paintings or sculptures, wear out over a very long time, and there is no direct connection between their use and their being used up. The *Mona Lisa* does not wear out more quickly when viewed by a hundred people rather than one person in the course of a day. Its physical deterioration depends on the conditions under which it is exhibited rather than the number of viewers. Other cultural forms are less closely tied to particular physical forms. For instance, a poem or a song can be learned and repeated, and cannot be used up no matter how often it is used to satisfy some want. The more frequently it is used, the greater its power of survival. The disc on which the song is recorded is the commodity form in this case, but want satisfaction may be independent of this form. The song can be transferred on to a tape, and serve equally well.

These differences between commodities of different kinds were not analysed by Marx, nor systematically by any subsequent Marxists. Yet they have consequences for the development of the commodity form in cultural production. Some of these consequences may be seen in the difficulties which capitalism has in placing essential marks of ownership upon such commodities, through copyright and its protection, difficulties which are compounded by certain forms of mechanical reproduction, as witness recent attempts to control illicit taping of records. The problem stems ultimately from the lack of intrinsic connection between the usefulness to the consumer of a particular type of cultural artifact, and the physical form of commodity under which it is sold. This example indicates the need for an investigation of the effects of the transformation of cultural products into commodities, the difficulty of pinning down cultural product to commodity form.

iii Cultural Production and Left Pessimism

The use-value of a commodity cannot be known in advance of investigation of actual use of that commodity. Marx has very little to say about the use-value of commodities, with the exception of the commodity labour-power. The reason for Marx's neglect is capitalism's own indifference. Capitalist commodity production is *per se* interested only in the production of *surplus-value*. The extent to which the production and sale of cultural products as commodities can generate surplus-value depends on their value-form and not their use-value. Their value-form depends on the labour they contain, not the use to which they are put. Of course commodities must also be repositories of use-value, otherwise they would not sell. The capitalist producer is keenly interested in the proliferation of wants which will lead consumers to seek out the commodities sold to satisfy those wants.

The focus on the transformation of cultural production into capitalist commodity production is not new, but has usually been associated with 'left pessimism' in the history of Marxism, for instance that of the Frankfurt School. Cultural production, from a left pessimist point of view, is the production of shoddy goods, once culture is transformed into commodities. It is argued that the constraints of reaching the largest possible market places a premium on blandness, inoffensiveness, the lowest common denominator of public taste.[1] Left pessimism cannot cull much support for this view from the writings of Marx, however. As we have seen, the capitalist producer of commodities must be keenly interested in the proliferation of wants, and Marx saw this as the chief justification of capitalism historically. He wrote of:

> ... the search for means to spur workers on to consumption to give [the] wares new charms, to inspire them with new needs by constant chatter, etc. It is precisely this side of the relation of capital to labour which is an essential civilising moment, and on which the historical justification, but also the contemporary power of capital rests.[2]

Where Marx, in this decidedly positive evaluation of capitalism, sees the civilising effects of the proliferation of wants, left pessimism sees only a loss of standards, a cultural downgrading process. There is no suggestion to be found in Marx's writings that commodities are, as such, second-rate goods, nor that the wants which they satisfy are not 'real' wants. For Marx there is no such category, essential to left pessimism, as 'false needs'.

While it is true that not all use-values can take the form of a commodity and that the development of the commodity form transforms use-values, it cannot be assumed that this automatically involves loss of quality. The cult of the hand-made craft product assumes that standardisation means loss. Good home-cooked meals are contrasted with degenerate TV dinners. Yet even in catering, standardisation may mean the raising of standards in general, in some respects. Traditional peasant cooking and Elizabeth David reconstructions thereof for middle-class dinner parties are worlds apart, and both in turn differ from Trust House Forte and TV dinners. But Elizabeth David cookery shares with the latter that it is a consequence of the development of the commodity form, and is misrepresented as a simple refusal of that form, a harking back to earlier, pre-capitalist use-values.

iv Some Contradictions of Capitalist Penetration of Cultural Production

The key to capitalist commodity production lay, for Marx, in the contradiction between the use-value and the value of the commodity labour-power. Labour-power is that commodity which has, as its use-value for its purchaser, the ability to create value. So long as the labour-power is used to produce greater value than the exchange-value (the wage) which was paid for it, then the result will be the production for its capitalist purchaser of *surplus-value*. Using this key example, we may infer that the use-value of a commodity may be in contradiction with its value. This potential contradiction can be seen in Marx's analysis of the capitalist system of production as a whole. Its operation requires that different commodities be produced in a certain proportion to each other and in relation to social necessity. In Volume II of *Capital*[3] he discusses this necessary proportion between what he terms 'Departments I and II' of production – production for individual consumption, and for 'productive consumption' (producer goods) respectively. In his analysis Marx shows how it is possible for this relationship between production in the two Departments to be in equilibrium. Ernest Mandel shows that this is a special case which cannot be assumed always to obtain[4] Capitalist production between the two Departments may be in disequilibrium, and the theory of combined and unequal development suggests that this greater or lesser disequilibrium must be the norm. In other words, there is no inbuilt mechanism to ensure that production overall is as much as and no more than is socially necessary, and in the required proportions.

'Social necessity' is a problematic concept in *Capital*. But we may assume that capitalism itself generates certain requirements for its own maintenance and well-being, some of which operate at the level of individuals, and others at the level of the social collectivity. For instance, there is a need for efficient systems of transport for the circulation of commodities which is essential to the capitalist commodity form. The very concept of ideology points to another area of the requirements of capitalism.

Some of these diverse needs of capitalism are met within institutions which are not, or not fully, penetrated by capital. They are needs which are not, or cannot be, met by the purchase and sale of commodities. Much ideological production takes place in schools, homes, the church, etc., and in all of these the production of 'the ideological effect' does not depend on the consumption of a commodity. What must be raised here is the question of what happens when, with the penetration of capital, the production of 'the ideological effect' does become dependent upon the consumption by individuals and groups, of commodities? The commodities in question – films, books, television programmes, etc. – have different use-values for the individuals who use and purchase them than they have for the capitalists who produce and sell them, and in turn, for capital*ism* as a whole. We may assume that people do not purchase these cultural artifacts *in order* to expose themselves to bourgeois ideology, the 'ideological effect', but to satisfy a variety of different wants which can only be guessed at in the absence of analysis and investigation. There is no guarantee that the use-value of the cultural object for its purchaser will even be compatible with its utility to capitalism as bourgeois ideology, and therefore no guarantee that it will in fact secure 'the ideological effect'. For example, the utility of a television programme for a producer who buys advertising time is the ability of that programme to enhance the sale of the advertised product, by giving the producer access to the audience which is watching the programme. But the viewer will be watching that programme for its entertainment value, and there is some evidence that these two interests may conflict. A programme which is a bestseller and which its audience rates very highly on entertainment value may actually be less effective as a vehicle for impressing advertised products and increasing their sales than a less entertaining programme.

This particular example illustrates conflicts which may occur between the use-value of a commodity and its unity for particular capitals. But this conflict may also obtain between the use-value in question and the interests of capitalism in general. Here the conflict may be compounded by the divergence of interest between particular capitals and capitalism as a whole. Particular capitals invested in the entertainment industry have an interest in maximising profits through maximising the popularity and therefore the sale of entertainment. They have only a common class interest in securing the ideological needs of capitalism. This collective class interest may cut across the interest in the search for surplus-value. If surplus-value can be extracted from the production of cultural commodities which challenge, or even subvert, the dominant ideology, then all other things being equal, it is in the interests of particular capitals to invest in the production of such commodities. Unless collective class restraints are exercised, the individual capitalists' pursuit of surplus-value may lead to forms of cultural production which are against the interests of capitalism as a whole.

v Use-Value, and the Pleasure of the Text

To examine this problem would require a shift from the point of view of capitalist commodity production, to that of consumption. Unfortunately we have no Marxist theory of capitalist commodity consumption. The only school of Marxist theory to address this question was the Frankfurt School, and for this reason it is a pity that its work has been dismissed as 'humanist' and 'historicist'. Despite its left pessimism, the Frankfurt School did raise important questions which other approaches have neglected.

Any Marxist theory of consumption would have as its central category 'use-value', and would focus on 'the pleasure of the text'. It is true that Althusserian and Lacanian currents in cultural studies have turned to this important question of pleasure, but its meaning has been restricted to the narrow Freudian sense. Cultural products are articulated structures of feeling and sensibility which derive from collective, shared experience as well as from individual desires and pleasures. The pleasure of the text stems at least in part from collective utopias, social wish fulfilment and social aspirations, and these are not simply the sublimated expression of more basic sexual desires.

Whatever the locus and nature of the use-values of cultural products, it remains certain that capitalist producers of those products must make and sell commodities which embody those use-values if they are to succeed in meeting the wants which they satisfy, and through doing so, generating surplus-value. The producer must 'give the public what it wants', and what it wants does not necessarily sit square upon bourgeois ideology.

Of course, care must be taken to avoid the suggestion that those wants are the independent expression of the random and varied desires of the sovereign consumer. Wants are systematically, socially produced, and their production is not independent of the dominant mode of production of the society in which they occur. In part they are produced and elicited by the products themselves, so that at a single stroke, a want is created and a commodity produced to meet that want. The market for commodities is too important to capitalism to be left to consumer whim. Along with capitalist commodity production a whole host of means of stimulating and proliferating wants has been developed. Wants are not natural or eternal. Again this points to an area of investigation to which Marx himself gives few clues, and which has been neglected by Marxism. The social production of wants under capitalism would constitute part of the absent Marxist theory of capitalist consumption. But it may be hazarded that the production of wants is never fully under the control of the dominant class. Capitalism generates, by its very nature, a rich variety of wants. The satisfaction of many of these would not be desirable for capitalism, and some would be inimical to its interests, while others would be impossible to meet, difficult to control.

The paradoxical effects of the capitalist penetration of cultural production are a matter of conscious concern for certain groups outside the point of production itself – the ideologues and the professional guardians of public morality who swell the ranks of Gramsci's 'traditional intellectuals'. Every successive penetration of capital into cultural production has produced an outbreak of 'moral panic' in its wake. In the eighteenth century the rise of the novel produced widespread attack, allegations that it was morally pernicious in its effects upon weak-minded women and servants who were avid consumers of the new form. It was universally slammed, from pulpit to review. The same spectacle was repeated in our century over film in the thirties, and television in the fifties. The panic this time centred on equally weak-minded children and adolescents, for fear they would indulge in an orgy of imitative violence on exposure to the media. Effects studies have been the meat and drink of media specialists ever since. But there has been relatively little interest in the question of how and whether the 'anarchy of capitalist production' is offset in the interests of securing its ideological safety. The history of censorship should be looked at from this point of view. Censorship at least indicates which areas are considered sensitive or taboo. The increasing role of the state in the various areas of cultural production outside of a strict capitalist nexus would also repay study. For instance, the independent cinema may be independent of capitalist production, but is in turn dependent on the capitalist state, through the support of state-funded bodies such as the Arts Council. The approach to Marxist cultural studies from the point of view of production has generated no greater interest in these questions than did reflection theories. When the concept of the social relations of production is reinstated, perhaps such questions will come into sharper focus.

Finally, it is clear that a Marxist perspective yields no *a priori* grounds for anticipating the results of ideological analysis of cultural production of the various media penetrated by capital, in the absence of any Marxist theory of capitalist *consumption*. The theory of *production* too shows that cultural commodities are likely to express a wide variety of ideas, emotions, values and sensibilities, only some of which will be drawn from and articulated with the dominant ideology, and many of which will originate in class experience and class aspirations which are antithetical to capitalism. This type of analysis leaves room for different strategies of class struggle, based on workers within the heartland of the mass entertainment industry and not centring entirely on an avant-garde which has no mass appeal. We cannot read off the effects of cultural production from the manner of its production – from the fact that much of it takes the form of capitalist commodity production and is subject to the law of value, Nor [. . .] can it be read off automatically from aesthetic form itself.

Notes

1. The work of P. Golding and G. Murdoch offers a contemporary example of this type of argument, see 'For a Political Economy of Mass Communication', *Social Register*, R. Milliband and J. Saville (eds), London, Merlin Press (1973).
2. Karl Marx, *Grundrisse*, Harmondsworth, Penguin (1973), p. 287.
3. Karl Marx, *Capital*, vols I and II, London, Lawrence & Wishart (1970).
4. Ernest Mandel, *Late Capitalism*, London, New Left Books (1972).

45 □ *The Practice of Everyday Life*

Michel de Certeau

This essay is part of a continuing investigation of the ways in which users – commonly assumed to be passive and guided by established rules – operate. The point is not so much to discuss this elusive yet fundamental subject as to make such a discussion possible; that is, by means of inquiries and hypotheses, to indicate pathways for further research. This goal will be achieved if everyday practices, 'ways of operating' or doing things, no longer appear as merely the obscure background of social activity, and if a body of theoretical questions, methods, categories, and perspectives, by penetrating this obscurity, make it possible to articulate them.

The examination of such practices does not imply a return to individuality. The social atomism which over the past three centuries has served as the historical axiom of social analysis posits an elementary unit – the individual – on the basis of which groups are supposed to be formed and to which they are supposed to be always reducible. This axiom, which has been challenged by more than a century of sociological, economic, anthropological, and psychoanalytic research (although in history that is perhaps no argument), plays no part in this study. Analysis shows that a relation (always social) determines its terms, and not the reverse, and that each individual is a locus in which an incoherent (and often contradictory) plurality of such relational determinations interact. Moreover, the question at hand concerns modes of operation or schemata of action, and not directly the subjects (or persons) who are their authors or vehicles. It concerns an operational logic whose models may go as far back as the age-old ruses of fishes and insects that disguise or transform themselves in order to survive, and which has in any case been concealed by the form of rationality currently dominant in Western culture. The purpose of this work is to make explicit the systems of operational combination (*les combinatories d'opérations*) which also compose a 'culture', and to bring to light the models of action characteristic of users whose status as the dominated element in society (a status that does not mean that they are either passive or docile) is

From de Certeau, M., *The Practice of Everyday Life*, University of California Press, Berkeley, 1984, pp. xi–xxiv.

concealed by the euphemistic term 'consumers'. Everyday life invents itself by poaching in countless ways on the property of others.

I Consumer Production

Since this work grew out of studies of 'popular culture' or marginal groups,[1] the investigation of everyday practices was first delimited negatively by the necessity of not locating cultural *difference* in groups associated with the 'counterculture' – groups that were already singled out, often privileged, and already partly absorbed into folklore and that were no more than symptoms or indexes. Three further, positive determinations were particularly important in articulating our research.

Usage, or Consumption

Many, often remarkable, works have sought to study the representations of a society, on the one hand, and its modes of behavior, on the other. Building on our knowledge of these social phenomena, it seems both possible and necessary to determine the *use* to which they are put by groups or individuals. For example, the analysis of the images broadcast by television (representation) and of the time spent watching television (behavior) should be complemented by a study of what the cultural consumer 'makes' or 'does' during this time and with these images. The same goes for the use of urban space, the products purchased in the supermarket, the stories and legends distributed by the newspapers, and so on.

The 'making' in question is a production, a *poiēsis*[2] – but a hidden one, because it is scattered over areas defined and occupied by systems of 'production' (television, urban development, commerce, etc.), and because the steadily increasing expansion of these systems no longer leaves 'consumers' any place in which they can indicate what they make or *do* with the products of these systems. To a rationalized, expansionist and at the same time centralized, clamorous, and spectacular production corresponds *another* production, called 'consumption'. The latter is devious, it is dispersed, but it insinuates itself everywhere, silently and almost invisibly, because it does not manifest itself through its own products, but rather through its *ways of using* the products imposed by a dominant economic order.

For instance, the ambiguity that subverted from within the Spanish colonizers' 'success' in imposing their own culture on the indigenous Indians is well known. Submissive and even consenting to their subjection, the Indians nevertheless often *made of* the rituals, representations, and laws imposed on them something quite different from what their conquerors had in mind; they subverted them not by rejecting or altering them, but by using them with respect to ends and references foreign to the system they had no choice but to accept. They were *other* within the very colonization that outwardly assimilated them; their use of the dominant social order detected its power, which they lacked the means to challenge; they escaped it without leaving it. The strength of their difference lay in procedures of 'consumption'. To a lesser degree, a similar ambiguity creeps into our societies through the use made by the 'common people' of the culture disseminated and imposed by the 'elites' producing the language.

The presence and circulation of a representation (taught by preachers, educators, and popularizers as the key to socioeconomic advancement) tells us nothing about what it is for its users. We must first analyze its manipulation by users who are not its makers. Only then can we gauge the difference or similarity between the production of the image and the secondary production hidden in the process of its utilization.

Our investigation is concerned with this difference. It can use as its theoretical model the *construction* of individual sentences with an *established* vocabulary and syntax. In linguistics, 'performance' and 'competence', are different: the act of speaking (with all the renunciative strategies that implies) is not reducible to a knowledge of the language. By adopting the point of view of enunciation – which is the subject of our study – we privilege the act of speaking; according to that point of view, speaking operates within the field of a linguistic system; it effects an appropriation, or reappropriation, of language by its speakers; it establishes a present relative to a time and place; and it posits a *contract with the other* (the interlocutor) in a network of places and relations. These four characteristics of the speech act[3] can be found in many other practices (walking, cooking, etc.). An objective is at least adumbrated by this parallel, which is, as we shall see, only partly valid. Such an objective assumes that (like the Indians mentioned above) users make (*bricolent*) innumerable and infinitesimal transformations of and within the dominant cultural economy in order to adapt it to their own interests and their own rules. We must determine the procedures, bases, effects, and possibilities of this collective activity.

The Procedures of Everyday Creativity

A second orientation of our investigation can be explained by reference to Michel Foucault's *Discipline and Punish*. In this work, instead of analyzing the apparatus exercising power (i.e. the localizable, expansionist, repressive, and legal institutions), Foucault analyzes the mechanisms (*dispositifs*) that have sapped the strength of these institutions and surreptitiously reorganized the functioning of power: 'minuscule' technical procedures acting on and with details, redistributing a discursive space in order to make it the means of a generalized 'discipline' (*surveillance*).[4] This approach raises a new and different set of problems to be investigated. Once again, however, this 'microphysics of power' privileges the productive apparatus (which produces the 'discipline'), even though it discerns in 'education' a system of 'repression' and shows how, from the wings as it were, silent technologies determine or short-circuit institutional stage directions. If it is true that the grid of 'discipline' is everywhere becoming clearer and more extensive, it is all the more urgent to discover how an entire society resists being reduced to it, what popular procedures (also 'minuscule' and quotidian) manipulate the mechanisms of discipline and conform to them only in order to evade them, and finally, what 'ways of operating' form the counterpart, on the consumer's (or 'dominee's'?) side, of the mute processes that organize the establishment of socioeconomic order.

These 'ways of operating' constitute the innumerable practices by means of which users reappropriate the space organized by techniques of sociocultural production. They pose questions at once analogous and contrary to those dealt with in Foucault's book: analogous, in that the goal is to perceive and analyze the microbe-like operations proliferating within technocratic structures and deflecting their functioning by means of a multitude of 'tactics' articulated in the details of everyday life; contrary, in that the goal is not to make clearer how the violence of order is transmuted into a disciplinary technology, but rather to bring to light the clandestine forms taken by the dispersed, tactical, and makeshift creativity of groups or individuals already caught in the nets of 'discipline'. Pushed to their ideal limits, these procedures and ruses of consumers compose the network of an antidiscipline[5] which is the subject of this book.

The Formal Structure of Practice

It may be supposed that these operations – multiform and fragmentary, relative to situations and details, insinuated into and concealed within devices whose mode of usage they constitute, and thus lacking their own ideologies or institutions – conform to certain rules. In other words, there must be a logic of these practices. We are thus confronted once again by the ancient problem: What is an *art* or 'way of making'? From the Greeks to Durkheim, a long tradition has sought to describe with precision the complex (and not at all simple or 'impoverished') rules that could account for these operations.[6] From this point of view, 'popular culture', as well as a whole literature called 'popular',[7] take on a different aspect: they present themselves essentially as 'arts of making' this or that, i.e. as combinatory or utilizing modes of consumption. These practices bring into play a 'popular' *ratio*, a way of thinking invested in a way of acting, an art of combination which cannot be dissociated from an art of using.

In order to grasp the formal structure of these practices, I have carried out two sorts of investigations. The first, more descriptive in nature, has concerned certain ways of making that were selected according to their value for the strategy of the analysis, and with a view to obtaining fairly differentiated variants: readers' practices, practices related to urban spaces, utilizations of everyday rituals, re-uses and functions of the memory through the 'authorities' that make possible (or permit) everyday practices, etc. In addition, two related investigations have tried to trace the intricate forms of the operations proper to the recompositon of a space (the Croix-Rousse quarter in Lyons) by familial practices, on the one hand, and on the other, to the tactics of the art of cooking, which simultaneously organizes a network of relations, poetic ways of 'making do' (*bricolage*), and a re-use of marketing structures.[8]

The second series of investigations has concerned the scientific literature that might furnish hypotheses allowing the logic of unselfconscious thought to be taken seriously. Three areas are of special interest. First, sociologists, anthropologists, and indeed historians (from E. Goffman to P. Bourdieu, from Mauss to M. Détienne, from J. Boissevain to E. O. Laumann) have elaborated a theory of such practices, mixtures of rituals and makeshifts (*bricolages*), manipulations of spaces, operators of networks.[9] Second, in the wake of J. Fishman's work, the ethnomethodological and sociolinguistic investigations of H. Garfinkel, W. Labov, H. Sachs, E. A. Schegloff, and others have described the procedures of everyday interactions relative to structures of expectation, negotiations and improvisation proper to ordinary language.[10]

Finally, in addition to the semiotics and philosophies of 'convention' (from O. Ducrot to D. Lewis),[11] we must look into the ponderous formal logic and their extension, in the field of analytical philosophy, into the domains of action (G. H. von Wright, A. C. Danto, R. J. Bernstein),[12] time (A. N. Prior, N. Rescher and J. Urquhart),[13] and modalization (G. E. Hughes and M. J. Cresswell, A. R. White).[14] These extensions yield a weighty apparatus seeking to grasp the delicate layering and plasticity of ordinary language, with its almost orchestral combinations of logical elements (temporalization, modalization, injunctions, predicates of action, etc.) whose dominants are determined in turn by circumstances and conjunctural demands. An investigation analogous to Chomsky's study of the oral uses of language must seek to restore to everyday practices their logical and cultural legitimacy, at least in the sectors – still very limited – in which we have at our disposal the instruments necessary to account for them.[15] This kind of research is complicated by the fact that these practices themselves alternately exacerbate and disrupt our logics. Its regrets are like those of the poet, and like him, it struggles against oblivion: 'And I forgot the element of chance introduced by circumstances, calm or haste, sun or cold, dawn or dusk, the taste of strawberries or abandonment, the half-understood message, the front page of newspapers, the voice on the telephone, the most anodyne conversation, the most anonymous man or woman, everything that speaks, makes noise, passes by, touches us lightly, meets us head on.'[16]

The Marginality of a Majority

These three determinations make possible an exploration of the cultural field, an exploration defined by an investigative problematics and punctuated by more detailed inquiries located by reference to hypotheses that remain to be verified. Such an exploration will seek to situate the types of *operations* characterizing consumption in the framework of an economy, and to discern in these practices of appropriation indexes of the creativity that flourishes at the very point where practice ceases to have its own language.

Marginality is today no longer limited to minority groups, but is rather massive and pervasive; this cultural activity of the non-producers of culture, an activity that is unsigned, unreadable, and unsymbolized, remains the only one possible for all those who nevertheless buy and pay for the showy products through which a productivist economy articulates itself. Marginality is becoming universal. A marginal group has now become a silent majority.

That does not mean the group is homogeneous. The procedures allowing the re-use of products are linked together in a kind of obligatory language, and their functioning is related to social situations and power relationships. Confronted by images on television, the immigrant worker does not have the same critical or creative elbow-room as the average citizen. On the same terrain, his inferior access to information, financial means, and compensations of all kinds elicits an increased deviousness, fantasy, or laughter. Similar strategic deployments, when acting on different relationships of force, do not produce identical effects. Hence the necessity of differentiating both the 'actions' or 'engagements' (in the military sense) that the system of products effects within the consumer grid, *and* the various kinds of room to maneuver left for consumers by the situations in which they exercise their 'art'.

The relation of procedures to the fields of force in which they act must therefore lead to a *polemological* analysis of culture. Like law (one of its models), culture articulates conflicts and alternately legitimizes, displaces, or controls the superior force. It develops in an atmosphere of tensions, and often of violence, for which it provides symbolic balances, contracts of compatibility and compromises, all more or less temporary. The tactics of consumption, the ingenious ways in which the weak make use of the strong, thus lend a political dimension to everyday practices.

2 The Tactics of Practice

In the course of our research, the scheme, rather too neatly dichotomized, of the relations between consumers and the mechanisms of production has been diversified in relation to three kinds of concerns: the search for a problematic that could articulate the material collected; the description of a limited number of practices (reading, talking, walking, dwelling, cooking, etc.) considered to be particularly significant; and the extension of the analysis of these everyday operations to scientific fields apparently governed by another kind of logic. Through the presentation of our investigation along these three lines, the overly schematic character of the general statement can be somewhat nuanced.

Trajectories, Tactics, and Rhetorics

As unrecognized producers, poets of their own acts, silent discoverers of their own paths in the jungle of functionalist rationality, consumers produce through their signifying practices something that might be considered similar to the 'wandering lines' (*'lignes d'eere'*) drawn by the autistic children studied by F. Deligny:[17] 'indirect' or 'errant' trajectories obeying their own logic. In the technocratically constructed, written, and functionalized space in which the consumers move about, their trajectories form unforeseeable sentences, partly unreadable paths across a space. Although they are composed with the vocabularies of established languages (those of television, newspapers, supermarkets, or museum sequences) and although they remain subordinated to the prescribed syntactical forms (temporal modes of schedules, paradigmatic orders of spaces, etc.), the trajectories trace out the ruses of other interests and desires that are neither determined nor captured by the systems in which they develop.[18]

Even statistical investigation remains virtually ignorant of these trajectories, since it is satisfied with classifying, calculating, and putting into tables the 'lexical' units which compose them but to which they cannot be reduced, and with doing this in reference to its own categories and taxonomies. Statistical investigation grasps the material of these practices, but not their *form*; it determines the elements used, but not the 'phrasing' produced by the *bricolage* (the artisan-like inventiveness) and the discursiveness that combine these elements, which are all in general circulation and rather drab. Statistical inquiry, in breaking down these 'efficacious meanderings' into units that it defines itself, in reorganizing the results of its analyses according to its own codes, 'finds' only the homogeneous. The power of its calculations lies in its ability to divide, but it is precisely through this ana-lytic fragmentation that it loses sight of what it claims to seek and to represent.[19]

'Trajectory' suggests a movement, but it also involves a plane projection, a flattening out. It is a transcription. A graph (which the eye can master) is substituted for an operation; a line which can be reversed (i.e. read in both directions) does duty for an irreversible temporal series, a tracing for acts. To avoid this reduction, I resort to a distinction between *tactics* and *strategies*.

I call a 'strategy' the calculus of force-relationships which becomes possible when a subject of will and power (a proprietor, an enterprise, a city, a scientific institution) can be isolated from an 'environment'. A strategy assumes a place that can be circumscribed as *proper* (*propre*) and thus serve as the basis for generating relations with an exterior distinct from it (competitors, adversaries, 'clientèles', 'targets', or 'objects' of research). Political, economic, and scientific rationality has been constructed on this strategic model.

I call a 'tactic', on the other hand, a calculus which cannot count on a 'proper' (a spatial or institutional localization), nor thus on a borderline distinguishing the other as a visible totality. The place of a tactic belongs to the other.[20] A tactic insinuates itself into the other's place, fragmentarily, without taking it over in its entirety, without being able to keep it at a distance. It has at its disposal no base where it can capitalize on its advantages, prepare its expansions, and secure independence with respect to circumstances. The 'proper' is a victory of space over time. On the contrary, because it does not have a place, a tactic depends on time – it is always on the watch for opportunities that must be seized 'on the wing'. Whatever it wins, it does not keep. It must constantly manipulate events in order to turn them into 'opportunities'. The weak must continually turn to their own ends forces alien to them. This is achieved in the propitious moments when they are able to combine heterogeneous elements (thus, in the supermarket, the housewife confronts heterogeneous and mobile data – what she has in the refrigerator, the tastes, appetites, and moods of her guests, the best buys and their possible combinations with what she already has on hand at home, etc.); the intellectual synthesis of these given elements takes the form, however, not of a discourse, but of the decision itself, the act and manner in which the opportunity is 'seized'.

Many everyday practices (talking, reading, moving about, shopping, cooking, etc.) are tactical in character. And so are, more generally, many 'ways of operating': victories of the 'weak' over the 'strong' (whether the strength be that of powerful people or the violence of things or of an imposed order, etc.), clever tricks, knowing how to get away with things, 'hunter's cunning', maneuvers, polymorphic simulations, joyful discoveries, poetic as well as warlike. The Greeks called these 'ways of operating' *mētis*.[21] But they go much further back, to the immemorial intelligence displayed in the tricks and imitations of plants and fishes. From the depths of the ocean to the streets of modern megalopolises, there is a continuity and permanence in these tactics.

In our societies, as local stabilities break down, it is as if, no longer fixed by a circumscribed community, tactics wander out of orbit, making consumers into immigrants in a system too vast to be their own, too tightly woven for them to escape from it. But these tactics introduce a Brownian movement into the system. They also show the extent to which intelligence is inseparable from the everyday struggles and pleasures that it articulates. Strategies, in contrast, conceal beneath objective calculations their connection with the power that sustains them from within the stronghold of its own 'proper' place or institution.

The discipline of rhetoric offers models for differentiating among the types of tactics. This is not surprising, since, on the one hand, it describes the 'turns' or tropes of which language can be both the site and the object, and, on the other hand, these manipulations are related to the ways of changing (seducing, persuading, making use of) the will of another (the audience).[22] For these two reasons, rhetoric, the science of the 'ways of speaking', offers an array of figure-types for the analysis of everyday ways of acting even though such analysis is in theory excluded from scientific discourse. Two logics of action (the one tactical, the other strategic) arise from these two facets of practicing language. In the space of a language (as in that of games), a society makes more explicit the formal rules of action and the operations that differentiate them.

In the enormous rhetorical corpus devoted to the art of speaking or operating, the Sophists have a privileged place, from the point of view of tactics. Their principle was, according to the Greek rhetorician Corax, to make the weaker position seem the stronger, and they claimed to have the power of turning the tables on the powerful by the way in which they made use of the opportunities offered by the particular situation.[23] Moreover, their theories inscribe tactics in a long tradition of reflection on the relationships between reason and particular actions and situations. Passing by way of *The Art of War* by the Chinese author Sun Tzu[24] or the Arabic anthology *The Book of Tricks*,[25] this tradition of a logic articulated on situations and the will of others continues into contemporary sociolinguistics.

Reading, Talking, Dwelling, Cooking, etc.

To describe these everyday practices that produce without capitalizing, that is, without taking control over time, one starting point seemed inevitable because it is the 'exorbitant' focus of contemporary culture and its consumption: *reading*. From TV to newspapers, from advertising to all sorts of mercantile epiphanies, our society is characterized by a cancerous growth of vision, measuring everything by its ability to show or be shown and transmuting communication into a visual journey. It is a sort of *epic* of the eye and of the impulse to read. The economy itself, transformed into a 'semeiocracy',[26] encourages a hypertrophic development of reading. Thus, for the binary set production–consumption, one would substitute its more general equivalent: writing–reading. Reading (an image or a text), moreover, seems to constitute the maximal development of the passivity assumed to characterize the consumer, who is conceived of as a voyeur (whether troglodytic or itinerant) in a 'show-biz society'.[27]

In reality, the activity of reading has on the contrary all the characteristics of a silent production: the drift across the page, the metamorphosis of the text effected by the wandering eyes of the reader, the improvisation and expectation of meanings inferred from a few words, leaps over written spaces in an ephemeral dance. But since he is incapable of stockpiling (unless he writes or records), the reader cannot protect himself against the erosion of time (while reading, he forgets himself and he forgets what he has read) unless he buys the object (book, image) which is no more than a substitute (the spoor or promise) of moments 'lost' in reading. He insinuates into another person's text the ruses of pleasure and appropriation: he poaches on it, is transported into it, pluralizes himself in it like the internal rumblings of one's body. Ruse, metaphor, arrangement, this production is also an 'invention' of the memory. Words become the outlet or product of silent histories. The readable transforms itself into the memorable: Barthes reads Proust in Stendhal's text;[28] the viewer reads the landscape of his childhood in the evening news. The thin film of writing become a movement of strata, a play of spaces. A different world (the reader's) slips into the author's place.

This mutation makes the text habitable, like a rented apartment. It transforms another person's property into a space borrowed for a moment by a transient. Renters make comparable changes in an apartment they furnish with their acts and memories; as do speakers, in the language into which they insert both the messages of their native tongue and, through their accent, through their own 'turns of phrase', etc., their own history; as do pedestrians, in the streets they fill with the forests of their desires and goals. In the same way the users of social codes turn them into metaphors and ellipses of their own quests. The ruling order serves as a support for innumerable productive activities, while at the same time blinding its proprietors to this creativity (like those 'bosses' who simply *can't* see what is being created within their own enterprises).[29] Carried to its limit, this order would be the equivalent of the rules of meter and rhyme for poets of earlier times: a body of constraints stimulating new discoveries, a set of rules with which improvisation plays.

Reading thus introduces an 'art' which is anything but passive. It resembles rather that art whose theory was developed by medieval poets and romancers: an innovation infiltrated into the text and even into the terms of a tradition. Imbricated within the strategies of modernity (which identify creation with the invention of a personal language, whether cultural or scientific), the procedures of contemporary consumption appear to constitute a subtle art of 'renters' who know how to insinuate their countless differences into the dominant text. In the Middle Ages, the text was framed by the four, or seven, interpretations of which it was held to be susceptible. And it was a book. Today, this text no longer comes from a tradition. It is imposed by the generation of a productivist technocracy. It is no longer a referential book, but a whole society made into a book, into the writing of the anonymous law of production.

It is useful to compare other arts with this art of readers. For example, the art of conversationalists: the rhetoric of ordinary conversation consists of practices which transform 'speech situations', verbal productions in which the interlacing of speaking positions weaves an oral fabric without individual owners, creations of a communication that belongs to no one. Conversation is a provisional and collective effect of competence in the art of manipulating 'commonplaces' and the inevitability of events in such a way as to make them 'habitable'.[30]

But our research has concentrated above all on the uses of space, on the ways of frequenting or dwelling in a place, on the complex processes of the art of cooking, and on the many ways of establishing a kind of reliability within the situations imposed on an individual, that is, of making it possible to live in them by reintroducing into them the plural mobility of goals and desires – an art of manipulating and enjoying.[31]

Notes

1. See M. de Certeau, *La Prise de parole* (Paris: DDB, 1968); *La Possession de Loudun* (Paris: Julliard-Gallimard, 1970); *L'Absent de l'histoire* (Paris: Mame, 1973); *La Culture au pluriel* (Paris: UGE 10/18, 1974); *Une Politique de la langue* (with D. Julia and J. Revel) (Paris: Gallimard, 1975); etc.
2. From the Greek *poiein*, 'to create, invent, generate'.
3. See Emile Benveniste, *Problèmes de linguistique générale* (Paris: Gallimard, 1966), I, 251–66.
4. Michel Foucault, *Surveiller et punir* (Paris: Gallimard, 1975); *Discipline and Punish*, trans. A. Sheridan (New York: Pantheon, 1977).
5. From this point of view as well, the works of Henri Lefebvre on everyday life constitute a fundamental source.
6. On art, from the *Encyclopédie* to Durkheim.
7. For this literature, see the booklets mentioned in *Le Livre dans la vie quotidienne* (Paris: Bibliothèque Nationale, 1975) and in Geneviève Bollème, *La Bible bleue, Anthologie d'une littérature 'populaire'* (Paris: Flammarion, 1975), 161–379.
8. The first of these two monographs was written by Pierre Mayol, the second by Luce

Giard (on the basis of interviews made by Marie Ferrier). See *L'Invention du quotidien*, II, Luce Giard and Pierre Mayol, *Habiter, cuisiner* (Paris: UGE 10/18, 1980).

9. By Erving Goffman, see especially *Interaction Rituals* (Garden City, NY: Anchor Books, 1976); *The Presentation of Self in Everyday Life* (Woodstock, NY: The Overlook Press, 1973); *Frame Analysis* (New York: Harper & Row, 1974). By Pierre Bourdieu, see *Esquisse d'une théorie de la pratique. Précédée de trois études d'ethnologie kabyle* (Geneva: Droz, 1972); 'Les Stratégies matrimoniales', *Anneles: économies, sociétés, civilisations*, 27 (1972), 1105–27; 'Le Langage autorisé', *Actes de la recherche en sciences sociales*, no. 5–6 (November 1975), 184–90; 'Le Sens pratique', *Actes de la recherche en sciences sociales*, no. 1 (February 1976), 43–86. By Marcel Mauss, see especially 'Techniques du corps', in *Sociologie et anthropologie* (Paris: PUF, 1950). By Marcel Détienne and Jean-Pierre Vernant, *Les Ruses de l'intelligence. La Mètis des Grecs* (Paris: Flammarion, 1974). By Jeremy Boissevain, *Friends of Friends: Networks, manipulators and coalitions* (Oxford: Blackwell, 1974). By Edward O. Laumann, *Bonds of Pluralism: The form and substance of urban social networks* (New York: John Wiley, 1973).

10. Joshua A. Fishman, *The Sociology of Language* (Rowley, MA: Newbury, 1972). See also the essays in *Studies in Social Interaction*, ed. David Sudnow (New York: The Free Press, 1972); William Labov, *Sociolinguistic Patterns* (Philadelphia: University of Pennsylvania Press, 1973); etc.

11. Oswald Ducrot, *Dire et ne pas dire* (Paris: Hermann, 1972); and David K. Lewis, *Convention: A philosophical study* (Cambridge, MA: Harvard University Press, 1974), and *Counterfactuals* (Cambridge, MA: Harvard University Press, 1973).

12. Georg H. von Wright, *Norm and Action* (London: Routledge & Kegan Paul, 1963); *Essay in Deontic Logic and the General Theory of Action* (Amsterdam: North Holland, 1968); *Explanation and Understanding* (Ithaca, NY: Cornell University Press, 1971). And A. C. Danto, *Analytical Philosophy of Action* (Cambridge: Cambridge University Press, 1973); Richard J. Bernstein, *Praxis and Action* (London: Duckworth, 1972); and *La Sémantique de l'action*, ed. Paul Ricoeur and Doriane Tiffeneau (Paris: CNRS, 1977).

13. A. N. Prior, *Past, Present and Future: A study of 'tense logic'* (Oxford: Oxford University Press, 1967) and *Papers on Tense and Time* (Oxford: Oxford University Press, 1968), N. Rescher and A. Urquhart, *Temporal Logic* (Oxford: Oxford University Press, 1975).

14. Alan R. White, *Modal Thinking* (Ithaca, NY: Cornell University Press, 1975); G. E. Hughes and M. J. Cresswell, *An Introduction to Modal Logic* (Oxford: Oxford University Press, 1973); I. R. Zeeman, *Modal Logic* (Oxford: Oxford University Press, 1975); S. Haacker, *Deviant Logic* (Cambridge: Cambridge University Press, 1976); *Discussing Language with Chomsky, Halliday, etc.*, ed. H. Parret (The Hague: Mouton, 1975).

15. As it is more technical, the study concerning the logics of action and time, as well as modalization, will be published elsewhere.

16. Jacques Sojcher, *La Démarche poétique* (Paris: UGE 10/18, 1976), 145.

17. See Fernand Deligny, *Les Vagabonds efficaces* (Paris: Maspero, 1970); *Nous et l'innocent* (Paris: Maspero, 1977); etc.

18. See M. de Certeau, *La Culture au pluriel*, 283–308; and 'Actions culturelles et stratégies politiques', *La Revue nouvelle*, April 1974, 351–60.

19. The analysis of the principles of isolation allows us to make this criticism both more

nuanced and more precise. See *Pour une histoire de la statistique* (Paris: INSEE, 1978), I, in particular Alain Desrosières, 'Eléments pour l'histoire des nomenclatures socio-professionnelles', 155–231.

20. The works of P. Bourdieu and those of M. Détienne and J.-P. Vernant makes possible the notion of 'tactic' more precise, but the sociolinguistic investigations of H. Garfinkel, H. Sacks, *et al.* also contribute to this clarification. See notes 9 and 10.
21. M. Détienne and J.-P. Vernant, *Les Ruses de l'intelligence*.
22. See S. Toulmin, *The Uses of Argument* (Cambridge: Cambridge University Press, 1958); Ch. Perelman and L. Ollbrechts-Tyteca, *Traité de l'argumentation* (Brussels: Université libre, 1970); J. Dubois *et al.*, *Rhétorique générale* (Paris: Larousse, 1970); etc.
23. The works of Corax, said to be the author of the earliest Greek text on rhetoric, are lost; on this point, see Aristotle, *Rhetoric*, II, 24, 1402a. See W. K. C. Guthrie, *The Sophists* (Cambridge: Cambridge University Press, 1971), 178–9.
24. Sun Tzu, *The Art of War*, trans. S. B. Griffith (Oxford: The Clarendon Press, 1963). Sun Tzu (Sun Zı) should not be confused with the later military theorist Hsun Tzu (Xun Zı).
25. *Le Livre des ruses. La Stratégie politique des Arabes*, ed. R. K. Khawam (Paris: Phébus, 1976).
26. See Jean Baudrillard, *Le Système des objets* (Paris: Gallimard, 1968); *La Société de consommation* (Paris: Denoel, 1970); *Pour une critique de l'économie politique du signe* (Paris: Gallimard, 1972).
27. Guy Debord, *La Société du spectacle* (Paris: Buchet-Chastel, 1967).
28. Roland Barthes, *Le Plaisir du texte* (Paris: Seuil, 1973), 58; *The Pleasure of the Text*, trans. R. Miller (New York: Hill & Wang, 1975).
29. See Gérard Mordillat and Nicolas Philibert, *Ces Patrons éclairés qui craignent la lumière* (Paris: Albatros, 1979).
30. See the essays of H. Sacks, E. A. Schegloff, etc., quoted above. This analysis, entitled *Arts de dire*, will be published separately.
31. We have devoted monographs to these practices in which the proliferating and disseminated bibliography on the subject will be found (see *L'Invention du quotidien*, II, *Habiter, cuisiner*, by Luce Giard and Pierre Mayol).

46 □ *The New Validation of Popular Culture: Sense and Sentimentality in Academia*

Michael Schudson

In the past generation, popular culture has attained a new legitimacy in American universities. Popular culture is now studied more often, in more different courses, in more departments, and with more sympathy than before. In literature, serious scholars can write on science fiction or on detective fiction or on romance novels, in short, on what is still often labeled as 'trash'. In history, the attention to popular culture has moved even further; the attention to the beliefs and practices of ordinary people actually has displaced studies of political, diplomatic, and military elites as the leading edge of historical writing. In the interpretive social sciences, now rubbing up against and taking inspiration from the humanities, there is also a new freshness and new importance to the study of popular cultural forms.

The concept of popular culture has been revised entirely, and revitalized, by these developments. The result has been, in my opinion, a salutary new valuation of popular culture combined with an undiscriminatingly sentimental view of it. In the pages that follow, I describe the main intellectual lines that have produced this change, and I suggest that the new study of popular culture now offers a serious challenge to the identity of the modern university.

[. . .]

The study of popular culture can be broken down as the study of (a) the production of cultural objects, (b) the content of the objects themselves, and (c) the reception of the objects and the meanings attributed to them by the general

From *Critical Studies in Mass Communication*, vol. 4, 1987, pp. 51–68.

population or subpopulations. In all three dimensions – the study of the production of culture, the study of texts, and the study of audiences – intellectual developments of the past generation have provided a new validation for the study of popular culture. This development raises a fundamental question that I will take up later in the essay: what rationale remains for distinguishing 'high' or 'elite' culture from popular culture? If popular culture is valid for serious study, is there still a high culture that is *more* valid? That is, what justification remains for teaching – and thereby legitimating, even enshrining – some texts rather than others in university courses in the humanities? There is new thinking on this question, too, that has come out of historical and sociological accounts of the development of popular and high culture traditions and the evolution of a distinction between them.

[. . .]

[U]niversity humanities departments have [always] been promoters of their favorite artists and authors. More than most departments in a university, humanities departments are, perhaps necessarily, employers of scholars *engagé*, people deeply involved in *making* the very thing – elite culture – that they study. Barbara Herrnstein Smith describes the process with respect to Homer:

> . . . the value of a literary work is continuously produced and reproduced by the very acts of implicit and explicit evaluation that are frequently invoked as 'reflecting' its value and therefore as being evidence of it. In other words, what are commonly taken to be the *signs* of literary value are, in effect, also its *springs*. The endurance of a classic canonical author such as Homer, then, owes not to the alleged transcultural or universal value of his works but, on the contrary, to the continuity of their circulation in a particular culture. Repeatedly cited and recited, translated, taught, and imitated, and thoroughly enmeshed in the network of intertextuality that continuously *constitutes* the high culture of the orthodoxly educated population of the West . . . that highly variable entity we refer to as 'Homer' recurrently enters our experience in relation to a large number and variety of our interests and thus can perform a large number of various functions for us and obviously has performed them for many of us over a good bit of the history of our culture. (1984, pp. 34–5)

This is the kind of observation that literary scholars in recent years have begun to accept as they adopt a loosely sociological view of their own institution, understanding it as a hierarchical social structure with larger social functions. Frank Kermode (1983), for instance, writes of literary studies as an institution, that 'professional community which interprets secular literature and teaches others to do so' (p. 168). It has authority (not undisputed, he observes) 'to define (or indicate the limits of) a subject; to impose valuations and validate interpretations'. It is, he says, 'a self-perpetuating, sempiternal corporation' (p. 169).

This skeptical stance toward the academic institution as an imposer of valuations has enlarged the number and kinds of texts acceptable for study in the humanities. More kinds of literary texts have been added to the reading lists. Further, the whole concept of textuality has been applied to materials not previously regarded as textual at all, and here anthropology has made the most notable contribution.

[. . .]

Compared to this radical extension of the notion of textuality, the inclusion of new literary forms into the acceptable canon for literary studies seems a minor footnote in intellectual history. Of course, it has not been experienced that way. The universities are conservators of tradition, protectors of what they regard as the best and most valuable monuments to human invention and creative expression. It is therefore in some ways easier to accept the cockfight for study than the popular romance or the codes of fashion than television soap operas. The cockfight is sufficiently exotic to be beyond our own culture's status ranking of cultural forms. The romance and the soap opera, in contrast, hold a place – a very low place – in this society's established hierarchy of literary taste.

Now that sociologists and literary scholars alike hold up for examination the social processes whereby hierarchies of taste get established, should the hierarchies be granted any remaining authority? If the 'lower' forms of culture deserve study, not just as data for social science but as literary texts meriting the same attention one might give Shakespeare, does this change what the university is supposed to be about? Does it call for a radical change or extension in what we take the mission of the university to be? This is a thorny and a fundamental issue. On the one hand, nothing that is human should be foreign to the 'humanities' in a university, and African or Asian or American Indian literature should have as much place as Shakespeare or Dickens in a university education; on the other hand, American universities are, and intend to be, carriers of and promoters of Western traditions of art and thought, and their curricula cannot and should not be encyclopedic. They must be pedagogic. That is, the selection of materials presented, let alone the ways of presenting them, are a vital part of the university's educational endeavor. Selection is *the* vital part, in the view of Bartlett Giamatti (1980), who argues that the main task of the teacher is the task of *choosing* where to begin and what to begin with. On the one hand, it seems perfectly appropriate to study formulaic literatures, romances or detective stories, to see how they work, to think about *why* so many people respond so eagerly to them, and to contemplate the meaning of form and formula and genre in literature generally. On the other hand, there is justifi-cation for a critical tradition that pays greatest tribute to work that challenges form, breaks or becomes self-conscious about formula, blurs the boundaries of genres, or seems to surpass the limits of meaning possible within a genre. Watchers of baseball are more interested in learning lessons from Pete Rose than from Joe Schmo, and people who enjoy eating pay greater attention to the Sunday dinner that someone takes hours to prepare than the Wednesday leftovers dumped on the table. The making of distinctions and the making of judgments of better or worse, more or less complex, more or less memorable or enduring or pleasing were not invented by power-hungry elites or greedy institutions (though elites and institutions certainly have taken advantage of their power to make *their* judgments the reigning judgments).

It may be – it certainly remains the common-sense intuition – that different qualities of art reside in the thing itself: some paintings or performances or poems are better than others. But it is now argued with equal vigor that the quality of art lies in how it is received, or in how it is created within the context of reception, rather than in some quality intrinsic to the art object itself. Roland Barthes argues we have moved from an emphasis on the Work (the pristine object with intrinsic quality) to engagement with the Text, something that is produced by reader as much as by writer, by critic or interpreter as much as by author. The quality of *reading* rather than the quality of the object then takes center stage and the critic is more producer than evaluator or consumer. Indeed, for Barthes, as long as a person reads passively, it matters little if the reading matter is Shakespeare or subway graffiti. The task is to read *playfully*, playing the text 'in the musical sense of the term' (Barthes, 1979, p. 79). And the task for the humanities in the university I would infer from this, is not to create hierarchies of Works but to educate readers in reading. If this can be done with Shakespeare, fine; if it is better achieved with newspaper cartoons, that's fine, too. The task is to diminish the distance between writer and reader, writing and reading, and encourage students to be players.

The notion of the ideal reader as a 'player' is not the only model of how a reader should read. Perhaps a more common understanding is that a good reader reads *critically*, reads 'against the text' in the terms of one critic or reads 'as a process of inaugurating disbelief' according to another (Altieri, 1984, pp. 60–61). Charles Altieri urges that good readers read through a text, submitting to 'its provisional authority' as a work of art. Without abandoning a sense of critical reading, this position comes close to Barthes's notion of play and recommends to the reader an attitude that the anthropologists [...] would recognize as resembling the 'subjunctive' mood. It emphasizes gaining familiarity and facility more than distance and perspective but none the less a kind of facility that presumes perspective.

Suppose that the university sees its task as one of educating students to read against texts and to be players of texts. At some point, the question will still arise about who is a better player and who a worse player and who is to judge and what rules of play need to be observed. The radical democratization that appears when the Work is demoted to the Text does not do away with the desire for distinctions; the university must still determine, in a redefined context, what values it should be promoting.

[. . .]

Sense and Sentimentality

So far, I have reviewed, generally approvingly, intellectual developments of the past two decades that have profound implications for our understanding of culture.

First, I have reviewed the sociological insight that cultural products are created by groups as well as by individuals and that, even with individual artists, cultural products are oriented to a small or large degree to a marketplace and to a socially constructed 'art world'. This insight relativizes or democratizes works of art and raises questions about the distinction that universities have made between high culture and popular or mass culture. Second, I have reviewed developments in the study of texts that vastly enlarge the range of texts appropriate for serious study. This trend suggests an equivalence across texts whereby judgments of quality do not have pride of place and may not have much of a place at all. Third, I have looked at changing views of the audience that give credit to the audience, any audience, as a privileged critic or reader, even, *creator* of the texts it reads or watches. Once again, the tendency is to relativize the concept of culture, to whittle away at the props that maintain some elements of culture as higher than others.

There is a lot of justifiable excitement about these developments. Barriers to the halls of academe are breached by cultural objects that never before had seen the inside of a classroom; hallways between departments where professors did not know one another existed are now well worn. There has been a real liberation in all of this, based, in my view, on very good intellectual sense.

But with each of the intellectual movements I have reviewed here, there is a corresponding danger. With the sociological approach to artistic production, there is the threat of cynicism; with the democratization of the number and kinds of texts worthy of study, there is a danger of obscuring the special features of *written* texts; and, most of all, with the recognition of the active role of audiences in constructing the works they engage, there is a danger of romanticizing and sentimentalizing audiences as they exist in certain inhumane social conditions.

Production. While it is true that all art is produced by someone or some ones, not all production aims to manufacture or manufactures art. Some organizations produce toothpicks or ball bearings or toilet paper, not textbooks or soap operas. And producing the textbooks or soap operas is different. Certainly useful things (toothpicks) may have meanings and just as surely meaningful things (soap operas) may be useful, but for most things there is no difficulty in distinguishing whether utility or meaning is the primary feature. That there are university departments and international conferences and bibliographies overflowing on William Shakespeare, who produced plays, and not on Clarence Birdseye, who produced frozen foods, is not just an accident nor just a prejudice of people who disdain mass culture. The difference between meaning and utility remains important; the sociologizing trend in the understanding of artistic production does not erase it but asks that it be understood more carefully.

Texts. The fact that an anthropologist or literary critic can read an evening meal or a fast food advertisement or the names of athletic teams or the design of Disneyland as a commentary or metacommentary on culture does not mean that participant natives also read the texts that way. There is some danger that the recent trends in the study of popular culture may inadvertently romanticize the semiotic process itself; the academy's professional interest and pleasure in the act of interpreting can be self-indulgent, and the readings of meals or ads may be only academic *études* if these objects are not privileged as signs by the general community. Anthropologist Bruce Kapferer has recognized this problem:

> Most anthropologists argue that rituals make metacommentaries, and thus are reflexive upon the nonritualized, paramount reality of everyday life. But the anthropologist is in a position that would lead to such an observation: the anthropologist is never completely part of the culture being studied, but always apart from it. The subjects of research, the people, are also objects; and this is demanded by the nature of the anthropological discipline. The anthropologist, in a sense, assumes the role of a critic, for particular events are placed in the context of other events, are interrelated, contrasted, and evaluated. Therefore, while rituals might typically be regarded as reflexive events by anthropologists, it does not necessarily follow that they will be similarly regarded by participants. (1984, p. 203)

There is something democratic about opening up the range of things taken to be textual and accessible to interpretation, but it is as presumptuous to offer critical readings of popular artifacts as it is to interpret high culture artifacts without reference to what the actual audiences may be thinking. Sometimes, as Kapferer suggests, the artifact may be one in which the natives invest a great deal of interpretive energy themselves; sometimes, however, it will be an object that the people in question do not, in fact, think with. Vincent Crapanzano (1986) has made this point about Geertz's celebrated cockfight, that Geertz offers no evidence that the Balinese themselves see the cockfight as a text to be read, no evidence that the cockfight is marked in Balinese culture as a cultural object to be interpreted. Geertz's own interpretive virtuosity, without such support, may then be an instance of the academy's semiotic aggrandizement.

But do we not think with *all* the objects in our environment? Yes, at some level we do. But cultures do not invest all objects with equal amounts of meaning. For urban Americans, say, the power of the distinctions among street/road/avenue/court/place is much greater than that among elm/oak/maple/spruce, even though both sets of categories are part of the culture. These natives may find it worthwhile to interpret both the Sunday comics and the Sunday sermon, but they will most likely find disagreements over the sermon more troubling and the task of interpretation more significant and the value of skilled interpreters correspondingly greater.

Moreover, there is with some objects in the culture a tradition of interpretation that is cumulative and, for this reason, has acquired a sophistication or refinement that everyday interpretation does not attain. While such cumulative traditions exist with respect to a number of kinds of objects, they are especially noteworthy with respect to *written* materials, and, not incidentally, the interpretations themselves are carried on in writing. Written texts provide something that most other objects do not: the possibility of a tradition of criticism that makes an enormous difference in developing and elaborating reflective thought (Goody, 1977). It is not that analysis and reflection are impossible or even unlikely without writing, but a *sustained* tradition of reflection is unlikely. Certainly there can be a connoisseurship with respect to cockfights or culinary arts that exists primarily in oral culture. But with all its richness, oral culture also has its limits. The celebration of cockfights and culinary arts and clown dances in the university is all to the good so long as we do not forget that the medium of that celebration, the medium that makes thinking about these objects so interesting and enables an enlargement of our vision about what human cultures are about, is still the written word.

Audiences. It is right to observe that audiences do not absorb culture like sponges. The popular audience is selective, reflective, and constructive in its use of culture. But this is not to say that the popular audience is always critical or creative in its responses any more than elite audiences are. Even within an individual, a person responds differently to different cultural experiences. Very critical and searching readers of fiction may let music wash right over them at a concert; a discerning reader of poetry may not be able to stand before a painting in a gallery for more than a few seconds. Some people who are discriminating consumers of theater may rely on 'name brands' for dance. Such people know very well, or should know, that they are more active, playful, critical, or creative in responding to some cultural objects than in responding to others.

If we can recognize such distinctions for individuals, then why not for groups? If we know, further, that in many of the areas where we *are* critical readers we have gone through a process of education, formal or informal, why can we not conclude that processes of education are central to critical and playful readings in general? And if we can say this, can we not also say, indeed, must we not affirm also that one of the tasks of education, not only in the schools and universities but in the structure of society as a whole, is, as Raymond Williams put it, 'to deepen and refine the capacity for significant responses' (1983, p. 62)? The fact that popular audiences respond actively to the materials of mass culture is important to recognize and understand, but it is not a fact that should encourage us to accept mass culture as it stands or popular audiences as they now exist. The fact that different subgroups in the population respond in different ways to common cultural objects or have developed refined critical temperaments with regard to some local or provincial cultural form unrecognized by elites is important to understand and should lead us to recognize a wide variety of connoisseurships and a plurality of educational forms that lead to them. But this is not or should not be to admit all cultural forms equal, all interpretations valid, all interpretive communities self-contained and beyond criticism.

The celebration of popular culture and popular audiences in the universities has been a political act; it could not have been otherwise. The challenge popular culture now presents the university is not a call to erase all boundaries to what is to be treated in a classroom. Rather, it is to force a self-conscious and sociologically self-aware defense of the boundaries the university draws. The challenge is not to deny a place for judgment and valuation but to identify the institutional, national, class, race, and gender-bound biases set deep in past judgments and to make them available for critical reassessment. The new validation of popular culture should not lead higher education to abandon its job of helping students to be critical and playful readers, helping to deepen and refine in them a capacity for significant response. Instead, it should enhance these efforts with new respect for how, in some spheres and in some ways and despite some limits, students (and others) have been critical and playful readers all along.

The essay should end there. It would have, if I thought I had resolved the problems I presented.

I do not. I end up caught between a belief that the university should be a moral educator, holding up for emulation some values and some texts (and not others), and a reluctant admission that defining the basis of moral education is an unfinished, often unrecognized, task. I know, of course, that the university is a moral educator whether this is intended or not. Students learn from teachers what we value, by what values we 'profess' to work, and what turns of mind or character we approve. But if we learn to be self-conscious about the implicit hierarchies of taste and value we live and teach by, will we locate adequate grounds for our moral claims? What ground can we stand on, especially when the trends that favor relativism are so much more powerful and cogent (to my own mind) than the rather arbitrary and ill-defended hierarchies of value they so pointedly confront?

If there is sentimentality on one side – would-be populists waving the banner of people's culture – there is piety on the other – ardent champions of a traditional curriculum wailing at the decline of literacy, values, morals, the university, or their students' ability to write (or even recognize) a good English sentence. Neither side seems to me very clear about the pass we have reached. We can all carry on, nevertheless: departments and professional associations will sustain the structures for individual careers; institutional and personal investments in things as they are will keep us from looking too closely at the intellectual crisis we have come upon. But if we ever come to separating sense from romance and standards from nostalgia in all of this, it is not going to be easy.

References

Altieri, C. (1984) 'An idea and ideal of a literary canon', in R. von Hallberg (ed.), *Canons*, Chicago: University of Chicago Press (pp. 41–84).

Barthes, R. (1979) 'From work to text', in J. Harari (ed.), *Textual Strategies: Perspectives in post structural criticism*, Ithaca, NY: Cornell University Press (pp. 73–81).

Becker, H. S. (1982) *Artworlds*, Berkeley: University of California Press.

Geertz, C. (1973) 'Deep play: notes on the Balinese cockfight', in C. Geertz (ed.), *The Interpretation of Cultures*, New York: Basic Books (pp. 412–453).

Giamatti, A. B. (1980, July) 'The American teacher', *Harper's*, pp. 24–9.

Gitlin, T. (1978) 'Media sociology: the dominant paradigm', *Theory and Society*, 6, 205–53.

Goody, J. (1977) *The Domestication of the Savage Mind*, Cambridge, MA: Cambridge University Press.

Herrnstein Smith, B. (1984) 'Contingencies of value', in R. von Hallberg (ed.), *Canons*, Chicago: University of Chicago Press (pp. 5–40).

Hirsch, P. (1972) 'Processing fads and fashions: an organization-set analysis of cultural industry systems', *American Journal of Sociology*, 77, 639–59.

Kapferer, B. (1984) 'The ritual process and the problem of reflexivity', in J. MacAloon (ed.), *Rite, Drama, Fesival, Spectacle*, Philadelphia: Institute for the Study of Human Issues (pp. 179–207).

Kermode, F. (1983) *The Art of Telling: Essays on fiction*, Cambridge, MA: Harvard University Press.

Lears, T. J. J. (1985) 'The concept of cultural hegemony: problems and possibilities', *American Historical Review*, 85, 567–93.

Mukerji, C. and Schudson, M. (1986) 'Popular culture', *Annual Review of Sociology*, 12, 47–66.

Peterson, R. A. (ed.) (1976) *The Production of Culture*, Beverly Hills, CA: Sage.

Peterson, R. A. (1979) 'Revitalizing the culture concept', *Annual Review of Sociology*, 5, 137–66.

Williams, R. (1983) *The Year 2000*, New York: Pantheon Books.

47 □ *The Popular Economy*

John Fiske

The Problem of the Popular

Popularity is seductively easy to understand if we persist in the fallacious belief that we live in a homogeneous society and that people are fundamentally all the same. But it becomes a much more complex issue when we take into account that late capitalist societies are composed of a huge variety of social groups and subcultures, all held together in a network of social relations in which the most significant factor is the differential distribution of power.

In this book I have argued against the common belief that the capitalist cultural industries produce only an apparent variety of products whose variety is finally illusory, for they all promote the same capitalist ideology. Their skill in sugar-coating the pill is so great that the people are not aware of the ideological practice in which they are engaging as they consume and enjoy the cultural commodity. I do not believe that 'the people' are 'cultural dopes'; they are not a passive, helpless mass incapable of discrimination and thus at the economic, cultural, and political mercy of the barons of the industry. Equally I reject the assumption that all that different people and different social groups have in common is baseness, so that art that appeals to many can only do so by appealing to what humans call 'the animal instincts'. 'The lowest common denominator' may be a useful concept in arithmetic, but in the study of popularity its only possible value is to expose the prejudices of those who use it.

More recent Marxist thinking rejects the notion of a singular or monovocal capitalist ideology in favour of a multiplicity of ideologies that speak capitalism in a variety of ways for a variety of capitalist subjects. Their unity in speaking capitalism is fragmented by the plurality of accents in which they speak it. Such a view posits a multiplicity of points of resistance or accommodations whose only unity lies in the *fact* of their resistance or accommodation, but not in the *form* it may take.

From Fiske, J., *Television Culture*, Routledge, London, 1987, pp. 309–26.

This is a model that has far greater explanatory power in late capitalism and is one that grants some power to 'the people'. Despite the homogenizing force of the dominant ideology, the subordinate groups in capitalism have retained a remarkable diversity of social identities, and this has required capitalism to produce an equivalent variety of voices. The diversity of capitalist voices is evidence of the comparative intransigence of the subordinate.

Any discussion of popularity must account for opposing forces within it. The definition that serves the interests of the producers and distributors of the cultural commodity is one of head counting, often with some demographic sophistication so that heads of a particular socioeconomic class, age group, gender, or other classification can be collected, counted, and then 'sold' to an advertiser. The greater the head count, the greater the popularity. Opposed to this is the notion that popular means 'of the people' and that popularity springs from, and serves the interests of, the people amongst whom it is popular. Popularity is here a measure of a cultural form's ability to serve the desires of its customers. In so far as the people occupy different social situations from the producers, their interests must necessarily differ from, and often conflict with, the interests of the producers.

The term 'the people' has romantic connotations which must not be allowed to lead us into a idealized notion of the people as an oppositional force whose culture and social experience are in some way authentic. We need to think rather of the people as a multiple and constantly changing concept, a huge variety of social groups accommodating themselves with, or opposing themselves to, the dominant value system in a variety of ways. In so far as 'the people' is a concept with any validity at all, it should be seen as an alliance of formations which are constantly shifting and relatively transient. It is neither a unified nor a stable concept, but one whose terms are constantly under reformulation in a dialectic relationship with the dominant classes. In the cultural domain, then, popular art is an ephemeral, multifarious concept based upon multiple and developing relationships with the practices of the dominant ideology.

The term 'people', then, refers to social groups that are relatively powerless and are typically interpellated as consumers, though they may not respond in this manner. They have cultural forms and interests of their own that differ from, and often conflict with, those of the producers of cultural commodities. The autonomy of these groups from the dominant is only relative, and never total, but it derives from their marginalized and repressed histories that have intransigently resisted incorporation, and have retained material, as well as ideological, differences usually through devalued cultural forms, many of which are oral and unrecorded. For some groups these differences may be small and the conflicts muted, but for others the gap is enormous. For a cultural commodity to be popular, then, it must be able to meet the various interests of the people amongst whom it is popular as well as the interests of its producers.

The Two Economies

The multiplicity and contradictory value of these interests does not mean that they cannot be met in the one commodity: they can, though only because the cultural commodity circulates in different though simultaneous economies, which we may call the financial and the cultural.

The workings of the financial economy cannot account adequately for all cultural factors, but it still needs to be taken into account in any investigation of popular art in a consumers' society. It is useful, if only up to a point, to be able to describe texts as cultural commodities, but we must always recognize crucial differences between them and other goods in the marketplace.

For instance, cultural goods do not have a clearly defined use-value, despite Marx's assertion that the production of aesthetic pleasure is a use-value, but this seems to be a metaphorical use of the term – the use-value of a work of art is different from that, say, of a machine gun or a can of beans, if only that it is very much more difficult to predict or specify. Cultural commodities do, however, have a more clearly identifiable exchange-value which the technology of reproduction has put under severe pressure. Photocopiers, audio and video recorders are agents of popular power, and thus the producers and distributors have had to argue for elaborations and extensions of copyright laws to maintain some control over exchange-value and its base in scarcity. Such legislation has largely failed: the copying of television programs and of records is not only widespread, but also socially acceptable.

The cultural commodity differs from other commodities in having comparatively high initial production costs and very low reproduction costs, so distribution offers a safer return on investment than production. Technical development and venture capital have, therefore, been concentrated on satellites, on cable and microwave distribution systems, or in the hardware of televisions, sound systems, and home entertainment centers.

But the cultural commodity cannot be adequately described in financial terms only: the circulation that is crucial to its popularity occurs in the parallel economy – the cultural. What is exchanged and circulated here is not wealth but meanings, pleasures, and social identities. Of course commodities primarily based in the financial economy work in the cultural economy too, consumer choice between similar commodities is often not between competing use-values, despite the efforts of consumer advice groups, but between cultural values: and the selection of one particular commodity over others becomes the selection of meanings, pleasures, and social identity for the consumer. With the shift of capitalist economies from production to marketing, the cultural value of material commodities has enormously increased in proportionate importance – one has only to look at the fashion industry, or the motor car industry, to find examples. None the less, such commodities, still circulate within a primarily financial economy that retains their bases in use-value.

We need to look in a little more detail at the interaction between these separate, though related, economies, the financial and the cultural. The financial economy offers two modes of circulation for cultural commodities: in the first, the producers of a program sell it to distributors: the program is a straightforward material commodity. In the next, the program-as-commodity changes role and it becomes a producer. And the new commodity that it produces is an audience which, in its turn, is sold to advertisers or sponsors.

A classic example of the interdependence of these two financial 'subeconomies' and the possibility of controlling them is provided by *Hill Street Blues*. MTM produces the series and sells it for distribution to NBC. NBC sells its audience (a higher socioeconomic group of both genders than most TV audiences) to Mercedes Benz, who sponsor the series. The show rates respectably, but not spectacularly. MTM could, if they wished, modify the format and content of the series to increase the size of the audience. But such an increase would be in a lower socioeconomic group, and this is not a commodity that Mercedes Benz wish to buy. So the show stays as it is, one of the few on American television that has a strong class basis, though noticeably little class conflict. Furillo and Davenport, those embodiments of middle-class *angst*, care and suffer for their team of working-class cops. The program is built around the yuppie view of class, social conscience, and moral responsibility, which form the basis of the meanings and pleasures that it offers in the cultural economy.

The move to the cultural economy involves yet another role-shift from commodity to producer. As the earlier role-shift changed the role of the program from commodity to producer, so the move to the cultural economy involves the audience in a role-shift which changes it also from a commodity to a producer: in this case a producer of meanings and pleasures. The gap between the cultural and the financial economies is wide enough to grant the cultural economy considerable autonomy, but not too wide to be bridgeable. The producers and distributors of a program can exert some, if limited, influence over who watches and some, though limited, influence over the meanings and pleasures that the audiences (and we must shift to the plural in the cultural economy) may produce from it. The upscale target audience of *Hill Street Blues* is far from its only audience and the variety of audiences will presumably produce a variety of pleasures and meanings. *Dallas* not only tops the ratings in the USA and thus must gain a wide diversity of American audiences, it is also widely exported and arguably has the largest range of audiences of any fictional TV program. [. . .] Ien Ang (1985) found a Dutch Marxist and a feminist who were able to find pleasure in the program by discovering in its excess of sexism and capitalism a critique of those systems that it was apparently celebrating. Similarly, Katz and Liebes (1984, 1985) found that members of a Jewish kibbutz were clear that the money of the Ewings did not bring them happiness, whereas members of rural North African cooperative were equally clear that their wealth gave them an easy life. Katz and Leibes's fifty different ethnic lower-middle-class groups produced a huge variety of meanings and found an equal variety of pleasures from the same show.

This book has argued that the power of audiences-as-producers in the cultural economy is considerable. This is partly due to the absence of any direct sign of their (subordinate) role in the financial economy which liberates them from its constraints – there is no exchange of money at the point of sale/consumption, and no direct relationship between the price paid and the amount consumed; people can consume as much as they wish and what they wish, without the restriction of what they are able to afford. But more importantly, this power derives from the fact that meanings do not circulate in the cultural economy in the same way that wealth does in the financial. They are harder to possess (and thus to exclude others from possessing), they are harder to control because the production of meaning and pleasure is not the same as the production of the cultural commodity, or of other goods, for in the cultural economy the role of consumer does not exist as the end point of a linear economic transaction. Meanings and pleasures circulate within it without any real distinction between producers and consumers.

In the financial economy consumption is clearly separate from production and the economic relations that bind them are comparatively clear and available for analysis. But the cultural economy does not work in the same way. Its commodities, which we call 'texts', are not containers or conveyors of meaning and pleasure, but rather *provokers* of meaning and pleasure. The production of meaning/pleasure is finally the responsibility of the consumer and is undertaken only in his/her interests: this is not to say that the material producers/distributors do not attempt to make and sell meanings and pleasures – they do, but their failure rate is enormous. Twelve out of thirteen records fail to make a profit, TV series are axed by the dozen, expensive films sink rapidly into red figures (*Raise the Titanic* is an ironic example – it nearly sank the Lew Grade empire).

This is one reason why the cultural industries produce what Garnham (1987) calls 'repertoires' of products; they cannot predict which of their commodities will be chosen by which sectors of the market to be the provoker of meanings/pleasures that serve *their* interests as well as those of the producers. Because the production of meaning/pleasure occurs in the consumption as well as the production of the cultural commodity, the notion of production takes on a new dimension that delegates it away from the owners of capital.

Popular Cultural Capital

Cultural capital, despite Bourdieu's (1980) productive metaphor, does not circulate in the same way as economic capital. Hobson's (1982) viewers of *Crossroads*, for example, were vehement that the program was theirs, it was their cultural capital. And they made it theirs by the pleasures and meanings they produced from it, that articulated their concerns and identities. There is a popular cultural capital in a way that there is no popular economic capital, and thus Bourdieu's institutionally validated cultural capital of the bourgeoisie is constantly being opposed, interrogated, marginalized, scandalized, and evaded, in a way that economic capital never is.

This popular cultural capital consists of the meanings and pleasures available to the subordinate to express and promote their interests. It is not a singular concept, but is open to a variety of articulations, but it always exists in a stance of resistance to the forces of domination. Like any form of capital, either economic capital or the cultural capital of the bourgeoisie, it works through ideology, for, as Hall (1986) points out, we must not limit our understanding of ideology to an analysis of how it works in the service of the dominant. We need to recognize that there are resistive, alternative ideologies that both derive from and maintain those social groups who are not accommodated comfortably into the existing power relations: 'an ideology empowers people, enabling them to begin to make some sense or intelligibility of their historical situation' (p. 16).

These ideologies that empower the subordinate enable them to produce resistive meanings and pleasures that are, in their own right, a form of social power. Power is not, according to Foucault, a one-way force, from the top down. When he talks of power coming from below, he alerts us to the fact that power is necessarily a two-way force: it can only work, in either direction, in opposition. This is just as true for 'top–down' power as it is for 'bottom–up' power.

If power is a two-way force, so, too, is the pleasure so closely associated with it.

> The pleasure that comes of exercising a power that questions, monitors, watches, spies, searches out, palpates, brings to light: and, on the other hand, the pleasure that kindles at having to evade this power, flee from it, fool it or travesty it. The power that lets itself be invaded by the pleasure it is pursuing: and opposite it, power asserting itself in the pleasure of showing off, scandalizing, resisting. (Foucault, 1978: 45)

Television participates in both these modes of power-pleasure. It exerts the power of surveillance, revealing the world, spying out people's secrets, monitoring human activity, but an integral part of this power is the resistance, or rather resistances, to it. The two-way nature of power means that its resistances are themselves multiple points of power. Power, paradoxically, can thus liberate people from its own force to subject and discipline them.

Play, besides being a source of pleasure, is also a source of power. Children's 'play' with television is a form of power over it. In incorporating its characters and scenarios into their own fantasy games they create their own oral and active culture out of the resources it provides. Sydney children in 1982 and 1983 were singing their own version of a beer commercial:

How do you feel
when you're having a fuck
under a truck
and the truck rolls off

I feel like a Tooheys', I feel like a Tooheys'
I feel like a Tooheys or two.

(Children's Folklore Archives, Australian Studies Centre, Western Australian Institute
of Technology)

The production of a scatological playground rhyme out of a television commercial
is a typical, and complex, cultural activity. At the most obvious level it is an
empowering, creative response to television and an oppositional one. It is a clear
example of 'excorporation', that process by which the powerless steal elements of
the dominant culture and use them in their own, often, oppositional or subversive,
interests. This is the verbal equivalent of Madonna's use of religious inconography
to convey her independent sexuality, and the opposite of the fashion industry's
incorporation of elements of punk or of working-class dress into its own *haute
couture*. It is also an example of Foucault's resistive power, the power to 'travesty'
the original power, the pleasure of 'showing off, scandalizing, resisting'.

This children's rhyme involves a powerful, playful, pleasurable misuse of
television, in that the signifiers are changed as well as the signifieds. [. . .] [We have]
noted a similar 'misuse' of *Dallas* (Katz and Liebes, 1985), in which the narrative
was distorted to meet the cultural needs of a particular audience. The Arab group
who 'rewrote' the program so that Sue Ellen returned with her baby to her father's
home instead of her former lover's were 'rewriting' or travestying television in a
fundamentally similar way to that of the Sydney schoolchildren, and for much the
same purposes. *Prisoner*, too, is easily rewritten in a way that allows school students
to travesty its meanings and to make it a representation not of prison but of school
(Hodge and Tripp, 1986). Their ideology, deriving from, and making sense of, their
social experience of subordination in both the school and the family, enabled them
to partake in an active ideological practice: they were not cultural dopes at the mercy
of the text or its producers, but were in control of their own reading relations. They
were active producers of their own meanings and pleasures from the text.

Of course, the semiotic excess and the producerly reading relations it requires are
not unique to television: any art form that is popular amongst widely differing
audiences must allow for this overspill. Thus Michaels (1986) shows that Aboriginal
viewers of *Rambo* found neither pleasure nor sense in his nationalistic, patriotic
motivation. Instead, they 'wrote' him into an elaborate kinship network with those
he was rescuing, thus making 'tribal' meanings that were culturally pertinent to
themselves. The fact that the film was popular with both them and Ronald Reagan
must not lead us to assume any similarity between the two, nor that the meanings
and pleasures they produced from it were similar.

Resistance and Semiotic Power

Resistance is a concept that has been woven throughout the argument of this book,
for it is central to an understanding of popularity in a society where power is

unequally distributed. As social power can take many forms, so too can the resistances to it. There is no singular blanket resistance, but a huge multiplicity of points and forms of resistance, a huge variety of resistances. These resistances are not just oppositions to power, but are sources of power in their own right: they are the social points at which the powers of the subordinate are most clearly expressed.

It may be helpful to categorize these resistances into two main types, corresponding to two main forms of social power – the power to construct meanings, pleasures, and social identities, and the power to construct a socioeconomic system. The first is semiotic power, the second is social power, and the two are closely related, although relatively autonomous.

The power domain within which popular culture works is largely, but not exclusively, that of semiotic power. One major articulation of this power is the struggle between homogenization and difference, or between consensus and conflict. The 'top–down' force of this power attempts to produce a coherent set of meanings and social identities around an unarticulated consensus whose forms serve the status quo. It attempts to deny any conflict of interest and to mobilize social differences in a structure of complementarity. It is a homogenizing, centralizing, integrating force that attempts to maintain semiotic and social power at the centre.

Volosinov argues that the multiaccentuality of the sign is crucial, for it is this that enables it to play an active role in the class struggle: its polysemic potential is always mobilized in and against a structure of domination, and the strategy of the dominant is to control polysemy, to reduce the multiaccentual to the uniaccentual.

> The ruling class strives to impart a superclass, external character to the ideological sign, to extinguish or drive inward the struggle between social value judgments which occurs in it, to make the sign uniaccentual. (Volosinov, 1973: 23)

Resisting this is the diversity of social groups with their diversity of social interests. Their power is expressed in the resistances to homogenization, it works as a centrifugal rather than a centripetal force, it recognizes conflict of interest, it proposes multiplicity over singularity and it may be summed up as the exercise of the power to be different.

This power to construct meanings, pleasures, and social identities that *differ* from those proposed by the structures of domination is crucial, and the area within which it is exercised is that of representation. Popular culture is often denigrated by its critics for appearing to offer not representations of the world, but avenues of escape from it: 'mere escapism' is an easy way of dismissing popular culture from the critical and social agenda. Underlying this is the notion that *representation* has a social dimension, whereas *escapism* is a merely personal flight into fantasy. Such an easy dismissal ignores the fact that escapism or fantasy necessarily involves both an escape from or evasion of something and an escape to a preferred alternative: dismissing escapism as 'mere fantasy' avoids the vital questions of *what* is escaped from, *why* escape is necessary, and *what* is escaped to.

Asking these questions gives escapism or fantasy as strong a sociopolitical dimension as representation, and begins to erode the difference between the two. But the differences are still commonly believed to exist, and I wish to challenge them because maintaining them serves the interests of the dominant by devaluing many of the pleasures of the subordinate. As with many of the experiences of the subordinate, fantasy or escapism is often 'feminized', that is, it is seen as a sign of feminine weakness resulting from women's inability to come to terms with (masculine) reality. It is a sort of daydreaming that allows women or children to achieve their desires in a way that they are never capable of in the 'real' world, a compensatory domain which results from and disguise their 'real' lack of power. Representation, however, is seen as a means of exercising power: not a means of escaping from the world but of acting upon it. Representation is the means of making that sense of the world which serves one's own interests: it is 'the process of putting into concrete forms (that is, different signifiers) an abstract ideological concept' (O'Sullivan *et al.*, 1983: 199). Its process of making ideology material, and therefore natural, is a highly political one that involves the power to make meanings both of the world and of one's place within it: it is therefore 'appropriately' thought of as dominant or masculine: it is seen as a site of struggle for power, in a way that fantasy is not. Such a simplistic distinction that is so much a part of the structures of domination needs challenging.

McRobbie (1984) articulates this challenge when she argues convincingly that fantasy is a private, intimate experience which can be interpreted as

> part of a strategy of resistance or opposition: that is, as marking out one of those areas that cannot be totally colonised. (p. 184)

She makes the point that the apparently obvious distinction between fantasy and reality is open to question:

> [fantasy is] as much an *experience*, a piece of reality, as is babysitting or staying in to do the washing. (p. 184)

Fantasy is a means of representation whose privacy and intimacy do not prevent its acting just as powerfully upon the meanings of social experience as do the more public representations of language and the media. Its inferiority does not disqualify it from political effectivity: the interior is, to coin a phrase, the political.

The argument that this is a pseudo-power that dissipates the drive to seize 'real' political or economic power underestimates the extent to which the construction of subjectivity is political. Part of the argument asserts that resistive fantasies that occur only in the interior experience of the subject are not finally resistive at all, for resistance can only occur at the level of the social or the collective. This argument is based upon the belief that the material social experience of the subordinate can, of itself, be the origin of resistance. Against this I would argue that the origins of resistance lie not just in the social experience of subordination, but in the sense people make of it. There are meanings of subordination that serve the interests of the dominant, and there are ones that serve those of the subordinated. But the crucial point is that the separation of material social experience from the meanings given to it is an analytical and theoretical strategy only. In everyday life, there is no such neat distinction: our experience *is* what we make of it. Similarly, distinctions between the social and the interior are finally unproductive particularly when they value one over the other: social or collective resistance cannot exist independently of 'interior' resistance, even if that is given the devalued name of 'fantasy'. The connections between the interior and the social cannot be modeled along the simple cause and effect lines that underlie the devaluation of interior resistance because it may not have the direct effect of producing resistance at the social level. The relationship between the interior and the social can only be explained by a model of a much more dispersed and deferred effectivity.

Popular culture that works in the interests of the subordinate is often a provoker of fantasy. These fantasies may take many forms, but they typically embody the power of the subordinate to exert some control over representation. Such a fantasy is no escape from social reality, rather it is a direct response to the dominant ideology and its embodiment in social relations. The challenge it offers lies both in *what* meanings are made and in *who* has the power and the ability to make them. Fantasy, at the very least, maintains a sense of subcultural difference, it is part of the exercise of semiotic power.

Diversity and Difference

The 'power to be different' is the power that maintains social differences, social diversity. The relationship between social diversity and a diversity of voices on television is one that needs to be carefully thought through. There is a familiar rhetoric that proposes that diversity of programs on television is a good thing, and few would take issue with that as a general principle. Conversely, homogeneity of programming is seen to be undesirable. The problem lies in deciding what constitutes homogeneity and what diversity and, equally problematically, what constitutes 'a good thing'. In one sense, the new technologies of distribution, satellites, cables, and optical fibers, can be viewed as potential agents of diversity, in that their economics demand that *more* be transmitted. But, as Bakke (1986) argues, in the European context, at least, new technologies such as satellites also permit a larger audience to be reached which produces a demand for noncontroversial content, a bland homogeneity that will offend no one and appeal in some, relatively superficial, way to everyone. Paradoxically, then, the increase in the means of distribution may actually decrease the variety of cultural commodities that are distributed.

But diversity is not simply to be measured in terms of the variety of programs transmitted: diversity of readings is equally, if not more, important. Paradoxically, diversity of readings may best be stimulated by a greater homogeneity of programming. A widely distributed single program, such as *Dallas*, whose openness makes it a producerly text, may not be such an agent of homogenization as it appears, for to reach its multitude of diverse audiences it must allow for a great deal of cultural diversity in its readings, and must thus provide considerable semiotic excess for the receiving subcultures to negotiate with in order to produce *their* meanings, rather than the ones preferred by the broadcasters. *Dallas* may be a singular, and highly profitable, commodity in the financial economy, but in the cultural it is a full *repertoire* of commodities: as Altman (1986) says, *Dallas* provides a 'menu' from which the viewers choose.

A diversity of programs is a diversity that is deliberately constructed by television producers and schedulers in an attempt to segment the audience into the markets required by the advertisers, which may or may not coincide with the subcultural formations constructed by the people. A greater variety of closed, readerly texts that impose their meanings more imperialistically and that deliver market segments to advertisers may not be as socially desirable as a narrower range of more open texts, where the diversity is a function of the people rather than of the producers.

Wilson and Gutierrez (1985) argue that the new technologies, particularly cable, allow the media to exploit subcultural diversity, and to commodify ethnic and minority audiences in order to sell them to advertisers. *Dallas*, for all its apparent homogeneity, may well be a more diversified program than the variety of offerings of such multiple special-interest channels, and in so far as its diversification is audience-produced rather than centrally produced, it is, I argue, more likely to maintain cultural differences and to produce subculturally specific meanings and pleasures.

The same dilemma confronts us in the attempt to understand television's role and effects in the international arena. Hollywood, and, to a lesser extent, Europe, may dominate the international flow of both news and entertainment programming, yet there is little evidence of a global surge of popularity for the Western nations and their values. The domination in the economic domain may not necessarily produce the equivalent domination in the cultural. Katz and Liebes (1987) have shown that Russian Jews, newly arrived in Israel, read *Dallas* as capitalism's self-criticism: 'consuming' the program did not necessarily involve consuming the ideology.

A national culture, and the sense of national identity which many believe it can produce, which is constructed by the cultural industries or by politicians or cultural lobbyists, may not coincide with the social alliances that are felt to be most productive by subordinate groups within the nation. Thus Aboriginal cultural identity within contemporary Australia may serve itself best by articulating itself not with an Australian nation, but with blacks in other white-dominated, ex-colonial countries. And Michaels (1986) has indicated that the recent popularity of reggae amongst Aboriginal peoples is explained by some Aboriginals as the perception of a common social alliance amongst black subjected cultures. Black music, produced within and against colonialism, has a cultural and political effectivity that traverses national boundaries. Hodge and Tripp's (1986) Aboriginal children who constructed a single cultural category that included themselves, American Indians, and American black children were similarly forging their own cultural alliances in a way that can be neither controlled nor predicted by the cultural industries. Such a cultural consciousness is a prerequisite for political action, though it will not, of itself, produce it. But without it, any political movement to improve the Aboriginal situation will be insecurely based. MacCabe (1986) makes the point well:

> The crucial necessity for political action is a felt collectivity. It may be that cultural forms indicate to us that politically enabling collectivities are to be located across subcultures, be they national or international. (pp. 9–10)

Hebdige (1979, 1982, 1987) has shown how American popular culture in the 1950s and 1960s was eagerly taken up by British working-class youth who found in its flashy streamlining a way to articulate their new class confidence and consciousness. Such symbolizations of their identity were simply not available in 'British' culture which appeared to offer two equally unacceptable sets of alternatives – the one a romanticized cloth-cap image of an 'authentic' traditional working-class culture, the other a restrained, tasteful, BBC-produced inflection of popular culture. The commodities produced by the American cultural industries were mobilized to express an intransigent, young, urban, working-class identity that scandalized both the traditional British working class and the dominant middle classes. The cultural alliance between this fraction of the British working class and their sense of American popular culture was one that served their cultural/ideological needs at that historical moment. Similarly, one might speculate about the cultural meanings of Madonna in Moscow (at the time of writing it is reported that her albums are changing hands for $75 on the black market).

In a similar vein, Worpole (1983) has shown how the style of pre-Second World War American fiction, particularly that of Hemingway, Hammett and Chandler, articulated a vernacular, masculine, critical stance towards urban capitalism that the British working class found pertinent to their social position. British popular literature, typified by the bourgeois rural milieu of Agatha Christie or the aristocratic, imperialist heroism of Bulldog Drummond, promoted a nostalgic class-specific Britishness that was more alien and hostile to the British working class than novels produced in America. Similarly, Cohen and Robbins (1979) have shown how Kung Fu movies play a positive role as articulations of the subcultural norms of working-class London boys. The economic origin of the cultural commodity cannot account for the cultural use-value it may offer in its moment and place of reception, and can neither control nor predict the variety of meanings and pleasures it may provoke. The dominant ideological interests of the society that produces and determines the industry may well be imbricated in the conventions and discourses of the text, but they cannot comprise all of the textual fabric. In order for the text to be popular amongst audiences whose social position produces a sense of difference from that ideology, it must contain contradictions, gaps, and traces of counter-ideologies. Its narrative structure and hierarchization of discourses may attempt to produce a resolution in favor of the dominant, but various moments of reading can reveal this resolution to be much more fragile than traditional textual analysis would suppose it to be. Indeed, texts that are popular amongst a wide variety of audiences must hold this balance between the dominant ideology and its multiple oppositions on a point of extreme precariousness: it is no willful misreading to find in *Dallas* a critique of patriarchal capitalism, nor in *Prisoner* an exposure of the insensitivities of institutional power.

The unpredictability of the market for cultural commodities has forced the cultural industries into certain economic strategies, particularly the production of a repertoire of products (Garnham, 1987), to ensure their profitability, and while these strategies have proved successful in maintaining the industries' domination in the financial economy, they necessarily weaken their ideological power in the cultural.

Those of us on the Left may deplore the fact that, with some exceptions, it is the commercially produced commodities that most easily cross the boundaries of class, race, gender, or nation, and that thus appear to be most readily accessible and pleasurable to a variety of subordinated groups. But alternative strategies are not easy to find, though the success of the BBC with working-class realist serials like *EastEnders* or the comedy series *Only Fools and Horses* does offer some hope. Otherwise, attempts to produce television by and for the working classes or other subordinate or minority groups have only partially succeeded, if at all. Ang's (1986) account of the problems faced by a proletarian progressive television channel in Holland is exemplary here, and Blanchard and Morley (1984) have given an equally thoughtful account of the difficulties faced by Britain's Channel 4. It may well be that the subordinate maintain their subcultural identity by means other than television (schoolyard culture for children, gossip for women, etc.), and that television is popular to the extent that it intersects with these other cultural forces.

Cohen and Robbins (1979) try to account for the popularity of Kung Fu movies with British urban working-class males via the coming together of two forms of 'collective representations', one of which is the oral tradition and interpersonal style of working-class culture, and the other is the industrially produced conventions of the genre. Morley (1981) summarizes the argument neatly:

> The oral traditions constitute forms of cultural competence available to these kids which make it possible for them to appropriate these movies – without forms of competence, the popularity of these movies would be inexplicable. (p. 11)

These points of intersection between mass and local or oral culture can only be activated by the viewers and cannot be deliberately or accurately produced by the cultural industries themselves, though they can, of course, be aimed at.

The industrial mode of production of television will necessarily separate its producers from its audiences culturally, socially, and ideologically: in the financial economy this gap clearly works to the advantage of the industry, which obviously would not like to see a series of popular, low-cost community stations develop, and thus it works to maximize the difference by developing more fully its high-cost production values. But in the cultural economy, the gap works to the industry's disadvantage and it seeks to close it, to stress its cultural closeness to its audiences. But in this it is rather like the lovesick suitor who can only hope to be chosen and who will never know if he will be, nor the reasons why he was or was not.

The attempt to produce a culture for others, whether that otherness be defined in terms of class, gender, race, nation, or whatever, can never be finally successful, for culture can only be produced from within, not from outside. In a mass society the materials and meaning systems out of which cultures are made will almost inevitably be produced by the cultural industries: but the making of these materials into culture, that is, into the meanings of self and of social relations, and the exchange of these materials for pleasure is a process that can only be performed by their consumer-users, not by their producers. Thus, in the sphere of a 'national' culture, it may be that *Miami Vice* is more 'Australian' than a mini-series that sets out to document and celebrate a specific movement in Australian history. *Miami Vice* is a cultural form of a late capitalist, consumerism, pleasure-centered society, where drugs, sex, sun, sensuality, leisure, music, and, above all, style are the order of the day; its depicted society is a racial cocktail where the white Anglo-Saxon hero only just maintains his position of narrative dominance; this world of *Miami Vice* may offer most contemporary Australians a more pertinent set of meanings and pleasures than any of the mini-series, so beloved of the Australian television industries, in which white, male, British immigrants open up the bush and in so doing build their own and their nation's character.

The reception of Hollywood cultural commodities into the cultures of Third World and developing nations may be a very different matter indeed, though the work of Katz and Liebes and of Michaels has hinted at similar active and discriminating viewing practices. A lot more work needs to be done on the international reception of both news and entertainment programs and ways that the developed nations can help the less developed to produce their own cultural commodities that can genuinely challenge Hollywood's in the arena of popular taste rather than of political or economic policy.

For this can be achieved. While it is clear that the most popular cultural commodities tend to be produced in and exported by Hollywood and other Western cultural industries, this tendency is far from total. The top twenty television programs (and records) in the USA, the UK and Australia may well exhibit striking similarities but they also contain very significant differences. There are locally popular cultural commodities as well as internationally popular ones.

We must also bear in mind that attempts to produce or defend a national culture, whether by a national broadcasting system or other means, have historically been dominated by middlle-class tastes and definitions of both nation and culture, and have shown remarkably little understanding of popular pleasures or popular tastes. Thus is it almost without exception that in countries that have both a national public broadcasting system and a commercial one, the commercial one will be more popular with the subordinate groups and classes, and the public one with the more educated middle classes. It is also generally true that the public channels will show more nationally produced programs, and the commercial channels more internationally produced, usually American, ones. The interesting exception to this is the public channel jn the United States, which tends to show more British programs, because in the United States 'British' culture is strongly associated with higher-class, educated tastes.

If those with a public or social motivation wish to intervene effectively in the cultural economy, they need to devote more attention to understanding popular tastes and pleasures than they have in the past. It is all too easy to arrive at a set of values that are deemed to be in the public interest, but submitting those values to the test of popular pleasure and subcultural pertinence is a much less comfortable enterprise. The reconciliation of a sense of the public good with the diverse demands of popular pleasure may not be easy, but those who wish to attempt it have much to learn from Hollywood and its ilk, for these industries are sometimes adept at achieving an equally difficult reconciliation – that between an industrially centralized, economically efficient mode of production and a multiplicity of dispersed, subculturally determined, as opposed to industrially determined, moments of reception.

There will always, in industrialized cultures, be a conflict of interest between producers/distributors on the one hand and the various formations of the people on the other. The two economies, the financial and the cultural, are the opposing sides of this struggle. The financial economy attempts to use television as an agent of homogenization: for *it* television is centered, singular in its functionality, and is located in its centers of production and distribution. In the cultural economy, however, television is entirely different. It is decentered, diverse, located in the multiplicity of its modes and moments of reception. Television is the plurality of its reading practices, the democracy of its pleasures, and it can only be understood in its fragments. It promotes and provokes a network of resistances to its own power whose attempt to homogenize and hegemonize breaks down on the instability and multiplicity of its meanings and pleasures.

Despite a generation of television, that most centrally produced and widely distributed popular art form, Western societies have resisted total homogenization. Feminists have shown that we do not all of us have to be patriarchs; other class, ethnic, age, and regional differences are also alive and well. Wilson and Gutierrez (1985), whose book is appropriately subtitled *Diversity and the end of mass communication*, show how ethnic minorities in the USA have maintained and even strengthened their separate identities, despite the homogenizing thrust of the mass media. Labov has shown, too, that the difference between black English and white English has widened over the past ten years, despite the white dominance of the media and educational systems.

Carey (1985) argues that any theory of the popular media must be able to account for the diversity of social experience within a contemporary society, and therefore the diversity of pleasures that the media offer:

> To strip away this diversity, even it if is described as relatively autonomous diversity, in order to reveal a deep and univocal structure of ideology and politics, is to

steamroller subjective consciousness just as effectively as the behaviorists and functionalists did. One does not, on this reading, wish to trade the well-known evils of the Skinner box for the less well-known, but just as real, evils of the Althusserian box. Any movement, therefore, toward encompassing elements of social structure – class, power, authority which explain away the diversity of consciousness is to head one down a road just as self-enclosing as the behaviorist terrain phenomenologists have been trying to evacuate for most of this century. (pp. 35–6)

Mercer (1986) also argues that the shift of critical attention from ideology to pleasure is one that rejects the supposed homogenizing power of the dominant ideology:

> The concern with pleasure then is a corresponding interrogation of the 'fact' of ideology. It suggests a rejection of the ascribed unity and omniscience, of its depth and homogeneity, of its stasis within a given cultural form.

Any theory of the popular must be able to account for this elaborate diversity of social formations.

The sort of diversity of programming that is often called for on television is one that diversifies the social positions of those who are granted access to it. This is unlikely to occur within a commercial broadcasting system, though cable networks in the USA and Channel 4 in the UK are making some moves in this direction. But however valuable these moves are, they still remain minority voices speaking to minority audiences. The political battle of popularity is fought in the arena of commercial broadcast television, and it is on this struggle that I have concentrated in this book.

In this arena, the inevitable (because profitable) homogenization of programming, which means that one financial commodity is sold to as many different audiences as possible, may not be such an agent of cultural domination as many fear. Indeed, I would argue the opposite. Diversity of readings is not the same as diversity of programs, and a diversity of readings and the consequent diversity of subcultural identities is crucial if the popular is to be seen as a set of forces for social change.

This brings us to the relationship between entertainment and politics. These are two separate cultural domains which, in Althusserian terms, are relatively autonomous though overdetermined. The resistive readings and pleasures of television do not translate directly into oppositional politics or social action. Relatively autonomous cultural domains do not relate to each other in simple cause and effect terms. But the absence of a direct political effect does not preclude a more general political effectivity [. . .]. Resistive reading practices that assert the power of the subordinate in the process of representation and its subsequent pleasure pose a direct challenge to the power of capitalism to produce its subjects-in-ideology. The way that people understand themselves and their social relations is part of the social system itself. Any set of social relations requires a set of meanings to hold it in place (Hall, 1984), and any set of social meanings has to be produced by, and in the interests of, a group or a formation of groups situated within a social system of power relations. The classes who dominate social relations also attempt to dominate the production of meaning that underpin them: social power and semiotic power are two sides of the same coin. Challenging meanings and the social group with the right to make them is a crucial part of asserting subcultural identities and the social differences that they maintain. The domain of entertainment is one of pleasures, meanings, and social identity: if this domain cannot maintain and promote the power of the subordinate to be different, there will be severely reduced motivation for change in the political domain. Maintaining subcultural diversity may not, in itself, produce any direct political effect, but at the more general level of effectivity its power is crucial.

And television is not neutral in this. Its success in the financial economy depends upon its ability to serve and promote the diverse and often oppositional interests of its audiences. In this sense it is the meanings and pleasures of the cultural economy that determine the extent of the economic return on that capital: the cultural economy drives the financial in a dialectic force that counters the power of capital. Television, as a mass-mediated popular art, must contain within it the opposing but linked forces of capital and the people if it is to circulate effectively in both financial and cultural economies. Far from being the agent of the dominant classes, it is the prime site where the dominant have to recognize the insecurity of their power, and where they have to encourage cultural difference with all the threat to their own position that this implies.

References

Altman, R. (1986) 'Television/sound', in T. Modleski (ed.), *Studies in Entertainment: Critical approaches to mass culture*, Bloomington and Indianapolis: Indiana University Press, 39–54.

Ang, I. (1985) *Watching Dallas*, London: Methuen.

Ang, I. (1986) 'The vicissitudes of "progressive television"', paper presented at the International Television Studies Conference, London, July 1986.

Bakke, M. (1986) 'Culture at stake', in D. McQuail and K. Siune (eds), *New Media Politics: Comparative perspectives in Western Europe*, London: Sage, 130–51.

Blanchard, S. and Morley, D. (1984) *What's This Channel Fo(u)r?*, London: Comedia.

Bourdieu, P. (1980) 'The aristocracy of culture', *Media, Culture and Society*, 2: 225–54.

Carey, J. (1985) 'Overcoming resistance to cultural studies', in M. Gurevitch and M. Levy (eds), *Mass Communications Review Yearbook, Volume 5*, Beverly Hills, CA: Sage, 27–40.

Cohen, P. and Robbins, D. (1979) *Knuckle Sandwich*, Harmondsworth: Penguin.

Foucault, M. (1978) *The History of Sexuality*, Harmondsworth: Penguin.

Garnham, N. (1987) 'Concepts of culture: Public policy and the cultural industries', *Cultural Studies*, 1: 1, 23–37.

Hall, S. (1984) 'The narrative construction of reality', *Southern Review*, 17: 1, 3–17.

Hall, S. (1986) 'On postmodernism and articulation: an interview with Stuart Hall' (edited by L. Grossberg), *Journal of Communication Inquiry*, 10: 2, 45–60.

Hebdige, D. (1979) *Subculture: The meaning of style*, London: Methuen.

Hebdige, D. (1982) 'Towards a cartography of taste 1935–1962', in B. Waits, T. Bennett, and G. Martin (eds), *Popular Culture: Past and present*, London: Croom Helm/Open University Press, 194–218.

Hebdige, D. (1987) *Hiding in the Light*, London: Comedia.

Hobson, D. (1982) *Crossroads: The drama of a soap opera*, London: Methuen.

Hodge, R. and Tripp, D. (1986) *Children and Television*, Cambridge: Polity Press.

Katz, E. and Liebes, T. (1984) 'Once upon a time in Dallas', *Intermedia*, 12: 3, 28–32.

Katz, E. and Liebes, T. (1985) 'Mutual aid in the decoding of *Dallas*: preliminary notes from a cross-cultural study', in P. Drummond and R. Paterson (eds), *Television in Transition*, London: British Film Institute, 187–98.

Katz, E. and Liebes, T. (1987) 'On the critical ability of television viewers', paper presented at the seminar 'Rethinking the Audience: New Directions in Television Research', University of Tübingen, February 1987.

MacCabe, C. (1986) 'Defining popular culture', in C. MacCabe (ed.), *High Theory/Low Culture*, Manchester: Manchester University Press, 1–10.

McRobbie, A. (1984) 'Dance and social fantasy', in A. McRobbie and M. Nava (eds), *Gender and Generation*, London: Macmillan, 130–61.

Mercer, C. (1986) 'Complicit pleasures', in T. Bennett, C. Mercer, and J. Woollacott (eds), *Popular Culture and Social Relations*, Milton Keynes and Philadelphia: Open University Press, 50–68.

Michaels, E. (1986) 'Aboriginal content', paper presented at the Australian Screen Studies Association Conference, Sydney, December 1986.

Morley, D. (1981) 'The *Nationwide* audience – a critical postscript', *Screen Education*, 39: 3–14.

O'Sullivan, T., Hartley, J., Saunders, D., and Fiske, J. (1983) *Key Concepts in Communication*, London: Methuen.

Volosinov, V. (1973) *Marxism and the Philosophy of Language*, New York: Seminar Press.

Wilson, C. and Gutierrez, F. (1985) *Minorities and Media: Diversity and the end of mass communication*, Beverly Hills, CA: Sage.

Worpole, K. (1983) *Dockers and Detectives*, London: Verso.

48 □ *Feminist Desire and Female Pleasure*

Ien Ang

Janice Radway's *Reading the Romance* does not exactly read like a romance. In contrast to the typical reading experience of the romance novel, it is difficult to go through *Reading the Romance* at one stretch. The text contains too many fragments which compel its reader to stop, to reread, to put the book aside in order to gauge and digest the assertions made – in short, to adopt an *analytical* position *vis-à-vis* the text. Contrary to what happens, as Radway sees it, in the case of romance novels, the value and pleasure of this reading experience does not primarily lie in its creation of a general sense of emotional well-being and visceral contentment (p. 70). Rather, *Reading the Romance* has left me, as one of its enthusiastic readers, with a feeling of tension that forces me to problematize its project, to ask questions about the kind of intervention Radway has tried to make in writing the book. Such questions generally do not present themselves to romance readers when they have just finished a particularly satisfying version of the romance genre. Radway has argued convincingly that it is precisely a *release* of tension that makes romance reading a particularly pleasurable activity for women. This release of tension is on the one hand accomplished by a temporary, literal escape from the demands of the social role of housewife and mother which is assured by the private act of picking up a book and reading a romance, and on the other hand by a symbolic gratification of the psychological need for nurturance and care that the romance genre offers these women – needs that, given their entrapment in the arrangements of 'patriarchal marriage', cannot be satisfied in 'real life'. This is elaborated by Radway in her characterization of romantic fiction as compensatory literature (pp. 98, 95). In other words, the value of romance reading for women is, in Radway's analysis, primarily of a *therapeutic* nature.

But this opposition – between the analytical and the therapeutic – invites a somewhat oversimplified view of the relationship between *Reading the Romance* and women reading romances. To be sure, in Radway's book, we can distinguish an overtly therapeutic thrust. For what is at stake for Radway is not just the

From *Camera Obscura*, vol. 16, 1988, pp. 179–90.

academic will to offer a neat and sophisticated explanation of the whys and hows of romance reading, but also a feminist desire to come to terms, politically speaking, with this popular type of female pleasure.

The enormous popularity of romantic fiction with women has always presented a problem for feminism. It is an empirical given that preeminently signifies some of the limits of feminist understanding and effectivity. One of the essential aims of *Reading the Romance*, then, is to find a new feminist way to 'cope' with this 'problem'. And I would suggest that it is precisely this therapeutic momentum of *Reading the Romance* that, paradoxically enough, produces the deep sense of tension I felt after having read the book. At stake in the therapy, as I will try to show, is the restoration of feminist authority. The result, however, is not an altogether happy ending in the romance tradition. This is not to say that the book should *have* a happy ending, for *Reading the Romance* belongs to a completely different genre than the genre it is trying to understand. But because all feminist inquiry is by definition a politically motivated theoretical engagement, it always seems to present a certain articulation of the analytical with the therapeutic, both substantially and rhetorically. What I will try to do in this review, then, is to explore some of the ways in which this articulation materializes in *Reading the Romance*.[1]

What sets Radway's book apart in a 'technical' sense from earlier feminist attempts to grasp and evaluate the meaning of female romance reading is her methodology. In contrast, for example, to Tania Modleski's well-known *Loving with a Vengeance*,[2] Radway has chosen to base her analysis upon oral interviews with a group of actual romance readers. Drawing on the insights of reader-response critics like Stanley Fish, she rejects the method of immanent textual analysis, which she criticizes as 'a process that is hermetically sealed off from the very people they [the romance critics concerned] aim to understand' (p. 7). According to Radway, 'the analytic focus must shift from the text itself, taken in isolation, to the complex social event of reading where a woman actively attributes sense to lexical signs in a silent process carried on in the context of her ordinary life' (p. 8). By leaving the ivory tower of textual analysis and mixing with actual readers, she pursues a strategy that aims at 'taking real readers seriously'. She thereby rejects the practice of treating them as mere subject positions constructed by the text, or as abstract 'ideal readers' entirely defined in terms of textual mechanisms and operations.

In her introduction to *Studies in Entertainment*, Tania Modleski has fiercely warded off Radway's criticism by arguing that conducting 'ethnographic studies' of subcultural groups may lead to a dangerous 'collusion between mass culture critic and consumer society':[3] in her view, it is virtually impossible for critical scholars to retain a 'proper critical distance' when they submit themselves to the empirical analysis of audience response. While I share Modleski's concern about the dangers and pitfalls of empiricism, I do not believe that the project of ethnography is necessarily at odds with a critical stance, both in relation to consumer society and with respect to the process of doing research itself. On the contrary, ethnographic fieldwork among audiences – in the broad sense of engaging oneself with the unruly and heterogeneous practices and accounts of real historical viewers or readers –

helps to keep our critical discourses from becoming closed texts of Truth, because it forces the researcher to come to terms with perspectives that may not be easily integrated in a smooth, finished and coherent Theory.[4] If anything, then, *Reading the Romance* is inspired by a deep sense of the contradictions and ambivalences posed by mass culture, and by a recognition of the profoundly unresolved nature of critical theory's dealings with it.

This does not mean, however, that ethnography is an unproblematic project. In every ethnographic study the researcher has to confront very specific problems of access and interpretation, which will have a decisive impact on the shape of the eventual account that is presented by the ethnographer: the text of the written book. In this review, then, I would like to examine the political motifs and strategies that are laid out in *Reading the Romance*. For Radway, ethnography is more than just a method of inquiry, it is an explicitly political way of staging a new feminist 'reconciliation' with 'the problem' of romantic fiction's popularity. For one thing, *Reading the Romance* is a report on the quite difficult, but apparently very rewarding, encounter between a feminist academic and (non-feminist) romance readers. Its broader significance thus lies in its dramatization of the relationship between 'feminism' and 'women'. It is the recognition that this relationship is a problematic one, not one of simple identity, that makes Janice Radway's book so important. Yet at the same time it is Radway's proposals for the resolution of the problem that make the tension I described above so painfully felt.

In the early chapters of the book, Radway's self-chosen vulnerability as an ethnographer is made quite apparent. In these chapters, the dialogic nature of the ethnographic project, which according to Radway is one of its central tenets, is more or less actualized. Of course, the narrative voice speaking to us is Radway's, but the limits of academic writing practice seem to make a more heterologic mode as yet almost unrealizable.[5] She describes her initial trepidation upon first contacting and then meeting 'Dorothy Evans', or 'Dot', her main informant and the impassioned editor of a small fanzine for romance readers, living and working in a small Pennsylvania community fictionalized by Radway into 'Smithton'. The gap between researcher and informants is apparently quickly surmounted, however:

> My concern about whether I could persuade Dot's customers to elaborate honestly about their motives for reading was unwarranted, for after an initial period of mutually felt awkwardness, we conversed frankly and with enthusiasm. (p. 47)

From this point on, Radway ceases to reflect on the nature of her own relationship to the 'Smithton women', and offers instead an often fascinating account of what she has learned from them. She quotes them extensively and is at times genuinely 'taken by surprise' by the unexpected turns of her conversations with Dot and the Smithton women. However, precisely because she does not seem to feel any real strain about the way in which she and her informants are positioned towards each other, she represents the encounter as one that is strictly confined to the terms of a relationship between two parties with fixed identities: that of a researcher/feminist and that of interviewees/romance fans. This ontological and methodological separation between subject and object allows her to present the Smithton readers as a pre-existent 'interpretive community', a sociological entity whose characteristics and peculiarities were already there when the researcher set out to investigate it. It may well be, however, that this group of women only constituted itself as a 'community' in the research process itself – in a very literal sense indeed: at the moment that they were brought together for the collective interviews Radway conducted with them; at the moment that they were invited to think of themselves as a group that shares something, namely, their fondness of romance reading, and the fact that they are all Dot's customers. An indication of this is offered by Radway herself:

> In the beginning, timidity seemed to hamper the responses as each reader took turns answering each question. When everyone relaxed, however, the conversation flowed more naturally as the participants disagreed among themselves, contradicted one another, and *delightedly* discovered that they still agreed about many things. (p. 48; emphasis added)

In relying on a realist epistemology, then, Radway tends to overlook the constructivist aspect of her own enterprise. In a sense, doing ethnography is itself a political intervention in that its activity helps to *construct* the culture it seeks to describe and understand, rather than merely reflect it. The concrete political benefit, in this specific case, could be that Radway's temporary presence in Smithton, and the lengthy conversations she had with the women, had an empowering effect on them, in that they were given the rare opportunity to come to a collective understanding and validation of their own reading experiences. Such an effect might be regarded as utterly limited by feminists with grander aims, and it is certainly not without its contradictions (after all, how can we ever be sure how such temporary, cultural empowerment relates to the larger stakes of the more structural struggles over power in which these women lead their lives?), but it is worth noticing, nevertheless, if we are to consider the value and predicaments of doing feminist research in its most material aspects.[6]

For Radway, however, other concerns prevail. The separation between her world and that of her informants becomes progressively more absolute towards the end of the book. In the last few chapters the mode of writing becomes almost completely monologic, and the Smithton women are definitively relegated to the position of 'them', a romance reading community towards which Radway is emphatically sympathetic, but from which she remains fundamentally distant. Radway's analysis first recognizes the 'rationality' of romance reading by interpreting it as an act of symbolic resistance, but ends up constructing a deep chasm between the ideological world inhabited by the Smithton women and the convictions of feminism:

> ... when the act of romance reading is viewed as it is by the readers themselves, from within the belief system that accepts as given the institutions of heterosexuality and monogamous marriage, it can be conceived as an activity of mild protest and longing

for reform necessitated by those institutions' failure to satisfy the emotional needs of women. Reading therefore functions for them as an act of recognition and contestation whereby that failure is first admitted and then partially reversed. . . . At the same time, however, when viewed from the vantage point of a feminism that would like to see the women's oppositional impulse lead to real social change, romance reading can also be seen as an activity that could potentially disarm that impulse. It might do so because it supplies vicariously those very needs and requirements that might otherwise be formulated as demands in the real world and lead to the potential restructuring of sexual relations. (p. 213)

These are the theoretical terms in which Radway conceives the troubled relationship between feminism and romance reading. A common ground – the perceived sharing of the experiential pains and costs of patriarchy – is analytically secured, but from a point of view that assumes the mutual exteriority of the two positions. The distribution of identities is clear cut: Radway, the researcher, is a feminist and *not* a romance fan; the Smithton women, the researched, are romance readers and *not* feminists. From such a perspective, the political aim of the project becomes envisaged as one of bridging this profound separation between 'us' and 'them'. In a recent article, Radway has formulated the task as follows:

> I am troubled by the fact that it is all too easy for us, as academic feminists and Marxists who are preoccupied with the *analysis* of ideological formations that produce consciousness, to forget that our entailed and parallel project is the political one of convincing those very real people to see how their situation intersects with our own and why it will be fruitful for them to see it as we do. Unless we wish to tie this project to some new form of coercion, we must remain committed to the understanding that these individuals are capable of coming to recognize their set of beliefs as an ideology that limits their view of their situation.[7]

Does this mean, then, that doing feminist research is a matter of pedagogy? The militant ending of *Reading the Romance* leaves no doubt about it:

> I think it absolutely essential that we who are committed to social change learn not to overlook [the] minimal but nonetheless legitimate form of protest [expressed in romance reading]. We should seek it out not only to understand its origins and its utopian longing but also to learn how best to encourage it and bring it to fruition. If we do not, we have already conceded the fight and, in the case of the romance at least, admitted the impossibility of creating a world where the vicarious pleasure supplied by its reading would be unnecessary. (p. 222)

Here, Radway's feminist desire is expressed in its most dramatic form: its aim is directed at raising the consciousness of romance reading women, its mode is that of persuasion, conversion even. 'Real' social change can only be brought about, Radway seems to believe, if romance readers would stop reading romances and become feminist activists instead. In other words, underlying Radway's project is what Angela McRobbie has termed a 'recruitist' conception of the politics of feminist research.[8] What makes me feel so uncomfortable about this move is the unquestioned certainty with which feminism is posed as the superior solution for all women's problems, as if feminism automatically possessed the relevant and effective formulae for all women to change their lives and acquire happiness. In the course of the book Radway has thus inverted the pertinent relations: whereas in the beginning the ethnographer's position ensures a vulnerable stance that puts her assumptions at risk, what is achieved in the end is an all but complete restoration of the authority of feminist discourse. This, then, is the therapeutic effect of *Reading the Romance*: it reassures where certainties threaten to dissolve, it comforts where divisions among women, so distressing and irritating to feminism, seem almost despairingly insurmountable – by holding the promise that, with hard work for sure, unity *would* be reached if we could only rechannel the energy that is now put in romance reading in the direction of 'real' political action. In short, what is therapeutic (for feminism) about *Reading the Romance* is its construction of romance readers as embryonic feminists.

I do agree with Radway that the relationship between 'feminism' and 'women' is one of the most troublesome issues for the women's movement. However, it seems untenable to me to maintain a vanguardist view of feminist politics, to see feminist consciousness as the linear culmination of political radicality. With McRobbie I think that 'to make such a claim is to uncritically overload the potential of the women's movement and to underestimate the resources and capacities of "ordinary" women – by virtue of *age, class, race,* and *culture* – to participate in their own struggles as women but quite autonomously.'[9] I am afraid, therefore, that Radway's radical intent is drawing dangerously near a form of political moralism, propelled by a desire to make 'them' more like 'us'. Indeed, what Radway's conception of political intervention tends to arrive at is the deromanticization of the romance in favor of a romanticized feminism!

This is not the place to elaborate on the practical implications of this political predicament. What I do want to point out, however, is how the therapeutic upshot of *Reading the Romance* is prepared for in the very analysis Radway has made of the meaning of romance reading for the Smithton women, that is, how the analytical and the therapeutic are inextricably entwined with one another.

Strangely missing in Radway's interpretive framework, I would say, is any careful account of the *pleasurableness* of the pleasure of romance reading. The absence of pleasure *as* pleasure in *Reading the Romance* is made apparent in Radway's frequent, downplaying qualifications of the enjoyment that the Smithton women have claimed to derive from their favorite genre: that it is a form of *vicarious* pleasure, that it is *only temporarily* satisfying because it is *compensatory* literature; that even though it does create 'a kind of female community', through it 'women join forces only symbolically and in a mediated way in the privacy of their homes and in the devalued sphere of leisure activity' (p. 212). Revealed in such qualifications is a sense that the pleasure of romance reading is somehow not really real, as though there were other forms of pleasure that could be considered 'more real' because they are more 'authentic', more enduring, more veritable, or whatever.

Radway's explanation of repetitive romance reading is a case in point. She analyzes this in terms of romance reading's ultimate inadequacy when it comes to the satisfaction of psychic needs for which the readers cannot find an outlet in their actual social lives. In her view, romance reading is inadequate precisely because it gives these women the *illusion* of pleasure while it leaves their 'real' situation unchanged. In line with the way in which members of the Birmingham Centre for Contemporary Cultural Studies have interpreted youth subcultures,[10] then, Radway comes to the conclusion that romance reading is a sort of 'imaginary solution' to real, structural problems and contradictions produced by patriarchy. (The real solution, one could guess, lies in the bounds of feminism.) All this amounts to a quite functionalist explanation of romance reading, one that is preoccupied with its effects rather than its mechanisms. Consequently, pleasure as such cannot possibly be taken seriously in this theoretical framework, because the whole explanatory movement is directed towards the *ideological function* of pleasure.

Are the Smithton women ultimately only fooling themselves, then? At times Radway seems to think so. For example, when the Smithton women state that it is impossible to describe the 'typical romantic heroine' because in their view, the heroines 'are all different', Radway is drawn to conclude that 'they refuse to admit that the books they read have a standard plot' (p. 199). In imposing such a hasty interpretation, however, she forgets to take the statement seriously, as if it were only the result of the women's being lured by the realistic illusion of the narrative text.[11] But perhaps the statement that all heroines are different says more about the reading experience than Radway assumes. Perhaps it could be seen as an index of the pleasure that is solicited by what may be termed 'the grain of the story': the subtle, differentiated texture of each book's staging of the romantic tale that makes its reading a 'new' experience even though the plot is standard. In fact, Radway's own findings seem to testify to this when she reports that 'although the women almost never remembered the names of the principal characters, they could recite in surprising detail not only what had happened to them but also how they managed to cope with particularly troublesome situations' (p. 201).

Attention to this pleasure of detail could also give us a fresh perspective on another thing often asserted by many of the Smithton women that puzzled Radway, namely that they always want to ascertain in advance that a book finishes with a happy ending. Radway sees this peculiar behavior as an indication that these women cannot bear 'the threat of the unknown as it opens out before them and demand continual reassurance that the events they suspect will happen [i.e. the happy ending], in fact, will finally happen' (p. 205). But isn't it possible to develop a more positive interpretation here? When the reader is sure *that* the heroine and the hero will finally get each other, she can concentrate all the more on *how* they will get each other. Finding out about the happy ending in advance could then be seen as a clever reading strategy aimed at obtaining maximum pleasure: a pleasure that is oriented towards the *scenario* of romance, rather than its outcome. If the outcome is predictable in the romance genre, the variety of the ways in which two lovers can find one another is endless. Cora Kaplan's succinct specification of what in her view is central to the pleasure of romance reading for women is particularly illuminating here, suggesting 'that the reader identifies with both terms in the seduction scenario, but most of all with *the process of seduction*'.[12]

This emphasis on the staging of the romantic encounter, on the details of the moments of seducing and being seduced as the characteristic elements of pleasure in romance reading, suggests another absence in the interpretive framework of *Reading the Romance*: the meaning of fantasy, or for that matter, of romantic fantasy. In Radway's account, fantasy is too easily equated with the unreal, with the world of illusions, that is, false ideas about how life 'really' is. It is this pitting of reality against fantasy that brings her to the sad conclusion that repetitive romance reading 'would enable a reader to tell herself again and again that a love like the heroine's might indeed occur in a world such as hers. She thus teaches herself to believe that men *are able* to satisfy women's needs fully' (p. 201; emphasis Radway's). In other words, it is Radway's reductionist conception of fantasmatic scenarios as incorrect models of reality – in Radway's feminist conception of social reality, there is not much room for men's potential capacity to satisfy women – that drives her to a more or less straightforward 'harmful effects' theory.

If, however, we were to take fantasy seriously as a reality in itself, as a necessary dimension of our psychical reality, we could conceptualize the world of fantasy as the place of excess, where the unimaginable can be imagined. Fiction could then be seen as the social materialization and elaboration of fantasies, and thus, in the words of Allison Light, 'as the explorations and productions of desires which may be in excess of the social possible or acceptable'.[13] This insight may lead to another interpretation of the repetitiveness of romance reading as an activity among women (some critics would speak of 'addiction'), which does not accentuate their ultimate psychical subordination to patriarchal relations, but rather emphasizes the rewarding quality of the fantasizing activity itself. As Radway would have it, romance fans pick up a book again and again because romantic fiction does *not satisfy them enough*, as it is only a poor, illusory and transitory satisfaction of needs unmet in 'real life'. But couldn't the related readings be caused by the fact that the romance novel *satisfies them too much*, because it constitutes a secure space in which an imaginary perpetuation of an emphatically utopian state of affairs (something that is an improbability in 'real life' in the first place) is possible?

After all, it is more than striking that romance novels always abruptly *end* at the moment that the two lovers have finally found each other, and thus never go beyond the point of no return: romantic fiction generally is exclusively about the titillating period *before* the wedding! This could well indicate that what repetitious reading of romantic fiction offers is the opportunity to continue to enjoy the excitement of romance and romantic scenes without being interrupted by the dark side of sexual relationships. In the symbolic world of the romance novel, the struggle between the sexes (while being one of the ongoing central themes of melodramatic soap operas)[14] will always be overcome in the end, precisely because that is what the romantic imagination self-consciously tries to make representable. The politics of romance reading, in other words, is a politics of fantasy in which women engage precisely because it does *not* have 'reality value'. Thus, the romance reader can luxuriate in never having to enter the conflictual world that comes after the 'happy ending'. Instead, she leaves the newly formed happy couple behind and joins another heroine, another hero, who are to meet each other in a new book, in a new romantic setting.

What is achieved by this deliberate fictional bracketing of life after the wedding, it seems to me, is the fantasmatic perpetuation of the romantic state of affairs. Whatever the concrete reasons for women taking pleasure in this – here some further ethnographic inquiry could provide us with new answers – it seems clear to me that what is fundamentally involved is a certain determination to maintain the *feeling* of romance, or a refusal to give it up, even though it may be temporarily or permanently absent in 'real life', against all odds. And it is this enduring emotional quest that, I would suggest, should be taken seriously as a psychical strategy by which women empower themselves in everyday life, leaving apart what its ideological consequences in social reality are.

If this interpretation is at all valid, then I am not sure how feminism should respond to it. Radway's rationalist proposal – that romance readers should be convinced to see that their reading habits are ultimately working against their own 'real' interests – will not do, for it slights the fact that what is above all at stake in the energy invested in romance reading is the actualization of romantic feelings, which are by definition 'unrealistic', excessive, utopian, inclined towards the sensational and the adventurous. That the daring quality of romanticism tends to be tamed by the security of the happy ending in the standard romance novel is not so important in this respect. What is important is the tenacity of the desire to feel romantically.

This is not to say that romantic fiction should be considered above all criticism. The ideological consequences of its mass production and consumption should be a continuing object of reflection and critique for feminism. Questions of sexual politics, definitions of femininity and masculinity, and the cultural meanings of the romance in general will remain important issues. However, all this should not invalidate the significance of the craving for and pleasure in romantic feelings that so many women have in common and share. In fact, I am drawn to conclude that it might be this common experience that could serve as the basis for overcoming the paralyzing opposition between 'feminism' and 'romance reading'. While feminists, as Elizabeth Wilson has noted,[15] have often dismissed romanticism, it has a psychical reality that cannot simply be banished. However, by taking the love for romantic feelings seriously as a starting point for engagement with 'non-feminist' women, the feminist researcher might begin to establish a 'comprehension of self by the detour of the comprehension of the other',[16] in a confrontation with other women who may have more expertise and experience in the meanings, pleasures and dangers of romanticism than herself. What could change as a result of such an ethnographic encounter – and to my mind it is this process-oriented, fundamentally dialogic and dialectical character of knowledge acquisition that marks the distinctive critical edge of ethnography – is not only 'their' understanding of what 'we', as self-proclaiming feminists, are struggling for, but, more importantly, the sense of identity that is constructed by feminism itself.

Notes

1. I would like to emphasize that in doing this I cannot do full justice to the accomplishments and problems of the book. Many aspects of Radway's distinctly innovative book, such as her discussion of the differences between the ideal romance and the failed romance, and her application of Nancy Chodorow's version of psychoanalysis to explain women's 'need' for romance reading, will therefore not be discussed here. I would also like to draw attention to Radway's preface to the new, British edition of *Reading the Romance* (London: Verso, 1987), in which she raises some of the issues I will go into in this review article. See Chapter 28 of this volume.
2. See, for a lengthy and insightful review of this book, Lynn Spigel, 'Detours in the search for tomorrow', *Camera Obscura*, 13/14 (Spring/Summer 1985), pp. 215–34.
3. Tania Modleski, 'Introduction', in Tania Modleski (ed.), *Studies in Entertainment* (Bloomington and Indianapolis: Indiana University Press, 1986), p. xii.
4. See Ien Ang, 'Wanted: audiences. On the politics of empirical audience studies', paper presented at the Symposium on 'Rethinking the Audience: New Directions in Television Research', University of Tübingen, February 1987; to be published in Ellen Seiter *et al.* (eds), *Rethinking the Audience* (Chapel Hill: University of North Carolina Press).
5. See James Clifford and George Marcus (eds), *Writing Culture: The politics and poetics of ethnography* (Berkeley/Los Angeles/London: University of California Press, 1986).
6. See, for a discussion of ths issue, Angela McRobbie, 'The politics of feminist research: between talk, text and action', *Feminist Review*, 12 (October 1982), pp. 46–57.
7. Janice Radway, 'Identifying ideological seams: mass culture, analytical method, and political practice', *Communication*, 9 (1986), p. 105.
8. McRobbie, 'The politics of feminist research', p. 52.
9. *Ibid.*, p. 53.
10. Stuart Hall *et al.* (eds), *Resistance Through Rituals* (London: Hutchinson, 1975); Dick Hebdige, *Subculture: The meaning of style* (London: Methuen, 1979).
11. It should be noted that Radway's discussion of the narrative discourse of romantic fiction is very similar to the theory of the 'classic realist text' as developed in film theory by Colin MacCabe and others.
12. Cora Kaplan, '*The Thorn Birds*: fiction, fantasy, femininity', in Victor Burgin, James Donald and Cora Kaplan (eds), *Formations of Fantasy* (London and New York: Methuen, 1986), p. 162. Emphasis mine.
13. Allison Light, '*Returning to Manderley*: romance fiction, female sexuality and class', *Feminist Review*, 16 (Summer 1984), p. 7. See, for a discussion of the concept of fantasy, Elizabeth Cowie, 'Fantasia', *m/f*, 9 (1984), pp. 71–105.
14. See Ien Ang, *Watching Dallas: Soap opera and the melodramatic imagination* (London/New York: Methuen, 1985), esp. chapter 4. See Chapter 27 of this volume.
15. Elizabeth Wilson, 'Forbidden love', in Elizabeth Wilson (with Angela Weir), *Hidden Agendas* (London/New York: Tavistock, 1986), p. 17.
16. Paul Rabinow, *Reflections on Fieldwork in Morocco* (Berkeley/Los Angeles/London: University of California Press, 1977), p. 5.

49 □ 'High Culture' Revisited

Jostein Gripsrud

Let's do away with critical distance! (John Fiske)[1]

The late 1960s and the 1970s brought about both a substantial increase in and new forms of scholarly interest in popular culture. New approaches were marked by an interdisciplinary and 'totalizing' conception of socio-cultural research, transcending traditional boundaries between economics, politics, and aesthetics. Research was supposed to contribute to a *general* critique of capitalist society-as-a-whole, in theoretical and methodological matters openly guided by what Habermas (1968) once called an 'emancipatory knowledge-interest'.

This approach was clearly linked to the contemporary revival of Marxist theory, and as political conjunctures changed, the various forms of Marxist-inspired research ran into severe problems. The theoretical developments between, say, 1975 and 1985 have proved fruitful in many ways. It seems to me, though, as if the hallmark of the tradition from the 1960s – research as a contribution to 'total' social critique – is about to get lost in certain current trends in media and cultural studies, in spite of retained 'emancipatory knowledge-interest'.

A critique of these trends sooner or later runs into the highly complex debates over 'postmodernity'/'postmodernism'. In this article, though, I will try to avoid a general discussion of the theoretical and political status of these concepts. Instead, a widely shared basic assumption within current critical media research will be looked into, and a critique of it attempted. I should at once stress that this is a highly problematic venture, and that my views are presented tentatively, open to further debate.

I should add that this article is an attempt at 'checking' the viability of certain ideas and perspectives developed during the 1960s and 1970s, consciously opposing the form of collective amnesia that a certain theoretical 'trendiness' in the fields of media and cultural studies seems to produce. The personal need to write something like this arose after spending six months in the United States, getting increasingly annoyed with the axiomatic status of certain fashionable but not entirely reliable observations on 'postmodern culture' within some academic circles. Regarding myself as in many ways some sort of 'postmodernist' in Norway, I was a bit surprised to realize that in view of certain Anglo-American discourses on media, culture, and politics, I would have to agree with Habermas that Modernity/Enlightenment is still an incomplete project.

The assumption I intend to criticize is that the distinction between high and low culture is 'in fact' outmoded and only kept alive in reactionary ideological rhetoric. In my view, the distinction is not only still alive as a social fact throughout the western world, even if the relationship(s) between the two spheres may differ considerably from one country to another and on the whole have undergone very important changes. It also seems pertinent that we have a closer look at the institutions and practices embraced by high culture, and discuss their relevance to critical research and analysis in our field(s). I then intend to argue that a total dismissal of the distinction between high and low culture may serve as an ideological veiling of the social positions of researchers and other academic intellectuals, hindering a recognition of the political limitations, obligations, and possibilities inherent in these positions.

I would like to start, though, by sketching how the tendency I am criticizing is directly linked to basic features of the 1960s' tradition. Thus I intend not only to signal my own degree of sympathy with my object of critique. The historical approach also allows for some important observations on the characteristics of the present generation of media researchers and students.

II

The early efforts of 'neo-Marxist' media research, especially within the humanities, may be labeled 'critique of ideology'. Its two main objectives represented a radical challenge to traditional notions of art and cultural heritage within academia. First, a (re)interpretation of cultural texts from both high and low culture was intended to show how the texts contained and conveyed ideology, forms of consciousness that supported social repression. Second, inextricably linked to the first, a rewriting of cultural history was undertaken which would expose class- and gender-based repression not only in society and culture in general, but in traditional academic research and writing as well. 'Digging up' artists, texts, and whole traditions of cultural expression that had been left out of traditional accounts of cultural history was a highly rewarding activity in this respect. It was easily demonstrated that the construction of cultural canons relied not only on something regarded as pure and socially neutral aesthetic and historical judgement, but also very much on certain clearly ideological notions.

Although much work on popular culture was devoted to exposing the bourgeois, misogynist etc. ideology of texts, this form of popular-culture criticism differed from earlier critical disavowal in at least two significant ways. First, popular-culture texts were analyzed with the same semiological/semiotic tools as the texts of the high culture canons – and for the same purpose: exposing ideology. Thus the methodology, based on a semiotic understanding of the nature of language and texts, in itself posed a critique of traditional aesthetic hierarchies. Second, and this may be even more crucial to an understanding of later developments, it soon became clear that the new scholarly critique of popular culture was to a considerable extent a 'critique from within'. The critical students and scholars were themselves consumers of the artifacts in question. Having grown up with pop music, movies, television etc., their position could hardly be one of totally detached, condescending distance. Their own pleasures in the consumption of popular or mass culture products had to complicate the ideological analyses sooner or later, not least because their political commitment in many cases was directly linked to their engagement with the mass mediated 'youth culture' of the 1960s, rock music in particular.[2] The uneasiness produced by these complications have in many cases led to a development Tania Modleski has formulated as follows:

> If the problem of some of the work of the Frankfurt School was that its members were too far outside the culture they examined, critics today seem to have the opposite problem: immersed in their culture, half in love with their subject, they sometimes seem unable to achieve the proper critical distance from it. As a result, they may unwittingly wind up writing apologias for mass culture and embracing its ideology. (Modleski, 1986: xi)

According to this line of thinking, the postwar baby-boomers had specific interests in a more appreciative view of mass-mediated low or popular culture. But this was not only in keeping with their own cultural experience of growing up in a society where the 'culture industry' and modern mass media dominated everyday life. To rally students and younger scholars a positive re-evaluation of 'mass culture' and its recipients could also serve as a solution to a certain, specific dilemma concerning their social identity.

This function is suggested by the fact that the radicalization of students that occurred in the 1960s coincided with an unprecedented growth in the number of students at institutions of higher learning. In Norway, for instance, the number of students at the universities tripled during this decade. Even if the recruitment was socially skewed in favour of sons and daughters of academic and upper-class parents, this rapid process also meant an unprecedented influx of students from working-class or non-academic petit-bourgeois backgrounds, also often from geographically 'peripheral' areas. These people entered the realm of high culture, in which the universities are central institutions with a newcomer's ambivalence. While university education might have been a conscious goal for most of them – and student life consequently in many ways a fulfilling experience – the prevailing complacency of the academic proponents of high culture would seem to many of them either offensive or stupid or both.

This type of cultural clash is of course not limited to the experience of students of this particular generation. It has probably been the experience every working- or peasant-class bookworm with similar careers since the dawning of modernity. Such upwardly-mobile subjects are placed in a sort of cultural limbo, not properly integrated in the lower-class culture they left, nor in the upper-class high culture they have formally entered. Since they are newcomers, they are faced with a need to make *choices* concerning what to do in and with their acquired position. This is not given by family tradition or upper-class consciousness. One solution here could be (1) to strive for or pretend full integration into upper-class high culture, simply taking the class position opened to them by their education. Another way out of the dilemma could be (2) to strive for or pretend re-integration into the classes they once left, preferably as 'leaders' in some sense, 'voices' for the people, etc. Various radical organizations could function for them as a 'home away from home'.[3] The third, most difficult, alternative would be (3) for them to *acknowledge their marginal position* and identify themselves as intellectuals in the sense once formulated by Jean Paul Sartre: 'un-assimilated everywhere' (Sartre, 1973), and start investigating the possibilities for *engagement* from there.

It seems to me that the strategy of 'siding with' the consumers of popular culture, by more or less uncritically legitimating their choices and their presumed tastes, is often motivated by the second alternative. It is not only an act of solidarity, but also functions more self-satisfactorily as a form of symbolic 'homecoming'. The strategy offers an imaginary way out of the newborn, radical intellectual's socio-cultural limbo, often regarded with suspicion by 'the people', who at least since Romanticism have learnt to distrust intellectuals pretending to be more 'popular' than the people themselves, pretending that all those books and schools haven't changed them in any significant way.

The hermeneutic nature of any attempt at analyzing and understanding culture and society necessitates acknowledgement of and critical reflection on the socio-cultural specificity of the researcher and his/her position. My impression is that much current work in Anglo-American media and cultural studies fails to do so, by implicitly denying both the privileged and the marginal aspects of the position of the researchers. The almost ritual denunciations of high culture in much writing (and talking) within this (these) field(s) can be seen as one expression of this dilemma.

III

The rhetorical dismissals of the notion of high culture that I have in mind fail to take into consideration that the concept has several meanings. It refers both to a set of institutions, to certain types of media and texts, and to discourses on these and other social phenomena. This complex material and cultural sphere is of course constantly undergoing changes, and some of the changes over the last decades have been fundamental.[4] But if we for the moment concentrate on the institutions and discourses of high culture, a few quite stable characteristics relevant to our discussion here do emerge.

Universities and other institutions of higher learning are still, as stated above, parts of the high-culture institutional realm. This is also true of the various discourses that circulate within academic and intellectual communities, constantly referring to and resupposing a couple of thousand years of 'high' cultural history within 'Western Civilization'. In this perspective, attacks on the notion of high culture in writings about, for instance, the complex subject positions in postmodern intertextuality, appear ludicrous in their ideological blindness. They represent an implicit denial of the social determination of discourses, not least their own very obvious belonging to a high-culture discourse on culture.

Such denial may also make it hard to grasp the implications of the differences between the discourses on soap operas in *Soap Opera Digest* and those in *Screen*. Denunciation of high culture, often accompanied by populist attacks on 'elitism' (as if unequal distribution of knowledge and other resources were just another reactionary ideological fantasy), may have the dubious function of presenting the writer or speaker in question as no-different-from-the-rest, as some sort of ordinary and authentic soap-watcher-in-general.

Presenting oneself as a soap-fan in scholarly circles could be considered daring or provocative some ten years ago. Nowadays it is more of a prerequisite for legitimate entry into the academic discourse on soaps in some Anglo-American fora. The demographic profiles of soap audiences consistently suggested by surveys are not seen as demanding social explanation, but often dismissed either as produced by slightly immoral administrative information-gathering for the industry, or as 'elitist' and 'empiricist' misrepresentations of 'reality' – for instance by pointing to the popularity of soaps among certain groups of college students and other marginal audiences.[5]

The writer/researcher/critic is then left with a classless, at the most gendered, subject with equally classless pleasures in the encounter with the soap text in question. By pretending that the academic critic's pleasure is the same as anybody else's, s/he not only erases the socio-cultural differences between the academic and the genre's core audiences, but also avoids analyzing the specificities of for instance the film scholar's pleasure in soap-watching. And soap-talking!

Such specific analysis would require considerations on the differences between, on the one hand, soap-watchers with years and years devoted to the accumulation of high cultural capital in Pierre Bourdieu's sense – and on the other hand soap fans less well-off in this respect. Such considerations might render the distinction between high and low culture harder to dismiss – or overlook – in cultural analysis.

IV

So far I have only tried to demonstrate the validity of the distinction between high and low culture by linking scholarly discourses on culture to the high-culture institutions which are their material basis. Examining the distinction more thoroughly requires a closer look at the obvious changes in the relationships between the two spheres that I briefly mentioned above.

Today's university students and teachers may be devoted rock fans – while at the same time being readers of James Joyce and Friedrich Nietzsche. This kind of floating between media and genres on both sides of the high/low border is often regarded as one of the hallmarks of the 'postmodern' cultural condition. In my view, it is a historically new situation. But *structurally* it is reminiscent of Peter Burke's (1978) outline of the relationship between 'high' (upper-class/learned) culture and 'low' (lower-class, folk/traditional) culture in the middle ages. The bearers of high/learned culture would also share and participate in the competences and practices of low/popular culture, until the onset of modern thought, scientific and geographical discoveries etc, rendered the split in terms of ways of thinking/'world views'/forms of consciousness too wide. Popular (*folk*) culture was then left to itself, until it was rediscovered as something exotically 'authentic' by the Romantic movement towards the end of the eighteenth century. The concrete, historical developments of the relationships between high and low culture will vary considerably from place to place,[6] and popular/low culture is split into folk (traditional, typically rural) and 'mass' ('industrial', typically urban) culture by the advent of industrial capitalism, further complicating the use of ahistorical parallelisms. Still, the structural similarity between the situation described by Burke in relation to Europe's middle ages and today's so-called 'convergence' between high and low culture remains helpful in conceptualizing what is going on.

What the presence of the PhD at the rock concert tells us is that the audiences of the two cultural spheres overlap. But what is often overlooked, is *how* they overlap. While the audiences in the opera almost certainly go to the movies and even watch television, the majority of movie and television audiences will never go to the opera; or visit places like museums of contemporary art, certain theatres, seminars on feminism and psychoanalysis, poetry readings, or lectures by Derrida. The point I am trying to make is simple as it is significant. Some people have access to both high and low culture, but the majority has only access to the low one. (A diminishing minority has only access to high culture – that should not be forgotten either!)

It can safely be assumed that the dividing lines between 'double-access' and 'single-access' audiences coincide with lines drawn on the basis of other significant social characteristics, such as income and education. (Age is also relevant here, as the most typical double-access audiences are probably younger than, say, 50.) In other words, the reception of high and low culture is still clearly linked to the social formations we call classes. The double access to the codes and practices of both high and low culture is a *class privilege*. Consequently, denial of the existence of significant differences between high and low culture is ideological in the most simplistic Marxist sense – it engenders ideas serving to conceal inequality in the distribution of power and other resources. Just like the traditional bourgeois wanted (wants!) us to believe that 'money means nothing, we're all equal', certain theorists of culture now want us to believe that 'knowing Aristotle, Shakespeare, Marx, Foucault and Godard means nothing, we're all equal'.

Admittedly, money (economic capital) is very different from cultural knowledge/capital. While money is universally recognized as a key to a better life, most people don't give a damn about Godard; or about Aristotle, Marx, or Foucault for that matter. And they are of course right, in the sense that you don't necessarily get a more secure, comfortable, or even enjoyable life out of having access to high culture, its codes and products. It may even be more probable that the more you know of it, the gloomier you get (one may think of Hegel's 'unhappy consciousness' and related forms of intellectual melancholia ...). So why bother?

V

This is where the harder part of my argument starts. I am supposed to argue that something not necessarily enjoyable is worth having. In other words, I am now moving into the *qualitative* aspect of the 'high-culture' concept. What I have done so far has only been to point to the existence of an inescapable hierarchy of classes and a roughly parallel hierarchy of cultural formations and forms which cannot be transcended by individual word-acts alone. The question of whether qualitative differences between cultural forms can be hierarchically ordered as well is far more complicated. It is a lot easier and also more rewarding (to me at least) to tear down socially constructed hierarchies (which I have tried to contribute to for years) than to defend them.

It would be impossible here to discuss the multiple attempts at establishing 'objective' criteria for the evaluation of aesthetic artifacts. But I do want to point out that the question of aesthetic quality has been neglected for too long within the various fields of critical media studies – not to mention traditional mass communication research.[7] As traditional canons and hierarchies of values have been rightfully deconstructed, a combination of programmatic relativism and tacit agreement on taste has made anything but very widely conceived *political* criteria of evaluation unspeakable. And even the political criteria are losing ground, in two ways. First, the 'discovery' that texts are not univocal but offer possibilities for 'oppositional', 'aberrant', or even 'subversive' readings has undermined any simplistic notion of texts as mere vehicles of ideology. Second, the current enthusiasm for ethnographic reception studies can produce some very odd conclusions. Thus a critical analysis of *Rambo* concluding that it is a reactionary movie might be argued, by ethnographers, to be somehow 'displaced' by their finding that a particular audience sub-group has produced a reading of the film as an enjoyable anti-establishment (?) epic.[8]

Even if most traditional notions of Art may seem more or less impossible to uphold, I would at least argue that the relationship between *knowledge* and *judgement* may be worth some further discussion.

Such a discussion could start with a commonsensical assumption: it is not improbable that a literary scholar's judgement about a piece of literature is in some sense more qualified than that of any individual reader without the critic's training and experience. This is only more or less equivalent to saying that a carpenter (or a designer, or someone professionally teaching carpenters and designers) is in some sense the best judge of carpentry. The possibility that individual readers' experience of the piece in question may differ completely from the scholar's does not contradict this principle, no more than my appreciation of a piece of furniture which a carpenter regards with contempt. The parallel between texts and furniture should of course not be taken too far, but the element of experience and knowledge in a critic's work should not be completely disregarded either. Pretending that years of specialized training in criticism has not taught us anything about how to distinguish a well-done piece of 'art' from a not-so-well-done one, is futile. More important, however, is that this training should also have taught us to explicate the various criteria for our judgement, thus making the evaluation accessible for discussion and contestation.

Furthermore, the academic critic's conclusions about a text are supposedly based on some sort of analysis of the text in question, an interpretative effort aimed at bringing to the fore dimensions of the text not necessarily consciously accessible through the normal, once-over reading. This is to argue that the outcome of a reading based on textual analysis can only be contested by other readings based on analytic work on/with the text. This elementary principle is of course terribly 'elitist', but still indispensable for any kind of socio-cultural analysis that wants to move beyond mere registration of 'facts': interpretative work necessarily privileges the interpreter. The validity of its results can not be determined by simple 'checking of the facts' or by counting the number of individuals who agree. Rather, it depends upon the sophistication of procedures and the quality of arguments – and on whether or not one shares the (preferably) explicated, moral, and political values the interpreting subject carries with her/him when encountering the text.

Aesthetic values always have moral and political components (cf. Mukarovsky, 1979). But they have other components too, criteria for the evaluation of various aspects of 'craftsmanship'. This is why anti-fascists are able to see that Leni Riefenstahl's *Triumph des Willens* is a well-done film – even though they may still find it ideologically repulsive. To draw the line(s) between 'craftsmanship' and ideology at a general, theoretical level is practically impossible, since texts in all media that are intended to voice something 'oppositional' in some sense (or just 'different from the rest') will often have to break with established uses of each medium's means of expression. But those of us who, like me, have done extensive research on 'forgotten' textual traditions (workers' literature, for example) will know that history is full of texts that are definitely lousy from almost every possible point of view, especially when they are extracted from their immediate socio-historical context. If someone sets out to write a sonnet, a strongly defined form of poetic expression, there should be a discernible/constructable artistic *idea* explaining or giving sense to breaks with the sonnet's form. If not, it's sheer sloppiness, a failure – no matter which philosophical, moral, or political values it may attempt to convey. Critical training should, in principle, increase the reader's ability to discern failure from creativity, a judgement that always requires a consideration of plausible intentions and of context. Valid judgements of this kind presuppose quite extensive knowledge of the medium in question and of the various relevant contextual elements. Feminist films may not (should not?) adhere to Hollywood standards, but a 'lousy shot' may be either just a lousy shot or an element in some kind of textual strategy relevant to the aesthetico-political project in question.

The point I am (tentatively) trying to make here, is that aesthetic judgements made by members of a more or less academic community of critics and/or practitioners may well be regarded as the most solidly founded, in the sense that they are based on specialized training and knowledge. The teaching of literature, theatre, film etc in schools at all levels also necessarily requires *choices* from the enormous mass of texts available, and if sales or audience figures are not to be the only criteria for the choices made, some standards for judging 'quality' or 'degree of interest' must be established, preferably based on a kind of knowledge not yet possessed by students.[9]

This does on the other hand *not* mean that these specialists should have some sort of social authority that gives them the unrestricted right to prescribe a certain cultural menu to people outside their own group or class outside the classroom, for instance through the public broadcasting channels that rule the airwaves in countries like the Scandinavian. But such a view of differences in aesthetic qualifications allows us to keep the distinction between more or less 'naive' and more or less 'informed' receptions of texts, even if a unilinear hierarchy of the texts themselves is considered an impossible idea.[10] It also implies that the kind of competence the critic possesses may be desirable for others, in so far as they want to know more about a particular area. The general musical competence of a musicologist may be of interest to young rock musicians who want to know more about what they are in fact doing and what they might be able to achieve by way of a 'technical' language. (The musicologist may be even more useful to rock musicians if he is aware of the limits of traditional musicology in dealing with the rock idiom.)

There is then, in my view, some general value in the kinds of knowledge that *also* distinguish people with 'cultural capital', that is, people with access to high culture's texts and discourses. There is power in this kind of knowledge as much as there is in others. Furthermore, the academic/intellectual discourses on culture and the arts are strongly linked to the more general discourses on society, politics, economics, health etc. – in a multitude of ways. The language(s) of high culture belong to the dominant discourses in society, specialized in refined abstract thought and (potentially) instrumental reason. Mastering them is part of general social mastery, of gaining and executing social power. This is *one* reason why high culture remains a sphere worth conquering for those in less powerful positions than ours, and why the traditional 'distributive' idea in the cultural politics favoured by the social democratic labour movement retains some political relevance.

Another reason might simply be that as lower classes still are, in practice excluded from much of the high-culture realm, the historical point once made about working-class appropriation of high culture still holds some truth. As long as the working class is excluded from high culture, then 'even the canonization of classical art and literature [by workers' organizations, JG] contained democratizing, antiauthoritarian, yes: heretic impulses' (Brückner and Ricke, 1974: 41).[11]

Such 'impulses' gain subversive significance at another level, when the process of appropriation of high culture by previously excluded groups produces insights both into cultural history in general and the concrete experiences and conditions of the subjects in question.[12] The appropriation of high culture might also be an appropriation of history, of an 'expanded' historical consciousness – provided that the process is of a critical, self-reflective kind. Such a perspective would raise a number of questions – what are the limitations of 'high culture'? how does it relate to our own social and existential experiences? how does the sensual and emotional 'impact' of the poem, performance, picture in question relate to the 'impact' of artifacts from other cultural traditions? Such questions can only be asked from an 'outsider's' position – an outsider in the process of establishing knowledge of the 'inside' and 'the insiders': questions asked by *critical intellectuals*.

VI

Pierre Bourdieu's work on the sociology of culture contains provocative and enlightening analyses of the 'economic' logic of the intellectual field. The analysis suggests that all struggles within this field are 'actually' just struggles for positions of power within the field, that nothing but the participants' positions and interests are at stake in cultural debates, research, etc. The energy and significance(s) of Bourdieu's own sustained efforts suggest something else, though, something his purely 'structural' approach cannot really thematize. His demystifying, critical research must not only be driven on by some kind of 'emancipatory knowledge-interest', but also be based on substantial knowledge of various forms of both high and low culture: his extraordinary amount of cultural capital. In my view, this clearly implies that 'cultural capital' is not 'empty', devoid of substance and quality, like the completely abstract exchange value of economic capital. Cultural capital is not reducible to its abstract function as vehicle for individual intellectual careers: it always has a use-value in which there are ties to more general social interests.

Another aspect of the use-value of cultural capital may be what Bourdieu calls 'pure' taste. While the 'barbaric' taste, which Bourdieu argues is characteristic of the lower classes, insists on 'the continuity between art and life, which implies the subordination of form to function', 'pure' taste has as its basic premise the separation of the aesthetic from other aspects of life, so that the aesthetic demands a particular form of distanciation, in order to be apprehended adequately (Bourdieu, 1984: 32). While 'barbaric' taste – and products directed at satisfying it – prefers direct emotional involvement, sensual pleasure, and priority to 'content' over 'form', 'pure' taste – and its corresponding products – demands detachment, distanciation, reflection, and tends to focus on 'form' rather than 'content'. D. W. Griffith's formulation of the difference between 'European' and 'American' films refers to the same difference in tastes – while the typically American film says 'come and *have* an experience', the typically 'European' film says 'come and *see* an experience' (Monaco, 1981: 36).

If pure taste may thus be said to demand a distanciating attitude, it seems to me that this parallels the intellectual distanciation which is a prerequisite for all forms of critical reflection (and thus for conscious, 'strategic' political action as well). Pure taste's distanciating critical discourse has, in the postwar period, been able to appropriate originally 'barbaric' cultural forms in film, music, and various print media. This indicates not only that the categorization of particular forms of texts on either side of the high/low border has something historically 'accidental' about it, that there is a fluidity between the high and low realms of culture in the area of 'artistic' texts. It also indicates the real freedom and power of the high-culture discourse. The everyday language used in everyday talk about soap operas, movies, and pop music is not useful as a means to a refined understanding of most high-culture texts. But, as Bourdieu's work shows, the high-culture discourse can even distanciate itself from itself.[13] This ability is its critical potential.

VII

To sum up my argument high and low culture are still separated cultural realms in terms of institutions, discourses, and, to a large extent, also in terms of traditions of cultural ('artistic') expression. Students and researchers of culture clearly have their base in the high-culture realm, and should reflect on this as a basic premise for critical work in their various fields. Our ability to take part in both high and low culture's codes and practices is a class privilege; it does not mean that the socially operative distinctions between the two spheres have ceased to exist. High culture remains a sphere worth conquering for those now excluded from it, not least because of the critical potential of its meta-languages. It is our task as critical intellectuals to draw on this potential in order to turn our inescapable social distance from other categories of people into a critical one, serving an 'emancipatory knowledge-interest'.

While doing so, we may as recipients of any available cultural product benefit from the pleasures of the hard-to-pin-down phenomenon 'art' (a three-letter-word in some recent forms of critical media studies), in accordance with Brecht's cunning statement:

> Even when there is talk of higher and lower forms of amusement, art keeps a straight face, because it wishes to move both high and low and be left alone, as long as it can entertain people by doing so. (Brecht, 1973: 111)

Notes

1. Enthusiastic remark by John Fiske in a discussion following a presentation by Ien Ang at the International Communications Association's conference in Montreal, May 1987.
2. I owe this last point, that rock and folk music, for large sections of the radical 1960s generation, were an integral part of becoming and being politically conscious, to Michael Schudson, who kindly gave valuable comments on an earlier draft of this article.
3. Stuart Hall wrote in a review of Raymond Williams' *Politics And Letters* (1979):

> I still feel a strong sympathy for that way in which the bright young lad from the 'periphery', coming to Oxbridge as the idealized pinnacle of an *intellectual* path, first experiences the actual social shock of discovering that Oxbridge is not only the apex of official English intellectual culture, but the cultural centre of the class system. I know at once what Williams means by remarking, in his usual understated way, that 'the class stamp of Trinity was not difficult to spot'; and also that inevitable path which led, in the search for some kind of refuge, to the discovery of the Socialist Club – 'a home away from home'. (Hall, 1980: 96)

   The utopian dream of successful reintegration as 'homecoming', carried by radical intellectuals with lower-class backgrounds, is the central figure of thought identified and discussed in my book on a nationalist-democratic mass movement in Norway, *Folkeopplysningas dialektikk* ('The Dialectics of Popular Enlightenment'), in press. The basic structure of this dream is that The People have borne a Son, who Leaves Home in order to acquire Knowledge, which The Son then brings back to The People, creating the dialectical *Aufhebung* which enables the People to realize their True Essence or Historical Role (*Wesen*). My book deals not least with the various problems that arise when this Dream is confronted with Reality, i.e. the *resistance* from The People against their self-appointed representatives.
4. I am here thinking of phenomena such as high-culture 'appropriation' of low-culture artifacts and textual traditions since the 1950s (jazz and Hollywood films, in France) and 1960s (for instance pop art, in the US and elsewhere); and the changes in the social composition of audiences within the two spheres which I discuss below.
5. Robert C. Allen's highly valuable book, *Speaking of Soap Operas* (1985), gives a very critical account of the quantitative research on soap-opera audiences. This research has, since the 1930s, demonstrated that soaps are relatively *more* popular with lower-class and female audiences than with upper-class and male audiences. Allen's point is that research also shows that soaps are enjoyed by people of all social classes and both genders, a fact investigators often have left out of consideration in order to 'collapse the entire soap opera audience into a single social and psychosocial category whose members could be regarded as "different" from everyone else' (p. 28). His argument for the complexity of the audience (and the soap opera itself) is acceptable, and especially understandable when regarded as polemic against the simplistic tradition of US empiricism in mass communication research. The problem is that Allen does not seem to regard the consistency of the audience pattern marking certain social categories as more interested in soaps than others as a phenomenon in need of a socio-cultural explanation. In less sophisticated versions than Allen's, the critique of empiricism may be turned into a dismissal of all reasoning on the significance of observed affinities between specific social categories/classes and specific genres like the soap opera.

6. Paul DiMaggio's (1986) admirably lucid and thorough account of the establishment of high-culture institutions in Boston in the second half of the nineteenth century demonstrates this. His analysis shows how a certain bourgeois group (the Brahmins) established distinct high-culture institutions, which brought an end to previous fora for mixed cultural presentations to equally mixed audiences. Still, pertinent to my argument: (a) DiMaggio's analysis does not show that the older mixed presentations of, for instance, 'high' and 'low' forms of music were not *experienced* as mixed, i.e. that the audiences at these 'pre-split' gatherings were not already split in terms of tastes; (b) the Brahmins' preference for 'high' culture forms may (should) be understood as part of a class strategy for establishing socio-cultural distinction, but the choice of high culture for this purpose is not accidental. It is related not only to the abstract social status of this culture (in this case imported from Europe), but *also* to *qualitative* characteristics of the various high-culture forms: their relatedness and affinity to the tradition of modern learned culture and advanced thought in general.

7. As Adorno (1973) pointed out in his *Résumé über Kulturindustrie*: 'Because of its [the culture industry's, JG] role in society, uneasy questions concerning its quality, concerning truth or untruth, concerning its aesthetic status are suppressed or at least kept out of the so-called sociology of communication.'

8. For a very different interpretation of this phenomenon see Fiske (1987: 316).

9. Cf. Schudson 1987, especially pp. 66f.

10. Something in the way of a 'multilinear hierarchy of genres' may be a tenable idea, though, i.e. an ordering of genres according to what they can and cannot 'do' or 'hold' in terms of themes and modes of dealing with themes. There are limits to what a soap opera can contribute to a serious discussion of Death And Its Implications.

11. I should stress here that Brückner and Ricke refer to the times (end of the nineteenth century) when the working class was *openly* excluded from various bourgeois cultural events, fora, and forms. It seems to me, though, that their argument may be valid for our times too, when exclusion is informal but still very real.

12. Such an exemplary educational 'use' of high culture is described by the German-Swedish writer Peter Weiss in his three-volume novel *Ästhetik des Widerstands* (The Aesthetics of Resistance) (1975–8, published also in the three Scandinavian languages). Jürgen Habermas' rendering of the example should demonstrate my point:

> Weiss describes the process of reappropriating art by presenting a group politically motivated, knowledge-hungry workers in 1937 in Berlin. These were young people who, through an evening high school education, acquired the intellectual means to fathom the general and social history of European art. Out of the resilient edifice of this objective mind, embodied in works of which they saw again and again in the museums of Berlin, they started removing their own chips of stone, which they gathered together and reassembled in the context of their own milieu. This milieu was far removed from that of traditional education as well as from the then existing regime. These young workers went back and forth between the edifice of European art and their own milieu until they were able to illuminate both. (Habermas, 1985: 13)

13. Cf. Bourdieu's closing remark in his preface to the English language edition of *Distinction*:

> At all events, there is nothing more universal than the project of objectifying the mental structures associated with the particularity of a social structure. Because it presupposes an

epistemological break which is also a social break, a sort of estrangement from the familiar, domestic, native world, the critique (in the Kantian sense) of culture invites each reader, through the 'making strange' beloved of the Russian Formalists, to reproduce, on his or her own behalf, the critical break of which it is the product. For this reason it is perhaps the only rational basis for a truly universal culture. (Bourdieu, 1984: xiv)

References

Adorno, T. W., 'Om kulturindustrien' (On the culture industry), in H. F. Dahl (ed.) *Massekommunikasjon*, Oslo: Gyldendal, 1973 (originally published 1967).

Allen, R. C., *Speaking of Soap Operas*, Chapel Hill: University of North Carolina Press, 1985.

Bourdieu, P., *Distinction*, Cambridge, MA: Harvard University Press, 1984 (originally published 1979).

Brecht, B., *Lille Organon for teatret* (Little Organon for the Theater), in B. Brecht, *Om tidens teater*, Copenhagen: Gyldendal, 1973 (originally published 1948).

Brückner, P. and Ricke, G., 'Über die ästhetische Erziehung des Menschen in der Arbeiterbewegung', in C. Bessel *et al.*, *Das Unvermögen der Realität. Beiträge zu einer anderen materialistichen Ästhetik*, Berlin: Verlag Klaus Wagenbach, 1974.

Burke, P., *Popular Culture in Early Modern Europe*, Hounslow: Temple Smith, 1978.

DiMaggio, P., 'Cultural entrepreneurship in nineteenth century Boston: the creation of an organizational base for high culture in America', in R. Collins *et al.* (eds) *Media, Culture and Society*, Beverly Hills, Newbury Park, New Delhi: Sage, 1986. Available here as Reading 43.

Fiske, J., *Television Culture*, London: Methuen, 1987.

Habermas, J., *Technik und Wissenschaft als 'Ideologie'*, Frankfurt: Suhrkamp Verlag, 1968.

Habermas, J., 'Modernity – an incomplete project', in H. Foster (ed.) *Postmodern Culture*, London: Pluto, 1985.

Hall, S., 'The Williams interviews', *Screen Education* 34, Spring, 1980, 94–104.

Modleski, T., Introduction in her (ed.) *Studies in Entertainment*, Bloomington: Indiana University Press, 1986.

Monaco, J., *How to Read a Film*, New York and Oxford: Oxford University Press, 1981.

Mukarovsky, J., 'Estetisk verdi som sosialt faktum' (Aesthetic value as a social fact), in A. Heldal and A. Linneberg (eds) *Strukturalisme i litteraturvitenskapen*, Oslo: Gyldendal, 1979 (originally published 1936).

Sartre, J. P., 'Forsvar for de intellektuelle', in *Vinduet* 23 (2), 1973, 3–23. (Norw. translation of two lectures, published in *Plaidoyer pour les intellectuals*, Paris: Gallimard, 1972).

Schudson, M., 'The new validation of popular culture: sense and sentimentality in academia', in *Critical Studies in Mass Communication* 4, 1987, 51–68. Available here as Reading 46.

50 □ *Symbolic Creativity*

Paul Willis

The institutions and practices, genres and terms of high art are currently categories of exclusion more than of inclusion. They have no real connection with most young people or their lives. They may encourage some artistic specializations but they certainly discourage much wider and more general symbolic creativity. The official existence of the 'arts' in institutions seems to exhaust everything else of its artistic contents. If some things count as 'art', the rest must be 'non-art'. Because 'art' is in the 'art gallery', it can't therefore be anywhere else. It is that which is special and heightened, not ordinary and everyday.

The arts establishment, by and large, has done little to dispel these assumptions. It prefers instead to utilize or even promote fears of cultural decline and debasement in order to strengthen its own claims for subsidy, institutional protection and privilege. In general the arts establishment connives to keep alive the myth of the special, creative individual artist holding out against passive mass consumerism, so helping to maintain a self-interested view of elite creativity.

Against this we insist that there is a vibrant symbolic life and symbolic creativity in everyday life, everyday activity and expression – even if it is sometimes invisible, looked down on or spurned. We don't want to invent it or propose it. We want to recognize it – literally re-cognize it. Most young people's lives are not involved with the arts and yet are actually full of expressions, signs and symbols through which individuals and groups seek creatively to establish their presence, identity and meaning. Young people are all the time expressing or attempting to express something about their actual or potential *cultural significance*. This is the realm of living common culture. Vulgar sometimes, perhaps. But also 'common' in being everywhere, resistant, hardy. Also 'common' in being shared, having things 'in common'. Where 'arts' exclude, 'culture' includes. 'Art' has been cut short of meanings, where 'culture' has not.

As Raymond Williams always insisted, culture is ordinary.[1] It is the extra-ordinary in the ordinary, which is extraordinary, which makes both into culture,

From Willis, P., *Common Culture*, Open University Press, Milton Keynes, 1990, pp. 1–29.

common culture. We are thinking of the extraordinary symbolic creativity of the multitude of ways in which young people use, humanize, decorate and invest with meanings their common and immediate life spaces and social practices – personal styles and choice of clothes; selective and active use of music, TV, magazines; decoration of bedrooms; the rituals of romance and subcultural styles; the style, banter and drama of friendship groups; music-making and dance. Nor are these pursuits and activities trivial or inconsequential. In conditions of late modernization and the widespread crisis of cultural values they can be crucial to the creation and sustenance of individual and group identities, even to cultural survival of identity itself. There is work, even desperate work, in their play.

The Arts Institution

The existence, reproduction and appreciation of the high arts or 'official arts' depends on institutions, from individual art galleries, museums, theatres, ballet companies to the Arts Council itself. But institutions include not only buildings and organizations, but also systematic and specific social values and practices. The appreciation of official art (its consumption) further depends on the acquisition of certain kinds of knowledge and therefore on a prior educational process lodged within its own kinds of institutions. That is, the taste for art is learned.

The conventional list of 'high art' includes classical music, ballet, opera, drama, poetry, literature, the visual and plastic arts. Within these branches of art are institutionalized canons which attempt to place the 'works' into finite hierarchies differentiating greater and lesser value. Of course these hierarchies are not fixed. In contradiction to the sense of the universal which is supposed to characterize 'great art', new works (by no means always newly created) are admitted over time, just as established ones slip down or out. But at all times there are a limited number only of 'great works'.

These different aspects of the institutionalization of art produce the physical organizational and cultural separation of 'art', but also the possibility of an *internal* 'hyperinstitutionalization' of 'art' – the complete dissociation of art from living contexts. This is where the merely formal features of art can become the guarantee of its 'aesthetic', rather than its relevance and relation to real-life processes and concerns: religious art installed in the antiseptic stillness of the museum. In the 'hyperinstitutionalization' of 'art', aesthetic appreciation can become so atrophied as to make culturedness only the knowledge of form. Expressions and artifacts become inert things. Seated in the opera stalls, knowing what to expect again, seeing themselves reflected all around, the elite may actually be bored through and through with only the shell of that which used to contain a passion of meaning.

When aesthetic communication and critique become rhetorical assemblies of clever allusions and of wholly self-contained and therefore usually vacuous artistic 'cross-references', 'art' can end up in a floating and sometimes charlatan aesthetic without its own associated human practices and transformations. But this floating aesthetic conceals the social process by which it is appreciated, a process relying largely on the prior institutions of liberal-arts education to supply the knowledge of the purely formal and internal history of 'art'. And here lies the rub, for in the hyperinstitutionalization of 'art' the 'others', the 'uncultured', merely lack the code, but they're seen and may sometimes see themselves as ignorant, insensitive and without the finer sensibilities of those who really 'appreciate'. Absolutely certainly they're not the 'talented' or 'gifted', the elite minority held to be capable of performing or creating 'art'.

The traditional function of the artist is seen to be in the production of a refined aesthetic in things, texts and artifacts. Cultural practices involve, to be sure, symbolic representations, and part of their creativity is in the critical and creative transformation of these representations. But representational work cannot claim the distinction of being involved in a creative aesthetic unless it is in some real productive relationship to what is represented, unless it is embedded in a process of consciousness and meaning-making – categories which are not 'internally coded' but are a result of symbolic creativity. The notion of the full-time artist – separate from the market and requiring subsidy – is, if anything, at the periphery of the field of symbolic creativity in common culture, not at its centre. But it can seem to be its centre, thus disorienting the whole field with respect to its own real cultural practices and functions. Furthermore, it may be that certain kinds of symbolic creativity in the expressive and communicative activity of 'disadvantaged' groups exercise their uses and economies in precisely eluding and evading formal recognition, publicity and the possible control by others of their own visceral meanings. In this case the decontextualized search for aesthetics is, by definition, doomed to endless labour, for the aesthetic will be wherever it isn't. Hyperinstitutionalization excludes but can also repel.

It seemed for a time that things might be different. In the phase of social reconstruction after the war, part of the welfare–capitalist pact was to widen out the appreciation and practice of the high arts from their traditional base in the leisured upper-middle class. The arts were part of those good things of life which were to be shared out more equally. As in other areas, the state was to be responsible for this sharing out. The formation of the Arts Council in 1945 and the BBC Third Programme in 1946 was to spearhead this democratization of the arts. But the 'raise and spread' motto didn't last very long or spread very far. The Arts Council withdrew very promptly from the sites of popular consumption, cutting back promotions in Butlin's holiday camps, exhibitions in schools, canteens, factories and shops. Local arts clubs, regional initiatives, subsidized symphonies – many of these too were soon abandoned.

In fact the state became the vehicle for the continuance and reinforcement of the traditional conceptions and institutions of high culture rather than a vehicle for cultural democratization and experimentation with new, altogether wider institutions. The 'spreading' of art became highly specific and essentially conservative: the leisure-class idea of 'good culture' maintained its dominance (if not the class itself) but now with a wider well-subsidized audience of the rising middle class of managers and professionals.

The current attempts by the Conservative government to abrogate the 1945 welfare pact, specifically in the cultural field, by forcing the arts to reconstitute themselves in market terms does not really attack the continuing minority basis, elite and exclusive definition of the high arts. It merely seeks to lessen or to remove their state subsidies – or even bring back patronage in the form of high-class corporate-image enhancement. If the post-1945 welfare-state arts policy had really been about democratic cultural development, if it had not given up so early on imaginative alternatives, if it had not so easily taken over the leisure-class view of art, then the current opposition to the government's cultural pre-Keynesianism might, itself, be much more broadly based.

Though subordinated and often marginalized, the many strands of the community arts movement continue to carry the torch. They share the continuing concern to democratize the arts and make them more a part of common experience. Their search for new or expanded publics can, however, suffer from the implicit assumption that such groups are, in some sense, 'non-publics', that they have no forms of their own, no culture, no common culture, except perhaps a very much debased version of elite culture or of mass culture passively consumed. There can be a final unwillingness and limit even in subversive or alternative movements toward an arts democracy. They may have escaped the physical institutions and academies, but not always their conventions – the forms must be kept more or less intact. If they must go, then so too does any notion of a specifically artistic practice. What is left is indistinguishable from other activities such as community action or politics itself. Some activists are, indeed, led by this logic to pure community action. But an approach which won't discard the conventions makes assumptions which presuppose effects which must be free. If it is to be free, creative activity must be allowed to be what it is, and to lead where it will.

There seem to be hidden questions behind even those arts initiatives and policies which genuinely seek cultural democratization – not 'What are their cultures?' but 'Why are their cultures not like ours?', 'Why are their cultures not as we think they should be?'

[. . .]

Commodities and Consumerism

The main cultural materials and resources used in the symbolic work of leisure are cultural commodities. They are supplied to the market overwhelmingly by the commercial cultural industries and media for profit. Indeed, it was the market discovery, exploitation and development in the 1950s and 1960s of a newly defined affluent and expanding consumer group of young people which produced the popular conception of 'the teenager'.[2] We're currently experiencing a renewed and, it seems, even less caring emphasis on market forces in cultural matters. The rise of leisure we've referred to is really the rise of commercialized leisure. Does this matter? Does their production in a commercial nexus devalue cultural commodities and the contents of the cultural media?

There is a strange unanimity – and ghostly embrace of their opposites – between Left and Right when it comes to a condemnation of consumerism, and especially of the penetration of the market into cultural matters. It is the profane in the Temple for the artistic establishment. For some left cultural analysts it constitutes a widened field of exploitation which is in and for itself unwelcome; now workers are exploited in their leisure as well as in their work. The circuit of domination is complete, with no escape from market relations.

We disagree with both assessments, especially with their shared underlying pessimism. They both ignore the dynamic and living qualities of everyday culture, and especially their necessary work and symbolic creativity. These things have always been in existence, though usually ignored or marginalized. They continue to be ignored even when an extraordinary development and transformation of them are in progress. For symbolic work and creativity mediate, and are simultaneously expanded and developed *by*, the uses, meanings and 'effects' of cultural commodities. Cultural commodities are catalyst, not product; a stage in, not the destination of, cultural affairs. Consumerism now has to be understood as an active, not a passive, process. Its play includes work.

If it ever existed at all, the old 'mass' has been culturally emancipated into popularly differentiated cultural citizens through exposure to a widened circle of commodity relations. These things have supplied a much widened range of usable symbolic resources for the development and emancipation of everyday culture. Certainly this emancipation has been partial and contradictory because the consumer industries have sought to provide some of the contents and certainly the forms as well as the possibilities for cultural activity. Consumerism continuously reproduces an image of, and therefore helps to encourage, selfishness and narcissism in individualized consumption and hedonism. But those tendencies are now given features of our cultural existence. It is the so far undervalued balance of development and emancipation which has to be grasped. As we shall see, the images and offers of consumerism are not always taken at face value, nor are 'individualized' forms of consciousness as socially isolated and self-regarding as the pessimists suppose. Meanwhile a whole continent of informal, everyday culture has been recognized, opened up and developed.

Capitalism and its images speak directly to desire for its own profit. But in that very process it breaks down or short-circuits limiting customs and taboos. It will do anything and supply any profane material in order to keep the cash tills ringing. But, in this, commerce discovered, *by exploiting*, the realm of necessary symbolic production within the undiscovered continent of the informal. No other agency has recognized this realm or supplied it with usable symbolic materials. And commercial entrepreneurship of the cultural field has discovered something real. For whatever self-serving reasons it was accomplished, we believe that this is an historical *recognition*. It counts and is irreversible. Commercial cultural forms have helped to produce an historical present from which we cannot now escape and in which there are many more materials – no matter what we think of them – available for necessary symbolic work than ever there were in the past.[3] Out of these come forms not dreamt of in the commercial imagination and certainly not in the official one – forms which make up common culture.

The hitherto hidden continent of the informal (including resources and practices drawn from traditional folk and working-class culture produces, therefore, from cultural commodities much expounded, unprefigured and exciting effects – and this is why, of course, commerce keeps returning to the streets and common culture to find its next commodities. There is a fundamental and unstable contradictoriness in commercial rationality and instrumentality when it comes to consumer cultural goods. Blanket condemnations of market capitalism will never find room for it or understand it.

For our argument perhaps the basic complexity to be unravelled is this. Whereas it may be said that work relations and the drive for efficiency now hinge upon *the suppression* of informal symbolic work in most workers, the logic of the cultural and leisure industries hinges on the opposite tendency: a form of *their enablement and release*. Whereas the ideal model for the worker is the good time kept, the disciplined and empty head, the model for the good consumer is the converse – a head full of unbounded appetites for symbolic things.

Oddly and ironically, it is from capitalism's own order of priorities, roles, rules and instrumentalities *in production* (ironically, of leisure goods and services too) that informal cultures seek escape and alternatives in capitalist leisure consumption. Commerce appears twice in the cultural argument, as that which is to be escaped from and that which provides the means and materials for alternatives. Modern capitalism is now parasitic not only upon the puritan ethic, but also upon its instability even its subversion.

There is a widespread view that these means and materials, the cultural media and cultural commodities, must appeal to the lowest common denominators of taste. Not only do they have no intrinsic value but, more disturbingly, they may have coded-in negative values which manipulate, cheapen, degrade and even brutalize the sensibilities of 'the masses'.

In contradiction we argue that there is no such thing as an autonomous artifact capable of printing its own intrinsic values, one way, on human sensibility. This is to put a ludicrous (actually crude Marxist) emphasis on *production* and what is held to be initially coded into artifacts.

What has been forgotten is that circumstances change cases, contexts change texts. The received view of aesthetics suggests that the aesthetic effect is internal to the text, and a universal property of its form. This places the creative impulse squarely on the material productions of the 'creative' artist, with the reception or consumption of art wholly determined by its aesthetic form, palely reflecting what is timelessly coded within the text. Against this we want to rehabilitate consumption, creative consumption, to see creative potentials in it for itself, rather than see it as the dying fall of the usual triplet: production, reproduction, reception. We are interested to explore how far 'meanings' and effects can change quite decisively according to the social contexts of 'consumption', to different kinds of 'de-coding' and worked on by different forms of symbolic work and creativity. We want to explore how far *grounded* aesthetics are part, not of things, but of processes involving consumption, processes which make consumption pleasurable and vital. Viewers, listeners and readers do their own symbolic work on a text and create their own relationships to technical means of reproduction and transfer. There is a kind of cultural production within all consumption.

Young TV viewers, for instance, have become highly critical and literate in visual forms, plot conventions and cutting techniques. They listen, often highly selectively, to pop music now within a whole shared history of pop styles and genres. These knowledges clearly mediate the meanings of texts. The fact that many texts may be classified as intrinsically banal, contrived and formalistic must be put against the possibility that their living reception is the opposite of these things.

The 'productive' reception of and work on texts and artifacts can also be the start of a social process which results in its own more concrete productions, either of new forms or of recombined existing ones. Perhaps we should see the 'raw materials' of cultural life, of communications and expressions, as always intermediate. They are the products of one process as well as the raw materials for another, whose results can be, in turn, raw materials for successive groups. Why shouldn't bedroom decoration and personal styles, combinations of others' 'productions', be viewed along with creative writing or song and music composition as fields of aesthetic realization? Furthermore, the grounded appropriation of new technology and new hardware may open new possibilities for expression, or recombinations of old ones, which the dominant culture misses because it does not share the same conditions and contradictory pressures of that which is to be explained or come to terms with.

Our basic point is that human consumption does not simply repeat the relations of production – and whatever cynical motives lie behind them. Interpretation, symbolic action and creativity are *part* of consumption. They're involved in the whole realm of necessary symbolic work. This work is at least as important as whatever might originally be encoded in commodities and can often produce their opposites. Indeed, some aspects of 'profanity' in commercial artifacts may be liberating and progressive, introducing the possibility of the new and the socially dynamic.

It is pointless and limiting to judge artifacts *alone*, outside their social relations of consumption, with only the tutored critic's opinion of an internal aesthetic allowed to count. This is what limits the 'Official Arts' in their institutions. People bring living identities to commerce and the consumption of cultural commodities as well as being formed there. They bring experiences, feelings, social position and social memberships to their encounter with commerce. Hence they bring a necessary creative symbolic pressure, not only to make sense of cultural commodities, but partly through them also to make sense of contradiction and structure as they experience them in school, college, production, neighbourhood, and as members of certain genders, races, classes and ages. The results of this necessary symbolic work may be quite different from anything initially coded into cultural commodities.

Notes

1. Raymond Williams, 'Culture is ordinary' (1958), reprinted in his *Resources of Hope*, Verso, 1988.
2. See the first major study of youth culture in Britain, Mark Abrams, *The Teenage Consumer*, London Press Exchange, 1959.
3. We're bending the stick of argument here to emphasize how cultural products are creatively *used*, rather than passively *consumed*. We should not, of course, ignore the continuing ubiquity of forms of direct cultural production such as writing, photography and 'storying' (c.f. D. Morley and K. Worpole, *The Republic of Letters*, Comedia, 1981; S. Beszceret and P. Corrigan, *Towards a Different Image*, Comedia/Methuen, 1986; S. Yeo, *Whose Story?*, Blackwell, 1990). Equally, against elitism, we should recall activities like knitting and gardening as combining both production and use. Our general argument here should not obscure that varieties of such 'home produce' are important fields for symbolic work and creativity.

51 □ *Pessimism, Optimism, Pleasure: The Future of Cultural Studies*

Duncan Webster

[...]

To reduce cultural studies to the study of popular culture narrows its range and places much interesting work outside the scope of my argument, but popular culture has been central to the emergence and development of the discipline, and their relation is at the core of criticisms of trends in contemporary cultural studies. A repeated accusation is that a notion of a democratised culture, a transformed and 'truly popular' culture, has been diluted to become a populist celebration of existing popular forms.

[...]

Martin Barker's review of [John] Fiske's *Reading the Popular* and *Understanding Popular Culture* [...] suggests, in the first issue of the *Magazine of Cultural Studies*, that 'the problems with Fiske's version of cultural studies are just those this magazine was born to oppose'. Fiske's books, student textbooks 'cashing in on a new market in America and elsewhere', represent a 'real threat to cultural studies'. The problems found in the books are 'their profound lack of any interest in history; their transmogrification of theory into hollow and mechanical epithets; their congratulatory domestication of culture, and their dulling of all politics of culture under the guise of advocating "semiotic resistance"'. What's more, they're 'bloody dull'. Fiske's work, Barker argues, 'represents all that is going bad in work on popular culture. It is the equivalent of cheering in the face of defeats, warming one's hands in the cold fog of the new conservatism'. It doesn't analyse or challenge the

From *News from Nowhere*, no. 8, 1990, pp. 81–103.

dominant right-wing culture and politics: 'People negotiate their readings – wow!' Barker concludes by saying that if this 'is cultural studies, let's write five books, draw our salaries and go back to bed'.[1]

If the tone and openness of Barker's review are rare, the feeling that something either is going wrong with cultural studies or has already gone wrong is widespread, and overlaps with anxieties expressed elsewhere about the loss of *critical* work. So Ann Gray in a review-essay of studies of TV viewing concentrates on 'the problem of the popular', taking issue with Jane Root's *Open the Box*. Gray worries that while Root challenges a 'left-middle class intellectual elitism', she also seems to suggest that, in this instance, the 'spontaneous' pleasure of *The Price is Right* studio audience is 'natural' and unmediated. There is, therefore, a danger of falling into 'the consumerism notion of popular culture which naturalises the meanings produced by capitalism', of accepting that television gives "the audience what it wants"'. This isn't seen as a particular flaw of Root's work but as a 'worrying trend': 'by celebrating on the one hand an active audience for popular forms and on the other those popular forms which the audience "enjoy", we appear to be throwing the whole enterprise of a cultural critique out of the window'. A populist polemic against the myth of TV audiences as passive zombies, combined with 'the subjectivity licensed by the postmodern ethos', leads to the loss of some fifteen years' hard labour around the *production of meaning* and the ideological and political significance of the cultural. These things do matter'. 'Distance', she argues, is a necessary part of the process of cultural critique if it is 'to go beyond a simple celebration of what is already there'.[2]

So, cultural critique and critical distance versus a populist celebration of the popular. A response from that populist perspective might focus on Gray's quotation marks around *enjoy* and the punitive sound of that 'fifteen years' hard labour', and argue that the popular is not a problem but 'the problem of the popular' is. In this analysis 'pleasure' might well replace 'ideology', but that should be presented not as a depoliticisation of cultural criticism but as a way of addressing not just the pleasures of the audience but also the position of the critic, the conditions of that 'distance' – class, education, 'cultural capital'. I will return to these issues, but it is important to emphasise different variations of this critique-versus-celebration opposition. Two pieces by Paul Willemen are of interest here since they stress that the 'problem' is seen as cultural theory in the last decade, not just specifically cultural studies. In a long piece on 'The Third Cinema question', Willemen offers a critique of current approaches to 'popular culture' and a polemic against 'post' theory.

He characterises such approaches as either 'hypocritically opportunist', as in the 'attempts to validate the most debilitating forms of consumerism, with academics cynically extolling the virtues of the stunted products of cultural as well as political defeat', or as degenerating into 'a comatose repetition of '70s deconstructivist rituals'. Instead, 'the question to be asked today in Britain is: how to induce people into adopting , critical-socialist ways of thinking'.[3] He continues this argument in a review of John Hill's *Sex, Class and Realism* in the same issue. Hill's book, rather like the Third Cinema, is praised as offering 'the way out of the main impasse currently incapacitating Anglo-Saxon criticism': the 'impossible choice' between deconstruction's claims that films are 'thoroughly plural' and 'the abdication of critical responsibilities in favour of the celebration of existing patterns of consumption'. The latter is seen to stem from a refusal 'to countenance the possibility that vast sections of the population have come to derive pleasure from conservative orientated media discourses'.[4] Note that 'have come to derive', which suggests changes either in popular culture or its audiences which are nowhere analysed.

Socialist film (and cultural) theory of the 1970s, according to Willemen, implied 'an image of what a socialist cultural practice might be, for producers as well as consumers', and 'operated with a socialist ideal ego as something yet to be attained'. He admits that this 'ideal ego' was 'a puritanical one', but argues that since Thatcher, 'large sectors of the apparently left-inclined intelligentsia' have abandoned any kind of goal to work towards. This has been done 'under the guise of criticising the shortcomings of '70s theory and its puritanical ideal ego which has to work for its gratifications'. Intellectuals in the 1980s no longer argue for 'a socialist cultural practice', since that was relocated in the ways that 'working-class people (and black people, and women, and gays, etc.) made sense of/with the material provided for them by the established media multi-nationals and our existing television regimes'. 'At best', this was seen in terms of resistance; 'at worst (and predominantly) existing patterns of consumption were legitimised and even celebrated'. Based on 'the (innocent?) misuse of certain aspects of '70s theory', such as 'textual plurality' and a socialist essentialism (if 'oppressed consumers' enjoy popular culture, then it must contain socialist elements), this was 'cloaked in an aggressively populist rhetoric aimed against intellectuals at a time when we need to keep our critical wits more than ever' (117).

'The tragic mistake of many left cultural commentators and academics is to connive' with the forces of commodification, 'wittingly or not'. Although he sees the pleasure question' as important, Willemen sees the role of 'pleasure' in the discussion of popular film and television as helping the 'commodity disguise itself as the ultimate object of enjoyment' (119). Furthermore, these ideas of subversive pleasures depend on 'a capitalist logic which creates and defines the sites of possible contestation. Merely to play around within those spaces with the material offered is to consent to that process of definition, not to challenge it' (118). One problem with Willemen's argument is the striking absence of history from a socialist analysis; deconstruction and populism are transcended rather than located. There is the coincidence of left cultural critics making a 'tragic mistake' and Thatcherism, but the only relation between them is some sense of guilt by association: cynical opportunists betraying socialism ('under the guise of . . .', 'innocent?', 'wittingly or unwittingly'). There's no discussion of any problems within socialism during a decade of the New Right's hegemony, nor is there any discussion of the problems of funding alternative cultural spaces since the 1970s. Nor is there much analysis of any of the problems within 1970s theory which may have shaped the positions he attacks. His discussion of pleasure not only overlooks work on pleasure and use-value (Terry Lovell's *Consuming Fiction*, for example), it also seems to surrender a great deal. If we give up struggles within spaces defined by capitalist logic, where is left? We return to a traditional picture of the left intellectual as mediator between socialist vanguard and artistic avant-garde. The starting point for a 'socialist critical-cultural practice' appears to be to inform people that their pleasure in popular culture is suspect, then to form them into an orderly crocodile and march them off to a retrospective of Cuban cinema.

Judith Williamson's recent criticisms of cultural studies at least place more of a stress on history. In 'The problems of being popular', she complains that the Left's vocabulary no longer includes words such as 'revolutionary' or 'reactionary', and instead, feminist and left academics are busy discovering 'subversion' in almost any aspect of popular culture. She sees the Left as becoming less and less *critical*, stemming from the Left's 'post-'79 awareness of the Right's successful populism, known to many as "Thatcherism"'. Two readings of this awareness are offered: a 'charitable' one which sees the Left trying to reappropriate 'popular pleasures' from the Right, and a more critical view where politically demoralised socialist academics sink into popular culture out of a mixture of pessimism and boredom. She argues that they should be offering radical and new ways of meeting popular demands and desires instead.[5]

[. . .]

The criticisms of cultural studies outlined so far reveal a pattern: a conflict between a socialist criticism and one that is seen as Left-populist, and behind that, at points overlapping with it, some notion of being 'for' or 'against' postmodernism, also a sense of an argument between cultural and political optimism and pessimism. This last opposition connects changes within cultural criticism to the diverse processes of 'rethinking' on the Left in the 1980s. So both Labour and the Communist Party have been accused of a pessimistic capitulation to Thatcherism, taking over the Right's agenda rather than transforming it [. . .]; just as, so the argument goes, cultural studies has capitulated to the existing cultural industries, in order to celebrate the couch potato rather than propose an alternative. [. . .] It might be useful here to turn to some perspectives from outside Britain, to follow the export of British theory but also to get a different viewoint on these debates.

[. . .]

If a typical cultural studies text of the past might be characterised by its strong sense of locality (from Hoggart through to subcultural theory), a text like Lawrence Grossberg's *It's a Sin* is possibly typical of cultural studies now: an American academic discusses contemporary American culture and the history of British cultural studies in front of an Australian audience.

Grossberg's first section on 'The Scandal of Cultural Studies' starts with cultural studies' success in the United States: 'its recent rise has all the ingredients of a made-for-TV movie', but it 'has been installed into the American academy at just the moment when its work – especially in the US – seems to be stalled'.[6] For Grossberg, cultural studies is powerful in so far as it sees theory historically, politically and strategically, but its success threatens to restrict its theoretical mobility. He argues that it is now failing to address links between political struggles and the national popular culture. His critique overlaps with the others outlined above, as he welcomes work on 'the politics of everyday life' (Modleski, Chambers, Fiske), but suggests that 'the everyday' is seen in this work 'as if it were absolutely autonomous, and its practices as if they were always forms of empowerment, resistance and intervention'. This approach 'simply answers too many questions ahead of time'; not only do terms like pleasure or resistance 'refer to complex sets of different effects which have to be specified concretely', but also the relations between them 'are themselves complex and never guaranteed in advance' (13).

However, Grossberg's worries about how effective cultural studies is relate problems in recent work back to its original emergence (Hoggart, Williams and Thompson in the usual shorthand) and its institutionalisation at the Birmingham Centre for Contemporary Cultural Studies. He argues that this initial step skewed cultural studies: 'first, a cultural theory of communication is transformed into a communicational theory of culture; second, the terms of the problematic – culture and society – are bifurcated and disciplinised into literary-textual studies and sociology'. As 'these two theoretical structures are mapped onto each other', cultural studies subsequently focuses on the ideological relationship between the production of meaning and experience' (15).

Thus cultural studies 'is always caught in the twin pulls of textual and sociological research'; reading 'experience off of texts' or reading 'texts through experience' with ideology as 'the ultimate object of research' for both traditions. This leads Grossberg to locate another problem, 'a populist politics based upon the identification of the popular with social position', arguing that this differs from Williams but resembles Thompson's criticism of him, which replaced ways of life with ways of struggle, 'that is, which identified cultural and political positions' (17).

In some ways, then, Grossberg reverses other criticisms of current cultural studies by relating problems with today's models to its initial conception. However, his argument is not that clear about where and when cultural studies stalled. The 'scandal' seems to be both its current political weakness and its initial theorisation as a discipline. By politicising theoretical questions it's possible that he's arguing that despite theoretical problems cultural studies 'worked' until meeting the transformed political and cultural terrain of the 1980s. The changed conditions of cultural analysis are thus both theoretical and historical.

Both theory and historically different conditions have undermined fixed notions of texts (19) and audiences (21). Apart from debates within cultural theory, there's 'the changing spatial and temporal complexity of the cultural terrain itself' (19): new technologies, the expansion of leisure, the difficulty in isolating one area of popular culture – his example is American television (20–21). Grossberg criticises cultural studies for reducing culture to ideology, suggesting that a focus on meaning misses the importance of 'complexly produced affective structures – structures of desire, emotion, pleasure, mood, etc.' (35). This is central to his analysis of the American New Right who have located the 'crisis of America' as 'neither economic nor ideological, but rather affective' (31). His discussion of Reaganism's attempt to produce a new national popular is an interesting analysis, and although I will not be able to discuss his argument, I will return to the postscript of *It's a Sin* to examine Grossberg's suggestions about the future of cultural studies rather than his quarrel with its past.

Grossberg refers to Williamson's 'Problems of being popular' and to Meaghan Morris' 'Banality in cultural studies', probably the two most-cited pieces in the debates about cultural studies now. Morris relocates the debates about cultural studies through an engagement with feminism and postmodernism. The range of her writing (movies, philosophy, art, the everyday), and her own position outside the academy, contribute to a constant awareness of the circulation of 'theory'. She is, for example, as interested in 'the theoretical debates that circulate in and as popular culture as I am in academically situated theoretical work *about* popular culture'. She also points to the 'shuttling' of people and discourses 'between pedagogical institutions and the cultural industries', as part of a process of the dissemination and commodification of ideas. The academy functions within a network of bookshops, TV chat-shows, interviews, reviews, exhibitions, and so on.[7] This stress on mobility across social sites and cultural spaces runs alongside an insistence on specificity, the cultural politics of space and place. 'Things to do with shopping centres', for instance, concerns the specificity of place, the history of particular Australian mall developments, but also addresses the place of the analyst.

The analysis of shopping centres involves 'exploring common sensations, perceptions and emotional states aroused by them', both positive and negative, but also working against those 'in order to make a place from which to speak other than that of the fascinated describer'. The latter can be 'outside' in the role of ethnographer or, 'in a pose which seems to me to amount to much the same thing', supposedly 'inside' as the 'celebrant' of popular culture. The first position belongs to the sociology of consumerism or leisure and the second corresponds to positions in cultural studies. Morris quotes Iain Chambers's argument that recognising 'the democratic "potential" of people's active appropriations of popular culture involves the "wide-eyed presentation of actualities"' that Adorno criticised in Walter Benjamin. Morris relocates this argument over a materialist account of Baudelaire's Paris to the Australian mall. Adorno declared that Benjamin's study was located '"at the crossroads of magic and positivism. That spot is bewitched"', but theory can break the spell. Morris rejects both the 'strategy of "wide-eyed presentation"' and the 'faith in theory as the exorcist'; neither meets 'the critical problems posed by feminism in the analysis of "everyday life"'. Feminist cultural studies pays more attention to 'everyday discontent' in shopping, 'anger, frustration, sorrow, irritation, hatred, boredom, fatigue', rather than consumerism as liberating (remember 'shopping for democracy'). Feminism's discontent with the everyday, 'and with wide-eyed definitions of the everyday as "the way things are"', thus 'allows the possibility of rejecting what we see and refusing to take it as "given"'.[8]

Morris comments on the vogue for emphasising the meanings for users/shoppers and the possible resistance inherent in contemporary practices of consumption.

Articles return to certain 'exemplary inaugural stories' (punk is her example); 'principles of cultural action – bricolage, cut-up, appropriation, assemblage and so on' are restated. But as 'time passes in shoppingtown, however, it's tempting to wonder how much longer (and for whom) these stories can do the rounds'. After the analyst has hung out at the mall, what happens next? There are two slides: 'from user to consumer to consumption, from persons to structures to processes'; and from 'notions of individual and group "creativity" to cultural "production" to political "resistance"'. Morris quotes a friend's parody of this slide as '"the discovery that washing your car on Sunday is a revolutionary event"' (213–14). Perhaps that point needs to be related back to the productionist aesthetics of the 1970s. Washing your car or queuing in Sainsbury's isn't revolutionary, but equally 'baring the device' in independent films didn't cause a rush to the barricades either. Instead, Morris challenges current theorisations of the production/consumption process, arguing that the opposition needs to be rethought and that assumptions that we know about 'production' and 'can move to the other side' are problematic. She suggests that an essay could be written on the slides she identifies; it could, she did – 'Banality in cultural studies'.[9]

Morris starts with her irritation with Baudrillard's use of 'banality' in theorising the media and with trends in the analysis of the popular and the everyday, which 'seems to be criticism that actively strives to achieve "banality"'. She doesn't oppose these positions 'as, say, pessimistic and optimistic approaches to popular culture', which admittedly avoids simplifying these debates but also, I think, misses a chance to historicise them (Baudrillard's relation to Marxism and situationism, for example). The *boom* in cultural studies is placed through the politics of intellectual work as it relates to, and moves in and out of, commodity circulation' (15). Recent work, with its ideas of 'cultural democracy', of 'mass culture not as a vast banality machine, but as raw material made available for a variety of popular practices (19), suggests to Morris that there's an English 'master-disk from which thousands of versions of the same article about pleasure, resistance, and the politics of consumption are being run off under different names with minor variations' (20). Ideas are not just repeated but exported, and an English left populism is decontextualised and 'recycled in quite different political cultures', Australia and America, for example, dulling any oppositional edge along the way (20).

She does not challenge the 'enabling theses' of theories of consumption that consumers are not '"cultural dupes"' (Stuart Hall), but 'active, critical users of mass culture'; that consumption can't be read off from production nor confined to the economic; and that consumption practices, like sexuality, are made up of 'a multiplicity of fragmented and contradictory discourses' (20). Instead she criticises the style and ways in which intellectuals inscribe their relation to the popular. An ethnographic approach cites 'popular voices', translates and comments on their pleasures, then introduces 'a play of *identification* between the knowing subject of cultural studies, and a collective subject "the people"'. In John Fiske's work, for example, Morris suggests that 'the people' are defined as negotiating their readings, reworking and interpreting culture: 'This is also, of course, the function of cultural studies itself'. 'The people' end up not just as 'the cultural student's object of study, and his native informants' but also as 'the textually delegated, allegorical emblem of the critic's own activity'. They are 'both a source of authority for a text and a figure of its own critical activity'; the 'populist enterprise' is seen as both circular and narcissistic (20).

Morris then moves on to another strategy, impersonating the popular. Referring to work on 'mass culture as woman', the conflation of stereotypes of femininity with the popular, Morris looks at Iain Chambers's *Popular Culture* as a text which invites this distracted skimming over the surfaces of the popular, and as an example of 'critical cross-dressing' (Elaine Showalter's phrase): 'the *white male theorist* as bimbo' (22). The problem of 'anti-academic pop-theory writing' shaped, she argues, by 'the vestigial anti-feminism of the concept of distraction', is that 'a stylistic enactment of the "popular" as distracted, scanning the surface, and short on attention-span' reproduces, 'at the level of *renunciative* practice', the notion of 'cultural dupes' that cultural studies opposes. Recycling the oppositions of contemplation/distraction, academic/popular, regardless of 'which of the terms we validate', limits critical and popular interventions in a 'return to the postulate of cultural dopism in the *practice* of writing' (22). She argues that cultural studies may have stalled now because its style contradicts its argument, and it can only motivate its repetitions through inscribing an Other ('grumpy feminists and cranky leftists') who needs to be reminded of the complexities of consumption. In her view, discrediting these other voices is 'one of the immediate political functions of the current boom in cultural studies' (23).

Morris announces her frustration at the choice in cultural theory between 'cheerleaders and prophets of doom'. She is 'equally uneasy about fatalistic theory on the one hand, and about cheerily "making the best of things"' and calling it cultural studies on the other (24). The problems of recent cultural studies are set out quite brilliantly here, but if that concluding stand-off between fatalists and cheerleaders captures elements of the present impasse, the piece avoids a sense of how this came about. Reintroduce history and those discredited voices get louder; the stand-off is no longer between cheery populists and apocalyptic postmodernists, other voices are heckling from the sidelines, and what they're shouting is: 'What's all this crap, then?' This takes us back to another Morris piece, but also suggests reasons for the populists' caricatures of those who 'misunderstand' popular culture.

In the conclusion to 'Banality in cultural studies', Morris suggests that seeing the need for a discriminating criticism of popular culture as pessimistic or elitist leaves us with a weaker, poorer critical language. I agree, but the associations that a word like 'discrimination' carries are not easily scraped off. If you wanted to locate another impasse within cultural studies, it's easily found in the history of (Left) Leavisite attempts to separate out good and bad popular culture, Marxist judgements of the 'progressive text', and feminist quests for 'positive images', and the depressing narrative of their interchanges. And that's a history of an *engagement* with popular culture, there's also simple dismissal. In 'Politics now' Morris talks of the inscription of politics 'as a perfect *non sequitur*': her example is an immediate response to a lecture by Juliet Mitchell after *Psychoanalysis and Feminism* was published, 'that nightmare voice of the Left, yelling boldly from the back of the room, "*Yeah, Juliet, what about Chile?*"' She adds that this is not a question of 'the gulf between intellectuals and the working class, but a matter of the way that petty-bourgeois intellectuals treat each other'.[10]

The conclusion to 'Politics now' introduces a topic often greeted with exactly this kind of dismissal – postmodernism. Using Jameson's analysis of postmodernism as 'the cultural logic of late capitalism', Morris argues that there's a 'practical insistence' that any 'critical political culture' must engage with these debates and take into account that the 'abolition of "critical distance"' makes 'the old tools of ideology-critique' ineffective. A further practical point is that 'in a mass-media society with mass-media cultures and mass-media politics, the relationship between *signifying* ... gestures and political ones' cannot easily be divided up between the cultural/aesthetic and the political. She argues against a kind of blackmail: a rhetoric of *urgency* which dismisses 'idle speculation, wild theorising, and lunatic prose'. She argues the opposite: 'things are too urgent now for the Left to be giving up its imagination, or whatever imagination the Left's got left.... The very last thing that's useful now is a return (as farce, rather than tragedy) to the notion of one "proper" critical style, one "realistic" approach, one "right" concern' (185–6). Bearing in mind Morris's critique of 'banality' and her warning against prescription, my concluding suggestions for 'the future of cultural studies' are offered as a way of reframing the debates outlined above, rather than an urgent demand for a change of direction.

Pistachio Shirts and Corsets: Intellectuals and the Popular

> It's always tempting these days – and especially at the end of
> long essays – to wheel on Gramsci as a 'hey-presto' man, as
> the theorist who holds the key to all our current theoretical
> difficulties.[11]

Echoing in the debates outlined above, there is a longer argument between cultural optimism and pessimism, often also connected to analyses of political possibilities. However, the position that the mass media have a 'progressive potential' currently deformed through existing social and economic relations has been eclipsed by a sense of the 'popular' which locates 'cultural democracy' here and now in the active resistance and negotiation of consumers. One reason for this radical relocation of that ideal from a socialist future to a capitalist present lies in a rejection of the cultural conservatism that intellectuals of the Left and Right have shared. Commenting on the parallels between Debray's *Teachers, Writers, Celebrities* and the work of the Leavises, Francis Mulhern points to the 'tense combination of fatalism and defiance' in both analyses. Debray's study could take as its motto either 'Gramsci's famous borrowing, "pessimism of the intelligence, optimism of the will"', or 'the perhaps more lucid Leavisian phrase, "desperate optimism"'.[12] Baudrillard's view of the masses turns this inside out – optimistic despair – staying in the terms of cultural conservatism (the masses as zombie consumers) but rejecting critique.

Gramsci's 'famous borrowing' suggests the qualities needed for digging in for a long struggle. Setting aside optimism and pessimism, what of will and intelligence? Where are they located?

[. . .]

I want to suggest that, in reaction to 1970s theory, what gets inserted into this pessimism/optimism, intelligence/will couplet is *pleasure*. Pleasure, the blind spot of much past Marxist and feminist analysis, introduces questions of desire, affective investment, fantasy and so on, shifting the focus to consumption rather than production. I think this was a necessary and productive move, but one which has faltered by locating pleasure in audiences (or in a poststructuralist delirious play of textuality), leaving the academic or critic as the secretary or analyst of these pleasures, transcribing, commenting, explaining, but disembodied.

'Pleasure' as poststructuralist *jouissance* or as populist fun inserts the body into cultural studies as a site of resistance, respectively reconstructing the propriety of power or empowering the consumer, but what is often invisible here is the intellectual's own body and power, not just intellectuals' desire but their position in regimes of power-knowledge. I'm basing this on a belief that the 'collapse of critical distance' is not just an epistemological question but a historical and material process, and also on a rejection of current positions: a nostalgia for a panoptical ivory tower, a left variant of that nostalgia, where the intellectual scans the horizon and confidently pronounces on progressive texts and forces, and the populist perspective that Morris uncovered, gazing at the popular in order to celebrate cultural studies' own reflection. What I'm suggesting instead isn't a position so much as a project, maintaining criticism while respatialising 'distance'. Some work on intellectuals and the popular can serve as signposts.

Grossberg adds a postscript to *It's a Sin* as he felt his conclusion was too pessimistic; it left 'little room for that "optimism of the will" which Gramsci thought necessary for political struggle'. He finds that optimism by relating the fanatic, utopian side of American history to the shifting terrain of popular culture, and exploring 'the postmodern gap' between fans, fanatics and ideologues (66). The differences between these have been produced by discourses of power-knowledge and by the drawing of 'distinctions' (Bourdieu). Postmodernity unsettles these differences, but Grossberg takes issue with many versions of 'the postmodern collapse of critical distance and the increasing uncertainty about the authority of intellectual and political voices/positions'. Since this has been articulated as 'an abstract epistemological problem', the answer has been seen as a 'need for reflexivity', defined as 'auto-critique and self-revelation, as a search for more autobiographical and dialogical writing forms' (66). But that move surrenders not just authority but also the possibility of intervention; 'it cannot rearticulate a new structure of authority appropriate to the contemporary context' (67).

Grossberg argues that the collapse of critical distance and 'the crisis of authority' are not epistemological questions 'but a concrete historical dilemma', shaped by the fact that we are a part of the terrain we write about (67). Our authority cannot rest on 'privileged distinctions of taste and distaste', so reflexivity needs to be rethought as the basis for a new form of critique. As fans and critics, 'we can be simultaneously on the terrain but not entirely of it', enabling 'an historically specific form of critical distance' (68). We may have to limit our claims but as 'intellectuals, we have the resources to articulate social possibilities': as 'critical fans', our task is not to define '"proper" cultural tastes' or '"proper" political positions', but to analyse 'specific investments' in the popular and their political possibilities. If 'we are fans, we are not only fans; nor are we only intellectuals' (68). Instead of reconstructing authority, we need 'to rearticulate new forms of authority which allow us to speak as critical fans'. He ends with a vision of a 'politics for and by people who live in the modern world, people who live in the world of popular tastes. An impure politics for pop people!' (69)

Grossberg's account of the contradictory spaces of contemporary popular culture can be complemented by Andrew Ross's *No Respect*, a history of the relation between American intellectuals and popular culture from early responses to mass culture to postmodernism. It's an important study precisely because that 'and' is a terrain of genuine debate and dialogue, linking, for example, arguments within the American Left to debates over modernism and kitsch, focusing on concepts that bridged the intellectual and the popular (hip, camp, and so on), ranging across cultural forms from the Rosenberg letters to pornography, examining the complex interactions between discourses and bodies, class and taste, and widening the definition of the intellectual by drawing on Gramsci and Bourdieu among others. Ross's approach is necessarily dialectical, for a history of popular culture cannot be just a history either of producers or of consumers, it must also be 'a history of intellectuals – in particular, those experts in culture whose traditional business is to define what is popular and what is legitimate'.[13]

Ross offers a 'postmodern picture of multiple and uneven activities, loyalties, obligations, desires and responsibilities' of intellectual work now, suggesting, like Grossberg, a sense of 'impure' political possibilities (230). Both arguments stem from a practical, local rather than apocalyptic, sense of postmodernism's dissolution of boundaries between popular and high cultures, with an awareness that power relations between intellectuals and popular culture do not simply dissolve in that process. Bearing Ross's argument that intellectuals and popular culture need to be thought of together, we can now turn from changes in the position of intellectuals to a transformed culture.

In a review-essay of work on popular culture, Geoffrey Nowell-Smith suggests that the term is now problematic: 'popular cultural forms have moved so far towards centre stage in British cultural life that the separate existence of a distinctive popular culture in an oppositional relation to high culture is now in question'.[14] The idea that 'the leading lights of British rock music would shortly be asked to perform before the Princess of Wales must have seemed a crazy pop-culturalists' dream in 1956, but this is what has happened' (83). Nowell-Smith historicises that shift, first by an interesting comparison between Britain and other European countries and their relation to American popular culture, then by turning to the late 1950s and the simultaneous emergence of cultural studies (Williams and Hoggart) and a new popular culture (rock 'n' roll and commercial television). Despite these changes and the expansion of leisure and popular culture in the 1960s, an assumption remained that class divisions were reflected in 'differential cultures'. It was assumed that 'the divide that seemed to exist between popular cultural forms and those of high culture was a permanent feature of the modern world', and that this division 'could be mapped sociologically and made to correspond to divisions in society at large. Two cultures had to exist, and they had to be the cultures of the dominant and dominated classes respectively' (82). He argues that this meant that differences 'between and within cultures' were overlooked. Also, that this is another instance of the 'peculiarities' of British culture, highly stratified and following 'class stratification more closely than in other countries' (82). Britain in the 1960s, then, did not provide an appropriate model for analysis of popular culture in other countries, nor do the critical assumptions of that period work for today's popular culture.

Today, Nowell-Smith argues, the choice is between saying that there is 'one culture (albeit with divisions in it) or several cultures (overlapping and rubbing up against each other) but no longer that there are two cultures, high and popular, divided from each other'. He suggests that there is 'one (multiply divided) culture' with the dominant forms being those 'traditionally designated as popular' (83). He feels that the use of 'popular' can itself be a distraction outside of an analysis of a form's producers or its public, and writing from within film studies rather than cultural studies proper, he uses that distanced engagement to call into question central assumptions of (popular) cultural studies. Although he seems to approve of the 'move away from the theoretical high ground into the empirical flatlands' in the work he reviews, he notes the absence of an 'implicit theory' of how 'the components of popular culture relate to each other' (90). He suggests that if the central project of seeing 'culture as a whole' is set aside, then cultural studies has lost its rationale, and he sees a weakness in the stress on consumption at the expense of production; 'the most striking absence' in the study of popular culture is, for him, 'any sense of artistic production'. When production 'comes in, or rather when it comes back, then the study of popular culture will have become the study of . . . culture' (90).

Dick Hebdige argues for a similar shift in both the study of popular culture and the field itself, in a piece that suggests the radical potential of 'banality' (post-Live Aid events, etc.). If in the 1950s and 1960s the 'artificial order of the classroom was built against the viral chaos' of the popular, those popular forms are now legitimate objects of study from schools to post-graduate research. The central assumption that '"pop/pap" was culture's Other' maintained a strictly policed frontier between the popular and a threatened culture ('classical, high, modernist even . . . folk, progressive rock or gritty working class'). 'Popular culture was an animal to be approached Barbara Woodhouse-style with firm voice and steady hand'. Now, in the West at least, the map has been redrawn: 'popular culture is no longer marginal, still less subterranean. Most of the time and for most people it simply *is* culture'. This needs to be recognised within cultural studies, and in a provocative paradox, Hebdige suggests that popular culture now 'may not actually exist anywhere except on the shelves of academic bookshops'.[15]

Hebdige suggests that the maps being used by academics, the popular as a knowable terrain crossed by class, race, and gender, are no longer as persuasive as the discourses of identity and desire offered by marketing and advertising practices. He's not suggesting that the consumerism paradise of endless individuation has arrived, nor that class, race and gender are irrelevant, but pointing to the weakness of current cultural studies: 'academics (I count myself among them) armed with semiotics, a truncated account of Gramsci and the remnants of Raymond Williams's culturalism have been staggering around the ruins of the sixties-in-the-eighties accompanied by their publishers trying to revive the fallen giant of the masses'. We return to the stand-off between 'gloomy, decadent Baudrillard' and 'optimistic, enabling cultural studies', but this time offered as a mirroring: Baudrillard 'is progressive British cultural studies back to front'. The way out is to smash that glass 'on to which generations of intellectuals have been projecting so many of their own largely unadmitted anxieties and desires'; to let go 'of our selves and the gravity traditionally accorded to intellectual projects'; to admit that 'disposable culture is *intrinsically* worth studying without trying to justify it by referring the analyses back to "proper" political concerns'; to give up 'speaking on behalf of the whole of humanity' and 'the quest of intellectuals either to merge with the imaginary masses or to triumph in their disappearance'.

While I'm not persuaded that the pop humanism of Live Aid is a great advance on the humanism of the universal intellectual, Hebdige's useful proposals link transformations within popular culture to a rethinking of the position of intellectuals. In a related piece, he again outlines a transfigured social mapped by post-Fordist marketing's vocabulary of desire, aspiration and identity, in order to argue that cultural studies, and the Left in general, must learn from both postmodern scepticism and the alternative definitions of race and national identity within popular culture. This vision of 'new times' escapes a universal model of postmodernism's 'logic' and the 'old language of the left'. To intervene within this changing world we need 'to abjure certain kinds of authority we might have laid claim to in the past, without losing sight of the longer-term objective, how to articulate a new kind of socialism, how to make socialism, as Raymond Williams might have said, without the masses'.[16]

My claims are more modest but could be summarised as the need to rethink the position of intellectuals; to follow the dissolution of 'popular culture' into 'culture' or 'the popular'; and to link that with the relation between the construction of a national-popular within an international popular culture and changing definitions of national identity. This last point raises the complex relations between 'Englishness' and its production through culture and leisure practices ('heritage', etc.), and the form of the nation-state within a context of multiculturalism, 'Europe', American popular 'cultural imperialism', and the political demands for a transformation of that form. This may provide a way of rethinking audiences and consumption, reframing them with questions of citizenship and the complex relations of power-knowledge that shape discussions of 'taste', 'standards' and 'quality' and which link these terms to the national – British television as the best in the world.

Rethinking the relations between intellectuals, popular culture and (cultural) democracy takes us back to Gramsci, the 'hey-presto' man. Alan O'Shea and Bill Schwarz ask what Gramsci has to offer:

> He had no liking for the Americanised popular culture of his own day, for all the originality of his cultural investigations he was never the slightest bit interested in its modern manifestations like the cinema and radio, he systematically subordinated self to politics, had nothing interesting to say on the symbolic forms of popular cultures or their elements of fantasy, wrote incomprehensibly on psychoanalysis, suffered nervous collapse if subjected for too long to the speediness of city life, and so on: a grizzled old Bolshevik about as far removed from the dynamics of contemporary popular cultures as one could possibly imagine.[17]

Such a critique could be extended, they argue, to the way that the study of the popular is institutionalised, specifically the externality of academic discourse and intellectuals when confronting this terrain.

Orwell is introduced here as a figure representing 'almost any explorer of popular culture of the past hundred years or so', sitting on a train, 'insulated from the culture he watches', seeing a woman clearing out a drain. That self-reflexivity, *The Road to Wigan Pier*'s awareness of the social relations implied by this kind of observation and description, is eclipsed as Orwell wriggles free in order to suggest that it's not himself who is 'caught up in all this after all, but *others*', and to 'castigate the deluded, pistachio-shirted intellectuals all around him'. O'Shea and Schwarz find a mirror-image of this move in Iain Chambers's mapping of the 'metropolitan experience', *Popular Culture*. By turning from the academy to the postmodern dazzle of the streets, Chambers 'can make it appear as if all the problems of knowledge and pedagogy lie with others in this bi-polar world: the monochrome guardians of official culture'. Chambers is the pomo Orwell, appearing to 'absolve himself from his own positions: only this time he champions the pistachio-shirts'. But externality, indeed social relations, can't simply be rhetorically shrugged off. O'Shea and Schwarz rightly refuse 'the choice between two planetary discourses – the one academic, totalising and external, the other lived and popular'. They suggest that a return to Gramsci might enable those discourses to be 'more fruitfully, and more justly' integrated. Gramsci's work, historicising both intellectuals and the popular, provides the terms for the critique of Gramsci. If Chambers's 'popular epistemology' does not resolve the problems of externality, 'it may be necessary –

wizened, miserable old Bolshevik that he was – to go back to Gramsci, to read him anew, to imagine or invent a Gramsci for our own bleak times (108–9).

Rosalind Brunt, discussing the 'politics of identity', does just that, arguing for a new image of the political activist. Instead of the activist as 'mole', tunnelling beneath capitalism in order to undermine it, she turns to Gramsci's suggestive metaphor for '"intellectuals of a new type"': they should become '"as it were, the whalebone in the corset"'. Her pleasure in this image stems from its idea of 'revolutionary stiffening and control while also being an intimate, indeed sensuously materialist figure of speech'. It's an image of discipline but support, of literally '"keeping in touch"' with the masses, while suggesting a non-vanguardist 'way of working: up front, open and close'.[18]

In the context of cultural studies, the 'whalebone in the corset' is an image that suggests both embracing the popular and shaping it. It may draw on images of 'mass culture as woman', but it also provides a figure for the problems of externality and distance, and suggests ways of linking the two. Madonna's lingerie, and the fierce arguments about the meaning of her embodiment of a female pop and desiring subject, could be seen as deconstructing an opposition between outside and inside, for example. As an image of *transition*, of new ways of relating intellectuals and the popular, it also suggests the ways that cultural studies is now seen as 'sexy' by publishers, as worryingly commodified and populist by critics, and potentially, as a way of rearticulating a critical practice within and outside the popular.

Notes

1. Martin Barker, *MOCS*, 1 (March 1990), pp. 39–40.
2. Ann Gray, 'Reading the audience', *Screen*, 28 (Summer, 1987), pp. 27–8, p. 30.
3. Paul Willemen, 'Notes and reflections', *Framework*, 34 (1987), p. 7, p. 37.
4. Paul Willemen, review of *Sex, Class and Realism*, *Framework*, 34, p. 115.
5. Judith Williamson, 'The problems of being popular', *New Socialist*, 41 (September 1986), pp. 14–15; Cora Kaplan, 'The culture crossover', *New Socialist*, 43 (November 1986); Duncan Webster, *Looka Yonder! The Imaginary America of Populist Culture* (London, 1988).
6. Lawrence Grossberg, *It's a Sin* (Sydney, 1988), p. 8.
7. Meaghan Morris, *The Pirate's Fiancée: Feminism, reading, postmodernism* (London, 1988), pp. 8, 9, 10.
8. Meaghan Morris, 'Things to do with shopping centres', in Susan Sheridan (ed.), *Grafts: Feminist cultural criticism* (London, 1988), p. 196–7.
9. *Ibid.*, p. 214; 'Banality in cultural studies', *Block*, 14 (1988).
10. Morris, *Pirate's Fiancée*, pp. 180–81.
11. Tony Bennett, 'Marxism and popular fiction', in Bob Ashley (ed.), *The Study of Popular Fiction: A source book* (London, 1989), p. 182.
12. Francis Mulhern, 'Introduction to Regis Debray', *Teachers, Writers, Celebrities* (London, 1981), p. xii.

13. Andrew Ross, *No Respect: Intellectuals and popular culture* (London, 1989), p. 5.

14. Geoffrey Nowell-Smith, 'Popular culture', *New Formations*, 2 (Summer 1987), p. 80.

15. Dick Hebdige, 'Banalarama, or can pop save us all?', *New Statesman and Society*, 9 December 1988, pp. 31–32.

16. Dick Hebdige, 'After the masses', *Marxism Today*, January 1989, p. 53.

17. Alan O'Shea and Bill Schwarz, 'Reconsidering popular culture', *Screen*, 28, 3 (Summer 1987), p. 106.

18. Rosalind Brunt, 'Bones in the corset', *Marxism Today*, October 1988, p. 23.

52 □ The Good, the Bad, and the Indifferent: Defending Popular Culture from the Populists

Simon Frith

In his book *Origins of the Popular Style*, musicologist Peter Van Der Merwe suggests that 'reviewing the popular music of the twentieth century as a whole, most people would probably agree that some of it is excellent, some unbearable and most of it very indifferent. What the good, bad and indifferent share is a musical language' (3). Most people would probably agree with this statement; disagreement would be about which songs or genres or performers were good, which bad, which indifferent. And, as Van Der Merwe points out, such aesthetic arguments and distinctions (including that between the 'high' and the 'low') are possible (and impassioned) only because they take place within a shared musical and critical discourse, because they rest on an assumption that we know what the music we like and dislike 'means'.

Take, for example, the following three authoritative statements. The first comes from the most famous middlebrow intellectual of the 1980s – Allan Bloom. 'Rock music', he wrote in *The Closing of the American Mind*, 'has one appeal only, a barbaric appeal, to sexual desire – not love, not *eros*, but sexual desire undeveloped and untutored ... these are [its] three great lyrical themes: sex, hate and a smarmy, hypocritical version of brotherly love' (73–4).

The second comes from a leftist cultural critic – Mark Crispin Miller. 'The rock critic', he wrote in the *New York Review of Books* in 1977, 'struggles to interpret something that requires no interpretation ... tries to appraise and explicate a music whose artists and listeners are anti-intellectual and usually stoned, and whose producers want more than anything to own several cars' (175).

The third comes from *The Shoe*, a novel by a young Scottish writer, Gordon Legge, the best book I've read about what it means to be a pop fan. 'How could people get so worked up about relatives and cars when there were records?', asks *The Shoe*'s central character.

Records cut so much deeper. For him *Astral Weeks*, *Closer* and *For Your Pleasure* (the three best LPs of all time, [he] said. No contest) articulated the mundanity, despair and joy of existence.... [He] said his records were the most important things in his life – more important than Celtic [football club] easily .... It's just that football was easier to talk about for five hours down the pub on a Saturday night. (36)

Several things could be said about these passages – not least about the remarkable assurance with which academics describe other people's pleasure – but I want to pick up immediately on Gordon Legge's point: the exercise of taste and aesthetic discrimination is as important in popular as in high culture but is more difficult to talk about. This means that the glib, professional talkers, the Blooms and Millers – and I could multiply examples of such confident accounts of the real worth or worthlessness of pop culture from both left and right – have the voices that are heard most often.

This is the case even after the rise of cultural studies as an academic concern. The aesthetics of popular culture is a neglected topic, and it is time we took it as seriously as Allan Bloom et al. One reason for this neglect is that cultural studies emerged from disciplines in which issues of taste and judgment are kept well away from issues of academic analysis and assessment: 'evaluation', as Barbara Herrnstein Smith notes, was long ago 'exiled' from literary criticism, and has yet to be admitted to studies of popular culture.[1]

In universities, then, just as in high schools, there is still a split between what Frank Kogan describes as the discourse of the classroom (with its focus on a subject matter) and the discourse of the hallway (with its focus on one's feelings about a subject matter) (3–4). In this respect (and despite first impressions) academic approaches to popular culture still derive from the mass cultural critiques of the 1930s and 1940s, particularly from the Marxist critique of contemporary popular culture in terms of the production and circulation of commodities. For the Frankfurt School, analyzing the organization of mass production on the one hand, and the psychology of mass consumption on the other, the value issue was, in a sense, straightforward – if it's popular it must be bad! – and Adorno and his colleagues developed a number of concepts (such as standardization) to show why this must be so.

On the whole, the analytic move since then has been to accept the Frankfurt reading of cultural production and to look for the redeeming features of commodity culture in the act of consumption. The task, beginning with American liberal sociologists in the 1950s, has been to find forms of mass consumption that are not 'passive' and types of mass consumers who are not stupified, to provide a sociology of watching and reading and listening. If it is in the act of consumption that contemporary culture is lived, then it is in the process of consumption that contemporary cultural values must be located.

In the cultural studies tradition with which I'm most familiar, British subcultural theory, this reworking took on the particular form of identifying certain social groups with what we might call 'positive mass consumption' (which became – and remains – the pithiest academic definition of 'popular' culture). The value of cultural goods could therefore be equated with the value of the groups consuming them – youth, the working class, women, and so forth.

There are two points to note about this move from the position 'if it's popular it must be bad' to the position 'if it's popular it must be bad, unless it's popular with the right people'. First, this remains a highly politicized notion of popular cultural value, whether explicitly, as in the British use of terms like *resistance* and *empowerment*, or implicitly, as in the American celebration of opinion leaders and taste publics in the name of a pluralist democracy. Other value terms – beauty, say – are notable by their absence. To put it another way, cultural value is assessed according to measures of true and false consciousness; aesthetic issues, the politics of excitement, say, or grace, are subordinated to the necessities of ideological interpretation, to the call for 'demystification'.

Second, because such reclamation of popular culture from the machinations of capital is politically selective, those consumers who aren't approved are still dismissed as 'dupes' in conventional Marxist terms. This is the fate, to which I will return, of the middlebrow: the easy listener and light reader and Andrew Lloyd Webber fan. Indeed, it would be quite easy to produce a canon of popular texts excluded from cultural studies, such exclusion reflecting a contempt for their consumers which derives, in turn, from assumptions about their class position and/or social passivity.

More recently, though, partly in response to the implicit elitism of this position, partly as an effect of the depoliticization of cultural studies as they enter the humanities curriculum, a new argument has emerged: if it's popular it must be good! I could point to specific examples of this approach – the Popular Culture Association, the work of John Fiske – but the questions that interest me here are whether a populist approach is the logical conclusion of subculturalism, and whether it is likely to be the norm of academic cultural studies in the 1990s. I fear that the answer to both questions is yes, that cultural studies will remain rooted in accounts of the consumer, every act of 'popular' consumption an excuse for celebration. This is the populist argument against which I want to defend popular culture, and I should begin my defense by sketching the problems I have with it. To begin with, it is based on inadequate empirical studies of consumption (and, indeed, production) as such. I suspect that less such empirical work is being done in cultural studies now than was done by positivist social scientists in the 1950s, and I'm not yet convinced that the so-called 'turn to ethnography', with its focus on select groups of valorized fans, is going to solve this problem.

This has two consequences. First, for all the talk about process and modes of circulation, the definition of 'popularity' by default refers to consumption as measured by sales figures and market indicators – Neilsen ratings, the music charts, box office returns, bestseller lists, circulation statistics, and so on (figures that in turn become the regulators of popular cultural history). Even if such figures were accurate (which is doubtful), they provide no evidence as to why such goods are chosen by their consumers nor whether they are actually enjoyed or valued by them (it is a common enough experience to go to a blockbuster film, watch a high-rated TV program, read a bestselling book, or buy a chart record that turns out to be quite uninteresting). The elision between what sells and what is popular (the assumption that what sells is therefore 'valuable') is obvious in John Fiske's account of 'popular discrimination', for example. He stresses rightly the inability of mass culture industries to predict or manipulate popular taste (as indicated by the vast number of 'failed' records, films, TV shows, magazines, and so forth) but does not question the assumption that a market failure is by definition unpopular or that a market success has by definition a popular audience [see Fiske]. In accounts of popular music, at least, this is to ignore the significant unpopularity of certain stars (Vanilla Ice, say) and the popular cult influence of such market failures as Velvet Underground or the Stone Roses. If nothing else, consumer research among pop fans immediately reveals the intensity with which musics and musicians are loathed as well as loved.

Second, because of its lack of sociological sophistication, academic cultural analysis remains for the most part textual analysis. The popular text (the TV show or shopping mall, the Madonna video or Springsteen CD) is read for the positive or 'transgressive' values the 'popular' audience must have found there, which is to end up (as in E. Ann Kaplan's book on MTV) with the familiar argument that cultural consumers and their values are somehow determined by the text, that what Kaplan calls the 'historical viewer' is irrelevant to a theory of popular values. 'Evidence of specific spectator behavior', she declares brazenly, 'in no way invalidates the theory of MTV as a postmodernist form' (159). This is an essentially condescending view of the people – Madonna fans, say – who are supposedly being celebrated (a condescension not tempered by the use of anachronistic terms like carnival to describe their fandom) and, in particular, has the effect of leveling the cultural experiences involved: the populist assumption is that all popular cultural goods and services are somehow the same in their empowering value (as they are in terms of exchange value); the populist suggestion is that we equate romance reading and *Star Trek* viewing, Madonna and metal fans, shoppers and surfers, each having their own form of 'resistance'. The aesthetic discrimination essential to cultural consumption and the considered judgments it involves are ignored.

It is hard to avoid the conclusion that the more celebratory the populist study, the more patronizing its tone, an effect, I think, of the explicit populist determination to deny (or reverse) the usual high/low cultural hierarchy. If one strand of the mass cultural critique was an indictment of low culture from the perspective of high art (as was obviously the case for Adorno, for example), then to assert the value of the popular is also, certainly, to query the superiority of high culture. Most populist writers, though, draw the wrong conclusion; what needs challenging is not the notion of the superior, but the claim that it is the exclusive property of the 'high'.

To deny the significance of value judgments in popular culture (to ignore popular taste hierarchies) is, if nothing else, hypocritical. How often, I wonder, do cultural studies theorists celebrate popular cultural forms which they themselves soon find boring? How are their own feelings for the good and the bad coded into their analyses? I'm sure in my own cultural practice that *Jane Eyre* is a better romance than a Mills and Boon or Harlequin title, just as I know that the Pet Shop Boys are a better group than U2 and that Aerosmith has no value at all. The problem is how best to argue this. To gloss over the ceaseless value judgments, the continuous exercise of taste, being made within popular audiences themselves is, in effect, to do their discriminating for them, to refuse to engage in those arguments which produce cultural values.

My defense of popular culture rests, then, on two assumptions: first, that the essence of cultural practice is making judgments and assessing differences.[2] Such judgments, distinctions, and choices are justified – to examine the question of value in popular culture is to examine the terms of such justifications. Second, there is no reason to believe *a priori* that such judgment processes work differently in different cultural spheres. There are obvious differences between operas and soap operas, between classical and country music, but the fact that the objects of judgment are different does not mean that the processes of judgment are. The conventional distinction between form (high culture) and function (low culture) is not sustainable for long, even in its populist reading as a contrast between measures of quality and aesthetics, on the one hand, and measures of relevance and productivity, on the other (for a discussion of these terms see Fiske).

In *Contingencies of Value*, her book about high cultural evaluation, Barbara Herrnstein Smith suggests that

> what we are doing in making an explicit judgement of a literary work is
> a) articulating an estimate of how well that work will serve certain implicitly defined functions
> b) for a specific implicitly defined audience
> c) who are conceived of as experiencing the work under certain implicitly X defined conditions. (13)

This could equally well describe what's going on in the judgment of pop songs or TV shows, shopping centers or newsreaders. The implication is that to understand popular cultural values we need to look at the social contexts in which value judgments are deployed, to look at the social reasons why some aspects of a sound or spectacle are valued over others. Musical value judgments, for example, are most significantly made in three contexts:

First, among *musicians*. The value complex here is fairly straightforward: values emerging from the constraints of collaboration (trust, professionalism, reliability); values emerging from the constraints of craft (skill, technique, technical and technological expertise); values emerging from the experience of performance (revolving around a sense of difference).[3]

Second, among *producers*, by whom I mean the broad range of people concerned to turn a music or musician into a profitable commodity. The obvious values of productive efficiency in this group are overlaid, perhaps unexpectedly, by a Romantic belief in genius and originality, in the 'mystery' of both musical creation and audience taste. The cliched opposition of art and commerce is, in this context, misleading. What is actually judged to be at stake is the production of value: commerce *as* art (see Stratton).

Third, among *consumers*. There are various sociological approaches to consumer values: via 'homologies' – musical genres are valued for their representation or expression of a group's nonmusical concerns; via fantasy – a song or star is an object available for identification and individual use; via social settings – music works as a soundtrack, a background noise for dancing, praying, shopping, and so on.

What interests me, though, is not the precise concepts involved, but the general point that from a functional perspective there is inevitably a tension between musicians' and consumers' value terms and procedures (which, from the musicians' point of view, leads almost invariably to both a contempt for their 'popular' audience and a sense that popular music making is a matter of compromise).[4] The gap between the evaluative principles of music makers and music listeners is equally apparent in classical music. In both pop and classical worlds this gap is bridged by producers, who seek to bring creators and consumers into profitable alignment (a productive tension), and by critics, who function both as experts, teaching audiences how to listen and look, and as representatives, interpreting audiences for artists.[5] The commodification of culture, in short, in constituting a tripartite structure of communication – creator/producer/consumer – also constructed a series of evaluative oppositions (art vs. commerce, art vs. craft, the amateur vs. the professional) and a series of evaluative processes that are common to all contemporary cultural forms, that play across high and low cultural practices alike. One effect of this has been the rise of the cultural go-between, the publishers and critics who now play a central role in the making of meaning. Indeed, from this perspective, we could define high culture simply as that form of mass culture which is mediated by academics.

The importance of the critic's role leads me to a second sociological issue: not the context of cultural judgments, but the terms in which they are made. As I have argued elsewhere (drawing on the work of Howard Becker and Pierre Bourdieu), three discourses seem to dominate cultural judgments (see Frith, 'What Is Good Music?'):

an *art* discourse – the ideal of cultural experience is *transcendence*; art provides a means of rising above the everyday, leaving the body, denying the significance of historical time and geographical place;

a *folk* discourse – the ideal of cultural experience is *integration*; folk forms provide a means of placement – in a space, a season, a community;

a *pop* discourse – the ideal of cultural experience is *fun*; pop provides routinized pleasures, more intense than the everyday but bound into its rhythms, and legitimized emotional gratification, a play of desire and discipline.

The point to stress about these discourses (and this is where I part company with both Becker and Bourdieu) is that they describe neither separate art worlds nor different class attitudes but are, rather, all at play across all cultural practices and indeed produce each other (the ideologies of art and folk are thus equally the legacy of Romanticism, and were both, in turn, redefined by the emergence of mass entertainment) (see Shiach). Value terms (most notoriously the concept of 'authenticity') are therefore shared. Aesthetically, there is no immediate reason to treat popular culture any differently from high culture (which is one reason, to return to Bourdieu, why class cultural rituals are so important: they mark out boundaries of taste that are, in fact, unstable).

In general, though, my argument is a deliberate departure from the claim that taste – the use of culture as a means of class differentiation, a mark of distinction – is specific to the bourgeoisie. Such a claim rests on dated evidence and an oversimple account of the class structure (for this argument see Bourdieu). It is certainly easy enough to trace the historical origins of what Bourdieu calls bourgeois culture. In *Highbrow/Lowbrow*, for instance, Lawrence Levine shows how the cultural flexibility of eighteenth-century America had to be denied by the aesthetic ideology that emerged in the mid-nineteenth century: 'A concert given in Baltimore on September 12, 1796, attests to the prevalence of a musical ethos quite divergent from the one we have come to know, an ethos that thought it quite proper to follow a Haydn overture with the song "And All For My Pretty Brunette", and a Bach overture with the song "Oh, None Can Love Like an Irish Man"' (107).

The development of a new musical ethos meant first promoting the concept of 'a sacralized art', an art 'that makes no compromises with the "temporal" world, an art that remains spiritually pure and never becomes secondary to the performer or to the audience, an art that is uncompromising in its devotion to cultural perfection' – the words are taken from *Dwight's Journal of Music* – and then marking off this sort of cultural experience from all others:

> Thus by the early decades of this century the changes that had either begun or gained velocity in the last third of the nineteenth century were in place: the masterworks of the classical composers were to be performed in their entirety by highly trained musicians on programmes free from the contamination of lesser works or lesser genres, free from the interference of audience or performer, free from the distractions of the mundane; audiences were to approach the masters and their works with proper respect and proper seriousness, for aesthetic and spiritual elevation rather than mere entertainment was the goal. This transition was not confined to the worlds of symphonic and operatic music or of Shakespearian drama; it was manifest in other important areas of expressive culture as well. (Levine 120, 146)

And Paul DiMaggio has shown how this aesthetic argument was tied into the development of a class-conscious American bourgeoisie: the distinction between high and popular culture, he writes, emerged in the second half of the nineteenth century 'out of the efforts of urban elites to build organisational forms that, first, isolated high culture and, second, differentiated it from popular culture'; his examples are the Boston Symphony Orchestra (which sloughed off the Boston Pops) and the Boston Museum of Fine Arts. What became high art rituals, connoisseurship, and so on were, then, as Bourdieu argued, an aspect of bourgeois 'distinction': if art had become the experience of the transcendent and the ineffable, then it was also the exclusive property of 'those with the status to claim that their experience is the purest, the most authentic' (DiMaggio 317).

But whatever the role of this artistic ideology in shaping the bourgeois aesthetic, or the role of the *haute bourgeoisie* in defining art, it is misleading to fix the discourse of transcendence in a single social position or to assume that the late nineteenth-century urban bourgeoisie is exactly the same thing as the late twentieth-century middle class. Even in the nineteenth century the increasing concern to define taste boundaries reflected the extent to which tastes were actually shared across classes – the problem was the control of public space; the threat was social intermingling. 'The art must not be degraded', complained a columnist in London's *Music World* in 1845 in response to an announcement of cheap concerts. 'To play the finest music to an audience which has been admitted at a shilling apiece is what I can never give consent to' (qtd. in Weber 26).

Despite such attempts to control taste by price, in England, at least, by the end of the nineteenth century 'something very close to a mass musical culture had emerged – a sharing of common taste across a broad social range'. On the one hand this meant 'popular musicians and audiences [drawing] upon what we tenuously call "art music"': 'through the people's concert, the concert-hall, the music-hall, the choral contest, the brass band performance and other routes, Handel, Wagner and Donizetti to name but three, were known to many "ordinary people": vaguely by some, intimately and expertly by a significant minority' (Russell 6–7).

On the other hand, it meant the broad popularity of what Van Der Merwe calls 'parlour music' among all sectors of the population. This is not to say there was not, by the end of the nineteenth century, a 'Great Musical Schism' between classical and parlor music, but, rather, that the differences could not easily be mapped onto the class structure. Just as professional musicians of the time moved easily between opera and music hall pit bands, between winter seasons in symphony orchestras and summer seasons in pier shows, so listeners from all social spheres could well be fans of Wagner and Vesta Tilley, choral music and comedy turns. 'Highbrow and lowbrow lived in the same world', as Van Der Merwe puts it, and 'quite often they were the same person' (3–4: and see Russell 7–8) – a fact that turn-of-the-century entrepreneurs were quick to exploit. In its 1934 obituary of the 'high' composer, Edward Elgar, the *Times* remembered what a 'rage' his first (1904) symphony had been: 'For some time the regular orchestras of London could not play it often enough, special concerts were arranged for it, [and] enterprising commercialists even engaged orchestras to play it in their lounges and palm courts as an attraction to their winter sales of underwear' (Crump 167).

To trace the social meaning of high and low culture, then, it is not enough to point to the aesthetic ideology of the nineteenth-century urban bourgeoisie; we also need to look at the effects of mass cultural production, which in key ways *followed* the emergence of bourgeois culture and worked on it (just as it worked on urban proletarian culture). The 'transcendent' meaning of classical music, for example, was both exploited and denied by its immediate use in the new movie houses, just as it has been since by radio and record and television companies, as the background sound of advertisements and airplanes and shopping malls.

I want to note three aspects of this approach to mass cultural history. First, if high culture is defined as bourgeois culture, it becomes a reflex to equate mass culture with the working class. In fact, though, mass culture (if we define it as the culture made possible by technological change, by the use of the means of mass cultural production) has always been a form of middle-class culture, characterized by middlebrow concerns. As Janice Radway has shown in her studies of the Book of the Month Club, the rise of mass culture at the beginning of this century actually meant a blurring of the distinctions between high and low, art and commerce, the sacred and the profane.

Second, if one aspect of the emergence of mass culture was the 'disciplining' of nineteenth-century 'unrespectable' culture, another, equally important, was the 'loosening up' of nineteenth-century respectable culture. There is, by now, much illuminating historical work on the former process. In *Rudeness and Civility*, for example, John F. Kassan shows clearly how the rise of consumer culture, the 'orderly spectacle', meant the decline of a participatory, communal leisure culture in American working-class neighborhoods, a move from 'enthusiasm' to 'disciplined spectatorship' (252–6). But the other side of this story is the development of 'safe' ways in which middle-class city dwellers (and the respectable working class) could enjoy proletarian patterns of sociability and noisy public behavior. Kathy Peiss, for example, suggests that the rise of mass culture (the cinema is a good example) meant developing those aspects of working-class leisure that the middle class found attractive and shedding those things of which they disapproved. Mass culture meant 'Polite Vaudeville', 'regulated pleasure' for all classes, organized especially around heterosociability and a new valorization of youth and youth consumption. Her example is Coney Island:

> Steeplechase incorporated into its notion of mass entertainment cultural patterns derived from working class amusements, street life and popular entertainment. Like them, the park encouraged familiarity between strangers, permitted a free-and-easy sexuality, and structured heterosocial interaction. This culture was not adopted wholesale, but was transformed and controlled, reducing the threatening nature of sexual contact by removing it from the street, workplace and saloon. Within the amusement park, familiarity between women and men could be acceptable if tightly structured and made harmless through laughter. At Steeplechase, sexuality was constructed in terms of titillation, voyeurism, exhibitionism and a stress on a couple and romance. (Peiss 136)

From this historical perspective twentieth-century popular culture describes a process in which class and other group values and conflicts are mediated rather than directly expressed, which is one reason why popular commodities (*Hustler*, say, or heavy metal) can be and often are simultaneously 'transgressive' (of 'respectable' values) and reactionary (see Kipnis). Third, if mass culture is not defined against middle-class culture, against art, but is a way of processing it, then the crucial high/low conflict is not that between social classes but that produced by the commercial process itself at *all* 'levels' of cultural expression, in pop as well as classical music, in sports as well as the cinema. High/low thus describes the emergence of consumer elites or cults, on the one hand (the bohemian *versus* the conformist), and the tension between artists and their audiences I've already described, on the other (the modernist and avant-gardist against the orthodox and the mainstream).[6]

Sometime in the opening decades of the twentieth century, notes Levin Schücking, the critical observation that 'the play succeeded with the public' became a standard line in the scathing review, as German theater critics sought to ally themselves with experimental playwrights (and the future) against audiences (and the past) (57). 'The crowd liked them', remains a standard line in a scathing rock review – the more their fans liked, say, Genesis, the more I, as *Sunday Times* rock critic, felt moved to dismiss them.

Thus the themes that haunted modernist writers and critics at the turn of the century (their 'high' cultural concern to be true to their art, to disdain mere entertainment, to resist market forces, their longing for a 'sensitive minority' readership, for what Ezra Pound called 'a party of intelligence', which meant, in practice, each other) have continued to haunt such low artists as jazz and rock musicians, such low audiences as pop fans.[7]

In Arnold Bennett's 1907 story 'The Death of Simon Fuge', the narrator describes 'one of the two London evening papers that a man of taste may peruse without humiliating himself. How appealing a morsel, this sheet new and smooth from the press, this sheet written by an ironic, understanding small band of men just for a few thousand persons like me, ruthlessly scornful of the big circulations and the idols of the people!' (196). This could equally well be a description of *Melody Maker* and its readers in the 1960s or *New Musical Express* and its readers in the 1970s, or *The Face* and its readers in the 1980s.

And in his 1893 story 'Greville Fane', Henry James remarks that his eponymous heroine, a decidedly middlebrow, commercial churn-'em-out novelist is, nevertheless, 'haunted by solemn spinsters who came to tea from Continental pensions, and by unsophisticated Americans who told her she was just loved in *their* country, "I had rather just be paid there", she usually replied; for this tribe of transatlantic opinion was the only thing that galled her. The Americans went away thinking her coarse' (160). Which reminds me irresistibly of my friend Louise, who came from Baltimore to London in 1967 to read her poetry to Donovan. He was coarse, too.

But perhaps the most striking (and recurrent) feature of the continuing standoff of the aesthete and the philistine (a necessary discursive counterpoint) is that for both sides the other is feminine. The woman as materialist corruptor of the artist is a consistent theme of James's stories and of subsequent bohemian mythology – of

Bob Dylan's early songs, for instance – just as the high cultural description of mass culture as 'feminine' by theorists from Adorno and Horkheimer to Baudrillard is echoed in rock fans' contemptuous dismissal of 'teenybop' music (see Huyssen).

Meanwhile, from the philistine side, the American bandmaster John Philip Sousa once stressed to a Houston reporter that 'the people who frequent my concerts are the strong and healthy. I mean healthy both of mind and body. These people like virile music. Longhaired men and shorthaired women you never see in my audience. And I don't want them' (qtd. in Levine 238). This equation of high art and sissiness and perversion is familiar today for us in Britain thanks to the efforts of Gary Bushall, punk-rock-writer-turned-TV-critic of the *Sun*.

But the point I want to stress here is that the sustenance of 'art' in Henry James's or Ezra Pound's terms became dependent, in the end, on the academy, and it is this institutional setting, rather than the value issues as such, that has come to differentiate high from popular culture. It is the academy, that is – the university, the conservatoire, the art school – that, as Pierre Bourdieu argues, nowadays sustains high culture and guarantees its reproduction: in the master/pupil relationship, in the continuity of knowledge and sense of tradition embodied in the library and gallery and concert hall, in the setting of the standards of creative skill and interpretative expertise. It is the academy that now provides the terms – the meaning – of high cultural experience; it is academic discourse that now shapes the newspaper review, the record sleeve note, the exhibition catalogue; it is the academic who makes possible the mass consumption of high culture (Henry James as a classic text). Matthew Arnold, who continues to hover over all discussions of cultural value, approvingly quoted Renan as saying that 'all ages have had their inferior literature, but the great danger of our time is that this inferior literature tends more and more to get the upper place. No one has the same advantage as the Academy for fighting against this mischief' (376–7]. Academy here means the Académie Française, which, in Arnold's words, had special facilities 'for creating a form of intellectual culture *which shall impose itself on all around*'.

By 1913, when Sir Arthur Quiller-Couch came to give his inaugural lecture as the first Professor of English at Cambridge, this notion of the academy had a more general currency. The purpose of studying English literature, suggested Quiller-Couch, was 'the refining of critical judgment', the Cambridge degree aimed to create 'a man of unmistakeable intellectual breeding, whose trained judgment we can trust to choose the better and reject the worse' (qtd. in Keating 456–7). The development of English literature as an academic discipline has become a familiar story, but it is still worth stressing that it involved not just a civilizing mission – sending discriminating readers out into the classroom and marketplace – but also a defensive move: the academy became a stockade within which the better and the superior could be defended from the philistines (and, in particular, from the philistines' literary representative, the journalist, the object of recurrent academic hostility).[8] Thus, to provide a random example of the embattled academic, defending the artist from commercial forces, here is a quote from Harvey Allen's 1938 introduction to the Modern Library edition of Edgar Allan Poe's complete tales and poems. Poe's 'misfortune', writes Allen, was that

> The results of a labour of a lifetime, two decades of continuous and persistent writing both in verse and prose, lay scattered in the pages of obscure, provincial, female and piffling – not to say downright eccentric – magazines, newspapers, weeklies, journals, remaindered and suppressed books and prospectuses – the very names of which are frequently productive of ribaldry or conducive to nausea. *Only the cast-iron constitution of professional scholars can solemnly digest their contents with the bowels of compassion.* (v; my emphasis)

The imagery is of the scholar as knight, riding forth to rescue the innocent artist from the clammy, corrupting hands of the popular paper, the popular magazine, the popular reader.

It is not only our cast-iron constitution that enables academics to consider mass culture dispassionately, but also our institutional position: we're free of the material implications of the art-vs.-market dilemma of writers like Henry James or musicians like the Gang of Four. It is not surprising, then, that high cultural values are by now inextricably entangled with academic practices, rather than with bourgeois consumption as such. This has had a number of consequences both for the teaching of cultural and literary studies (hence, for example, the peculiar suggestion in every monthly magazine I read at present that changes in university reading lists mean the end of civilization as we know it) and, indeed, for pop culture itself (in the influence of art schools on British pop music, for example). But I want to make two rather different points about culture, the academy, and popular taste.

First, the equation of high and academic culture helps explain why the high/low culture distinction is still so consistently read as a mind/body split. This can be traced back to the mental/manual division of labor built into the Industrial Revolution and the consequent organization of education, and overlies the original Romantic dichotomy between feeling and reason – feelings, that is, are now taken to be best expressed in mental terms, in silent contemplation of great art or great music. Bodily responses are, it seems, by definition, mindless. 'The brain', wrote Frank Howes in the *British Journal of Aesthetics* in 1962, is associated with art music; 'brainlessness' with pop. Popular music, agreed Peter Stadler in the same journal a couple of issues later, is music requiring 'a minimum of brain activity'.

By 1971 the same argument was still being made in the journal but now, by Raymond Durgnat, to the opposite effect. He was *celebrating* rock and roll for its sensual effects. This has become a familiar strand in the populist academic account of pop culture, as intellectuals fantasize about the pleasures of mindlessness, and echoes similar intellectual arguments about the thrills of sensational literature, the emotional impact of film and TV melodrama (see Durgnat; and Frith, 'Cultural Studies'). 'In show business', wrote the Hungarian musicologist Janos Marothy in his exhaustive Marxist history of high and low music, 'audience demands ... are determined by the taste of the bourgeoisie. With ... a kind of romantic longing, the bourgeoisie lays claim to the popular in an attempt to compensate for the emptiness of its life by means of "exotic" stimulants' (530–31). In cultural studies, we might add, audience demands are determined by the taste of academics. With a kind of romantic longing, the academy lays claim to the popular in an attempt to compensate for the eggheadedness of its life by means of sensual stimulants. Academics have bodies, that is, even if the theoretical effects of this are carefully hidden.

Even more important, 'the people' have minds. 'Here, in reading together', writes Levin Schücking about nineteenth-century German culture (and these days we would add, in going to the movies together, watching TV together, playing music together), 'the opportunity was gained [especially for the young] of securing from the other's judgement of men and things an insight into [their] thoughts and feelings: an insight likely to become the first bond between kindred souls' (Schücking 32). Exactly the same point is made in Gordon Legge's pop novel, *The Shoe*, in which a pub newcomer's character (his slobbishness, his conservatism, his potential violence) is immediately revealed to drinkers and readers alike by his jukebox choice: Jeff Beck's 'Hi Ho Silver Lining'.

As academics, it seems, we don't actually know much about such aesthetic alliances and distinctions or about their implications (though we live them ourselves all the time). Even when we claim to know what people like, we rarely have much interesting to say about how such liking is organized from the inside (an inside untrammeled by sociological questionnaires and unpatrolled by subcultural cheerleaders). Among the few studies I know that give a sense of the popular aesthetic in action are the Mass-Observation surveys of British film tastes in 1938 and 1943 (Richards and Sheridan).

In these essays in popular criticism there are several obvious evaluative themes:

– films are assessed in terms of technique, skill and craft; with reference to things (acting, lighting, staging – *details*) done well.

– films are assessed in terms of expense and spectacle; cheapness and tackiness are words of abuse.

These are judgments (echoed in popular music discourse) of what is perceived to have *gone into the production*; they measure the extent to which the audience (the viewer, the listener) is being taken seriously.

– films are assessed for their believability, their truth-to-life; the realist impulse (the pop concern for sincerity) means judging a film's (or song's) narrative against one's own 'reality' (and vice versa), a judgment commonly made via identification with a character or performer.

– films are assessed for their ability to take one out of oneself, a quality of experience measured by its intensity (thrills), its presence (laughter), its difference from the everyday, its quality, that is, as entertainment.

These apparently contradictory demands are brought together in an assessment of films according to the *range* of experiences they offer – a good laugh and a good cry, the believable and the unbelievable – and the most common complaint is that a film (or record or TV show or holiday resort or haircut) is disappointing, doesn't live up to expectations or else meets them all too well. Such judgments rest on various sorts of prior knowledge (about genre distinctions, for example) but also on implicit aesthetic hierarchies: the popular consumer too distinguishes between the easy and the difficult, between trash and quality, between indulgence and education; the popular consumer too makes different sorts of demand (more or less aesthetic, more or less functional) of different sorts of cultural commodity.

I will end – appropriately – with another Mass-Observation theme, the suggestion that to be valuable a film should have a 'moral' (a word that substitutes, I suppose, for meaning). 'I don't know what that was about', said someone behind us at *The Grifters*. 'What was the moral?' 'Never throw something at someone who's drinking', her friend suggested. The pursuit of a moral (a point, a closure) is, in academic cultural studies, seen as naive if not reactionary; it ensures that commercial popular culture, whatever its supposed content, remains orderly. On the other hand, in pursuit of such order, a popular reading often has to ask what Jonathan Culler once called (with reference to the popular story of the Three Little Pigs) 'improper questions', just as in their concern for the real the popular reader or viewer or listener is often in pursuit of improper detail, of gossip, anecdotal truth (Ray 284) . How many children had Lady Macbeth? Elvis Presley? Paul de Man?

The compulsion to explain the inexplicable, a recurring theme of popular narrative, has the effect of making the remarkable banal and thus, literally, even more remarkable. This is not a political impulse (politics starts from the material conditions in which people live, not with the cultural strategies that make those conditions livable), but it does generate a certain critical momentum, and, as I began with two quotes from high cultural positions which dismissed low culture as having no intellectual interest at all, I want to end with two quotes from equally high positions which suggest that what's at stake in exploring popular cultural values is not just something out there (in the body), but involves a common culture, something in which we share, in the mind as well.

'When we love a book', Catherine Stimpson wrote recently,

> we read energetically. We believe that if a beloved book were human it would embrace us. Our feeling is more intense than easy pleasure, more dashing and ferocious than delight, more gorgeous than distraction. We are grateful to the beloved text for being there .... [Such books] provide some of love's relational and terrifying thrills ... [provide] the sensation of inhabiting a world apart from the world that normally inhibits one; an oscillation between control and self abandonment; a dance with the partners of amusement and consolation; the gratification of needs that [have been] concealed. (1958)

To which I'd just add that the romance of reading defines popular culture too: records and films, cars and TV shows, sports teams and designer clothes are loved.

'When we study the great classics of literature', notes Northrop Frye in his essays on popular romance,

we are following the dictates of common sense, as embodied in the author of Ecclesiastes: 'Better is the sight of the eye than the wandering of desire.' Great literature is what the eye can see, it is the genuine infinite as opposed to the phony infinite, the endless adventures and endless sexual stimulation of the wandering of desire. But I have a notion that if the wandering of desire did not exist, great literature would not exist either. (30)

And I have a notion – here's my moral – that if desire has, for a moment, wandered into the classroom we should now be ready to follow it out again.

Notes

1. This has led, among other things, to the relentless drive of film, TV, and pop music studies to develop canons of texts-for-study even less open to challenge than the literary canon. For a general discussion of these issues see Smith.
2. One sign of this is the ubiquitous use of competitions in the popular arts.
3. For a useful survey of musicians' day-to-day assessment of their work see Wills and Cooper.
4. The classic discussion of popular musicians' attitudes toward popularity remains Becker.
5. For a brilliant account of the evaluative consequences of this 'gap' in classical music see Cook.
6. For the significance of bohemianism for pop culture see Frith and Horne.
7. For an entertaining and helpful account of these arguments among turn-of-the-century writers see Keating.
8. Most recently expressed in the arguments around Paul de Man and deconstruction.

References

Allen, Harvey, 'Introduction', *Edgar Allan Poe: Complete Tales and Poetry*, New York: Modern Library, 1938.

Arnold, Matthew, 'The literary influence of academies', *Matthew Arnold: Poetry and prose*, ed. John Bryson, London: Hart-Davis, 1954.

Becker, Howard, *Outsiders: Studies in the sociology of deviance*, New York: Free Press, 1963.

Bennett, Arnold, *The Grim Smile of the Five Towns*, Leipzig: Tauchnitz, 1907.

Bloom, Allan, *The Closing of the American Mind*, New York: Simon and Schuster, 1987.

Bourdieu, Pierre, *Distinction: A social critique of the judgement of taste* (1979), London: Routledge, 1984.

Cook, Nicholas, *Music Imagination and Culture*, Oxford: Clarendon, 1990.

Crump, Jeremy, 'The identity of English music: the reception of Elgar 1898–1935', *Englishness: Politics and culture, 1880–1920*, ed. Robert Colls and Philip Dodd, London: Croom Helm, 1986.

DiMaggio, Paul, 'Cultural entrepreneurship and Nineteenth Century Boston, Part II: The

Classification and Framing of American Art'. *Media Culture and Society* 4.4 (1982): 303–22.

Durgnat, Raymond, 'Rock, rhythm and dance'. *British Journal of Aesthetics* 11 (1971): 28–47.

Fiske, John, 'Popular Discrimination', *Modernity and Mass Culture*, ed. James Naremore and Patrick Brantlinger, Bloomington: Indiana University Press, 1991.

Frith, Simon, 'What is good music?', *Canadian Universities Music Review* 10.2 (1990): 92–102.

Frith, Simon, 'Cultural Studies and Popular Music'. Grossberg *et al.* 174–86.

Frith, Simon and Horne, Howard, *Art into Pop*, London: Methuen, 1988.

Frye, Northrop, *The Secular Scripture: A study of the structure of romance*, Cambridge: Harvard University Press, 1976.

Grossberg, Lawrence *et al.*, *Cultural Studies Now and in the Future*, London: Routledge, 1991.

Howes, Frank, 'A Critique of Folk, Popular and "Art" Music', *British Journal of Aesthetics* 2.3 (1962): 239–48.

Huyssen, Andreas, 'Mass culture as woman: modernism's other', *After the Great Divide*, Bloomington: Indiana University Press, 1986.

James, Henry, *Stories of Writers and Artists*, 1903, New York: New Directions, 1944.

Kaplan, E. Ann, *Rocking Round the Clock: Music, television, postmodernism and consumer culture*, New York: Methuen, 1987.

Kassan, John F., *Rudeness and Civility: Manners in nineteenth century urban America*, New York: Hill and Wang, 1990.

Keating, Peter, 'Readers and novelists', *The Haunted Study: A social history of the English novel, 1875–1914*, London: Secker and Warburg, 1989.

Kipnis, Laura, '(Male) desire and (female) disgust: reading *Hustler*', Grossberg *et al.*, 373–91.

Kogan, Frank, *Why Music Sucks* 7 (1991).

Legge, Gordon, *The Shoe*, Edinburgh: Polygon, 1989.

Levine, Lawrence M., *Highbrow/Lowbrow*, Cambridge: Harvard University Press, 1988.

Marothy, Janos, *Music and the Bourgeois: Music and the proletarian*, Budapest: Akademiai Kindo, 1974.

Miller, Mark Crispin, 'Where all the flowers went', *Boxed In: The culture of TV*, Evanston: Northwestern University Press, 1989.

Peiss, Kathy, *Cheap Amusements: Working women and leisure in turn-of-the-century New York*, Philadelphia: Temple University Press, 1986.

Radway, Janice, 'The scandal of the middlebrow: The Book of the Month Club, class fracture and cultural authority', *South Atlantic Quarterly* 89.4 (1990): 703–36.

Ray, Robert B., 'The twelve days of Christmas: a response to Dudley Andrew', *Strategies* 3 (1990): 268–85.

Richards, Jeffrey and Sheridan, Dorothy (eds), *Mass-Observation at the Movies*, London: Routledge, 1987.

Russell, Dave, *Popular Music in England, 1840–1914*, Manchester: Manchester University Press, 1987.

Schücking, Levin L., *The Sociology of Literary Taste*, 1931, London: Kegan Paul, 1944.

Shiach, Morag, *Discourse on Popular Culture*, Cambridge: Polity, 1989.

Smith, Barbara Herrnstein, *Contingencies of Value*, Cambridge: Harvard University Press, 1988.

Stadler, Peter, 'The Aesthetics of Popular Music', *British Journal of Aesthetics* 2.4 (1962): 351–61.

Stimpson, Catherine R., 'Reading for love: canons, paracanons, and whistling Jo March', *New Literary History* 21 (1990): 957–76.

Stratton, Jon, 'Capitalism and romantic ideology in the record business', *Popular Music* 3 (1983): 143–56.

Van Der Merwe, Peter, *Origins of the Popular Style*, Oxford: Clarendon, 1989.

Weber, William, *Music and the Middle Class*, London: Croom Helm, 1975.

Wills, Geoff and Cooper, Cary L., *Pressure Sensitive: Popular musicians under stress*, London: Sage, 1988.

53 □ *Trajectories of Cultural Populism*

Jim McGuigan

[...]

Here we begin to see the drift into an uncritical populism, of which I shall take John Fiske's work on television and popular culture as a revealing instance.[1]

Fiske's agenda, it should be noted, borrows some items from feminist cultural studies, including rejection of the simplistic binary of positive/negative imaginary and the exploration of feminine empowerment in media and consumer culture, but it carries the revisionist logic of those emphases to an outer limit that, I believe, few feminists would wholly agree with. The much-debated case of Madonna is indicative. When she burst upon the scene in 1985, several British feminists sought to make sense of Madonna. Diana Simmonds disputed the authenticity of her earthy image (*Marxism Today*, October 1985), whereas Judith Williamson stressed the irony of Madonna's self-presentation and her sly complicity with ordinary women's feelings: 'It is this flaunting of her fame that ties Madonna so firmly to other women and girls' (*New Socialist*, October 1985). And Cheryl Garratt observed, 'men are terrified of Madonna, which is part of the reason why other women love her so' (*Women's Review*, March 1986).[2] It is interesting, then, that Fiske chose Madonna's videos and her youthful female fans to demonstrate the respective merits of '*Screen* theory' and 'cultural ethnography' in his summary of British cultural studies approaches to television (1987a). '*Screen* theory' here stands for structuralist, linguistically based textual analysis of how texts position subjects; and 'cultural ethnography' stands for the interpretation of ordinary people's experiential accounts and pleasures. Fiske analysed the punning strategies of Madonna's early videos like *Material Girl*, and he interviewed young girls about what they thought of Madonna, her actual meaning for them. He say 'Cultural analysis reaches a satisfactory conclusion when the ethnographic studies of the historically and socially located meanings that are made are related to the semiotic analysis of the text' (1987a: 272). A pleasing symmetry indeed: meaning is conceived of as a transaction

From McGuigan, J., *Cultural Populism*, Routledge, London, 1992, pp. 70–85.

between semiotic structures and interpretative subjects, but, in spite of Fiske's reference to 'historically and socially located meanings', comparatively decontextualised, at least in terms of the dialectic of cultural production and consumption, and isolated from time–space co-ordinates. Fiske's often quite acute analyses are largely confined to the hermetic encounter between the consumer and the commodity, the reader and the text, qualified only by a broad definition of 'text' and a free-floating 'intertextuality' borrowed from poststructuralism.

Significantly, in a book-length study of television (1987b), Fiske says next to nothing about institutional change in television during the 1980s: vital issues to do with de-regulation/re-regulation and technology, for instance, are simply banished since, for Fiske, they are not pertinent to questions of interpretation. That there is no discussion of the policy clash between public service and free market principles over the organisation of broadcasting, especially in the British context from which Fiske and his approach originally hail, is a sad omission in the work of a theorist claiming to provide a critical understanding of television.

Thus, following Bourdieu, Fiske separates 'the cultural economy' (symbolic exchange between texts and audiences) from 'the financial economy' (where the television industry is located). Fiske believes it is completely unnecessary to interpret the meaning of the former in relation to the commercial operations of the latter: 'In this book I have argued against the common belief that the capitalist cultural industries produce only an apparent variety of products whose variety is finally illusory for they all promote the same capitalist ideology' (1987b: 309). This is a routine objection to the mass culture critique and the alleged cultural homogenisation and ideological closure said, by some radical critics, to result automatically from capitalist media production and distribution. Fiske, alternatively, stresses the variety and openness of mainstream television texts, enhanced rather than diminished by commercially populist imperatives (for instance, he makes a great deal of *Dallas*'s appropriation by people of widely divergent cultures during the 1980s).

A satisfactory theory of television, I would suggest, needs to account for the multidimensional interaction of production and consumption at both economic and symbolic levels, giving due weight to textual diversity and audience differences, as Fiske rightly recommends. Yet, in practice, Fiske merely produces a simple inversion of the mass culture critique at its worst, thereby reducing television study to a kind of subjective idealism, focused more or less exclusively on 'popular readings', which are applauded with no evident reservations at all, never countenancing the possibility that a popular reading could be anything other than 'progressive'. Fiske's television viewers, unlike Madonna, do not live in the material world or, for that matter, in a world where sexism, racism and xenophobia circulate amongst ordinary people.

Fiske's two-volume book on popular culture (1989a and 1989b) makes the rationale for bracketing off history, macro-politics and economics even more explicit. He recruits several not entirely compatible theoretical authorities to support his views (Bakhtin, Barthes, Bourdieu, de Certeau, Foucault, Gramsci, Hall, to mention a few). They are raided and sanitised in order to help him beat the drum against those whom he argues cannot see the micro-politics of popular culture in consuming practices and reading pleasures because they are so hopelessly fixated on macro-politics and the machinations of the cultural industries. Which is not to say that Fiske himself has any illusions about where the products actually come from. In various selections and combinations throughout *Understanding Popular Culture* (1989a) and *Reading the Popular* (1989b) the ultimate provider is named: 'white patriarchal bourgeois capitalism'. This empty rhetorical hybrid, however, has no real analytical function to perform because, in Fiske's scheme of things, 'the people' are not at all ground down or denied by the reified monster that supplies the goods. In effect, there is a striking homology between Fiske's 'semiotic democracy' and the ideal of 'consumer sovereignty' in free market economics, in spite of his extreme aversion to economistic reasoning. Repressed materials will always return, if only in symptoms open to differential decoding.

Under modern conditions, according to Fiske, there is no way in which the material (artifacts of popular culture can be made by 'the people': that folkish practice is a thing of the past. But contemporary popular culture is indeed 'produced' by 'the people' metaphorically speaking, in the transaction between the dominant culture's products and their consumption by subordinate groups: working-class, female, black, and so on. Apparently, 'popular readings' of commodity texts are by virtue of social subordination never complicit with any kind of domination: '[t]here can be no popular dominant culture, for popular culture is formed always in reaction to, and never as part of, the forces of domination' (1989a: 43). Ordinary people persistently 'evade' and 'resist' the oppressive and make their own personally liberating meanings through consumption. Hence, shopping malls, video arcades, the beach, TV game shows, jeans and many other products of 'white patriarchal bourgeois capitalism' become sites and artifacts for pleasures that are 'progressive' through not, of course, 'radical'. Mass culture critics of Right and Left were wrong to assume that such forms are in any way pacifying. Fiske insists that the opposite view is mistaken too, in effect undermining his own position: unqualified celebration of popular culture is blind to the power relations, the dialectic of domination and subordination. That insight is what distinguishes the radical theorist like Fiske from the mere populist, according to him. There are plenty of examples in Fiske's work, however, to suggest the contrary. Drawing especially on Michel de Certeau's *The Practice of Everyday Life* (1984), Fiske's ordinary human being is a tricky customer, negotiating and manoeuvring the best out of any conceivable situation. For example, Fiske tells us admiringly that '[t]he young are shopping mall guerrillas par excellence' (1989a: 37). Unemployed youth's 'trickery' (changing price tags on clothing, and so forth) and 'tactics' (such as trying on a jacket and walking off with it) are compared with the survival tactics used by the Vietcong against the US Army in the 1960s, a comparison of astonishing insouciance that does justice neither to the perils of guerrilla warfare in a swamp nor to petty theft in a shop.

Fiske's conception of popular culture, with its ostensibly critical pedigree, represents a dramatic narrowing of vision: the gap between 'popular' and 'mass' culture is finally closed with no residual tension; the relation between interpretative cultural studies and the political economy of culture is obliterated from the surface of the argument. The critical purview of cultural analysis is effectively reduced to a pinpoint seen through the wrong end of a telescope. Fiske's outer limit position represents a kind of neo-Benthamite radicalism, combining utilitarian pleasure-seeking implicitly, and in fact quite consistently, with *laissez-faire* economics, but does not, curiously enough, include Foucault's (1977) paranoid obsession with the panopticon, the political technology of surveillance actually invented by Jeremy Bentham in the early nineteenth century. Fiske backs popular culture study into a narrow corner of the field, breaking with any effort to explore the complex circuits of culture, including production as distinct from productive consumption, and the temporal and spatial contexts of culture in a conflictful world.

One can overestimate the importance of Fiske in the study of popular culture. He is essentially a good populariser of difficult ideas and a bowdleriser of their subversive implications, not by any means an original thinker. His work, however, is symptomatic of a general trend: that of 'the new revisionism'. Philip Schlesinger (1991) characterises this as 'a collapse into subjectivism . . . a hermeneutic model of media consumption' that 'forces a breach between politico-economic arguments about the production of culture and the ways in which it is consumed and interpreted' (pp. 148–9). The provenance of the new revisionism, observes Schlesinger, is contemporary cultural studies, which as we have seen was at one time cohered by neo-Gramscian hegemony theory.

James Curran (1990), concentrating on 'mass communication research' rather than 'popular culture' in the broadest sense, has traced in detail the emergence of the new revisionism and suggested that it is not as new as it seems. Reacting against the critical paradigms of both political economy and hegemony theory, several leading students of the media turned towards a much more diffuse concept of power, sometimes inspired by an optimistic reading of Foucault (1977 and 1979), but actually reminiscent of many themes associated with the liberal pluralist paradigm of American mass communication research from the 1940s onwards and promoted in Britain, since the 1960s, by the 'uses and gratifications' school. For Curran, the new revisionism is concerned specifically with *audience* and *cultural value*. In audience research, 'the focus of attention shifted from whether media representations advanced or retarded political and cultural struggle to the question of why the mass media were so popular' (Curran, 1990: 146). And '[t]he other notable contribution of revisionist thinking has been to reject the elitist pessimism about mass culture that was a significant strand within the radical tradition, represented by the Frankfurt School (p. 154).

This is entirely consistent with the view expressed here that the new revisionism is the latest trajectory of British cultural populism: themes of audience empowerment, pleasure and 'popular discrimination', a term used quite constructively by Fiske, are fundamental to it. My own attitude to this research trajectory is ambivalent. It is genuinely illuminating in the better work of writers like Angela

McRobbie and David Morley, but it also involves a retreat from more critical positions. In many ways such a trajectory is understandable, considering how difficult it has become to challenge present conditions with theoretical and political conviction. None the less, there are questions of critique, quality and explanation to be revisited and developed further if we want to avoid abjectly uncritical complicity with prevailing 'free market' ideology and its hidden powers. The exemplary figure in this respect, John Fiske, is frankly self-conscious about overstating the case in his fashionable disdain for anything which is not immediately 'popular'. Concluding a recent essay, Fiske remarks:

> The challenge offered by popular culture . . . comes from outside this social, cultural, and academic terrain [of 'high or bourgeois art']: the structure of this essay around the antagonism between dominant and popular culture is intended to emphasize this challenge and to help resist its incorporation. If, as a result, I am charged with oversimplifying the dominant, then this is a price which my academic politics lead me to think is worth paying. (1991: 115)

It is a curious conception of 'the dominant' in the cultural field that confines it to the official terrain of 'high or bourgeois art' and has no sense of a much more dominant set of market-based arrangements that were not, in the past, treated so favourably by academics. 'High or bourgeois art' has arguably become too easy a target, and perhaps something of a straw man, for a new generation of intellectual populists to attack. Fiske's politics is actually quite a pervasive 'academic politics' and, for this reason, his work should not be simply ignored as a peculiar aberration or considered in isolation from more substantial work, such as that of Paul Willis's (1990a and b) 'common culture' research [.] [. . .]

In this chapter I have traced two trajectories of cultural populism: the first, leading to a *productionist* view of popular culture; the second, leading to a *consumptionist* view. On the cusp of the mass culture critique, the cultural democracy movement tried and failed to establish a kind of dual power in the cultural field based on a popular system of production opposed to the dominant system. This project fell foul of the rightward turn in Britain from the late 1970s, which reconstructed the conditions of political and cultural hegemony, undermining the public sector and applying free market ideology across the institutional practices of British society. Radical populism had a contradictory love/hate relationship to social democracy but, more seriously, it underestimated popular powers of cultural consumption. The second trajectory, by contrast, was eventually to reach a position which vastly overestimated consumer power, falling into an uncritical populism not entirely different from right-ring political economy.

Between these two extremes, neo-Gramscian hegemony theory aimed to account dialectically for the interplay of the 'imposed from above' and the 'emerging from below'. Within contemporary cultural studies this continues to be a residual position and perhaps, if Angela McRobbie (1991) is right, the preferred one. However, as I [have] argued [...], the field of study has fragmented, with leading positions restructuring around the opposition and interactions between postmodernist theory and new revisionist thought and practice (Morris, 1988). To some extent, McRobbie is right to argue that hegemony theory offers a means of cohering the field but it has never done so adequately due to the original schism with the political economy of culture. Although it is possible, and desirable, to have a situation of methodological pluralism, the uncritical drift of popular cultural study is encouraged by the failure to articulate consumption to production. Hegemony theory bracketed off the economics of cultural production in such a way that an exclusively consumptionist perspective could emerge from its internal contradictions: that is one of the reasons why it ceased to be the organising framework it once was.

My doubts concerning this trajectory are not unique. Several other commentators have also questioned the drift into uncritical populism from a number of different perspectives. To conclude this chapter, I shall briefly survey the extant arguments around three themes: *political critique*, *qualitative judgement* and *social scientific explanation*.

In 1987, Paul Willemen, the film theorist, noted

> the abdication of critical responsibility in favour of the celebration of existing patterns of consumption based on a principled refusal to countenance the possibility that vast sections of the population have come to derive pleasure from conservative oriented media discourses. (1990: 105)

He suggested that formerly radical critics were now conniving, in effect, with the intensified commodification of culture by affecting disingenuous solidarity with ordinary people and their preferences. Willemen's tone is harsh and moralistic, but perhaps justifiably so when one considers the knowledge and choices open to the highly educated in comparison with most people (Bourdieu, 1984). Approaching the issue from a rather different angle than Willemen, Jostein Gripsrud (1989) argues that an unquestioning endorsement of 'the popular' is downright hypocritical on the part of critics who are themselves well endowed with cultural capital and possess privileged access to both 'high' and 'popular' culture. Their specialised competences are undeniable and should, therefore, be used in the service of an 'emancipatory knowledge interest' (Habermas, 1972), not abrogated.

This general line of argument was initiated on the British Left by Judith Williamson's much-debated polemic in the February 1985 issue of *New Socialist*, where she said:

> The original context of any product is that of its production. The one feature shared by Hoggart, whose argument is limited to the sphere of leisure and domestic culture, and the post-punk stylists within cultural studies, whose concern is with the meaning of consumerism alone, is an absence of any sense of a relationship between the spheres of production and consumption. (1985: 19)

Williamson did not deny the power and meaning of 'consuming passion' but she did stress that consumption is unequal; not everyone has the same material access to commodities or an equivalent range of choices: 'The idea that ideologies including consumer fads are increasingly "cut loose" from the economic "base" has become more and more fashionable on the left at a time when these levels have rarely been more obviously connected' (1985: 20). Pre-empting Mica Nava, Williamson pointed out that sections of the radical intelligentsia were bored with the puritanical zeal of revolutionary politics, and wanted to enjoy themselves and become relevant again. Eighteen months later, Williamson resumed her attack, prompted by recent tributes to Mills and Boon romances, the joys of TV game shows and the subversiveness of (Princess) Sarah Ferguson's public image. She saw all this as symptomatic of a postmodern populism:

> One of the big tenets of 'post-modernism' is subjectivity. People are 'allowed' to be subjective 'again', to enjoy, to say what they feel. But the new yuppie-left pop culture craze is peculiarly phoney and non-subjective, for while it centres on *other* people's subjectivity (all those TV watchers who love *The Price is Right* or *Dynasty*) it allows the apparently left-wing practitioners of it to conceal theirs. How about a radical left critique of *The Price is Right*? With all our education, have we nothing more to say than 'people like it'? (1986a: 19)

Polemical and vulnerable to counter-attack, Williamson none the less posed some of the key questions, mainly concerning the politics of cultural analysis, and she reminded radical intellectuals of a certain critical responsibility. In some quarters she was misconstrued as having reverted to an early Frankfurt School position, most notably by Cora Kaplan (1986a), who replied in the pages of *New Socialist*. Kaplan put the elementary semiological argument that textual meanings change according to reception contexts. For instance, outside its American context of production, *Dallas* was likely to be read ironically, particularly by British viewers, amused by the excessive display of opulence, whereas the meaning of *Dallas* in the United States would be more conservative. Kaplan had a point [...] but as a challenge to Williamson's argument concerning the institutional structures of production/consumption, cultural and material inequality, it rather missed the point. Kaplan's chosen example is significant for another reason: her belief that Williamson was merely re-running the old elitist attack on 'American' popular culture, a favourite theme of the mass culture critique. Kaplan's main example, against Williamson's presumed anti-Americanism, was Steven Spielberg's film version of Alice Walker's novel *The Color Purple*. In an unguardedly literary moment of textual essentialism, Kaplan said the film de-radicalised the novel's meaning (namely, it was not so 'good'). Despite its faults, however, the film succeeded in communicating a black feminist sensibility hitherto unfamiliar to British audiences (Kaplan, 1986b). It is very odd that Kaplan should select a comparatively unusual 'serious' film version of a 'serious' novel to make her case concerning the progressiveness of Hollywood cinema abroad.

Commenting on the Williamson–Kaplan debate, Duncan Webster (1988) opined that Williamson, like many British Leftists, allowed opposition to US foreign policies to cloud her appreciation of American popular culture. Both Kaplan's and Webster's arguments are perplexing, since Williamson did not criticise *American* popular culture specifically in the first place: she questioned the uncritical endorsement of mass popular culture, full stop. And, as Webster himself registered, Williamson (1986b) has made sophisticated and appreciative analyses of popular culture, including American-produced: witness her enthusiasm for Madonna quoted earlier in this chapter. So, what was the counter-attack about? One of the most pervasive dogmas of cultural populism: the remotest hint of anti-Americanism instantly brands the critic a European elitist and, therefore, out of order. Like all easily taken-for-granted domain assumptions, this populist reflex suppresses important questions. For example, does questioning the United States's 'global culture' and raising issues of, say, identity and self-determination in subordinate nations really constitute grounds for being judged a snob? And, furthermore, why should such considerations be construed as necessarily contemptuous of ordinary people's tastes? Incidentally, Williamson never ventured on to such treacherous terrain, though she might have done.

Another issue, and partially separable from political critique, is the crisis of qualitative judgement, not exclusively in communication, cultural and media studies but throughout the humanities. Cultural populism, in one way or another, disputes absolutist criteria of 'quality'. Who is to say whether a text is good or bad, or whether a reading practice is adequate to the text or deficient? By and large, mass culture critics had no doubts on these matters: they were confident in their capacity, usually legitimated by academic position and participation in the networks of 'serious' culture. They felt able to pass judgement on mass cultural consumption, to denounce it comprehensively or to make evaluative discriminations between the authentically popular and the usual rubbish foisted upon most people. Undiluted cultural elitism no longer washes. Cultural populism dealt it a fatal blow: opening up the range of 'texts' worthy of study (from grand opera to soap opera, from lyric poetry to disco dancing), evincing humanity towards popular tastes and installing the active audience at the centre of the picture. None of this is *unpolitical*. It challenges the traditional academic politics of the humanities, as Michael Schudson (1987) quite rightly notes with some dismay, surveying recent developments in the US university system. The drift into relativising populism could put professional critics like himself out of work. Schudson's response is not, however, that of a conservative academic only worried about his job. For him, the present situation poses genuine dilemmas. Schudson welcomes the sociologising of cultural analysis from both the production and consumption ends of the circuit, yet he regrets the decline of the university's moral authority:

> I end up caught between a belief that the university should be a moral educator, hold-
> ing up for emulation some values and some texts (and not others), and a reluctant
> admission that the basis for defining moral education is an unfinished, often

unrecognised taste. . . . [I]f we learn to be self-conscious about the implicit hierarchies of taste and value we live and teach by, will we locate adequate grounds for our moral claims? What ground can we stand on, especially when the trends that favor relativism are so much more powerful and cogent (to my own mind) than the rather arbitrary and ill-defined hierarchies of value they so pointedly confront? (1987: 66–7 [see Chapter 47: above])

The dilemmas are real enough. Although Schudson does not resolve his own dilemmas, he is courageous to have mentioned them at all, since the pitfalls are so enormous that silence on these matters is undoubtedly the safest and most common option. Like Gripsrud (1989), Schudson slides back into a position where he is obliged to defend the superior judgements of professional criticism on more or less traditionalist grounds. They are both admirably circumspect about doing so. Some others are not, however, like the English critic Tony Dunn. In a notoriously provocative and perhaps tongue-in-cheek *Guardian* article, Dunn (1987) recommended a recovery of uncompromising Wildean elitism as the best alternative to taking 'the path of populism' which meets 'not the people but video promoters, fashion editors and Arts Council bureaucrats'.

Introducing a collection of essays on 'quality' in television which try to unblock the judgemental impasse, Geoff Mulgan (1990) argues that 'an alternative to the stale debate between a crude populism . . . and an equally crude elitism' (p. 6) must be sought. I agree with him, but it is easier said than done. One of the most promising signs, however, is that some latter-day cultural populists have begun to voice self-doubt: for example, Charlotte Brunsdon. Addressing an American audience, she asked: '*What is good television?* This has not been a very fashionable question for television scholars in the UK' (1990a: 59). In that paper, Brunsdon roamed around why the question had been neglected, reviewed literary reception studies, ethnographic and subcultural approaches, and the 'redemptive reading' of popular texts. Wisely perhaps, from her position, she avoided answering the question. In a second stab at the problem, Brunsdon (1990b) mentioned a 'marked populism' (p. 71) in British television studies, a refusal to judge which eventually winds up in political quietism, especially when faced with urgent policy debates over 'quality television'. So, in order to clarify what might be at stake, she ran through various discourses on 'quality', discarding each in its turn, and reaching no satisfactory solution.

Brunsdon's discursive survey covered traditional aesthetics, professional codes, realist paradigms, entertainment and leisure codes and moral paradigms. Concluding that cultural populists should reveal their own surreptitious judgements and 'talk about them' (p. 90), Brunsdon (1990b) effectively proposed greater academic self-consciousness and scholarly reflexivity so that students of popular culture might again be able to speak, at least subjectively, about the unavoidable problem of judgement. Going somewhat further than Brunsdon was prepared to do, John Mepham (1990) has suggested boldly that 'quality television' is indeed identifiable, if not objectively then intersubjectively. Whatever the programme category, 'serious' or 'popular', quality programming is socially recognisable as *diverse*, *usable* and *truthful* – ethical rather than purely aesthetic criteria [...].

Circulating around the 'quality' problem for cultural populism is the residual issue of 'progressiveness'. At one time, judgemental practice in the field of study concentrated heavily on either identifying textual forms that were thought to be intrinsically 'progressive' or, in a more complex version, institutional and historical contexts that were conducive to the reception and activation of potentially 'progressive' meanings (Caughie, 1980). This fitted with hegemony theory's emphasis on perpetual 'struggle', not to mention radical populism's contestatory cultural politics. However, in the 1980s, some were to argue that 'progressivism' was far too politically earnest and of doubtful popularity (Ang, 1987). It had been assumed that opportunities for alternative and oppositional representations were more favourable in the area of 'serious' rather than 'popular' television, for institutional and ideological reasons (Murdock, 1980). This assumption was also widely rejected in cultural populist circles during the 1980s.

In my view, the excessively audience-orientated and one-dimensional consumptionist perspectives have led to a lamentable foreclosure on questions concerning both 'quality', in the broadest sense, and the narrower sense of 'progressiveness', resulting in confused and hopeless silence. Production and textual determinations were too readily dissolved into uncritical constructions of 'popular reading'. However, one also has to remember that earlier positions were excessively political and sometimes tended towards restrictive judgementalism.

Finally, there are explanatory issues that are, in part, separable from political critique and qualitative judgement. This is obvious in a social scientific framework yet not always so evidently the concern of cultural criticism. For example, in his incisive critique of the British monarchy and its role in maintaining an archaic and comparatively undemocratic state, *The Enchanted Glass*, Tom Nairn remarks:

> People enjoy the Monarchical twaddle, and show very little sign of being robotized or 'brain-washed'. They relish the weird mixture of cheap fun, exalted moments and great spectacles, and come back for more. Whatever it all means, that meaning is sustained and apparently continually refreshed by a genuine, positive will more significant that any amount of peevish grousing around cost. (1988: 53)

Nairn is a republican abolitionist, but he believes the monarchy's popularity has to be understood, not only critiqued or judged. An interpretative, non-judgemental approach, such as that of cultural populism at its best, is indispensable but not, however, sufficiently explanatory.

In a similar vein, Geoffrey Nowell-Smith says, with a crystal clarity often lacking in discussions of popular culture: 'the term popular culture retains its value when one is talking about the people who make it popular – that is, when one is talking about the people who keep a particular cultural form going by being the public for it or being its producers' (1987: 87). That observation summarises the territory traversed in this chapter. Nowell-Smith went on to argue, however, that an exclusive attention to 'the popular' may distract critical analysis from focusing upon how the cultural field works in general. Accordingly, when 'the popular' is suspended, two major realities come sharply into focus:

1 Modern culture is capitalist culture . . .
2 Modern culture also takes the form of a single intertextual field, whose signifying elements are perpetually being recombined and played off against each other. (1987: 87)

Contemporary cultural objects are mainly commodities produced and circulated for financial valorisation through exchange and consumption. That is not confined to 'popular' culture. 'High' cultural objects are also caught up in the process of capital accumulation, however much traditionalists may wish to ignore the fact. Of special interest is the postmodern interaction of forms and meanings across once heavily policed borders of cultural value and politics; and the complex relations between symbolic and material configurations at national, global and local levels. The old sociocultural distinctions and hierarchies have not disappeared, but they are becoming less important. Under these conditions, the rediscovery of popular culture is not so daring after all. Nobody is going to be shocked in the Senior Common Room or in the Student Union Bar if you talk about the textual playfulness and popular appeal of the latest Madonna film: it's probably already on the curriculum.

In the world syncretic culture of postmodernity nothing is sacrosanct; no boundary, either hierarchical or spatial, is forever fixed. There are, none the less, persistent tensions between centrifugal and centripetal forces, most importantly between globalisation and experimentally situated cultures. Culture in general is of heightened significance in a world of international information flows and shared forms of popular entertainment, all of which is greatly enhanced by the new technologies, especially satellite communications (Robins, 1989). A crucial analytical task now is to reconnect interpretation and understanding, of one's own culture and of others, with explanation of the structures and processes that are recomposing these cultures. As Graham Murdock (1989a), for instance, has rightly observed, the 'interplay between the symbolic and the economic' (p. 45) has never been more pronounced and demanding of critical attention. Murdock (1989b) also calls for a renewal of interdisciplinarity, a breaking down of intellectual barriers between theoretical disciplines and methodologies to address changing material conditions and cultural locations, broadening out rather than narrowing in.

Notes

1. John Fiske's position is not only indicative of the critical decline of British cultural studies, for which he is considered a leading representative in Australia and the United States, though not so much in Britain. Fiske's own brand of uncritical populism goes back much further, at least to his association with John Hartley at the Polytechnic of Wales. Their

1978 book *Reading Television*, for instance, extolled television's 'bardic function' in contrast to the then more influential critiques of broadcasting's function as an apparatus of dominant ideology.

2. Madonna is a rather problematic case for exclusively consumptionist analysis since she is not just any old pop star but a generally recognized 'author' and controller of her own commodified image. She is, moreover, prepared to take creative and calculatedly commercial risks with her popularity. The 1990 'Blond Ambition' Tour, which was subsequently exploited by her film *In Bed with Madonna* (1991), broke the bounds of respectability and brought the censure of the Vatican down on Madonna's deliberately subversive head. See Skeggs (1991) for a defence of Madonna's erotic politics against feminist criticisms.

References

Ang, I. (1987) 'The vicissitudes of "progressive television"', in *New Formations* 2, London: Methuen.

Brundson, C. (1990a) 'Television – aesthetics and audiences', in P. Mellencamp (ed.), *Logics of Television*, London: British Film Institute.

Brunsdon, C. (1990b) 'Problems with quality', *Screen*, 31 (1).

Caughie, J. (1980) 'Progressive television and documentary drama', *Screen*, 21 (3); reprinted in T. Bennett. S. Boyd-Bowman, C. Mercer and J. Woollacott (eds), *Popular Television and Film*, London: British Film Institute.

de Certeau, M. (1984) *The Practice of Everyday Life*, Berkeley: University of California Press.

Dunn, T. (1987) 'Take a walk on the Wilde side', *Guardian* (10 February).

Fiske, J. (1987a) 'British cultural studies and television', in R. Allen (ed.), *Channels of Discourse*, London: Methuen.

Fiske, J. (1987b) *Television Culture*, London: Methuen.

Fiske, J. (1989a) *Understanding Popular Culture*, London: Unwin Hyman.

Fiske, J. (1989b) *Reading the Popular*, London: Unwin Hyman.

Fiske, J. (1991) 'Popular discrimination', in J. Naremore and P. Brantlinger (eds), *Modernity and Mass Culture*, Indianapolis: Indiana University Press.

Foucault, M. (1977) *Discipline and Punish: The birth of the prison*, London: Allen Lane.

Foucault, M. (1979) *The History of Sexuality*, vol. 1, Harmondsworth: Penguin.

Gripsrud, J. (1989) '"High culture" revisited', in *Cultural Studies* 3 (2), London: Methuen.

Habarmas, J. (1972) *Knowledge and Human Interests*, London: Heinemann.

Kaplan, C. (1986a) 'The culture crossover', in *New Socialist* (November).

Kaplan, C. (1986b) *Sea Changes: Culture and feminism*, London: Verso.

McRobbie, A. (1991) 'New times in cultural studies', in *New Formations* 13 (Spring), London: Routledge.

Mepham, J. (1990) 'The ethics of quality in television', in Mulgan (1990); reprinted in *Radical Philosophy*, 57 (spring 1991).

Morris, M. (1988) 'Banality in cultural studies', *Block*, 14, reprinted in Mellencamp (1990).

Mulgan, G. (ed.) (1990) *The Question of Quality*, London: British Film Institute.

Murdock, G. (1980) 'Authorship and organisation', *Screen Education*, 35.

Murdock, G. (1989a) 'Cultural studies at the crossroads', *Australian Journal of Communication*, 16.

Murdock, G. (1989b) 'Critical inquiry and audience activity', in B. Dervin *et al.* (eds), *Rethinking Communications*, vol. 2, *Paradigm Exemplars*, London: Sage.

Nairn, T. (1988) *The Enchanted Glass*, London: Radius Books.

Nowell-Smith, G. (1987) 'Popular culture', in *New Formations* 2, London: Methuen.

Robins, K. (1989) 'Reimagined communities? European image spaces, beyond Fordism', in *Cultural Studies* 3 (2), London: Methuen.

Schlesinger, P. (1991) *Media, State and Nation: Political violence and collective identities*, London: Sage.

Schudson, M. (1987) 'The new validation of popular culture: sense and sentimentality in academia', *Critical Studies in Mass Communication*, 4 (March).

Skeggs, B. (1991) 'A spanking good time', *Magazine of Cultural Studies*, 3 (spring).

Webster, D. (1988) *Looka Yonder!: The imaginary America of populist culture*, London: Routledge.

Willemen, P. (1990) 'Review of John Hill's "Sex, class and realism: British cinema 1956–1963"', in M. Alvarado and J. Thompson (eds), *The Media Reader*, London: British Film Institute; originally published in *Framework*, 35 (1987).

Williamson, J. (1985) 'Consuming passion', *New Socialist* (February); reprinted in Williamson (1986b).

Williamson, J. (1986a) 'The problems of being popular', *New Socialist* (September).

Willis, P. (1990a) *Common Culture*, Milton Keynes: Open University Press.

Willis, P. (1990b) *Moving Culture*, London: Calouste Gulbenkian.

54 □ *Political Economy and Cultural Studies: Reconciliation or Divorce?*

Nicholas Garnham

In his recent book, *Cultural Populism*, Jim McGuigan (1992, p. 244) identifies 'a discernable narrowing of vision in cultural studies, exemplified by a drift into an uncritical populist mode of interpretation'. He locates the source of this drift in bracketing off economic determinations, 'because of some earlier traumatic encounter with the long redundant base-superstructure model of "orthodox" Marxism, a trauma represented symptomatically by a debilitating avoidance syndrome' (p. 245).

We can find examples of what McGuigan means in two recent statements by leading cultural studies scholars. Stuart Hall put it like this:

> British cultural studies ... begins, and develops through the critique of a certain reductionism and economism, which I think is not extrinsic but intrinsic to Marxism: a contestation with the model of base and superstructure, through which sophisti- cated and vulgar Marxism alike had tried to think the relationship between society, economy, and culture. It was located and sited in a necessary and prolonged and as yet unending contestation with the question of false consciousness (Hall, 1992, p. 279).

These sentiments are echoed by Angela McRobbie (1992, pp. 720, 719) in the same collection:

> Cultural studies emerged as a form of radical inquiry which went against reduction- ism and economism, which went against the base and superstructure metaphor, and which resisted the notion of false consciousness .... The return to a pre-postmodern Marxism as marked out by critics like Fredric Jameson and David Harvey is untenable because the terms of that return are predicated on prioritizing economic relations and economic determinations over cultural and political relations by positioning these latter in a mechanical and reflectionist role.

This article explores the implications of this founding antagonism between

Marxist political economy and cultural studies. I will argue that the antagonism is based on a profound misunderstanding of political economy and that the project of cultural studies can only be successfully pursued if the bridge with political economy is rebuilt. I say 'rebuilt' because cultural studies as an enterprise came out of a set of assumptions about political economy. It continues to carry that paradigm within itself as its grounding assumption and its source of legitimation as a 'radical' enterprise, even if this paradigm is often suppressed or disguised behind a rhetorical smoke screen in order to avoid the dread accusation of economism or reductionism.

What do I mean? The founding thrust of cultural studies in the work of Raymond Williams and Richard Hoggart – itself drawing on the legacy of Leavis – was, first of all, the revalidation of British working class or popular culture against the elite, dominant culture. It was situated within the context of a class structure formed by industrial capitalism and an increasingly commercialized system of cultural production, distribution, and consumption. But this was not just a revalidation of popular culture for its own sake. It was an oppositional, broadly socialist political movement which saw the cultural struggle as part of a wider political struggle to change capitalist social relations in favor of this working class. The revalidation of working class culture was a move to rescue this culture and those who practiced it from what E. P. Thompson called 'the immense condescension of posterity' and to provide this class with the self-confidence and energy to assert its own values – 'the moral economy of the working class' – against those of the dominant class. Thus cultural studies took for granted a particular structure of domination and subordination and saw its task as the ideological one of legitimation and mobilization. It clearly viewed itself as part of a wider political struggle, even if many of its practitioners saw education as a key site for their contribution to that struggle. It knew both the enemy and its friends.

I want to argue that cultural studies as a meaningful political enterprise is unsustainable outside this founding problematic. One can clearly see in contemporary writing from both British and US cultural studies that most of the current practitioners still assume, indeed assert, that cultural studies is a broadly oppositional political enterprise. It is to this that Stuart Hall (1992, p. 278) refers when he talks about cultural studies' worldly vocation: 'I don't understand a practice which aims to make a difference in the world, which doesn't have some points of difference or distinction which it has to stake out, which really matter.' It is to this idea that the cultural studies literature constantly refers in its mantric repetitions of struggle, empowerment, resistance, subordination, and domination.

Two Developments

In the history of cultural studies there have been two main developments. First, the question of ideology has been immensely complicated by developments within the analysis of textuality. This analysis has brought into question the concepts of truth and falsity, of intentionality and interpretation. It has incessantly posed the difficult but unavoidable problem of the relationship between symbolic representations and social action. Secondly and crucially, the concepts of domination and subordination have widened from referring only to class to also include race and gender. The enemy is now not just capitalism but what Fiske (1992, p. 161) calls 'white patriarchal capitalism'. The question for my purposes is whether these developments invalidate the original links of cultural studies with political economy.

To answer this question, it is necessary to explain what I think political economy means. I want to rescue the concept from the false image that circulates largely unquestioned within cultural studies, to rescue it from the immense and damaging condescension of cultural studies.

The roots of political economy can be traced to the Scottish Enlightenment, to the writings of Adam Ferguson and Adam Smith. Witnessing the early impact of capitalist relations of production, they argued that societies could be distinguished on the basis of their 'modes of subsistence'. They insisted that without a functioning mode of subsistence a society and its members could not survive and that it was in this sense foundational, or the society's base. For them modes of subsistence had key structural characteristics – whether in terms of the dominance of pastoral, agricultural, or industrial modes of production or in terms of differing relations of production (feudal or capitalist or a combination of the two). Here the crucial difference in analytical traditions has been and remains over what each tradition holds as the source of historical change and the key defining characteristic of modes of production. On one side are those who stress technology and organizational forms of production, while on the other are those who emphasize collaborative social relations.

Three crucial aspects of political economy follow from the perspective that collaborative social forms are the key characteristic of production. First, such collaboration requires a set of institutional forms and cultural practices – legal and political forms, family structures, and so forth (what became known as the superstructure) – in order to function. Moreover, different modes of production will have different sets of superstructural forms and practices. Second, this necessary structure of social collaboration is the form through which individual social agents are shaped and relate to one another. Thus, identity formation and culture practices are not random. They are, in some sense, to be analyzed, determined. Thirdly, given the necessarily collaborative and supra-individual nature of the mode of production, the normative question of justice must be addressed. That is to say, how can inequitable distributions of the resources produced by the mode of production be either justified or changed. Thus, the question of the distribution of the surplus was central to political economy from the start. By what mechanisms was it distributed and how was it justified? This was as crucial to Adam Smith as to Marx. For Smith, rent and the unfair share of surplus being taken by landed capital was the problem. For Marx, the problem was profit and the exploitation of wage labor. Both attempted to develop a labor theory of value in order to explain the existing pattern of distribution and the ways in which it diverged from the ideal of social justice.

Classical sociology from Smith through Marx to Weber understood that the distribution of social resources was not natural but resulted from political struggle. Moreover, the positions that people took in such struggles were usually related to the sources of their income or the nature of their stake in the given mode of production. Thus, from the beginning, class was not simply an abstract analytical category. It was a model of the link via ideology between relations of production and political action. The link between base and superstructure was material interest. The question for our purposes is whether this model is any longer valid and whether it is compatible with the project of cultural studies.

It seems clear that most cultural studies practitioners do in fact accept the existence of a capitalist mode of production. Although Fiske (1992, p. 157), for instance, wishes to sever any determining link between 'the cultural economy' and 'the financial economy', he nonetheless constantly refers to something called capitalism as the source of domination:

> The social order constrains and oppresses the people, but at the same time offers them resources to fight against those constraints. The constraints are, in the first instance, material, economic ones which determine in an oppressive, disempowering way, the limits of the social experience of the poor. Oppression is always economic.

This sounds dangerously economistic to me. Similarly Larry Grossberg (1992, p. 100), while arguing for radically distinct 'economies of value' – money, meaning, ideology, and affect – with no necessary determining relationship, at the same time argues that the fact that 'people cannot live without minimal access to some material conditions ensures only that economics (in a narrow sense) must always be addressed in the first instance'. He talks elsewhere in the same book, in a very deterministic manner, of the 'tendential forces' of capitalism, industrialism, and technology (p. 123).

The first problem in the relation between political economy and cultural studies, then, is the refusal of cultural studies to think through the implications of its own claim that the forms of subordination and their attendant cultural practices – to which cultural studies gives analytical priority – are grounded within a capitalist mode of production. One striking result has been the overwhelming focus on cultural consumption rather than cultural production and on the cultural practices of leisure rather than those of work. This in turn has played politically into the hands of a Right whose ideological assault has been structured in large part around an effort to persuade people to construct themselves as consumers in opposition to producers. Of course, they are themselves at the same time producers, who must enter into an economic relation of production in order to consume. While not wishing to be economistic, would cultural studies practitioners actually deny that the major political/ideological struggles of the last decade in advanced capitalist countries have been around, for better or worse, narrowly economic issues –

taxation, welfare, employment, and unemployment? Would they deny that much so-called identity politics, and the cultural politics of lifestyle associated with it, has its roots in the restructuring of the labor market – the decline of white male manual labor, increased female participation, the failure to incorporate blacks into the wage labor force, the growth of service employment, and so on?

By focusing on consumption and reception and on the moment of interpretation, cultural studies has exaggerated the freedoms of consumption and daily life. Yes, people are not in any simple way manipulated by the dominant forces in society. Yes, people can and often do reinterpret and use for their own purposes the cultural material, the texts, that the system of cultural production and distribution offers them. Yes, it is important to recognize the affective investment people make in such practices and the pleasures they derive from them. But does anyone who has produced a text or a symbolic form believe that interpretation is entirely random or that pleasure cannot be used to manipulative ends? If the process of interpretation were entirely random, and if, therefore we had to give up entirely the notion of intentionality in communication, the human species would have dropped the activity long ago.

Political economists recognize with Marx that all commodities must have a use-value; they must satisfy some need or provide some pleasure. There is no simple relationship between the unequal power relations embedded in the production, distribution and consumption of cultural forms as commodities – the overwhelming focus of cultural studies analysis – on the one hand, and the use-value of that commodity to the consumer on the other. But there is some relationship. A delimited social group, pursuing economic or political ends, determines which meanings circulate and which do not, which stories are told and about what, which arguments are given prominence and what cultural resources are made available and to whom. The analysis of this process is vital to an understanding of the power relationships involved in culture and their relationship to wider structures of domination. As Grossberg (1992, p. 94) rightly argues,

> Daily life is not the promised land of political redemption . . . . By separating structure and power it [the focus on daily life] creates the illusion that one can escape them. But such fantasies merely occlude the more pressing task of finding ways to distinguish between, evaluate and challenge specific structures and organizations of power.

Certainly the cultural industries are such specific structures and organizations of power. Where in the contemporary cultural studies literature or research program are examinations of the cultural producers and of the organizational sites and practices they inhabit and through which they exercise their power?

There are two issues at stake here. First, what explanatory force does such economic analysis have at the cultural level? And second, in what way do people come to understand and act upon their conditions of existence through cultural practices? Both of these issues are linked to the question of false consciousness.

While in the past, some from within political economy may have argued for a narrow reflectionist or determinist relationship between the mode of production and cultural practices, such a position is not necessarily entailed by the general approach. Political economy certainly does argue that some institutional arrangements, involving specific cultural practices, necessarily accompany a capitalist mode of production. Two examples are laws of private property and the legal practices within which such laws are enacted. These legal practices in turn require forms of legitimated coercion and definitions of criminality to support them. The cultural link between ownership and identity, so central to many consumption and lifestyle studies, will be part of such a formation. On the other hand, it is clear that while some political institutions and practices will be necessary – and the mode of production may place limits on the range of their viable forms – the capitalist mode of production does not demand, require, or determine any one form of politics. Some capitalist apologists have made that argument in relation to representative democracy, but it is obvious from the historical record that capitalism has been and is compatible with a range of political forms.

Nor is political economy a functionalism. It does not claim that certain superstructures will be created because the mode of production requires them. Again, it is clear from the historical record that the capitalist mode of production can grow within a variety of inherited superstructural forms. All that is required is that they be compatible with the mode of production. Thus, in addition to political systems, a range of kinship systems, religious beliefs and practices, and aesthetic traditions may happily coexist with the capitalist mode of production. Political economy does argue that once a mode is established, the general interest of the human agents living within it in their own material survival and reproduction will tend to coordinate human actions so as to ensure their maintenance. For this reason, critics of the dominant ideology thesis – such as Abercrombie *et al.* (1980) – have argued that the 'dull compulsion of economic relations', not ideological hegemony, explains the relative stability of the capitalist structure of domination, in spite of manifest inequalities. Thus, there is a strong inertia in modes of production. This in turn will entail the modification of cultural practices to maintain the dominant structure. Where these stress-points between base and superstructure will come and what forms of cultural change they will entail are matters for historical analysis. The historical analysis of the development of time discipline is a good example of this. So too are current analyses by scholars such as Giddens and Harvey of the impact of global post-Fordism on people's sense of space and time.

Political economy does not argue that attempts by human agents to maintain the system will be successful. The mode of production may well face insurmountable or unresolved tensions or contradictions between its various practices. For this reason, the regulation school argues that every regime of accumulation – the particular set of structural arrangements that at any time constitute the mode of production, involving the various possible relationships between labor and capital, and the associated patterns of distribution – will entail a corresponding mode of regulation. For instance, varying forms of welfare capitalism and social democracy developed to support the Fordist regime of accumulation. I should note in passing that the recent work of Stuart Hall contains the strange cohabitation of a post-Fordist regulation school analysis of the so-called New Times with a denial of economic determinism. He cannot, in my view, have it both ways.

This relative autonomy of cultural practices from the mode of production entails the fact that – from the perspective dear to cultural studies of resisting, challenging, or changing the structure of domination based upon that mode of production – many cultural practices will simply be irrelevant. One of the problems with much cultural studies writing is that in fact it assumes a very strong form of the base/superstructure relationship, such that all the cultural practices of subordinate groups necessarily come into conflict with the structure of domination. As Fiske (1992, pp. 161, 163) puts it, 'popular differences exceed the differences *required* by elaborated white patriarchal capitalism .... . Without social difference there can be no social change. The control of social difference is therefore *always* a strategic objective of the power bloc' (emphasis added).

False Consciousness and Intellectuals

This brings me to the question of the need – for purposes of the political project of cultural studies – for discriminating among cultural practices on the basis of their likely effectiveness, that is, their contribution to the general project of overthrowing domination. Such a project entails an analysis of the structure of domination to identify those practices that sustain domination and those that do not. This is what I take Grossberg (1992, p. 143) to mean when he writes: 'Identifying the politics of any struggle ultimately requires a map, not only of the actors and agents, but of what I shall call the agencies of this struggle.' This in turn brings us to the thorny problem of false consciousness and the role of intellectuals.

Cultural studies was founded on a turn from the analysis of dominant or elite cultural practices towards the analysis of popular cultural practices. There were two reasons for this turn. The first was to aid the working class struggle by giving the working class a sense of the importance of its own experience, values, and voices as against those of the dominant class. In short, it was seen as a contribution to a classic Gramscian hegemonic struggle. But it assumed that the values embedded or enacted in these cultural practices were progressive and sprung directly from the experience of subordination. This was a classic Marxist view. A revolutionary consciousness would be produced by the direct experience of subordination. The problem was to mobilize it. This model was later used in the context of colonialism and race by Fanon and his followers and also within the feminist movement. It still runs powerfully through cultural studies, in particular through its increasing stress on the study of daily life. The project is then to give a voice to subordinate groups, a voice which stems from experience and therefore, is, by definition both authentic and progressive.

The second reason for the turn to popular culture derived from a different analytical tradition and from a different definition of the political problem. Here while rejecting their elitism, cultural studies shared the preoccupations of the Frankfurt School as well as those of Gramsci. The problem was the demonstrable lack of revolutionary consciousness, and the purpose of cultural studies was to analyze the mechanisms by which people are mobilized or not behind those emancipatory projects that aid progressive and combat reactionary action. There is, of course, nothing original in this position. It merely recognizes Marx's own view that in the ideological forms of the superstructure people become conscious of economic conflicts and fight them out.

It does, however, have important consequences for the argument I am conducting here. First, once political and cultural values are divorced from the necessary authenticity of experience, some grounds for identifying positions as either progressive or reactionary must be found. In short, we have to discriminate among cultural practices. This in turn requires an analysis of the structure of domination, which may be distinct from the perception of that domination by the social agents subject to it. The concept of false consciousness makes people uncomfortable because it seems to imply a rejection of the cultural practices of others as inauthentic and the granting to intellectuals – or, more pertinently in the history of cultural studies, a vanguard party – a privileged access to truth. However, once one accepts the idea that on the one hand, our relations to social reality are mediated via systems of symbolic representation and, on the other hand, that we live within structures of domination – the mechanisms and effects of which are not immediately available to experience – then a concept like false consciousness becomes necessary. Moreover, only such a concept gives intellectuals a valid role. First, organic intellectuals, in a necessary and legitimate division of labor, create the consciousness of a class out of the fragments of that class's experience. Second, intellectuals provide a political strategy by providing a map of the structure of domination and the terrain of struggle.

In fact, most practitioners of cultural studies tacitly accept this; otherwise their practice would be incomprehensible. But they have a debilitating guilty conscience about it. Of course, this is not to say that the consciousness of subordinate groups is necessarily false. That would be absurd. Whether a given consciousness is false or not is a matter for analysis and demonstration and, politically, it entails acceptance by a given subordinate group. For that moment of recognizing false consciousness is the basis for empowerment. At this moment, one lifts oneself out of one's immediate situation and the limits of one's own immediate experience and begins to grasp the idea of dominating structures. In this sense, the model of the intellectual as a social psychoanalyst is both powerful and useful. And it is indeed strange that a tradition of thought such as cultural studies, which has been and remains so deeply influenced by psychoanalytical modes of thought, should refuse to recognize false consciousness while recognizing repression in the psycho-analytical sense.

This is not to deny the tensions implicit in the position of intellectuals as a specific class fraction within the mode of production. But I am sure, if we are honest, that we can all recognize the existence of false consciousness and thus the fact that we do not always either know or act in our own best interest. I am sure, in fact, we all recognize that there are those who know more about a subject than we do and whose advice about how to cope with a given problem we would accept. I am sure also that we are all aware of the ways in which the pressures of everyday existence – of earning a living, of maintaining relationships, of bringing up children – lead us to act in ways which we recognize, at least in retrospect, as irrational and, to put it mildly, socially and personally suboptimal. The interesting question is why people, out of a misplaced sense of guilt or political correctness, choose to forget this when they put on their scholarly hats.

The refusal to recognize the possibility of false consciousness, the associated guilt about the status of intellectuals, and the fear of elitism have all contributed to undermining cultural studies' role within education. In its origins – and not just because its practitioners were located in academia – it saw education as a key site for its intervention. Educational policy and reform were a key focus of its activity.

Certainly, in the case of Williams, participation in the workers' education movement was formative and crucial. There were two aspects to this movement that cultural studies inherited. On the one hand, cultural studies wished to make education relevant to the experience of working people by recognizing their experiences, including their cultural practices, as valid subjects for study and as resources to draw upon in the classroom. Hence cultural studies' close association in its early days with the local and oral history movement as represented, for instance, by the journal *History Workshop*. But on the other hand, the movement by its very stress on education acknowledged that it was both possible and important politically to learn things that were not immediately available in experience and to reflect on that experience from the necessary distance that the classroom provides. The things to be learned included the valuable skills and knowledge which until then had been the reserve of the dominant class. Such a view of education – and of the role of cultural studies within it – claimed the whole of culture, including dominant cultural practices, for its field, provided a legitimate and valued role for intellectuals, and was not afraid to discriminate. Unfortunately, in my view, the educational influence of cultural studies has become potentially baleful and far from liberating because it has pursued the role of introducing popular cultural practices into the classroom indiscriminately at the expense of the wider political and emancipatory values of intellectual inquiry and teaching. The situation reminds me of a cartoon I saw some years ago in which two toddlers were playing in a sandpit overseen by a young female teacher. One toddler says to the other, 'Why is it always the ones with PhDs who want us to make mud pies?' Whatever the reason, the tendency of cultural studies to validate all and every popular cultural practice as resistance – in its desire to avoid being tarred with the elitist brush – is profoundly damaging to its political project.

The rejection of false consciousness within cultural studies goes along with the rejection of truth as a state of the world, as opposed to the temporary effect of discourse. But without some notion of grounded truth the ideas of emancipation, resistance, and progressiveness become meaningless. Resistance to what, emancipation from what and for what, progression toward what? The cultural studies literature plays much with the word 'power'. The problem is that the source of this power remains, in general, opaque. And this vagueness about power and the structures and practices of domination allows a similar vagueness about resistance.

Here we need to make a distinction between resistance and coping. Much cultural studies literature focuses, quite legitimately and fruitfully, on the ways in which cultural practices can be understood as responding to and coping with people's conditions of existence. For Angela McRobbie and others, shopping grants women a space for autonomous self expression. For others, romance literature and soap operas provide the same function through fantasy. In the bad old days, we called this escapism; in those ascetic, puritan, socialist days escapism was a bad thing. Today, while it may be an understandable response to constrained social circumstances, and while it is clearly neither manipulated nor merely passive, and while these social subjects are not given any other options, escapism does little, it seems to me, to resist the structure of domination in which these subjects find themselves. In fact, escapism may (understandable as the practice is) contribute to the maintenance of that structure of power. This surely is Foucault's main theme – the widespread complicity of victims with the systems of power that oppress them. It is not a question of either patronizing this group or imposing one's own cultural standards on them, but of recognizing the systemic constraints within which they construct their forms of cultural coping and how unemancipative these can be. Surely the aim should not be to bow down in ethnographic worship of these cultural practices, but to create a social reality in which there are wider possibilities for the exercise of both symbolic and (in my view more importantly) material power. Can we not admit that there are extremely constrained and impoverished cultural practices that contribute nothing to social change? We may wish to salute the courage and cultural inventiveness shown in such circumstances, but at the same time still wish to change them.

Structures of Domination

Let me return to the question of power and the structure of domination, because here I think is possibly the main point of contention between political economy and cultural studies as it is presently constituted. To put the matter simply, political economy sees class – namely, the structure of access to the means of production and the structure of the distribution of the economic surplus – as the key to the structure of domination, while cultural studies sees gender and race, along with other potential markers of difference, as alternative structures of domination in no way determined by class.

That patriarchal and ethnically based structures of domination preexisted the capitalist mode of production and continue to thrive within it is not in question. It is equally plausible to argue that forms of domination based on gender and race could survive the overthrow of capitalist class domination. Nor is the fact in question that until recently much political economic and Marxist analysis was blind to such forms of domination. But to think, as many cultural studies practitioners appear to do, that this undermines political economy and its stress on class is to profoundly misunderstand political economy and the nature of the determinations between economic and other social relations for which it argues.

There are two issues here. First, in what ways are the forms of this racial and gendered domination – and the awareness of and struggle against them – shaped determinately by the mode of production? Second, what might be the connections, if any, between the struggles against forms of domination based on class, gender, and race? Might there be any strategic priorities between them? Another way of putting this question is to ask whether the overthrow of existing class relations would contribute to the overthrow of gender-and-race based domination (or vice-versa) and to ask which forms of domination, if overthrown, would contribute most to human liberty and happiness.

It is hard to argue against the proposition that modern forms of racial domination are founded on economic domination. This is true in the slave trade and its aftermath in North America, in the form of immigrant labor in Western Europe, and in the various forms of direct and indirect colonialism throughout the world. While the forms of awareness of and struggle against such domination have been culturally varied, and will be so in the future, little dent will be made in domination if black is recognized as beautiful but nothing is done about processes of economic development, unequal terms of trade, global divisions of labor, and exclusion from or marginalization in labor markets.

The same goes for gender. Again, it would be hard to argue against the proposition that the forms of patriarchy have been profoundly marked by the ways in which the capitalist mode of production has divided the domestic economy from production as a site of wage labor and capital formation, by the ways in which women have been increasingly incorporated into the wage labor force often and increasingly at the expense of white male labor, and by changes in and struggles over the mode of reproduction and disciplining of labor power. It is plausible to argue, indeed I would argue, that contemporary feminism developed largely as a response to the growing tension between changes in the structure of the labor market and in the mode of reproduction of labor, driven by changes in the mode of production on the one hand and more traditional, inherited forms of patriarchy on the other. Again the cultural forms in which women and their allies come to recognize and struggle against this domination will be varied and of varying efficacy. But I am sufficiently old fashioned to believe that no empowerment will mean much unless it is accompanied by a massive shift in control of economic resources. It is an interesting but open question whether such a shift is compatible with the existing class structure of developed capitalism.

In short, I would argue that one cannot understand either the genesis, forms, or stakes of the struggles around gender and race without an analysis of the political economic foundations and context of the cultural practices that constitute those struggles. The political economy of culture has never argued that all cultural practices are either determined by or functional for the mode of production of material life. But it has argued, and continues to do so, that the capitalist mode of production has certain core structural characteristics – above all that waged labor and commodity exchange constitute people's necessary and unavoidable conditions of existence. These conditions shape in determinate ways the terrain upon which cultural practices take place – the physical environment, the available material and symbolic resources, the time rhythms and spatial relations. They also pose the questions to which people's cultural practices are a response; they set the cultural agenda.

Political economists find it hard to understand how, within a capitalist social formation, one can study cultural practices and their political effectiveness – the ways in which people make sense of their lives and then act in the light of that understanding – without focusing attention on how the resources for cultural practice, both material and symbolic, are made available in structurally determined ways through the institutions and circuits of commodified cultural production, distribution, and consumption. How is it possible to study multi-culturalism or diasporic culture without studying the flows of labor migration and their determinants that have largely created these cultures? How is it possible to understand soap operas as cultural practices without studying the broadcasting institutions that produce and distribute them, and in part create the audience for them? How is it possible to study advertising or shopping, let alone celebrate their liberating potential, without studying the processes of manufacturing, retailing, and marketing that make those cultural practices possible? How at this conjuncture is it possible to ignore, in any study of culture and its political potential, the development of global cultural markets and the technological and regulatory processes and capital flows that are the conditions of possibility of such markets? How can one ignore the ways in which changes in the nature of politics and of struggle are intimately related to economically driven changes in the relationship of politics to the institutions of social communication such as newspapers and broadcasting channels, and to the economically driven fragmentation of social groups and cultural consumers? If this is reductionist or economistic, so be it. It is, for better or worse, the world we actually inhabit.

References

Abercrombie, N., Hill, S. and Turner, B. S., *The Dominant Ideology Thesis*. London: George Allen and Unwin, 1980.

Fiske, J., 'Cultural studies and the culture of everyday life', in L. Grossberg, C. Nelson and P. Treichler (eds), *Cultural Studies* (pp. 154–73), New York: Routledge, 1992.

Grossberg, L., *We Gotta Get Out of This Place*. New York: Routledge, 1992.

Hall, S., 'Cultural studies and its theoretical legacies', in L. Grossberg, C. Nelson and P. Treichler (eds), *Cultural Studies* (pp. 277–94), New York: Routledge, 1992.

McGuigan, J., *Cultural Populism*. London: Routledge, 1992.

McRobbie, A. 'Post-marxism and cultural studies: a post-script', in L. Grossberg, C. Nelson and P. Treichler (eds), *Cultural Studies* (pp. 719–30), New York: Routledge, 1992.

55 □ *Cultural Studies vs. Political Economy: Is Anybody Else Bored with this Debate?*

Lawrence Grossberg[1]

There is something disingenuous in the title of Nicholas Garnham's critique of cultural studies. The familial alternatives – reconciliation or divorce – imply that cultural studies and political economy were, at one time, 'married' and, having recently separated, must now decide what to do.[2] But cultural studies and political economy were never so intimate; after all, intimacy is itself a powerful social determinant. They were more like cousins who tolerated each other. And Garnham's essay reads like it is 'addressed to the failings of a wayward child who is seen to be in need of stern parental (patriarchal) discipline'.[3] Garnham is correct that cultural studies writers commonly and almost ritualistically distinguish themselves from their 'reductionist' cousins. But he fails to acknowledge that every few years, some political economist – usually one involved with *Media, Culture, and Society* in Britain – writes the latest version of their attack on cultural studies, although the articles have not changed much since the mid-1970s. And they raise the same two criticisms:[4] First, because cultural studies ignores the institutions of cultural production, it celebrates popular culture and gives up any oppositional role; second, because cultural studies ignores economics, it is incapable of understanding the real structures of power, domination, and oppression in the contemporary world.

I want not only to contest these criticisms, but also to challenge Garnham's history of the relation between cultural studies and political economy, for they have always been divided over the terms of an adequate theory of culture and power. The issue has always been how one thinks about the relationships or links between the different domains (forms and structures of practices) of social life. Cultural studies did not reject political economy *per se* – discussions of capitalism have always figured centrally in its work; rather it rejected the way certain political economists practice political economy. At the same time, I agree that there are particular positions in cultural studies that have become too celebratory of culture, in part because the commitment to the local and the specific have overshadowed any sense of the broader social context of unequal power relations. And I agree that there has been a tendency in some cultural studies to avoid detailed attention to the economic, in part because of the fear of falling back into reductionist models. But without a careful analysis of these developments and their place within the broader assumptive and political grounds of cultural studies, the value of such criticisms all but disappears.

Garnham's argument uses a number of conjoined discursive strategies that have become increasingly common weapons in political discourse (not only of the right against the left, but of factions of the left against one another). First, to some extent, Garnham is criticizing cultural studies for being cultural studies rather than political economy – for holding positions that it admits to holding – although Garnham's descriptions are usually just enough off the mark to make the positions sound silly. Thus, it is true that 'cultural studies sees gender and race along with other potential markers of difference, as alternative structures of domination' to class, although I doubt that many people in cultural studies would argue that such differences are 'in no way determined by those of class'. In fact, what they are likely to argue is that any difference, and how it is lived – whether race, gender, class, sexuality and so forth – is articulated to and by other differences. And the ways in which they are articulated make a difference in the formation of specific capitalisms (in particular countries, for example) rather than to some abstract capitalism. Garnham's political economy becomes ahistorical at just the points that matter: If capitalist societies (rather than modes of production) are variable, how does one understand those variations? Why is it that the USA is not the UK or Japan? These are not just superstructural problems, but issues about the ways social relations develop beyond a simple binary distinction between owners of the means of production and waged labor. But Garnham is unable to consider such questions precisely because he refuses to engage the question of articulation, which is, of course, the principal way in which the relations between production, consumption, politics, and ideology are theorized in cultural studies.

Second, his interpretation and indictment of cultural studies depend on what I would describe as sampling by convenience. The arguments of particular authors are selectively presented, and the range of work in cultural studies is alternatively narrowed (systematically ignoring others) or expanded beyond the scope of any recognizable notion of cultural studies. An example of the latter: Garnham's judgment of the 'baleful' educational influence of cultural studies depends upon an expansion of the terrain to include those who simply equate cultural studies with the study of popular culture sans politics. An example of the former: While arguing that cultural studies ignores economics, Garnham seems to have conveniently forgotten that he has already mentioned the collective New Times project and my own analysis of the relationship between capitalism and culture in the New Right. But one could add others here – such as the important work of John Clarke, Meaghan Morris, Arjun Appadurai, Gayatri Spivak, Marcus Breen, and many others – as well as the wide-ranging discussions of globalization taking place. In fact, cultural studies is both narrower and broader than Garnham assumes, but that is, of course because he never defines cultural studies nor identifies exactly whom he is criticizing. Instead it is simultaneously reified and selectively embodied.

Third, Garnham's interpretations of particular authors seem to operate by a *reductio ad extremis* – that is, by juxtaposing two authors writing about related topics, the more complex and moderate position can be equated to the more extreme and simplistic position. For example, I find it difficult to see how anyone can equate the following two bodies of work. On the one hand is work on consumption (and reception) in cultural studies, which looks at the complex and even contradictory nature of consumption and yes, often concludes that consumption can produce pleasures, that it can be, in some ways empowering, but which need not and does not deny the exploitative, manipulative, and dominating aspects of the market. Such work attempts to place local practices into the wider context of the social structures of power, even as it attempts to see how those structures are lived and felt locally. On the other hand is work which, for whatever reasons, argues that any act of consumption that is pleasurable, by definition is an act of resistance. Both bodies of work exist in cultural studies, but they are not the same. It is this misequation which appears to legitimate much of Garnham's critique, as well as that of McGuigan, whom Garnham cites. While I may agree that some work in cultural studies has been caught up in a rather celebratory mode of populism, I think it is absolutely necessary to distinguish this from the more prevalent and nuanced position of cultural studies. Moreover, Garnham ignores the fact that similar critiques of such extreme positions have been made by writers, especially feminists, within cultural studies itself (including Angela McRobbie, Meaghan Morris, John Clarke, Judith Williamson, and myself).

Finally, Garnham's indictment of cultural studies is often built on a critique by absence. This tendency is particularly common in the contemporary culture of the Left: Criticize a position for what it does not do or say. Obviously, it is one thing to claim that a position cannot talk about something, but it is quite another to claim that it has not talked about it. Thus, Garnham accuses cultural studies of paying too much attention to consumption, leisure, and everyday practices and not enough to production work, and institutions: 'Where in contemporary cultural studies are the studies of the cultural producers and the organizational sites and practices they inhabit and through which they exercise their power?' On the one hand, I am tempted to answer that they are in political economy; that is, after all, what political economists do, so why should they want cultural studies to do it? One could after all, just as easily ask of political economy: Where are the studies of consumption and everyday life? But, on the other hand, it is important to answer: They are there in the works of people you have not cited, including Dorothy Hobson, Angela McRobbie (on the fashion industry), Sean Nixon, Jody Berland, and so forth. And they are also in the work of people studying organizational cultures. But perhaps the problem runs deeper, for what is assumed here is a rather narrow and abstract conception of production. If the very notion and practice of production are themselves culturally produced,[5] and if the relations between production and consumption are more complex and less stable than Garnham suggests, then the model of cultural analysis based on a separation of production and consumption is itself problematic, as is the reduction of production to waged labor (which ignores what Marx himself had pointed out: the production involved in consumption/reproduction).[6]

It is in fact rather telling that production here is so tightly equated with the 'cultural industries' as if the commodification of culture were somehow complete. Part of what cultural studies has always been about (especially in the very tradition of Williams/Hoggart/Thompson of which Garnham is so fond) is the self-production of culture – the practices by which people come, however imperfectly, to represent themselves and their worlds. Important work (for example, by Mike Apple, Henry Giroux, Cameron McCarthy, Peter McLaren, in education; by Bourdieu and his followers; by Foucauldians looking at state discourse, and so forth) has also been done on cultural production in what used to be called the 'ideological state apparatuses'. Production cannot simply be the capitalized manufacture of cultural commodities. Consider the ANC's decision to extend the cultural boycott to people as well as commodities, apparently recognizing that the embodied and personified practice of production is as important as the commodities themselves.[7]

Obviously, there is more than simply rhetoric at stake here. Perhaps cultural studies has paid too much attention to consumption, but I fear that what is operating behind such claims is the tendency to dismiss consumption (or leisure) as somehow less important than production, perhaps even as trivial. Production, narrowly understood as the practices of manufacturing, and abstractly understood as the mode of production is too easily assumed to be the real bottom line. Perhaps cultural studies has overemphasized the pleasure, freedom and empowerment of consumption (and reception), but again, I fear that what is operating behind such claims is the desire to return to a simpler model of domination in which people are seen as passively manipulated 'cultural dupes'. Certainly, some people in cultural studies have overemphasized the capacity for resistance in popular cultural practices, although I still see value in this work, not only as a provocation in the face of a still-puritanical Left, but also as a strategy for helping people see that things are not always the way authorities describe them, and moreover, that things do not have to be the way they are. Certainly, cultural studies often writes more about how systems of domination are lived than about the systems of domination themselves, and I agree that more work on the latter needs to be done. But without such work on how domination is lived, the Left is likely to fall back on old assumptions – and old generalizations at fairly high levels of abstraction – about the masses and everyday life.

On the other hand, it is simply not true to say that cultural studies does not look at dominant cultural practices; in fact, I am not sure what 'dominant' – as opposed to popular – means in the contemporary capitalist context. Does Garnham mean elite or legitimate (via particular institutions of cultural capital)? Such differences are themselves institutionally constructed as both forms and expressions of power. Garnham claims that the capitalist structure of ownership prevents certain meanings from circulating. While I agree that not all meanings circulate equally along the same paths, I also think that there is little or nothing that is commercially unthinkable, although increasingly, it may be regulated by the state, moral agencies, and so forth. Of course, the fact is that different meanings may be differently sought out, taken up, and invested in. Once again, Garnham glosses over the real theoretical differences between the assumptions that, on the one hand, production is determining in the last instance, and on the other hand, production has its political and discursive conditions and vice versa.

Nor is it true to say that, in general, cultural studies adopts an uncritical populism. Most of the work in cultural studies that I read does not equate the popular with pleasure and resistance. It does not assume that all pleasure is good or politically progressive; on the contrary, it often recognizes that pleasure can be manipulated by or at least articulated to repressive forms of power and existing structures of inequality. And it recognizes that pleasures may themselves be repressive and regressive – for example those derived from relations of domination over other groups in formations of racism. Certainly this is a basic premise of most cultural studies work in feminism, postcolonialism, and critical race studies.

Cultural studies does not assume that opposition, resistance, struggle, and survival (coping) are the same; but it does assume that the possibilities for the first two depend in complex ways on the realities of the last two. The question of the relations and tensions among these forms of effectivity is important and needs to be explored. Perhaps most important is the question of what it is that mobilizes opposition. But I see no evidence that Garnham is either interested in addressing these questions, or capable of doing so. For cultural studies, the fact that people do use the limited resources they are given to find better ways of living, to find ways of increasing the control they have over aspects of their lives, is significant, not only in itself, but also in terms of understanding the structures of power and inequality in the contemporary world and the possibilities for challenging them. Cultural studies does assume that people live their subordination actively; that means, in one sense, that they are often complicit in their own subordination, that they accede to it, although power often works through strategies and apparatuses of which people are totally unaware. Be that as it may, cultural studies believes that if one is to challenge the existing structures of power, then one has to understand how that complicity, that participation in power, is constructed and lived, and that means not only looking at what people gain from such practices, but also at the possibilities for rearticulting such practices to escape, resist, or even oppose particular structures of power. Cultural studies refuses to assume that people are cultural dupes, that they are entirely and passively manipulated, either by the media or by capitalism. But it does not deny that they are sometimes duped, that they are sometimes manipulated, that they are lied to (and believe the lies, sometimes knowing that they are lies).

In both cases, Garnham's version of political economy, while apparently advancing a classical Marxist position, refuses in practice to think about the contradictory nature of social practices. For Garnham, apparently, capital determines in a mechanical way from start to finish. Political economy thus has no way of thinking about contradiction (except in the most abstract, ahistorical form, such as the class contradiction) and therefore it has no way of thinking about why things change. This, in my opinion, is not Marxist in the least!

Thus Garnham's position still leaves unanswered many important questions about how this domination, consent, and so forth, are accomplished and why they are successful (that is, how such attempts are able, sometimes, to help people occupy the positions they want). Perhaps some people in cultural studies exaggerate the possibilities or the freedom to interpret and use popular practices. But the choice is not, as Garnham would have it, between freedom and determination. Certainly economic practices and relations determine the distribution of practices and commodities (although not entirely by themselves), but do they determine which meanings circulate and which do not? I doubt it. Those articulations are much more complex and difficult to describe. The fact that certain institutions (and individuals) would like to control how people interpret texts or what they do with them does not mean that such 'intentions' actually determine what people do and think, that is, the effects of practices. Are the real effects determined? Of course, but in very complex ways, across a multiplicity of planes and dimensions, of codes and structures, as the result of particular struggles to articulate particular sorts of practices to particular sorts of effects. This relation between origins and effects is, as we shall see, a crucial issue between political economy and cultural studies.

Here we are beginning to get to the crux of the matter: Cultural studies believes that culture matters and that it cannot simply be treated (dismissed) as the transparent – at least to the critic – public face of dominative and manipulative capitalists. Cultural studies emphasizes the complexity and contradictions not only within culture, but in the relations between people, culture, and power. Now I am sure that Garnham would quickly respond that political economy also believes that culture matters, but it is obvious from Garnham's paper that culture matters only as a commodity and an ideological tool of manipulation. And it is clear as well that political economy has little room for complexity and contradiction – odd for a Marxist position. Here I want to consider two moments in Garnham's argument which, I think, demonstrate the very real difference between political economy and cultural studies.

The first is what I would describe as Garnham's intentional misreading of the origins of British cultural studies. Garnham is certainly correct to describe the emergence of cultural studies as part of an oppositional, broadly socialist, political movement. But Garnham seems to equate 'broadly socialist' with political economy. Cultural studies may have been (and I would hope still is) opposed to capitalism, its structures of inequality and exploitation, but that does not mean that it ever bought into political economy as a model of cultural explanation. On the contrary, there is plenty of evidence that its founding figures (especially Hoggart and Williams) quite intentionally distanced themselves from any attempt to explain culture in purely economic terms. Both cultural studies and the New Left, with which many of its leading figures were affiliated, distanced themselves from Marxism and its various models of culture, even while they operated within the space that it opened. And while it may be true that Thompson Williams, and Hoggart all assumed that power in British society was organized entirely on the single dimension of class relations, this was not true of other important figures, such as Stuart Hall, nor of the New Left in general (which was, for example, concerned with issues of race and imperialism). And even the fact that they may have held such a view does not make it either correct nor constitutive of cultural studies. In fact, as early as 1968, the Centre for Contemporary Cultural Studies was exploring issues of the gendered relations of power, without assuming that these were merely epiphenomenal expressions of deeper, more real, bottom-line economic or class relations. Nor do I think that the founders of cultural studies as a group were as confident as Garnham suggests about who their friends and enemies were.[8] In fact Garnham fundamentally misunderstands the nature of cultural studies when he asserts that 'cultural studies as a meaningful political enterprise ... is unsustainable outside the founding problematic'. In fact, cultural studies as a meaningful political enterprise is sustainable only so long as its problematic is defined contextually, and thus is constantly open to challenge and change. Cultural studies is not a stable and closed enterprise; of course, unlike Garnham, I would also argue that political economy is also neither stable nor closed, that it is itself contested terrain.

Again, I am not denying the importance of a critique of capitalism to cultural studies, nor am I denying the prescriptive view that cultural studies should be 'broadly socialist'. I am denying, however, that such commitments should or even did entail particularly strong links to political economy, at least as I understand it or as Garnham defines it here. It is impossible that the two developments that Garnham identifies as central to contemporary cultural studies – more sophisticated theories of textuality and ideology and the widening of the concept of domination and subordination from class to include race and gender, and so forth – should 'invalidate' the original links with political economy, since those links were not there in anything like the way Garnham needs for his argument. Moreover, even if they were, it would not matter; for the fact that cultural studies starts with a particular position cannot define its future – that is indeed one of its peculiarities and strengths.

This leads me to the second site that illustrates Garnham's dismissal of culture: namely, the extraordinarily off-hand way he dismisses issues of identity and difference other than class, while ignoring that class itself is a culturally constructed identity. Here the concept of class conflates an abstract relation (defined at the level of the mode of production), a social relation, and an empirical referent. I do not quite know how to describe the glib way Garnham glosses decades of sustained intellectual and political work, as if it added up to nothing more than the recognition that black is beautiful – a recognition that, I might add, has in fact had important effects, despite Garnham's sarcasm. And then he glibly adds, 'the same goes for gender'. It is telling that Garnham's view of labor recomposition is that women entered waged work 'increasingly at the expense of white male labor'; this is a telling indicator of what 'class' is really about for Garnham – 'at the expense of' indeed.[9]

Garnham's protests to the contrary, his position here strikes me as quite reductionist, as if class and economics (Garnham, by the way, conflates these) were all that really mattered.[10] He assumes a universal answer to the question of the nature of the determination between economic and other social relations. This avoids what McRobbie (in press) describes as the 'more awkward theoretical questions such as the nature of the political relationships which can and do exist between emergent social identities .... . Much of the left prefers instead to rely on the assumed centrality of class as providing a kind of underpinning for the politics of race or sexuality'. Thus, Garnham asks whether 'cultural studies practitioners [would] deny that the major political/ideological struggles of the last decade in advanced capitalist countries have been around ... narrowly economic issues'. In fact, of course, all sorts of issues having to do with race, gender, and sexuality come to mind – as well as issues of indigenous peoples, of disabled persons, of ecology and environmentalism – but that is beside the point. Garnham goes on to claim that such issues of 'identity politics' are themselves rooted in 'the restructuring of the labor market', and later he claims that modern forms of racial and gendered domination – in their genesis, forms, and stakes – are 'founded' on economic domination. If race and gender are 'economic' as well as social relations, I wonder what sort of economic relations they are? And how would Garnham account for them theoretically? That they are not detached from issues of capitalism is clear, but that they are 'narrowly economic' is far from clear.

Obviously the changes, not only in the labor market but in the forms of labor, are one of the conditions of possibility (determinants) of the various contemporary 'identity' issues. And the distribution of economic capital is absolutely crucial to the creation and maintenance of inequality. But does that mean that economics and class are in any sense adequate descriptions of all structures of power? The fact that modern forms of race and gender relations are themselves articulated in complicated ways by and to capitalist relations (including but not limited to class) does not mean that they are only or even primarily economic. No one in cultural studies denies the economic realities of racism or sexism, although they are likely to think that such inequalities cannot be directly mapped by or onto class relations. Moreover, they may also think that those inequalities are constructed in a variety of ways, along a variety of dimensions, besides the distribution of labor and capital, and that some of those other ways centrally involve cultural practices. The real issue is what it means to say that something is grounded or founded in something else: It need not be a description of origins, since as Garnham admits racism and sexism preceded capitalism but it also need not define a sufficient condition or explanation. That is, the fact that race and gender are articulated to economics (and may be articulated to class) does not say much about the appropriate ways of accounting for, or struggling against, structures of domination organized around race and gender.

Thus, while I do agree with Garnham (along with a number of key figures in cultural studies like Meaghan Morris) that too much work in cultural studies fails to take economics seriously enough, I am also convinced that political economy – at least this version of it – fails to take culture seriously enough. And ironically, I think it also fails to take capitalism seriously enough. Moreover, the way in which cultural studies takes economics seriously must be radically different from the assumptions and methods of political economy. For cultural studies does not believe that all forms of power can be explained by capitalist relations or in economic terms.[11]

Despite Garnham's denials that political economy is either reductionist (whether economist or classist) or reflectionist (built on a base/superstructure model), I think his argument at least establishes that his version of political economy is too reductionist and reflectionist for cultural studies. (I apologize if this merely continues the 'immense and damaging condescension of cultural studies', but then, I am not the one accusing someone of being complicitous with the Right.) No one in cultural studits denies that economic relations and practices 'shape in determinate ways the terrain upon which cultural practices take place' – they may even in part help to shape the cultural agenda, but always and only in part. The question is, what follows from such statements? For the fact of the matter is, that for political economy, in every instance, in every context, somehow, almost magically, the economic appears to be the bottom line, the final and real solution to the problem, the thing that holds everything together and makes everything what it is. That is why, I believe, Hall argues that such reductionism and reflectionism are intrinsic to Marxism (and by extension, to political economy). Everything seems to be locked into place, guaranteed by, economic relations. Garnham's own vocabulary betrays this: The fact is that 'different modes of production will have a different set of ... superstructural relations'. Consequently, and somewhat ironically, Garnham castigates Hall for using the Regulation School. The problem is that Hall reads them as anti-reductionists who refuse to assume a necessary correspondence between regimes of accumulation and modes of regulations (which do not exactly correspond to base and superstructure), while Garnham seems to think that as political economists, they must assume necessary correspondences, and hence, they must be reductionists in Hall's terms. The question is not whether Hall's reading is correct but whether it is possible to have a political economy theorized around articulation rather than strict determination or necessity.

And while Garnham denies the charge of functionalism – denies that superstructures are created 'because the mode of production requires them' – he does assume a preexistant compatibility between the base and superstructure. Moreover, he speaks about the economy 'entailing' particular modifications of cultural practices to particular ends. This sounds pretty close to functionalism to me. Finally, Garnham claims that rather than the superstructure merely reflecting the base, they are 'linked' (presumably mediated) through the category of material interest; but presumably this is itself determined by and functional for the mode of production. For cultural studies, on the other hand, it is precisely because no specific fit or pregiven compatibility can be discerned between the base and the superstructure that the questions of cultural studies (and of cultural politics) become important. How can the variability of actually existing capitalism (and the practices within them) be explained? Thus, cultural studies argues that interests are themselves culturally produced, that part of what is involved in political struggles is the articulation of particular subject groups (particular identities) to particular interests. There are no originary and authentic interests, immediately and unproblematically defined by economic position, capable of linking the base (economics – or is it merely production for Garnham?) to the superstructure (or does consumption fall here under culture?). But this is precisely what Garnham seems to assume and needs in order to then differentiate between such interests and the sort of needs and interests that are produced through cultural practices.

Thus the category of false consciousness returns – actually it has never left political economy. According to Garnham, without such a notion (and the related notion of truth), intellectuals have no valid role. And cultural studies of course rejects such notions. As I have said, cultural studies does not deny that, at times, people are duped, that they come to believe things that they ought not to believe. The question is whether this can serve as an adequate theory of ideology and/or culture, whether the vanguardist claims of Garnham's political economist – to know 'the' truth – can be legitimated, or even whether they constitute a particularly effective political strategy. If people are so easily manipulated, how can they be educated, or is the leftist critic merely to remanipulate people? A great deal has already been written in cultural studies on its refusal of notions of false consciousness. For Garnham to merely assert that such a notion is necessary for any politics is the height of condescension, to say nothing of ethnocentrism. My point here is not to defend the rejection of false consciousness, or merely to attack it once again (as elitist, and so forth). Rather my point is that Garnham's insistence on false consciousness merely reaffirms the readings of political economy he so vehemently claims to challenge.

But in the end, what is at stake is not so much the relations between cultural studies and political economy, but rather the ways in which questions of economics – and of contemporary capitalism in particular – are to be articulated into analyses of the politics of culture. For in a sense, cultural studies did not reject political economy, it simply rejected certain versions of political economy as inadequate. And such versions are characterized, not merely by their logic of necessary correspondences (reductionist and reflectionist), but by their reduction of economics to the technological and institutional contexts of capitalist manufacturing (with occasional gestures – and little more – to marketing, distribution and retailing), by their reduction of the market to the site of commodified and alienated exchange,[12] and by their rather ahistorical and consequently oversimplified notions of capitalism. After all, to describe contemporary capitalism as dependent on waged labor and commodity exchange is, well, rather uninformative, as is the observation that contemporary culture is increasingly commodified. To point to the conditions of existence of capitalism as providing an adequate explanation of anything is to forget that Marx described them as 'what every child knows'. Such a political economy seems to assume that capitalism is a universal structure which, despite minor variations (for example, in what is being commodified), remains unchanged and stable. In fact, cultural studies did not reject political economy's interest in capitalism. It rejected this political economy; it rejected both its description of the economy and its vision of the place of the economic in cultural and political analyses.

Contemporary cultural studies is, I believe, returning to questions of economics in important and interesting ways. Such work needs to be encouraged and developed even further. What cultural studies does not need is to return to some relationship that never actually existed (and would not have been very good if it had). So I must decline the invitation to reconcile, and point out that we don't need a divorce because we were never married. I would hope instead that we could learn to live together, if not in the same neighborhood, at least in the same region. We might not like each other's taste or travel the same routes, but we can share a sense of the geography of power and the power of geography. We can criticize particular versions of each other's projects. More generally, we can criticize each other's assumptions; we can even criticize each other's political positions. But when we start accusing each other of evacuating politics all together, of being traitors to the Left (that is, playing into the Right), then we have truly forgotten who the enemies are and where our allies (who may or may not be our friends) are to be found.

Notes

1. I am grateful to Stuart Hall, Angela McRobbie, and especially John Clarke for their invaluable advice and suggestions.
2. Of course, the details and implications of this metaphor – the particular set of gendered, heterosexual relationships – are left unexamined.
3. John Clarke, personal correspondence.
4. Interestingly, US political economists, especially in the field of communication, for the most part, have been so dismissive of cultural studies that they ignore it entirely.
5. See discussion of Sean Nixon's work in McRobbie (1996).
6. Garnham's use of the 'circuits' arguments (regarding the relation of production and consumption) is decidedly disappointing and unproductive. He would have been well advised to look at John Clarke's argument (1991) that consumption is not the same as exchange. 'Consumption involves social practices after and beyond the exchange relation (including forms of production to realize specific use values). There is a significant issue about whether capitalists care about use values beyond their ability to realize exchange values' (John Clarke, personal correspondence).
7. This paragraph is largely a paraphrase of arguments made to me by John Clarke in his comments on an earlier draft of this paper.

8. In fact, my guess is that most people in cultural studies remember the 1960s and 1970s as a time when cultural studies had virtually no friends. Perhaps the problem today is that cultural studies has too many 'friends' who are happy to tell us what it should be or what it is doing wrong.

9. I am grateful to John Clarke for this observation.

10. As Stuart Hall has pointed out (personal correspondence), this position is 'pre-Althusserian, pre-Gramscian'. It seems to have ignored the various attempts within political economy of the 1970s and 1980s to save it from its own crude reductionisms.

11. For example, in my own work (Grossberg, 1992) I have argued that while capitalism does not explain either the emergence or the efficacy of particular cultural formations, it is the case that the formations are currently being rearticulated to and by (that is, being deployed in the service of) particular contradictions and struggles of contemporary capitalism.

12. Angela McRobbie (1996) has described the marketplace as the 'collision place of capitalist commerce with popular desires', and as 'an expansive popular system'.

References

Clarke, J., *Old times and new enemies*. New York: Routledge, 1991.

Grossberg, L., *We gotta get out of this place: popular conservatism and postmodern culture*. New York: Routledge, 1992.

McRobbie, A., 'Looking back at New Times and its critics', in D. Morley and K. H. Chen (eds), *Stuart Hall: critical dialogues in cultural studies*. London: Routledge, 1996.

Bibliography

Adorno, T. W. (1991) *The Cultural Industry: Selected essays on mass culture*, ed. with intro. J. M. Bernstein, London: Routledge.

Adorno, T. W. (1994) *The Stars Down to Earth and Other Essays on the Irrational in Culture*, ed. S. Crook, London Routledge.

Adorno, T. W. and Horkheimer, M. (1979) *Dialectic of Enlightenment*, London: Verso.

Agger, B. (1992) *Cultural Studies as Cultural Theory*, London: Falmer Press.

Allen, R. (ed.) (1992) *Channels of Discourse, Reassembled*, London: Routledge.

Althusser, L. (1966) *For Marx*, London: Penguin.

Althusser, L. (1971) *'Lenin and Philosophy' and Other Essays*, London: New Left Books.

Althusser, L. and Balibar, E. (1970) *Reading Capital*, London: New Left Books.

Alvarado, M. and Thompson, J. (eds) (1990) *The Media Reader*, London: British Film Institute.

Anderson, P. (1969) 'Components of the national culture', in A. Cockburn and R. Blackburn (eds), *Student Power*, London: Penguin.

Ang, I. (1985) *Watching Dallas: Soap opera and the melodramatic imagination*, London: Methuen.

Ang, I. (1990) *Desperately Seeking the Audience*, London: Routledge.

Ang, I. (1991) *Watching Television*, London: Routledge.

Ang, I. (1995) *Living Room Wars*, London: Routledge.

Angus, I. and Jhally, S. (eds) (1989) *Cultural Politics in Contemporary America*, London and New York: Routledge.

Appignanesi, L. (1986) *Postmodernism*, London: ICA.

Arato, A. and Gebhardt, E. (eds) (1978) *The Essential Frankfurt School Reader*, Oxford: Blackwell.

Arnold, M. (1932) *Culture and Anarchy*, London: Cambridge University Press.

Baehr, H. and Dyer, G. (eds) (1987) *Boxed In: Women and television*, New York: Pandora.

Bailey, P. (ed.) (1986) *Music Halt: The business of pleasure*, Milton Keynes: Open University Press.

Bakhtin, M. (1981) *The Dialogic Imagination*, Austin: University of Texas Press.

Bakhtin, M. (1984) *Rabelais and His World*, Bloomington: Indiana University Press.

Baldick, C. (1983) *The Social Mission of English Criticism*, Oxford: Clarendon Press.

Balsamo, A. (1991) 'Feminism and cultural studies', *Journal of the Midwest Modern Language Association*, 24(1), pp. 50–73.

Balsamo, A. and Treichler, P. A. (1990) 'Feminist cultural studies: questions for the 1990s', *Women and Language*, 13(1), pp. 3–6.

Barker, M. (1989) *Comics: Ideology, power and the critics*, Manchester: Manchester University Press.

Barker, P. (1993) *Michael Foucault*, Hemel Hempstead: Harvester Wheatsheaf.

Barker, M. and Beezer, A. (eds) (1992) *Reading Into Cultural Studies*, London: Routledge.

Barrett, M. (1980) *Women's Oppression Today: Problems in Marxist feminist analysis*, London: Verso.

Barrett, M., Corrigan, P., Kuhn, A. and Wolff, J. (eds) (1979) *Ideology and Cultural Production*, London: Croom Helm.

Barthes, R. (1972) *Mythologies*, London: Jonathan Cape.

Barthes, R. (1975) *The Pleasure of the Text*, New York: Hill and Wang.

Barthes, R. (1977) *Image-Music-Text*, London: Routledge.

Baudrillard, J. (1988) *Selected Writings*, ed. M. Poster, Cambridge: Polity Press.

Benjamin, W. (1969) *Illuminations*, New York: Schocken Books.

Bennett, T. (1979) *Formalism and Marxism*, London: Methuen.

Bennett, T. (1990a) *Outside Literature*, London: Routledge.

Bennett, T. (ed.) (1990b) *Popular Fiction*, London: Routledge.

Bennett, T. Boyd-Bowman, S., Mercer, C. and Woollacott, J. (eds) (1981a) *Popular Television and Film*, London: BFI Publishing in association with the Open University Press.

Bennett, T., Martin, G., Mercer, C. and Woollacott, J. (1981b) *Culture, Ideology and Social Process*, London: Batsford Academic and Educational Ltd in association with the Open University Press.

Bennett, T., Mercer, C. and Woollacott, J. (1986) *Popular Culture and Social Relations*, Milton Keynes: Open University Press.

Bennett, T. and Woollacott, J. (1987) *Bond and Beyond: The political career of a popular hero*, London: Macmillan Education.

Best, S. and Kellner, D. (1991) *Postmodern Theory*, London: Macmillan.

Betterton, R. (ed.) (1987) *Looking On: Images of femininity in the visual arts and media*, London: Pandora.

Bhabha, H. (1983) 'The other question – the stereotype and colonial discourse', *Screen*, 24(6), pp. 18–36.

Boime, A. (1990) *The Art of Exclusion: Representing Blacks in the nineteenth century*, London: Thames Hudson.

Bourdieu, P. (1986) *Distinction: A social critique of the judgement of taste*, trans. R. Nice, Cambridge, MA: Harvard University Press.

Bourdieu, P. (1993) *The Field of Cultural Production*, Cambridge: Polity Press.

Boyne, R. and Rattansi, A: (eds) (1990) *Postmodernism and Society*, London: Macmillan.

Brake, M. (1985) *Comparative Youth Culture*, London: Routledge & Kegan Paul.

Bramson, L. (1961) *The Political Context of Sociology*, Princeton, NJ: Princeton University Press.

Brantlinger, P. (1990) *Crusoe's Footsteps: Cultural studies in Britain and America*, New York: Routledge.

Brunsdon, C. (1981) 'Crossroads: notes on soap opera', *Screen*, 22, pp. 32–7.

Brunsdon, C. (1991) 'Pedagogies of the feminine: feminist teaching and women's genres', *Screen*, 32(4), pp. 364–81.

Brunsdon, C. and Morley, D. (1978) *Everyday Television: 'Nationwide'*, London: British Film Institute.

Buckingham, D. (1987) *Public Secrets: 'EastEnders' and its audience*, London: British Film Institute.

Budd, M., Entman, R. and Steinman, C. (1990) 'The affirmative character of U.S. cultural studies', *Critical Studies in Mass Communication*, 7, pp. 169–84.

Callinicos, A. (1985) 'Postmodernism, post-structuralism and post-Marxism?', *Theory, Culture and Society*, 2(3), pp. 85–102.

Canclini, N. (1988) 'Culture and power: the state of research', *Media, Culture and Society*, 10(4), pp. 467–97.

Carey, J. (1989) *Communication as Culture: Essays on media and society*, Boston, MA: Unwin Hyman.

Carter, E., Donald, J. and Squires, J. (1994) *Reading the Popular: Theories of politics and culture*, London: Verso.

Centre for Contemporary Cultural Studies (1982) *The Empire Strikes Back*, London: Hutchinson.

Certeau, M. de (1984) *The Practice of Everyday Life*, Berkeley: University of California Press.

Cham, M. and Andrade-Watkins, C. (eds) (1988) *Blackframes: Critical perspectives on black independent cinema*, Cambridge, MA: MIT Press.

Chambers, I. (1985) *Urban Rhythms: Pop music and popular culture*, London: Macmillan.

Chambers, I. (1986) *Popular Culture: The metropolitan experience*, New York: Methuen.

Chambers, I. (1990) *Border Dialogues: Journeys in postmodernity*, New York: Routledge.

Chambers, I., Clarke, J., Cornell, I., Curti, L., Hall, S. and Jefferson, T. (1977) 'Marxism and culture' [reply to Rosalind Coward], *Screen*, 18, pp. 109–19.

Clarke, G. (1990) 'Defending Ski-jumpers: A critique of theories of youth subculture', in Frith, S. and Goodwin, A. (eds).

Clarke, J. (1991) *New Times and Old Enemies: Essays on cultural studies and America*, London: HarperCollins Academic.

Clarke, J. and Critcher, C. (1985) *The Devil Makes Work: Leisure in capitalist Britain*, London: Macmillan.

Clarke, J., Critcher, C. and Johnson, R. (1979) *Working Class Culture: Studies in history and theory*, New York: St. Martin's Press.

Cohen, E, (1989) 'The "hyperreal" vs. the "really real": If European intellectuals stop making sense of American culture can we still dance?', *Cultural Studies*, 3(1), pp. 25–37.

Collins, J. (1989) *Uncommon Cultures: Popular culture and post-modernism*, London: Routledge.

Conner, S. (1989) *Postmodern Culture: An introduction to theories of the contemporary*, Oxford: Blackwell.

Coward, R. (1977) 'Class, "culture" and the social formation', *Screen*, 18(1), pp. 75–105.

Coward, R. (1984) *Female Desire*, London: Pandora.

Coward, R. and Ellis, J. (1977) *Language and Materialism: Developments in semiology and the theory of the subject*, London: Routledge & Kegan Paul.

Crane, D. (1992) *The Production of Culture*, London: Sage.

Creekmur, C. K. and Doty, A. (eds) (1995) *Out in Culture: Gay, lesbian and queer essays on popular culture*, London: Cassell.

Cruz, J. and Lewis, J. (eds) (1994) *Viewing, Reading, Listening: Audiences and cultural reception*, Boulder: Westview Press.

Cunningham, H. (1980) *Leisure in the Industrial Revolution*, London: Croom Helm.

Curran, J. and Gurevitch, M. (eds) (1991) *Mass Media and Society*, London: Edward Arnold.

Curran, J., Gurevitch, M. and Woollacott, J. (eds) (1977) *Mass Communication and Society*, London: Edward Arnold.

Dahlgren, P. and Sparks, C. (eds) (1992) *Journalism and Popular Culture*, London: Sage.

Davis, H. and Walton, P. (eds) (1983) *Language, Image, Media*, London: Blackwell.

Day, G. (ed.) (1990) *Readings in Popular Culture*, London: Macmillan.

de Lauretis, T. (1984) *Alice Doesn't*, Bloomington: Indiana University Press.

de Lauretis, T. (ed.) (1986) *Feminist Studies/Critical Studies*, Bloomington: Indiana University Press.

de Lauretis, T. (1987) *Technologies of Gender: Essays on theory, film and fiction*, Bloomington: Indiana University Press.

Derrida, J. (1973) *Speech and Phenomena*, Evanston: Northwestern University Press.

Derrida, J. (1976) *Of Grammatology*, trans. G. Spivak, Baltimore: Johns Hopkins University Press.

Derrida, J. (1978) *Positions*, London: Athlone Press.

Derrida, J. (1978) *Writing and Difference*, London: Routledge & Kegan Paul.

Docherty, T. (1992) *Postmodernism: A reader*, Hemel Hempstead: Harvester Wheatsheaf.

Docker, J. (1994) *Postmodernism and Popular Culture*, Cambridge: Cambridge University Press.

Dorfman, A. and Mattelart, A. (1975) *How to Read Donald Duck*, New York: International General.

Doyle, B. (1989) *English and Englishness*, London: Routledge.

Dreyfus, H. L. and Rabinow, P. (1983) *Michel Foucault: Beyond structuralism and hermeneutics*. Second edition. With an afterword by and an interview with Michel Foucault, Chicago: University of Chicago Press.

During, S. (1992) *Foucault and Literature*, London: Routledge.

During, S. (ed) (1993) *The Cultural Studies Reader*, London: Routledge.

Dyer, R. (1979) *Stars*, London: British Film Institute.

Dyer, R. (1986) *Heavenly Bodies: Film stars and society*, New York; St. Martin's Press.

Dyer, R., Geraghty, C., Jordan, M., Lovell, T., Paterson, R. and Stewart, J. (1981) *Coronation Street*, London: British Film Institute.

Eagleton, T. (1983) *Literary Theory: An introduction*, Oxford: Blackwell.

Easthope, A. (1986) *What a Man's Gotta Do: The masculine myth in popular culture*, London: Paladin.

Easthope, A. (1991a) *British Post-structuralism*, London: Routledge.

Easthope, A. (1991b) *Literary into Cultural Studies*, London: Routledge.

Easthope, A. and McGowan, K. (eds) (1992) *A Critical and Cultural Theory Reader*, Milton Keynes: Open University Press.

Eco, U. (1979) *The Role of the Reader: Explorations in the semiotics of texts*, Bloomington and London: Indiana University Press.

Ellis, J. (1982) *Visible Fictions*, London: Routledge & Kegan Paul.

Featherstone, M. (1991) *Consumer Culture and Postmodernism*, London: Sage.

Fiske, J. (1984) 'Popularity and ideology: a structuralist reading of Dr Who', in W. Rowland and B. Watkins (eds), *Interpreting Television: Current research perspectives*, Beverly Hills: Sage, pp. 165–98.

Fiske, J. (1987a) *Television Culture*, New York: Routledge.

Fiske, J. (1987b) 'British cultural studies and television', in Storey, J. (1996b), pp. 115–46.

Fiske, J. (1989a) *Understanding Popular Culture*, Boston, MA: Unwin Hyman.

Fiske, J. (1989b) *Reading the Popular*, Boston, MA: Unwin Hyman.

Fiske, J. (1993) *Power Plays, Power Works*, London: Verso.

Fiske, J. (1994) *Media Matters*, Minneapolis: University of Minnesota Press.

Fiske, J. and Hartley, J. (1978) *Reading Television*, London: Methuen.

Fiske, J., Hodge, B. and Turner, G. (1987) *Myths of Oz: Reading Australian popular culture*, Sydney, London, Boston, MA: Allen & Unwin.

Forgacs, D. (1989) 'Gramsci and Marxism in Britain', *New Left Review*, 176, pp. 70–90.

Fornas, J. (1995) *Cultural Theory & Late Modernity*, London: Sage.

Foster, H. (1983) *Post-modern Culture*, London: Pluto Press.

Foucault, M. (1978) *The History of Sexuality. Volume one: An introduction*, trans. R. Hurley, New York: Pantheon.

Foucault, M. (1979) *Discipline and Punish*, Harmondsworth: Penguin.

Foucault, M. (1980) *Power/Knowledge: Selected interviews and other writings 1972–77*, New York: Pantheon.

Franklin, S., Lury, C. and Stacey, J. (eds) (1991) *Off-Centre: Feminism and cultural studies*, London: HarperCollins.

Frith, S. (1983) *Sound Effects*, London: Constable.

Frith, S. (1988) *Music for Pleasure: Essays in the sociology of pop*, New York: Routledge.

Frith, S. and Goodwin, A. (eds) (1990) *On Record: Rock, pop and the written word*, New York: Pantheon.

Frith, S., Goodwin, A. and Grossberg, L. (eds) (1991) *Sound and Vision: The music television reader*, Boston, MA: Unwin & Hyman.

Frow, J. (1995) *Cultural Studies & Cultural Value*, Oxford: Clarendon Press.

Frow, J. and Morris, M, (eds) (1994) *Australian Cultural Studies: A reader*, St. Leonards: Allen & Unwin.

Gallop, J. (1985) *Reading Lacan*, Ithaca, NY: Cornell University Press.

Gamman, L. and Marshment, M. (eds) (1988) *The Female Gaze: Women as viewers of popular culture*, London: Verso.

Gans, H. (1974) *Popular Culture and High Culture: An analysis and evaluation of taste*, New York: Basic Books.

Garnham, N. and Williams, R. (1980) 'Pierre Bourdieu and the sociology of culture: an introduction', *Media, Culture and Society*, 2, pp. 209–23.

Geraghty, C. (1991) *Women and Soap Opera*, Cambridge: Polity Press.

Gillespie, M. (1995) *Television, Ethnicity and Cultural Change*, London: Routledge.

Gilroy, P. (1987) *Their Ain't No Black in the Union Jack*, London: Hutchinson.

Gilroy, P. (1993a) *The Black Atlantic: Modernity and double consciousness*, London: Verso.

Gilroy, P. (1993b) *Small Acts: Thoughts on the politics of black culture*, London: Serpent's Tail.

Giroux, H. (1994) *Disturbing Pleasures*, London: Routledge.

Giroux, H. and Simon, R. (eds) (1989) *Popular Culture, Schooling, and Everyday Life*, New York: Bergin & Garvey Press.

Giroux, H., Shumway, D., Smith, P. and Sosnoski, J. (1984) 'The need for cultural studies: resisting intellectuals and oppositional public spheres', *Dalhousie Review*, 64(2), pp. 472–86.

Gitlin, T. (1983) *Inside Prime Time*, New York: Pantheon.

Gledhill, C. (ed.) (1987) *Home is Where the Heart Is: Studies in melodrama and the woman's film*, London: British Film Institute.

Goodwin, A. (1991) 'Popular music and postmodern theory', *Cultural Studies*, 5(2), pp. 174–203.

Gramsci, A. (1971) *Selections from Prison Notebooks*, ed. and trans. Q. Hoare and G. Nowell-Smith, London: Lawrence & Wishart.

Gramsci, A. (1985) *Selection from Cultural Writings*, ed. D. Forgacs and G. Nowell-Smith, London: Lawrence & Wishart.

Gray, A. and McGuigan, J. (eds) (1993) *Studying Culture: An introductory reader*, London: Edward Arnold.

Greer, G. (1971) *The Female Eunuch*, London: Paladin.

Grossberg, L. (1986b) 'Teaching the Popular', in C. Nelson (ed.), *Theory in the Classroom*, Urbana: University of Illinois Press, pp. 177–200.

Grossberg, L. (1988) (with) Fry, T., Curthoys, A. and Patton, P., *It's a Sin: Essays on postmodernism, politics and culture*, Sydney: Power Publication.

Grossberg, L. (1989a) 'The formations of cultural studies: An American in Birmingham', *Strategies*, 2, pp. 114–49.

Grossberg, L. (1989b) 'The circulation of cultural studies', *Critical Studies in Mass Communication*, 6(4), pp. 413–20.

Grossberg, L. (1992) *We Gotta Get Out of this Place: Popular conservatism and postmodern culture*, London: Routledge.

Grossberg, L., Nelson, C. and Treichler, P. (eds) (1992) Cultural Studies, London: Routledge.

Gurevitch, M., Bennett, T., Curran, J. and Woollacott, J. (eds) (1982) *Culture, Society and the Media*, London: Methuen.

Hall, S. (1977) 'Culture, the media and the "ideological effect"', in J. Curran, Gurevitch, M. and Woollacott, J., *Mass Communication and Society*, London: Arnold.

Hall, S. (1980a) 'Cultural studies and the centre: some problematics and problems', in S. Hall *et al.* (eds), *Culture, Media, Language*, London: Hutchinson-CCCS, pp. 15–47.

Hall, S. (1980b) 'Encoding and decoding', in S. Hall *et al.* (eds), *Culture, Media, Language*, London: Hutchinson-CCCS.

Hall, S. (1982) 'The rediscovery of "ideology": return of the repressed in media studies', in Gurevitch, M., Bennett, T., Curran, J. and Woollacott, J. (1982), pp. 56–90

Hall, S. (1983) 'The problem of ideology – Marxism without guarantees', in B. Matthews (ed.), *Marx 100 Years On*, London: Lawrence & Wishart.

Hall, S. (1985) 'Signification, representation, ideology: Althusser and the post-structuralist debates', *Critical Studies in Mass Communication*, 2(2), pp. 91–114.

Hall, S. (1986) 'On postmodernism and articulation: An interview with Stuart Hall', *Journal of Communication Inquiry*, 10:2, 1986.

Hall, S. (1987) 'Minimal selves', in *The Real Me: Postmodernism and the question of identity*, London: ICA, pp. 44–6.

Hall, S. (1990a) 'The emergence of cultural studies and the crisis of the humanities', *October*, 53, pp. 11–90.

Hall, S. (1990b) 'Cultural identity and diaspora', in J. Rutherford (ed.) (1990), pp. 222–37.

Hall, S. (1996) 'Cultural studies: two paradigms', in Storey, J. (1996b), pp. 31–48.

Hall, S., Critcher, C., Jefferson, T., Clarke, J. and Roberts, B. (1979) *Policing the Crisis: Mugging, the state and law and order*, London: Macmillan.

Hall, S. Hobson, D., Lowe, A. and Willis, P. (1980) *Culture, Media, Language*, London: Hutchinson.

Hall, S. and Jefferson, T. (eds) (1976) *Resistance Through Rituals: Youth subcultures in post-war Britain*, London: Hutchinson.

Hall, S. and Whannel, P. (1964) *The Popular Arts*, London: Pantheon Books.

Harris, D. (1992) *From Class Struggle to the Politics of Pleasure: The effects of Gramscianism on cultural studies*, London: Routledge.

Harvey, D. (1989) *The Condition of Postmodernity*, Oxford: Blackwell.

Hawkes, T. (1977) *Structuralism and Semiotics*, Berkeley: University of California Press.

Hebdige, D. (1979) *Subculture: The meaning of style*, New York: Routledge.

Hebdige, D. (1987) *Cut 'n' Mix*, London: Comedia.

Hebdige, D, (1988) *Hiding in the Light: On images and things*, London: Routledge.

Held, D. (1980) *Introduction to Critical Theory: Horkheimer to Habermas*, London: Hutchinson.

Hirschkop, K. and Shepherd, D. (eds) (1989) *Bakhtin and Cultural Theory*, Manchester: Manchester University Press.

Hobson, D. (1982) *Crossroads – The Drama of a Soap Opera*, London: Methuen.

Hoggart, R. (1958; rpt. 1970) *The Uses of Literacy*, New York: Oxford University Press.

Hollows, J. and Jancovich, M. (eds) (1995) *Approaches to Popular Film*, Manchester: Manchester University Press.

hooks, b. (1989) *Talking Back: Thinking feminist, thinking black,* London: Sheba Feminist Publishers.

hooks, b. (1991) *Yearning: Race, gender, cultural politics*, Boston, MA: South End Press.

hooks, b. (1994) *Outlaw Culture: Resisting representations*, New York: Routledge.

Horkheimer, M. (1941) 'Art and mass culture', *Studies in Philosophy and Social Science*, IX.

Huyssen, A. (1986a) *After the Great Divide: Modernism, mass culture and postmodernism*, London: Macmillan

Institute of Contemporary Arts (1987) *Identity: The Real Me*, London.

Jameson, F. (1981) *The Political Unconscious: Narrative as a socially symbolic act*, Ithaca, NY: Cornell University Press.

Jameson, F. (1984) 'Postmodernism, or the cultural logic of late capitalism', *New Left Review*, 165, pp. 53–92.

Jeffords, S. (1989) *The Remasculinization of America,* Bloomington and Indianapolis: Indiana University Press.

Jenkins, H. (1992) *Textual Poachers*, London: Routledge.

Jhally, S. (1987) *The Codes of Advertising: Fetishism and the political economy of meaning in the consumer society*, London: Frances Pinter.

Johnson, R. (1987) 'What is cultural studies anyway?', in Storey, J. (1996b), pp. 75–114.

Jones, S. (1988) *Black Culture, White Youth*, London: Macmillan.

Jordan, G. and Weedon, C. (1994) *Cultural Politics*, Oxford: Blackwells.

Kaplan, C. (1986) *Sea Changes: Culture and feminism*, London: Verso.

Kaplan, E. A. (ed.) (1983) *Regarding Television – Critical Approaches: An anthology*, American Film Institute Monograph Series, vol. 2. Frederick, MD: University Publications of America.

Kaplan, E. A. (1987) *Rocking around the Clock: Music television, postmodernism, and consumer culture*, New York: Methuen.

Kaplan, E. A. (1988) *Postmodernism and Its Discontents: Theories, practices*, New York: Verso.

Lacan, J. (1977) *Ecrits: A selection*, London: Tavistock.

Laclau, E. (1977) *Politics and Ideology in Marxist Theory*, London: New Left Books.

Laing, S. (1986) *Representations of Working-class Life, 1959–64*, London: Macmillan.

Laplanche, J. and Pontalis, J. B. (1973) *The Language of Psychoanalysis*, New York: Norton.

Latimer, D. (1984) 'Jameson and postmodernism', *New Left Review*, 148, pp. 116–28.

Lazere, D. (ed.) (1987) *American Media and Mass Culture*, Berkeley: University of California Press.

Leavis, F. R. (1930) *Mass Civilisation and Minority Culture*, Cambridge: Minority Press.

Leavis, F. R. and Thompson, D. (1933) *Culture and Environment*, London: Chatto & Windus.

Leavis, Q. D. (1978) *Fiction and the Reading Public*, London: Chatto & Windus.

Lefebvre, H. (1984) *Everyday Life in the Modern World*, trans. S. Rabinovitch. New Brunswick: Transaction Books.

Lefebvre, H. (1991) *Critique of Everyday Life*, vol. 1, London: Verso.

Levine, L. (1988) *Highbrow/Lowbrow: The emergence of cultural hierarchy in America*, Cambridge, MA: Harvard University Press.

Levine, S. (1972) 'Art values, institutions and culture', *American Quarterly*, 24(2), pp. 131–65.

Lévi-Strauss, C. (1963) *Structural Anthropology*, New York: Basic Books.

Lewis, L. (1990) *Gender, Politics, and MTV: Voicing the difference*, Philadelphia: Temple University Press.

Lewis, L. (ed.) (1992) *The Adoring Audience: Fan culture and popular media*, London: Routledge.

Long, E. (1987) 'Reading groups and the postmodern crisis of cultural authority', *Cultural Studies*, 1(3).

Longhurst, D. (ed.) (1989) *Gender, Genre and Narrative Pleasure*, London: Unwin Hyman.

Louvre, A. and Walsh, J. (eds) (1988) *Tell Me Lies About Vietnam*, Milton Keynes: Open University Press.

Lovell, T. (1983) *Pictures of Reality*, London: British Film Institute.

Lury, C. (1996) *Consumer Culture*, Cambridge: Polity Press.

Lyotard, J.-F, (1986) *The Postmodern Condition: A report on knowledge*, Manchester: Manchester University Press.

MacCabe, C. (ed.) (1986) *High Theory/Low Culture: Analyzing popular television and film*, Manchester: Manchester University Press.

McGuigan, J. (1992) *Cultural Populism*, London: Routledge.

Macherey, P. (1978) *A Theory of Literary Production*, London: Routledge & Kegan Paul.

McRobbie, A. (1980) 'Settling accounts with subcultures', *Screen Education*, 34.

McRobbie, A. (1982) 'The politics of feminist research: between talk, text and action', *Feminist Review*, 12.

McRobbie, A, (1991a) 'New times in cultural studies', *New Formations*, Spring, pp. 1–17.

McRobbie, A. (1991b) 'Moving cultural studies on – post-modernism and beyond', *Magazine of Cultural Studies*, 4, pp. 18–22.

McRobbie, A. (1994) *Postmodernism and Popular Culture*, London: Routledge.

McRobbie, A. (ed.) (1997) *Back to Reality? Social experience and cultural studies*, Manchester: Manchester University Press.

McRobbie, A. and Nava, M. (eds) (1984) *Gender and Generation*, London: Macmillan.

Marris, P. and Thornham, S. (eds) (1995) *Media Studies: A reader*, Edinburgh: Edinburgh University Press.

Marx, K. (1976) *Preface and Introduction to A Critique of Political Economy*, Peking: Foreign Languages Press.

Marx, K. and Engels, F. (1970) *The German Ideology*, London: Lawrence & Wishart.

Marx, K. and Engels, F. (1977) *Selected Letters*, Peking: Foreign Languages Press.

Masterman, L. (ed.) (1984) *Television Mythologies: Stars, shows and signs*, London: Comedia/UK Media Press.

Mellancamp, P. (ed.) (1990) *The Logics of Television*, Bloomington: Indiana University Press.

Mercer, C. (1988) 'Entertainment, or the policing of virtue', *New Formations*, 4, pp. 41–71.

Mercer, K. (1994) *Welcome to the Jungle: New positions in black cultural studies*, London: Routledge.

Middleton, R. (1990) *Studying Popular Music*, Milton Keynes: Open University Press.

Miller, D. (ed.) (1995) *Acknowledging Consumption*, London: Routledge.

Milner, A. (1994) *Contemporary Cultural Theory: An introduction*, London: UCL Press.

Modleski, T. (1984) *Loving with a Vengeance*, London: Methuen.

Modleski, T. (1986a) 'Femininity as mas(s)querade: a feminist approach to mass culture', in C. McCabe (ed.), *High Theory, Low Culture: Analyzing popular television and film*, New York: St. Martin's Press, pp. 37–52.

Modleski, T. (ed.) (1986b) *Studies in Entertainment: Critical approaches to mass culture*, Bloomington: Indiana University Press.

Mohanty, C. (1988) 'Under western eyes: feminist scholarship and colonial discourses', *Feminist Review*, 30, Autumn, pp. 60–88.

Moores, S. (1993) *Interpreting Audiences*, London: Sage.

Morley, D. (1980) *The 'Nationwide' Audience: Structure and decoding*, London: British Film Institute.

Morley, D. (1986) *Family Television: Cultural power and domestic leisure*, London: Comedia.

Morley, D. and Chen, K.-H, (1996) *Stuart Hall: Critical dialogues in cultural studies*, London: Routledge.

Morris, M. (1988a) 'Things to do with shopping centres', in Sheridan, S. (ed.) (1988).

Morris, M. (1988b) 'At Henry Parkes Motel', *Cultural Studies*, 2(1), pp. 1–47.

Morris, M. (1988c) *The Pirate's Financée*, London: Verso.

Morris, M. (1996) 'Banality in cultural studies', in Storey, J. (1996b), pp. 147–67.

Mort, F. (1996) *Cultures of Consumption*, London: Routledge.

Mukerji, C. and Schudson, M. (1991) *Rethinking Popular Culture: Contemporary perspectives in cultural studies*, Berkeley: University of California Press.

Mulvey, L. (1989) *Visual and Other Pleasures*, London: Macmillan.

Munns, J. and Rajan, G. (eds) (1995) *A Cultural Studies Reader*, London: Longman.

Naremore, J. and Brantlinger, P. (eds) (1991) *Modernity and Mass Culture*, Bloomington & Indianapolis: Indiana University Press.

Nava, M. (1987) 'Consumerism and its contradictions', *Cultural Studies*, 1:2.

Nelson, C. and Grossberg, L. (eds) (1988) *Marxism and the Interpretation of Culture*, Urbana: University of Illinois Press.

Nicholson, L. J. (ed.) (1990) *Feminism/Postmodernism*, New York: Routledge.

O'Connor, A. (1989) 'The problem of American cultural studies', in Storey, J. (1996b), pp. 187–96.

Open University (1982) *Popular Culture (U203)*, Milton Keynes: Open University Press.

O'Shea, M. and Schwartz, B. (1987) 'Reconsidering popular culture', *Screen*, 28 (3), pp. 104–9.

O'Sullivan, T., Hartley, J., Saunders, D., Montgomery, M. and Fiske, J. (1994) *Key Concepts in Communication and Cultural Studies*, second edition, London: Routledge.

Palmer, J. (1991) *Potboilers: Methods, concepts and case studies in popular fiction*, London: Routledge.

Parmar, P. (1990) 'Black feminism: the politics of articulation', in J. Rutherford (ed.), pp. 101–26.

Pawling, C. (ed.) *Popular Fiction and Social Change*, London: Macmillan.

Penley, C. (ed.) (1988) *Feminism and Film Theory*, New York and London: Routledge/BFI Publishing.

Pribram, E. D. (ed.) (1988) *Female Spectators: Looking at film and television*, New York and London: Verso.

Punter, D. (ed.) (1986) *Introduction to Contemporary Cultural Studies*, London: Longman.

Radway, J. (1984) *Reading the Romance: Women, patriarchy and popular literature*, Chapel Hill: University of North Carolina Press; London: Verso, 1997.

Radway, J. (1986a) 'Reading is not eating: mass culture, analytical method, and political practice', *Communication*, 9(1), pp. 93–123.

Radway, J. (1986b) 'Identifying ideological seams: mass culture, analytical method, and political practice', *Communication*, 9(1), pp. 93-123.

Radway, J. (1988) 'Reception study: ethnography and the problems of dispersed audiences and nomadic subjects', *Cultural Studies*, 2(3), pp. 359–67.

Radway, J. (1990) 'The scandal of the middlebrow: the Book-of-the-Month Club, class fracture, and cultural authority', *South Atlantic Quarterly*, Fall, pp. 703–7.

Ransome, P. (1992) *Antonio Gramsci: A new introduction*, Hemel Hempstead: Harvester Wheatsheaf.

Regan, S. (1993) *Raymond Williams*, Hemel Hempstead: Harvester Wheatsheaf.

Robbins, D. (1991) *The Work of Pierre Bourdieu*, Milton Keynes: Open University Press.

Roman, L. G., Christian-Smith, L. K. and Ellsworth, E. (1988) *Becoming Feminine: The politics of popular culture*, London: Falmer Press.

Rosenberg, B. and White, D. W. (eds) (1957) *Mass Culture: The popular arts in America*, New York: Macmillan.

Ross, A. (ed.) (1988) *Universal Abandon? The politics of postmodernism*, Minneapolis: University of Minnesota Press.

Ross, A. (1989) *No Respect: Intellectuals and popular culture*, London: Routledge.

Rutherford, J. (ed.) (1990) *Identity, Community, Culture, Difference*, London: Lawrence & Wishart.

Ryan, M. and Kellner, D. (1988) *Camera Politica: The politics and ideology of contemporary Hollywood film*, Bloomington: Indiana University Press.

Rylance, R. (1993) *Roland Barthes*, Hemel Hempstead: Harvester Wheatsheaf.

Said, E. (1978) *Orientalism*, New York: Random House; (1995) Harmondsworth: Penguin.

Samson, A. (1992) *F. R. Leavis*, Hemel Hempstead: Harvester Wheatsheaf.

Samuel, R. (ed.) (1991) *People's History and Socialist Theory*, London: Routledge & Kegan Paul.

Sarup, M. (1993) *An Introductory Guide to Post-Structuralism and Postmodernism*, second edition, Hemel Hempstead: Harvester Wheatsheaf.

Saussure, F. de (1974) *Course in General Linguistics*, London: Fontana.

Schwartz, B. (1985) 'Gramsci goes to Disneyland: postmodernism and the popular', *Anglistica* (Naples), 28(3).

Schwartz, B. (1989) 'Popular culture: the long march', *Cultural Studies*, 3(2), pp. 250–4.

Seiter, E., Borchers, H., Kreutzner, G. and Warth, E.-M. (eds) (1989) *Remote Control: Television, audiences, and cultural power*, London: Routledge.

Sheridan, A. (1980) *Michel Foucault: The will to truth*, London: Tavistock.

Sheridan, S. (1988) *Grafts: Feminist cultural criticism*, London: Verso.

Shiach, M. (1989) *Discourse on Popular Culture*, Cambridge: Polity Press.

Silverman, (1983) *The Subject of Semiotics*, New York and Oxford.

Sim, S. (ed.) (1995) *The A–Z Guide to Literary and Cultural Theorists*, Hemel Hempstead: Harvester Wheatsheaf.

Slater, P. (1977) *Origin and Significance of the Frankfurt School*, London: Routledge.

Sontag, S. (1966) *Against Interpretation*, New York: Deli.

Sontag, S. (1982) *A Susan Sontag Reader*, New York: Farrar, Straus & Giroux.

Spivak, G. C. (1987) *In Other Worlds: Essays in cultural politics*, London and New York: Methuen.

Stacey, J. (1994) *Star Gazing: Hollywood and female spectatorship*, London: Routledge.

Stallybrass, P. and White, A. (1986) *The Politics and Poetics of Transgression*, London: Methuen.

Stephanson, A. (1987) 'Regarding postmodernism – a conversation with Fredric Jameson', *Social Text*, 17, pp. 29–54.

Storey, J. (1996a) *Cultural Studies and the Study of Popular Culture: Theories and methods*, Edinburgh: Edinburgh University Press.

Storey, J. (ed.) (1996b) *What is Cultural Studies: A reader*, London: Edward Arnold.

Storey, J. (1997) *An Introduction to Cultural Theory and Popular Culture*, second edition, Hemel Hempstead: Harvester Wheatsheaf.

Strinati, D. (1995) *An Introduction to Theories of Popular Culture*, London: Routledge.

Tallack, D. (ed.) (1995) *Critical Theory: A reader*, Hemel Hempstead: Harvester Wheatsheaf.

Tasker, Y. (1991) *Feminist Crime Writing: The politics of genre*, Sheffield: Pavic.

Taylor, H. (1989) *Scarlett's Women*, London: Virago.

Thompson, E. P. (1961) 'Review of The Long Revolution', *New Left Review*, 9, pp. 24–33.

Thompson, E. P. (1963; rpt. 1966) *The Making of the English Working Class*, New York: Vintage.

Thompson, E. P. (1978) *The Poverty of Theory and Other Essays*, London: Merlin Press.

Thompson, J. B. (1984) 'Symbolic violence: language and power in the writings of Pierre Bourdieu', in *The Theory of Ideology*, Cambridge: Polity Press, pp. 42–72.

Thornham, S. (1997) *Feminism and Film Theory*, London: Edward Arnold.

Thwaites, T., Davis, L. and Mules, W. (1994) *Tools for Cultural Studies: An introduction*, South Melbourne: Macmillan.

Tolson, A. (1996) *Mediations: Text and discourse in media studies*, London: Edward Arnold.

Traube, E. (1992) *Dreaming Identities: Class, gender, and generation in 1980s Hollywood movies*, Boulder: Westview Press.

Tulloch, J. and Alvarado, M. (1983) *'Doctor Who': The unfolding text*, London: Macmillan.

Turner, G. (1988) *Film as Social Practice*, London: Routledge.

Turner, G. (1996) *British Cultural Studies: An introduction*, second edition, London: Routledge.

Urry, J. (1990) *The Tourist Gaze: Leisure and travel in contemporary societies*, London: Sage.

Volosinov, V. N. (1973) *Marxism and the Philosophy of Language*, London: Seminar Press.

Waites, B., Bennett, T. and Martin, G. (eds) (1982) *Popular Culture Past and Present*, London: Croon Helm – Open University Press.

Webster, D. (1988) *Looka Yonder: The imaginary America of popular culture*, London: Comedia/Routledge.

Weedon, C. (1987) *Feminist Practice and Poststructuralist Theory*, Oxford: Blackwell.

Williams, P. (1993) *Colonial Discourse and Past-Colonial Theory: A Reader*, Hemel Hempstead: Harvester Wheatsheaf.

Williams, R. (1958) *Culture and Society 1780–1950*, London: Chatto & Windus; (1963) Harmondsworth: Penguin.

Williams, R. (1961; rpt. 1965) *The Long Revolution*, London: Penguin.

Williams, R. (1975) *Television: Technology and cultural form*, New York: Schocken Books.

Williams, R. (1976) *Keywords*, London: Fontana.

Williams, R. (1977) *Marxism and Literature*, Oxford: Oxford University Press.

Williams, R. (1979) *Politics and Letters*, London: Verso.

Williams, R. (1981) *Culture*, London: Fontana.

Williams, R. (1989) *The Politics of Modernism: Against the new conformists*, London: Verso.

Williamson, J. (1978) *Decoding Advertisements: Ideology and meaning in advertising*, London: Marion Boyars.

Williamson, J. (1986a) 'The problems of being popular', *New Socialist*, September, pp. 14–15.

Williamson, J. (1986b) *Consuming Passions: The dynamics of popular culture*, London and New York: Marion Boyers.

Willis, P. (1977) *Learning to Labour: How working class kids get working class jobs*, Farnborough: Saxon House.

Willis, P. (1978) *Profane Cultures*, London: Routledge & Kegan Paul.

Willis, P. (1990) *Common Culture*, Milton Keynes: Open University Press.

Winship, J. (1987) *Inside Women's Magazines*, London: Pandora.

Wolmark, J. (1993) *Aliens and Others: Science fiction, feminism and postmodernism*, Hemel Hempstead: Harvester Wheatsheaf.

Women's Studies Group, Centre for Contemporary Cultural Studies (1978) *Women Take Issue: Aspects of women's subordination*, London: Hutchinson.

Wright, W. (1975) *Sixguns and Society*, Berkeley: University of California Press.

Acknowledgements

Grateful acknowledgement is made to the following sources for permission to reproduce material in this book previously published elsewhere. Every effort has been made to trace copyright holders, but if any have been inadvertently overlooked the publisher will be pleased to make the necessary arrangement at the first opportunity.

Reading 4: © Richard Hoggart, 1957; reprinted by permission of Jonathan Cape. Reading 5: © Raymond Williams, 1961; reprinted by permission of Chatto & Windus. Reading 6: © 1963 by E. P. Thompson; reprinted by permission of Pantheon Books, a division of Random House, Inc. Reading 7: © Stuart Hall and Open University, 1964. Reading 8: © *Journal of Social History*, 1973–74. Reading 9: © Routledge, 1987. Reading 11: © Roland Barthes, 1972; reprinted by permission of Chatto & Windus. Reading 12: © University of California Press, 1975. Reading 13: © Routledge, 1978. Reading 14: © Verso/Editions La Decouverte, 1971. Reading 15 © 1976 by Éditions Gallimard; reprinted by permission of Georges Borchardt, Inc. Reading 16: © Blackwell Publishers, 1987. Reading 17: © Lawrence & Wishart, 1971. Reading 21: © Lawrence & Wishart, 1971. Reading 22: © The Open University Press, 1986. Reading 24: Christine Gledhill, 1988. Reading 26: © Routledge, 1985. Reading 27: © Gordon and Breach Publishers, 1986. Reading 28: from *Reading the Romance: Women, Patriarchy, and Popular Literature*, Janice A. Radway; © 1984 by the University of North Carolina Press; used by permission of the publisher. Reading 29: © Jacqueline Bobo, 1988. Reading 30: © Blackwell Publishers, 1991. Reading 31: © Yvonne Tasker, 1991. Reading 32: © Blackwell Publishers, 1991. Reading 34: © Screen, 1987. Reading 35: Meaghan Morris, 1988. Reading 36: © Dick Hebdige and *Journal of Communication Inquiry*, 1986. Reading 37: © Edinburgh University Press, 1988. Reading 38: from *Postmodernism and Society*, Boyne and Rattansi © Boyne and Rattansi; reprinted with permission of St. Martin's Press, Incorporated, and Macmillan Press, 1990. Reading 39: © Routledge, 1991. Reading 41: © Routledge, 1984. Reading 42: © Routledge, 1981. Reading 43: from *Media, Culture and Society*, vol. 4, pp. 33–50; © reprinted by permission of Sage Publications Ltd. Reading 44: © The British Film Institute, 1983. Reading 46: © the Speech Communication Association, 1987; reproduced by permission of the publisher. Reading 47: Routledge, 1987. Reading 48: © Indiana University Press, 1988. Reading 49: from *Cultural Studies*, vol. 3.2 (1989): 194–207; © Routledge, 1989. Reading 50: The Open University Press, 1990. Reading 52: from *Diacritics*, vol. 21.4 (1991): 102–115; © the Johns Hopkins University Press. Reading 53: © Routledge, 1992. Reading 54: from *Critical Studies in Mass Communication*, March 1995, pp. 62–71; © the Speech Communication Association, 1995; reproduced by permission of the publisher. Reading 55: from *Critical Studies in Mass Communication*, March 1995, pp. 72–81 © the Speech Communication Association, 1995; reproduced by permission of the publisher.

Index